Fifth Edition

Personality

Marc Setterlund
Alma College

Seymour Feshbach
University of California, Los Angeles — Emeritus

Bernard Weiner
University of California, Los Angeles

Arthur Bohart
California State University, Dominguez Hills — Emeritus

Academic Media Solutions
Affordable - Quality Textbooks, Study Aids, & Custom Publishing

Cover photos: HelgaLin/Shutterstock

Paperback (black/white):	ISBN-13: 978-1-942041-57-3
	ISBN-10: 1-942041-57-8
Paperback (color):	ISBN-13: 978-1-942041-56-6
	ISBN-10: 1-942041-56-X
Loose leaf version (B/W):	ISBN-13: 978-1-942041-58-0
	ISBN-10: 1-942041-58-6
Online version:	ISBN-13: 978-1-942041-59-7
	ISBN-10: 1-942041-59-4

Printed in the United States of America by Academic Media Solutions.

Brief Contents

Preface xvii
About the Authors xx
Introduction xxi

PART 1 INNATE AND ENVIRONMENTAL DETERMINANTS OF PERSONALITY   1

1   Genetic Determinants of Personality   3
2   Contextual Aspects of Personality and Behavior   25

PART 2 THEORIES OF PERSONALITY   39

3   Freud's Psychoanalytic Theory of Personality   43
4   Psychoanalytic Dissidents and Descendants   61
5   Learning Theory Approaches to Personality   85
6   Phenomenological Theories   107

PART 3 THE STRUCTURE OF PERSONALITY   125

7   Foundations of Personality Measurement   127
8   Personality Assessment   141
9   Traits, Situations, and Their Interaction   157

PART 4 PERSONALITY DEVELOPMENT   173

10   The Development and Functions of the Self   175
11   Identity   193
12   Social Development and Patterns of Childrearing   215
13   Development Through the Life Span   241

PART 5　PERSONALITY DYNAMICS 259

14　The Dynamics of Behavior 261

15　Emotion and Stress 277

16　Consciousness 297

PART 6　COMPLEX PERSONALITY PROCESSES 317

17　Perceived Causality and Control 319

18　Love and Hate 345

19　Summing Up 377

Glossary 389
References 397
Index of Names 449
Index of Concepts 457

Contents

Preface xvii
About the Authors xx
Introduction xxi

PART 1   INNATE AND ENVIRONMENTAL DETERMINANTS OF PERSONALITY   **1**

1   Genetic Determinants of Personality   **3**

All Humans Are Alike 4
The Question of Instincts 5
Instinctive Patterns of Behavior 5
Evolutionary Psychology 7
Facial Expressions and Emotions 9
The Need to Belong and Survival 10

All Humans Are Unique 12
The Experimental Study of Heritability 12
The Study of Heritability Through Human Research 13
Heritability Estimates Depend on the Sample 19
The Nonshared Environment Effect 21
Molecular Genetics 22
Criticisms of Genetic Views of Personality 22

Summary 23 ■ *Key Terms 23* ■ *Thought Questions 23*

2   Contextual Aspects of Personality and Behavior   **25**

The Person and Situation 26
The Social World 27
Social Class 27
Culture 28
The Physical World 33
The Natural Environment 33
Constructed Environments 36

Behavior Settings 36
Privacy 37
Summary of Environmental Effects 37

Summary 38 ■ *Key Terms 38* ■ *Thought Questions 38*

PART 2   THEORIES OF PERSONALITY   39

3   Freud's Psychoanalytic Theory of Personality   43

Biography 44
Basic Theoretical Concepts 46
  Homeostasis and Hedonism 46
  Psychological Energy 47
  The Instincts 48
  Psychological Determinism 48
  Libido and Developmental Stages 49
  Personality Structures 51
Anxiety 53
Defense Mechanisms 54
  Repression and the Unconscious 54
  Childhood Sexual Abuse and Repression 56
  Other Defenses 57
  Individual Differences in Defensive Preferences 58
  Defense Mechanisms May Be Necessary 59
General Evaluation 59

Summary 60 ■ *Key Terms 60* ■ *Thought Questions 60*

4   Psychoanalytic Dissidents and Descendants   61

Rivals to Freud 61
  The Analytic Psychology of Carl Jung 62
  Alfred Adler's Individual Psychology 67
  Karen Horney 68
  Erich Fromm 70
Psychoanalysis Since Freud 72
  Erik Erikson 73
  Psychoanalytic Ego Psychology 75
  Object Relations Theory 77
  Narcissism and the Self 80
Psychoanalysis in Flux 81

Summary 82 ■ *Key Terms 83* ■ *Thought Questions 83*

5 Learning Theory Approaches to Personality 85

Associationist (Stimulus-Response) Learning Theory 86
Habits and Drives 87
Personality Development 88

Reinforcement Theory 91
Radical Behaviorism 92
Lawfulness and Control 92
Increasing or Maintaining Behavior 93
Decreasing Behavior 94
Applications of Reinforcement Theory 95
Limitations of Reinforcement Theory 97

Social Learning Theory 98
Expectancy-Value Theory 98
Bandura's Social Learning Theory 99
Limitations of Social Learning Theory 103

Cognitive Behavior Modification 104
Conditioning New Associations 104
Other Cognitive Changes 105

Summary 105 ■ *Key Terms 106* ■ *Thought Questions 106*

6 Phenomenological Theories 107

Humanistic Theory 108

The Person-Centered Theory of Carl Rogers 109
Self-Actualization 109
Client-Centered Therapy 111

Maslow's Organismic Humanism 112
The Need Hierarchy 112
The Actualized Person 114

Existential Humanism 115

Kelly's Personal Construct Theory 116
The Human as Scientist 117
Constructive Alternativism 118
Formal Theory 119
The Role Construct Repertory (REP) Test 120
Emotions 121
Overview of Kelly's Theory 122

Implicit Psychology 122
A Concluding Comment 123

Summary 123 ■ *Key Terms 124* ■ *Thought Questions 124*

PART 3 THE STRUCTURE OF PERSONALITY   125

7 Foundations of Personality Measurement   127

    The Prescientific Era 128
    The Scientific Era 129
    Reliability and Validity 131
        Reliability 131
        Validity 135
        How Low Reliability Affects Validity 139

    Summary 140 ■ *Key Terms 140* ■ *Thought Questions 140*

8 Personality Assessment   141

    Objective Personality Tests 142
        Tests Based on Face Validity 143
        Empirical Approaches 144
        Factor Analysis 146
        The Theoretical Model 147
    Projective Personality Tests and Methods 148
        The Rorschach Inkblot Test 148
        The Thematic Apperception Test (TAT) 150
    Other Approaches to Personality Assessment 152
        The Interview 153
        Self-Report 154
        Observers 154
        Physiological Assessment 154

    Summary 155 ■ *Key Terms 156* ■ *Thought Questions 156*

9 Traits, Situations, and Their Interaction   157

    Personality Types 158
    Trait Theories 159
        Cattell and Factor Analysis 159
        Eysenck's Hierarchy 159
        The Big Five 161
    Trait and Situational Theories 163
        Mischel's Argument 163
        Attribution Theory 164
    Alternative Assessment Strategies 166
        The Interactionist Position 166
        The Moderator Variable Approach 167
        Aggregation Techniques 168

Trait Psychology Revisited 169
State versus Trait 170
Conceptualizing Traits 171

Summary 172 ■ *Key Terms 172* ■ *Thought Questions 172*

PART 4 PERSONALITY DEVELOPMENT 173

10 The Development and Functions of the Self 175

The Self 176
Culture and the Self 176
Definitions of Self 176
The Self as a Concept 177
Self as Agent 178

Development of the Self-Concept 178
Self-Awareness 178
Further Developments of the Self-Concept 179
Self-Esteem 183

Self-Processes 184
Self-Monitoring 185
Self-Control 186
Positive and Negative Effects of Self-Awareness 186

Self-Motives 187
Self-Protection and Self-Enhancement 187
Self-Consistency 189

Personality Theories and the Self 190
The Self in Personality Theories 190

Summary 191 ■ *Key Terms 191* ■ *Thought Questions 191*

11 Identity 193

Stages of Identity Formation: Erikson and Marcia 194
Beyond Four Statuses 197

Racial and Ethnic Identity 197

Sexual Orientation Identity Development 199

Gender Identity, Gender Typing, and Gender Differences 201
Gender Identity 201
Gender Differences 202
Gender Typing: Development of Gender Differences
and Gender Identity 205

Narrative and Identity 209

Summary 213 ■ *Key Terms 213* ■ *Thought Questions 213*

12 Social Development and Patterns of Childrearing   215

Issues in Personality Development 216
Nature or Nurture? 216
Continuity or Stages? 217

Attachment Theory 218
Characteristics of Attachment 219
Mary Ainsworth and The Strange Situation 222
Caregiving and Attachment 223
Childhood Outcomes 224
Measurement in Adults 226

Socialization and the Family 228
Child-Rearing Patterns 228

Moral Development 231
The Superego and Moral Development 231
Stages of Moral Development: The Cognitive Approach 232
The Social Learning Approach 233

Prosocial Behaviors 234
Evolution of Positive Social Behaviors 234
Cooperation 235
Generosity and Caring 237
Empathy 237

Summary 239 ■ *Key Terms 239* ■ *Thought Questions 239*

13 Development Through the Life Span   241

Personality Continuity and Change 241
Adolescence and Emerging Adulthood 245
Biological Changes 246
Individual Variations 247
Autonomy and Conformity 247
Trait Level Changes 248
Continuity Between Adolescents and Parents 248

Adult Development 249
Adult Developmental Stages 250
Midlife "Crisis" 251
Continuity and Change in Adulthood 252

Old Age 254
Trait Stability into Old Age 254
Aging and Health 255
Competence and Survival 256

To Disengage or Not to Disengage 256
Demography 257

Summary 258 ■ *Key Terms 258* ■ *Thought Questions 258*

PART 5   PERSONALITY DYNAMICS   259

14 The Dynamics of Behavior   261

A Historical Introduction 261
Psychodynamics from a Psychoanalytic Perspective 261
Behaviorism 262
Gestalt Psychology 263

Topics in the Study of Personality Dynamics 263

Conflict 264
Temporal, Spatial, and Discriminative Conflict 265
Lewin's Classification System 265
Miller's Conflict Model 266

Impulse Control and Delay of Gratification 268
Imaginary Images 269
Learning Theory Approaches 270
Expectancy and Delay of Gratification 270

Substitution 271

Frustration 273

Goals and Life Tasks 273

Summary 275 ■ *Key Terms 275* ■ *Thought Questions 275*

15 Emotion and Stress   277

Emotion 277
Definition 278
Areas of Study 279

The Body as the Source 279

Two Factor Model 280

Cognitive Theories 282
An Attributional Approach to Emotions 283
Appraisal Approach to Emotions 284

The Structure of Emotion 285
Basic Emotions 285
Individual Differences in Emotional Reactivity 286

Mood 286

Stress 287

Life-Event Stress 287

Effects of Stress on Thinking 291

Coping with Stress 291

Appraisal and Problem-Focused Coping 292

Social Support 292

Individual Differences in Stress Reactions and Hardiness 294

Conclusion 294

Summary 295 ■ *Key Terms 295* ■ *Thought Questions 295*

16 Consciousness   297

The Relationship of Consciousness to Nonconscious Information Processing 298

Mindlessness 299

Automaticity 300

Priming 301

The Relationship of the Self to Consciousness 302

Are Nonconscious Processes "Smart" or "Dumb?" 303

Altered States of Consciousness 304

Sleep 304

Dreams 306

Hypnosis 309

Drugs 312

The Divided Self: Split-Brain Experiments and Consciousness 313

Fantasy and Consciousness 315

Summary 316 ■ *Key Terms 316* ■ *Thought Questions 316*

PART 6   COMPLEX PERSONALITY PROCESSES   317

17 Perceived Causality and Control   319

Perceived Control 320

Locus of Control 320

Learned Helplessness 322

Optimism 325

Efforts to Preserve a Sense of Personal Control 326

Self-Determination Theory 329

Achievement Motivation 330

The Measurement of Achievement Needs 331

Achievement Needs as a Personality Structure 331

Achievement Motivation and Economic Development 332

The Development of Achievement Needs 334
Atkinson's Theory of Achievement Motivation 334
Attribution Theory and Achievement Strivings 336

Competence 339
Mindset 339
Integrating Perceived Control with Achievement Motivation and Competence 340

Attributions of Responsibility 340
Evaluation 341
Helping Behavior 342

Conclusion 342

Summary 342 ■ *Key Terms 343* ■ *Thought Questions 343*

18 Love and Hate

345

Love's Infinite Variety 346

Research on Love 347

A Triangular Model of Love 347

Passionate Love 349

Companionate Love 350

Intimacy 351
Attachment Styles 351

Choosing a Partner 353

Love and Sex 353

Love and Hate 354

Aggression 356
What Is Aggression? 356
Biological Aspects of Aggression 357
Physiological Influences 359
Genetics and Aggression 360

Cultural Influences 361

The Physical Environment 362

Personality Theories and the Antecedents of Aggression 364
Psychoanalytic Theory 364
Learning Theory Models of Aggression 365

Developmental Influences 371
Child-Rearing Practices 371
Child Abuse 372

Aggression as a Personality Trait 372
Hostile Attribution Bias 373
Narcissism 373

Catharsis and the Regulation of Aggression 374

Catharsis 374
Cognitive Control Mediators and Prosocial Expression of Anger 375
Altering Stimulus Meaning 375

Summary 375 ■ *Key Terms 376* ■ *Thought Questions 376*

19 Summing Up
377

Interactionism 377

The Multidimensionality of the Person 380

The Self 381

Personality as a Science 382

The Future 383
Personality Structure 384
Individual Differences and Their Development 385
Personality Dynamics 385
An Integrated Theory of Personality 386

Summary 387 ■ *Thought Questions 387*

Glossary 389
References 397
Index of Names 449
Index of Concepts 457

Preface

In a sense, we are all personality psychologists. We are making an inference about the genetics of personality when we say, "She has her father's personality." We are judging child-rearing practices when we note, "They're good parents." We are noticing the stability of personality when we complain that, "He has always been stubborn."

Personality is intended for an undergraduate audience at two- and four-year colleges and universities. An extensive background in psychology is not a prerequisite for the use of the book. We have tried to produce a text written for students at the college level. We have tried to respect most students' ability and have not written down to them.

More so than most topics in psychology, personality psychology textbooks can be described in terms of style, rather than content. Some focus on grand theories, others focus on recent research. This textbook includes some of both perspectives. Most chapters in the second half of the book address topics from the perspective of the theories laid out in the first half. This approach provides an integrative framework for understanding these issues. It is likely that some approaches will work better or be more intuitive than others. However, it is useful to take the time to understand the approaches that aren't so intuitive in that context. It is also a good exercise to critically evaluate those approaches.

Often the problem with the grand theories is that they tend to not be parsimonious and fail with regard to empirical validity. The grand theories tend to be older and the style is quite different from the more recent, and often smaller, theories. The grand theories do contribute heuristic value; that is, they give the reader a way to think about how and why people behave as they do. The psychoanalytic approach is referred to often in the book, and has some serious problems, but there is no doubt that was a crucial theory for developing psychotherapy.

The new research approach tends to be smaller in aims, and more grounded in empirical validity. A textbook that focuses on new research, however, tends to neglect some of the classic but very important and useful theory and research. Learning theory approaches to personality have great explanatory power and are very useful for behavior change. The conflict models and frustration-aggression models are both parsimonious and empirically supported. But the reference dates sure do look old. Remember that old research, well conducted, is still good research.

This edition has updates to every chapter, but the basic format has been maintained from previous editions. Given the comprehensive coverage of the book, it is likely the instructor may want to choose which chapters to assign. As a student, you are certainly welcome to read the unassigned chapters.

This book offers a range of features and tools to help students develop and test their understanding of core concepts and topics.

- *An accessible and relevant text that offers a unique narrative*—A natural and relaxed writing style promotes a sense of a conversation between the authors and student.

- *Comprehensive coverage of current topics and scholarly research*—The text has been thoroughly updated to reflect recent research, theories, and scholarship from across the discipline.

- *Flexible format and organization*—The text provides the core theoretical foundations of Personality while offering instructors the flexibility to incorporate a variety of outside course materials and cases.

- *Extensive use of real-world examples*—Each chapter contains a wide variety of real-world examples that illustrate text concepts and demonstrate the connection between theory and applications.

- *Student-friendly pedagogy and features*—Chapter outlines, key terms and on-page marginal key-term definitions, "*Highlight*" box inserts, numerous photos, graphs, tables, figures, chapter summaries, and Thought Questions, and key terms support student learning, retention, and critical analysis.

- *Complete Instructor's Support Package*—The support package includes the Instructor's Resource Manual, Test Item File, and PowerPoint Lecture Slides.

Online and in Print

Student Options: Print and Online Versions

This fifth edition of *Personality* is available in multiple versions: online, in PDF, and in print as either a paperback or loose-leaf text. The content of each version is identical.

The most affordable version is the online book, with upgrade options including the online version bundled with a print version. What's nice about the print version is that it offers you the freedom of being unplugged—away from your computer. The people at Academic Media Solutions recognize that it's difficult to read from a screen at length and that most of us read much faster from a piece of paper. The print options are particularly useful when you have extended print passages to read.

The online edition allows you to take full advantage of embedded digital features, including search and notes. Use the search feature to locate and jump to discussions anywhere in the book. Use the notes feature to add personal comments or annotations. You can move out of the book to follow Web links. You can navigate within and between chapters using a clickable table of contents. These features allow you to work at your own pace and in your own style, as you read and surf your way through the material. (See "Harnessing the Online Version" for more tips on working with the online version.)

Harnessing the Online Version

The online version of *Personality*, 5e, offers the following features to facilitate learning and to make using the book an easy, enjoyable experience:

- *Easy-to-navigate/clickable table of contents*—You can surf through the book quickly by clicking on chapter headings, or first- or second-level section headings. And the Table of Contents can be accessed from anywhere in the book.

- *Key terms search*—Type in a term, and a search engine will return every instance of that term in the book; then jump directly to the selection of your choice with one click.

- *Notes and highlighting*—The online version includes study apps such as notes and highlighting. Each of these apps can be found in the tools icon embedded in the Academic Media Solutions/Textbook Media's online eBook reading platform (http://www.academicmediasolutions.com).

- *Upgrades*—The online version includes the ability to purchase additional study apps and functionality that enhance the learning experience.

Instructor Supplements

In addition to its student-friendly features and pedagogy, the variety of student formats available, and the uniquely affordable pricing options that are designed to provide students with a flexibility that fits any budget and/or learning style, *Personality, 5e,* comes with the following teaching and learning aids:

- *Test Item File*—An extensive set of multiple-choice, short answer, and essay questions for every chapter for creating original quizzes and exams.

- *Instructor's Manual*—An enhanced version of the book offering assistance in preparing lectures, identifying learning objectives, developing essay exams and assignments, and constructing course syllabi.
- *PowerPoint Presentations*—Key points in each chapter are illustrated in a set of PowerPoint files designed to assist with instruction.

Student Supplements and Upgrades (Additional Purchase Required)

- **Lecture Guide**—This printable lecture guide is designed for student use and is available as an in-class resource or study tool. Note: Instructors can request the PowerPoint version of these slides to use as developed or to customize.

Acknowledgments

We are grateful to those who reviewed the manuscript for previous editions: Sylvia Santos, California State University, Dominguez Hills; Hal Arkowitz, University of Arizona; Etzel Cardena, Uniformed Services University of the Health Sciences; Paul M. Fromson, Elon College; Stella D. Garcia, University of Texas, San Antonio; Bill C. Henry, Colby College; Anita E. Kelly, University of Notre Dame; Carolyn C. Morf, University of Utah; Robert W. Newby, Tarleton State University; Michael F. Shaughnessy, Eastern New Mexico University; T. Gale Thompson, Bethany College; Bill Thornton, University of Southern Maine; and Paul H. Wright, University of North Dakota We also want to thank Virginia Harrelson Lilian Gonzales and Lorraine Woods for their assistance in tracking down relevant articles.

Finally, we would like to thank Mark Covey, Concordia College; Gwyneth Beagley, Alma College; Wally Beagley, Alma College; and Paula Niedenthal, University of Wisconsin; for support at various points in the project. We would also like to thank Emily Kirby, Kilee DeBrabander, and Megan Setterlund for their extensive help. We would also like to thank Dan Luciano for development of the concept of affordable college textbooks and his encouragement to write the book, and Victoria Putman of Putman Productions for the production and editorial direction she provided to make this book a reality.

About the Authors

Marc Setterlund is a Professor of Psychology at Alma College. He has served as the associate provost of the college, as well as department chair. He earned his B.A. from Gustavus Adolphus College, and his Ph.D. from The Johns Hopkins University. He has been teaching Personality Psychology for over twenty years to students at liberal arts colleges. In addition, he has taught social psychology, human sexuality, research methods, statistics, and a travel-abroad course about the origins of psychology in Vienna and Germany. He has published and conducted research on the self-concept, self-esteem, emotion, sexual decision making, and the effects of ostracism.

Seymour Feshbach earned his B.A. from the City College of New York (CCNY), after being discharged from the army, and his Ph.D. from Yale University. After receiving his Ph.D., he was recalled to active duty and served in the Korean War. He is a professor emeritus at the University of Pennsylvania and at the University of California, Los Angeles. His major area of interest was the dynamics of aggressive behavior, especially the reduction of aggression. His later research focused on other areas, particularly the analysis of patriotism and nationalism.

Bernard Weiner received his undergraduate degree from the University of Chicago and his Ph.D. from the University of Michigan. Since 1965, he has been at the University of California, Los Angeles, where he is currently Distinguished Professor of Psychology. He has written, coauthored, or edited 16 books, including *Judgments of Responsibility* (1995), and *Social Motivation, Justice, and the Moral Emotions* (2006), as well as published more than 225 articles. He has been awarded the Donald Campbell Research Award and the Edward L. Thorndike Lifetime Achievement Award from the American Psychological Association, the Distinguished Scientist Award from the Society of Experimental Social Psychology, and is a member of the National Academy of Education. In addition to a Distinguished Teaching Award, he holds honorary degrees from the University of Bielefeld, Germany; Turku University, Finland; and the University of Manitoba, Canada.

Arthur C. Bohart received his undergraduate degree in mathematics and psychology from the University of California, Santa Barbara. He received his Ph.D. from the University of California, Los Angeles. He is a retired professor emeritus at both California State University Dominguez Hills and at Saybrook University. He is the coauthor or coeditor of several books, including *How Clients Make Therapy Work: The Process of Active Self-Healing, Constructive and Destructive Behavior, Empathy Reconsidered, and Humanity's Dark Side*. His work has focused on the nature and effects of empathy, the client's role in psychotherapy, psychotherapy integration, and evidence-based practice in psychotherapy.

Introduction

Source: HelgaLin/Shutterstock

Definition of *Personality*

The field of personality is enormously complex and diverse. As a student taking this class, you may be interested in questions such as What is my personality—what are my fundamental characteristics? How changeable is my personality? How did I acquire my personality? How is my personality organized? What factors determine my behavior—my motives, my self, my traits, my thoughts, my emotions? How do all those factors interact and interrelate? How can I understand others' personality? Are all aspects of my personality conscious, or are some parts determined by unconscious forces—how well can I know myself? What role do my emotions play in my personality and my behavior? Why are some people more able than others to handle stress and conflict? Are humans basically aggressive or basically loving?

The field of personality addresses the most basic questions of what it means to be a functioning human being. Because many writers and theorists have taken different approaches and emphasized different aspects, it is difficult to define *personality* in a way that will satisfy everyone. For the person on the street, personality most fundamentally refers to what is distinctive about an individual. People describe themselves and their friends in terms of what is distinctive about them: he is shy, quiet, and sensitive; she is outgoing, friendly, and open to different experiences. In addition, people often use the term *personality* to refer to someone who is not only distinctive but interesting in a positive way. Thus, they might say that someone "has a lot of personality," meaning that the person stands out in charm, colorfulness, or interesting characteristics. When people say that someone has "no personality," they mean that there is little about the person that is distinctive, interesting, or colorful.

For some psychologists, *personality* is largely defined in terms of the enduring characteristics that differ from person to person, that is, in terms of individual differences. Thus, for many, personality is typically equated with personality traits. However, personality can also be considered to include one's motives, thoughts, emotions, beliefs, and values. Further, one's personality may depend on how all these things are organized.

In this text, we adopt a broader view of personality than simply the focus on individual differences. For us, the field of personality consists of the study of all the issues and topics we have mentioned, and how they interrelate. In essence, it deals with the study of all the factors that play a role in how an individual's overall functioning is organized.

The study of personality intersects with other aspects of psychology. Just as how we perceive and learn is relevant to our overall functioning, so is our genetic endowment. Our overall functioning is also influenced by social and cultural variables. What distinguishes the study of personality from the study of social and cultural psychology is that we focus on how those many variables influence the functioning of the individual. How our personalities develop is also a topic of relevance, and, therefore, the field of personality intersects with that of developmental psychology. Finally, how personality functioning can go awry is an important part of personality. Therefore, the field of personality overlaps with the fields of abnormal and clinical psychology as well.

In sum, for us, personality refers to (1) the relatively enduring behavior patterns that distinguish individuals from one another, (2) the overall organization and structure of individuals' behavior patterns, and (3) the patterns of interactions between this organization and both external factors—such as cultural, environmental, and social variables—and internal factors—such as motivations, emotions, and thoughts.

The Field of Personality and the Structure of This Textbook

Because of its great complexity and diversity, the field of personality presents a great challenge to both the student and the psychologist. Many individuals associate this field of study with grand theorists, such as Sigmund Freud and Carl Jung, who postulated comprehensive schemes that attempted to explain phenomena as far ranging as war, neurosis, and dream symbolism. But the formulation of a general theory of personality is just one aspect of a vast mosaic. Other personality psychologists focus on less ambitious, and more attainable, goals. A number of personality psychologists have been concerned with the structure of personality—identifying basic traits, such as introversion or the need for achievement, and ascertaining how they can be best assessed. Others have examined how these characteristics come into existence—that is, the genetic and experiential determinants of personality development. Still other personality psychologists are interested in personality dynamics, or how personality structures interact with the environment to generate behavior. Issues such as stress, conflict, and frustration are part of the study of the dynamics of personality.

The four main divisions in the study of personality—theory, structure, development, and dynamics—are not completely separate. For example, Freud's general theory includes a discussion of personality structure (such as the "anal" character), how such a trait might develop (conflict with parents during the period of toilet training), and its effects on later behavior (the tendency to hoard money or to be compulsively clean). Nevertheless, the four major areas within personality do have somewhat separate histories and did not develop simultaneously. They therefore provide the organizing framework for this book.

In the ensuing chapters we examine contemporary theoretical and empirical efforts that address the viability of a general theory of personality; traits, their measurement, and development; and the manner in which these traits influence an individual's actions in particular environments.

We are sympathetic to many theoretical positions and types of empirical investigations because of the enormous complexity of the problems with which they attempt to deal. Thus, our discussion of personality research and theories will be from the perspective of psychologists who are not limited to one particular theory but draw upon a number of them. In our framework, the individual both acts and reacts, has unique aspirations and fantasies, and is conscious of the future as well as the past and the present. We will consider personal behavior within a broad social-cultural context, for one must be sensitive to the powerful effects that the values of the culture, the family, and the larger society exert on behavior. Individuals are social beings, functioning in particular cultural settings. At the same time, one must have some appreciation of the role of genetics and evolution in human behavior. We are also biological creatures shaped by evolution.

Psychology cannot yet provide the answers to many of the difficult questions regarding personality. The relatively objective and systematic study of personality is still in its infancy, less than seven decades old. Our scientific tools are still quite limited. We have no magical procedures that will reveal the inner depths of our minds. For ethical reasons, we cannot and should not freely experiment with infants, raising them under carefully controlled, laboratory conditions. We do not have the power to alter culture, socioeconomic structures, and other significant features of the human environment that play an important role in personality. Nor do we have the power to alter the human body. For these reasons, we cannot reach the precision of measurement and experimental control in the study of human behavior that characterizes research in physics and chemistry.

Nevertheless, much can be learned by examining personality from an empirical, scientific perspective. At the very least, adoption of a scientific approach enables one to think about personality issues in a more analytic, discriminating manner. There are a great many, often conflicting, current assertions regarding personality. For example, "One's basic personality is formed in the first two years of life" versus "We are constantly changing and growing"; "Personality changes as the situation changes" versus "We are who we are, regardless of context"; "Sex and aggression are the basic human drives" versus "The basic human goal is self-actualization." Research provides us with the data to discriminate between valid and unfounded assertions, between assertions that have yet to be tested and those that are probably not testable.

We also apply a scientific approach to the examination of theories of personality. Because personality theories typically attempt to account for different aspects of human behavior, it is often difficult to call one "better" than another. But one must also be critical when evaluating the relevant evidence and the logic of each theory. We are able to use common scientific criteria to evaluate and compare theories. These criteria include the breadth and comprehensiveness of the theory (how much of the data on personality is explained); the testability of the theory; its degree of empirical support; and its heuristic or generative value.

Chapter Topics

Our view of personality dictates the organization of this text. The two most basic aspects that influence the development and functioning of personality are biological and genetic factors, and environmental and sociocultural factors. In Part 1, we consider these two basic influences. In Part 2, we turn to a consideration of the three major groups of theories that have influenced how we think about the functioning of the whole person:

psychodynamic theories, behavioral and social learning theories, and phenomenological theories. In Part 3, we examine the basic structure of personality and consider the issue of traits. We also consider the tests and procedures used to assess personality. In Part 4, we consider developmental aspects of personality, including the development of the self and identity. In Parts 5 and 6, we consider a variety of specific topics related to personality functioning: the dynamics of conflict, emotion and stress, consciousness, perceived control and achievement motivation, and love and hate.

That various sections of the book overlap and are interrelated will be evident. For example, in our discussion of personality development in Chapter 13, we must return to issues raised in Chapter 1 regarding the roles of nature and nurture in shaping the person. And in Chapter 14, which addresses conflict and frustration, we must return to issues raised by the broader personality theorists, as examined in Chapters 3–6. Although we must break the whole into parts to present details, we trust our approach will be clear to our readers; that is, we do perceive the field of personality as an integrated whole.

Innate and Environmental Determinants of Personality

PART 1

CHAPTER 1
Genetic Determinants
of Personality

CHAPTER 2
Contextual Aspects
of Personality and
Behavior

Source: Ollyy/Shutterstock.com.

A key question for personality psychologists is: "Are we what we are because of nature or because of nurture?" When the question is phrased in this manner, neither answer can be correct, for the answers are not mutually exclusive. The premise of the question itself is wrong. We are what we are because of how nature and nurture interact; it is not a question of either/or. There clearly are both inborn and social-cultural influences on the individual. Genetics and environment—nature *and* nurture—regulate and guide each person.

In Chapter 1 we examine some of the innate determinants of personality and behavior. We observe that, as products of a long evolutionary history, human beings are predisposed to certain patterns of behavior. In addition, specific genetic blueprints provide the foundation for personality and behavior.

But it is evident that individuals' personalities are greatly influenced by the contexts that surround them and by the experiences they have had. Individuals brought up in different cultures or social classes behave differently. If one wants to predict what an individual is doing or thinking at a given time, some of the best predictors are the point in history when the individual was born and where he or she is living. In Chapter 2 we examine some of these social and cultural influences as well as other kinds of environmental influences.

Culture not only influences individuals; it also influences psychological theories themselves. There is increasing reason to believe that the "grand theories" of Western psychology reflect certain biases about the nature of people that characterize Western culture.

Chapters 1 and 2 do not attempt to give complete accounts of the genetics of personality or the social determinants of action; full courses are devoted to these topics. Rather, we introduce the context of the person: an individual with unique predispositions who is nevertheless modifiable and shaped by surroundings.

Genetic Determinants of Personality

CHAPTER 1

Source: Kenneth Sponsler/Shutterstock.com.

Chapter Outline

All Humans Are Alike

All Humans Are Unique

Charles Darwin introduced the idea that the human species is the product of a long period of evolution in *The Origin of Species* and *Descent of Man*. His arguments had an enormous influence on the field of personality. First, his theory of evolution assumed scientific determinism—that is, the theory assumed that the most complex aspects of behavior in all species are subject to scientific and rational analysis and are not due to accident or divine intervention. This principle was accepted by psychologists in their study of both nonhuman and human behavior. Second, Darwin focused attention on the function or adaptive value of biological structures and behavior. Psychologists have been guided by this viewpoint as they search for the usefulness of a particular pattern of action. Still another implication of Darwin's work for the study of human personality is the importance of species differences and of individual differences within species. These issues are addressed in this chapter.

Darwin proposed a simple yet powerful theory to explain the process of evolution that linked the development of species with the concept of inheritance—the transmission of characteristics from one generation to another. He stated: "Any variation, however slight and from whatever cause proceeding, if it be in any degree of profitability to an individual . . . will tend to the preservation of that individual, and will generally be inherited by its offspring. The offspring, also, will thus have a better chance of surviving" (1869, p. 61).

Nearly every theory of personality tries to describe why people are the way they are. Personality theories are going to make the claim that all humans are alike and the propositions apply to everyone. Simultaneously, personality theories are going to try to explain why each human is different. In our exploration of the influence of genetics on personality, we will see this fully on display. We will start with the ways in which we understand how people are alike, and then we will explore the ways in which people are unique.

In this chapter we examine some of the genetic determinants of personality structure and behavior. Although neurotransmitters and hormones, brain mechanisms, and other biological factors influence personality, we focus here on the topic of genetics because of the vast research in this area and because it well illustrates the role of biological givens in behavior.

It is helpful to frame a genetic approach to personality within the context of evolutionary theory. Among the questions we discuss in this chapter are: What limitations do inherited characteristics place on learning? Do humans have instincts, or innate urges and unlearned patterns of behavior? Are there universal facial expressions or behaviors that are exhibited across cultures? And can it be demonstrated scientifically that personality characteristics and behavioral problems are in part genetically influenced? We will present evidence that the answers are yes and that a complete theory of personality must consider innate factors.

genome The organized set of DNA that every living thing has.

All Humans Are Alike

The human genome is made up of 23 chromosomes, which are then made up of a molecule called deoxyribonucleic acid (DNA). DNA has four bases: adenine, thymine, guanine, and cytosine. These are often denoted just by their first letter: A, T, G, and C. These four letters provide the instructions for making amino acids that then make up the various proteins and enzymes that make up living organisms. The process by which this happens is beyond the scope of this book, but it is important to understand some of the basics.

DNA is copied via another molecule called ribonucleic acid (RNA). In the process of copying, mistakes can be made. Furthermore, mutations can also occur due to exposure to radiation and other things in the environment. Most of the time, the mutations are harmless; some of the time, the mutations are harmful. Importantly, sometimes the mutation leads to positive outcomes and increases the chances of the organism or its offspring surviving.

Through the instructions on how to build the amino acids and how to arrange the amino acids into proteins and enzymes, the DNA provides the information needed to create brain structures, neurotransmitters, and hormones. These then become the building blocks of behavior. All humans have a **genome** that codes for these things, but there will be subtle differences among each person, as everyone (except monozygotic twins) has a slightly different genome. However, unrelated humans still share somewhere between 99% to 99.5% of their DNA. The general pattern is what makes us human and will therefore make us similar in many ways.

It is important to recognize that most of what we will be examining will not be the result of a single gene, but rather

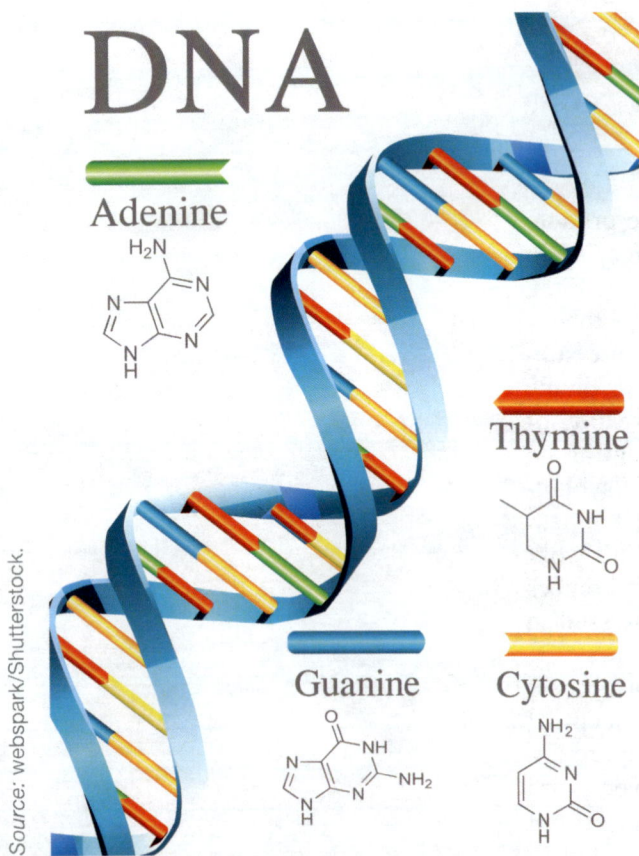

Adenine

H_2N

Thymine

O

NH

O

N
H

Guanine

O

NH

N

NH_2

N
H

Cytosine

NH_2

N

O

N
H

Our DNA is made up of four molecules: adenine, thymine, guanine, and cytosine.

the result of several genes acting together. The genes may be all pointing in a particular direction, or a few genes may point in one direction while the others point in the opposite direction. Consider the genes that are involved in height. Some genes may promote being tall, whereas other genes may promote being short. Some people will get many genes that point toward being tall; some people will get many genes that point toward being short. Most people will get a combination and end up somewhere in the middle. Traits that are made up of several genes are likely to be revealed as something that is normally distributed.

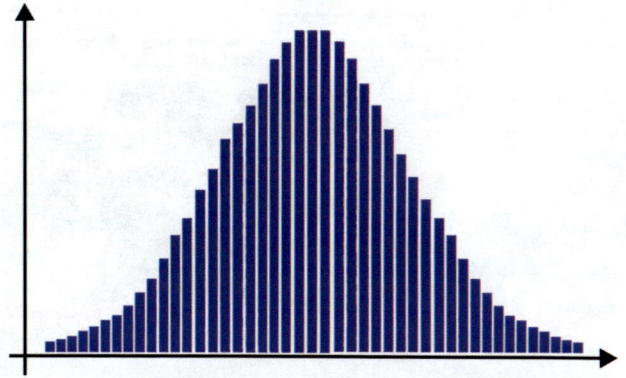

Traits that are due to multiple genes are likely to be distributed in a bell-shaped curve. People who get all the genes pointing toward being tall are likely to be tall; however, most people have a combination and are toward the middle of the distribution. Could we expect that people who have all their genes pointing toward shyness to be at one tail of the distribution of extraversion?
Source: Shahreen/Shutterstock.

The Question of Instincts

Instincts are regarded as genetic givens. An **instinct** or, more appropriately, instinctive behavior can refer to either (1) an unlearned, fixed pattern of activity found in all members of a species, such as nest building in birds and web spinning by spiders; or (2) a specific motivational tendency that is inferred from overt behavior. An instinct in this second sense is a potential toward action and is considered an unlearned "want" or "urge" built into the structure of the organism. Although the ends, or goals, of instincts (urges) are presumed to be fixed, the means of expression can be quite diverse.

instinct An innate, biologically based mode of response to certain stimuli.

Instinctive Patterns of Behavior

Recall that instinct, in addition to meaning a genotypic urge, also refers to an unlearned pattern of behavior that is characteristic of all members of a species of the same sex at the same level of development. Birds' responses to mating calls and squirrels' hoarding of food are examples of such unlearned patterns of responses. These behaviors are caused primarily by genetically transmitted physiological states and function they are akin to the built-in behaviors exhibited by plants, such as movement toward light. These instinctive behaviors frequently are not single responses, but are action sequences that follow a predetermined, predictable course. Furthermore, the observed behaviors often are crucial for survival and therefore are interpreted in an evolutionary sense. For example, it is known that the stickleback fish will attack any other fish of its color or even any object of this particular color. This behavior results in **species-spacing**, or spreading species members apart so that there is sufficient food available for survival. Distinctive birdsong often also has a species-spacing function.

species-spacing Spreading members of the same species across environment to enhance survival.

An interesting set of studies that combines instinct and learning was conducted with Rhesus monkeys (Cook and Mineka, 1989; 1990). One group of monkeys was trained to fear either snakes or flowers. A different group of monkeys watched film of the first group while the first group was trained to fear that stimuli. The monkeys that observed the other monkeys learning to fear snakes acquired a fear of snakes, whereas those that watched the flower condition did not learn to fear flowers. This would seem to indicate that they have an instinctual predisposition to learn to fear things that may threaten survival.

It often is difficult to prove with certainty that a response is innate or unlearned rather than learned and experience-based. In addition, the higher the organism is in the nonhuman-human scale the more likely that the behavior is influenced by learning. Among human beings one might expect to find few unlearned patterns of behavior, other

Source: Eric Isselee/Shutterstock

Source: Monika Vosahlova/Shutterstock

Source: Zdravinjo/Shutterstock

Source: Stuart Jenner/Shutterstock

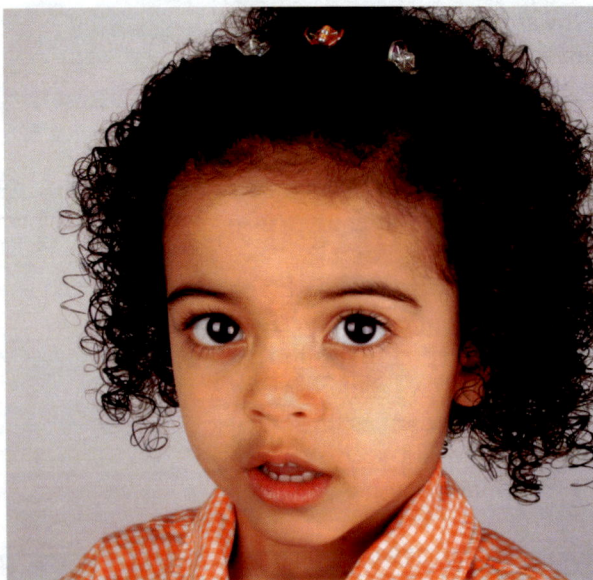
Source: Young Nova/Shutterstock

Source: ptnphoto/Shutterstock

Childlike faces elicit positive responses. This is true in humans as well as pets, like puppies and kittens.

than reflexive responses such as the eye blink or knee jerk. However, it is quite possible that there are innate reactions—fears, aversions, preferences for particular stimulus situations—that have significance for human personality. Fear of the grotesque or a child's responsiveness to the mother's breast and the warmth of her body are possible examples of such reaction tendencies.

Infant Features and Maternal Care

Whether behaviors such as maternal care among humans have genetic determinants cannot be demonstrated with certainty, although it is reasonable to suppose that they do. Such an inborn tendency would have great survival value for the species, in that the young would be protected from danger and starvation. It has been speculated that certain features of the young, particularly facial characteristics, operate as social signals and innately elicit complex emotions and behaviors (Berry and McArthur, 1986). A variety of facial features distinguish infants from adults. Infants have large heads in relation to their bodies, their faces are hairless and smooth—skinned, and they have a relatively large forehead and small chin so that the vertical placement of features is low in the infant's face. In addition, infants' eyes are large, their nose is small.

Berry and McArthur (1986) have shown that these infant facial features may elicit helping responses and positive emotions that, in turn, promote survival. Consider, for example, your reactions to the faces of infants, as opposed to their adult counterparts. It is evident that infant features call forth approach reactions and warmth. It has been contended that these features also influence responses toward adults. In one startling finding, it was reported that baby-faced criminal defendants were judged less harshly than mature-faced defendants, even when they had committed the same criminal offense (Berry and McArthur, 1986).

Evolutionary Psychology

Evolutionary psychology has sought to establish that even such social behaviors as conformity, altruism, and cheating have a biological or genetic basis using principles laid out by E. O. Wilson (1975, 1977). Wilson called his model Sociobiology, which helped lead to a field in psychology called Evolutionary Psychology. Evolutionary psychologists have noted that Darwinian principles account well for aggressive behavior. Aggressive individuals are likely to receive food and also may engage in more mating behavior. Hence, it is argued, those most aggressive will survive and pass on this trait to their offspring. However, it is difficult for Darwinian principles to account for altruism. Those with altruistic tendencies decrease their own "fitness" relative to others, and thus altruism would tend to extinguish over time.

Like Darwin, evolutionary psychologists also accept the view that survival-promoting behavior is passed on from one generation to another. But they contend that survival of the genes, rather than the individual organism, is the prime evolutionary tendency. This belief enables them to account for apparently altruistic actions. For example, a bird may risk its own life to warn the rest of the flock of impending danger. In so doing, the individual bird might not survive, but the survival of others with like genes is aided. Why do human beings help others who apparently are not related to them? Evolutionary psychologists argue that an agreement of "reciprocal altruism" has evolved because mutual help-giving augments the genetic pools of all participating parties.

These ideas have been invoked to explain a vast array of puzzling facts. For example, why should female ants devote their lives to helping the queen to breed, instead of breeding themselves? Wilson (2000) has pointed out that female ants actually share more genes in common with their sisters than they would with their own offspring. Thus, in order to perpetuate genes identical to their own, it is in their self-interest to assist the queen in producing more daughters.

1840   1881   1854

Charles Darwin.

Evolutionary psychology concepts have also led to reinterpretation of various facets of human sexual behavior. The male, evolutionary psychologists may argue, has one prime goal: to transmit as many of his own genes as possible to the next generation. On the other hand, the female must invest a great deal of time in each birth and can have only a very limited number of offspring. Thus, males are in general more promiscuous than females because their promiscuity has a genetic payoff. Furthermore, because females must invest more of themselves in each pregnancy, they are important resources that males must "purchase." As a result, in many cultures older males (who have more resources) marry younger women (who have many years of childbearing and child caring left), and women prefer men who are "good providers" (Buss, 2003, 2005; Fales et al., 2016). However, we should also examine this phenomena from a cultural vantage point. Historically, it has been difficult for women to accumulate wealth on their own, so the only way for them to get it was through a husband. Thus, a behavior of looking for a husband with access to wealth and resources can be explained through an evolutionary approach or a cultural approach.

It has been suggested that men might use two different reproductive strategies, sometimes referred to as "dads" and "cads" (Draper and Harpending, 1982). The first strategy involves finding a reproductive partner and investing time and resources in helping to raise their children. The second strategy is the promiscuous strategy mentioned in the previous paragraph: find as many reproductive partners as possible and not invest strongly in raising the children.

Likewise, women likely use two strategies. In one strategy, a woman looks for a reproductive partner who will invest in the offspring; thus, she is looking for a man who is using the dad strategy. In the other strategy, the woman is looking for a reproductive partner who will provide high-quality genes and will lead to "sexy sons" (Gangstead and Simpson, 1990; Weatherhead and Robertson, 1979). Those sexy sons could then conceivably use the cads reproductive strategy. Interestingly, women who are ovulating are more likely to misperceive a cad as a dad (Durante, Griskevicius, Simpson, Cantú, and Li, 2012). There is evidence that there are consistent changes in reproductive partner choices during the ovulatory cycle such that women prefer the sexier cads during fertile parts of their ovulatory cycle (Gildersleeve, Hasselton, and Fales, 2014). This pattern has been named **ovulatory shift** (Gangestead, Thornhill, and Garver-Apgar, 2005).

Evolutionary psychologists are not reluctant to extend their ideas to explain seemingly unrelated phenomena. For example, they anticipate that child abuse will be most prevalent toward stepchildren because not only do these offspring not carry the genes of the abuser (most typically the stepfather), but they even decrease the "survival fitness" of the stepfather (Daly and Wilson, 1996). Interestingly, data from Sweden (Temrin, Buchmayer, and Enquist, 2000) does not support this hypothesis.

Evolutionary psychologists point out that males have only one great disadvantage in breeding: they cannot be certain that the offspring are their own. Thus, sexual jealousy is aroused and courtship rituals have emerged to monopolize the female's time. During this extended courtship the male also can determine if the female is already pregnant. Evolutionary psychologists suggest that the maternal grandparents (the parents of the mother) will be more attached to the offspring than the paternal grandparents (the parents of the father) because of uncertainty regarding the "true" father. It is generally accepted that the mother's mother has prerogatives, such as the first visit to the baby!

Needless to say, these ideas have been controversial (Archer, 1988). The controversy involves primarily the extension of evolutionary psychology principles to complex human social behaviors. It is obvious that cultural factors greatly influence human actions. For example, how can evolutionary psychology account for the fact that today many men undergo voluntary sterilization and the birthrate in many countries is falling so rapidly that there is zero population growth? In spite of difficulties in explaining such facts, advocating this extreme biological view has proved exceedingly provocative and has spurred the interpretation and reinterpretation of a variety of phenomena.

ovulatory shift A woman's preference for attractive healthy partners who may not invest in offspring during ovulation.

Facial Expressions and Emotions

Darwin argued that human facial expressions are inherited and are modified very little by cultural experience. For example, he pointed out that the baring of teeth by humans in situations of anger and contempt is similar to the display of teeth among carnivores prior to a hostile attack or during an aggressive defense.

A number of studies have attempted to verify Darwin's insight. These studies bear on the biological basis of emotional experience as well as on the universality of emotional displays. Two basic paradigms have been followed in this research area: (1) examining the facial expressions of children born deaf and blind; and (2) analyzing the agreement concerning identification of emotions in different cultures.

Investigations reveal that blind and deaf children do display quite normal facial expressions (Eibl-Eibesfeldt, 1970, Freedman, 1964). Hence, these observations tend to support the universalistic, Darwinian explanation of facial expression. Of course, culture plays some role in the control of facial expression and in determining which situations are appropriate for eliciting and displaying particular emotions and facial expressions.

The cross-cultural research has been guided by identification of the so-called basic human emotions. Ekman and Friesen (1975) isolated six primary emotions—happiness, sadness, fear, anger, disgust, and surprise—and also identified the facial muscles associated with these emotional states. Photographs showing the facial expressions associated with these emotions were then shown to people in five different countries—the United States, Brazil, Chile, Argentina, and Japan—and the subjects were asked to identify the emotion portrayed. The percentage of agreement with the labels supplied by Ekman and Friesen was quite high across all countries used.

A baboon in full threat gesture, with teeth bared. Darwin pointed out that a human snarl has a similar facial pattern and suggested that emotional displays are genetically programmed.

In addition, natives of New Guinea, who had very little exposure to Western culture and were not subject to the possible confounding of media exposure, responded similarly to people in the other five countries. (However, it must be noted that individuals are more adept at this labeling task when selecting the appropriate emotion from a given list, rather than supplying their own interpretation without the aid of a preselected list.) In sum, it appears that facial expressions of some emotions are to a large extent a genetically based characteristic of the species (Ekman, 1993, 2016). Although these appear to be the six facially displayed emotions across cultures, it does not mean they are the only emotions. There are likely to be emotions that are unique to different cultures (Niiya, Ellsworth, and Yamaguchi, 2006) and other emotions that are more effective if not facially displayed.

The Need to Belong and Survival

Humans are a social species and survive and reproduce most successfully when they are part of a group. In the past, exclusion was likely to lead to death. Exclusion from a group is usually described using words associated with pain (MacDonald and Leary, 2005). Functional magnetic resonance imaging (fMRI) research has found that the same part of the brain is active when a person is in physical pain or experiences social exclusion (Eisenberger, Lieberman, and Williams, 2003).

Fear of exclusion also helps to explain one of the major fears that many people experience: public speaking. If a person speaks in such a way that he or she loses status or belonging, there will be negative survival or reproductive consequences. Because of these perceived high stakes, people who believe that public speaking could have this consequence are likely to experience anxiety (Baumeister and Tice, 1990).

Leary and his colleagues (Leary and Baumeister, 2000; Leary, Tambor, Terdal, and Downs, 1995) have suggested that self-esteem acts as a way to monitor the extent to which a person belongs and is important to social groups. In this model, self-esteem measures social belonging in the same way that a thermometer measures temperature; thus, they term this the **sociometer** theory of self-esteem. People who have a strong sense of

sociometer A theory that suggests the function of self-esteem is to measure the extent to which people fit in their social environment.

Source: Chaiyaporn Baokaew/Shutterstock

Source: guruXOX/Shutterstock

Source: Zurijeta/Shutterstock

Source: chainarong jaykeaw/Shutterstock

Source: Lapina/Shutterstock

Source: Serdar Tibet/Shutterstock

The facial expressions of emotion that were identified across cultures are happiness, sadness, anger, fear, disgust, and surprise.

belonging will have high self-esteem, whereas people who do not feel as if they belong will have low self-esteem. Self-esteem is, therefore, an evolved mechanism by which humans are consistently checking belongingness.

Interestingly, there appear to be genetic differences in the ways in which people respond to social exclusion (Gallardo-Pujol, Andrés-Pueyo, and Maydeu-Olivares, 2013). They found that people with one gene respond strongly to being excluded, whereas those with the other version of the gene do not.

All Humans Are Unique

Despite cross-cultural similarities and the universality of some behaviors, it can equally be said that each human is genetically unique. Given the billions of possible inherited gene patterns, each individual is provided with an idiosyncratic genetic configuration. The resulting variability in genetic structure is manifested in individual differences in characteristics and behavior. Two basic procedures have been followed in studying the genetic determinants of individual differences. One method is experimental, involving the selective breeding of nonhumans. The other is nonexperimental in the sense that there is no intervention in the lives of its human subjects. The nonexperimental procedures include both twin and adoption designs. Finally, there are new approaches looking at loci on the genome that are associated with behavior.

The Experimental Study of Heritability

selective breeding Choosing organisms with positive characteristics to reproduce.

For many years **selective breeding** has been unsystematically performed on domestic animals to enhance certain temperamental or behavioral characteristics, such as ferocity, docility, hunting ability, and so on. In more systematic laboratory settings, animals exhibiting a high or low degree of a certain behavior, such as emotionality, are selectively bred for generations and the emotionality of subsequent generations is then compared. The experimenter thus performs on a compressed time scale what natural selection is presumed to do during the course of evolution. In natural selection, high or low extremes of a characteristic or **directional selection**, may be favored. For example, natural selection in opossums evidently favored inertness in the face of danger; visual aggressive displays or strength and speed are favored in other species. In nature, as in the laboratory, there may also be **balancing selection**, which favors intermediate values of the characteristic in question.

directional selection An extreme version of a trait or behavior may be preferred in some instances of natural selection.

balancing selection An intermediate version of a trait of behavior may be preferred in some instances of natural selection.

heritability The degree to which genetics plays a role in the development of a particular aspect of a trait or behavior.

The logic of breeding experiments is straightforward and nicely illustrates what is meant by the concept of **heritability**—the degree to which genetics plays a role in the development of a particular aspect of behavior in a particular population. Assume, for example, that we observe a group of animals learning a maze and that they attain scores of 1–10, based on the number of trials before success. That is, one animal learns the maze in a single trial, another takes two trials, a third requires three trials, and so on. Now, for example, we take the "brightest" animals, which require only one trial to learn, and we inbreed them. Of their offspring, we again inbreed the fastest learners. Assume that this procedure is continued for thirty generations. Now, if the thirtieth generation of animals still gives us scores of 1–10 in maze learning, we know that the ability to learn this maze has no heritability. Rather, the differences among the animals are due entirely to environmental factors. Conversely, assume that for this thirtieth generation, all the animals learn the maze in one trial. In that case, we would assume that maze learning was due entirely to genetic factors; heritability is the determining factor. In actuality in this situation, the variability among the animals, i.e., their differences in how many trials it took them to learn, will most likely decrease over generations, but will not disappear entirely. Thus, there will be both genetic and environmental determinants of learning, with the decrease in variability indicating the degree to which this behavior is influenced by genetic factors.

A representative study of selective breeding for a particular ability is illustrated in an investigation by Thompson (1954). Thompson measured the speed with which rats learned a maze for a food reward. Then he bred the low-error (maze-bright) rats with other maze-bright rats, and the high-error (maze-dull) rats with other maze-dull rats. The offspring of these matings were then tested on the maze. This procedure continued for six generations; by the sixth generation, the error scores of the two breeding populations were dramatically different. It is interesting to note that rats superior in maze learning do not necessarily master other problems as rapidly. Maze learning appears to be a specific ability.

Although the research by Thompson indicates that maze learning is influenced by heredity, this should not be taken to mean that environmental factors have no effect on such learning. Cooper and Zubek (1958) took the strains of rats bred by Thompson and reared them in either enriched or impoverished conditions. The enriched environment contained ramps, tunnels, and many movable objects, whereas the restricted environment included only a food box and a water tin. When the maze learning of the rats was assessed, the experimenters found that when the groups were reared in either extreme environment, their performance did not differ greatly. The enriched environment primarily raised the performance of the dull rats, while the restricted environment chiefly lowered the performance of the bright rats. Only in the normal environment were there differences due to an innate ability factor. Hence, *there is nothing absolute about heritability*; an organism's individual sensitivity to disparate environmental conditions may either mask or exacerbate inborn tendencies. What is inherited, then, is the way in which the organism responds to the environment, and heritability is in turn a function of the environment in which the behavior is studied.

Very similar conclusions regarding heritability have been reached in the study of emotionality. Broadhurst (1961) inbred high- and low-emotionality rats, selected on the basis of their defecation in an open field test. In this procedure, rats are placed in an unfamiliar environment, and emotional responses are inferred from the well-documented fact that fear causes defecation and urination. After six generations of inbreeding, there were dramatic differences between the populations, with the data resembling those reported by Thompson (1954) in terms of the magnitude of group differences and the increasing inequality in emotionality over the generations.

While it seems reasonable that learning ability and even emotionality may have a genetic basis, it is perhaps less sensible to believe that preferences or incentive values have a genetic component, as opposed to being entirely learned. However, breeding experiments have demonstrated that alcohol preference also may be inherited. It has been documented that particular strains of mice choose an alcohol solution over a water solution (Rodgers, 1966), while other strains avoid alcohol and prefer water. Furthermore, when strains with high and low alcohol preference are interbred, the offspring display an intermediate desire for alcohol as opposed to water (Rodgers and McClearn, 1962). Later in this chapter we will suggest that alcoholism among humans might also be determined in part by inborn tendencies.

The Study of Heritability Through Human Research

In contrast to studies of nonhumans, research using human populations is non-experimental in the sense that there is no intervention or manipulation of variables because of obvious ethical constraints. Rather, individuals who vary in their degree of genetic relationship, such as foster parents and their children, natural parents and their children, siblings, dizygotic twins, and monozygotic twins, are compared and contrasted. Genetic similarity is a function of degree of kinship, so for genetically influenced characteristics, similarity in behavior and character should increase with biological relatedness.

Source: Geoffrey Kuchera/Shutterstock

Source: Mick Gast/Shutterstock

Many dog breeds were bred to be predisposed to particular skills. Border collies were bred for their herding instincts. Golden retrievers were bred to retrieve birds from the water; they even have webbed feet, which make it easier for them to swim.

Correlations

One of the most important statistics that is used in personality psychology is the correlation coefficient. The correlation coefficient allows the similarity between two variables to be quantified. The correlation coefficient has two components: sign and magnitude. The sign, positive or negative, tells us the direction of the relationship. If it is a positive correlation, as one variable goes up, the other variable also tends to go up; as one variable goes down, the other tends to go down. Height and weight are typically positively correlated: tall people typically weigh more than short people. For a negative correlation, as one variable goes up, the other variable tends to go down. We might expect classroom absences to be negatively correlated with grades; as absences increase, grades tend to go down. The magnitude can range from 0 to 1.0. When two variables are closely related, the magnitude will be near 1.0; when they are unrelated, they will be near 0. Considering both sign and magnitude, correlation coefficients can range from +1.0 to −1.0.

To create a simple example, let's imagine that researchers have people take each of the following measures: a measure of shyness, a measure of extraversion, and a measure of emotionality. They might want to know whether a relationship exists between the measure of shyness and the measure of extraversion. Using the correlation coefficient, they can answer that question. They might find that the correlation between the measure of shyness and extraversion is −0.78. This would indicate that there is a strong relationship between the two measures, and as shyness goes up, extraversion tends to goes down. They could then investigate whether extraversion and emotionality are related, and they might find the correlation to be +0.08. This would indicate that there is a very weak, or no, relationship between the two variables.

By squaring the correlation coefficient, we can quantify how much of the variability is predicted by one variable to the other. Remember, we are squaring decimals, .90 squared is .81, .50 is .25, and .30 is .09. If we find a correlation of .30, then .09 of the variance is predicted—less than 10%.

Chapters 7 and 8 discuss these ideas further, but it is necessary to understand the basics to understand the research on twins. Most of the time in personality research, the same person provides both variables. However, in investigating heritability of personality, different people would be measured on the same scale. So both twins might take an IQ test, or a parent and child might both take a measure of shyness, or siblings would be measured on extraversion.

The basic shortcoming of human genetic research is that the environments are not controlled. As a result, it is often impossible to infer with certainty that observed behavioral similarity is a function of biological relatedness and is due to inborn characteristics. In nonhuman research using inbreeding techniques, the environments are controlled and identical for each group.

Consider, for example, a hypothetical research study demonstrating that emotional mothers have highly emotional children, whereas non-emotional mothers have children with low emotionality. These data might be interpreted as demonstrating that emotionality is heritable. However, it is quite possible that these children had different home environments; perhaps highly emotional mothers create unstable environments which produce highly emotional children, whereas non-emotional mothers establish stable environments which give rise to children low in emotionality. In this investigation, the learning and the genetic contributions to emotionality cannot be separated. To help interpret the ambiguous results of such family studies, twin and adoption studies are often employed to disentangle genetic and environmental contributions.

The central research separating genetic from environmental contributions to human behavior involves a comparison between twins from different eggs (fraternal, or **dizygotic twins**) with those from the same egg (identical, or **monozygotic twins**). The latter type share completely identical gene pools; dizygotic twins, *on average*, share only about 50% of their genes. Hence, monozygotic (MZ) twins should be more alike in behavior than dizygotic (DZ) twins, if the behavior under study has a genetic component. This hypothesis assumes that the environments of DZ twins are as identical as the environments of MZ twins. However, such an assumption, although reasonable, is not always warranted. Identical twins may have more similar social learning histories; it has been found that they are more likely to dress alike, have common friends, and spend more time together than fraternal twins (Smith, 1965). However, this factor may be of limited importance, as parents of twins often incorrectly classify their children as MZ or DZ (Scan and Carter-Saltzman, 1979). See Table 1.1.

Identical (monozygotic, MZ) twins. Evidence indicates that many aspects of their temperament and behavior also will be similar.

Source: Blend Images/Shutterstock.

dizygotic twins Twins that develop from two fertilized eggs.

monozygotic twins Twins who develop from a single fertilized egg.

TABLE 1.1

Relationship	(A) Shared genes	(C) Common environment
MZ together	100%	100%
MZ apart	100%	0%
DZ together	50% on average	100%
DZ apart	50% on average	0%
Siblings together	50% on average	<100%
Siblings apart	50% on average	0%
Half-siblings together	25% on average	<100%
Half-siblings apart	25% on average	0%
Parent-child	50%	<100%
Grandparent-grandchild	25%	<100%
Adopted siblings	0%	<100%

By knowing the genetic relatedness, it is possible to begin making estimates about the contributions of the genotype to the phenotype. Different degrees of family relatedness lead to different amounts of shared genes. Again, remember we are examining only those genes that vary.

In principle, it is possible to study the effects of shared genes by comparing identical twins reared in similar versus different environments. Although such a sample is seldom available, some investigations have examined the similarities of siblings adopted in infancy and reared in foster homes, compared with unrelated individuals reared in these same homes. Any differences in the similarities within these two groups, given that all else is equal, are logically attributable to the genetic similarity of the sibs. Conversely, any differences in the behavior of the identical twins shows environmental and experiential influences on behavior.

phenotype The totality of observed characteristics or behaviors of an organism that result from the interaction between genotype and environmental influences.

The **phenotype** is going to be expressed as a function of the genotype and the environment. If we consider monozygotic twins raised together, the genotype is going to be the same, and the environment is going to be very similar, but there are likely to be differences in their experiences. One twin may have fallen and hit her head, another may have read more books, or one twin may have punched the other. These differences are known as nonshared environment.

Researchers often use the "ACE model" to describe the proportional influence on the phenotype (see Figure 1.1). The genetic contribution is labeled "A." The next component is the shared common environment, which is labeled "C." The shared environment includes things like experiencing the same parenting style, eating the same foods, being in a household with many or few books, attending the same school. As a simplifying assumption, it is assumed that people living together are going to share many of those things. The final component is the nonshared environment, which is labeled "E." The nonshared environment is the unique experiences that each person has. Even people living together are likely to have different experiences; in fact, some people have argued that all experiences are unique to one person.

Another way of estimating the heritability is to double the difference in the correlations of monozygotic twins raised together, to the correlations of dizygotic twins raised together (this method is usually represented as h^2). Remember the assumption is that the shared

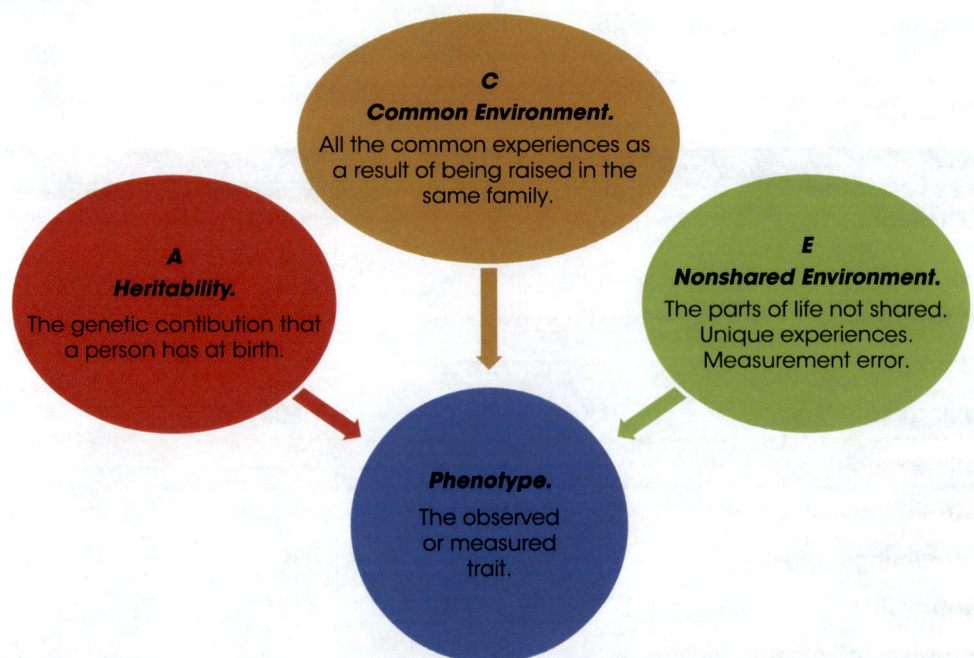

FIGURE 1.1 The ACE Model Specifies the Phenotype as Being a Function of A—Heritability, C—Common Environment, E—Nonshared Environment

environment is the same for monozygotic and dizygotic twins raised together, so the difference is due to genetic effects. A meta-analysis examined 50 years of twin studies that looked at a variety of human traits (Polderman et al., 2015). The studies examined physical traits, diseases, and psychological traits. The correlation for all the temperament and personality traits included in this analysis was .47 for MZ twins and .234 for DZ twins. For the computation of our heritability estimate, we would use $h^2 = 2(.470 - .234) = 2(.236) = .472$. This method is still used; however, many researchers in the field also use more sophisticated methods.

Temperament

". . . we now turn to the question of whether differences in human personality are heritable. We can be mercifully brief, yes." (Turkheimer, Pettersson, and Horn, 2014, p. 517.)

The role of genetics in the development of temperament has long been noted. In his studies of conditioning experiments, Pavlov examined individual dogs for long periods of time and observed striking differences in temperament that he attributed to inborn, neurological inequalities. **Temperament** may be defined as the "characteristic phenomena of an individual's nature, including his susceptibility to emotional stimulations, his customary strength and speed of response, and the quality of his prevailing mood, and all the peculiarities of fluctuation and intensity of mood" Allport, 1961, p. 34). Buss, Plomin, and Willerman (1973) selected four temperaments to study: emotionality, activity, sociability, and impulsivity. Twenty-item questionnaires were constructed, with five items for each temperament. These questionnaires were given to mothers of fraternal (DZ) or identical (MZ) twins. The mothers rated items such as "Child cries easily" on a scale of 1 (a little) to 5 (a lot). They found that on virtually all the items the correlations were higher for the MZ than for the DZ twins of both sexes. Toddlers and preschool children also show a genetic influence on temperament (Goldmith, Buss, and Lemery, 1997). In general, most dimensions of temperament tend to show heritability in the .20 to .60 range (Saudino, 2005).

temperament Behavioral characteristics that are present at an early age and that are believed to have some basis in biological processes partly determined by heredity.

Shyness

Kagan (Kagan, 1989; Kagan and Saudino, 2001; Kagan and Snidman, 1991) and his colleagues have argued for the heritability of a trait which leads to the behavior that we call shyness. They suggest that about 10% of healthy white children are born with a predisposition to act in an "inhibited" fashion in the presence of new stimuli such as strange individuals or strange situations. Another 10% are born to be more adventuresome and "disinhibited" in such situations.

Kagan and Snidman (1991) say that the antecedents of this cautiousness are present at around 4 months of age and can be seen in both high levels of motor activity and crying to stimuli. These predispositions have a tendency to persist into later life. While about 50% of the children studied at age 4 months no longer showed extreme fears at age 8 years, 80% were still not spontaneous. Additionally, about 75% of the shy children at age 8 had one or more unusual fears—such as fear of speaking in class or fear of attending summer camp—compared to 25% of those rated as disinhibited. Generally, shy children also exhibited a variety of physiological correlates such as more motor tension. Kagan (1989) suggests that these are based on brain activity that is easily aroused by unfamiliarity.

Finally, in line with our previous discussion on the difference between phenotype and genotype, Kagan, Arcus, and Snidman (1993) review data indicating that about 35% of the variability in the fear score of children at age 14 months is due to parenting behaviors. Parents who do not comfort their shy and fearful infants too much when they are upset (but who are not harsh) and who set limits have infants who show significantly lower fear scores. Thus both nature and nurture play a role in how fearful an older child is. Many children with an inhibited disposition can learn, for the most part, not to act shyly, although subtle signs of their tendency to act inhibited in strange situations may still be observed.

polymorphism Different
versions of a gene.

At the molecular genetic level, a **polymorphism** (the technical way of referring to different versions of the gene) of the 5-HTTLPR has been identified in multiple studies as being associated with anxiety (Lesch et al., 1996; Miu et al., 2013; Schinka, Busch, and Robichaux-Keene, 2004). Arbelle and colleagues (2003) found that this polymorphism contributed about 7% of the variability in shyness among grade school children in their sample.

Introversion-Extraversion and Other Personality Traits

It has been suggested that introversion-extraversion may be the most genetically influenced of the personality traits. Introverts are defined as quiet, retiring, introspective, and not very socially active. Extraverts, on the other hand, are characterized as being outgoing, impulsive, and uninhibited, having many social contacts, and frequently taking part in group activities (Eysenck and Eysenck, 1964).

The best-known theory of introversion-extraversion relates this personality dimension to inherited differences in the functioning of the reticular activating system (RAS). This neurological activating system is located in various areas of the cortex and is responsible for an organism's level of arousal or degree of internal stimulation. Eysenck (1967) has suggested that under normal conditions introverts are more highly aroused than extraverts. Somewhat paradoxically, high arousal results in restraints or inhibited behavior because the cortex is exercising control over the more primitive brain centers (see Wilson, 1978). Extraverts on the other hand, being less normally aroused, are also subject to less cortical control.

Given this physiological conception, one might anticipate a high degree of heritability in this personality dimension; the twin studies support this belief. Several investigations have compared the similarity of MZ and DZ twins on self-report measures of extraversion (see Shields, 1976; Rose et al., 1988). These measures contain such items as:

- Do you often long for excitement?
- Are you mostly quiet when you are with people?
- Generally, do you prefer reading to meeting people?

Based on a review of over 25,000 pairs of twins, Henderson (1982) has concluded that the typical correlations between tests scores of MZ twins is about $r = .50$, while for DZ, the correlation is about $r = .20$. In one study, Shields (1976) found that identical twins separated from each other actually had slightly more similar scores on the extraversion scale than identical twins reared together, as if parents reacted to the twins or they reacted to each other in a manner that would enhance their differences.

Loehlin and Nichols (1976), making use of personality inventory responses, reported data that support the above conclusion. The subjects, twins who had taken the National Merit Scholarship Qualifying Test, were administered a variety of measures, including the California Psychological Inventory (CPI), which consists of eighteen different scales, some of which relate to the introversion-extraversion dimension. On virtually all of these scales the correlations of the scores for the MZ twins approximated $r = .50$; those for the DZ pairs were $r = .20 - .30$.

The dominant model of traits (see Chapter 9) suggests that there are five major traits, of which the extraversion dimension is one. The other four are agreeableness, conscientiousness, neuroticism, and openness to experience. Because of the importance of these traits, there have been many studies examining their heritability. In general, the five trait dimensions appear to have a heritability estimate in the range of .40 to .60 (see Table 1.2).

Altruism and Aggression

It already has been suggested that aggression and altruism are products of long evolutionary histories. Rushton et al. (1986) examined the heritability of these behaviors in a large study of twins. They mailed questionnaires to adult twin pairs assessing altruism, empathy, nurturance, aggression, and assertiveness. The altruism scale, for example, included

TABLE 1.2 The Heritibility Estimates for Five Personality Traits

Source	E	A	C	N	O
Loehlin, McCrae, and Costa (1998)	.57	.51	.52	.58	.56
Jang, McCrae, Angleitner, Riemann, and Livesley (1998)	.50	.48	49	.49	.48
Riemann, Angleitner, and Strelau (1997)	.60	.57	.71	.61	.81
Waller (1999)	.49	.33	.46	.42	.58
Johnson and Krueger (2004)	.49			.56	
Floderus-Myrhed, Pedersen, and Rasmuson (1979)	.60			.54	

items such as: "I have given directions to a stranger" and "I have donated blood." The findings are similar to those already presented in that the correlations for the MZ pairs were near $r = .50$, while for the DZ pairs the correlations approximate $r = .15$.

It appears from the research that many personality traits may have a genetic component. This same research, however, clearly shows that genes do not account for all variations in behavior and that environments also determine personality.

Heritability Estimates Depend on the Sample

One of the most important caveats when considering the genetic contribution to heritability of behavior is that the heritability estimate is based on the population from which the sample is drawn. Variability in the experiences of the population will lead to lower heritability estimates than populations that experience a more similar environment during development.

Let's use an example that may be familiar from grade school. If we take a bunch of different seeds for different types of corn and plant them, we are likely to get corn stalks of different height. If we take a single strain of seed corn that is nearly identical and plant those seeds, we would see less variability in the height of the corn stalks. Now, let's create a few different conditions for our thought experiment. In one condition, we mix up all the seeds, and then we plant them in a mix of good and bad soils, with variable exposure to light and rain, and some we give fertilizer, and some we do not. If we find variability in the height of the corn stalks, is it due to the seed (the genes)? Or is it due to the soil, water, and fertilizer (the environment)? We really do not know. In a different condition, we use our mixed-up seeds in the same soil, receiving the same water and fertilizer. Now, if we see a difference in the height, it is likely to be due to the difference in the seeds (the genes). We would see the greatest heritability estimate in the last case. One of the ironies of heritability estimates is that the environment changes the heritability estimate, with more uniform environments producing higher heritability estimates. After all, if the environment is the same, the only thing that will vary is the genes.

Interesting research revealing this point is work by Turkheimer and his colleagues (2003). From a large sample, they used MZ and DZ twins who had completed the Weschler Intelligence Scale for Children. The twins were also identified as coming from either low or high socioeconomic status (SES) backgrounds. Socioeconomic status reflects the wealth and prestige of one's family. In this research, for the low SES group the correlation for MZ twins was .68, and for DZ twins it was .63. The heritability estimate was .1, while the estimate for common environment was .58. For the high SES group, the correlation on intelligence for MZ twins was .87, and for DZ twins it was .51, giving a heritability estimate of .72 and a common environment estimate of .15. To use the metaphor from the beginning of the highlight, the wealthy children had good soil and fertilizer, so the genes determined the outcome. For the poorer children, the things that happened in their environment such as parental attention, good or bad nutrition, school quality, and so on, had a great impact on the observed intelligence scores. Thus, SES interacts with the gene. To add to the complexity, in countries in which access to health care and education is more uniform, the interaction goes away (Trucker-Dobbs and Bates, 2016). So, it appears that this interaction interacts with the nation in which the data were collected. If you remember nothing else, heritability estimates depend on the population from which they are drawn.

In addition to the heritability estimate depending on the sample, it is important to remember that the estimate is drawn from the full sample, and not from a single individual. It would be inappropriate to say that 72% of the intelligence for someone in the sample is due to genes. The heritability estimate does not apply to an individual.

Other Genetic Aspects of Personality and Behavior

Research on the genetics of behavior has become a vigorous and expanding area in recent years. There are now studies which have reported finding genetic aspects of how much television we watch (Plomin, Corley, De Fries, and Fulke, 1990), the likelihood of our getting divorced (McGue and Lykken, 1992), whether we believe in God or not (Tesser, 1993). There has even been a study that used twins and siblings, and found that a person's attitudes about exercise appear to have a genetic contribution in the .4 to .5 range (Huppertz et al., 2013).

Mental Illness and Social Problems

The twin studies of heritability of personality required the assignment of quantitative degrees of the trait under investigation to the individuals being compared. This quantitative trait score was derived from reports of others, self-reports, or actual observations of behavior. Examination of the genetic determination of mental illness and social problems, on the other hand, involves the assignment of individuals to a category, such as schizophrenic, alcoholic, criminal, and so on. Then the rates of **concordance** (both twins classified in the same category) and **discordance** (twins in different categories) are examined. The genetic hypothesis concerning social problems is corroborated when higher concordance rates are displayed as a function of biological relatedness.

concordance The rate at which pairs of individuals share a trait, status, or diagnosis.

discordance The rate at which pairs of individuals do not share a trait, status, or diagnosis.

The mental illness that has been most extensively investigated from a genetic perspective is schizophrenia. Gottesman (1993) has provided a summary of the nine studies comparing monozygotic and dizygotic twins. The mean concordance rate for monozygotic twins was 39%, while for dizygotic twins it was 10%. Gottesman suggests that estimates of the heritability of schizophrenia range from .42 to .63, with estimates for the effects of the environment ranging from .29 to .53.

In addition to twin studies, investigations utilizing entire families and adoption studies also support the genetic hypothesis. The logic of the family study approach is straightforward—if schizophrenia is an inherited disorder, relatives of schizophrenics should also exhibit a higher incidence of schizophrenia. Further, the closer the relative in terms of genetic relatedness, the higher should be the concordance rate. It has been estimated that the risk of schizophrenia for first-degree relatives (e.g., parents of a schizophrenic) is about 8% and about 2.5% for second-degree relatives (e.g., uncles and aunts), as compared to the general population base rate of 1%.

In addition, adoption studies reach the same conclusion. The adoption study design removes the possibility of post-natal environmental interaction between the adopted child and biological relatives. One study has shown that when children of a schizophrenic mother are raised by normal mothers, over 10% of the adoptees become schizophrenic (see Faraone and Tsuang, 1985; Plomin, 1989).

The data from another study (Cardno et al., 1999) indicates that of 49 MZ twin pairs in which one twin was diagnosed with schizophrenia, 20 of the co-twins were also diagnosed with schizophrenia, a concordance rate of 40.8%. For the DZ twins, the concordance rate was only 5.3%. Schizoaffective disorder showed an MZ concordance rate of 39.1%, while the concordance rate for DZ twins was 4.5%.

These findings have resulted in a search for the specific chromosome that may be carrying the schizophrenic gene. However, given that different types of schizophrenia have different concordance rates, the search for a single gene seems unlikely to be successful. In fact, it is generally believed (Gottesman, 1993) that schizophrenia involves more than one gene.

In a similar manner, manic-depressive psychoses and affective disorders appear to have a genetic component. Recent research has shown the same pattern of data as discussed for schizophrenia, although the strength of the genetic contribution is controversial (see Plomin, 1989).

In addition to mental illness, a variety of social problems, including criminality and alcoholism, have some biological bases. Data are quite clear that crime virtually everywhere and throughout history is a young man's pursuit. That is, in greatly diverse cultures, age and sex influence crime rates. There also is evidence that there are general sex differences in aggression that appear to be at least in part traced to biological factors (male sex hormones). In support of the biological approach, twin studies have revealed that identical twins are more similar in delinquency than are fraternal twins, independent of amount of shared activities. In addition, adoption studies have shown that boys with criminal biological parents and noncriminal adopting parents were more likely to have criminal records than those with noncriminal biological parents and criminal adopting parents (Chapter 18)! These studies do not demonstrate that there is a "criminal gene." Rather, other inherited traits such as temperament and intelligence are likely contributors to the tendency to commit criminal acts (Mednick, Brennan, and Kandel, 1989; Mednick, Moffitt, and Stack, 1987; Wilson and Herrnstein, 1985).

Finally, recall that the preference for alcohol differed greatly among strains of mice. Humans also apparently have inborn preferences or susceptibility to alcoholism, for investigations reveal a marked heritability of this problem. (Of course, preference for alcohol among rats and alcoholism among humans should not be considered identical phenomena.) It has long been recognized that alcoholism is a familial disorder in that rates of alcoholism are far higher among relatives of alcoholics than among the general population. Goodwin et al. (1973) even found that where children have been separated from their biological parents at birth or shortly thereafter, the presence of alcoholism in the biological parents is of far greater predictive significance for the development of this disorder in the children than is the presence of alcoholism among the adoptive parents. An offspring of an alcoholic parent is more likely to become an alcoholic even when raised by nonalcoholic foster parents than is an offspring of nonalcoholic parents when raised by alcoholic foster parents. In general, the data have revealed a threefold to fourfold increased risk for this disorder in sons and daughters of alcoholics, even when raised by nonalcoholic adoptive parents (see Schuckit, 1987). McGue (1999) estimates that there is a 50% to 60% genetic contribution toward alcoholism. At the molecular level, two candidate genes appear to be associated with metabolism of alcohol, and three other genes may also play a role (Edenberg and Foroud, 2013).

It is likely that what is inherited is only a predisposition in which social-cultural factors play a role in the manifestation of alcoholism. The relative roles of genetics and culture are exceedingly complex. For example, it has been suggested that the Chinese drink little because of a genetic propensity to become ill with alcohol intake. Clearly, then, the disentanglement of genetic from cultural factors cannot be readily resolved, and simple instances of a genetic or a cultural influence, on closer inspection, reveal contributions from the other source.

The Nonshared Environment Effect

One of the most startling findings to come out of recent genetic research is the suggestion that the shared environments that siblings grow up in may have very little effect on their personalities (Rowe, 1994). That is, two genetically different siblings growing up in the same family will be no more alike in personality than if they had grown up in different families. This conclusion is based on a variety of researchers' finding of very low correlations between siblings on measures of various personality traits (Loehlin, 1989; Plomin, Chipuer, and Loehlin, 1990; Reiss, 1993).

Low correlations mean that although siblings may share the same family in a general, physical sense, their psychological environments may nonetheless be different. Interest is now shifting to an examination of the impact of nonshared environments on personality. Both Plomin et al. (1990) and Reiss (1993) have suggested that family dynamics play a role. One child is not treated the same as another child, and relationships among siblings vary. In addition, other aspects of the child's environment, such as relationships with peers outside the home or with teachers, probably differ among siblings brought up in the same home.

Molecular Genetics

One of the most exciting recent developments has been the ability to scan the entire genome to find polymorphisms that may be associated with characteristics and behavior. The success of this enterprise has been mixed, however. As researchers find correlations between genes and personality, there has often been a failure to replicate the finding. One researcher will find the effect, and then another, or even the same research group, will be unable to find the same effect. Another problem with this approach has been termed "the chopsticks gene" (Hamer and Sirota, 2000), where the cultural effect of eating with a particular utensil is correlated with a gene. With these caveats in mind, there is interesting research investigating polymorphisms and personality.

Genome Wide Association Studies (GWAS) scan the entire genome to identify candidate loci that are correlated with a measured aspect of personality. The researchers use one sample to scan for the association between genes and behavior and then use another sample to replicate the finding. Commercial sites like 23andMe.com and Ancestry.com allow people to investigate aspects of their own DNA. A person can send in DNA samples by swabbing the inside of his or her own cheek. Researchers have used some of these databases along with purely research-based databases to have access to really large samples of different people's DNA. Of course, they can only investigate the aspects of personality that happened to be reported at the same time that people submit their request for their analysis.

As indicated earlier in the chapter, most traits will be based on several polymorphisms (Chabris, Lee, Cesarini, Benjamin, and Laibson, 2015), not just a single one. Using GWAS, Reitveld and colleagues (2016) identified three candidate single nucleotide polymorphisms (SNP) that were associated with years of schooling. The discovery sample was based on over 95,000 people. They then used replication samples of over 23,000, 3,000, and 6,000 people. Importantly, the results replicated. These three SNPs together seem to account for 2% to 4% of the variance in years of education.

Criticisms of Genetic Views of Personality

Few would now debate that genetics play a role in personality development. What is debated, however, is the question of how much of a role and how that role is played. Findings that genetics contribute to divorce, belief in God, television watching, and the like would suggest that large proportions of our lives are genetically influenced.

However, this issue is more complex than it seems. First, there is no gene for television watching (how would it have manifested itself 100 years ago?). Further, two to three centuries ago in western Europe divorce was much more uncommon than it is today. It is likely that if genetic studies had been done on divorce at that time no effects would have been detected because divorce was such a rarity. While genetic causes for behaviors such as television watching and divorce can be found, it is likely that such behaviors are actually mediated by other genetic factors such as personality (McGue and Lykken, 1992). It is clear that there is a genetic influence, but what does "influence" even mean (Turkheimer, 2016)? The attempts at finding the exact genes leading to a particular trait have been met with failures to replicate or account for exceedingly low amounts of the variance.

A number of writers have criticized the concept of heritability, the idea that one can give a percent figure to the degree to which a trait is inherited. Bronfrenbenner and Ceci

(1993) have pointed out that the degree of heritability of a trait depends on the environment, and others have noted that an estimate of heritability from a given research study holds only for the sample of subjects studied in that investigation. One cannot generalize heritability estimates for the whole population. Others have pointed out that genetically oriented researchers do not adequately measure the environment in their studies and so are not really able to assess the impact of the environment. This has led to the possibility that heritability estimates of various traits are inflated. For instance, in adoption studies twins are separated at birth and adopted by different families. To estimate the heritability of a trait, such as television watching, one then correlates the degree of television watching in each adopted twin. However, twins are typically adopted into families of similar social class that are likely to provide similar environments. While this similarity might not affect the finding that television watching has a genetic component, it might inflate the magnitude of the heritability estimate.

Summary

1. A characteristic or a predisposition can be both inherited and modified by environmental factors and experience.
2. The genome is made of 23 chromosomes, and unrelated humans are 99.5% genetically similar to each other.
3. *Instinct* has two meanings: (a) an unlearned, fixed pattern of activity such as nest building in birds, and (b) an inner "want" or "urge."
4. *Evolutionary psychology* seeks to establish that complex social behavior has a biological or genetic basis.
5. Some facial expressions appear to be universal. This observation supports the Darwinian belief that expressions are inherited behaviors.
6. *Selective breeding* experiments have demonstrated that specific abilities such as maze learning and traits such as emotionality have genetic components. The

offspring in such studies tend to behave similarly to their parents.
7. Twin and adoption research has demonstrated that temperament and personality traits have genetic components.
8. Studies have demonstrated a genetic basis for mental illnesses like schizophrenia and for social problems like criminality and alcoholism.
9. Molecular genetics has shown the relationship between gene loci and some aspects of personality. However, the variance has been rather small.
10. The nonshared environment effect, that siblings growing up in the same family environment appear to have little in common in terms of their personalities, suggests that siblings may actually experience different environments within the same family.

Key Terms

balancing selection (p. 12)
concordance (p. 20)
directional selection (p. 12)
discordance (p. 20)
dizygotic twins (p. 15)
genome (p. 4)
heritability (p. 12)
instinct (p. 5)

monozygotic twins (p. 15)
ovulatory shift (p. 9)
phenotype (p. 16)
polymorphism (p. 18)
selective breeding (p. 12)
sociometer (p. 10)
species-spacing (p. 5)
temperament (p. 17)

Thought Questions

1. Can you think of any apparently instinctive patterns of behavior in pets you have observed? Do you think you can read their emotions?
2. Why might women pursue different reproductive strategies at different points in their ovulatory cycle?
3. Why can't heritability estimates be applied to the individual?
4. If the genes are discovered for shyness, would parents consider genetic engineering to change those genes?

Contextual Aspects of Personality and Behavior

CHAPTER 2

Source: Odua Images/Shutterstock.com

Chapter Outline

The Person and Situation
The Social World
The Physical World

In Chapter 1 we contended that personality structure and behavior are determined in part by a long evolutionary history that predisposes individuals to act in certain ways. People come into the world with genetic givens that influence who and what they are and what they become.

In this chapter we examine the same questions from a totally different perspective: how aspects of the environment influence us. These determinants of behavior, which are not genetically transmitted, are part of the impinging physical, social, and cultural milieu. Human beings are versatile in their patterns of adaptation to a variety of physical and social conditions: they dwell in hot or cold climates; they have contrasting social roles; they are brought up in cultures with widely disparate customs and mores. All of these factors produce different modes of behavior. Indeed, it has been said that humans have no nature, only history. It should come as no surprise that environmental conditions influence personality. We know, for example, that even in the plant world such environmental conditions as the composition of soil and amount of rainfall have a significant effect on the characteristics of a plant's root system and leaf structure. In the human world, we may surely expect an even more significant influence from the environment.

In this chapter we examine how personality interacts with a person's situation, at the small scale, then the influence of culture, and then finally the influence of the natural and built environment.

The Person and Situation

Behavior is a function of both the person and the situation (Lewin, 1936). Although this text is primarily concerned with the personality aspect of that formula, as psychologists, we are interested in behavior and need to understand the ways that situation and personality interact. The "situation" can vary from the micro to the macro. The situation can vary from a dorm room to cafeteria to family to country to culture. The interaction of behavior, personality, and situation is truly an interaction. They influence each other. A personality can change a situation. A situation may demand particular behavior. Personality may influence the situations a person selects.

An important critique by Walter Mischel in 1968 pointed out that personality psychology was not considering the situation. Consequently, personality psychology was doing a rather poor job of predicting behavior because of the neglect of the situation and the ways in which people interpret the situation. This critique caused personality psychologists to take a close look at their methods and the ways they approached the topic. Mischel's critique laid a foundation for improvement of personality psychology as a science.

One of the ways we would want to consider the interaction of the person and situation is in terms of the *strength of the situation*. Situations vary in the demands for particular behaviors (Price and Bouffard, 1974). Strong situations demand near uniformity in behavior. Think of a courtroom or a religious service. Weak situations allow for a variety of behaviors. In a park, people can do many different things. In a private dorm room, people can do even more things. We would expect that personality would be a better predictor of behavior in weak situations, whereas the situation would be a better predictor of behavior in strong situations. A review by Cooper and Withey (2009) suggests that this is true under some circumstances, but it does appear that the situation and personality interact. As they point out, some aspects of personality can be revealed only in the strong situation. After all, one can be brave only in a situation in which nearly everyone else is afraid.

self-monitoring The degree to which individuals regulate their social behavior in order to make a particular social impression.

Another way in which we can consider the interaction of personality and situation is via a meta-trait called **self-monitoring** (Snyder, 1974). Self-monitoring is an individual difference through which people who are high self-monitors evaluate a situation to determine the appropriate behaviors. People who are low in self-monitoring use their own traits to guide their behaviors. Thus, for high self-monitors, the situation is the best predictor of behavior, whereas for low self-monitors, personality is the best predictor of behavior (Snyder, 1987). This topic is discussed in more depth in Chapter 10.

situational selection The environments and situations people choose to fit their personalities.

Personality and situations will interact in terms of the situations people choose. This is called **situational selection**. We are more likely to find an introvert in the library on a Friday night than an extravert. People who like exciting things are more likely to become firefighters and skydivers (Roberti, 2004; Zalesky, 1984).

Situations are likely to have dimensions, just as personality has dimensions. Rauthman and colleagues (2014) have suggested that situations have eight dimensions. They identify situations as having dimensions of duty, intellect, adversity, mating options, positivity, negativity, deception, and sociality, which they call DIAMONDS. To clarify a few of the dimensions, duty means that a job needs to be done. Intellect means that a situation provides an opportunity to demonstrate intelligence. Mating means that potential romantic partners are present. Situations will vary in the amount each of these dimensions is present or noticeable. For example, a party will have some of these dimensions present to a high degree while other dimensions are quite low. A scientific symposium will probably have some quite different dimensions apparent. By describing these dimensions, the researchers hope to provide a basis by which the person and situation interaction can better be explored.

The person-situation debate dominated personality psychology for nearly 40 years, but in many ways, the debate has come to a close. The situation is often the best predictor of immediate behavior, but personality is the better predictor of trends of behavior across time and multiple situations (Fleeson, 2004).

The Social World

The physical world of climate, terrain, material structures, and space provides the background for diverse cultures, customs, social structures, and roles. We will treat the social world as if it were independent of the physical world, but in fact the two are as intimately connected as nature and nurture. The structure of a society and its cultural traditions exert powerful influences on the personalities of individuals born into it. Social groups and cultures may live in similar physical settings but display quite different behaviors.

The influence of the social world is especially impressive when one considers that the members of quite different social groups can still be quite similar biologically. The infant born into a preliterate New Guinea tribe and the infant born to a sophisticated Parisian family are genetically more alike than different. Indeed, unrelated individuals share more than 99% of their genes. After all, all humans have two eyes, one nose, a mouth, and so on. Hence, it remains clear that genetic differences between groups are minor compared with the wide range of behaviors exhibited between social classes and cultures. It is primarily social, not biological, factors that cause members of a social group to behave uniquely.

Because of our flexibility, because humans are adjustable and changeable, the disparate norms and values of a society can be transmitted to and accepted by succeeding generations, ensuring the survival of the culture. Each generation must learn to function within the confines and according to the rules of a given society and social group. Our families, peers, schools, churches, and mass media are among the social agents and institutions that determine who and what we are, or our socialization. Some of these influences will be examined in later sections of the text where we analyze personality development and specific behavioral patterns. For the present, we again choose an illustrative topic, social class, and consider the relation between this key social variable and personality to demonstrate the binding of the individual and the social world.

Social Class

All societies are to some extent stratified. Social stratification is a relatively stable, hierarchical arrangement of groups of individuals, with the "higher" classes within this hierarchy receiving more social and material rewards than the "lower" classes. Individuals within a class typically perform similar occupations and face the same life conditions and problems. As a result, individuals can be assigned to a social class by using indexes such as education, occupation, income, and prestige. All of these class indicators are intertwined, for education provides access to job opportunities, while jobs, in turn, bring increased income, prestige, and power.

The concepts of social class and social status are so complex that some scholars even differentiate between the two, contending that class has implications for one's *chances* in life, while status has implications for one's *style* of life. Here we will not differentiate between the terms, but assume that assignment to a particular class may reveal place of residence, type of job, level of property ownership, amount of education, friends' social status, and related attributes. Class is also associated with such personal characteristics as values, mode of dress, and even style of speech. Because of the pervasive influence of class membership, knowledge of just this variable can reveal much about an individual's personality. Disparate social classes also expose children to different methods of child rearing, which influence a variety of personality traits.

Although social class membership can be a revealing indicator of a person's life style, speech patterns, and even certain personality attributes, one must keep in mind two cautions when interpreting social-class differences in abilities and behavior:

1. In essentially all instances in which social class differences have been demonstrated, there is a great deal of variation between individuals within a particular social class. For example, lower-class children typically obtain, on the average, lower scores on intelligence tests than middle-class children (Hart, Petrill, Deckard, and Thompson, 2007; Scan and Carter-Saltzman, 1985). However, there are wide differences in

intelligence test scores *within* each social class, so that many lower-class children will obtain higher scores than many middle-class children.

2. Style and personality differences that have been observed between lower-and middle-class individuals are not fixed forever. As the challenges that face different social groups change, and as people change from one social class to another, their life styles, language, and even personality attributes will change also.

Middle versus Working Class

There are many contrasts between and implications of middle- and working-class membership in the United States. The upper middle class is made up of well-paid, often university-educated professionals like doctors, lawyers, and upper management. The middle class includes people like teachers, nurses, electricians, and plumbers (Gilbert, 2015). The middle class often earns income sufficient to permit savings and has both advanced education and marketable skills. Its members have what is called a conceptual orientation (Miller and Swanson, 1960), using their mental capacities to solve problems, with their jobs often involving the manipulation of symbols rather than objects. Their working life focus is on occupational advancement and competent performance, and their jobs are often quite specialized and responsible.

The working class includes many retail workers, along with unskilled office and factory workers (Gilbert, 2015). Members of the working class typically have more serious financial concerns and not enough salary to permit savings. They are more likely to have on-the-job training than a formal education. Their orientation toward life is considered to be *motoric*, in that they manipulate objects rather than symbols.

It might be expected that the varied and subtle effects of social class would be evident in the self-concept and self-esteem of the members of the disparate classes; those in the upper classes would be expected to have higher self-esteem than those in the lower classes. However, the relation between social class and sense of self-worth is complex and determined by a multiplicity of factors.

One determinant of a person's sense of self-worth is comparison with others. Children are likely to believe that their external environment is homogeneous and that others are like themselves. On the other hand, adults recognize the differentiations within the larger social environment. Consistent with this fact, among children there is virtually no relation between class and self-esteem, whereas among adults those of the higher classes at times score higher in sense of self-worth than those of the lower classes (Rosenberg and Pearlin, 1978; Twenge and Campbell, 2002). However, it also has been reported that *within* groups of men with either a high school education or a college education, the self-esteem of successful groups is higher than the self-esteem of unsuccessful groups.

Interestingly, being a member of a stigmatized group usually does not result in a decrease in self-esteem (Crocker and Major, 1989). Those of lower class may ascribe their relative failure in life to barriers imposed by others, thus maintaining their own self-worth. Or they may tend to devalue material gains and value other characteristics that they do possess, such as friends.

Finally, changing economic status at various points in life might affect feelings toward oneself, adding still further complexity to any simple relation between class and psychological variables. For example, it has been reported that mother's background status, status at a child's birth, and status before the child is in school all contribute to the child's performance and behavior at age five (Furstenberg, Brooks-Gunn, and Morgan, 1987).

Culture

Personality differences between nations and ethnic groups are popularly recognized; there are stereotypes that the people within a particular group or nation are believed to follow. These differences are ascribed to disparities in **culture**: the modes of acting and feeling, or the set of norms and ideals, that are customary for an entire group. Culture therefore involves consistency in the actions of a larger number of people than does social class.

culture The modes of acting and feeling, or the set of norms and ideals, that are customary for an entire group.

Not all customs that distinguish one culture from another are equally relevant to personality. The fact that it is taboo in some cultures to eat pork while in other cultures it is taboo to eat beef is probably not germane to personality. It is also important to recognize that there is much more variability in personality than in social customs in any society. Consequently, one finds that only on the average are people in one culture more aggressive, ambitious, courageous, or conforming than people in another culture. When such common attributes are found, one can speak of a "national character type," recognizing that there are many individuals within that culture who may not conform to that type.

In certain instances the description of the resources or practices of a culture virtually ensures that there will be personality and behavioral differences between cultural groups. Indeed, our own observations and experience suggest that people in different cultures appear to be dissimilar in certain essential ways. Crossing borders in Europe, one is met with differences in people, from the laconic Finn to the loquacious Italian. Clearly, an individual's character is determined by time and place of appearance in history. Let us now briefly consider some examples of cultural differences pertinent to personality that have been documented from the study of psychopathology.

Cultures that honor age, like Ghana, do not show a worsening of some mental illnesses due to age.

Psychopathology

Symptoms of mental disorder vary greatly, depending on the cultural context of the disturbed individual. For example, the hysterical symptoms that were so frequent in Vienna at the time of Freud, and so central in the development of Freudian theory, are now rarely in evidence. Similarly, the incidence of manic-depressive psychoses has greatly decreased in America, but not in England. Although care must be taken in all such comparisons because diagnoses are also subject to change, it is quite clear that there are different rates of mental illness between cultures over time.

Mental disorders may vary between cultures because different cultures give rise to different types of conflict and stress. For example, Weisz and his colleagues (1987) reported that in Thailand, in which children's aggression and other uncontrolled behaviors are severely disapproved, overcontrolled behavioral problems (e.g., fear, worry, nervous movements) are particularly frequent in children. It appears that the traditional emphasis on quietness and inhibition, and the concomitant child-rearing practices, foster the development of problems regarding overcontrol.

In addition, disparate cultural values may result in disparate pathologies. For example, the aged in Ghana have secure positions within the family and are not relegated to a lower status as they grow old. This is not the case in our culture. Thus, in Ghana the tendency toward mental illness is not made worse by aging, while in our culture the aged exhibit a variety of specifically age-related disturbances such as depression.

In sum, cultural differences in psychopathology illustrate the impact of culture on personality.

Culture and the Study of Personality

It is important to consider how culture influences the study of psychology itself. Smith and Bond (1993) have reviewed attempts to replicate important research findings across cultures. They note that many of the "classic" findings of American psychology do not replicate in other cultures. For instance, in the United States, when individuals work together in groups, a phenomenon called *social loafing* occurs; that is, individuals exert less effort than they do when they work alone. However, this is not found in Taiwan (Gabrenya et al., 1985) or China (Early, 1989). In these cultures individuals work *harder* when they are in groups.

In recent years a rising chorus of voices has been arguing that many of our ideas about personality are based on a view of the individual that is largely a product of Western

"Know thy self" was inscribed on a temple in Delphi, Greece. The emphasis on the self has been present in Western culture for millennia.

culture. Furthermore, it is a view that is more reflective of masculine rather than feminine experience. Finally, it has been argued that these cultural biases have also influenced our models of research.

In particular, critics have focused on the Western view of the self and of the individual. Landrine (1992) has noted that in Western culture an unequivocal distinction is drawn between the self on the one hand and the nonself on the other. Our Western view of the self tends to treat it as a ghostly entity inside which has, or should have, absolute power to regulate the individual. The self is thus separate, encapsulated, and godlike, in that it is presumed to be the "originator, creator, and controller of behavior" (p. 402). Such a view of the self puts an enormous emphasis on mastery and control, and healthy individuals are seen as exercising self-control as well as control of any situations they are in.

This self is also seen as having its own stable identity that it maintains independent of the contexts it is in. Therefore, it has a structure consisting of traits which are themselves free of contexts. Such a self can be described without reference to other people or to the situations it is in. Such a self can also be reflected on, and Western culture places a high value on abstract self-reflection. Thus there is a premium on ideas such as self-awareness, self-criticism, self-consciousness, self-actualization, self-fulfillment, and self-determination. Finally, this self also puts a premium on rationality (Triandis, 1989).

This view of the self is not only a Western one but is also based more on masculine than on feminine experience (Jordan et al., 1991). It goes hand in hand with a stance that leads to the kind of research model that emphasizes distance, objectivity, the study of relatively static objects, and control. In contrast, Gilligan, Brown, and Rogers (1990) argue for a research model that stresses connection, receptivity, understanding, and the flow of interaction over time. In particular they stress the importance of researchers hearing the "voice" of the people they are studying, reflecting the idea that researchers and subjects are more interconnected than our typical models of research assume.

In a recent study of the development of adolescent girls, Brown and Gilligan (1992) repeatedly interviewed girls in a private school over several years. Initially, they tried to follow a formal, rigid interview format, so that they would maintain "objectivity," so that the data-collecting conditions would be the same for all subjects, and so that interviewers could not bias the results by leading subjects in one direction or the other. However, they discovered that they introduced a different kind of bias. By following a formal interview format, they created an inauthentic relationship with the girls, who then did not open up in the ways Brown and Gilligan wanted. Once the interviewers stopped worrying about objectivity and related to the girls in more informal ways, they were better able to hear the voices of the girls, and to obtain data more truly reflective of the girls' experiences.

The Western, masculine view of the self as separate, encapsulated, bounded, existing free of contexts, and controlled from within, is a view of the self not shared by the majority of cultures in the world. In contrast, most cultures hold an interconnected view of the self. This view sees the self as fundamentally interdependent and as existing within a field of forces. Markus and Kitayama (1991) note that the "interdependent view is normative in most cultures . . . seeing oneself as part of an-encompassing social relationship and recognizing that one's behavior is determined, contingent on, and, to a large extent organized by what the actor perceives to be the thoughts, feelings, and actions of others in the relationship . . . the view of the self and the relationship between the self and others features the person not as separate from the social context but as more connected and less differentiated from others" (p. 227). This view of the self is more characteristic of the African-American (Stevenson, 1993), Hispanic-American (Ramirez, 1991), and Asian-American cultural experiences (Markus and Kitayama, 1991) as well as the experiences of many others, including Native Americans (Markus and Kitayama, 1991).

In Japan, for instance, the word for the self—*jibun*—refers to an individual's share of the shared life space rather than to a substance or attribute with a constant oneness. The self is not a constant, like the ego, but rather a fluid concept which changes as a function of the person's interpersonal relationships (Markus and Kitayama, 1991). To quote Markus and Kitayama, "the Japanese nightmare is exclusion, meaning that one is failing at the non-native goal of connecting with others. This is in sharp contrast to the American nightmare, which is to fail at separating from others, as can occur when one is unduly influenced by others, or does not stand up for what one believes, or when one goes unnoticed or undistinguished" (p. 228).

An implication of the interdependent view of the self for personality theory is that many of our Western concepts, such as the idea of enduring individual traits, motives, and desires, are revealed to reflect our Western, individualistic view of the self. Landrine (1992) notes that the sociocentric self found in most cultures "has no enduring, trans-situational characteristics, no traits or desires or needs of its own in isolation from its relationships and contexts." Further, self-reflection is not necessarily valued, especially since in some cultures the self is an illusion. In reply to a comment such as "Tell me something about yourself," a person from an interdependent culture would not be likely to give an abstract self-description in terms of personality traits and enduring likes and motivations (for example, "I'm outgoing, I like sports, I'm a high achiever."). Rather, they would be likely to give several long, detailed, concrete descriptions of their interactions with others (for example, "The other day a friend of mine and I were arguing and I lost my temper . . ."). In the process, they might be seen by a Western psychologist as "lacking insight."

Another implication of this discussion for personality theory is that our Western view biases us to see certain kinds of personality traits as more healthy than others. Pederson (1987) has noted that we tend to view independence as more valuable than dependency. Many of our concepts of psychopathology, such as that of co-dependence, revolve around ideas of being excessively dependent, or enmeshed, with others. Yet what a Western therapist sees as excessive dependency would be seen as both healthy and absolutely necessary in many cultures. In a similar manner, Ramirez (1983, 1991) has criticized the idea that those whose perceptions are heavily influenced by their context ("field dependence," Witkin and Goodenough, 1981) are "less than" those whose separate their perceptions and judgments out from the context ("field independence"). He has suggested that field dependence is more appropriately thought of as "field sensitivity" and has argued that as a "cognitive style" field sensitivity is more characteristic of non-Western cultures.

Triandis (1989) has studied the differences between cultures that hold **individualistic** notions about the self and cultures that hold interdependent or "*collectivist*" notions. In the West, selves have personal names, while in **collectivistic** cultures they are often referred to relationally (for example, mother of X). Individualistic cultures see the self in terms of what it *owns*—its possessions, its own experiences, its accomplishments—while in collectivist cultures identity is defined in terms of relationships. In individualistic cultures, to be distinct and different is highly valued. In contrast, in collectivist cultures people try to conform to others in public settings, for instance, ordering the same food at a restaurant.

individualistic A culture that focus on the unique and independent aspects of the self and members of a group.

collectivistic A cultural focus on sociability, family, and the importance of in-groups.

Two studies point out the differences. In one study, G. V. Mann, Mann, Otero-Sabogal, Sabogal, and Perez-Stable (1987, as referenced in Triandis, 1989) studied individuals' responses to the question of why they should not smoke. Hispanics (from a collectivistic culture) in the United States gave answers emphasizing concern for others, including the negative effects of cigarette smoke and setting a bad example for children. The individualistic sample was more concerned with the effects of smoking on their own physiology.

In a second study of the differences between individualistic and collectivistic cultures, Stipek, Weiner, and Li (1989) asked Chinese and American subjects to describe situations in which they got angry. Americans described situations in which something negative had happened to them personally, while Chinese subjects described situations in which something had happened to others.

Triandis points out that the kind of self valued by a culture depends on its ecology. As cultures become more complex and more affluent, they tend to become more individualistic.

However, the more complex the culture, the more confused the individual's identity is likely to be. Other variables that affect whether a culture is individualistic or collectivistic are the degree of population and whether the culture is agricultural or industrialized. Densely populated cultures and agricultural cultures are more likely to be collectivistic in their view of the self.

There is a difference between the culture and the people within a culture (Triandis, 2002). A culture may be individualistic, but that does not mean every person in that culture is that way. It is important to differentiate the culture (individualistic versus collectivistic) from the person (**ideocentric** versus **allocentric**). People who are ideocentric focus on uniqueness, self-reliance, and competition. People who are allocentric focus on sociability, family, and the importance of in-groups. As expected, however, people tend to fit their culture, with about 60% of people in collectivistic cultures being allocentric, and about 60% of the people in individualistic cultures being ideocentric (Triandis, et al, 2001).

In sum, the separate, encapsulated, individualistic self of Western culture is not representative of the self of most other cultures, which emphasize a relational, interdependent view. Many of our notions about personality, such as the idea that individuals' behavior primarily reflects individual personality traits that exist independent of situations, or that internal self-control is good, may reflect certain cultural biases. The kind of self a culture values appears to be a function of the ecological nature of that culture.

ideocentric A person's focus on individuality, independence, and uniqueness, as opposed to sociability, family, and the importance of in-groups. This is at the individual level, not the cultural level.

allocentric A person's focus on sociability, family, and the importance of in-groups, as opposed to individuality, independence, and uniqueness. This is at the individual level, not the cultural level.

Cultural Demands and Mental Health

Not only have critics pointed out that psychology's ideas about self and personality may be culturally biased, but also have a number of critics argued that our culture's emphasis on individualism is the source of some of our mental health problems. Baumeister (1993) argues that in our individualistic culture the self has taken over as the major source of meaning, as other sources of meaning (such as religion and family) have declined. In accord with this, Seligman (1990) has argued that our society has moved toward a value of the "maximal self." The self has come to be the repository of all our hopes. No longer do larger institutions such as family, subgroup, religion, or nation provide a context of meaning for individuals. Now, all meaning must come from the self. Seligman argues that this is too great a burden to place on individual selves, and he blames the recent rise in depression in the United States on this overemphasis on the individual self.

Some studies have looked at questionnaires that ask whether individuals hold more individualistic or more collectivistic values, and they have found that higher individualism scores correlate with higher (more pathological) scores on the Minnesota Multiphasic Personality Inventory (Johnson and Norem-Hebeisen, 1977; Norem-Hebeisen and Johnson, 1981). On the other hand, Waterman (1981) found that individuals who scored highly on a scale of traditional Western measures of psychological health and development, such as identity achievement, Kohlberg's morality scale, and internal locus of control (all associated with the Western individualistic emphasis on a firm, autonomous, self-chosen identity and set of values), were also rated as more cooperative and altruistic.

Cultures make demands about how we manage our emotions. Some cultures allow displays of nearly all emotions, whereas other cultures limit those displays. Cultures may allow some emotions for one gender while not allowing it for another gender. In Western cultures, it is often expected that "boys don't cry" while women are not allowed to show anger. Control of those emotions is accomplished via emotion regulation. Among the ways in which emotion may regulated is reappraisal (which has the individual reframe his or her experience and perception of the situation or emotion) or suppression (controlling the expression of the emotion). Matsumoto and colleagues (2008) predicted that cultural differences would tend to lead to more reappraisal or suppression of emotion. They did find that more egalitarian countries tended to use emotion suppression more and countries that valued people being able to express their own emotions tended to use suppression less. At the country level, suppression is negatively correlated with happiness (Matsumoto et al., 2008). Interestingly, the rates at which countries use suppression is negatively correlated with depression, anxiety disorders, and alcohol use. So people are less happy but also less depressed and anxious in countries that tend to suppress expression of emotion.

No matter what the outcome of the debate over the nature of the self, and whether one view of the self is healthier than another view, current challenges to our traditional Western perspective should lead to a broader and more comprehensive view of personality.

The Physical World

The ultimate situation in which we find ourselves is the physical world. It is convenient to distinguish between two aspects of the physical world: (1) the natural environment, including the climate, availability of resources, existence of nearby bodies of water, and similar factors; and (2) constructed environments such as offices, homes, and hospitals (Altman, 1976).

The Natural Environment

The natural environment makes demands, sets constraints, and provides resources. In short, it has a great deal to do with how we live our lives and thus tends to affect personality greatly. For example, families in extremely cold climates are more likely to sleep in one bed. This sleeping pattern could influence the closeness of the family, sexual attitudes, and related aspects of personality development. Individuals typically are not consciously aware of the importance of physical factors as determinants of personality. Thus, both the natural environment and the biological givens discussed in Chapter 1 exert their effect often without the immediate knowledge of those affected.

Climate, Subsistence, and Settlement Patterns

Cross-cultural investigations of the influence of climate on personality nicely illustrate the interlocking of the physical and social worlds. Climate is just one example among many (e.g., physical resources, topography, amount of daylight, ionization of the atmosphere) we could have selected to demonstrate personality's broad environmental context. Climate is particularly appropriate for discussion, however, because its effects on personality and behavior have been clearly documented.

Berry (1976) has shown that one manner in which climate affects personality is through the causal chain of climate → settlement pattern → individuals' personalities. Anthropologists have identified four settlement patterns of societies: fully nomadic (move continuously); seminomadic (move regularly but occupy a fixed settlement for a season); semi sedentary (move regularly but less often); and fully sedentary (occupy one settlement for a long period of time). These patterns of adaptation are directly related to the manner in which the society subsists. Societies that live by hunting and gathering are semi- or fully nomadic; agricultural societies are semi- or fully sedentary.

Two climatic variables influence both the means of subsistence and the settlement pattern within a society: the average temperature and the amount of rainfall. The temperature level and amount of rain permit organisms to satisfy their subsistence and shelter needs in diverse ways. In the case of both low rainfall and low temperature, as in polar regions, agriculture is impossible. Hence, the means of satisfying basic nutritional needs are hunting and/or fishing, activities that typically require a nomadic existence. Given low rainfall but high temperature, as in desert regions, neither agriculture nor fishing is possible, but hunger can be satisfied by hunting and gathering; this, too, requires mobility. Given high rainfall, however, agricultural activities are possible for the satisfaction of basic needs.

In sum, the natural environmental factors of temperature and rainfall influence the manner in which food needs are met and, in turn, influence patterns of settlement. Furthermore, these disparate methods of need satisfaction require different personality types in order for the society to survive. In agricultural societies, according to Barry, Child, and Bacon (1959, p. 52):

> Carelessness in performance of routine duties leads to a threat of hunger, not for the day of carelessness itself but for many months to come. Individual initiative attempts to improve techniques may be feared because no one can tell immediately whether the changes will lead to a greater harvest or to a disastrous failure. Under those conditions, there might well be a

Source: siribao/Shutterstock

Climate will affect the way food is gathered, which in turn may affect personality.

premium on obedience to the older and wiser, and on responsibility in faithful performance to the routine laid down by custom for one's economic role.

Furthermore, "growing and harvesting crops on a large scale requires teamwork, and rigid organization may be needed to mobilize and direct the people's efforts toward the common goal of an abundant harvest" (Pelto, 1968, p. 40). On the other hand (Barry, Child, and Bacon, 1959, p. 52):

> At an opposite extreme is subsistence through hunting or fishing with no means for extended storing of catch. Here individual initiative and development of high skill seem to be at a premium. Where each day's food comes from that day's catch, variations in the energy and skill exerted in food-getting lead to immediate reward or punishment.

To summarize, societies must cope with disparate environmental demands and may require disparate personality types in order to be successful. Agricultural societies need to bring up children to be reliable and obedient, whereas hunting societies require that their members be self-reliant and autonomous. The research indicates that societies do indeed tend to beget appropriate personalities.

socialization The process of developing the motivations and behaviors that are appropriate in one's culture.

The research (Berry, 1976) suggests relationships among the natural environment, means of need satisfaction, food accumulation, settlement pattern, and **socialization** practices. Although it seems farfetched and requires an understanding of many mediating variables, it is not entirely incorrect to say that personality is influenced by the culture, which is influenced by the amount of rainfall! In one investigation (Berry, 1967), individuals from high and low food-accumulating cultures (respectively, the Temne and Eskimo peoples) were tested for conformity in a controlled laboratory setting. The participants were asked to match the length of various lines and in one condition were given false information about others' responses. It was found that only the Temne (high food accumulators) tended to agree with the alleged responses of others, regardless of the information's correctness. Of course, there may be many interpretations of the observed differences in conformity.

Another theory that relates forms of agriculture to personality is laid out by Nisbett (1993). Different forms of agriculture and mercantile culture develop in different locations. Some people plant and harvest crops. Other people herd animals. He suggests that cultural norms will develop differently if it is easy to steal another person's wealth. It is difficult to steal a field, but relatively easy to steal some cattle or sheep. "Their livelihoods can be lost in an instant through the theft of their herds" (Nisbett, 1993, p. 442). Because of this, a culture of honor develops that requires extreme reactions, to the point of murder, to any threat to a person's honor. A person living in that culture needs to make it clear that he is not one to be trifled with so that people would be afraid to steal his property.

Even though the conditions that gave rise to that aspect of the culture may be gone, the tradition of protecting one's honor is still maintained (Cohen and Nisbett, 1994). They suggest that a difference in a culture of honor exists between the northern United States and southern and western United States based on who settled the lands, and the type of agriculture in their previous cultures. In a study conducted at the University of Michigan, participants were insulted by someone working for the researchers. Compared to participants raised in the American north, participants who were raised in the American south reacted by acting more aggressively afterward and showed greater physiological reactions related to stress and aggression (Cohen, Nisbett, Bowdle, and Schwarz, 1996).

Climate and Aggression

We are all familiar with the stereotype that individuals living in a warm climate are much more impulsive and tempestuous than persons living in a cold climate. The phrase *hot-tempered* illustrates this common association between heat and anger. Similarly, tempers are said to "flare" when we fight; we get "hot under the collar" when frustrated; and we might do a "slow burn" when angered. Thus, anger and aggression are often depicted with a heat metaphor.

A great deal of psychological research has explored whether there is a relationship between environmental temperature and aggression. Some studies examine differences in aggressive crime rates as a function of differences in temperatures of geographic regions. Other studies consider crime rates during various time periods, such as season, month, and day. Still other investigations, conducted in laboratories, examine the effects of temperature on the behavior of the participants (see review in Anderson, 1989).

Anderson (1987) examined the effects of both yearly temperature, and temperature between the four seasons of the year, on violent crime. The data clearly revealed that

Source: Lukas Gojda/Shutterstock

Aggression tends to be higher when the weather is hotter.

Lunacy and the Moon

It has often been suggested that the moon directly influences human behavior. The moon has been thought to increase sexual powers, affect births and deaths, cause the onset of epilepsy, promote mental disturbances, and, of course, be responsible for werewolves. These effects have been written about throughout history and in fictional literature. Inasmuch as the moon provides light at night and exerts a powerful gravitational force that influences the tides and weather, these effects could be thought of as having physical mediators.

To examine possible lunar effects on mental disturbances, Campbell and Beets (1978) reviewed the psychological literature related to psychiatric hospital admissions, suicides, and homicides. They found no correlation between a full moon and any of these indicators of psychological disturbance. Perhaps the widespread use of electric lights masks the influence of the presence or absence of a full moon. But, for whatever reason, it seems that a full moon has no significant consequences for mental stability. On the other hand, there are data suggesting a relation between the absence of sunlight and depression.

violent crimes were most prevalent in the second and third quarters of the year (the hottest periods). In addition, the differences between violent and nonviolent crimes were highest in these seasons. Violent crime was greatest in years that had the hottest number of days, and that the increase in violent crime as a function of yearly temperature exceeded the increase in nonviolent crimes. Anderson (1989) concluded that hot temperatures increase aggressive tendencies, and this is documented in the fact that hotter regions of the world are associated with more aggression, as are hotter years, quarters of the years, seasons, months, and days. Aggressions, including murders, rapes, assaults, riots, and wife beatings, all occur more frequently given augmented temperature.

Constructed Environments

The nature of a physical setting promotes a multitude of human actions and feelings. Consider the consequences of working in a windowless office; being confined to a small, dark room; or staying in a cold, impersonal hospital. There are many more research studies about the psychological effects of such constructed physical surroundings than about the natural environment, perhaps because social engineers can change offices and classrooms more readily than the climate or the availability of resources. Again, because of space limitations, we have selected just one example that illustrates the relationships between behavior and a person's physical context.

Behavior Settings

Roger Barker (1960, 1965, 1968) said that the best way to predict human behavior is to know where a person is. In a post office, a person behaves "post office–like"; in church, one's behavior is "churchy"; and in classrooms, one acts like a student (or a teacher). Post offices, churches, and schools are all *behavior settings*. A behavior setting has spatial properties and a geographical location, but it also has social properties, such that the setting exists only when people are gathered there to perform certain activities. Hence, a shutdown post office is no longer a behavior setting, even though its physical properties might remain unchanged. Behavior settings vary greatly, from bridge clubs and restaurants to baseball fields and offices. They can be part of the natural environment, such as parks and lakes, or constructed environments, such as schools and offices.

Wicker and Kirmeyer (1977) have described a behavior setting as a place where

1. One of a number of regularly occurring human activities takes place, such as playing bridge at a bridge club or praying in a church.

2. A behavior is coordinated with inanimate objects within the setting, such as card tables at a bridge club or pews in a church.

3. People inhabiting the setting are interchangeable and replaceable. Anyone arriving at a bridge club can enter a game, and Sunday services continue as congregations change. Hence, the behavior exhibited is independent of the particular people within the setting.

Within these settings, a variety of personal motivations are satisfied. The motivations of bridge players can vary from aggression and affiliation to achievement and power; the unity of the setting is not derived from the unity of the participants' motivations. But, in spite of motivational differences, the individuals in the setting engage in the same general pattern of behavior.

Privacy

A number of other key concepts have been identified in the study of the relation between the physical world and behavior; among them are privacy, territoriality, and density (Altman, 1975).

Privacy refers to an individual's freedom to choose what is communicated about the self, to control when this communication will take place, and to limit incoming stimulation. It is evident that when large families live in one or two rooms, or even when houses in good neighborhoods are placed too close to one another, feelings of privacy are sacrificed. In such situations, one gives up control over unwanted intrusion (see Ittelson, Proshansky, Rivlin, and Winkel, 1974).

Privacy has a number of functions, including the opportunity for self-evaluation, reflection, and planning. Hence, the absence of sufficient privacy can have serious psychological consequences. It comes as no surprise, then, that cultures provide mechanisms for ensuring privacy, such as locks on doors, curtains, and Do Not Disturb signs. Even primitive cultures have privacy mechanisms, including huts that only one sex or one person is allowed to inhabit. Given some opportunity for privacy, cultures differ markedly in their physical arrangements affecting privacy.

Societies that require economic cooperation and shared decision making tend to have physical arrangements that reduce privacy. The Israeli kibbutz is a modern example of such an arrangement where privacy is hard to come by. Societies that emphasize economic competition and individualism, on the other hand, are more likely to have tall fences to separate different families.

Summary of Environmental Effects

Our initial discussion has examined the relationship between the physical or geographical environment and personality. Natural factors such as average temperature and rainfall influence personality by limiting the available means of subsistence and, in turn, determining what personality types are best suited to survive within these environmental constraints. Constructed environments also influence behavior directly. For example, the placement of furniture or the size of a working area can affect interpersonal communication and friendship patterns.

Another aspect of the environment that shapes behavior is the *behavior setting*. Behavior settings can be characterized by the number of people available to perform important functions. If a setting is undermanned, for instance, more tension and uncertainty are aroused, but there is also a greater sense of responsibility and personal acceptance. A total institution is a particular type of behavior setting where communications with the external world are severely restricted.

Finally, the concepts of privacy, or the freedom to choose and control one's communications, are aspects of the physical environment that have far-reaching psychological consequences on both immediate behavior and long-term adjustment patterns.

Summary

1. Behavior is a function of the person and the situation.
2. The person and situation may interact through things like the strength of the situation, self-monitoring, and situational selection.
3. The person-situation debate improved personality psychology as a science.
4. The effects of social stratification into classes are complex but may not influence the self-esteem of children because of the many factors that influence self-esteem and because of the different kinds of social comparison that are or are not possible.
5. The importance of cultural variables in how we conceive of and study personality has become increasingly important. In particular, the Western view of the self as individualistic, autonomous, bounded, and separate has been found to be culture-specific.
6. Climatic conditions of rainfall and temperature in part determine a society's means of subsistence, which in turn affects settlement patterns and the characteristics of individuals needed for the society to survive. Agricultural societies need obedient and responsible members, whereas hunting societies require self-reliant and autonomous members.
7. Climate also affects behaviors such as aggression.
8. A culture of honor that developed because of the type of agriculture required a person to have a reputation.
9. Privacy, the freedom to choose and control incoming communications; and territoriality, the claim to a particular space, are aspects of the physical environment that also have profound psychological effects.

Key Terms

allocentric (p. 32)
culture (p. 28)
collectivistic (p. 31)
ideocentric (p. 32)

individualistic (p. 31)
self-monitoring (p. 26)
situational selection (p. 26)
socialization (p. 34)

Thought Questions

1. Do you think about your self in Western terms as an "individualistic" self or in terms of a "collectivistic" self? Which way of looking at your self do you prefer?
2. List some of the behavior settings in which you act. Are they settings that make demands on your behavior? Has this influenced your behavior in the settings?
3. Would we expect aggression to increase along with global temperatures?
4. Do you act consistently from situation to situation? Do your friends?

Theories of Personality

Source: Ollyy/Shutterstock

CHAPTER 3
Freud's Psychoanalytic Theory of Personality

CHAPTER 4
Psychoanalytic Dissidents and Descendants

CHAPTER 5
Learning Theory Approaches to Personality

CHAPTER 6
Phenomenological Theories

Part 2 presents some of the best-known and most influential theories of personality. Among them are Freudian psychoanalytic theory (Chapter 3); descendants of and dissidents from the psychoanalytic conception, including Jung, Adler, Horney, Fromm, Erikson, Kohut, and Horowitz (Chapter 4); learning theory (Chapter 5); and cognitive approaches to personality as in the work of Carl Rogers, Abraham Maslow, George Kelly, and other phenomenological theorists (Chapter 6). These theories differ in many respects, but at the heart of the differences are contrasting basic assumptions about human nature or the essence of human beings.

Psychoanalytic theorists such as Freud and his followers believed that individuals strive to reduce inner tension, keeping internal agitation to a minimum at all costs. Humans are, in their view, irrational and instinctive biological beings. Psychoanalytic theorists generally believe that:

1. Inasmuch as individuals are unaware of their need states, personality assessment is best conducted by means of indirect or projective techniques.
2. Biological and historical factors play an essential role in behavior, and individuals progress through a fixed sequence of developmental stages.
3. Personality change must deal with the unconscious and the irrational desires of individuals.
4. Conflicts concerning sexual and aggressive instincts and social inhibitions form the heart of the psychoanalytic study of behavioral dynamics. In addition, the frustration experienced because of unsatisfied desires is directly linked with psychopathology.

Learning theory, on the other hand, traditionally asserted in its most extreme form that individuals are mere machines and that the study of personality is part of the more general examination of input-output associations or stimulus-response bonds. Given this basic view of humans, personality assessment, development, change, and dynamics all focus on specific associations:

1. Personality assessment involves the direct recording of behaviors in specific situations.
2. Personality development is based on the formation and strengthening of habits or stimulus-response bonds.
3. Personality change is accomplished by altering stimulus-response connections through the use of rewards to foster acquisition of more functional responses and punishments to extinguish maladaptive responses.
4. Behavioral dynamics involves conflicts between competing habits or response tendencies. Different and incompatible responses may be called forth by the same situation.

In its less extreme, more modern form, which we primarily examine in this book, learning theorists accept the fact that humans are not robots. Many see humans as thinking organisms whose thoughts influence their actions. However, only a few of the higher mental processes are actually incorporated into their theories. The more moderate learning theorists also believe that, although reward and punishment do influence performance, learning can take place through mere observation of others, without the direct influence of reward and punishment. Nevertheless, even these less extreme positions reflect a more mechanistic orientation than do the psychoanalytic and cognitive approaches.

Gestalt, *phenomenological*, and other *cognitive approaches* to personality often start with the assumption that individuals are scientists seeking to understand their world and to fulfill their innate potentials. Thus:

1. Personality assessment is concerned with understanding how individuals view the world or ascertaining individuals' subjective experiences.
2. Personality development is synonymous with cognitive growth, accompanied by a movement in the direction of higher goals.
3. Personality change involves altering one's view of the world and oneself. A variety of techniques from group therapy and role playing to more radical forms of sensitivity training that enhance self-awareness can be employed.
4. Personality dynamics considers the influence that beliefs have on actions, focusing on the functional significance of cognitions and subjective meanings.

The theories presented here differ in a number of other respects. Primary among these differences are the phenomena on which they focus and the research methods they have used. Freudian theory led to an examination of defense mechanisms, free associations, dreams, and sexual behavior; social learning theory has examined the effects of different rewards, punishments, and role models on social behaviors; and Gestalt, phenomenological, and other cognitive approaches have been especially concerned with self-concept, self-esteem, self-actualization, and overall human potential. The theories stand side by side, each with unique abilities to account for certain observations. As a result, there is not a clear hierarchical ordering of theories, with one "better" in every respect than the others.

Table (P) 2.1 summarizes some points of comparison in the theories examined in the next four chapters. It will help you to return to this table as you progress through the chapters and the remainder of the text. Some of the terms in the table may be unfamiliar to you now, but they will be introduced and discussed in subsequent chapters.

TABLE (P) 2.1 Comparison of the Major Theories of Personality

Theory	Chapter	Some major contributors	Focus	Main concepts*	Assessment goal	Assessment instruments	Goals for change
Psychoanalytic	3	Freud	Sexual motivation	Energy, instinct, libido, cathexis, id, ego, superego	Reveal basic unconscious desires	Projective techniques	Insight into desires; new coping techniques
Psychoanalytic Dissidents	4	Jung, Adler, Horney, Sullivan, Fromm, Erikson	Personal growth, social motivations	Archetype, compensation, inferiority, neurotic trend, attachments, authoritarianism	Reveal basic unconscious desires	Projective techniques	Insight into desires; new coping techniques
Learning	5	Miller, Skinner, Bandura, Mischel, Rotter	Learning and the stimulus situation	Reinforcement, expectancy, value, model	Reveal typical ways of responding and their eliciting stimuli	Behavioral observation and objective instruments	Change habits; develop new responses
Cognitive-Phenomenological	6	Rogers, Maslow, Kelly	Humans as scientists; subjective experience	Unconditional regard, positive self-regard, personal constructs	Reveal perceptions of the world	Objective instruments, open-ended questionnaires	Alter cognitions or views of the world

* Not descriptive of all theorists within a category.

Freud's Psychoanalytic Theory of Personality

CHAPTER 3

Source: ArtFamily/Shutterstock

Chapter Outline

Biography

Basic Theoretical Concepts

Anxiety

Defense Mechanisms

General Evaluation

The greatest figure among personality theorists is Sigmund Freud, the creator of psychoanalysis. Freud's psychoanalytic theory is the most general and best-known conception of personality. His contributions range far beyond psychology; one cannot understand twentieth-century intellectual thought without some knowledge of psychoanalytic theory. Certainly Freud plays a less central role in psychological thinking today than 40 to 50 years ago, but he is by no means relegated to history. Many of his ideas have been absorbed by other personality theorists and incorporated within their theoretical frameworks.

Freud's conception is so vast that it is meaningless to ask whether it is "correct" or "incorrect." Some aspects of the theory have been shown to have reasonable validity, others have no empirical support at all, and still others are beyond empirical test. In this chapter, we present an overview of many of Freud's theoretical concepts and examine in detail the area of defense mechanisms in order to illustrate the experimental testing of some of Freud's ideas.

Biography

Sigmund Freud was born in Freiburg, Moravia (now Pribor, Czechoslovakia), on May 6, 1856, and died in London on September 23, 1939. Most of his life was spent in Vienna, which he left only when the Nazis invaded in 1938.

When Freud decided to devote himself to patients suffering from disorders in thought, emotions, and behaviors, the prevailing view in medicine was that the cause of illness—whether mental or physical—was fundamentally biological in origin e.g., a defect in the nervous system. The notion of a psychological basis for psychological symptoms—that traumatic events, internal conflicts, or poor parenting can be the primary cause of many mental and behavioral abnormalities—is a twentieth century concept. This radical change in how mental illness is perceived was introduced primarily by Sigmund Freud, who also introduced radical changes in the conception of the bases of human behavior. These changes are so fundamental that they have been likened to the changes in scientific thought brought about by Darwin's theory of evolution and Einstein's theory of relativity.

Freud began his scientific career as a neurologist and quickly established a reputation in neurological research and medical investigations. In his medical practice, he treated patients with various "nervous" disorders by using conventional medical and physical procedures. But he soon became disillusioned with these treatments. In his autobiography (Freud, 1935), he writes:

> My knowledge of electrotherapy was derived from W. Erb's textbook, which provided detailed instructions for the treatment of all the symptoms of nervous diseases. Unluckily I was soon driven to see that following these instructions was of no help whatever and that what I had taken for an epitome of exact observations was merely the construction of phantasy. The realization that the work of the greatest name in German neuropathology had no more relation to reality than some "Egyptian" dream-book, such as is sold in cheap bookshops, was painful, but it helped to rid me of another shred of the innocent faith in authority from which I was not yet free. So I put my electrical apparatus aside, even before Mobius had solved the problem by explaining that the successes of electric treatment in nervous disorders (in so far as there were any) were the effect of suggestion on the part of the physician. (pp. 27–28)

In an effort to discover new perspectives, he traveled to Paris in 1885 where he attended the lectures of Jean Martin Charcot, a very eminent neurologist. Charcot was a skilled hypnotist whose dramatic demonstrations of the effects of hypnotic treatments so impressed Freud that he made subsequent trips to France to attend the demonstrations of hypnotism by another French physician, Hippolyte Bernheim. But Freud soon became disenchanted with hypnosis as well; many patients were not susceptible to hypnosis, and the effects of treatment frequently did not carry over to the waking state.

Nevertheless, this period was extremely important in Freud's development. First, it was a hypnotic demonstration that provided Freud with key insights into the dynamics of personality. During an experiment conducted by Bernheim, a woman was given the posthypnotic suggestion that, after waking, she should walk to the corner of the room and open an umbrella. Upon awakening, and after the designated time had elapsed, she did exactly that. When questioned about the reason for her behavior, she said that she wanted to see if the umbrella was hers. On the basis of this demonstration, Freud realized that conscious reports do not always indicate the real motivation for an act; that is, an action can be determined by forces that are *unconscious*. A second consequence

Sigmund Freud (1856–1939) with his mother, Amalia Freud, in 1925.

Anna O.: The Founding Case of Psychoanalysis

In mid-November, 1882, Joseph Breuer told Freud about Anna O., a highly intelligent twenty-one-year-old woman who presented a diverse array of symptoms. Initially, she suffered from headaches, partial paralyses, intervals of excitement, and visual disturbances. Her symptoms then became more exaggerated—mental lapses, hallucinations about black snakes, skulls and skeletons, speech disturbances, and split personalities.

"The turning point in her 'talking cure' came during the spring of 1882, when Anna O. underwent a spell resembling hydrophobia. Though parched with thirst, she was unable to drink until one evening during her hypnotic state she told Breuer she had seen her English lady-companion, whom she disliked, letting her little dog drink out of a glass. Once her suppressed disgust came out into the open, the hydrophobia disappeared" (Gay, 1988, p. 65).

Although Anna's symptoms were not completely relieved through this process, Freud was very impressed by the effectiveness of the "talking" procedure.

Source: Photographee.eu/Shutterstock

Freud and Breuer's ideas about talking as a cure formed the foundation of much of modern psychotherapy.

of Freud's introduction to hypnosis was that he began to use a treatment technique, developed by Joseph Breuer, in which hypnotized patients talked about their symptoms. In the process, patients often recovered disturbing memories that seemed to be the unconscious causes of their illnesses.

From this beginning, Freud gradually discovered the method of *free association*, during which patients are asked, under normal waking conditions, to tell the analyst everything that comes to mind, regardless of how trivial or embarrassing it may seem. Freud found that these free associations could be systematically related to patients' underlying conflicts and overt symptoms. By listening carefully to verbal associations, he was able to detect consistent themes that were manifestations of unconscious wishes and fears. These themes often involved sexual conflicts. The discovery that much of individual behavior is a compromise between wishes and anticipated fears is another of Freud's central contributions.

Freud and Breuer soon parted ways after disagreements over Freud's beliefs about the importance of sexual desires in the development of mental illness. Thereafter, Freud primarily worked alone to formulate startling and original ideas about child development, the incest taboo, the interpretation of dreams, the unconscious, and a wealth of other psychological processes and phenomena. Freud initially surrounded himself with talented individuals, including Carl Jung from Switzerland and Alfred Adler from Austria (see Chapter 4), who were attracted to this new discipline that he was formulating. But his interpersonal relationships were often stormy, and friendships were aborted. His fascinating life history includes his self-analysis, the controversies surrounding his ideas, the founding of the International Psychoanalytic Association, and an invitation to Clark University in Massachusetts (1909) that paved the way for his acceptance after a long period of scientific ostracism. There were a number of reasons why Freud was not initially accepted by the scientific community (see Shakow and Rapaport, 1964). He did not communicate openly with other scientists, having virtually no academic correspondence and alienated others because of his strong opinions. Furthermore, he did not present carefully accumulated evidence in support of his ideas, even gathering his data in a mysterious and secretive atmosphere closed to all but his patients. Finally, he came from an unknown Jewish family at a time of religious discrimination that probably contributed to the delay in his being offered a university position.

It is interesting to note that Freud was part of a continuing trend toward relegating humans to lower and lower status levels. First, Copernicus took Earth and its inhabitants from the center of the universe; then Darwin established that humans are not unique; finally, Freud contended that individuals are irrational and unaware of their own motivations. Perhaps the next step, currently in progress, will be to make inanimate objects more intelligent than their makers!

Basic Theoretical Concepts

Homeostasis and Hedonism

It is useful to consider Freud's theories within the context of a biological survival model. For Freud, people are biological creatures driven by fundamental biological needs that produce psychological tensions until the needs are satisfied. Given this viewpoint, which borrows much from Darwin, individuals are viewed as striving to satisfy personal needs within a world of limited resources. To satisfy these needs, behaviors must be undertaken that lead to the desired goals—virtually all of which are located in the external world. Thus, individuals must function within the constraints imposed by the real world in which they find themselves, and acquire a mode of adaptation that will enable them, insofar as possible, to reduce these need-produced tensions.

More specifically, consider a psychological analysis of how behavior is governed by the need for food (although Freud was concerned more with sex and aggression than with tissue deficits). All organisms have a biological need to ingest food, a need made known to the organism because its presence causes discomfort. There is a limited supply of food in the external world, and organisms must compete for these resources. After the organism has engaged in appropriate activities and has eaten, the internal stimulation and pain (e.g., hunger pangs) that accompany food deprivation cease. The organism then feels satisfied and remains in an unmotivated state (at rest) until the next onset of hunger pangs, which follow a cyclical pattern, again generating food-seeking behavior. Freud conceived a similar cyclical model of sexual and aggressive desires and satisfactions.

The model of human behavior proposed by Freud reflects two broad theoretical principles: homeostasis and hedonism. The first is drawn from biology, the second from philosophy. *Homeostasis* is the tendency toward the maintenance of a relatively stable internal environment. That is, there is a propensity for an organism to remain in a state of equilibrium. If, for example, there is a condition of deprivation because food is absent, then a state of disequilibrium exists, and food-related actions are initiated to return the organism to balance, or equilibrium. *Hedonism*, a doctrine associated with the philosopher

Jeremy Bentham (1779), asserts that pleasure and happiness are the chief goals in life. If homeostasis is the governing principle of behavior, then pleasure is the by-product of being in a state of equilibrium, where all one's needs are satisfied. Freud accepted the doctrine of hedonism, which is expressed in his theoretical language as the *pleasure principle*.

In Freud's theory, the principle of homeostasis, which is reflected in efforts to reduce tension, is the basis for human action. For Freud, the satisfied individual typically does not pursue any stimulation, since activity indicates some type of dissatisfaction. On the contrary, the presumed ultimate goal of human striving is the absence of tension or need, which is accompanied by quiescence. One logical extension of this position was Freud's postulating a death instinct or death wish, for in death there are no unsatisfied desires. This is similar to the alleged desire to "return to the womb," where all needs are fulfilled.

Psychological Energy

One of the most difficult and debatable features of Freud's theory is his concept of psychological energy. Freud was greatly influenced by Hermann von Helmholtz, the German physicist who argued that physiological events could be explained with the mechanical principles of physics and chemistry. Freud contended that all psychological work, whether attaining a goal or just thinking about it, requires the use of energy. Three energy-related concepts are useful in understanding his explanation of human behavior: conservation of energy, entropy, and a distinction between bound (kinetic) and free (potential) energy.

Freud conceived of humans as closed energy systems. That is, there is a constant amount of energy (**libido**) for any given individual. This idea was derived from the principle of the conservation of energy, which states that energy is neither created nor destroyed. One corollary of this law is that if energy is spent performing one function, then it is unavailable for other functions. It will be seen that this corollary plays an important role in Freud's theory.

Entropy refers to the amount of energy that is not available for doing work. According to Freud, some energy is *bound*, kinetic, or "cathected." A *cathexis* (from the Greek *kathexo*, meaning "to occupy") involves an attachment to some desired but unattained object. The attachment or cathexis does not mean that energy literally leaves the person. Rather, there is a feeling of "longing" for the object, and there are repeated thoughts, images, and fantasies about him or her or some substitute object. A cathexis might be only temporary, for if the desired goal is attained, then there is a freeing of energy. As a result of goal attainment, bound energy is transformed into *free (potential) energy* that is then available for use in other functions. If all one's desires are fulfilled, then all energy is free. Thus, energy distribution is related to subjective satisfaction or happiness.

Consider, more specifically, how Freud might analyze the situation in which a loved one must go away for a period of time. Because that person is no longer available as a need satisfier, he or she becomes an object of cathexis. Energy is now bound, and the unsatisfied individual might fantasize about being with the loved one, daydream of their reunion, and so on. The binding of energy is unpleasant, reflecting the fact that needs have not been fulfilled. In addition, the bound energy is not available for other activities. The individual might therefore experience a lack of interest in other friends and hobbies. When the longed-for person returns, then needs are again satisfied, the cathected energy is freed to do other work, and there is a state of subjective pleasure. Note, then, how closely the concepts of homeostasis, hedonism, and the various forms of energy are linked in Freud's theory. If an organism is in equilibrium (homeostasis), then all energy is free, and the maximum pleasure is being experienced (hedonism).

Freud's statements about energy must be considered basic postulates in his conception; they are not amenable to proof or disproof. In other words, it is not possible to test the

Sigmund Freud (1856–1939) while training as a physician.

libido Freud's term of psychic energy, derived primarily from the sexual, pleasure-seeking instincts of the id.

notion that there is libidinal energy, or that happiness is associated with free energy, or that we are closed energy systems. While these energy concepts have had some utility in enhancing understanding of some aspects of human behavior, modern psychoanalytic theory tends to assign less importance to them.

The Instincts

The hedonistic goals that individuals wish to reach are instinctive, in the sense that instincts are considered internal urges. Freud contended that instincts drive the organism toward action and are represented in the mind as wishes or desires. The *source* of the instincts is bodily metabolism; their *aim* is immediate discharge; and their *objects* typically are external satisfiers.

Freud vacillated in his ideas about instincts, at times postulating one, and at other times two, basic instincts. Initially, he suggested that there are two classes of instincts: those meant to preserve life (hunger) and those directed toward the attainment of pleasure (sex). The sexual instincts also were related to the preservation of the species. In his final analysis he reaffirmed that there are indeed two instincts, but that they are somewhat different from the two he at first postulated. He contended that one instinct represented a life force (*Eros*, or love), while the second represented a death force (*Thanatos*, or death). Freud contended that aggressiveness is one manifestation of the death instinct turned outward. However, the notion of a death instinct, as contrasted with an aggressive instinct, has been accepted by few psychoanalysts. The life instinct, or sexual motivation, was incorporated within Freud's drive-discharge view of behavior. Sexual drives were conceived as biologically rooted, persistent internal stimuli that demand satisfaction. Gratification of sexual desires leads to a state of quiescence, while lack of satisfaction, usually because of an opposing force, could result in maladaptive behaviors and neurotic symptoms.

It is often contended that Freud's concentration on sexual motivation was a result of his living circumstances: repressive Vienna of the late 1800s. But the importance of sexual dilemmas and conflicts appears to be universal, which suggests that powerful drives for sexual expression must be operative in the face of social inhibitions. In addition, Freud pointed to certain clinical findings to defend his concentration on sexual motivation, including his beliefs that neurotic symptoms could be traced to unfulfilled sexual urges and that infants and children also exhibit great interest in sexual matters (Klein, 1969).

Psychological Determinism

Psychological determinism refers to the axiom that thoughts and actions have causes. Freud carried this principle to its extreme, stating not only that *all* psychological events are caused, but also that most of them are caused by unsatisfied desires or drives. Freud maintained that, in order to understand any behavior—be it a neurotic symptom, a free association, or a social act—one must attempt to analyze the motivational function of the behavior. Behavior, moreover, is typically *overdetermined* in that the behavioral act, such as a symptom, serves to satisfy two or more motives, thereby establishing a *compromise* between a wish and fear, or guilt over expressing the wish.

In one of his earliest publications, Freud singled out three apparently different aspects of normal human behavior—humor, slips of the tongue, and dreams—for special attention. According to Freud, all three behaviors serve the same function: vicarious gratification of a forbidden impulse or an unfulfilled wish. They are hidden means of tension reduction. Consider, for example, the following joke: Standing on a green, one golfer is vigorously choking another to death. A third party arrives on the scene and says casually to the aggressor, "Excuse me, but your grip's all wrong." Freud believed that such a joke evokes laughter because unconscious aggressive urges that are usually prevented from expression are being satisfied through the socially acceptable outlet of a joke. In addition, "A good joke needs a listener; its aim is not only to bypass a prohibition, but also to implicate the listener via laughter, to make the laughing listener an accomplice and, as it were, socialize the transgression." (Volosinov, 1976, pp. 58–59.)

Similarly, such mental lapses as slips of the tongue and forgetting also have psychological determinants.

> An error of this sort is said once to have crept into a Social-Democratic newspaper, where, in the account of a festivity, the following words were printed: "Amongst those present was His Highness, the Clown Prince." The next day a correction was attempted. The paper apologized and said: "The sentence should of course have read, the Clown Prince." Again, in a war-correspondent's account of meeting a famous general whose infirmities were pretty well-known, a reference to the general was printed as "this battle-scared veteran." Next day an apology appeared which read "the words of course should have been, the bottle-scarred veteran"! (Freud, 1915, p. 35)

In Freudian theory, dreams are also wish fulfillments, or at least attempts at wish fulfillment, having their origin in sexual and aggressive impulses. Freud argued that the true meaning of a dream, or its latent content, is often masked. The *manifest* content of the dream, or what the dreamer reports, is typically a distortion of the "real" dream contents. However, with proper analysis, Freud believed that the latent meaning of a dream could be uncovered. He therefore thought that dreams provided the "royal road to the unconscious." Freud also stated that the vicarious satisfaction provided by dreams has the function of preserving sleep. He thought that, in the absence of dreams, unpleasant impulses would disturb and awaken the sleeper.

Here again one can raise such empirical questions as: Must a "good" joke tap unconscious aggressions and sexual wishes? Are all "Freudian slips" related to unconscious wishes? If I miss an appointment with my girlfriend or with a professor, does it necessarily mean that I did not want to meet with them? Must dreams always fulfill wishes? The answer to these questions appears to be an unqualified "no," but *some* jokes, *some* slips, and *some* dreams do have a motivational basis that are amenable to a Freudian interpretation. Furthermore, Freud's creation of a theory that could interrelate and offer common explanations for such diverse behaviors as jokes, slips of the tongue, and dreams (to which might be added neurotic symptoms, religion, family rivalry, and other behaviors) was a remarkable achievement.

Libido and Developmental Stages

Freud used the term *libido* (Latin for "lust") to stand for the pleasure-seeking instinctive energy that drives human behavior. Freud proposed that sexual impulses undergo four developmental stages: oral, anal, phallic, and genital (see Table 3.1). During the first year of life, the infant is in the *oral stage*, with libidinal impulses being gratified through the mucous membranes of the mouth (note, then, that Freud might be seen as concerned with

TABLE 3.1 Freud's Psychosexual Stages and Outcomes for Personality

Stage		Years	Source of pleasure	Possible outcomes
Oral	Birth to 1	Mouth	Oral incorporative (believes everything, gullible)	Oral sadistic (uses the mouth to hurt others, biting, sarcastic, gossipy)
Anal	1 to 3	Anus	Anal expulsive (messy and destructive)	Anal retentive (excessively orderly and neat)
Phallic	3 to 5	Penis	Experience of Oedipal conflict, resulting in development of the superego	Over- or undersexualized
Latency	5 to Puberty			
Genital	Puberty	Penis or Vagina	Mature adult sexuality	

sensual pleasure in the broader sense, rather than in the more narrow sexual sense). During the child's second and third years, the *anal-stage* pleasures stemming from the excretion and retention of feces dominate the child's erotic life. Sometime toward the end of the third year and the beginning of the fourth year, the *phallic stage* of development takes place, in which excitation and stimulation of the genital area provides the primary source of erotic pleasure. This stage ends with the resolution of the so-called Oedipal conflict and is followed by a *latency period* during which children appear relatively unconcerned with sexual matters. Finally, after around the age of twelve, the child enters the *genital stage*, which corresponds to adult sexual concerns and pleasures.

The Oedipal Conflict

The psychoanalytic theory about the development of the Oedipal situation is clearest in the case of the male. Around the age of five or six, a boy's sexual impulses are directed toward his mother, and he resents his father, who is perceived as a rival for the mother's affections. Freud labeled this classic rivalry the **Oedipal conflict**, after Sophocles' play in which Oedipus unwittingly kills his father and marries his mother. According to Freud, the boy also fears that his father will retaliate against these sexual impulses by castrating him. Freud considered this fear, labeled *castration anxiety*, to be the prototype of all subsequent anxieties, in which one is flooded with internal stimulation. To reduce castration anxiety and at the same time gratify his feelings toward his mother, the boy identifies with his father, thereby internalizing his idealized perception of his father's attitudes and values. Clearly, the incest taboo is associated with the resolution of the Oedipal situation.

The same process in a girl—the **Electra complex**—takes an analogous, but more complicated form with the girl jealous of her mother's relationship with her father and ultimately identifying with her mother. This identification is not as complete as the boy's identification with his father, in part because of an already absent penis consequently, it is presumed in orthodox psychoanalytic theory that women do not develop as strong a moral sense as do men. Freud also asserted that, because of their lack of a penis, women envy men. Indeed, women emerge as the inferior sex in Freud's theorizing a facet of the theory that is more a figment of male chauvinism than a result of scientific inquiry and certainly not supported by any empirical evidence. In Freud's defense, however, it must be recalled

Oedipal conflict (Oedipus complex for boys; Electra complex for girls) In Freud's psychosexual theory of development, sexual attraction to the opposite-sex parent, and jealousy and hostility toward and fear of punishment from the rival, same-sex parent.

Electra complex In Freud's psychosexual theory of development, sexual attraction to the father, and jealousy and hostility toward and fear of punishment from the rival, mother.

HIGHLIGHT 3.2

Freud and Fliess

Freud writes in his *The Interpretation of Dreams*, "An intimate friend and a hated enemy have always been necessary requirements of my emotional life." At different times in some of his relationships, the same person came to perform both functions. The critical role which such persons came to play in his professional development is epitomized in the close friendship that he formed with Berlin ear, nose, and throat specialist Wilhelm Fliess, whom he first met in the fall of 1887. Fliess was a very bright, cultivated, and scientifically learned individual who at the same time was given to some unusual medical theories that strike us as peculiar today and were even a bit strange in the latter part of the nineteenth century. He believed that the nose was the dominant human organ affecting health and sickness in other parts of the body. Even less credible were his convictions that males and females are governed by biorhythmic cycles of 23 and 28 days and his numer-

ological manipulation of symptom duration and other time indices to conform to these cycles. Yet Fliess also entertained ideas that were consonant with some of Freud's thinking at that time. He proposed that people were fundamentally bisexual, and he also entertained notions of sexual energy. More significant, however, was his role as Freud's confidant, someone to whom Freud could communicate his struggles, insights, and concerns during the period of his great creative efforts in the 1890s. Freud became so uncritically attached to Fliess that he even placed the responsibility for a surgical mistake that Fliess had made on a patient, whom Freud had referred to Fliess, on the patient herself! However, as Freud became intellectually and emotionally independent of Fliess, the relationship cooled and essentially terminated in 1900 in a very emotional quarrel as each man attacked the validity of the other's beliefs (Gay, 1988).

that at his particular point in history there was great sexual inequality. In addition, Freud clearly was ahead of his time in recognizing and accepting female sexuality at all. Arid, on a more personal note, Freud used his influence to ensure that women no less than men were eligible to be candidates for psychoanalytic training (Gay, 1988).

Freud's reconstruction of the Oedipal situation from the free associations of his adult clients has provided profound theoretical and clinical insights into the nature of family dynamics. Freud may have been incorrect in assuming that the Oedipal conflict is universal and that sexual jealousy is the primary basis for the child's feelings of rivalry. He certainly failed to take into account the effect of such factors as variations in family structure and the death or absence of a parent on the Oedipal situation. Also, Freud's interpretation of the childhood seductions reported by his patients as being a reflection of early sexual fantasies has been challenged (Masson, 1984). It has been argued that these reports of childhood seduction are not indicative of Oedipal feelings but rather are accounts of actual incestuous episodes. This was Freud's original impression, which he subsequently changed after more extensive experiences with patients.

However, although there may be disagreement regarding Freud's theory of Oedipal conflict, there is little doubt that even in the most loving of households there are rivalrous elements in the family triangle. How the young son resolves the conflict between his envy and fear of his powerful father and his attachment to his mother, and how the young daughter integrates her envy of a mother to whom she is strongly attached with her desire to be the center of her father's attention, play a central role in subsequent personality development.

Fixation

Many adult emotional problems were traced by Freud to specific disturbances during the oral, anal, and phallic stages. As a result of these disturbances, libidinal energies become tied up, or *fixated*, at a particular stage of development. It is assumed that the greater the **fixation** at a given psychosexual stage, the less energy the person has available for mature relationships. Freud used the analogy of an advancing army, with the more troops stationed in the rear guard, the fewer troops available to meet new dangers. When defeated, the more likely the army is to retreat to where it has the greatest number of rear-guard troops (i.e., fixated energy). For example, a child with a strong oral fixation who encounters a major source of frustration during the phallic stage—say, the birth of a sibling—may revert to such oral behaviors as thumb sucking, exaggerated dependency, and, in some cases, nursing.

fixation (psychoanalytic) A disturbed focus of libidinal energy at a particular psychosexual stage preventing full maturation through the other stages.

You might well ask, "Do children really have to pass through such a developmental sequence? Is the retention of feces really the primary source of sensual or libidinal satisfaction for two-year-old children?" Such questions related to developmental stages and sequences will be examined in more detail in Chapters 11 and 12, which focus on the growth of personality. However, at this point it can be said that the experiences of feeding, toilet training, and genital exploration are of major significance for the child's development. What is debatable, however, is Freud's hypothesis that these three areas of bodily activity reflect a common sexual motivation. It is also questionable that oral, anal, and phallic transitions are more central to the child's development than are experiences in other areas, such as attachment and independence training.

Personality Structures

According to Freud, human personality has three components: the id, the ego, and the superego. These structures have specific unique functions as well as distinct operating processes. The id, ego, and superego are not to be found in a specific location in the brain or in the body. Rather, they represent interacting, hypothetical structures, proposed by Freud to explain his observation that behaviors result from compromises between libidinal needs and desires, the restrictions of the environment, and the conscience, or internalized moral values.

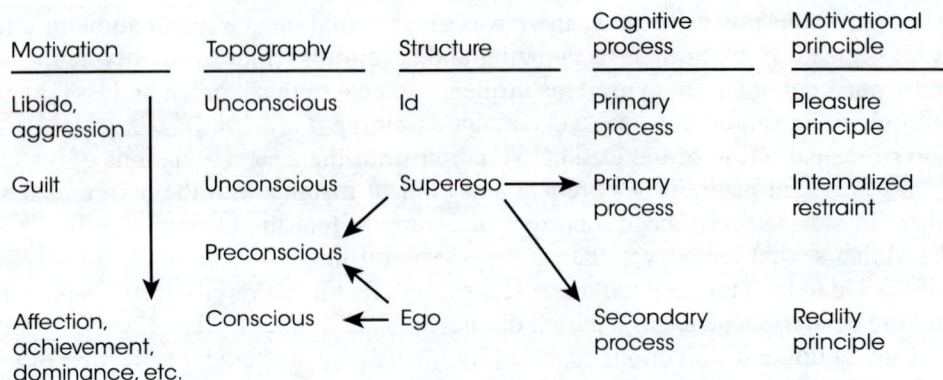

Motivation	Topography	Structure	Cognitive process	Motivational principle
Libido, aggression	Unconscious	Id	Primary process	Pleasure principle
Guilt	Unconscious	Superego →	Primary process	Internalized restraint
	Preconscious			
Affection, achievement, dominance, etc.	Conscious ←	Ego	Secondary process	Reality principle

FIGURE 3.1

Concepts in the same row are all linked to each other. The arrow from Libido, Aggression denotes Freud's proposition that all human motivations are derived from instinctual libidinal and aggressive impulses. The other arrows indicate that ego processes also can be preconscious and unconscious, and superego processes can be preconscious and conscious and both primary and secondary. Thus guilt has unconscious, preconscious, and conscious components.

The Id

id In Freudian theory, the most primitive and inaccessible part of the personality, made up of sexual and aggressive instincts, which strive continually for gratification.

Freud conceived of the **id** as the first system to develop within the person. It is most closely related to the biological realm of sexual and aggressive drives. Since the individual is unaware of these inborn drives, the contents of the id are primarily unconscious (see Fig. 3.1).

The id is the reservoir of all psychological energy, or libido. The availability of this energy allows the id to be directly responsive to bodily needs. Internal bodily tension cannot be tolerated by the id, which functions to discharge any internal tension immediately. Thus, the id operates according to the pleasure principle, or the doctrine of hedonism, seeking immediate pleasure through homeostatic processes and tension reduction. For example, a hungry infant will reflexively suck at a bottle or breast, thus reducing its hunger. Although it must be remembered that Freud was concerned primarily with sexual and aggressive instincts, this automatic action, designed to return the organism to equilibrium, reasonably captures Freud's idea of an id-instigated action.

Id functioning is also characterized by *primary process thought*, a mode of thinking perhaps best known to us through our dream experiences. Primary process thought is illogical and timeless, with reality not distinguished from irreality and hallucinations. For example, a dream is not distinguished from actual occurrences. Thus, in the absence of external goal gratification, internal mental acts can be called on to fulfill wishes. The infant, according to Freud, can imagine that it is ingesting milk to reduce tension (see Chapters 14 and 16 for a discussion of imagery). Extensions of this idea suggest that we might dream about great accomplishments in order to satisfy some of our achievement desires, or daydream of attacking someone in order to gratify aggressive needs.

Freud's view that human beings are driven by biologically rooted id impulses that seek immediate gratification has profound implications for the relationship between the individual and society. From the Freudian perspective, society must inculcate and provide checks to restrain individuals from savagely acting out their unconscious sexual and aggressive urges.

The Ego

It is evident that organisms must learn to differentiate between milk and the idea or the image of milk if they are to survive. Fantasy must be distinguished from reality. In addition, immediate goal gratification sometimes leads to more pain than pleasure, as when sexual or aggressive actions are later punished by society. To handle the problems of discrimination and the necessity of delay, the id develops a new structure that can come to terms with the objective world. Freud labeled this structure the **ego**.

The ego is governed by the reality principle rather than the pleasure principle. This does not mean that hedonism is given up. The ego serves the id in its pursuit of pleasure and tension reduction, but also takes the demands of reality into account. The ego follows the rules of *secondary process thought*: adult thinking that is characterized by logic, time orientation, and a distinction between reality and irreality. The ego also has access to the tools of memory, attention, and the control of motor activity. Thus, its existence provides a means for delaying gratification and planning long-term goals.

The contents of the ego are partially conscious (see Fig. 3.1), but the individual is still not aware of all aspects of ego functioning. Most experience is preconscious (not in consciousness), but nevertheless available from memory storage. The ego also includes the defense mechanisms, such as repression, that protect one from psychic pain. These defenses, which are generally not part of the conscious experience, will be examined more fully later in this chapter.

ego In Freudian theory, the part of the personality that mediates between the demands of id impulses, superego, and external reality.

The Superego

According to Freud, the **superego** is the last of the three personality structures to develop. The superego has two main functions, both based on built-in reinforcement processes: (1) to reward individuals for acceptable moral behavior and (2) to punish actions that are not socially sanctioned, by creating guilt. The superego thus represents internalized moral codes, often called the conscience. The superego opposes the expression of unacceptable impulses, rather than merely postponing them, as does the ego.

superego In Freudian theory, the part of the personality representing the morals, values, and ideals of one's society.

Freud contended that the development of the superego occurs when the child identifies with the same-sex parent. In doing so, the child internalizes moral ideals, takes on appropriate sex-role behaviors, and resolves the Oedipal conflict with the same-sex parent for the affection of the opposite-sex parent (see also Chapter 12).

Integration of the Structures

Freud was greatly influenced by his training in neurology, where he observed a hierarchical ordering of neural structures. For example, just as the onset of some neural firings can inhibit other neural firings, so can the ego inhibit the strivings of the id. Freud conceived of the ego as the executive agency or "highest" structure in a person, which is responsible for final behavioral decisions. In this capacity it must act as a mediator to satisfy the constant demands of the id, be bound by the constraints of reality, and pacify the ideals of the superego.

anxiety A state of unrealistic fear.

Anxiety

The concept of **anxiety** is of central importance in psychoanalytic theory, inasmuch as the dynamics of behavior revolve around the notion of a conflict between expression and inhibition. Inhibition is an ego function that is intimately associated with the experience of anxiety and, in turn, the defense mechanisms.

To understand the relationships among inhibition, anxiety, and the defense mechanisms, it is useful to trace Freud's changing analysis of these concepts. Freud's earliest theorizing argued that anxiety is the result of undischarged libidinal energy. The lack of sexual gratification, which could arise from any number of sources—the absence of wished-for objects, poor relations with others, or, most importantly, inhibitions and repressions—was believed to result in an accumulation of drive energy. The unexpressed libido was then "explosively released in a transformed state, the state of anxiety" (Monte, 1977, p. 120). Anxiety therefore was considered a product of the id, automatically arising

Dealing with anxiety is one of the most important parts of Freud's theory.

from unfulfilled sexual urges. Freud initially considered hypnosis a good therapeutic technique because the patient could relive experiences and discharge libidinal energy when in a hypnotic state, thereby reducing anxiety.

As Freud gave the ego greater importance in his theory, he reversed this sequence of "repression produces anxiety" to "anxiety produces repression" (Freud, 1926). In a later period in his thinking, Freud contended that when drive expression will lead to more pain than pleasure, the ego "inoculates" itself with anxiety. This anxiety serves as a warning that, if the individual engages in the forbidden activity, then the ego will experience a much greater amount of anxiety than it just felt in very modulated form. The anxiety that will be experienced will be similar to that of an earlier danger situation: the "birth trauma," or the overwhelming helplessness that is first experienced when one leaves the protection of the womb. In order to avoid this state, the ego initiates action, activating defense mechanisms that interfere with and delay drive expression. Freud thus made anxiety an ego signal rather than an id discharge.

Stated somewhat differently, whenever an instinct pushes for expression that might lead to significant punishment, pain, or guilt, the organism reacts with alarm in the form of anxiety. A defense will then arise, both to prevent immediate goal gratification and to help resolve the conflict by permitting the urge to be expressed in a socially acceptable form. Thus, anxiety can be directly linked to inhibition and psychological defenses.

Defense Mechanisms

It has just been suggested that the ego protects the individual from pain that might be experienced as a consequence of direct sexual or aggressive expression. Because the mechanisms used by the ego have a protective function, some of them are called **defense mechanisms**, or simply *psychological defenses*. Psychological understanding of these defenses was one of Freud's major insights and also one of the important contributions of his daughter, Anna Freud.

defense mechanisms In psychoanalytic theory, unconscious strategies that enable a person to avoid awareness of unpleasant or anxiety-arousing experiences.

The psychological defenses that protect an individual from overwhelming anxiety, punishment, and other unpleasant experiences are sometimes quite obvious. For example, fainting is one mechanism that prevents continued exposure to such aversive sensations as the sight of blood or the feelings that accompany the death of a significant other. Any observer can recognize a faint, and the fainter can later readily comprehend what happened, if not the underlying reason for the loss of consciousness. Thus, Freud would not have considered fainting to be a typical psychological defense, although Freud himself fainted on two occasions in uncomfortable interactions with Jung (Gay, 1988), and its function in avoiding unpleasantness was evident to him. Although it is now accepted that not all defenses must be unconscious, Freud contended that defense mechanisms usually operate on an unconscious level, with individuals not consciously aware of the defenses or their functional significance.

Repression and the Unconscious

One of the more provocative, better-known aspects of psychoanalytic theory is the assertion that a significant part of our behavior is governed by forces of which we have no awareness. Our choice of marriage partner, vocation, and even hobbies may reflect the influence of impulses and fears that remain unconscious. Memories associated with unacceptable feelings may also be excluded from awareness. When Freud encouraged his patients to recall painful memories and to confront unacceptable feelings, they appeared to resist his efforts. Freud hypothesized that this resistance was a function of an active force that he called **repression**, which acted to keep thoughts unconscious. The unconscious, of course, is not a place or object situated deep in the recesses of the brain; it is, rather, a property of thought and behavior. People are conscious of some of their thoughts and actions and their underlying reasons, while they may be completely unaware of other thoughts, motivations, attitudes, and actions. (See also Chapter 16.) Freud believed that repression is the most significant defense mechanism, upon which all the other defenses are based.

repression A defense mechanism in which an anxiety-arousing memory or impulse is prevented from becoming conscious.

Several different kinds of clinical and experimental observations support the belief that unconscious forces may exert significant influences on human behavior. Freud's analyses of his patients' symptoms, dreams, and associations convinced him that they were usually not conscious of the underlying reasons for their actions. They would repeat the same disastrous relationships, the same failures, and the same self-destructive life patterns (e.g., alcoholism and drug addiction) without any awareness of the motivational bases for their behavior. Freud further observed that some people were unconsciously attracted to activities or ideas to which they consciously objected. It has been suggested, for example, that those who lead crusades against pornography and spend a good deal of time reading and viewing pornographic material are often unconsciously drawn to such literature.

There are numerous clinical reports of instances of repression. One dramatic autobiographical example has been provided by the distinguished psychologist Elsa Frenkl-Brunswick. In one session of her psychoanalysis, undertaken in her early twenties, the analyst commented that her conflict and anxiety reflected a kind of "Cordelia" complex, referring to King Lear's youngest daughter. (Shakespeare's King Lear did not appreciate Cordelia's love for him until late in life.) Frenkl-Brunswick, puzzled by the reference to Cordelia, said that she was unfamiliar with the play, and the analyst had to summarize its highlights. Several years later, when sorting through her personal belongings, she came across some old high school notes on *King Lear*. She had not only studied the play, but also copied down the part of Cordelia, word for word!

The Experimental Study of Repression

In addition to clinical sources of data bearing on unconscious phenomena, there has been a very active study of repression in experimental settings (see Rapaport, 1942; Weiner, 1966). Freud was not very encouraging toward such laboratory investigations, for he felt that his clinical observations provided sufficient evidence and that tests of his ideas could be conducted adequately only during therapeutic sessions. However, others more fully recognized the limitations of drawing inferences where relevant variables are not controlled and where there is opportunity for observer bias.

Much of the modern research on repression will use the term **suppression** instead of repression. Using the term *repression* brings along all the implications of Freudian theory, whereas suppression does not. Wegner (1994) developed a model of suppression that he termed *Ironic Process*. The Ironic Process model proposes that there are two components to suppressing thoughts. The first component is an operating process that suppresses the unwanted thoughts and behaviors. The second component is a monitoring process that tests whether the first process is successful. Under most circumstances the first process successfully suppressed both the unwanted activity and the monitoring process. However, under conditions that increase cognitive load, the operating process does not have enough capacity to suppress both the unwanted activity and the monitor, so just the unwanted activity is suppressed. Ironically, this allows the monitor to bring to mind the unwanted activity. Wegner's classic demonstration is to ask participants to not think about a white bear. The active process would suppress both the thoughts of the white bear and the monitoring of whether a white bear has been brought into memory. However, under stress, the suppression processes would be working hard to keep the bear out of memory, while the monitoring process would be sitting there asking, "Have you thought of a white bear? Have you thought of a white bear?" In an additional level of irony, when a person is allowed to think about the suppressed activity, there is a rebound effect, causing the person to think about it more.

Freudian slips, which can be understood as a failure of repression, can be understood in this model as well. The thought that is not to be spoken—a racial epithet, for instance—is held back by the active process, while the monitor is making sure the word is not spoken (Galinsky and Moskowitz, 2007). When cognitive load is added, the monitor is still working while the active process is overwhelmed, making the unwanted word more likely to be spoken. Ironically, the people trying hardest to suppress the words are more likely to make the mistake.

suppression The process of keeping uncomfortable thoughts and feelings out of conscious awareness.

Cognitive psychologists have used a task in which participants learn to associate two words together—for instance, *ordeal* and *roach*. Participants then do a task in which they are given a signal about whether to recall roach after seeing ordeal, or to suppress roach. When they are repeatedly signaled to suppress, they are even less likely to recall roach on later trials (Anderson and Green, 2001). Perhaps most interesting from the Freudian perspective, researchers using the same paradigm were unable to create this effect for positive associations but did show suppression for negative stimuli (Lambert, Good, and Kirk, 2009), which fits entirely with the way that Freud would have described what we would repress.

Childhood Sexual Abuse and Repression

We have previously mentioned that there are those who now believe in Freud's original view that actual childhood sexual abuse was the basis of psychological dysfunction. Recently, the controversy over the existence of repression has resurfaced with respect to the issue of childhood sexual abuse. Victims of childhood sexual abuse are often perceived to be unable to recover the memories of such abuse because it has been repressed.

Briere and Conte (1993) found that 59% of a sample of 450 women and men who eventually reported forced sexual contact before age sixteen reported amnesia for sexual abuse at some point before age eighteen. This was more likely in those individuals who had been abused at an earlier age, who had been abused over a longer period of time, and whose abuse had been more violent.

Williams (1992) studied one hundred women who had been sexually abused as children and whose abuse had been carefully documented. The children had been brought to city hospital emergency rooms for treatment and collection of forensic evidence. About seventeen years later, the women were located and interviewed. It was found that 38% of them did not report memory of the abuse. Williams asserts that qualitative analysis of the interview data suggests that most actually did not remember, and it was not a matter of their simply failing to report on it. In one case, for instance, a woman did not remember that she had been abused by her uncle. What she did remember, however, was that her uncle had sexually assaulted "someone," but not her.

This evidence seems to suggest that many individuals who have been sexually abused as children either partially or completely lose memory of the abuse. Is this evidence of repression? It is not possible to say at this point. Memory is notoriously tricky, and at this point we do not know enough about how memory operates to say what possible mechanisms may be involved in this loss of memory, although repression is certainly one viable explanation.

On the other hand, the fact that many individuals in therapy recover memories of having been abused as children cannot necessarily be taken as evidence of repression. There is now concern that therapists are capable of implanting false memories in their clients. In this regard Loftus, (1993) reports a study in which she was able to successfully implant in a fourteen-year-old boy a false memory of an early traumatic experience of being lost in a shopping mall. As part of the research, the boy was told by his older brother that he had been lost in a mall when he was five years old, when in fact this had never happened. The brother offered some general details, including that the boy had been found by an older man wearing a flannel shirt. Within a couple of days the boy began to report more detailed memories of his feelings of being lost, of the man who found him, and of the mall itself. For instance, he described the man who found him as bald with grey hair and glasses, as well as his own feelings of being very scared.

Don't think about this white bear.

The concept of false memory is highly controversial, and more research is needed to clarify this important phenomenon.

Other Defenses

There are many other defenses against painful, anxiety-producing thoughts and feelings in addition to repression and perceptual defense, such as *rationalization, intellectualization* of impulses to strip them of their emotionality, and *isolation* of ideas to separate them from unacceptable related thoughts and attitudes. College students, because of their generally high verbal abilities, are frequently given to intellectualization: discussing threatening topics such as atomic warfare, future careers, and sexual inadequacy in an overly elaborate, rational manner which spares them the anxiety associated with these topics.

Defenses do not have precisely the same meaning or function for each individual. They differ in their consequences, generality, centrality to an individual's personality organization, degree of usage, and many other key dimensions. Suffice it to say that the manner in which one copes with unacceptable impulses is a key area of concern in the fields of personality and abnormal psychology. A few of the more familiar defense mechanisms are discussed in the following paragraphs.

Denial

In **denial**, impulses and associated ideas reach awareness, but their implications are rejected or denied. For example, an unwillingness to check on medical symptoms could indicate the presence of denial, as does "gallows humor," the tendency of soldiers to engage in banter and jest as they near an engagement with the enemy. While denial may be functional for soldiers marching off to combat, it can be damaging for the individual. To deny the possible diagnostic implications of a persistent swelling that may be symptomatic of cancer is to risk the possible consequences of failing to take advantage of early treatment. Denial can also result in profound psychological consequences as, for example, when one refuses to acknowledge negative traits in a potential spouse.

denial A defense mechanism in which a person refuses to acknowledge the truth, or the implications of that truth.

Reaction Formation

Reaction formation is the manifestation of behavior that is directly opposite to unconscious feelings and attitudes. A parent who defends against unconscious feelings of resentment toward an unwanted child by reacting with overwhelming affection is exhibiting a reaction formation. A few studies have demonstrated a relationship between homophobia and arousal with exposure to homosexual erotica (Adams, Wright, and Lohr, 1996; Zeichner and Reidy, 2009) and high degrees of sex guilt with higher arousal when exposed to sexual stimuli (Morokoff, 1985). Since it is nearly the opposite of genuine expression of feeling, reaction formation is often exaggerated, inflexible, and inappropriate.

reaction formation In Freud's theory, a defense mechanism in which a person behaves in a way directly opposite from some underlying anxiety-provoking impulse.

Projection

Projection consists of attributing one's own unacceptable, repressed feelings and ideas to others. Experimental studies have shown that perception of others' motives and feelings can be greatly influenced by the perceiver's own feelings and attitudes (Tagiuri, 1969). For example, frightened children are more likely to see other children as frightened (Feshbach and Feshbach, 1963; Murray, 1933). In the strictest definition of projection, the individual is completely unconscious of the impulse that is projected. However, although lack of awareness may facilitate projection, it is not a necessary condition for the attribution of one's own feelings and desires to others.

projection In Freud's theory, a defense mechanism involving the unconscious attribution of one's own unacceptable feelings or motives to others.

Displacement

The defense of **displacement** refers to repressed or blocked feelings and actions that are expressed toward an innocent target. In one well-known early study concerned with frustration effects, it was found that children at camp, who were prevented by the camp directors from engaging in a pleasurable activity, attributed fewer favorable traits to

displacement A defense mechanism in which a person shifts a reaction from an original target person or situation to some other person or situation.

minority-group members when judging their characters (Miller and Bugelski, 1948). This defense will be examined in more detail in Chapter 14.

Sublimation

sublimation In Freudian theory, a defense mechanism in which libidinal (sexual) energy is redirected from an unacceptable to a socially approved mode of expression.

Sublimation is a form of displacement in which an unacceptable, unsatisfied impulse is expressed in a socially acceptable form. Freud suggested, for instance, that unsatisfied sexual impulses could be expressed in highly approved artistic ways. Baumeister, Sommer, and Dale (1998) reviewed evidence for many of the defense mechanisms, finding support for many but wrote they "were unable to find any evidence for the theory of sublimation" (p. 1104). Lack of evidence does not disprove the theory, but positive evidence works far better than simply indicating that it hasn't been found yet.

Individual Differences in Defensive Preferences

repression-sensitization continuum An approach-avoidance stylistic dimension of individual differences in defense reactions.

As might be anticipated, individuals differ in their defensive reactions to threatening stimuli. Defensive preferences can be distinguished in many ways, according to their complexity, generality, effectiveness, and degree of reality distortion. One individual difference that has received much attention from psychologists is **repression-sensitization** (see Byrne, 1961). It is reasoned that some individuals respond to particular kinds of threats with repression and perceptual defense. In so doing, they avoid anxiety-laden information. Hysterical reactions, including symptoms such as blindness and limb paralysis, are generally associated with the use of repressive defenses. Conversely, it appears that one may cope with a particular threat by using sensitizing defenses. The person then becomes more vigilant to threat and remains in close contact with the stressful material. He or she may then be better able to monitor and control the threat. The constant worrier and the obsessive-compulsive neurotic are examples of the use of sensitizing defensive orientations.

Individual differences in repression-sensitization are generally assessed by means of a true/false, self-report inventory called the R-S scale (Byrne, 1961). Some typical items on the scale, with "True" answers indicating repression, are:

- I don't seem to care what happens to me.
- Often I feel as if there were a tight band about my head.

The items on this measure were taken from the Minnesota Multiphasic Personality Inventory (MMPI, see Chapter 8), and many of the items are also included in popular measures of general anxiety, such as the Manifest Anxiety Scale (MAS). Many investigations have examined the behavioral correlates of different responses to the scale items. It has been found, for example, that repressors, as opposed to people labeled as sensitizors, require longer tachistoscopic exposure before recognizing threatening words, remember more successful tasks than failed tasks, and are slower at learning a list of affective arousing words. Thus, the scale has some empirical validity (see Byrne, 1961).

A more recent individual difference approach to the categorization of individuals as repressors has employed two personality scales: a measure of anxiety and a measure of the tendency to respond in a socially desirable fashion (Weinberger, Schwartz, and Davidson, 1979). Individuals who display a pattern of low anxiety coupled with high scores on the social desirability measure are considered to be repressors: There have been a number of studies providing empirical support for this personality index of repressive tendencies; for example, individuals classified as repressors have fewer memories of their feelings and activities (Davis and Schwartz, 1987).

Two other examples follow of individual differences in repressive and defensive tendencies. Morokoff (1985) showed female subjects an erotic videotape and assessed the degree of sexual arousal both by asking them how aroused they were and by measuring their vaginal response with a special vaginal instrument. Women who had previously reported having a lot of guilt over sex reported being less sexually aroused by the videotape than women who reported low sex-guilt, although the women who reported a lot of guilt actually exhibited higher levels of physiological arousal. In a similar fashion, people who report being in excellent mental health, but who are rated by expert clinicians as denying mental distress, respond to stressful experimental procedures with higher levels of blood pressure than individuals who report feeling mentally distressed (Shedler et al., 1993).

Defense Mechanisms May Be Necessary

Defense mechanisms are important ways for us to cope with stressful situations (Coifman, Bonanno, Ray, and Gross, 2007). Defense mechanisms allow us to deal with our anxieties. The surgeon who holds someone's life in her hands is not going to be a very good surgeon if she focuses on that detail; instead, she would repress that thought and focus on the details of the surgery. Some defense mechanisms are going to be more appropriate and mature than other defense mechanisms (Cramer, 2000). A child may make use of denial when standing over the mess he just made: "It wasn't me." Using the same defense when caught in a sexual affair might make for a funny song but not a very mature defense mechanism. Blaming your professor for your grades (displacement), claiming she hates you (projection), isn't going to do anything except protect your own ego. Taking the time to inspect what problems you have with the course (intellectualization) is going to be a far more mature and effective defense mechanism.

General Evaluation

What, then, can we conclude about Freud's theory of personality? As was stated at the beginning of the chapter, it is useless to ask whether the theory is "correct" or "incorrect." Some of its concepts, such as that of defense mechanisms, have led to a great deal of research and have gained general acceptance. Other concepts, such as the death wish or the postulation of a closed energy system, have generated no research and have few adherents. In general, the theory's most significant contribution is that it provides a language with which to examine human action. It is therefore a most important step toward the development of a theory of personality, a step that builds a foundation for further work. But it is also just a first step and one with many shortcomings. The theory is often vague and without empirical support, concentrating excessively on particular facets of behavior and neglecting other aspects. As a result, it often leads to false interpretations and overgeneralizations.

There is a tendency to ask too much of this theory. People use it to try to explain why we engage in sports, why we are doing poorly in our interpersonal relationships, and why wars take place. At present, it is impossible for any single theory to account for such diverse phenomena with any degree of accuracy. Thus, rather than criticizing and rejecting Freud's theory out of hand, we should accept it for what it is and was: a monumental attempt to account for a great variety of human behavior by means of a few basic concepts and ideas. Many aspects and modifications of his ideas have been so widely incorporated in psychology and in contemporary thought that they may seem almost commonplace, for example, that we may be often unaware of important motivations that influence our behavior; that we engage in defensive thoughts and behaviors that serve to ward off anxiety and guilt; that experiences in childhood can have a profound effect upon the personality that we display as adults; that family relationships are characterized by anxieties and rivalry as well as by support and love; that disturbances in psychological functioning can have a psychological as well as biological basis; that our dreams, our fantasies, art, literature, and even many of our cultural beliefs and practices, may reflect unconscious impulses and motivations. Whether the overriding importance that Freud placed on libido theory will survive the test of time is questionable. But there is no doubt that Freudian theory has provided abundant insights and will influence psychology and social thought for many years to come.

Summary

1. Freud's ideas were spurred by a hypnotic demonstration that motivations are not always conscious and by the use of *free association*, a method initially derived from having hypnotized subjects talk about their symptoms.
2. *Homeostasis* refers to organisms' tendency to maintain a relatively stable internal environment; the doctrine of *hedonism* asserts that pleasure is the chief goal in life. Freud included both homeostasis and hedonism as basic principles in his conception of human behavior.
3. In Freud's system, if all psychological energy is *free*, then all wishes have been attained and there is a subjective state of pleasure.
4. Instincts are primarily sexual internal urges that strive for expression. They have a source (bodily metabolism), an aim (immediate discharge), and objects (satisfiers residing in the external world).
5. According to Freud, all behavior is determined, including jokes, slips of the tongue, and dreams. This is known as the principle of *psychological determinism*.
6. Humans progress through a fixed developmental sequence of oral, anal, phallic, and *genital stages*. The *Oedipal conflict*, which concerns the rivalry between a child and the same-sex parent, is resolved during the phallic stage. *Fixation* can result from specific disturbances during any one of the stages.
7. Freud conceived of personality as composed of three structures: *id*, *ego*, and *superego*. These structures represent the idea that behavior is in part determined by personal (biological) needs, social reality, and internalized ideals. The ego is the "executive" of these structures, responsible for the individual's overall adaptation.
8. *Repression* is the most important of the psychological defenses. Freud represented repression as a force active in keeping thoughts from consciousness. Many experimental investigations have tested this concept, but only a very few well-conceived studies have provided confirming evidence.
9. *Ironic process* is a way in which we suppress unwanted thoughts and actions that requires use of an active executive process and an automatic monitoring process.
10. There are many *defense mechanisms*, including *denial*, *reaction formation*, *projection*, *displacement*, and *sublimation*.
11. Individual differences on the *repression-sensitization* continuum have been identified by means of personality questionnaires.

Key Terms

anxiety (p. 53)
denial (p. 57)
defense mechanisms (p. 54)
displacement (p. 57)
Electra complex (p. 50)
ego (p. 53)
fixation (p. 51)
id (p. 52)
libido (p. 47)

Oedipal conflict (p. 50)
projection (p. 57)
reaction formation (p. 57)
repression (p. 54)
repression-sensitization (p. 58)
sublimation (p. 58)
superego (p. 53)
suppression (p. 55)

Thought Questions

1. Has psychoanalytic theory helped you to understand yourself? In what way?
2. Is repression necessarily "bad" for mental health? When, if at all, can repression facilitate psychological adaptation?
3. Freud maintained that hedonism is the chief goal in life. Can you think of times when you acted in a way that did not maximize pleasure? Could Freud have accounted for your behavior?
4. We have all had the experience of closing our eyes to avoid looking at something terrible or frightening. Can you think of any other methods you have used to avoid anxiety and stress?

Psychoanalytic Dissidents and Descendants

CHAPTER 4

Source: Monkey Business Images/Shutterstock

Chapter Outline

Rivals to Freud
Psychoanalysis Since Freud
Psychoanalysis in Flux

Although psychoanalysis began with Freud, it certainly did not end there. Psychoanalytic theory has undergone significant change since Freud's death, and Freud himself introduced major theoretical revisions during the course of his lifetime. Thus, any response to the question, "What is psychoanalytic theory?" depends on whether one refers to the early writings of Freud, the later writings of Freud, or more contemporary psychoanalytic theory. To complicate matters further, not only has Freud's theory of psychoanalysis undergone substantial revision, but also several similar, but significantly different, rival theories have emerged. Many contemporary modifications of psychoanalytic theory have been introduced in response to criticisms from these rival theories.

Rivals to Freud

Several of Freud's first rivals were early associates, including Carl Jung and Alfred Adler, who were prominent physicians in their own right. Because of their dissent on basic issues, they separated (or were asked to separate) from Freud with the request that they not call their theories "psychoanalytic." It is not always clear why some of Freud's adherents who proposed theoretical changes were able to retain their identification with classic psychoanalysis, while others decided to separate or were excluded from the psychoanalytic movement. In some instances, both personality and theoretical conflicts appear to have been involved. However, one common element in all the dissident movements is the rejection of libido or sexual motivation as the primary source of human conflict, anxiety, and neurosis. The alternatives to libido theory proposed by Jung

Basic Human Motivations as Perceived by Psychoanalytically Oriented Theorists

Carl Jung
Striving for self-actualization, as reflected in integrating the "wisdom" of the personal and collective unconscious with the products of conscious experience.

Alfred Adler
Will to power, feelings of inferiority, and striving toward superiority or perfection.

Karen Horney
Basic anxiety, as reflected in exaggerated needs for love (moving toward people), independence (moving away from people), and destruction (moving against people).

Erich Fromm
The expression of one's human, as contrasted to animal, nature; identity and a stable frame of reference for perceiving and comprehending the world, as reflected in the needs for relatedness to and transcendence of other people and physical nature.

(1916) and Adler (1927), as well as by such later dissidents as Horney (1937) and Fromm (1941), are diverse. (Highlight 4.1 provides a brief statement of some of these alternative motivations.) In response to their proposals, Freud would not deny that people are motivated by inferiority feelings (Adler) or by a need for relatedness to others (Fromm). But for Freud sexual motivation was primary. The possibility that human beings might have different central motives—with libidinal striving primary for some but ambition, pride, or need for affection dominant for others—was an unacceptable solution for Freud.

There are several possible reasons Freud held so tenaciously to libido theory. First, there is a certain theoretical simplicity and elegance in proposing one basic motive governing all human behavior, from which all desires and goals emerge. Second, transformations in libidinal or sexual impulses and the management and distribution of that energy, as discussed in Chapter 3, were basic premises in Freud's theory; lessening the importance of these impulses would have required substantial modification of the theory. Third, and here we are speculating about Freud's own psychodynamics, Freud had undergone enormous personal sacrifice in bringing the sexual basis of neurotic symptoms to the attention of medical colleagues and in suggesting the radical notion that young children may have sexual fantasies about their parents. Having sacrificed so much for libidinal theory, he must have been strongly motivated to defend that theory in the face of subsequent criticism.

In this chapter we will review some of the major psychoanalytically based alternative theories as well as some of the developments that have taken place in psychoanalytic theory itself subsequent to Freud. We first consider the work of Jung, Adler, Horney, and Fromm. We then move on to consider some of the more recent developments, such as that of ego psychology, the views of Erik Erikson, object relations theory, Kohut's Self Psychology, and Horowitz's concept of states of mind.

A word of precaution, though, before we review these alternatives: most did not arise from systematic empirical research. Most reflect mainly insights, speculations, and assumptions based on each theoretician's own clinical and life experiences. In addition, these theories do not lend themselves to critical empirical comparison, in large part because each stresses a different motivation. Thus, the theories are, in many respects, not *commensurate* (i.e., comparable with one another so that one theory may be judged "correct"). Rather, each theory explains some aspects of human behavior better than the other theories do.

The Analytic Psychology of Carl Jung

It would be wrong to presume that the only difference between Freud and his dissenters lay in the motivation believed to be central to human striving. Other revisions, innovations, and concepts were introduced by each theorist. The most comprehensive and formal alternative to Freudian theory is that proposed by Carl Gustav Jung (1875–1961). Jung, like Freud, has had a significant impact on modern thought and was a prolific writer and erudite scholar. Before he pursued a medical and then a psychiatric career, Jung's education and interests lay primarily in humanistic theology, philosophy, anthropology, and archaeology. This orientation became increasingly evident as Jung developed and expounded his own conception of human nature and the limits as well as the possibilities of human potential.

Freud and Jung

Jung had already begun a promising career as a leading young psychiatrist in Zurich, Switzerland, when he first became attracted to Freud's writings. It was Freud's interpretation of dreams that particularly intrigued him. Jung had had a long-standing interest in dreams, visions, and other manifestations of human fantasies. In addition, Freud's use of free association to unravel the unconscious meaning of dreams fit with Jung's exploratory investigation of word associations as a means of determining areas of internal conflict. After a lengthy correspondence with Freud, Jung came to visit him in Vienna in 1906. Freud's relationship with Jung had special personal as well as professional meanings for each. For Freud, concerned about the future of the fledgling psychoanalytic discipline, Jung's involvement represented the most important extension of the psychoanalytic movement outside of the Vienna circle. Freud, who was nineteen years Jung's senior, felt paternal toward Jung, an attitude and expectation that facilitated their interaction in the short run but did not bode well for their relationship in the long run.

Freud recognized Jung's brilliance and soon decided that Jung was to be his "crown prince," his successor as head of the psychoanalytic movement. When the International Psychoanalytic Association was founded in 1910, Jung became its first president at Freud's request. But growing theoretical differences began to affect their professional and personal relationship, and Jung withdrew as a member of the association only four years later. Freud thought that Jung's dissent was an expression of Jung's own unresolved Oedipal problem! (See Alexander, 1982.)

There is a sense in which Freud's diagnosis of the basis of his rift with Jung probably has some validity. But it is oversimplified. Jung did have personal difficulties in his relationship with a domineering mother and a troubled father, a pastor who was uncertain about his religious beliefs. He also felt that he was a failure. But Freud's paternalism tended to stimulate any negativism that Jung may have transferred to Freud from his feelings toward his father. In addition, Freud had a history of establishing close relationships with professional peers and then breaking the relationship. This was the case with Breuer and with Fliess (Gay, 1988). Finally, apart from any interpersonal issues, there were genuine and important theoretical differences between Jung and Freud.

Analytic Psychology

Jung saw human beings as guided as much by aims and aspirations as by sexual urges. Jung's formulation of a basic human striving for growth and self-actualization was probably the major factor in his rift with Freud. When Freud asked Jung to become the permanent president of the International Psychoanalytic Association, he also asked for a commitment to the overriding importance of the libido, requesting, "Promise me never to abandon the sexual theory. This is the most essential thing of all. You see, we must make a dogma of it, an unshakable bulwark" (Campbell, 1971, p. xviii). But Jung believed that the unconscious instinctual life embraces more than simply sex and aggression; it includes other urges such as the need to create and to self-actualize. These ideas were subsequently incorporated by humanistic psychologists in America, to the extent that Gordon Allport, one of the original leaders of this movement, spent a year under Jung's tutelage.

To distinguish his approach from classic psychoanalysis, Jung called his theory of personality **analytic psychology**. A basic assumption of this theory is that the personality consists of competing forces and structures that must be balanced. For example, each of us, according to Jung, has both masculine and feminine tendencies; however, an integrated

analytic psychology Jung's personality theory that deviates from psychoanalysis in its emphasis on the collective unconscious and on the human striving toward self-fulfillment.

personality balances its more masculine aggressiveness with a more feminine sensitivity. In a similar manner, there must be balance between our conscious and our unconscious. Jung thus emphasized conflicts between opposing forces *within* the individual, rather than between the individual and the demands of society or between the individual and reality. For Jung, a self-actualized individual emerges out of the struggle to balance and integrate the various opposing forces that make up the personality. Moreover, for Jung, the process of development and growth is not resolved in childhood but continues into maturity and later years.

The Collective Unconscious

Jung's interest in archaeology and in ancient cultures and mythology led him to take a much more positive view than Freud of the function of symbols, dreams, and related unconscious processes. One of the most original and controversial concepts in Jung's theory is that of the collective unconscious, which, according to Jung, is the source of much of our vitality, creativity, and neurosis. Jung differentiated the *ego*, or the conscious mind; the *personal unconscious*, which contains repressed memories and desires; and the **collective unconscious**, which includes the psychological residue of the human species' ancestral past. The collective unconscious consists of universal tendencies to respond selectively to particular situations and figures with particular kinds of feelings. Jung contended that "the collective unconscious contains the whole spiritual heritage of mankind's evolution, born anew in the brain structure of each individual" (Campbell, 1971, p. 45).

collective unconscious In Jungian theory, the site of inherited primitive, universal attitudes and ideals (archetypes) of which we are not conscious.

archetypes In Jungian theory, the primeval contents of the collective unconscious.

The collective unconscious is made up of powerful, primordial elements called **archetypes**. Among the many archetypes postulated by Jung are the hero, the wise man, the sun god, the demon, and even each key member of the family. Each archetype is associated with an instinctive tendency to have a particular kind of feeling or thought toward a corresponding object or experience. For example, an infant's image of its mother will consist of aspects of the actual mother infused with the preformed conception of the mother archetype.

A statue representing Heracles in Kassel, Germany. Heracles is an example of Jung's idea of dual birth.

Two especially significant archetypes are the animus and anima. The *animus* is the male archetype that is experienced by a woman, while the *anima* is the female archetype experienced by a man. These archetypes imply that, to some extent, women have innate dispositions toward particular ideas and attitudes about men and that men have analogous innate ideas about women. Thus, for example, a woman's response to a man is, according to Jung, a function of her animus archetype as well as a function of the actual man. The same holds true of a male's perceptions of and reactions to a female.

Two additional archetypes that warrant special mention are the shadow and the persona. The *shadow* is the lower, animal side of human nature, or our darker instincts. The passions and impulses associated with the shadow, not unlike those of Freud's id, give rise to socially unacceptable thoughts and behaviors. The *persona*, in contrast, is the socially acceptable mask that each person wears public. The persona archetype, in conjunction with social conventions, makes individuals tend to adopt masks and conceal their real nature. If this archetype too powerful, then the individual becomes shallow, playing a role and detach from genuine emotional experience. There must be a balance among the person the shadow, and the other archetypes. The archetype of the *self* signifies the innate tendency to balance and integrate the diverse components of the person. The primary symbolic representation of the self archetype, according to Jung, the magic circle, or *mandala*. This symmetrical circle symbolizes human striving for unity and wholeness. An important component of the path to self-actualization is the development of understanding of and sensitivity to these archetypes that comprise the collective unconscious. It further includes their integration with other facets of one's personality and with the actual attributes of particular me and women with whom one interacts.

It is interesting to consider the specific examples that Jung invoked as evidence for the archetypes. For example, Freud interpreted a da Vinci painting Saint Anne with the Virgin Mary and the Christ Child as meaning that Leonardo himself had two role mothers. Jung, on the other hand, contended that it was manifestation of the collectively shared and inherited archetype of the dual mother, or rebirth. There are many myths about dual descent from both human and divine parents. Heracles, according to Greek legend, was born of mortal parents, but unwillingly adopted by the goddess Hera; and Christ, through his baptism in the Jordan, was reborn (Jung, 1936). According to Jung, the practice giving children godfathers and godmothers is another example of the dual-birth motif.

Archetypes are reflected in the universal symbols, images, themes, myth and art of Eastern and Western cultures, as well as in dreams and even in the visions and symptoms of psychotics. Archetypes "create myths, religions, and philosophies that characterize and influence whole nations" (Jung, 1936, p. 6) and influence individual behaviors. These vast sources provided Jung with the needed "proof" for the existence of archetypes. Note again how Jung's training in archaeology and philosophy influenced his ideas, in contrast with the natural sciences that formed Freud's background.

The construct of archetypes is not readily reconcilable with modern psychological science, a factor contributing to the limited input that Jung has had on contemporary psychology. However, the phenomena that the construct of archetypes was invented to explain—the apparent universality of particular attitude conflicts, feelings, and images—may well be of fundamental significance and warrant systematic investigation and analysis.

Complexes

Another of Jung's important, but less controversial, contributions is the concept of the complex. Our common reference today to a "mother complex or a "guilt complex" are some examples of how Jung has influenced our everyday vocabulary. A **complex** consists of a set of feelings, ideas, memories, and behaviors organized around a common nuclear element that provides the binding power and "pull" of the complex. For example, an adolescent girl seen in a local clinic was unusually attracted to older men. At the same time, she experienced a great deal of conflict and guilt over these relationships. When directly questioned about her late father, she could relate very few memories of him. And when given a word association test, in which she was to respond with the first association that came into her mind, in response to her father's name she blushed and finally uttered a barely audible sound. This cluster of behaviors is a manifestation of what would be called a father complex.

Jung (1904) discovered evidence of these complexes through a clever adaptation of the word association procedure first devised by Galton. Jung presented lists of words to his patients and determined which words produced irregularity in breathing and changes in skin resistance. From an analysis of the content of these words, he was able to infer the existence of specific complexes. There are now a variety of modern word association procedures based on Jung's method. Typically, participants are asked to give a verbal response to each stimulus in a list of words. Delays in response time and unusual associations are taken to indicate that the stimulus has special meaning for the participant.

Personality Types

One of Jung's best-known contributions is his personality typology of two basic attitudes, or orientations, toward life: **extroversion** and **introversion**. Both orientations are viewed as existing simultaneously in each person, with one usually dominant. The extrovert's energy is directed toward external objects and events, while the introvert is more concerned with inner experiences. The extrovert is outgoing and makes friends easily; the introvert frequently prefers solitude and cultivates few relationships. Most investigators now view extroversion-introversion as a single personality dimension along which people vary, in

complex In Jung's theory, a group of feelings, ideas, memories, and behaviors organized around a significant object.

extroversion From Jung, the tendency to be strongly oriented toward other people and social situations.

introversion In Jung's theory, the tendency to be attentive and interested in one's own thoughts and feelings.

contrast to Jung's conception of a pair of opposing attitudes. There is a substantial amount of empirical evidence indicating that extroversion-introversion is indeed a significant personality dimension (e.g., Dicks-Mireaux, 1964; Eysenck, 1947; Wilson, 1978). The current dominant models of personality traits include this major dimension (Ashton and Lee, 2010; McCrae, Costa, and Martin, 2005).

What happens when introverts and extroverts are paired with partners sharing the same versus opposite personality traits? In a study in which the effects of this variation were explored, extroverts matched with each other had the most upbeat and expansive conversations of all the paired groups (Thorne, 1987). The introverts tended to have more serious discussions that were focused on fewer topics.

Jung extended his typology to include two other pairs of opposing tendencies: *thinking* versus *feeling* and *sensing* versus *intuiting*. These were considered to be psychological functions describing different ways in which extroverts and introverts deal with and perceive their experiences. *Thinking* is intellectual, leading one to ask how things work. Its opposite function, *feeling*, leads one to ask whether an experience feels good or bad. When the feeling function is dominant, one is oriented toward such emotional responses as love, anger, and pleasure. *Sensing* is a reality function; when it is dominant, one deals with the external world in terms of appearance, as if one were a photographer. On the other hand, when the *intuitive* function is prominent, one is responsive to unconscious images, symbols, and the mysteries of experience. Thus, the perceptive functions of sensation and intuition are contrasting ways for the individual to gather data—literal or symbolic—whereas the judgment functions of thinking versus feeling relate to how these data are evaluated.

An Overview of Jung's Theory

In sum, it is evident that most of Jung's theory remains at the level of conjecture. In contrast to Freudian theory, which stimulated an enormous and varied body of research, Jung's work (with the exception of introversion-extroversion) has given rise to little systematic research. In addition, his concepts of the collective unconscious and archetypes are difficult, if not impossible, to test empirically. Nevertheless, Jung has deepened and expanded our conception of cross-cultural themes, human experience, and human potential. He recognized the positive implications of religious, spiritual, and even mystical experiences for personality growth and can truly be said to be the forerunner of the humanistic movement in psychology (see Chapter 6).

In deviating from Freud's theory, Jung looked further inward, amplifying and reconceptualizing the contents and structure of the psyche. On the other hand, other analysts trained in the psychoanalytic tradition looked outward, maintaining that social motivations, such as the desire for status, approval, and power, can supercede biological urges. Included in this group are such figures as Alfred Adler, Karen Horney, Harry Stack Sullivan, and Erich Fromm. These analysts differ in the particular motivations they believe to be central in human behavior and in how much attention they give to social influence as a determinant of personality. However, these "social theorists" are all sensitive to the role of society in influencing personality and provide valuable, creative insights into personality structure and dynamics.

Alfred Adler's Individual Psychology

Alfred Adler (1870–1937) was a Viennese physician who became associated with Freud shortly after the turn of the century. However, he never fully accepted psychoanalytic theory, and Freud found Adler's criticism difficult to tolerate. Although Adler served as president of the Vienna Psychoanalytic Association in 1910, he severed all relations with psychoanalysis just one year later (Ansbacher and Ansbacher, 1956, 1964). He frequently visited the United States, finally settling in New York in 1933.

A basic tenet of Adler's *individual psychology* is that human beings have an innate social interest (Adler, 1927): it is in the nature of humans to be cooperative and interested in the welfare of other people. This positive, socially oriented image of human nature is in sharp contrast to Freud's depiction of the individual as driven by biological urges that are inevitably in conflict with the requirements of social living. According to Adler, people develop problems because of mistaken goals and patterns of living that block the expression and realization of their social interest—a far cry from Freud's ideas about repression of libidinal impulses.

Striving for Superiority

Closely related to the idea of innate positive social motivation is Adler's assumption of a basic human tendency to strive for superiority. Superiority, for Adler, does not necessarily entail power over others or competitive success, but refers to a more general goal of perfection and self-realization. The human being, in his view, constantly strives to move upward. There is a close similarity between this characterization of human motivation and Jung's postulation of a creative energy force motivating the organism toward wholeness and integration. In the neurotic or emotionally disturbed individual, this positive force is misdirected, manifesting itself in the pursuit of power, prestige, and other selfish goals.

Adler's conception of a force moving individuals in the direction of higher goals was the outcome of his own gradual evolution in thinking. Shortly after his association with psychoanalysis, Adler concluded that aggression was a more significant drive than sexuality. However, whereas aggression alone assumed greater importance in Freudian thought, Adler eventually came to view other motivations as more profound and ultimate. Adler replaced aggression with the striving for power, and both power and aggression were subsequently seen as distortions of a more basic urge for superiority or perfection. Adler coined the term *masculine protest* to describe exaggerated, power-oriented behaviors by men or women in response to feelings of inadequacy and inferiority.

Inferiority

The concept of inferiority appeared quite early in Adler's writings. Adler noted that many individuals seem to engage in constant efforts to overcome feelings of inferiority. Initially, he interpreted these as reactions to organ inferiority. As a practicing physician he encountered people who attempted to overcome a physical deficit by intensive exercise of the affected organ or by development of a compensatory skill; e.g., the development of acute hearing as a compensation for poor vision. A famous historical example of compensation for organ inferiority is Demosthenes, who stuttered as a child and is said to have practiced speaking with pebbles in his mouth to overcome his handicap. Thus, in spite, or perhaps because of his handicap, Demosthenes became an outstanding Greek orator.

Adler extended the concept of inferiority to its modern usage, which refers to feelings of psychological and social, as well as physical, inadequacy. Feelings of psychological or social inferiority, like those of physical inferiority, might also have positive consequences, as when a young child's feelings of inadequacy compared with an older sib might lead him or her to learn new skills. Adler, it may be noted, had much more experience working directly with children than Freud did. His focus on ego motivations such as inferiority feelings in contrast to Freud's emphasis on id impulses, coupled with his orientation to the social situation, was reflected in his therapeutic approach, which tended to be more practical and reality oriented than classic psychoanalytic therapy.

Style of Life

The individual's efforts to compensate for real or imagined inferiorities may affect a specific behavior, as in the case of Demosthenes, or the entire organization of personality. Adler referred to the distinctive personality that each of us develops in response to our inferiorities as our *style of life*. Each person is said to have a unique style of life, formed by the age of five, that characterizes the person throughout life and becomes the distinguishing feature of the personality. A related concept is that of the *creative self*, the facet of the individual that provides direction for life by organizing, transforming, and integrating one's experiences. This concept, like some of Jung's notions, is more an affirmation of the human spirit than an explanation of behavior.

An Overview of Adler's Theory

In sum, Adler presents a positive image of human nature and its potential. People are motivated by social interest and by creative efforts to attain perfection and overcome inferiority. These positive urges can turn destructive or neurotic because of deficient child-rearing practices, like rejection or overindulgence, or because of deficiencies in the larger society. Freud, in comparison, presented a more pessimistic, tragic view of development and considered Adler's psychology shallow and superficial. Although Freud recognized social and familial influences, he believed that people are destined to experience conflict between biological urges and the requirements of a civilized society regardless of the mode of child rearing or the organization of society.

Freud's and Adler's contrasting assumptions about human nature do not lend themselves to empirical examination. Which image one considers more valid depends on one's personal experience and worldview rather than on scientific findings. However, Adler's views concerning the importance of such ego or self-based motives as power strivings and inferiority feelings have found acceptance in contemporary views of personality dynamics and psychopathology. Also, Adler's more pragmatic, reality-based approach to psychotherapy is reflected in the work of a number of psychotherapists (Beck, 1976; Ellis, 1967). In addition, some of Adler's more limited and clinically based observations have been subject to empirical test and are among his most enduring contributions to psychology (see Highlight 4.3).

Karen Horney

Karen Horney (1885–1952) was a European-trained physician and psychoanalyst who had been psychoanalyzed by a disciple of Freud and emigrated to the United States from Berlin in 1932. Horney's first book, *The Neurotic Personality of Our Times*, was published in 1937 and provoked enormous controversy among psychoanalysts. Her departures from Freudian theory were no less striking than Adler's, and it was evident, from the perspective of Freud's adherents, that she had left the fold to join the ranks of the heretics.

President Theodore Roosevelt overcame early physical weaknesses to become an assertive, physically active adult.

Birth Order and Personality Development

One of Adler's most acute clinical observations was of the importance of birth order in determining personality development. The oldest child, having received the parents' individual attention, has the problem of coping with the birth of the second child. Because one common reaction is concern with maintaining power and the status quo, oldest children are likely to be more conservative, responsible, and socially oriented. The second child, competing to be "number one," is likely to be ambitious; the youngest child is often the family "pet," overindulged and spoiled. Although earlier research failed to provide support for these hypotheses, a classic study by Schachter (1959) reawakened interest in this Adlerian hypothesis and stimulated a large body of research indicating that birth order, in conjunction with such variables as family size and sex, does affect personality. Schachter conducted a number of experimental studies on the effect of anxiety on the need to affiliate with others. Participants who were led to believe that they would be shocked in a coming experimental session chose to wait for the session with people in a similar situation more often than they chose to wait alone. Of special relevance for Adler's views concerning birth order was the finding that, of first-born participants, 80 percent chose to wait with others while only 31 percent of later-borns chose to do so. This was believed to demonstrate the greater social orientation of the first-borns. Healy and Ellis (2007) found that first-borns were more conscientious and achievement oriented, whereas later-borns were more rebellious and open to new experiences.

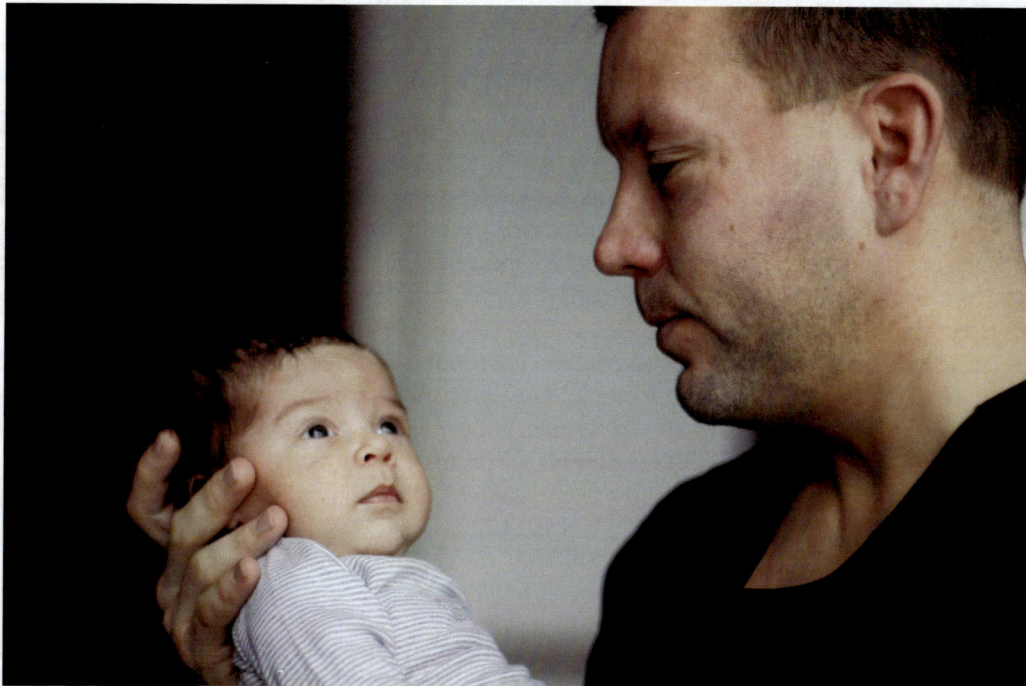

According to Horney, infant helplessness does not need to lead to anxiety, rather is influenced by parental warmth and affection.

Source: Mardoyan Anaida/Shutterstock

Horney's and Adler's ideas were fundamentally very similar. Horney was optimistic about the possibilities for human growth, satisfaction, and self-realization. She placed greater emphasis on the role of self-enhancement, personal security, and interpersonal (social) motives than on sexual and biological urges as the principal determinants of adjustment and neurosis. However, the specific interpersonal motives and mechanisms that Horney suggested as central to personality differ from those stressed by Adler. For Horney, **neurosis** was best understood as a pattern of response to basic anxiety, a concept which has some similarity to Adler's notion of inferiority feelings. Horney described basic

neurosis An emotional, nonpsychotic disorder characterized by anxiety and other symptoms and resulting in partial impairment of functioning.

anxiety as "the feeling a child has of being isolated and helpless in a potentially hostile world" (Horney, 1945, p. 41). The infant's feeling of helplessness is not inevitable but is dependent on the extent of parental warmth, affection, consistency, and other behaviors that contribute to a child's feeling of security.

Just as she felt that basic anxiety is not inescapable, Horney also took exception to the Freudian notion that penis envy in women is preordained by their biological nature. In general, she disagreed with Freud's psychology of women, contending that he failed to appreciate how the socialization of women fosters problems in self-confidence and leads to an exaggerated dependence on the love relationship.

Horney was sensitive to the various neurotic patterns that frequently exist in adult relationships, which she perceived as strategies that the child develops to reduce the distress of feelings of insecurity and helplessness (that is, of basic anxiety). Finding security in trying to please others, manipulating and exploiting others, and even devaluing oneself are examples of such neurotic patterns. What makes these patterns of behavior neurotic or maladaptive is that they are exaggerated and cannot produce satisfaction. In addition, although one of these modes of behavior might be dominant, they tend to conflict with one another, causing additional tension and distress.

Horney categorized neurotic patterns according to three fundamental types:

1. *Moving toward people*—a neurotic need for approval and affection from others; a need to please and defer to others.
2. *Moving against people*—a neurotic need for power; a need to exploit others and constantly feel superior.
3. *Moving away from people*—a neurotic need to be aloof, detached, uninvolved, completely self-sufficient, and independent of others.

All three neurotic patterns result in self-images that are impossible to live up to and trap both the person and those with whom he or she is involved. These patterns may maintain security, but they also serve as ways of expressing the unconscious hostility and rage to which feelings of helplessness give rise. Horney contended that there is a thin line between acting aloof in a social relationship and rejecting someone. Furthermore, one can control and even injure or psychologically destroy another person by excessive demands for affection, help, and support.

Horney neither formulated a comprehensive theory of personality nor attracted a large group of disciples to promote her ideas. However, her descriptions of neurotic patterns and their underlying mechanisms have been incorporated into many contemporary personality theories that address the problems of neurosis and psychopathology. Her views on the importance of the child's early experience of affection and security are reflected in a wealth of research (Bowlby, 1969; Harlow, 1971; Spitz, 1945; see Chapter 12).

Erich Fromm

The last of the theorists we will consider in this chapter is Erich Fromm (1900–1980). Fromm, like Adler, Horney, and Sullivan, had psychoanalytic training but, unlike the others, came to psychoanalysis with advanced training in sociology rather than with a medical degree (for a succinct description of differences among these theorists, the reader may refer back to Highlight 4.1). Fromm's background in sociology and the related disciplines of philosophy and political science is reflected in his contribution to the understanding of human personality. Fromm's views present an unusual combination of tough-minded Marxist analysis of the impact of economic institutions on personality structure, with warm, almost romantic humanism. While Freud saw social institutions as a mirror or consequence of basic psychological needs, Fromm perceived the individual as essentially victimized by a harmful society. Fromm, a refugee of Nazi Germany, believed that the attraction of so many Germans to extreme political forms was a consequence of the structure of German society, rather than a reflection of uninhibited biological urges.

Personality and Society

Fromm's first book, *Escape from Freedom* (1941), linked changes in basic personality to change in Western society. Fromm suggested that human beings strive for freedom and autonomy but that this very struggle may result in feelings of alienation from nature and society. People need to be free and autonomous, but they also need to feel connected and related to others. The intensity of this conflict and the different ways in which it is resolved, according to Fromm, are dependent on the economic organization of the society.

In preliterate cultures and feudal societies, the individual had few choices. Behavior and opportunity were fully prescribed by one's tribe or one's social and economic position in society. There was little freedom, but also little alienation. With the Renaissance, however, an individual striving for freedom and independence came to the fore. The Protestant Reformation and the rise of capitalism enhanced and emphasized individual opportunity, freedom of choice, and personal responsibility, but the price for this, Fromm argued, was intense feelings of isolation and loneliness.

How do individuals cope with alienation? One way is to surrender individuality and choice. Fromm described a number of personality mechanisms that are unconsciously adopted to "escape freedom." The first of these, *authoritarianism*, is manifested in either masochistic or sadistic tendencies, terms that do not have sexual connotations, as Freud used them, but refer to ways of relating to authority. The masochist behaves in an excessively helpless, submissive, and dependent manner, whereas the sadist strives to control, dominate, and exploit others. Both strivings are typically found in the same person. A highly authoritarian military structure may foster both traits, with the same individual behaving sadistically toward soldiers of lower rank and masochistically in relation to superior officers. Another escape mechanism that Fromm described is *destructiveness*, in which case a person no longer attempts to relate to others but reduces feelings of powerlessness and alienation by seeking to weaken others. Finally, one can escape through excessive *conformity* to social rules; by being completely conventional and exactly like others, one can reduce feelings of separateness.

Fromm's concept of authoritarianism arose, in large part, from an effort to explain the growth of fascism in pre–World War II Europe and the psychological attraction the Nazi ideology had for many individuals. It provided the stimulus for an extensive body of research on the authoritarian personality that was initiated shortly after that war (Adorno, et al., 1950).

The Basic Needs

As Fromm (1955, 1964) developed and elaborated on these ideas in his later work, his humanistic orientation became more evident. The conflict between striving for freedom and striving for security centered on five basic human needs:

1. *A need for relatedness*—to have, care for, share with, and be responsible for others.
2. *A need for transcendence*—to become more creative and rise above one's more animal nature.
3. *A need for rootedness*—to replace our separation from nature with feelings of kinship with others.
4. *A need for identity*—to achieve distinctiveness through one's own efforts or through identification with another person or group.
5. *A need for a frame of reference*—to have a stable structure or framework that will aid in organizing and understanding one's experiences.

Each of these needs can be satisfied in neurotic ways or in a personally and socially productive manner. In Fromm's later work, one finds a consideration of human needs in the context of existential issues such as awareness of death and one's separateness from others (see discussion of humanistic, existential approaches in Chapter 6). Again, the social and economic structure of the surrounding society is critical.

We have already seen, in Chapter 2, that social differences can influence personality. However, there is little evidence indicating that Fromm's character structures are linked with particular social structures. Nevertheless, Fromm's theoretical views are stimulating and appealing. In the tradition of social reformers, he argued that through radical change in the social structure one can create a society in which both the individual's and the society's needs can be met. Particularly in his later writings, Fromm proposed that humans are essentially good but become corrupted by civilization, a theme reminiscent of Rousseau's "noble savage." For Fromm, true self-love and the love of others are sides of the same coin. In deriving a humanistic code of ethics, Fromm put the matter most succinctly: "Evil constitutes the crippling of man's powers; vice is irresponsibility toward himself" (Fromm, 1947, p. 20). A judgment on whether this positive and optimistic view of human nature is more "correct" than Freud's pessimistic view will have to await the verdict of posterity.

Psychoanalysis Since Freud

Classic psychoanalysis has never been a static theory. It underwent regular and major changes during the course of Freud's lifetime. For example, the concepts of id, ego, and superego were not introduced until the 1920s, well after Freud had laid the major foundations of his theory. Since Freud's death, psychoanalytic theory has continued to evolve, with new concepts introduced, old ones revised, and new directions taken.

These more recent changes have come from a number of sources. First, psychoanalysis has not been immune to the contributions and criticisms of its dissidents, and efforts have been made to accommodate some of these critiques without altering the basic structure of the theory (Erikson, 1950; Anna Freud, 1946; Kardiner, 1945). Second, psychoanalysis was recognized even by Freud as incomplete. Because it still has areas of inconsistency and, ambiguity, a good deal of work has been directed toward making the theory more logical and coherent (Hartmann, 1964; Rapaport, 1959; Schafer, 1976). Third, as psychoanalysts experimented with therapeutic techniques and expanded their range of patients, new ideas were introduced to account for their observations (Erikson, 1950; Anna Freud, 1946; Fairbairn, 1952; M. Klein, 1937; Kohut, 1971). Perhaps surprisingly, experimental research has played a very minor role in these changes, even though an enormous number of studies have been directed to the investigation of psychoanalytic propositions (Kline, 1972).

We cannot hope in a few pages or even a few chapters to do justice to the development of psychoanalytic theory during the years since Freud's death. Many of these changes are either technical or involve esoteric controversies of concern only to psychoanalysts. Other changes, however, are of major significance, including a shift in emphasis away from instinctual drive conflicts to the problems posed by social attachments and maintaining one's individuality. There are several directions being taken in contemporary psychoanalytic theory that are of particular interest to students of personality.

1. *The growth of psychoanalytic ego psychology.* Increasing attention is being paid to defense mechanisms; to ego functions such as thinking, perception, and mastery; and to the development of the self and related ego structures. For example, analysts have become as much concerned with coping strategies and modes of adaptation as with basic id-instigated drives; that is, there is as much interest in the ways in which people deal with conflicts and with the effectiveness of their responses or strategies as there is in the motivational source of the conflict. A particularly significant component of this new direction has been object relations theory, which deals with the child's attachment to and thoughts about people, the effect of these attachments and thoughts on the child's individuality and feelings about the self, and how these factors change during the course of development. For example, a question of interest to objects relations theorists would be the developmental effects of a disturbed relationship with the mother when an infant is six months old versus the same disturbed relationship when the infant is eighteen months old. Note that the focus here is on relationships, not solely on impulse frustration or gratification.

2. *Disenchantment with psychic energy and drive therapy.* Modern psychoanalysts do not reject the importance of libidinal impulses and the psychosexual development of the child. However, there has been dissatisfaction with Freud's theory of libidinal energy and its supposed distribution and expenditure. These concepts are far removed from experiences that individuals report and from their perceived sources of conflict. Thus, there have been efforts to bring the theory closer to the perceived world of the patient in therapy.

3. *Greater recognition of the influence of culture and the family.* Although modern psychoanalytic thinking does not attribute the same importance to social variables, as do such dissidents as Fromm, Horney, and Sullivan, there is increased acknowledgment of the influence of social institutions on personality. There has been particular interest in the effects of cultural variables on the development of ego functions and self-processes, as evidenced in the writings of Erik Erikson and other psychoanalysts.

The writings of contemporary psychoanalytic theorists reflect these three trends in varying degrees. There is considerable ferment and debate among psychoanalysts over the significance of these theoretical developments. It will become clear in the following pages that contemporary psychoanalysis does not speak with the same unified voice as when Freud was alive and functioning as its principal arbitrator and innovator.

Erik Erikson

Of all the psychoanalytic writers to modify and expand psychoanalytic theory, the best known is German-born Erik H. Erikson (1902–1994). There is some question about whether he should be included among psychoanalytic descendants or psychoanalytic dissidents, with the choice depending on whether one emphasizes the similarities or the differences between his views and those prevailing among post-Freudian analysts. Since Erikson perceived his own views as expanding rather than radically altering Freudian theory, he has been included in this section of the chapter, rather than in the earlier section on alternatives to psychoanalysis.

Before being trained in psychoanalysis by Anna Freud, Erikson was an art teacher in a progressive private school and a graduate of a training program for teachers in the Montessori method. Erikson's educational background, his direct teaching experiences with children, and the Montessori emphasis on the child's development of initiative through play and work are evident in his later theoretical writings. Following the completion of his psychoanalytic training in Vienna, Erikson emigrated to the United States. At various times he held positions at Yale, at the University of California in Berkeley, at the Austin Riggs Center (a leading psychoanalytically oriented institute), and at Harvard University. His first book, *Childhood and Society* (1950), was a landmark volume, an impressively creative extension of psychoanalytic theory. It contains the essential ideas that provided the framework for his subsequent theoretical writings (1964, 1968, 1976) and his biographies of Luther (1958) and Gandhi (1969). We see in Erikson's writings an emphasis on ego processes and cultural influences, although the significance of libidinal development and biological factors is not denied.

The Stages of Development

The notion of developmental stages was central to Erikson's thought. He viewed the early stages of development in terms similar to Freud's, but he examined these stages from the perspective of the particular kinds of ego processes involved, rather than in terms of biologically determined libidinal tensions. An emphasis on ego processes leads naturally to consideration of social and cultural forces, for the ego is the mediator between personal needs and the demands of social reality. In addition, Erikson did not view the pattern of personality as essentially completed and unchangeable by the time the child enters school. His analysis of development embraced the full life span, from infancy to maturity.

Source: wavebreakmedia/Shutterstock

In Erikson's model, people continue to experience personality development across the life span. Each person in the photo would be experiencing a different psychosocial stage.

TABLE 4.1 Erikson's Eight Stages and Their Implications for Personality Structure

Psychosocial stages	Personality dimensions
1. Oral-sensory (first year)	Basic trust versus mistrust
2. Muscular-anal (ages 2–3)	Autonomy versus shame and doubt
3. Locomotor-genital (ages 3–5)	Initiative versus guilt
4. Latency (ages 5–12)	Industry versus inferiority
5. Puberty and adolescence	Identity versus role confusion
6. Early adulthood	Intimacy versus isolation
7. Adulthood	Generativity versus stagnation
8. Maturity	Ego integrity versus despair

psychosocial stages In Erikson's theory of personality, the periods from birth to maturity posing particular developmental tasks and providing the basis for specific personality characteristics.

Erikson proposed eight **psychosocial stages** in personality formation, each stage critical for developing certain fundamental personality characteristics and preparing the individual for later ones. Table 4.1 shows how basic personality dimensions are related to the psychosocial stages. Each stage involves a crisis or developmental problem; if the crisis is adequately resolved, then the individual acquires a healthy component of personality (e.g., trust or personal initiative); if the crisis is not adequately reconciled, then a negative quality (e.g., mistrust or guilt) is acquired. For example, in the earliest, oral-sensory stage the infant interacts mainly with its mother, and the goal of the interaction is primarily the supplying of food. It is the infant's first interaction with the social world, in which it finds out either that basic needs are fulfilled generously and with affection, or that the world is harsh and unpredictable, giving supplies grudgingly and without love. According to Erikson, the infant develops a sense of trust or mistrust toward the world during this period. That is, the infant is becoming a trusting or a mistrustful person. Although later events can alter the basic disposition that has been established, the first experience of fulfilled or unfulfilled expectations is nevertheless of critical importance.

In later work, Erikson (1976) introduced the concept of *ritualization* to describe a culturally patterned activity or social ritual which each stage fosters. In the oral-sensory stage, the mother recognizes the child through personal but culturally ritualized touching, feeling, and other interactions. This constitutes a significant affirmation of the child and of the mutuality between mother and child. This relationship is believed to form the foundation for subsequent adult ritualizations, such as certain religious ceremonies.

An Overview of Erikson's Work

Erikson's theoretical formulations are especially appealing to contemporary readers because of his emphasis on factors that underscore a sense of identity and relationships with others. If sexual problems can be said to have been the predominant "hangup" in the Victorian era, then problems of confusion over self-identity can be said to be the predominant concern in modern, technologically advanced Western societies.

Like Freud, Erikson thought that conflict was inevitable in the human struggle, but he had a less tragic and pessimistic conception of the outcome of conflict resolution. Self-insight and control, he felt, are important in coping with the dilemmas of living. In addition, the ability to resolve conflict is substantially augmented by the attributes acquired during development, given a positive resolution of each developmental stage. The mature person evolves the attributes, or "virtues," that help him or her to cope with problems: hope, will, purpose, and competence (the rudiments of virtue developed in the four childhood stages); fidelity (the adolescent virtue); and love, care, and wisdom (the central virtues of adulthood) (see Erikson, 1964).

Erikson's work contains a sensitivity to the problems encountered in the course of development that lends credence to his views. Problems of identity and of intimacy are indeed central to many adolescents and young adults as they struggle to determine what they will do with their lives and to establish their independence while, at the same time, they experience a need for close relationships with others. Although there have been a number of investigations regarding issues of identity, intimacy, and other personality dimensions to which Erikson has ascribed importance, his theory has stimulated surprisingly little research that directly address his hypotheses regarding stage-personality linkages. There is some evidence provided by a study of South Africans of an increase in intimacy from adolescence to adulthood. However, this trend did not hold for black males whose intimacy scores were already relatively high in adolescence (Ochse and Plug, 1986). Whether the process of developing intimacy follows a different path for South African black males (and possibly for other cultural groups) than that proposed by Erikson remains to be investigated.

Erikson has been criticized for emphasizing ego attributes and conscious impulses while neglecting sexual and aggressive motivations and unconscious forces. But, in spite of these empirical and theoretical criticisms, Erikson's rich, compassionate, and well-articulated views have had wide-ranging influence, far beyond the sphere of psychoanalysis. In addition, he has compelled psychoanalysis to pay greater attention to cultural factors influencing personality, as well as to the developmental problems that individuals must master at every age in the life span. As we shall see in subsequent chapters, problems of identity are particularly central to the study of development.

Psychoanalytic Ego Psychology

In its early formulation, psychoanalytic theory addressed primarily the issues of libidinal dynamics, psychosexual development, and the expression of unconscious desires in dreams, neurotic symptoms, slips of the tongue, and a variety of other behavioral phenomena. Following World War I, Freud turned his attention to other dimensions of personality and introduced the psychological structures of the id, ego, and superego. The ego, by instigating danger signals, became critical in his concept of defense. Anna Freud then developed and elaborated on the notion of ego defense against threat and considered in detail a variety of mechanisms that children and adults use to reduce threat.

These changes made the ego more central to psychoanalytic theory, but its theoretical status remained unsatisfactory. In classic psychoanalytic theory, all thoughts and actions were derived initially from id desires. Such functions as thinking, perceiving, and mastery, which Freud assigned to the ego system, were secondary processes that arose because of a conflict between reality and the immediate gratification of id impulses. Tying ego functions to the id created theoretical complexities for psychoanalysis, whereas other theories were able to deal with ego functions in a much more straightforward manner. Also, viewing the ego functions as a consequence of conflict and defense tended to make one look at those functions in terms of degree of impairment, rather than as positive, healthy mechanisms for coping with and mastering the environment.

Conflict-Free Ego Functions

Heinz Hartmann (1958) recognized that for psychoanalysis to become a general psychology, it was necessary to conceive of ego functions as independent of the id-reality conflict. He proposed that some ego functions are conflict-free and should be viewed as biological processes that enable human beings to master the various developmental tasks of walking, thinking, concept formation, and motor coordination that are required for effective growth and adaptation. He suggested that ego processes, rather than being derivatives of the id, emerge independent of the id. Because these ego processes were then no longer dependent on drives or conflicts, Hartmann said they had *primary autonomy*. Individuals were believed to derive satisfaction from the pure exercise of their limbs and from acts of perceiving and attending that were analogous to, but independent of, the libidinal pleasure derived from erogenous zones. These ideas provided the theoretical framework for what is currently referred to as *psychoanalytic ego psychology*.

Ego processes become organized into systems or structures that can serve a defensive function, satisfy libidinal impulses, or become instrumental in the satisfaction of other goals. For example, talking can serve a defensive function by obscuring one's true feelings and blocking direct action; satisfy libidinal or oral-sadistic functions, as in the case of sarcasm; and satisfy other goals by serving as an instrument to fame and success, as in the case of a national newscaster. When used instrumentally, these functions are said to acquire *secondary autonomy*. They can become free of the situations and drives that gave rise to them and become significant behaviors in their own right.

Hartmann's work on ego processes and related ideas offered by other psychoanalytic writers (e.g., Rapaport, 1960) contributed significant revisions to psychoanalytic theory. They helped resolve inconsistencies in the theory and provided a more integrated and logical account of normal psychological development. However, in general, psychoanalytic ego psychology has not offered an empirically tested set of hypotheses and predictions. Rather, its theoretical structure permits the study of curiosity, mastery, and perceptual and cognitive processes without relating these activities to id desires. Thus, researchers with a psychoanalytic ego psychology orientation have turned their attention to the ways in which individuals cope with internal feelings and the external world in nondefensive, as well as in threatening contexts.

Cognitive Styles

cognitive styles A person's consistent way of perceiving similarities and differences in relation to himself or herself and the surrounding world.

As an example of this type of research, George Klein and his associates (see Gardner, et al. 1959) contended that there are systematic individual differences, or **cognitive styles**, in the ways stimuli are perceived. For example, a distinction can be made between *levelers*, who are believed to gloss over perceptual differences, and *sharpeners*, who accentuate these differences. This contrast in cognitive styles is assessed by using a simple perceptual task; levelers, for example, take longer than sharpeners to notice changes introduced by experimenters in the size of simple geometric shapes. There is some debate concerning the generality of this style and its importance for the study of personality; ego psychologists feel that repression is aided by a cognitive style of leveling, although the empirical evidence supporting this belief is weak. Nevertheless, the point to be made is that these studies can stand without reference to classic psychoanalysis.

Psychoanalytic ego psychology, in contrast with traditional psychoanalytic theory, has also led to interesting and productive research in ego processes in infants and very young children. It has helped psychoanalysts go beyond oral, anal, and genital issues and look at the influence of the type of mothering; the infant's attachment to the mother, and the environment in which the infant is raised on the infant's cognitive and social development. Although the research is not uniquely psychoanalytic in method and implications, the pioneering work in this area has been conducted by psychoanalysts (Escalona, 1968; Mahler, 1958; Ribble, 1943; Spitz, 1945). For example, René Spitz (1945), an early psychoanalytic ego psychologist, drew the attention of psychologists, social workers, and the larger society to the potentially deleterious effects of early institutionalization on the cognitive and emotional development of children. In a classic study, Spitz followed two groups of infants: one raised in an institution where unmarried mothers or adequate substitutes cared for the babies, the other raised in a foundling home with a limited nursing staff (each nurse cared for about ten infants). The foundling home had good hygienic facilities and the infants were not mistreated; Nevertheless, Spitz found dramatic psychological and physical disturbances in this group of children. Thirty-four of the ninety-one babies in the foundling home died within a five-year period, while others displayed various deficits in speech, motor coordination, and other ego functions. While there is some question about the comparability of the babies in the two groups, subsequent work with both humans and nonhumans (Bowlby, 1969; Harlow, 1971) has strongly supported the finding that early attachment plays a critical role in later development.

Object Relations Theory

The core of much of object relations theory is the infant's attachment to the mother and other figures. The term *object* refers to these important people in the infant's life. These early attachments provide the basis for the infant's ego development from intense attachment to the mother to a distinct, autonomous self. The characteristics of these attachments are believed to provide the basis for the child's subsequent interpersonal relationships.

The theory of object relations is, in part, an aspect of development in psychoanalytic ego psychology and, in part, reflects other influences in contemporary psychoanalytic theory. Not all features of object relations theory are accepted by all psychoanalysts. There are even subgroups or "schools" that are divided according to which features they accept and the importance placed upon these features relative to other principles in psychoanalytic theory. There are debates about the extent to which object relations are indicative of libidinal investment or are independent of id motivations. However, what is most important is the recognition, by all of the theorists in this area, of the significance of the child's attachment to people and even to inanimate objects in the environment.

This change has profound implications for the way in which psychoanalysts view neuroses and personality development. Instead of focusing on internal conflicts between the id drives and the ego and superego, the question becomes one of the nature of the individual's relationships to other people. Although modern psychoanalysts have not rejected the concept of libido and its oral, anal, and phallic expressions, there is now at least an equal interest in such questions as the degree of psychological separateness from parents; the ability to perceive both positive and negative attributes in the same parent versus perceiving one parent as all "good" and the other parent as all "bad"; and the degree of attachment to and involvement with other people versus self-preoccupation. The question of the nature of one's

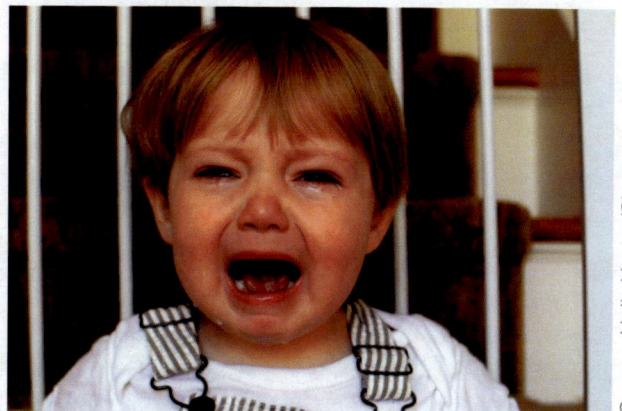

In Melanie Klein's model, infant development can be disrupted by unmet needs. Meanwhile, the infant tries to destroy the mother.

relationship to others also brings to the fore issues regarding the self—such as the fragility of one's self-concept and the degree of autonomy and independence.

Melanie Klein

The potential importance of the infant's early attachments was noted by a number of Freudian analysts who worked with young children. The first systematic theoretical propositions on the role of the infant's social attachments in the development of personality were presented by Melanie Klein (1937). Klein emphasized pre-Oedipal interpersonal experiences, especially mother-child attachment. According to Klein, the infant must pass through two stages of attachment and objects relations during approximately the first year of life. In the first phase, the infant is believed to develop attachments to part objects, such as the mother's breast, and to relate to these objects in terms of gratifications, frustrations, and fears.

Klein agreed with Freud's view on the role of libidinal impulses, but placed even more emphasis than Freud on the importance of aggressive impulses during this period. According to Klein, the child both wishes for the maternal object and is hostile and fearful toward it. The child resolves this conflict by categorizing the world into good and bad objects. This categorization is postulated as a necessary step in the child's ego development. During the next phase, the child begins to integrate objects, no longer splitting them into good and bad components. For instance, the infant now recognizes the mother and relates to the maternal object as a whole rather than as part objects. When the child comes to the realization that good and bad experiences stem from the same object, it must then struggle with feelings of ambivalence. Recognition of the mother as a whole object implies both awareness that she is a separate figure, upon whom one is dependent, as well as awareness of one's separateness. The developmental progress of the infant through these early phases can go awry and become disrupted by hostility and envy if the infant is unloved or if its needs are not gratified.

There is much more to the theoretical views of Klein and her adherents than this brief description of early object relations and ego development. Other aspects of Kleinian theory—the importance of dyadic (mother-child) relationships rather than the triangular (mother-father-child) relationships stressed by Freud, the assumption of pre-Oedipal envy of the parent, the projection of unacceptable impulses onto an object, and subsequent identification with that object—extend beyond the scope of this introduction to object relations theory.

Melanie Klein's theoretical views caused a rift within the Freudian psychoanalytic movement. Her principal rival was Freud's daughter, Anna Freud, who maintained that Klein's elaboration of the internal psychic life of the infant was unwarranted. Both Melanie Klein and Anna Freud, with Freud's encouragement, worked directly with children and derived their theoretical views from observations of children. While Anna Freud focused on the Oedipal and post-Oedipal period and on the ego defenses the child developed and manifested at this stage, Melanie Klein stressed earlier stages. She contended that during the pre-Oedipal period, the child internalized its representation of people and bodily parts and that these internalizations could be loving, envious, or destructive. Some sense of the intensity and complexity of the rivalry between Klein and Anna Freud is conveyed by Melanie Klein's daughter, who was analyzed by her mother and became a psychoanalyst herself, siding with Anna Freud (Grosskurth, 1986).

While Melanie Klein is a significant figure among psychoanalysts, she has had very little impact on the mainstream of developmental psychology because her views on the infant's emotional life are so extreme. She conceived of "an infant from six to twelve months trying to destroy its mother by every method at the disposal of its sadistic endeavor—with its teeth, nails, and excreta and with the whole of its body, transformed by imagination into all kinds of dangerous weapons" (1937, p. 187). This image rightly elicits skepticism and, like many other psychoanalytic conjectures, is not accompanied by empirical support.

Margaret Mahler

The child not only has feelings toward or libidinal investment in significant objects such as bottle, breast, mother, and father, but also has cognitive images or representations of these objects. These representations may be viewed as the *internalization* of object relations. Feelings and attitudes toward the object become elicited by a representation of the object. However, in the earliest phase, the infant is believed to be unable to differentiate itself from the object (Rapaport, 1950). Mahler (1968) views this primitive level as a period of symbiosis in which the infant is attached to and dependent on the mother and cannot differentiate between mother and self. Elements of symbiosis can sometimes be observed in adult relationships; for example, in some marital relationships the partners can no longer determine which feelings and values are their own and which are their spouses'.

Mahler provides a detailed description of the process of separation-individuation through which the infant achieves differentiation and autonomy from its mother, a primary need-satisfying object. Beginning at about four to five months of age, the infant engages in a series of activities characterized by exploration of the environment and seeking security from the mother. By about two years of age, a child who has achieved adequate separation will have established what Mahler refers to as a *rapprochement* between the dependent need for emotional support from the mother and the need to be independent. The attainment of this rapprochement enables the child to consolidate its individuality and develop a permanent sense of self. However, the struggle between dependence-independence is a lifelong one.

Object Representation

Object representations are believed to provide the necessary basis for separation between self and other. They permit the child to tolerate the absence of the mother and of immediate gratification and are the foundation for the development of thinking and symbolic activity. One important element in the process is the development of object constancy. *Perceptual constancy* refers to the recognition and maintenance of a constant perception of a stimulus, even though it is presented at different angles and distances and in varying environments. From a psychoanalytic standpoint, *object constancy* refers to the capacity to evoke a constant representation of an object in its absence, regardless of variations in need for and feelings toward the object. Imagine the child's world if the mother who feeds the child appears different from the mother who disciplines the child, or if each time the mother wears a new dress, she becomes a different person. There is evidence that infants who display greater constancy in their perception of people as compared to their perception of objects have mothers who engage in frequent communication with their offspring and are active in stimulating infant achievements (Chazan, 1981). For psychoanalytic ego psychology, disturbances in object relations are an important antecedent of subsequent neurosis and psychosis.

Empirical Research on Object Representations

Westen et al. (1990) have studied predictions of object relations theory with respect to object representations. Adolescents who were diagnosed as borderline personality disorder were administered the Thematic Apperception Test (TAT). In this test, participants make up stories in reference to various pictures. A group of nonborderline patients and a control group were also given the test. Object relations theory predicts that borderline personality disorder, a disorder characterized by instability in mood and behavior and unclarity in identity, is derived from developmental problems from early childhood. Therefore, people diagnosed with borderline personality disorder should have more disturbed representations of relationships with people. Scoring of the TAT stories revealed that they were significantly more likely to represent an object world that was threatening and dangerous; to represent the motives of others in simple, idiosyncratic, and illogical ways; and to portray themselves as investing in others only in terms of getting their own needs met.

Transitional objects provide security in a changing environment.

Transitional Objects

Infants develop attachments to their caregivers, but they also have to separate and learn to function, without them. For many infants and toddlers, attachments to *transitional objects* appear to help them bridge this separation (Winnicott, 1953). Blankets, diapers, and teddy-bears are familiar examples of transitional objects that psychologically seem to have the same function as the mother or another caregiver. These objects are soothing and provide security to the child. As Eagle (1984) notes, "the child knows that the blanket or teddy-bear is not the mother and yet he reacts affectively to these objects and derives comfort from them as if they were the mother. Giving external objects the capacity to soothe and comfort permits a freer and safer exploration of and interest in the external world" (p. 194).

Donald Winnicott (1953), the British pediatrician and psychoanalyst who first gave systematic attention to these phenomena, has argued that interests in transitional objects provide a basis for the later development and internalization of cultural interests and values. Whether Winnicott's speculations concerning the relationship between interest in transitional objects and interest in cultural activities are valid or not, it is likely that transitional objects serve a useful function during the periods of separation throughout the life span. A college freshman, living in a completely new setting, may not react to the disappearance of a favored object brought from home with the same intense distress as that of an infant whose blanket has been removed. Nevertheless, that object, though it might be an inexpensive stuffed animal, an old trophy, or even a favorite recording, may have an important transitional function during this period of initial separation and adaptation.

Many children do not develop these early object attachments. How do they differ from those who do? In one study (Passman and Weisberg, 1975), children attached or unattached to a blanket displayed equal stress while playing alone when their mothers were present. The unattached children, however, were much more upset when playing alone, while their mothers were absent. Some data suggest that emotionally disturbed adults had less-than-average transitional object attachments during childhood, but these findings are not consistent (Hong, 1978). Another study relating personality traits of college students to early transitional object attachments indicated that students without such attachments in early childhood tended to be more reserved and aloof as young adults than those with early transitional object attachments. However, the latter group displayed more tension and impatience. It appears that the nature of early transitional object attachments—their intensity, duration, and related characteristics—need to be taken into account in order to determine their adaptive functions.

Narcissism and the Self

Another major deviation from traditional psychoanalytic theory is entailed in the emphasis on the "self" in the work of Heinz Kohut (1971, 1977). For Kohut, the attainment of a cohesive, integrated self takes precedence over psychosexual issues, although the latter remain important. As with other psychoanalytic innovators, Kohut's theoretical views arose out of his work with a particular kind of patient, one who suffers from what Kohut has described as a *narcissistic personality disorder*. These are individuals who feel empty, powerless, and look to others to carry Out functions that one normally does for oneself; yet they are given to feelings of primitive grandiosity and boastfulness. Kohut found that traditional psychoanalytic therapy was not effective with these patients, but that he could obtain positive outcomes through manifesting a positive regard for and acceptance of the patient. (It will become evident in Chapter 6 that this approach owes much to the work of Carl Rogers.)

The patient's pathological narcissism stems from parental failure to fully accept the child, so the patient does not develop a truly positive self-regard or healthy narcissism.

For the self-structure to develop properly, the child requires admiration and acceptance together with an opportunity to idealize a figure with whom it can identify. Effective parents provide these dual functions. Since the parent is not always available to reflect and accept the child's feelings and to soothe and comfort the child, these minor or optimal frustrations, according to Kohut, result in the child internalizing these structures so that it can admire and soothe itself. In this way, self-esteem and internalized values and ideals develop. To this dual or bipolar component structure of the self, Kohut later added a third constituent resulting from the need to be with a similar-age person with shared interests as contrasted with an authority or parental figure (Kohut, 1984).

Kohut's (1984) perspective on the Oedipus complex is different than Freud's. For Freud, the five-year-old child has sexual feelings towards the parent of the opposite sex and aggressive, rivalrous feelings toward the parent of the same sex. For Kohut, this child is interested in exercising his or her capacities for assertion and affection. A male child will practice being assertive with his father and being affectionate with his mother. If the parents respond appropriately to the child, no Oedipus complex develops. However, if the mother has conflicts over the relationship of sex and affection and if the father gets threatened by the son's assertion, the child's assertive tendencies may degenerate into aggressive feelings and the affectionate impulses may become sexualized. For Kohut, Freud's Oedipus complex is not an inevitable aspect of early childhood experience but rather only occurs when parents handle normal developmental processes dysfunctionally.

Kohut's view of the therapeutic process is quite different from that of classical psychoanalysis. For Kohut, the therapist replaces the parent, as it were, and functions as a kind of mirror for the patient. Through the positive mirroring process, the patient's inadequate and wounded self can be restored to a cohesive self with genuine self-esteem. For Kohut, the change from pathological to healthy narcissism makes possible a self-reliant pursuit of one's own talents, ambitions, and values. These, presumably, are the attributes of the genius and the hero. But whether the genius and hero, by virtue of their accomplishments, are the best models for mental health is a matter of some debate.

Psychoanalysis in Flux

The one statement about contemporary psychoanalytic theory that can be made with confidence is that it is in the process of change. One of the most radical departures from traditional psychoanalytic theory has been proposed by Roy Schafer (1976) Schafer stresses the distinction between Freud's clinical insights and his theory (see Klein, 1967). He accepts Freud's theory of infantile sexuality, the importance of the Oedipal situation, the use of defense mechanisms, and similar propositions that are closely related to the reports of people in therapy. However, he rejects Freud's use of psychic energy constructs, of drive, and of terms that imply separate places or entities in the mind. He proposes that "we should not use phrases such as a 'strong ego,' the 'dynamic unconscious,' 'the inner world,' 'libidinal energy,' 'rigid defense,' 'an intense emotion,' 'autonomous ego function,' and 'instinctual drive'" (1976, p. 9). Such phrases make the error of *reification* that is making *things* or objects out of psychological processes experiences, and behaviors that are essentially *actions*. We should use verbs and adverbs, he contends; to designate these as processes. For example, instead of saying, "He cannot control his sex drive," we should say, "He readily engaged in sexual actions even when he knew it would be wise not to do so" (1916, p. 28). This reformulation substitutes sexual behavior for the energy construct of drive and provides a specific meaning—acting despite one's best judgment—for the ambiguous phrase, "cannot control." Phrases such as "internalize an object" and "deeply repressed" attribute to the mind spatial qualities that are properties of physical objects, and such common expressions as conflict between id and ego also require translation into action terms.

These changes in language would alter the entire theoretical framework of psychoanalysis. They eliminate a whole array of theoretical structures and mechanisms many of which are either controversial or simply vague and ill defined. Needless to say many of the changes proposed by Schafer have not been acceptable to the main body of psycho-analysts One problem is that Schafer, in his effort to discard surplus theoretical baggage, seems also to have discarded structural concepts such as ego or self that are needed in or-der to account for the organization and consistency of behavior. Furthermore, by adhering so closely to an action language, one tends to turn a theory into a collection of descriptive statements rather than an organized set of propositions that lead to specific deductions, predictions, and analytic interpretations.

Schafer (1992), along with Donald Spence (1982) and others, has been a contributor to the recent development of narrative approaches to psychoanalysis. Spence and a number of other writers have questioned the idea that the memories recovered in psychoanaly-sis represent historical truth. Spence has argued that psychoanalysis deals with narrative truth. That is, psychoanalysis is not an archeological enterprise in which one digs into one's past to uncover real, buried memories. Rather it is a storymaking enterprise in which the patient develops new, more functional stories about his or her past and its relationship to the present. We shall have more to say about the narrative approach in Chapter 11.

Although psychoanalysis has profoundly deepened our insight into human experience and behavior, much of the theory is loosely stated and needs to be rooted in clear oper-ations or behavior. In addition, much of the theory has been unresponsive to research. Psychoanalysts do refer to scientific findings, and some are engaged in research inquiries, but psychoanalysts typically do not drop or significantly change a theoretical conjecture simply because of lack of empirical support. They have generally not attempted to sep-arate those aspects of the theory for which there is sound scientific evidence from those portions that remain largely speculative.

Summary

1. According to Jung's *analytic psychology*, each indi-vidual has opposing personality tendencies, such as masculine-feminine and introversion-extroversion. The self-actualized individual emerges out of the bal-ance and integration of these opposing forces.

2. The *archetypes* that make up the *collective unconscious* are inherited by all human beings. They are reflected in universal symbols, images, myths, and dreams.

3. According to Adler, people are basically motivated by positive social interest and efforts to overcome in-feriority. Distortions of positive urges can take place through exaggerated compensation for feelings of inferiority.

4. Horney described three fundamental patterns of response to basic anxiety: moving toward people (exaggerated need for approval); moving against peo-ple (hostility, dominance); and moving away from people (aloofness, lack of involvement).

5. In Fromm's view, human beings are basically positive, loving creatures whose positive impulses can be warped by society, particularly by an alienating eco-nomic system.

6. Erikson described eight *psychosocial stages* from birth to maturity, each of which poses a particular developmental task. The manner in which develop-mental problems are resolved provides the basis for specific personality characteristics such as basic trust versus mistrust, initiative versus guilt, and identity versus role confusion.

7. One of the consequences of *psychoanalytic ego psychology* has been an increased emphasis on the infant's early attachment to the mother. This attach-ment and other *object relations* provide the basis for the child's ego development and subsequent interper-sonal relationships.

8. Melanie Klein emphasized the pre-Oedipal period of development, proposing that the young infant resolves its ambivalent feelings toward its caretaker by psycho-logically splitting that person into good and bad part objects.

9. Heinz Kohut proposed that, for many patients, the primary goal of psychoanalytic therapy should be rep-aration of the injured self-structure.

Key Terms

analytic psychology (p. 63)
archetypes (p. 64)
cognitive styles (p. 76)
collective unconscious (p. 64)
complex (p. 65)

extroversion (p. 65)
introversion (p. 65)
neurosis (p. 69)
psychosocial stages (p. 74)

Thought Questions

1. Do you socially present the "real" you and, if not, how do you think your real self differs from your persona?

2. Do you support the Freudian position that society inhibits desires and that people are basically antisocial, or the Adlerian position that society can facilitate personal development and that individuals have social concerns? Why?

3. Assuming that family rivalry is quite common, what other interpretations can you offer of the Oedipal and Electra conflicts besides Freud's hypothesized sexual envy?

4. Do you feel that American society promotes alienation? How might this be changed?

5. Do you think development primarily revolves around sex as Freud thought or around relationships and the development of the self as object relations theory and self-psychology hold?

Learning Theory Approaches to Personality

CHAPTER 5

Source: Rawpixel.com/Shutterstock

Chapter Outline

Associationist (Stimulus-Response) Learning Theory

Reinforcement Theory

Social Learning Theory

Cognitive Behavior Modification

Learning theories of personality have their origins in the laboratory, unlike psychoanalytic theories, which are rooted in the clinical interactions between therapists and patients. However, as we will see, the applicability of these learning theories to personality and clinical problems has become the primary source of their vigor and popularity.

Learning theorists have undertaken the ambitious task of not only accounting for personality development on the basis of principles established in the laboratory, but also applying these principles to changing emotionally disturbed, maladaptive behavior patterns. As we will see, therapeutic procedures based on learning theories have indeed been implemented successfully in clinical situations. In fact, one of the most significant developments in the field of clinical psychology has been the vigorous growth of therapies based on learning principles.

In previous chapters, we have seen how a group of psychodynamic, clinically based theories explained personality development and functioning using complex concepts that were difficult to define and evaluate. The concepts used by the learning theorists, however, are simpler and more readily tied to observable events. Thus, the learning theorists have in a real sense undertaken a difficult challenge: explaining the phenomena of human personality with a restricted, empirically based vocabulary and a set of well-defined principles. How they have approached this task, the ways in which vocabulary and principles have had to be expanded, and the adequacy of their theoretical accounts of personality are some of the questions to be considered in this chapter.

The learning theories reviewed in this chapter, share a number of characteristics, several of them noted earlier (see the introduction to Part 2):

1. The use of concepts and methods that are closely linked to the laboratory, particularly to the experimental analysis of learning.

2. The assumption that the principal behaviors constituting personality are acquired, or learned, during the course of development. More specifically, an individual's behaviors in a given situation are believed to have been acquired through a history of being rewarded or punished in the same or similar situations. For example, the difference in timidity and aggressiveness between two boys, Robert and John, may be accounted for by differences in their learning histories. Robert may be inhibited and timid because his retreats from threatening social encounters have been rewarded by adults, and his abortive attempts at self-defense have met with punishment from peers. However, John may be a bully at school because his aggressive behavior has been reinforced by his resultant control of others, by his gaining possessions, and by the attention he receives for it. Learning theorists acknowledge that genetic and biological factors may influence individual differences but believe that these are secondary to learning experiences.

3. A theoretical emphasis on observable stimuli and responses. All but the learning theories of personality locate the basic processes of personality inside the individual. Learning theories, however, differ on this point. Some, like Skinner's (1953) operant reinforcement theory, are concerned solely with observables and make no inferences about the mind or what might be occurring inside the organism. Others, like the learning theories of Miller and Dollard (1941) and Bandura (1977), do propose a variety of internal processes that intervene between the onset of the stimulus and the subsequent overt behavior. Nevertheless, even these theories prefer to focus on stimuli and behaviors that are observable to the scientist. They make as few assumptions as possible about mediating elements such as thoughts, feelings, and desires. They particularly try to explain behavior solely in terms of the organism's past learning history and in terms of current circumstances (Hineline, 1980).

4. An emphasis on the importance of the situation as a determinant of action. Personality theorists have mostly paid attention almost exclusively to the attributes of the person; learning theorists have helped to balance this emphasis by demonstrating the influence of situational or environmental factors on behavior. Some learning theorists may have pushed this balance between the situation and the person too far to the other extreme by minimizing the role of personality variables.

Although there are many similarities among learning theories, these are also major differences among them. These differences, which are in some instances as great as those among the various psychoanalytic and psychodynamic theories, will be considered in detail as we review the major learning theory approaches to personality.

In this chapter we begin by considering traditional stimulus-response approaches to learning theory, including the application of Dollard and Miller's work to psychoanalytic theory. We next consider Skinner's radical behaviorist position. We then consider two of the most currently influential perspectives, those of social learning theory and cognitive behavior modification.

Associationist (Stimulus-Response) Learning Theory

The period from the 1930s through the 1960s was one of ferment and controversy surrounding a few major psychological theories, each one offering hope of explaining much of psychology. One of the most influential of these theories was proposed by Clark Hull (1943, 1951, 1952). Hull and other theorists of this period aimed to formulate a theory of behavior that would adequately encompass most species, from the laboratory rat to the human. Indeed, much of the research support for these theories came from studies of the laboratory rat. Hull was not oblivious to the differences between rats and humans, but he believed that there are common requirements imposed on every living organism to satisfy biological needs and to adapt to the environment. Clearly, Darwin was an important influence on Hull, who further assumed that for mammals—whether rats or human beings—the mechanisms governing learning are basically identical. Humans as well as lower animals, according to Hull, are creatures of habit.

Habits and Drives

Habits are stable stimulus-response connections. A dog attacking an intruder on sight, a dolphin soaring above the water in response to a verbal command, and a preschooler regularly crying at the sight of another child with a toy he wants are all exhibiting habits. Hull proposed that habits are acquired and strengthened whenever a response that occurs together with a stimulus is accompanied or shortly followed by drive reduction. Drive reduction is thus required for a response to be reinforced. **Drive reduction** refers to a decrease in the intensity of a drive, as when hunger, thirst, or sex is partially or fully satisfied, or when fear is reduced after a threat is overcome. In addition, the effects of drive reduction work automatically. This lowering of drive strengthens any response that happens to be occurring in that particular stimulus situation. It is important to note that the response is strengthened whether the response is adaptive or nonadaptive.

Hull's own research examined the effects of the reduction of such primary drives as thirst and hunger. Since drive reduction in these instances meant that the organism has obtained water when thirsty or food when hungry, the reinforced response was biologically adaptive, aiding the organism in survival. But the reinforced response does not have to be related to the attainment of a reward, according to the theory. Irrelevant responses occurring in conjunction with relevant behavior are also expected to be reinforced. For example, a hungry rat that scratches its snout while pressing a bar that releases a food pellet will be more likely to scratch its snout the next time it is hungry and is placed in the same apparatus. B. F. Skinner has suggested that the same mechanism responsible for a hungry rat's pawing at its snout for food, when that response has nothing to do with obtaining a reward, is the basis for superstitious behavior in humans.

habits Stable stimulus-response connections.

drive reduction A decrease in the intensity of a motive or need force, which, according to associationist learning theory, also strengthens the stimulus-response connection.

Crossing one's fingers is a superstitious behavior that has been associated with positive outcomes often enough that the behavior is maintained.

The situation is more complex for humans because, in addition to such primary drives as hunger and thirst, there are many acquired, or secondary, drives such as our desires for love, power, achievement, and money. In addition, people have many learned fears. These secondary drives might even conflict with one another or with primary drives, so that the drive reduction of one motivation may lead to the reinforcement of a behavior that thwarts the satisfaction of other motivations. For example, the response of drinking alcohol may be reinforced by the reduction of painful fears and anxieties. However, habitual drinking may also result in economic loss, family disruptions, and social disgrace; thus, the overall effect of a drinking habit is maladaptive.

Personality Development

Hull provided the basis for a formal theory of learning that could be used to account for both maladaptive and adaptive behavior in humans and nonhumans. Thus, his theory was attractive to psychologists and other behavioral scientists with interests in animal behavior, human personality, and social interaction.

Dollard and Miller

Among Hull's associates and students at Yale were John Dollard, a sociologist with an extensive background in cultural anthropology and psychology, and Neal Miller, an experimental psychologist then known for his studies of drive acquisition and reinforcement. These two pioneered in systematically extending and elaborating on Hull's principles to account for personality development, social behavior, and psychopathology (Dollard, et al., 1939; Dollard and Miller, 1950; Miller and Dollard, 1941). In recent years the personality theory formulated by Dollard and Miller has declined in popularity, paralleling the decline of Hullian theory from the central position it once occupied in psychology. However, the Dollard-Miller analysis is still useful and has substantially influenced other learning approaches to personality.

It is helpful to consider how the important concepts in the Dollard-Miller analysis—cue (or stimulus), drive, response, and reinforcement—apply to a concrete situation. Assume that a professor typically responds with sarcasm whenever a student answers a question incorrectly. Even after receiving complaints about his behavior, the professor finds it difficult to change. According to the concepts of Dollard and Miller, the *cue* in this situation is an incorrect answer; the *response* is sarcasm. While the cue and the response are obvious, the operative *drive* in this situation and the *reinforcement* are less apparent. The drive could be a need to impress the class and the reinforcement, class laughter; or the drive could be a need for power and the reinforcement, student fear and docility; or the drive might be aggression and the reinforcement, the expression of pain on the face of the unfortunate student. In examining behavior from the perspective of Dollard and Miller, one seeks to establish the cue that is eliciting a response, the drive that has been gratified in the situation, and the reinforcement that reduces the drive.

Cues

Although the cue that elicited the professor's sarcasm is evident, cues are often so subtle and disguised that neither the respondent nor an outside observer can pinpoint the stimulus that is actually eliciting the behavior. Most of us have experienced feelings anxiety and have engaged in binge eating without being able to identify the stimuli that elicited, or caused, this behavior. An important task for the clinician dealing with symptoms such as fear, uncontrollable thoughts, and compulsive rituals is to determine the cues that evoke these symptoms. Cues exert a powerful effect on a person's behavior; they "can determine when one will respond and which response one will make" (Dollard and Miller, 1950, p. 32).

Cues can also elicit **mediating responses**: internal, nonobservable responses that are believed to intervene (mediate) between observable stimuli and overt responses. Thoughts, feelings, and the anticipation of events are potential mediating responses which can then serve as cues, eliciting other mediating or overt responses.

mediating response Any unobservable internal response that intervenes between the observable stimulus and the overt response.

Observable stimulus cue → Mediating response → Mediating drive stimulus, → Overt response
(dark area)   (fear)   or cue, of fear   (lighting room)

FIGURE 5.1 A Mediating Response with Cue Functions

Mediating responses can have drive as well as cue functions. For example, for a child who was once frightened in a dark room by an intruder, any dark area came to elicit the mediating response of fear, through a process of conditioning. Because fear is aversive, the child was driven to reduce the fear, in this case by lighting the room. Thus, the child insisted on sleeping in a well-lit room, never entered a dark area, looked for a flashlight before opening a large closet, and was reluctant to leave the house at night. This process is shown in Figure 5.1.

Acquired Drives

Fear, as a learned response, is one example of a secondary, or acquired, drive. Acquired drives are similar to such primary drives as hunger and thirst in that the organism will strive to reduce them. A response that results in drive reduction will then be reinforced; that is, the probability of that response occurring again in the same situation is increased. This holds true whatever the acquired drive; fear, say, or a need for fame or affiliation.

The cue, or stimulus value, for the fear drive is illustrated by the habits that the darkness-fearing child subsequently developed. He asked his mother to bring along a flashlight whenever he was taken to the dentist, and the dentist found that permitting him to shine a flashlight or placing a bright lamp near the drill helped relax the child. The mediating response of fear was therefore common to both the dental situation and the dark room, and the response of illuminating the area became attached to both the internal cue of fear and the external cue of darkness (see Figure 5.2). That is, when the internal cue (fear) occurred in a context other than that in which it was first learned (the dark), the previously learned fear-reducing response (bright light) became generalized to the new context. This process is referred to as mediated generalization. Through mediated generalization, very different stimuli—for example, a dark room or a dentist's chair—may come to elicit the same response: use of a flashlight.

From the learning theory perspective of Dollard and Miller, individual differences in personality can be described in terms of differences in the kind and intensity of acquired drives that influence a person's behavior, and in the responses or habits the person has acquired to reduce those drives. One difference between Dollard and Miller and other learning theorists such as Skinner and Bandura is that because of Dollard and Miller's focus on mediating responses, the acquired drives and habits that distinguish individuals may be expressed in

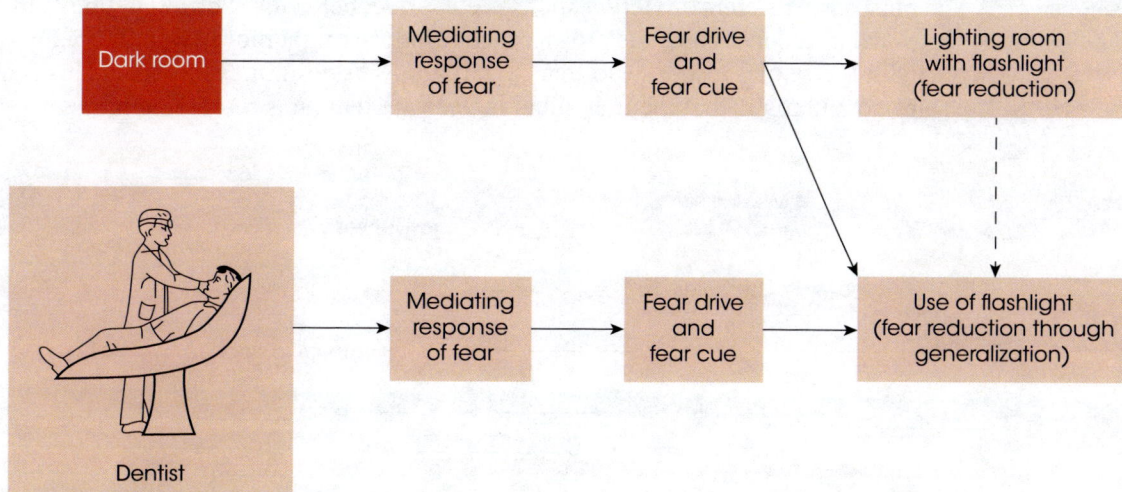

FIGURE 5.2 The Process of Mediated Generalization

a wide range of situations rather than being situation specific. Thus, the concept of personality traits is quite compatible with Dollard and Miller's theoretical orientation. A person may be conscientious because being conscientious has resulted in drive reduction (perhaps a reduction of anxiety) and the behaviors have been generalized to a variety of situations.

Comparison with Psychoanalytic Theory

The previous examples illustrating the concepts of cue, drive, response, and reinforcement suggest the applicability of Hull's and Dollard and Miller's learning theory to various aspects of psychoanalytic theory. Although stimulus-response learning theory and psychoanalytic theory come from far different traditions, employ different concepts, and differ sharply in methodology, they share several assumptions about human nature. Psychoanalytic propositions can therefore be translated into the language and structure of learning theory. Indeed, that translation was one of the goals of Dollard and Miller.

Dollard and Miller's learning theory, like psychoanalytic theory, allows for unconscious determinants of behavior; that is, motivations of which the individual is unaware that affect thought and action. In addition, both learning theory and psychoanalytic theory assert that the ability to label these motivations, or the achievement of insight, will produce more adaptive behavior. Both theories also emphasize the role of drives in governing behavior and the significance of motivational conflict as a cause of psychopathology. Still another point of consistency between the two theoretical approaches is their common assumption of the necessity of drive reduction for reinforcement. Both Hull and psychoanalytic theorists see the organism as striving to reduce tension and as acquiring and maintaining tension-reducing behaviors. Finally, both camps believe that behavior follows laws and is determined, thus providing the basis for scientific analysis and prediction of behavior.

Language and Repression

It is illuminating to examine the Dollard-Miller analysis of repression because it introduces the role of language in their theory and concepts that experimentally based learning theories use to explore complex psychoanalytic propositions and observations. We use an example of a man who, through his learning history, has come to feel anxious about sexuality.

Figure 5.3 depicts a number of possible responses that this man might make when confronted with a sexually attractive woman. Between the observable cue of an attractive female stimulus and the observable response, different chains of mediating responses might take place. The overt goal response at the end of the chain reduces the experienced anxiety and is therefore reinforced by anxiety reduction. The figure shows that different overt responses are often mediated by disparate covert cognitive statements. For example, a response of indifference might be preceded by the covert statement of "She bores me"; an aggressive remark might be mediated by the covert appraisal, "I don't like her"; and so on. These different anxiety responses can affect behavior at different points in the motivational sequence. Thus, the indifference response might move up in the chain and interfere with the sexual response so that sexual arousal does not even occur. This process might be so automatic that the individual is unaware that he is repressing his sexual feelings.

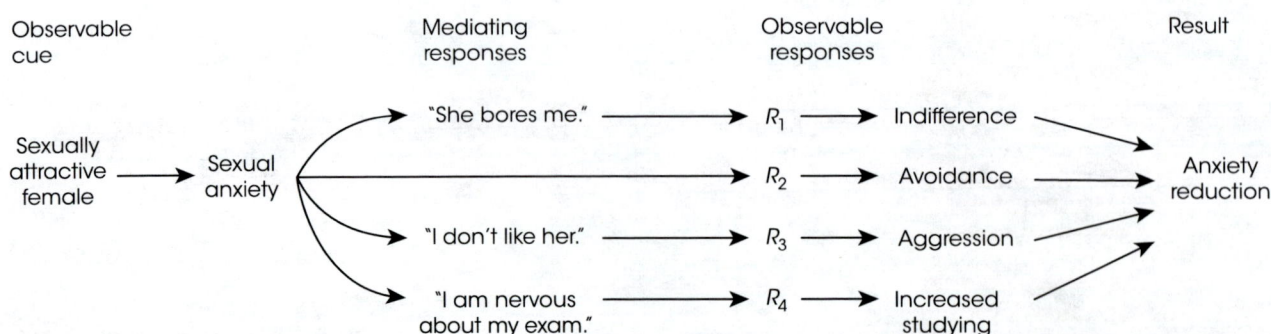

FIGURE 5.3 Alternative Stimulus-Response Mediating Response Chains Leading to Repression

This is one type of activity not explained by the concept of drive reduction.

Dollard and Miller's incorporation of covert verbal responses in their theoretical analysis anticipated current interest in cognitive behavioral modification, an approach considered later in this chapter. In general, the relative flexibility of their interpretations of Hullian theory has permitted investigators and theorists operating within this framework to address many major issues in the study of personality, including frustration, aggression, and conflict. The same flexibility, however, made the Dollard and Miller theory vulnerable to criticism that there are too many unobservable concepts that can be made to fit any behavioral outcome. There was also considerable objection to the principle of drive reduction as a prerequisite for learning. A number of apparent exceptions were noted in which people appeared to seek an *increase* in drive, such as excitement and activity, with these experiences themselves being reinforcing. There was so much dissatisfaction with the drive concept that attention shifted to the analysis of reinforcement. Nevertheless, although the popularity of the Dollard-Miller theory as a whole has waned, many of its concepts have been incorporated into other learning approaches to personality.

Reinforcement Theory

Learning theorists distinguish between **operant conditioning** and **classical conditioning**. In operant conditioning, a response that operates on the environment so as to change it is controlled or strengthened by the consequences that follow (for example, a rat pressing a bar receives a food reward). In classical conditioning, a conditioned stimulus, such as a bell, is sounded just before an unconditioned stimulus, such as food, is presented. The unconditioned response of salivating to the food becomes associated with the bell, which consequently elicits a conditioned response of salivation.

While some learning theorists have emphasized classical conditioning mechanisms in personality development and behavior change, Skinner's principal interest was in the variables governing operant behavior. The primary factor that he investigated was scheduling of, or the frequency and patterning of, reinforcement. A reinforcement can be administered after every response, after a specific or variable number of responses, or after a specific or variable time interval. In his first, groundbreaking book, *The Behavior of Organisms*, Skinner (1938) demonstrated lawful, predictable, and quantifiable relationships between different reinforcement schedules and the response rates of the organisms being reinforced. For example, organisms reinforced following every relevant response responded more frequently per unit of time than did organisms given a reward after specified time intervals.

operant conditioning A type of learning that emphasizes learning that a behavior leads to reinforcement or punishment.

classical conditioning A type of learning in which an organism learns to pair a stimulus with a response.

The behavior of humans operates under the same processes as rats, mice, and pigeons.

Skinner's learning theory dispensed with the mediating, unobservable processes that Hull, Miller, and Dollard posited as occurring inside the organism. The task of psychology, according to Skinner, is to establish lawful relationships between behavior and events in the objective world. Skinner was very precise about what he meant by "lawful" and "objective." Concepts such as tension, feeling, desire, drive, attitude, and intention do not refer to objective, physical events that can be directly observed; they are attributes of a vague entity called the "mind." For Skinner, it was scientifically inappropriate to use nonobjective events as explanations of behavior.

Radical Behaviorism

The *radical behaviorist* position advocated by Skinner had two fundamental components. One asserted that scientific explanation should depend on as few assumptions as possible. Consequently, before assuming the existence of hidden psychological processes, one should first explore the explanatory power of a system based on observables, one that requires no additional assumptions. Skinner noted that when we attribute the "cause" of a behavior to an internal event or tendency, we are doing little more than restating the behavior, instead of explaining it. For example, to say that a child assaults his peers because he is aggressive does not add to our understanding of the assaultive behavior. To say that your friend talks to many different people because she is extraverted is to simply label the behavior, not explain it.

The second aspect of the radical behaviorist position was more profound in its implications. Skinner's position was that what we commonly refer to as "mind" is either fictional or *irrelevant* as an explanation of behavior. Skinner contended that human behavior is subject to the same laws as the movement of physical objects and that a sophisticated science, whether of physics or of psychology, should not appeal to mysterious, hidden, inner forces.

Skinner felt that psychology should primarily be concerned with understanding the functional relationships between events in the environment and behaviors of the organism. Skinnerians do not ignore private events such as thoughts, emotions, choices, or decisions; rather they consider private events to be behaviors under the control of the environment (Hineline, 1980) and not caused by internal factors. What Skinnerians reject is not the existence of internal, private aspects of experience, but rather the idea that these internal aspects are the *causes* of overt behavior. In other words, they reject the idea of mind as a cause. Instead, their focus is on how environmental contingencies cause behavior. Through a functional analysis of the relationship between specific environmental events and specific reactions, one can explain behavior without referring to mechanisms operating within the organism. Hence, if we observe someone eating, instead of asserting that the person is eating because of hunger, we should link the eating to an antecedent environmental event such as hours of food deprivation, the lunch bell's ringing, or the appearance of appetizing food. The objective of functional analysis is to determine which features of the environment are regularly linked to particular behaviors. Thus, the key question becomes which environmental situation, hours since eating, the lunch bell, or presence of the appetizing food, is regularly associated with eating.

Lawfulness and Control

Regularity, the hallmark of a lawful relationship, is the basis for asserting that a particular event is the cause of a particular behavior. Human behavior may often appear chaotic, spontaneous, or free, but according to Skinner, that appearance is only because we have not discovered the events that control the behavior. Skinner deliberately used the word *control* to convey that human behavior is completely determined and predictable, given knowledge of the stimulus events that are lawfully related to the behavior. A simple example of predictability and control concerns a four-year-old boy who was referred to a clinic because of frequent tantrums. When the child's parents were interviewed, it immediately became evident that the boy threw a tantrum whenever a wish he expressed was denied. His desperate parents ultimately acceded to his demands, permitting him, for example, to stay up late and watch television. The behavior (tantrum) was reinforced (under the control of) his parents' acquiescence. In a similar manner, the parents' acquiescent behavior was reinforced by the child's stopping the tantrum. When the parents learned to ignore the tantrums, they very rapidly disappeared, or *extinguished*.

Increasing or Maintaining Behavior

The concept of reinforcement is one of Skinner's main theoretical ideas. A *reinforcer* is typically defined as any stimulus that follows a behavior that increases the behavior's frequency. Through the manipulation of reinforcement contingencies, dramatic changes in behavior may be brought about. Removing reinforcements from previously reinforced responses leads to extinction, while the reinforcement of a response will increase the future likelihood of that response.

A behavior becomes more likely to the degree that it has been reinforced. Reinforcement occurs in two different forms: **positive reinforcement** and **negative reinforcement**. Positive reinforcement occurs when something positive has been added to the situation. In the example of the tantrums, the boy receives more television time. Positive reinforcements can take many forms—for instance, water, food, candy, money, attention, or smiles. Behavior that results in receiving these things will tend to reoccur.

positive reinforcement Receiving a positive reward for behavior, leading to a greater probability of that behavior in the future.

Negative reinforcement is the removal of something aversive. In the earlier tantrum example, when the parents give in to the child's tantrum, the tantrum stops. In this situation, the tantrum is aversive; when the parents engage in the behavior of allowing more television, the tantrum stops and the parents are reinforced for their behavior. We can even differentiate two different types of negative reinforcement: escape learning and avoidance learning.

negative reinforcement Having something aversive or undesirable removed as a result of behavior, leading to a greater probability of the same behavior in the future.

In **escape learning**, the individual is in the aversive situation and removes the aversiveness through her behavior. For instance, if a teenager arrives home after curfew, and her parent is yelling at her, but then she lies about why she is late and the yelling stops, she has now been reinforced for the behavior of lying. She is being yelled at (the aversive situation), and she lies (the behavior) and escapes (negative reinforcement) from the aversive situation.

escape learning A form of negative reinforcement in which the organism learns to escape ongoing punishment by particular behaviors.

The other type of negative reinforcement is **avoidance learning**. In avoidance learning, the organism learns to avoid environments that lead to aversive outcomes. A rat will learn to avoid the part of the cage where it would be shocked. A person will avoid interacting with another person if he expects the other person to yell at him. A college student may avoid picking up a bad exam. In each of these examples, the individual removes the aversive possibility by avoiding the environment.

avoidance learning A form of negative reinforcement, in which the organism has learned to avoid punishment by avoiding particular situations, people, or behaviors.

Partial Reinforcement

Although it is frequently argued that the principles of operant reinforcement are less valid because they were derived from studies of rats and pigeons, there is both informal and experimental evidence that humans also respond differentially to different schedules of reinforcement. The effects of **partial reinforcement** certainly apply to humans as well as to nonhumans. Partial reinforcement occurs when the behavior is not reinforced every single time. Sometimes the behavior is reinforced, but sometimes it is not. Extensive research literature indicates that many partially reinforced responses are *even more difficult* to extinguish than responses that have had a history of constant reinforcement. Hence, parents who finally decide to ignore, rather than pick up, a child who cries after being put

partial reinforcement An intermittent reward schedule that strengthens a response.

Gambling is a behavior thought to be determined by partial reinforcement.

to bed will find that crying will persist much longer if the child was *not* picked up every time they cried previously. This consequence of partial reinforcement can also account for the seemingly paradoxical behavior of gamblers who keep betting despite heavy losses; they, too, are intermittently reinforced for their behavior.

Partial reinforcement increases the persistence of positive behaviors as well as such problems as crying and gambling. Given certain tasks, a history of successes interspersed with failures leads to greater persistence in the face of subsequent failures than does a history of 100 percent success. This phenomenon has been observed in the laboratory (Nation, Cooney, and Gartrell, 1979), as well as in everyday life. Compare two politicians, for example: one who has met with both success and defeat in running for political office and one who has always been successful. Suppose that they are both then repeatedly defeated at the polls. According to the partial reinforcement effect, the politician with a history of unmixed success will probably give up political life sooner than the politician who experienced failure as well as success. In other words, the "trait" of persistence can be developed by providing the learner with tasks that are neither too easy nor too difficult. Intermediate-level tasks allow learners to experience the pain and challenge of frustration, as well as the pleasure and satisfaction of success.

Discriminative Stimuli

The pattern of reinforcement, or reinforcement schedule, which determines the degree of persistent behavior, can vary with different stimulus conditions. Thus, one might have received 100% reinforcement when requesting help from one's mother, 50% reinforcement from one's father and 0% from one's sibling! Mother, father, and sibling then function as

discriminative stimuli A stimulus that indicates the probability of punishment or reinforcement.

discriminative stimuli that elicit different patterns of behavior. According to Skinnerian principles, one is then most likely to ask one's mother for help. However, if all three refuse after experiencing these reinforcement contingencies, then one is likely to be most persistent in seeking help from the father.

The fact that some partial reinforcement effects generalize to very dissimilar tasks suggests that there are cognitive factors mediating the effects. For example, the subject may be learning an expectancy or a rule, such as, "If I wait long enough, I will eventually succeed." However, from a Skinnerian standpoint, the important question is *whether* particular reinforcement schedules lead to predictable effects, not how they produce their effects. This is particularly true if the "how" requires reference to private events.

Decreasing Behavior

In our tantrum example, the goal was to eliminate the tantrums. The process used was extinction. **Extinction** occurs when a behavior is no longer reinforced. The parents stopped reinforcing the tantrums, and the behavior eventually stopped. If a pigeon pecks at a window that used to lead to food but no longer does, the pigeon will stop pecking at the window. If a child is not reinforced for asking for candy at the checkout of a grocery store, the child will stop asking. Extinction can occur relatively rapidly, or the behavior can maintain for some time if there had been partial reinforcement in the past. An interesting behavior, called *extinction burst*, will often occur during the process of extinction. The organism will often engage in very extreme versions of the behavior. A common example occurs when someone puts money in a vending machine, but the machine does not produce the product. The person is likely to push the buttons harder or even hit the machine. A rat that is used to being reinforced for pressing a bar will repeatedly hit the bar harder after it stops being reinforced for the behavior. In our tantrum example, we would probably expect the tantrum to be even more extreme when it is no longer reinforced, just as we would for the child who no longer gets candy while at the checkout of the grocery store.

extinction A behavior decreasing in likelihood due to no longer being reinforced.

Corporal punishment can decrease some behaviors but is associated with so many negative effects that the American Psychological Association recommends against it.

It is possible to decrease behavior through the use of **punishment**. Punishment may take the form of adding something aversive (for instance, pain) or removing something pleasant (for instance, being grounded). The organism can learn to not perform behaviors if the likely outcome is punishment but may simultaneously learn other behaviors through escape or avoidance learning. If a child expects to be hit, the child is likely to learn behaviors that result in not being hit. Often the child learns to avoid the parent or to lie to the parent. Notice that not engaging in the behavior that leads to being hit is not the thing the child learns. In a classroom, the child may engage in behaviors that result in punishment—for instance, responding inappropriately to a teacher—but there might also be reinforcing properties such as attention or the laughter of peers.

Corporal punishment is the use of spanking or slapping a child. A meta-analysis by Gershoff (2002) found that the use of corporal punishment does tend to result in immediate compliance but also results in higher levels of aggression, delinquency, abuse of spouse or child, and lower levels of mental health. The evidence is strong enough that many experts recommend entirely against spanking children (Gershoff, 2013; Smith, 2012).

What has all this to do with personality? Skinner and his students have attempted to demonstrate that through appropriate manipulation of reinforcement, one can control which responses a human will make and how frequently and vigorously these responses will be made. Personality, then, is viewed simply as the collection of these reinforced operant responses. For Skinner, individual differences in personality are primarily a function of the differences in behaviors that have been reinforced and in the reinforcement schedules governing the emission of those behaviors. Since we are likely to see people in similar situations, it also likely that we will notice the reinforced behaviors consistently, leading to our own perceptions of the consistency of that person's behavior, and conclude that it is part of their personality.

punishment An outcome to behavior that can be either adding something aversive or removing something positive.

Applications of Reinforcement Theory

Skinnerian psychology is functional and pragmatic. In an important sense, it is less a theory of personality than a system for behavior change and social engineering. Why, then, should one include Skinner's theory in a text on personality? The answer is that Skinner's approach represents an important theoretical perspective from which to view and analyze the behaviors that are considered to constitute "personality." It views many of the theoretical processes with which the psychoanalytic and other psychodynamic theorists have been concerned to be irrelevant and illusory. However, Skinner sought to explain in Skinnerian terms some of the phenomena observed by Freudians. Skinnerian theory primarily addresses regularities in behaviors and changes in behavior. It proposes a set of procedures for controlling and shaping behavior and has had a profound impact on a variety of areas, including education, clinical psychology, and animal training. Skinnerian methods, sometimes referred to as *behavior modification*, have been used for many different types of behavior difficulties.

Autism

One often finds Skinnerian principles applied to difficult cases that have been unresponsive to other forms of therapy. Work with autistic children, who suffer serious impairment in language and social attachment, is illustrative (Eikeseth, Smith, Jahr, and Eldervik, 2007; Whalen and Schriebman, 2004). Especially distressing to parents is the child's apparent unresponsiveness to and failure to display affection. Other symptoms of autism include stereotyped, ritualized gestures and behaviors (whirling around) and extreme attachment to certain objects. The initial task of determining the environmental stimuli and reinforcements that "control" such behavior has proven very difficult in these cases. A great deal of effort is spent simply determining what is reinforcing for the child, say, a favorite food. An experimenter's "yes" or smile might be paired with food so that the experimenter's response can also be used as a reinforcer. Through the use of such techniques, detailed shaping procedures, and many learning trials, it has become possible to train autistic children to acquire some speech and some social skills (Gaylord-Ross et al., 1984; Lovaas, 1968).

Token Economies

token economy A behavior modification technique in which desired behaviors are reinforced with tokens that can be exchanged for desired objects and activities.

Procedures based on Skinnerian principles have also been applied in such social settings and organizations as schools, prisons, and hospitals to foster desired behaviors. The **token economy** is one such innovation in organizational rules and procedures, where tokens are used as interim reinforcers that can eventually be exchanged for a preferred reinforcer. The great advantage of tokens is that they allow for great flexibility in reinforcers—from privileges to material objects—thereby permitting individualization of the reinforcement. The first implementation of a token economy, by Ayllon and Azrin (1965), has become a prototype for numerous programs. Schizophrenic patients in a psychiatric ward were reinforced for a designated set of behaviors including grooming themselves, serving meals, and washing dishes. The tokens the patients received when performing the desired responses could be exchanged for such rewards as passes, television privileges, selection of roommates, candy, and cigarettes. As is characteristic of Skinnerian studies, the responses and reinforcers were carefully specified and objectively recorded and quantified through systematic observation procedures. The results demonstrated substantial improvement in patient behavior with the implementation of a token economy. As soon as the reinforcement procedure was discontinued, however, the patients' behaviors deteriorated, returning almost to their initial levels.

The dependence of new behaviors on the maintenance of reinforcement also illustrates one of the limitations of token economies and other behavior modification techniques. The behavior is frequently dependent on being in the same stimulus situation; that is, positive changes do not generalize to new situations (e.g., the home) where the stimulus conditions are different. For these reasons, investigators working with highly aggressive youngsters have implemented behavioral change programs directly in the home, the setting in which the most difficulty occurred for these children (Patterson, Chamberlain, and Reid, 1982; Patterson, Cobb, and Ray, 1973). The experimenters attempted to modify the family systems of interaction, altering the patterns of provoking stimuli and the ineffective reinforcements employed by both children and parents.

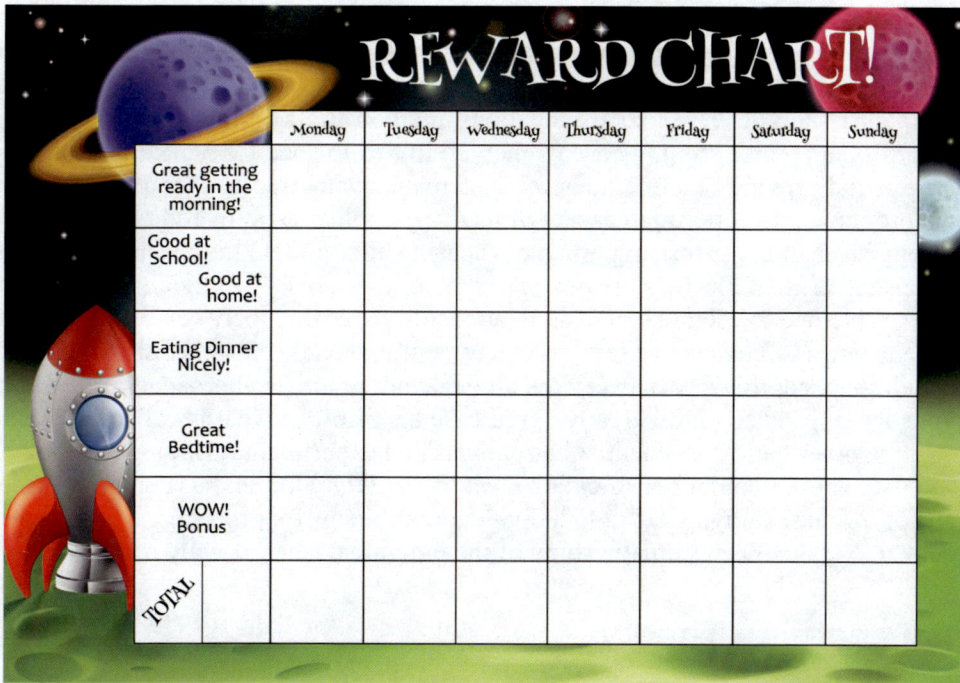

REWARD CHART!

	Monday	Tuesday	Wednesday	Thursday	Friday	Saturday	Sunday
Great getting ready in the morning!							
Good at School! Good at home!							
Eating Dinner Nicely!							
Great Bedtime!							
WOW! Bonus							
TOTAL							

Parents may use a chart to keep track of the behaviors they want to reinforce.

Limitations of Reinforcement Theory

It is evident that many clinical psychologists find Skinnerian techniques to be useful; research using operant theory and methodology is both vigorous and salient. At the same time however, there are serious limitations in the Skinnerian model as a comprehensive theory of personality and behavior. One fundamental difficulty is the arbitrary relationship it establishes between the particular response to be reinforced and the particular reward used as a reinforcement. Given a particular reinforcer, such as food, the Skinnerian assumption is that this reinforcer will work equally well or poorly for any individual organism, regardless of the response to be learned. However, as was discussed in Chapter 1, this is not the case. Food is an excellent reinforcer to condition the pecking of a pigeon, but a poor reinforcer when one wants to condition wing movements. Organisms are biologically organized so that there are natural reinforcing consequences for particular behaviors (Breland and Breland, 1961). In a similar manner and more germane to present concerns, reinforcing a child for excellent performance with such external rewards as money or candy may not increase subsequent achievement strivings if his or her goals were intrinsic mastery of the task or a desire for parental affection.

A related theoretical difficulty is the failure to consider factors other than external reinforcers that maintain a preferred response. It may be possible, given patience and a sufficient number of reinforcements, to train a child who is temperamentally introverted to be socially outgoing and extroverted (see also Chapter 1). This child might be superficially indistinguishable from a child who responds quickly to reinforcements for extroverted responses. However, there may be costs to the introverted child that would remain hidden unless explicitly assessed. A child whose behavior was difficult to shift might be less happy and spontaneous and have a lower threshold for frustration as an extrovert. Because Skinnerians have ignored the structural or organizational aspects of personality, they have given too little attention to the consequences of behavior modification for aspects of personality other than the specific behaviors that are undergoing modification.

In addition, Skinnerians have failed to ask what some psychologists consider to be a central question in personality, namely: Why are particular events or experiences reinforcing? For example, why is one individual attracted to particular kinds of mates, why is peer approval a powerful reward for child A but not for child B, and so on?

Nevertheless, whatever one's position on the merits of Skinner's ideas as a theory of personality and human behavior, there is no doubt that Skinner's operant reinforcement theory has made important contributions to psychology. In the area of methodology, it has fostered painstaking observations of situations and behaviors so that one can determine and quantify the precise stimulus events that are linked to specific behaviors. It has also encouraged and provided the methods for systematic evaluation of therapeutic and educational programs, just one small aspect of its many applications. In addition, Skinnerian psychology has had the surprising effect of focusing attention on the detailed study of an individual, rather than on the statistical average of a number of individuals. Skinnerian methods enable one to establish precise relationships over time between changes in individual behavior and changes in reinforcement contingencies and other stimulus events. In the traditional controversy between the clinical and scientific approaches, the clinician has typically emphasized individually based case histories, or what is called *idiographic data*. On the other hand, the scientist has emphasized experimental findings that are normative for an entire population, so-called *nomothetic data*. Skinner has combined aspects of both approaches, studying a single individual with scientific procedures. He has therefore helped to make the systematic study of the individual scientifically respectable.

Social Learning Theory

Although Skinnerians, along with Dollard and Miller, have applied learning principles to complex social behavior, they have been criticized by those learning theorists who are concerned primarily with social behavior. This criticism is based in part on the fact that their analyses are derived from the study of nonhumans. In addition, these critics find fault with Dollard and Miller's emphasis on drives and drive reduction and are especially unsympathetic toward Skinner because of his neglect of cognitive factors in regulating behavior. These shortcomings have been addressed by several related personality approaches which are collectively referred to as social learning theory.

Expectancy-Value Theory

Reinforcement Value and Expectancy

expectancy A belief that a particular behavior will lead to a reward or goal.

The theory proposed by Julian Rotter (1954, 1972) emphasizes the construct of **expectancy**, or an individual's belief in the probability that a specific behavior will lead to satisfactions or valued goals. For example, on the basis of prior experience, a student may have the simultaneous expectancies that diligent study will bring the approval and affection of her parents and the disapproval of her fiancé, who wants to spend more time with her. To predict how hard she will study, one has to know the reinforcement values of the goals represented by parental approval and avoidance of her fiancé's disapproval. Each of us has our own hierarchy of values for such common human goals as money, affection, status, entertainment, sex, and power.

The likelihood that a particular behavior will occur, according to Rotter, is a joint function of the person's expectancy that the behavior will lead to one's goals and the values attached to those goals. In other words, people will generally choose actions that, based on previous experience, they expect will lead to valued goals. Hence, children are likely to say "please" in requesting something if previous experience has shown that there is a high probability (expectancy) of getting what they want (highly valued goals) when they do so. Behaviors with low expectancies of satisfaction are not likely to be engaged in unless, under some circumstances, they are associated with high reward. For example, twelve-year-olds are not likely to cry when trying to convince their parents to do something; at this age, they have found that such behavior has low expectancy of bringing satisfaction. However, they might cry if crying could result in obtaining some very great satisfaction, such as permission to stay overnight at a friend's house. Characteristics of the specific situation also play a central role in Rotter's theory, inasmuch as expectancy and reinforcement vary according to one's specific environment.

Needs

Reinforcement value and expectancy are terms that Rotter uses to refer to specific goals and behaviors. These specific goals commonly cluster into broader categories that are conceptualized as needs, such as the needs for recognition and status, dominance, independence, love and affection, physical comfort, and protection-dependency. For any individual these needs will vary in their need value, or the value of their satisfaction for that individual. Personality differences can be described in terms of individual differences in need value. Also contributing to personality differences are differences in the likelihood, or expectancy, of the behavior one has learned to rely upon to achieve satisfaction of a need, referred to as *freedom of movement*. Low freedom of movement coupled with high need value results in a very frustrated individual who feels ineffective in satisfying an important goal. This particular constellation of factors could result in maladaptive and neurotic behavior, such as engaging in excessive amounts of nonproductive fantasy.

The concepts of need and need value link Rotter's model to psychoanalytic theories, while the expectancy concept provides links with more cognitive motivational theories. Rotter has been critical of psychoanalytic theorists for not recognizing the role of expectancy as a determinant of behavior. No matter how intense a specific desire or instinct postulated by psychoanalysts might be, if an action has zero subjective likelihood of leading to one's goals, then that action will not be undertaken.

Locus of Control

Rotter's formulation of the concept of freedom of movement was associated with the development of a scale for measuring generalized expectancy concerning the efficacy of one's efforts. This scale has been intensively used to study the properties of a personality dimension labeled internal versus external control of reinforcement. Internal control refers to the individual's belief (expectancy) that he or she can significantly determine whether or not a goal will be reached, while external control refers to the belief that fate, or external agents, rather than personal factors, are the most important determinants of goal attainment. The research and applications stimulated by the concept of **locus of control** will be examined in more detail in Chapter 17.

locus of control A perception of the influence that one has on the attainment of reinforcement.

Bandura's Social Learning Theory

Another prominent social learning theory was first proposed by Bandura and Walters (1963) and subsequently developed by Bandura and his students, as well as a number of others (e.g., Mischel, 1968; Wolpe, 1958). It now vies with Skinner's operant reinforcement theory as the principal representative of learning theory approaches to personality. The model places great emphasis on the consequences of a response—that is, the feedback provided by reinforcement or punishment of a behavior. Bandura (1986) has revised and expanded the model to incorporate a rich array of cognitive processes such as attention, covert rehearsal of instructions, self-motivation, self-reinforcement, and self-efficacy. For Bandura, people are actively involved in regulating their behavior as well as responding to situational cues that are in turn affected by the consequences of the behavior. This process of mutual interaction between person, situation, and behavior is referred to by Bandura as **reciprocal determination**.

reciprocal determination Mutual interactions between the person, situation, and behavior.

Observational Learning

A number of different learning mechanisms, especially observational learning, are used to account for the social development of the child. Observational learning refers to the acquisition of new behaviors through observation of another person performing them. Many social responses and personality characteristics are acquired simply by imitating or copying the behavior of the models one observes. Bandura and his students have carried out a systematic series of studies investigating the process of imitation or modeling; they assigned this process a central role in social learning theory.

Modeling

modeling The process of acquiring new behaviors through observation of another person performing them.

When we see a three-year-old boy carrying a briefcase, putting it down, and saying to his mother, "It's been a hard day at the office," we know that the child was not directly taught those behaviors. Rather, he acquired them through observation of a parent's behavior, through **modeling**. The mechanism of modeling has three properties that give it special significance for the understanding of personality development:

1. Modeling typically involves a social situation (the model and the imitator) and a social relationship. The model can be an actual person or a film or cartoon representation.
2. Modeling is a means by which complex behaviors can be readily acquired. The reinforcement methods proposed by Skinner require careful, time-consuming efforts to shape a complex social behavior. In contrast, imitation can produce very rapid acquisition of social behaviors.
3. Direct reinforcement of imitated behavior is not required for learning to take place.

These properties of modeling have significant consequences for our understanding of behavior change and the process by which children are socialized. According to Bandura (1969, p. 188), "virtually all learning phenomena resulting from direct experiences can occur on a vicarious basis through observation of other persons' behaviors and its consequences to them." Thus, while Skinner would look for reinforcement contingencies in the environment to explain a child's aggressive behavior, Bandura would examine important figures in the child's environment, such as parents, peers, or television heroes, who may serve as aggressive models. In what has become a classic study (Bandura, Ross, and Ross, 1961) nursery school children Individually observed an adult engaging in aggressive behavior toward a Bobo doll (a large, inflated plastic clown that uprights itself when knocked down). The adult struck the doll with a mallet and made a number of predetermined aggressive statements such as, "POW! Kick him sock him down sock him in the nose!" The child was then mildly frustrated and given an opportunity to play with the Bobo doll while the adults left the room. The degree of modeling displayed by the children was striking, with the children often hitting the doll with exactly the same motions as the model, using precisely the same verbal comments. A comparison of their responses with those of a control group of preschoolers who had merely observed the adult playing

Source: George Rudy/Shutterstock

In the social learning approach, behaviors may occur through the process of observing other people's behavior.

with a construction toy revealed much more aggressive behavior in the children who had observed the aggressive model.

A wide variety of behaviors from self-control and altruistic responses to aggression, can be acquired through modeling. For example, the influence of a model on aiding a "person in distress" was examined by stationing a woman next to a car with a flat tire. Approximately one-quarter mile closer on the same road, experimenters placed another car with a flat, but this time a young man was helping the female to fix it. The young man thus served as a model. Compared to a control condition without a model, a significantly greater number of drivers stopped to offer assistance to the second woman (Bryan and Test, 1967).

Response Acquisition and Performance

Children do not automatically or consistently imitate. Modeling, like other learning processes, is affected by a number of factors. Bandura and his colleagues have found that among the variables that facilitate modeling are similarity in gender between model and observer; the control of the model; and observation of reinforcement of the model's response. In evaluating the effects of these variables, it is essential to distinguish between acquisition and performance of the response. Different factors determine whether the response is acquired and, if it is acquired, whether it is performed. Learning, or response acquisition, is influenced by attention to the model and by how well one interprets and rehearses the model's behavior. Performance, however, depends much more on the nature of the reinforcing consequences to the model and the observer.

In a study bearing directly on this acquisition-performance distinction, preschool children observed a filmed model exhibiting aggressive responses. Under one condition, the model was praised and rewarded with treats, while in a second condition the model was severely punished for the aggressive display. A control condition was included in which there were no response consequences to the model. A test of the degree of imitation following the different modeling conditions revealed significantly less modeling by children in the punished-model condition, compared with children observing the model when reward or nothing followed the behavior. To demonstrate that this effect was not due to differences in learning of the response, the children in all three groups were offered highly attractive incentives to reproduce the responses of the model. When positive incentives were introduced, children in all groups performed the response they had observed. Thus, all three groups learned the model's responses equally, but their performance of the response was dependent on the anticipated consequences of that behavior. (See Bandura, 1965.) It will be noted that although the rewards and punishments were administered only to the model, they nevertheless influenced the observer's behavior. These vicarious consequences—*vicarious reward* and *vicarious punishment*—influence the observer's subsequent behavior through providing information about the effect of an action.

Verbalization and Rules

In contrast to Skinner, social learning theorists emphasize the importance of verbalization, rules, and related symbolic processes that are believed to mediate behavior. Rewards and punishments for behaviors are more effective when they are accompanied by explicitly verbalized rules (Liebert and Allen, 1967; Parke, 1970). To demonstrate the role of verbalization in observational learning, children witnessed a model engaging in a complex sequence of behaviors. They were asked to verbalize the model's novel responses, watch attentively, or count rapidly. The last condition was included to prevent implicit verbal coding of the model's actions (Bandura, Grusec, and Menlove, 1966). Modeling was highest in the verbalization group, next highest in the attentiveness group, and lowest in the rapid-count condition. Verbal statements that are silently rehearsed also have a significant effect on behavior.

Self-Reinforcement

Social learning theorists do not limit reinforcements to external rewards or punishments, but also include self-imposed reinforcing consequences (Bandura, 1977a; Kanfer and

Marston, 1963). Human beings have internalized standards of performance, which they utilize to evaluate their actions. The self-evaluative statement, "I did well," following a particular test performance is a reinforcement for that performance. One student might make such an evaluation only for a grade of A; another might feel such evaluation was accurate if the grade was C. Conversely, some individuals may be very self-critical, administering self-punishment even though performance might appear excellent to an observer. Depressed adults, for example, tend to evaluate their performances as poorer than the nondepressed do, even for identical accomplishments (Loeb, Beck, Diggory, and Tuthill, 1967).

Self-Efficacy

self-efficacy A person's expectation that he or she can effectively cope with and master situations and bring about desired outcomes through personal efforts.

Feedback from internal and external reinforcements affects one's sense of **self-efficacy**, a concept that has gradually assumed a central role in Bandura's (1977a) thought. Self-efficacy refers to the expectation that one can effectively cope with and master situations, and that one can bring about desired outcomes through one's own personal efforts. This clearly relates to Rotter's concept of locus of control, briefly introduced in the previous section.

Bandura maintained that the effects of conditioning and modeling therapies are mediated by the change that occurs in one's sense of self-efficacy, or the belief that "I can." One's perceived degree of self-efficacy, according to Bandura, is influenced by a variety of behaviors in regard to a particular task—e.g., the goals that are set for oneself, the degree of competence or accomplishment in the task, the degree of persistence displayed, and if the task involves something fearful, the degree of fear that is experienced. Thus, through changing self-efficacy, one can hope to bring about significant changes in behavior.

In an illustrative experiment demonstrating the role ascribed to self-efficacy, adults with a snake phobia (severe fear of snakes) were assigned to either a low, medium, or high efficacy-induction experimental condition (Bandura, Reese, and Adams, 1982). The efficacy treatment was conducted by a female experimenter using modeling and prompting procedures with tasks involving a boa constrictor. The tasks on which the subjects rated their ability to perform—that is, indicated their self-efficacy—were graded into eighteen progressively more threatening activities that ranged from approaching, to touching, to freely handling the boa. Subjects in the low self-efficacy group were treated until they made the judgment that they could place their hands in the cage near the snake. In the medium self-efficacy group, the criterion was the judgment that they would be able to touch and lift the snake inside the cage. In the high self-efficacy group, they were treated until they felt that they could let the snake loose and allow it to crawl in their laps. Following the experimental treatments, the participants" responses to a corn snake were recorded.

There have been a number of applications of self-efficacy theory to behavior problems besides fear reduction. For example, in a study of participants in a Weight Watchers' program designed to reduce weight, each week subjects were asked a self-efficacy question regarding their degree of confidence that they would eventually reach their goal weight (Mitchell and Stuart, 1984). Those who dropped out of the program reported significantly lower feelings of self-efficacy than those who remained in the program, despite the fact that their rates of weight loss were generally comparable. In the realm of health, self-efficacy training has been used to increase movement in assisted-living facilities for older adults (Chao, Scherer, Wu, Lucke, and Montgomery, 2013), self-care for people with diabetes (Gao et al., 2013), and rates of breast-feeding (Otsuka et al., 2014).

Source: In The Light Photography/Shutterstock

Even people with a snake phobia can hold a snake if they observe others handling the snake and believe they have high self-efficacy about handling the snake.

Self-Efficacy Issues

While there is no doubt that self-efficacy is related to a wide range of mastery behaviors, there remains a question as to its causal role. Perception of self-efficacy is closely related to past performance on a task, and both are related to future performance. What is cause and what is effect? Although this question remains to be fully resolved, there are data indicating that while past performance influences both self-efficacy and future performance, self-efficacy has an independent effect on future performance (Bandura and Wood, 1989). A second issue has to do with the difficulty of separating one's expectation of mastery of a behavior (self-efficacy) from one's **outcome expectancies**, that is, the success of the behavior. You may feel incomplete mastery of a subject matter, but still feel uncertain as to the outcome of an oral examination in that subject if you believe the instructor is biased. It is possible, but difficult, to get independent estimates of self-efficacy and outcome expectations (Maddux, Norton, and Stoltenberg, 1986; Manning and Wright, 1983). Moreover, features of the environment that affect outcome expectations can also influence perceived self-efficacy. Thus, varying information as to the controllability of a situation—in one study, the responsiveness of a group of employees to managerial control—has been shown to have a marked effect on both self-efficacy and performance. Studies show that high controllability elicits greater perceived self-efficacy and better performance than low controllability (Bandura and Wood, 1989). It should be noted that self-efficacy, in Bandura's framework, is significantly related to performance in a specific situation and is not conceived of as a generalized personality trait.

outcome expectancies The beliefs about whether a particular behavior will accomplish a particular goal.

The Situation and Discriminative Cues

One of the major tenets of social learning theory is that behavior is a function of the situation in which it takes place. Walter Mischel (1968, 1973) has argued cogently and vigorously that the consistency in behavior implied by such concepts as traits or motives is largely illusory. He stated (1968, p. 177), "response patterns even in highly similar situations often fail to be strongly related. Individuals show far less cross-situational consistency in their behavior than has been assumed." If a man is highly aggressive with his peers but docile with his father and other authority figures, social learning theorists would contend that he should not be considered a fundamentally aggressive individual who masks his aggression when dealing with individuals in positions of authority. Rather, they argue, he is more appropriately described as someone who displays different response patterns in situations that present different *discriminative cues*.

For Mischel, behaving the same way in the same situation, or temporal consistency, is much more characteristic of behavior than behaving the same way in different situations (Mischel, 1984). We tend to have similar goals and expectancies when we are in very similar situations; thus, we are likely to utilize similar cognitive strategies and display similar behaviors. We may believe people display cross-situational consistency because we tend to overgeneralize from some temporally consistent behavior. In addition, according to Mischel, we tend to overgeneralize from behavior that we view as representative of, or prototypical of, a particular trait. For example, if a classmate smiles warmly whenever he encounters an acquaintance, we are likely to label him as "friendly." Smiling serves as a *cognitive prototype* of the trait category "friendliness." We might miss or overlook his lack of other friendly behaviors, e.g., welcoming newcomers or expressing interest in other people.

In short, for Mischel, trait generality is not found in actual behaviors, but is a distortion stemming from temporal consistency and our tendency to use cognitive prototypes. Where Mischel finds the concept of personality to be useful is in regard to the strategies that individuals use to encode information about people and significant objects in their environment. We discuss the issue of traits versus situations in depth in Chapter 9.

Limitations of Social Learning Theory

Social learning theory, like operant theory, lacks concepts that deal with the organization and structure of personality, concepts that help predict the pattern of interrelationships among the significant components of personality. In general, social learning theory is concerned with the conditions influencing the acquisition and performance of specific responses, rather than with the factors that determine which behaviors or reinforcers are central to the organism. Such questions as the psychological significance of affection, sexuality, the family triangle formed by parents and child, and the development shifts in human striving, remain far outside the scope of social learning theories.

Cognitive Behavior Modification

The approaches that have been grouped together under the label of cognitive behavior modification stress the role of cognitive factors in mediating behavior and attempt to bring about change through alteration of these cognitions (Mahoney, 1974). There is clearly substantial overlap between cognitive behavior modification and social learning theory, and the two approaches are quite compatible. Their difference lies in emphasis and historical background. Cognitive behavior modification was guided by, yet significantly deviates from, Skinner's operant theory. Although Skinner's radical behavioral position either excludes or minimizes the relevance of internal events, the cognitively oriented behaviorists maintained that one can adhere to the objective spirit of Skinner's approach while investigating the role of such internal processes as images, self-monitoring responses, and perceived responsibility.

For example, in one study problem drinkers were taught to be aware of different facets of their drinking behavior by learning to self-monitor their drinking, compute their blood-alcohol level, establish weekly goals for total alcohol consumption, and intersperse drinking of nonalcoholic beverages with alcoholic beverages (Alden, 1988). The experimental treatment resulted in a significant decline in alcohol consumption, which was maintained over a two-year follow-up period. Other strategies may involve systematic efforts to alter the individual's thinking and problem-solving strategies, as in treatments of depressed patients which focus on alteration of patient's illogically negative interpretations of their experiences and their negative views of themselves (Beck, 1976, 1984).

Conditioning New Associations

Wolpe (1958), in his pursuit of behavioral alternatives to psychoanalytic treatment, pioneered a process called **systematic desensitization** of anxiety. Wolpe's objective was to train anxious patients to relax while in the presence of anxiety-provoking stimuli. He theorized that the relaxation response inhibits anxiety and therefore will weaken the bond between the anxiety response and threatening stimuli: a process considered to be an example of the more general principle labeled reciprocal inhibition.

Wolpe's treatment requires initial training of the client in deep-muscle relaxation and the construction of an **anxiety hierarchy**, consisting of a series of related situations that are graduated according to the degree of evoked anxiety. The patient first imagines the least anxiety-provoking situation in the hierarchy while maintaining a relaxation response, with the procedure then followed successively for each item in the hierarchy until the patient can relax fully while visualizing the situation that had evoked the most anxiety. Wolpe reported substantial clinical success with this treatment and, in the process, stimulated an extensive clinical and experimental literature applying this technique to a variety of problems. Clinically effective variations of Wolpe's approach include combining his procedures with imagery of pleasurable, relaxing stimuli or with imagery of successful coping with the anxiety-arousing stimuli (Crits-Christoph and Singer, 1983, 1984). Another variation, used with patients who experienced marked anxiety in social situations, entails relaxation training plus the practice of relaxation skills during role-playing of social situations. The new skills are then used in the natural environment (Jerremalm, Jannson, and Ost, 1986).

Cognitive behavioral treatment programs commonly employ combinations of training in cognitive strategies, self-monitoring, relaxation, behavioral alternatives, and related skills that help individuals to cope with their pain and fears and to reduce problem behaviors. It has been found to be especially useful for treatment of anxiety, bulimia, anger control, and general stress (Hofmann, Asnaani, Vonk, Sawyer, and Fang, 2012).

Other Cognitive Changes

The enormously complex world of images, anticipations, self-perceptions, beliefs, and information offers rich opportunities for changing behavior. We have previously referred to the technique of self-instruction. For example, reminding oneself to count to ten before responding in anger is one way in which self-instruction is used to control behavior. Imagery, another cognitive process just discussed in the context of desensitization, can also be used to condition fears and avoidance. For example, one treatment program for obesity required that obese clients visualize appetizing food coupled with a disgust-producing image, a procedure referred to as aversive imagery (Cautela, 1977). Aversive imagery has also been used in the treatment of alcoholism (Miller, 1959), smoking (Tongas, 1979), and sexual deviation (Davison, 1968).

The attribution, or **causal attribution**, that individuals make for their success and failure provides another promising area of cognitive intervention. The tendency to attribute failure to one's incompetence, rather than to lack of effort, task difficulty, or luck, is linked to a variety of maladaptive behaviors, ranging from depression (Abramson, Seligman, and Teasdale, 1978; Beck et al., 1979) to poor school achievement (Dweck and Leggett, 1988). In one study, children with poor frustration tolerance and who were having difficulties in school were trained to ascribe their failures to a lack of effort. Effort, as opposed to ability, is under volitional control and can thus be modified and increased. This perception resulted in a substantial improvement in persistence and performance in the face of failure, compared with children not receiving the attributional retraining (Dweck, 1975, 2000).

Source: leungchopan/Shutterstock

Systematic desensitization can be used to treat fear of flying.

causal attributions A term used in achievement-related contexts to connote beliefs about the reasons for one's success or failure—for example, ability, effort, task ease or difficulty, or luck.

Some Limitations

Cognitive behavior modification programs vary in their effectiveness, depending upon the behavior to be modified and the length and content of the procedures. Behaviors such as smoking and drug addiction may be so habitual or reinforcing as to be highly resistant to cognitive efforts at modifying them, so that even changes in beliefs and the recognition that the behavior is harmful may not produce a behavioral change. There is no doubt that there are significant links among cognitions, desires, feelings, and behavior. But the direction of these links—which elements are causes and which are effects—is a difficult issue. In fact, they may be linked in complex and reciprocally causal ways. Finally, cognitive behavior modification runs the risk of introducing thoughts and responses that are as difficult to define and measure as some of the psychoanalytic concepts that the behavior theorists have so roundly criticized.

Summary

1. Hullian theory asserted that *habits* are acquired when a stimulus-response pairing is followed by *drive reduction* for both *primary* and *secondary*, or *acquired*, *drives*.
2. *Drive, cue, stimulus, response*, and *reinforcement* are the key concepts in Dollard and Miller's theory.
3. Through a process of *mediated generalization*, dissimilar situations can come to have an equivalent effect because they elicit common *mediating responses*.
4. According to the Dollard-Miller model, the psychoanalytic mechanism of repression can be explained in terms of such overt responses as mislabeling and

avoidance which are elicited by anxiety-evoking stimuli because they reduce the mediating response of anxiety.

5. For Skinner, the concept of "mind" is illusory. Behavior, according to the radical behaviorist position, is a function of reinforcement. Reinforcement of selected responses determines the kinds of behavior elicited in response to a stimulus, and the schedule of reinforcement determines the rate and persistence of responding.

6. *Behavior modification* procedures based on Skinnerian principles have been applied in cases of severely disturbed children and adults. Autistic children have been taught to respond to social reinforcers, while schizophrenic patients have shown significant improvement in social behaviors through the application of these principles.

7. One limitation of Skinnerian theory is the assumption that any reinforcer should augment any response. In fact, organisms are biologically and developmentally organized so that certain reinforcers are more appropriate for particular behaviors.

8. Among Rotter's significant contributions are the analyses of the constructs of *expectancy*, *reinforcement value*, and the *internal* versus *external control* of reinforcement.

9. An important property of *observational learning* (*modeling*) is that it makes possible the very rapid acquisition of complex social behaviors.

10. A distinction must be made between learning and performance. A child may not display a response that has been acquired through modeling if the model was punished for that behavior, but may display that response given situations in which the fear of punishment is reduced.

11. According to Bandura, one's perception of self-efficacy in regard to a particular task or problem is a major determinant of one's mastery of and ability to cope with the task or problem.

12. The development of *cognitive behavior modification* procedures offers a less radical Skinnerian approach to behavioral problems. Cognitive processes such as imagery, *self-instruction*, and *attribution* are utilized in clinical procedures applying Skinnerian and related methods.

Key Terms

anxiety hierarchy (p. 104)
avoidance learning (p. 93)
causal attribution (p. 105)
classical conditioning (p. 91)
discriminative stimuli (p. 94)
drive reduction (p. 87)
escape learning (p. 93)
expectancy (p. 98)
extinction (p. 94)
habits (p. 87)
locus of control (p. 99)
mediating response (p. 88)

modeling (p. 100)
negative reinforcement (p. 93)
operant conditioning (p. 91)
outcome expectancies (p. 103)
partial reinforcement (p. 93)
positive reinforcement (p. 93)
punishment (p. 95)
reciprocal determination (p. 99)
self-efficacy (p. 102)
systematic desensitization (p. 104)
token economy (p. 96)

Thought Questions

1. A student who received a poor grade on an exam began to avoid studying. Analyze this situation using the key concepts of Dollard and Miller.

2. Would you want to live in a society based on Skinner's principles? What might it be like?

3. Can you think of ways in which you control your own behavior through covert self-instructions?

4. Why would a friend look at the evidence against corporal punishment and say, "I don't believe it. I was spanked and I turned out OK"?

5. What types of behavioral problems seem most amenable to learning theory treatments? Which ones might be better treated with a psychoanalytic approach?

Phenomenological Theories

CHAPTER **6**

Chapter Outline

Humanistic Theory

The Person-Centered Theory of Carl Rogers

Maslow's Organismic Humanism

Existential Humanism

Kelly's Personal Construct Theory

Implicit Psychology

Source: Olga Danylenko/Shutterstock

Many types of personality theories fall within the category of **phenomenology**—the study of subjective experience, or the "meaning" that one gives to events. What these theories have in common is a primary concern with the mental or cognitive aspects of behavior and experience. Although most social learning theories have incorporated cognitive variables into their theoretical models, reinforcement mechanisms that influence observable actions remain central to these theories. This is not the case for the phenomenologists. Phenomenological theories are concerned with the "now" of experience. They address the present situation and its meanings rather than the past and how things came to be the way they are (a central quest for both psychoanalytic and learning theories). Humanistic psychology, exemplified in the work of Carl Rogers, Abraham Maslow, and the existentialists, sees the constraints and fears that block full awareness of the "now" of one's experiences as major contributors to neurotic behavior. An important goal of humanistic theories is thus expansion of the individual's consciousness of the present environment and subjective experience.

Theories based on how individuals make sense of the world and themselves are also embraced by phenomenology. One of these theories was formulated by George Kelly, who assumed that individuals go about their everyday activities like scientists, formulating hypotheses about their environments and themselves, gathering information to test these hypotheses, and drawing inferences from the obtained information. Kelly's theory is subsumed within a literature known as **implicit psychology**, which deals with the perceived laws of behavior held by what the researchers termed "naïve observers." These naïve observers may actually have a very complex and accurate theory about how

phenomenology The study of subjective experience, or the "meaning" that a person gives to events.

implicit psychology The perceived laws of behavior held by naive observers, or the personality theories of individuals who are untrained psychologists.

humans and their personalities are organized and how it influences behavior; the person is naïve only in the sense that he or she is untrained as a psychologist.

One difference between humanistic approaches and the cognitive approach of Kelly stems primarily from their different views on how we "know" the world. While both humanistic theories and Kelly's cognitive theory deal with how people process meaning in their lives, these processes are seen differently. Kelly bases his theory on a model of humans as thinking scientists. He assumes that individuals are always thinking at some level, forming concepts or constructs, sorting data, and so on. This thinking may occur quickly and nonconsciously, so quickly that we are not aware that we are perceiving our worlds through our constructs. In contrast, humanists emphasize ways of knowing that are based on direct "felt" experience, emotions, and intuitions. They do not assume these processes are necessarily based upon thinking (Bohart, 1993). In essence, humanistic theories emphasize how people perceive and experience themselves and their worlds; Kelly's cognitive theory emphasizes how people *think about* themselves and their worlds.

Humanistic Theory

Sociologists of science suggest that the development of theoretical perspectives is greatly influenced by cultural factors. If we look at the psychoanalytic theory, we have a theory that originated in the supposedly repressive society of Vienna around the beginning of the twentieth century, a social milieu that may have accounted in part for the psychoanalytic emphasis on repression, conflict, and neurosis. On the other hand, behaviorism was spawned in early 1900s' America. It embraced Darwin's concern with adaptation and function, as well as the belief that behavior is completely modifiable, an assumption consistent with the optimistic psychological climate in America at that time.

Around 1960, a so-called third force in psychology came into existence. This third force, **humanistic psychology**, focused not only on what a person is, but also on what a person has the potential to become. Humanism emerged at a time when people were experiencing alienation and dissatisfaction, despite (or perhaps because of) economic and technological success. Many individuals began questioning traditional values, including striving for success and achievement. This emphasis on existential problems—basic problems of human values and existence—gave rise to a more humanistic psychology. This psychology focused on problems of the experiencing person living in an uncertain world. Thus, the three major theoretical positions we consider, each having the status of a movement, appear to have arisen directly from the social and cultural themes of their times.

The social precursors to humanistic psychology were in evidence when the Association of Humanistic Psychology was founded. Four interrelated principles were adopted by the humanists to guide their pursuits:

1. *The experiencing person is of primary interest.* Humanistic psychology begins with the study of individuals in real-life circumstances. Humans are real people, rather than merely being the object of study. Psychological research, the humanists contend, cannot be modeled after early physics, in which the objects of study were "out there." The person must be examined and described in terms of personal consciousness, which includes subjective experience and how the individual perceives and values himself or herself. The basic question with which each individual must grapple is "Who am I?" Individuals, as travelers in life, must determine where they are and where they wish to go. As a result, the humanists follow a holistic approach in which experiences are not broken down into component parts like single frames within a film, but the entirety of life is considered.

2. *Human choice, creativity, and self-actualization are the preferred topics of investigation.* Humanists argue that the study of psychologically dysfunctional people has led to a dysfunctional psychology, while the study of lower organisms has yielded an incomplete psychology, devoid of consciousness. The humanists believe that psychologists should study wholesome and healthy individuals, people who are creative and fully functioning. People have a real need to push forward in life and to develop their potentials and capabilities. Growth, rather than mere adjustment, is

humanistic psychology The system of psychology that focuses not only on what a person is, but also on what a person has the potential to become.

the criterion of health. These self-actualizing tendencies are of particular significance to the humanists.

3. *Meaningfulness must precede objectivity in the selection of research problems.* Psychological research, according to the humanists, has in the past centered on methods rather than on problems. Often research topics have been selected chiefly because objective and convenient methods are available. However, research projects should be undertaken because they are significant and pertinent to human issues, even if the methods available are weak. Research cannot be value free; psychologists must study the important issues of people's lives.

4. *Ultimate value is placed on the dignity of the person.* Above all, humans are accepted as unique and as having the potential to be noble. Psychologists must understand people, rather than predict or control their behavior. Individuals are believed by the humanists to have a higher nature with a need for meaningful work, responsibility, and the opportunity for creative expression.

Many prominent psychologists, representing different theoretical viewpoints but sharing a common belief in the importance of the individual's need for meaning and self-actualization, have been attracted to the humanistic movement. They include figures as diverse as Gordon Allport, who, as previously indicated, spent time with Jung; Erich Fromm, whose social psychological deviation from classic psychoanalysis was reviewed in Chapter 4; and Carl Rogers and Abraham Maslow, whose theoretical views lie at the center of the humanistic movement.

The Person-Centered Theory of Carl Rogers

Carl Rogers ranks among the most influential psychologists. Born in 1902, he functioned as an active spokesperson for the "third force" in psychology until his death in 1987. His conception of personality emerged from his work in psychotherapy and reflects the influence of both an early religious background and his early adolescent experience with the study of scientific principles of farming. In contrast to the psychoanalysts, Rogers communicated a fundamental faith and trust in human nature. While Freud viewed human beings as struggling with destruction and lustful impulses, Rogers believed that by providing love and fundamental acceptance, we can help our fellow human beings recognize and ultimately realize the potential for goodness that is in them. He also believed that the fully functioning person acted like a good scientist—continually testing personal ideas and values against experience.

Self-Actualization

For Rogers, as for the other humanists, a core tendency of a person is to actualize his or her own potential. The motive of **self-actualization** implies that there is an internal force that works to develop one's capacities and talents to the fullest. The individual's central motivation is to learn from experience and grow. Growth occurs when individuals confront problems, struggle to master them, and through that struggle develop new aspects of their skills, capacities, and views about life. Life is therefore an endless process of creatively moving forward, even if it is only in small ways. Fully functioning people are people who are continually learning and developing, much as Rogers, Freud, and Skinner continually learned and developed their own theories. Even if personality were to consist of basic traits, how one expressed and actualized these traits could be continually refined in more and more adaptive directions, and in that sense life is a process of continual growth and change (Bohart and Watson, 2011).

From the perspective of scientific inquiry, the actualization tendency is a vague, general concept that has not proven to be amenable to measurement or tests. The reality of an actualization tendency is an axiom of humanistic psychology which is not subject to proof or disproof. Whereas other motivations vary in intensity between individuals and fluctuate within an individual as a function of physiological or situational changes, this is not the case for actualization. Moreover, the form that actualization takes is unique to each individual, making it impossible to establish criteria for the presence or absence

self-actualization A principle of human behavior stating that individuals strive to develop their capacities and talents to the fullest—that is, growing and enhancing the basic self.

of actualization. Despite these methodological limitations, Rogers and other humanists (Maslow, 1971) found the actualizing tendency to be conceptually essential for the understanding of human striving and development.

However, there is evidence for a similar concept, that of a "self-righting tendency," from researchers who have studied the phenomenon of resilience. A number of investigators have now found that many children seem to not only survive but also thrive despite the obstacles of adverse circumstances such as poverty or a dysfunctional family life (Werner, 2013). That is, they seem able to "right themselves" and to continue to grow despite adversity. Masten, Best, and Garmazy (1990) conclude from their research that "studies of psychosocial resilience support the view that human psychological development is highly buffered and self-righting" (p. 438). And Werner and Smith, from their studies of disadvantaged children, conclude that "As we watched these children grow from babyhood to adulthood we could not help but respect the self-righting tendencies within them that produced normal development under all but the most persistently adverse circumstances" (1982, p. 159). While the concepts of self-righting and self-actualization are not identical, they are closely related, as can be seen from the fact that many of Rogers' examples of self-actualization are also examples of self-righting.

Rather than focusing on the source or strength of the actualizing tendency, Rogers found it more useful to consider what might stand in the way of, or inhibit, this basic human motivation. Rogers (1959) was particularly concerned with blockage of the tendency toward self-actualization, which is one component of the more general actualizing tendency. Rogers (1959, p. 200) defined the self as the "organized . . . [whole] . . . of the 'I' or 'me.'" It consists of one's self-perceptions (e.g., attractiveness, abilities, achievements, relationships with others) and the range of values attached to these perceptions (e.g., good-bad, worthy-unworthy). Thus, one's self-concept is very dependent on one's learning experiences, especially the kind of feedback and acceptance one receives from others. According to Rogers, human beings have a basic need for others' positive regard in the form of warmth, love, and acceptance. This regard and acceptance, however, is usually offered on a conditional basis. Typically, an individual receives love or recognition as a result of some particular action. Consequently, one's perception of oneself as a valuable human being often depends on these actions and on the resulting evaluations of other people. In contrast, the truly healthy personality perceives his or her whole self in a positive manner. Specific actions can be regarded as good or bad, but the self is always unconditionally valuable.

Positive Regard

unconditional positive regard Rogers' term for the accepting and valuing of a person per se, regardless of the degree to which he or she exhibits specific behaviors that are approved or disapproved.

To attain this level of adjustment, the individual needs the experience of **unconditional positive regard**, of being valued for oneself regardless of the degree to which specific behaviors are approved or disapproved. The love of a parent for a child often has such an unconditional quality. A mother may disapprove of her four-year-old's hitting a younger sibling or of the child's sloppy table manners, but she will nevertheless communicate her fundamental love and acceptance of the child. According to Rogers, one should criticize the action, not the person.

conditions of worth The conditional positive regard—the "do's" or "don'ts," "shoulds" and "shouldn'ts" - that people live by in order to feel appreciated and accepted by others.

Conditional positive regard, that is, acceptance that is dependent on the positive or negative evaluation of a person's actions, leads to the development of **conditions of worth**. The person experiences "do" or "do not" and "should" or "should not" as necessary in order to feel appreciated and accepted. A condition of worth, in turn, leads to defensive functioning, or to the closing off of experiences. The person loses contact with real experiences, reporting what one "should" feel, not what was actually felt. It is quite normal to behave in a way that is incongruent with the way one feels in order to avoid the disapproval of friends, parents, and other important figures. For instance, you may act as if you enjoy a particular movie or a rock group that you actually dislike because you fear that your friends would think less of you if you expressed your real feelings. The clinical problem arises when one begins to deceive oneself and dissociate the true feelings. This generates discrepancies between the objective and the subjective worlds, producing anxiety and threat, which in turn block self-actualization.

The warmth and affection displayed by this elderly couple convey the feeling of unconditional positive regard advocated by Rogers.

Source: Pressmaster/Shutterstock

Client-Centered Therapy

Corresponding to Rogers's theory of personality is a psychotherapeutic approach he developed, known as client-centered therapy. A key element in this therapy is the therapist's manifestation of unconditional positive regard for the client. The Rogerian therapist is trusting, accepting, and empathic, conveying to the client an understanding and acceptance of the client's perception of and feelings about the problem. Through the therapist's acceptance and empathy, the client becomes better able to accept real feelings that may have been previously distorted or denied because they conflicted with self-perceptions based on the conditional regard of others.

One of Rogers's most important contributions was his initiation of efforts to evaluate client-centered therapy. While studies of the effectiveness of various forms of therapy are now quite common, prior to Rogers's pioneering studies (Rogers and Dymond, 1954), assessment of psychotherapy depended primarily on unsystematic patient and therapist reports. Rogers's investigations both helped stimulate research in psychotherapy and contributed to personality theory.

Self-Concept

The investigations by Rogers's research group of the efficacy of client-centered therapy focused on the self-concept. Rogers and Dymond (1954) were in part concerned with changes during the course of therapy in the discrepancy between the client's self-concept and *ideal self*—the person the client would like to be, who possesses certain positive attributes and does not have certain negative characteristics. One of the instruments most frequently used to access both self-concept and ideal self is the Q-sort (Stephenson, 1953). In the Q-sort, a large number of statements, such as:

- I am satisfied with myself.
- I have a warm emotional relationship with others.
- I have few values and standards of my own.
- I don't trust my emotions.

are presented to the person. These descriptive statements are written on separate cards, which the test taker then sorts into categories from "least like me," to "most like me," under either "self" (as one is) or "ideal" (as one would like to be) instructions. Typically, there are from nine to eleven categories, each one assigned a number of points (e.g., from one to eleven). The respondent is required to place a certain number of cards in each category. This procedure permits specific percepts about both the self and the ideal self to be quantified. It is then possible to compare numerically the sorts for the self and the ideal self. The difference between the two sorts is called the self-ideal discrepancy. Large discrepancies, a lack of correlation, or a negative correlation reveal feelings of low self-esteem and lack of personal worth, one index of maladjustment.

The idea of discrepancy between the actual self and the ideal self are core ideas in Higgins's (1987) self-discrepancy theory. Higgins finds a relationship such that greater actual self to ideal self discrepancies are associated with experiencing more dejection-related emotions. This will be discussed more in Chapter 10, which focuses on the self-concept.

Therapeutic Processes

Rogers, along with his collaborators and students, addressed the process of psychotherapy in great detail and attempted to link therapeutic processes, or what is done during therapy, with therapeutic outcomes. Scales were developed that could be used to assess the openness of the therapists' communications with the client and the degree of acceptance of the client by the therapist (Rogers et al, 1967). The question of the therapist's ability to empathize with the client, to experience the world as the client experiences it, has important implications for the selection of therapists as well as for understanding the process and progress of client-centered therapy.

Rogers extended his basic ideas concerning self-actualization and unconditional positive regard to a variety of settings. The principle that self-acceptance and self-actualization are facilitated by full acceptance from others and impeded by conditional regard holds true, in small-group situations, in educational programs, and in families. In short, it applies to any interpersonal interaction: openness to experience and acceptance of others foster effective interpersonal relations, as well as personal growth (Rogers, 1980, 1983).

In opposition to Freud's belief that some repression is essential for mental health, Rogers argued that defenses help neither adaptation nor successful functioning in life. On the contrary, they interfere with satisfaction. In addition, Rogers was much less pessimistic than Freud regarding the inevitability of conflict between personal growth and society's needs. Society need not be restrictive, but can instead enhance mental health through the development of institutional attitudes of acceptance and trust.

Maslow's Organismic Humanism

Unlike Rogers, whose theory grew out of his mode of therapy, Abraham Maslow (1908–1970), another major contributor to humanistic psychology, did not form a specific therapy. When Maslow first embarked on a psychological career, he was drawn to behaviorism and carried out studies on primate sexuality and dominance. He gradually left the confines of the behaviorist method and, after the birth of his first child, remarked that "anyone who [observes] a baby could not be a behaviorist." He was influenced by psychoanalysis, but eventually became critical of the psychoanalytic theory of motivation as well. In developing his own model of motivation and behavior, he incorporated the humanistic notion of self-actualization and eventually embraced humanistic philosophy totally.

The Need Hierarchy

Rather than postulating just one source of motivation, Maslow acknowledged a multiplicity of need systems. More specifically, he delineated a hierarchy of five basic classes or categories of needs, which he defined as physiological, safety, love, esteem,

FIGURE 6.1 Maslow's Needs Hierarchy

Needs at the bottom will usually be fulfilled before the needs above them.

and self-actualization. Arkes and Garske (1977) have pointed out that these needs have common characteristics, such as:

1. Failure to gratify a need results in a related form of dysfunction or disturbance. For example, just as lack of vitamins can produce malnutrition, lack of love can produce depression.
2. Restoration of gratification remedies the dysfunction.
3. In a free-choice situation, gratification of lower needs will usually take precedence over gratification of higher needs. Maslow (1943, p. 372) stated:

If all needs are unsatisfied, and the organism is then dominated by physiological needs, all other needs may become simply nonexistent or pushed into the background. It is then fair to characterize the whole organism as saying simply that it is hungry, for consciousness is almost completely preempted by hunger. . . . The urge to write poetry, the desire to acquire an automobile, the interest in American history . . . are . . . forgotten or become of secondary importance.

Figure 6.1 shows the hierarchy of needs postulated by Maslow. As already suggested, there is a prepotency of needs, with the lower, physiologically based needs having greater strength, whereas the higher, psychologically based needs are relatively weaker. Hence, lower needs must be satisfied before higher ones can be fulfilled. Schultz (1976, pp. 221–222) listed a number of other distinctions between the higher- and lower-order needs:

1. The higher needs appeared later in the evolutionary development of mankind. All living things need food and water, but only humans have a need to self-actualize and to know and understand. Therefore, the higher the need the more distinctly human it is.
2. Higher needs are less necessary for sheer survival, hence their gratification can be postponed longer. Failure to satisfy a higher need does not produce as much of an immediate emergency or a crisis reaction as failure to satisfy a lower need.
3. While they are less necessary for survival, the higher needs nevertheless contribute to survival and growth. Higher-level need satisfaction produces better health, longer life, and a generally enhanced biological efficiency. For this reason, the higher needs are also called growth needs.

4. Higher-need satisfaction is productive or beneficial not only biologically but psychologically as well, because it produces deeper happiness, peace of mind, and fullness in one's inner life.
5. Higher-need gratification involves more preconditions and greater complexity than lower-need satisfaction. The search for self-actualization, for example, has the precondition that all the other needs have first been satisfied and involves more complicated and sophisticated behavior and goals than, say, the search for food.
6. Higher-need gratification requires better external conditions (social, economic, and political) than lower-need gratification. For example, greater freedom of expression and opportunity are required for self-actualization than for safety.

D Values versus B Values

The pyramid seems to indicate that lower and higher needs are, in some respects, qualitatively distinct. Maslow characterized the lower needs as deficit (D) values: attainment of their desired goal results in tension reduction and returns the organism to a state of equilibrium. Freud was concerned exclusively with D values.

Maslow also postulated that there are being (B) values. B values are associated with growth motivation, increased tension, and expanded horizons. Among the B values identified by Maslow are wholeness, perfection, justice, beauty, uniqueness, creativity, and truth. One experiences tension from the need to create or to produce beauty, but this tension, Maslow asserted, is associated with positive rather than negative affect.

The Actualized Person

Maslow's wide appeal both within and outside the psychological community has been due largely to his description and elaboration of self-actualization. The B values are associated not only with self-actualization, but also with such qualities as spontaneity and peak experiences, the latter being moments of great ecstasy or awe. Maslow believed that the **peak experience** is elicited by the achievement of real excellence or the movement toward perfect values, not by the "high" attained through the use of drugs.

peak experience A moment of great ecstasy or awe that is experienced without the use of drugs or other stimulants.

Maslow attempted to demonstrate the properties of self-actualization by studying individuals who he believed best displayed the qualities of the actualized person. Maslow (1971, P. 7) contended:

> If we want to answer the question of how tall the human species can grow, then obviously it is well to pick out the ones who already are tallest and study them. If we want to know how fast a human being can run, then it is no use to average out the speed of a "good sample" of the population; it is far better to collect Olympic gold medal winners and see how well they can do. If we want to know the possibilities for spiritual growth, or moral development in human beings, then I maintain that we can learn most by studying our most moral, ethical, or saintly people. [Maslow identified anthropologist Ruth Benedict and the Gestalt psychologist Max Wertheimer as two of these "saintly people."]

There are a number of characteristics associated with such self-actualizing or fully functioning individuals. They include such positive qualities as self-awareness, creativity, spontaneity, openness to experience, self-acceptance, and the more specific qualities of democratic character structure and social interest. Adjectives such as *happy* and *satisfied* are less appropriate in describing the lives of these individuals, Maslow contended, than are words like *challenging*, *exciting*, and *meaningful*.

One may well question whether these characteristics are a consequence of a psychological process called self-actualization or merely are reflections of the particular value systems held by Rogers and Maslow. One might also wonder whether anyone displays these idealized attributes in a consistent manner. Nonetheless, the descriptions of actualizing behavior provided by Rogers and Maslow have called attention to significant aspects of experience and behavior that other personality theorists have neglected.

A self-actualizing person tends to show creativity, openness to experience, and self-acceptance.

Existential Humanism

We now turn to existential personality theory. This is an outgrowth of the existentialist philosophy developed by Sören Kierkegaard (1813–1855) and subsequently expanded by a number of twentieth-century philosophers and writers, including Paul Tillich, Martin Heidegger, Jean Paul Sartre, Albert Camus, and Martin Buber. We will touch only briefly on the major psychological ideas reflected in these philosophical writings and in the work of personality theorists and clinicians who are identified with the existentialist approach.

Key words for the existentialists are freedom, choice, anxiety, meaning, authenticity, responsibility, and struggle. By virtue of our capacity for self-reflection and to perceive our uniqueness and our mortality, we are able to make choices that affect our fate and, thus, must also assume responsibility for the decisions we make. The German term *Dasein* is used to denote this higher, human level of consciousness that captures the whole psychological person. To face the future and contemplate change creates *existential anxiety*: to review the past and one's errors creates guilt. While either excessive anxiety or excessive guilt can be crippling, the experiences of anxiety and guilt are conditions of human existence. To change, to grow, and to choose entails anxiety, but the willingness or courage to confront anxiety and choose to change is the basis for personal development and the attainment of true maturity, or authenticity.

The existential psychologists do not permit us to escape responsibility for our actions, as might the psychoanalysis and the Skinnerians, by attributing the cause for our actions to some past experience or early conditioning. Rather, the cause lies in our present experience. Two Swiss psychiatrists, Ludwig Binswanger (1881–1966) and Medard Boss (1903–1990) pioneered in the development of a form of psychotherapy referred to as existential analysis (Binswanger, 1963), or *Daseinanalysis* (Boss, 1963), which is based on existential ideas. The existential therapists view their primary task as the analysis and clarification of the client's subjective world, the meanings that the client attributes to events and relationships, and the alternatives that they believe are available. Existentialists make use of the psychoanalytic method, but they reject psychoanalytic theory, maintaining that theoretical concepts such as the superego and the Oedipus complex, bias the therapist's perceptions and diminish openness to the reality of the client. In addition, the existentialists contend that Freud's views *justify* pathology, rather than giving the person responsibility and choice.

Frankl asserted that people who could find meaning in their lives were better able to survive the privations of concentration camps.

It is the person's existence, his or her "being-in-the-world" (Binswanger, 1963) or consciousness that defines what it is to be human. The person's experiences of the external world of people and objects and of his or her psychological self and body are the essence of being human. From some existential perspectives, there should be a unity or wholeness between the human being and the environment. This notion of oneness with the physical world reflects the influence of Eastern religious thought on existential psychology. Other existentially oriented psychologists point to the feelings of loneliness and separation from others and nature, which may accompany a full existential awareness of one's connectedness and separateness. From either perspective, there are certain conditions that diminish the achievement of authority or existential maturity. These include being treated as a thing or object by social institutions, self-preoccupation interfering with full awareness of people and of nature, and unwillingness to face the anxiety of making difficult choices. These conditions lead to feelings of alienation, loneliness, and despair.

To be authentic, the human being must be willing to recognize his or her unique potentials, desires, and freedom of choice. Authenticity also entails consciousness of the limitations imposed by the environment and one's personal capacities. All things are not possible for all people, but there are individual meanings and choices that can be made even in very limiting circumstances such as in prison or when facing impending death. Viktor Frankl (1963) is a well-known existential theorist and therapist whose views were formulated following his experiences in a concentration camp during World War II. His observations led him to conclude that prisoners who were reflective, fully conscious of their experience, and capable of finding personal meaning in even these extreme circumstances were best able physically and psychologically to survive the concentration camp ordeal.

The existentialist's emphasis on personal struggle, courage, and the unavoidability of anxiety and guilt distinguishes their views from those of self-actualization theorists. Rogers's portrayal of personal growth makes the assumption of a biologically programmed self-actualizing tendency that will result in self-fulfillment if the individual receives unconditional positive regard. The existentialists, however, see the individual as a much more active agent for whom struggle and anxiety are necessary precursors of authenticity. These theoretical differences between the existentialist and self-actualization theorists are a matter more of assumptions and worldviews than of issues that can be put to empirical test. In general, the existentialists see the empirical approach of psychology as irrelevant. However, one can find occasional examples of research efforts guided by existentialist theory.

The personality style of *hardiness*, as formulated and developed by Kobasa and Maddi (1977), is a reflection of existential ideas. Hardiness includes three elements—commitment, the feeling that some part of what you are doing is interesting and worthwhile, as compared to alienation; a sense of control rather than powerlessness; and the experience of life changes as a challenge rather than a threat. There have been a number of studies indicating that hardiness helps buffer the impact of stress and moderate its influence on physical illness (Kobasa et al, 1986), although the significance of the different components of hardiness remains at issue. While research on hardiness does not address the major principles of existential psychology, the role of personal choice and responsibility has assumed increasing importance in the study of personality (Singer and Kolligian, 1987).

personal construct theory Kelly's personality theory that focuses on how a person, as perceiver, organizes his or her world and interprets, or construes, events.

Kelly's Personal Construct Theory

Humanistic psychologists are particularly concerned with how individuals feel about and perceive themselves in terms of personal value or worth, and with the consequences of disparate self-concepts. **Personal construct theory** addresses how the perceiver organizes his or her world and interprets, or construes, events. Thus, personal construct theory is as much a part of the phenomenological approach in psychology as is humanism. However, in contrast to humanistic psychology, thought, rather than feeling, is stressed and affect is considered simply one of the consequences of particular thought processes.

The Human as Scientist

George Kelly (1905–1966), the originator of personal construct theory, contended that the underlying goal of the individual is to predict and control their experiences. Thus, he conceived of individuals as scientists seeking to understand and forecast the events around them.

Nancy's beliefs that John will act negatively toward her may be disproved by John acting friendly. Nancy would need to change her theory about John's behavior.

Kelly noted that it is puzzling that, while psychologists try to explain the behavior of their clients or of people in general, the theories they have formulated cannot account for their own scientific activity. For example, if people are impelled by sexual and aggressive instincts and if all behavior is directed toward the reduction of these primary urges, as the Freudians argue, then what motivated Freud to formulate his theory of personality? Freud did contend that higher intellectual activities, such as scientific pursuits, are derivatives of instinctual drives and are in service of these basic drives. But this analysis is far from convincing. In a similar manner, if humans are mere robots, as behaviorists like Skinner would have us believe, then how did the new ideas formulated by Skinner originate? In sum, the psychoanalytic and strict behaviorist theory that dominated psychology for so many years cannot readily account for the scientific behavior of Freud and Skinner.

As intimated above, Kelly's theory of personal constructs can explain scientific endeavors, for Kelly considered the average person to be an intuitive scientist with the goal of predicting and understanding behavior. To accomplish this aim, naïve individuals formulate hypotheses about the world and themselves, collect data that confirm or disconfirm these hypotheses, and then alter their theories to account for the new data. Hence, the average person operates in much the same manner as a professional scientist, although professional scientists may be more accurate and self-conscious in their attempts to achieve cognitive clarity and understanding. Just as scientists sometimes hold bad theories, individuals may entertain bad theories, that is, beliefs that hinder effective behavior and lead to bias in data collection and interpretation. For example, assume that a woman (Nancy) believes that a man (John) has strong negative feelings toward her. When Nancy meets John at a party, she expects that he will ignore her, make an insulting remark, or embarrass her in front of her friends. However, assume that, to Nancy's surprise, John acts friendly and seems happy to see her. Assume, too, that this disconfirmation is repeatedly experienced so that John's displayed friendliness cannot be due to some temporary mood state or to the immediate social pressures of acting "nice." On the basis of these new data, Nancy should reformulate her hypothesis and perceive that John really likes her. The new construction more accurately predicts behavior and allows Nancy to correctly anticipate her interactions with John.

In discussing his conception of the person as a seeker of truth, Kelly (1955, p. 5) asserted:

It is customary to say that *the scientist's ultimate aim is to predict and to control*. This is a summary statement that psychologists frequently like to quote in characterizing their own aspirations. Yet, curiously enough, psychologists rarely credit the human subjects in their experiments with having similar aspirations. It is as though the psychologist were saying to himself, "I, being a *psychologist*, and therefore a *scientist*, am performing this experiment in order to improve the prediction and control of certain human phenomena; but my subject, being merely a human organism, is obviously propelled by inexorable drives welling up within him, or else he is in gluttonous pursuit of sustenance and shelter.

Many other psychologists besides Kelly implicitly accept the conception of the individual as an intuitive scientist. Of great concern to experimental psychologists is the possibility that the participant will infer what the experimenter is trying to discover and then will consciously or unconsciously comply with this hypothesis. The demand characteristics of an experiment therefore must be carefully controlled or concealed in many psychological investigations. But the reason for the existence of such controls is because the participants search for meaning in their environment, formulate hypotheses, and act on the basis of these belief systems. Of course, if a participant were to perceive the experimenter as a nasty or intrusive person, then he or she might try to "ruin" the experiment by disproving the experimenter's hypothesis. This behavior is also in service of the participant's goal and is based on a particular belief system, as well as on inferences about the purpose of the investigation.

Bannister and Fransella (1971, p. 16), commenting on the human-as-scientist formulation, noted:

> One of the effects of this is to make the model man of personal construct theory look recognizably like you: that is, unless you are the very modest kind of man who can see himself as the stimulus-jerked puppet of learning theory [or] the primitive infant of psychoanalytic theory. . . . If you do not recognize yourself at any point in personal construct theory, you have discovered a major defect in it and are entitled to be suspicious of its claims.

One of the interesting similarities between humanistic theory and personal construct theory is a consequence of the human-as-scientist model. Both the psychologist and the client or an experimental participant are now equal parts of a dyad. That is, the psychologist is no "higher" than the so-called naïve person. Hence, psychology is now a metadiscipline, seeking to make sense out of the way that individuals make sense out of the world. The psychologist therefore is engaged in the same interpretive endeavor as nonpsychologists.

Note then that Kelly proposes a rational image of humans: to understand thoughts is to understand the person. Bruner (1956) speculated that this theory of personality was in part a product of the particular clinical experiences that Kelly encountered. For many years Kelly was a counselor of college students. Rather than facing patients with hysterical paralysis or bizarre dreams, "the young men and women of Professor Kelly's clinical examples are worried about their dates, their studies, and even their conformity" (Bruner, 1956, p. 357). Hence, Kelly spent relatively little time considering the unconscious, deep-seated urges, or even defenses. Like many of the approaches presented in this book, the theory was able to account adequately for some aspects of behavior. However, he could not readily explain a number of other phenomena.

Constructive Alternativism

Source: wavebreakmedia/Shutterstock

Kelly's theories were likely influenced by his time as a counselor of college students.

Kelly labeled his basic philosophical assumption constructive alternativism. Kelly asserted meaning is not inherent in an event, but depends on how a person construes or interprets that event. Thus, the only reality is the reality the person creates. Reality truly exists in the eyes of the beholder. Further, people can always revise their constructs—or ideas—about reality, and thus change how they experience it. As a result some of Kelly's ideas are, perhaps surprisingly, associated with the psychoanalytic notion that needs and values influence our perception of the world.

Because meaning is subject to change Kelly reasoned that individuals are personally responsible (able to respond) for their own future. Nature does not dictate one's life or, as Kelly contended "No one needs to be the victim of his biography." This position again links personal construct theory with humanistic and existentialist thinking by placing change processes within the grasp of the individual. Thus, either credit for a successful life or blame for an unsuccessful one is placed directly on the actor. Each person controls the course of his or her life.

Formal Theory

Kelly outlined a formal theory with one fundamental postulate and eleven corollaries. Here we examine only the postulate and three of the corollaries, selecting those that shed the most light on Kelly's conception of personality and behavior.

Fundamental Postulate

Kelly stated that an individual's life or conduct is guided by how the world is construed. Furthermore, the predictive power of that construal is demonstrated or proved by how much sense one has made out of the world, or the accuracy with which one is able to predict future events. Confirmation or disconfirmation of predictions was accorded much greater significance in Kelly's thinking than, for example, drives and drive reduction or reward and punishment. The core issue is whether or not a person's construal of the world allows that person to successfully predict and control his or her experience of the world.

Individual Corollary

Kelly asserted that people differ from one another in their construction of events. For example, one person might judge others according to their sincerity or wit, while another might use intelligence or kindness as bases for perceiving others. Furthermore, there are individual differences in the complexity of one's construal system; some individuals perceive or use more dimensions in their construals than others.

Because individuals perceive the identical objective situation in a different manner, it follows that behavior will also differ between individuals. Furthermore, since no two constructions are exactly alike, each person is unique. This position is in keeping with the humanist position.

Range Corollary

A given construction is not appropriate for all events. For example, the construct "tall-short" maybe appropriate for anticipating play on a basketball court but is likely to be quite irrelevant in predicting an individual's honesty. Kelly distinguished between the range of convenience and the focus of convenience of a construct. The range of convenience indicates the breadth of different phenomena to which a construct may be applied. The focus of convenience refers to the area in which the construct is maximally useful.

Scientists frequently employ the range and focus notions when describing and evaluating psychological theories. Freudians, for example, would argue that the range of convenience of their theory includes war, wit, and slips of the tongue; such generalizability is a positive attribute of any theory. But the Freudian model's focus of convenience concerns sexual and aggressive conflicts. A similar description of the range and focus of convenience of all the theories presented in previous chapters could be made and would prove instructive for comparison and evaluation (and would probably make a great essay question for your next exam).

Experience Corollary

A person's construct system is subject to change as a result of successful or unsuccessful construal of events. Given Kelly's perspective, psychotherapy is a process in which one's construct system is altered with the aid of a therapist. The therapist must first discover how the client perceives the world and then assist the client in reorganizing the old system and finding new, more functional constructs. The therapist might help the client to design and implement "experiments" to test particular hypotheses. For example, if an individual perceives a parent or a spouse as aggressive or dominating, then special behaviors might be suggested to test whether this perception helps rather than hinders the anticipation of events. Role playing and modeling are frequently used to help alter construct systems.

Each individual has a unique personal construction of the world based on his or her own experiences.

The therapist might suggest, for example, that the client act as if the parent or the spouse were not aggressive or dominant, in order to test an alternative hypothesis. (At an earlier time in his life Kelly was a drama coach, which may account in part for his selection of role playing as a technique for altering construct systems.)

In one social experiment involving the change of constructs, the participants were teachers who believed the children in their classrooms were not learning because they were "lazy" (Kelly, 1958). The experimenters suggested that the teachers give the children nothing to do in the classroom and see what happened. Of course, the pupils would not sit still without any activity. On the basis of this contradictory evidence, the teachers began to consider the school environment and their own inadequacy as causes of poor learning, rather than blaming the problems entirely on the children.

The Role Construct Repertory (REP) Test

Kelly devised an ingenious testing instrument to ascertain an individual's personal construct system. The test reflects Kelly's belief that the tester should not impose his or her

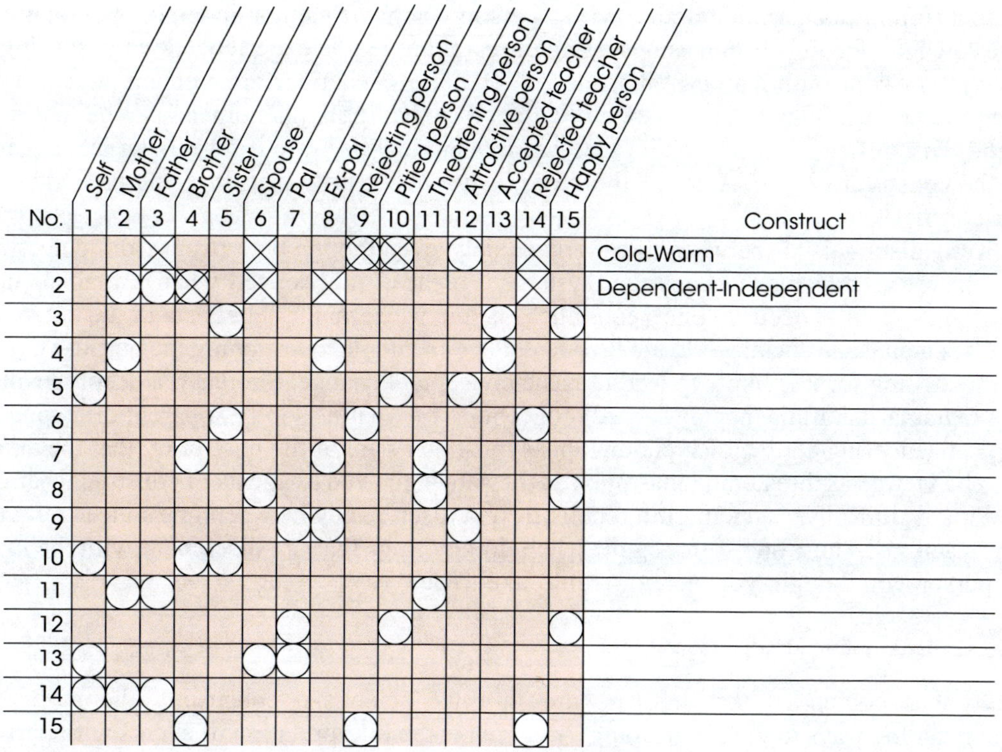

FIGURE 6.2 Simplified Grid Form of the REP Test

constructs on the test taker. Rather, the testee should be allowed to display constructs that are naturally used to give meaning to the world.

In the **REP test**, the test taker first lists the names of individuals who play or have played certain roles in his or her life, such as mother, father, rejecting person, threatening person, and so on (see Figure 6.2). On the standard REP grid, shown in Figure 6.2, the three circles in each row designate three roles that each participant is to consider as a group. For each triad, the participant determines the construct, such as cold-warm or dominant-submissive, in which two members of that triad are similar yet different from the third. The construct selected by the test taker is assumed to represent a dimension of thought or a construct along which significant people in the respondent's life are ordered or compared. In row 1 of the grid, for example, a respondent might perceive individuals identified as rejecting and pitied to be cold, while attractive people are warm. The respondent then judges the remaining twelve people as having or not having the quality (coldness) of the two linked individuals in the triad, placing an X in the box of that row if that particular characteristic is possessed. Figure 6.2 shows that father, spouse, and rejected teacher are perceived as cold. The remaining fourteen rows are completed in this manner, with a different construct selected for each triad. Using mathematical techniques, the tester reduces the chosen constructs to a few basic ones representing the respondent's typical way of perceiving and classifying others.

REP test Kelly's way of measuring and eliciting the role constructs that people use to predict and understand their world.

Emotions

Kelly focused brief attention on certain specific emotions, namely, anxiety, guilt, threat, fear, and anger; however, he defined them all as consequences of construct systems that are in transitional states. Anxiety, according to Kelly, occurs when one's construct system provides no means for dealing with an experience. Bannister and Fransella (1971, p. 35) elaborated on anxiety as follows:

> We become anxious when we can only partially construe the events which we encounter and too many of their implications are obscure. Sex for the chaste, adulthood for the adolescent, books for the illiterate, power for the humble and death for nearly all of us tend to provoke anxiety. It is the unknown aspect of things that go bump in the night that give them their potency.

In a similar manner, interacting with a person whom we cannot understand often gives rise to vague feelings of uneasiness. Even greater anxiety is experienced when starting a new job or confronting a new environment. If anxiety reactions are frequent and severe, then the range of constructs must be broadened so that more phenomena can be incorporated. Disconfirmation of a belief also arouses anxiety because it reveals an inadequacy in the construct system. Anxiety, therefore, is not necessarily bad. It is one precondition for construct change.

Kelly distinguishes between threat and anxiety, even though both result from defective, and therefore transitional, construct systems. Threat is experienced when a fundamental change is about to occur in one's construct system, when major beliefs about the nature of one's personal and social world are invalidated. For example, questioning the purpose of life is threatening for it is likely to lead to basic conceptual change. Similarly, a deeply involving extramarital affair may alter one's conception of what it is to be a parent or a spouse, thus engendering a threat. Psychotherapists must be aware of the possibility that they may also be viewed as threatening inasmuch as they are perceived as agents of construct change.

Finally, in Kelly's system guilt results from a discrepancy between one's ideal self and one's actions. Thus, one suffers guilt when doing things that are discrepant with the kind of person you thought you were or would like to be.

Overview of Kelly's Theory

Kelly has contended that humans are intuitive scientists, construing the world in idiosyncratic ways to give it meaning. Meaning is the interpretation of events with particular constructs, enabling one to predict, or anticipate, the future. One's construct system is not immutable. Individuals have alternative construction possibilities and are personally responsible for their own well-being. Finally, certain emotions, such as anxiety, threat, and guilt, are products of inadequate and changing construct systems.

Kelly's conception is unique among the theories of personality and provides an alternative language for understanding or construing human action. It has not generated a great deal of research, but it has produced new and valuable insights, as well as a novel method of measurement, and is gaining in popularity.

Implicit Psychology

Compatible with Kelly's theory are the implicit theories that people use to guide their behavior. This interest leads to the distinction between *science* and *ethnoscience*: the reasons people behave the way they do versus perceived reasons they behave the way they do, or what is known positively as "folk wisdom" and negatively as "grandma psychology" (see Wegner and Vallacher, 1977). It is evident that individuals have ideas and often elaborate theories about what people are like and what motivates them. Although these theories are "implicit" (Bruner and Tagiuri, 1954), they nevertheless determine social reality.

Implicit theories concerning the interrelationships of traits or attributes have already received much attention from psychological researchers (see Schneider, 1973). Beliefs like "Fat people are jolly," "People who wear glasses are introverts," and "Intelligent people are witty" are examples of such implicit theories of personality. People are often unaware that they hold such theories and thus do not put them systematically to test. Nevertheless, such notions greatly influence expectations and actions. These implicit theories of personality may influence one's responses on a personality scale or one's judgments of another's personality. They can contribute to interrelationships among personality variables that do not exist in reality (Mischel, 1984).

Kelly's REP test represents one attempt to measure implicit theories of person perception by ascertaining the constructs people employ as well as the perceived interrelationships among these constructs. Indeed Kelly's entire theory rests on the presumption that people are naïve scientists, formulating their own idiosyncratic psychological theories.

Kelly further contended that at times these theories do not work and that the individual must be aided in the construction of better theories.

In addition to implicit theories of person perception; there are implicit theories of child psychology, abnormal psychology psychodynamics and virtually any other area within the broad domain of personality psychology. For example, we exhibit our implicit ideas about children in the ways in which we communicate with them. As Wegner and Vallacher (1977, p. 303) state:

> The hostess at a dinner party is not likely to say "Hot, hot!" when she places a steaming dish before a guest but often makes similar remarks to her five-year-old. She does not say Look both ways now when she sends the guests across the street to their cars but often will repeat this warning to her child. . . . Many of these wholesome and insipid expressions would be totally inappropriate in adult conversation. [See Gleason, 1973]

In a similar manner, implicit theories of abnormal psychology abound. Since the layperson has been introduced to Freudian theory, often through pop psychology sources, early childhood experiences are typically perceived as an important cause of abnormal adult behavior. The naïve psychology of the layperson and the "true" laws of personality, child psychology, and abnormal psychology may or may not be identical.

A Concluding Comment

While psychoanalytic theory and its offshoots have focused on unconscious forces and the learning theories on overt behavior, the phenomenological theories have been concerned with the individual's subjective experience. The research that has been stimulated by phenomenological approaches fills an important gap in the description of human personality functioning. The ways in which individuals construe their environment, and themselves and the reasons for their actions, are major determinants of individual differences in behavior. The phenomenologists' depiction of the individual as an active, striving, developing organism, seeking meaning and growth or mastery, has also served as an important theoretical corrective. The difficulties with the phenomenological approach stem in part from an overemphasis on the "here and now." In general, they have neglected developmental and learning influences. Phenomenology is vulnerable in areas where the other theoretical approaches are strong; that is, insufficient attention is given to unconscious processes and to the relationship between experience and behavior. There is often a discrepancy between people's verbalized intentions and their actions; also, the reasons that people give for their behaviors are sometimes rationalizations for rather than causes of the behavior. Nevertheless, phenomenology provides a needed perspective in our efforts to describe and understand personality.

Summary

1. *Humanistic psychology* is governed by the tenets that the experiencing person is of primary interest, that creativity and self-actualization are the preferred topics of investigation, that meaningful research topics should be selected, and that the dignity of the person is an essential aspect of research inquiry.
2. *Self-actualization* denotes the internal driving force to develop one's capacities and talents to the fullest. It is central in the theory of Carl Rogers.
3. *Unconditional positive regard*, or being valued for oneself, facilitates self-actualization. On the other hand, *conditions of worth* where acceptance is dependent on particular actions decrease the possibility of self-actualization.
4. The *self-ideal discrepancy* refers to the differences between how one perceives oneself and how one would like to be. There is some evidence that this discrepancy decreases following *client-centered therapy*.
5. Maslow postulated a need hierarchy with physiological needs at the bottom and self-actualization needs at the highest level. Lower needs must be gratified prior to the full pursuit of higher-order needs. Higher needs, although aiding adjustment and satisfaction, are not necessary for survival.

6. There is a distinction between *deficit* (D) and *being* (B) *values*, the former associated with tension reduction and the latter with increased tension and expanded horizons.
7. Existentialists contend that we must assume responsibility for our actions and that we cannot escape anxiety and guilt.
8. *Personal construct theory* as formulated by George Kelly addresses the issue of how a person construes (perceives, organizes) his or her world. It is based on the assumption that individuals act as scientists, formulating hypotheses and gathering data relevant to those hypotheses.
9. Individuals differ in their construction of events and these constructions are not fixed. The REP test was devised to assess construct systems.
10. The emotions of *anxiety* and *threat* have been interpreted by Kelly with the aid of personal construct theory. Anxiety indicates that one's construct system does not allow one to deal with an experience, while threat is experienced when the construct system is about to undergo fundamental change.
11. *Implicit psychology* refers to the theories of behavior held by untrained psychologists or laypersons.

Key Terms

conditions of worth (p. 110)
humanistic psychology (p. 108)
implicit psychology (p. 107)
peak experience (p. 114)
personal construct theory (p. 116)

phenomenology (p. 107)
REP test (p. 121)
self-actualization (p. 109)
unconditional positive regard (p. 110)

Thought Questions

1. Who among your acquaintances is the most self-actualized? On what evidence do you base this judgment?
2. What do you think of the humanistic belief that people are fundamentally good? How do the humanists account for evil?
3. Many psychologists believe that the humanistic approach to personality can never attain the status of a science. Do you agree with this belief and, if so, is it a "fatal" flaw?
4. Do you believe that our significant behaviors are primarily (1) conscious and rational, (2) conditioned and mechanistic, or (3) unconscious and irrational?

The Structure of Personality

Source: Ollyy/Shutterstock

PART **3**

CHAPTER 7
Foundations of Personality Measurement

CHAPTER 8
Personality Assessment

CHAPTER 9
Traits, Situations, and Their Interaction

The word *personality* connotes what one is "like": the characteristics, traits, or general manner of thinking and behaving that define who one is. Psychologists sometimes refer to this as the structure of personality. The next three chapters, then, are concerned with this construction of the parts of the person. This rather analytic aspect of the study of personality contrasts with the explanation of how personality traits develop, which has just been discussed, and with the manner in which personality structures influence behavior, which falls under the dynamics of personality, analyzed in the next part of the text.

The study of the structure of personality is closely linked with the measurement of personality. To determine the degree to which one is introverted, aggressive, or high in need for achievement, there must be appropriate instruments to measure these concepts. In Chapter 7 the basic principles of measurement are introduced. **Reliability**, which refers to how well a concept is being measured, and **validity**, which is concerned with whether a test is measuring what it is supposed to measure, are examined in detail. This is followed, in Chapter 8, by a discussion of the types of instruments used to assess personality. **Objective tests** are distinguished from **projective tests**; other ways to measure personality are suggested; and the reliability and validity of these different approaches are considered. Then, in Chapter 9, traits are examined in detail. While trait approaches are sometimes considered in the context of theories of personality, we consider them in this part because they are so intimately linked to issues of measurement and assessment and because they tend to be empirically based.

In sum, the chapters in this part of the text progress from the basics of measurement, to an examination of specific measures being employed, to a discussion of traits, or what is being measured. The field of personality structure is exceedingly complex. Because so many issues remain to be resolved, it is one of the most active areas in the field of personality.

Foundations of Personality Measurement

CHAPTER 7

Source: marekuliasz/Shutterstock

Chapter Outline

The Prescientific Era
The Scientific Era
Reliability and Validity

In earlier chapters we frequently referred to specific studies of personality, describing the measures used in these studies and the results obtained. To interpret these results properly, however, it is necessary to be able to evaluate the measures and how well they assess whatever it is they are supposed to assess. One must also have an understanding of the meaning of the numerical relations that are reported. In the next three chapters, we will discuss some of the methods that psychologists use to measure aspects of personality, with measurements typically expressed in terms of scores, ratings, and other quantitative values. Quantitative methods allow us to evaluate theories and hypotheses more systematically. As a result, they also allow us to learn more about characteristics of individuals as well as how these characteristics are the same as or different from those of other individuals.

In this chapter we present some of the foundations for research in the measurement of personality. First, we discuss some of the history of personality assessment. Next, we discuss the reliability and validity of psychological assessment procedures.

Before considering these issues, remember that one of the most important purposes of personality assessment is to help investigators make decisions about people. Thus, a college student may be asked to take a test to help a counselor decide what career to recommend; a clinician may administer a test to help decide whether or not a person should be hospitalized or simply placed under psychiatric care. But such decisions involving selection or classification must take the risks and benefits into account. For example, a test score may classify an individual as suicidal. The therapist must then determine whether the person should be placed in a hospital, which is quite costly and has serious implications for both the individual and the community. While making this decision,

reliability The consistency, or degree of accuracy, of a measuring instrument.

validity The degree to which a test actually measures what it is intended to measure.

projective tests A test consisting of ambiguous stimuli, to which an individual produces spontaneous responses; scoring is often subjective.

the therapist takes into account the fact that suicide is quite rare (it has a low "base rate"). Because even good tests are imperfect and the chances of suicide are in general so low, usually the best prediction concerning this individual, regardless of his or her test score, is that suicide will not be attempted. Given only probability or likelihood as the basis for a decision, it would be best not to recommend hospitalization; but in view of the severity of loss in the event of suicide, the therapist may suggest hospitalization in spite of the low probability of that behavior. That is, the clinician would much rather err in the direction of hospitalizing a patient who would not have attempted suicide than in not hospitalizing a client who later does attempt suicide. In sum, testing must be considered within the broader context of decision making and cannot be divorced from the overall values of society.

The Prescientific Era

The prescientific era in the examination of personality structure, which extended to the middle of the nineteenth century, produced a number of interesting ideas that provided the foundation for modern personality testing. The origins of testing for mental abilities actually go back more than 2,000 years, to the practices of the Chinese emperors of the Qin or early Han dynasties, roughly around 150 B.C. It is said that the emperor himself gave written examinations to all nominees for government offices, and it is thought that the tests were more for literacy than for knowledge. These examinations then fell into disuse for several hundred years, but reappeared around 900 A.D. Modern scholars believe that the system ensured a supply of talented men from the provinces to serve in the national government and also formed a power group the emperor controlled as a counterbalance to the hereditary aristocracy. The tests were quite elaborate and required the use of abstract arguments and word games (Bowman, 1989).

Better known to us are the developments that first took place in Europe. Consider, for example, the interesting and creative conception of Theophrastus (372–287 B.C.), Aristotle's successor as head of the Lyceum in Athens, who is best known for his collection of personality sketches called "characters." Theophrastus was struck by the observation that, while all of Greece had the same climate and Greeks had the same general upbringing, they did not all have the same personality. He proposed a set of thirty personality types, each one presented in the form of a character vignette with one outstanding personality attribute. Each sketch opened with a brief definition of the dominant characteristic and continued with examples of this style in action. Among the characters sketched were the Liar, the Surly Man, the Tasteless Man, and the Flatterer. These exaggerated, unidimensional depictions of character also became common literary devices, as in the romantic heroism of Cervantes's Don Quixote and the blind loyalty of his vassal, Sancho Panza. The depictions have became stock characters in television and film.

Despite our sense that we know people who fit some of these character types, there are many difficulties with Theophrastus's approach. Some of these same difficulties apply to modern character typology. One obvious problem with these unidimensional sketches is that they are caricatures, appropriate perhaps for dramatic purposes but grossly inadequate for objective scientific description. The concept of type has an either-or quality; one is or is not a particular personality type. In contrast, the concept of trait implies a continuum of the quality in question, with some people displaying very little of the trait, others more, and so on. Individuals are more appropriately and accurately described by their position on a continuum of trait dimensions rather than as belonging to one particular type.

Aside from the unidimensionality of Theophrastus's character types, one has no way of knowing whether the number of types should be ten or one hundred or one thousand. Five centuries later, in fact, the physician Galen (A.D. 130–200) proposed only a fourfold classificatory system based on Hippocrates's doctrine of the four basic "humors" of the body (see Figure 7.1): black bile, yellow bile, phlegm, and blood. Galen's

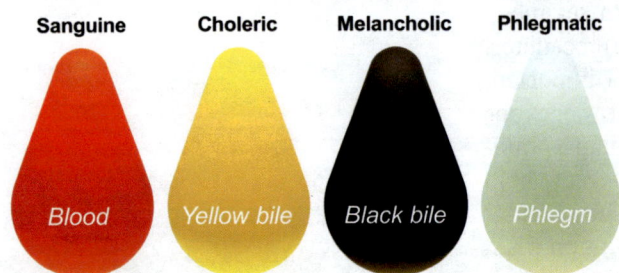

Sanguine — Blood
Choleric — Yellow bile
Melancholic — Black bile
Phlegmatic — Phlegm

FIGURE 7.1 The Four Humors of Hippocrates and Galen

A woodcut of the great teachers of medicine, including galen and hippocrates.

theory of **temperament** asserted that an excess of black bile makes a person melancholic; an excess of yellow bile produces a choleric temperament, quick to anger and action; the predominance of phlegm results in a phlegmatic (calm and dependable) individual; and the predominance of the fourth humor, blood, makes one sanguine (warm-hearted and confident). Although the terms are not especially common anymore, they still exist in our language. Someone prone to a light depression may be called melancholy, or someone who is feeling optimistic may say he or she is sanguine. Or we may hear that someone is "full of piss and vinegar," implying that this person has that choleric temperament. Galen's effort to relate biological characteristics to personality traits anticipates modern theories of the relationship between physique and temperament and the role of biochemical factors in personality. But Galen like Theophrastus failed to provide any evidence in support of his particular physical and psychological typology. There was no way to determine or measure the dominant humor or temperament, much less demonstrate that particular humors were associated with particular temperaments (also see Chapter 9).

Unfortunately, measurement in itself does not guarantee a scientific basis for a theory; that basis depends on how the measurements are obtained and the ability of other investigators to produce the same findings. When the measurement of personality is based on the judgments of a human observer, then the measurements are subject to serious distortion by possible observer bias An observer, when viewing an event or another person, does so selectively, attending to some stimuli in the situation and not to others. There is always a danger that the observer may attend primarily to those events and stimuli that support any hypotheses or biases that may be brought to the situation

temperament Behavioral characteristics that are present at an early age and that are believed to have some basis in biological processes partly determined by heredity.

The Scientific Era

The scientific era in the testing of individual differences may have begun with the work of Sir Francis Galton (1822–1911), a cousin of Charles Darwin, both of whom were the grandsons of the eminent philosopher Erasmus Darwin. In 1869 he published the first edition of *Hereditary Genius*, in which he marshaled evidence that eminence ran in families. He then assumed that this familial pattern was due to the inheritance of ability. Galton investigated many aspects of individual differences, such as the richness and range of verbal associations, and developed mental tests to measure these differences. He also proposed the use of physiological measures of blood pressure and heart rate to assess individual differences in emotionality and temperament.

Galton was able to accomplish his work through the establishment of a laboratory in the South Kensington Museum in London. Each visitor to the museum paid three pence for his or her assessment on a variety of attributes, including strength, breathing capacity, eyesight, and so on. This provided data for over 17,000 individuals, and increased Galton's preoccupation with measuring almost everything. To describe these data quantitatively, Galton invented the concepts of the median and percentiles (see Johnson, et al., 1985).

Later, work in France with children with intellectual disabilities led in 1905 to Alfred Binet's (1857–1911) development of a test of intelligence to establish a more accurate diagnosis of this disorder. Intelligence testing had a profound effect on the field of personality in that it highlighted the possibility and the importance of assessing *individual differences.*

World War I served as an impetus to the development of personality tests. To screen and classify soldiers, army psychologists constructed the first group-administered intelligence test: the Army Alpha. While previously it would have been necessary for each recruit to be interviewed individually, now recruits could answer 100 "yes" or "no" questions, such as "Do you ever walk in your sleep?" (Hollingworth, 1920). If a recruit responded in a way that might indicate psychopathology, he would be interviewed by a psychiatrist.

The 1920s and 1930s witnessed the development of a great variety of personality tests, some designed to assess psychological disturbance and others to measure individual differences in intelligence, personal values, and personality traits. These tests used increasingly sophisticated techniques, including complex methodologies that supposedly permitted the investigator to uncover the basic structure of personality.

Among the obstacles faced by test developers is that the "data" are typically provided by verbal reports of the respondents. These verbal reports may be distorted by the respondents because the truth either is consciously withheld or is not consciously known. Thus, test developers had to construct tests that would overcome these difficulties. The methodology in the area of psychological testing has become more sophisticated over time because of our increasing scientific knowledge; such advancement is less characteristic of the area of general personality theory. Psychological testing is now one of the major subdivisions within the field of personality.

One of the hallmarks of science is measurement. Psychologists, no less than physicists, chemists, and biologists, need to quantify the variables they wish to investigate. That quantification can consist of crude statements of mere "presence" or "absence" or quite precise terms such as "twice as much." When one deals with traits such as dependency and introversion, the task of measurement becomes especially difficult and challenging. Indeed, some would argue that the task is impossible. According to one eminent scholar (Barzun, 1954, p. 143), "the love of a parent for a child, or any other kind of attachment, repulsion, fear, joy, faith . . . these are realities that are visible, non-material and non-measurable." Yet these are precisely the "realities" that are at the very heart of the study of personality. In fact there is an entire literature that examines that attachment between child and parent (Ainsworth, Blehar, Waters and Wall, 2015; Berscheid, 2010; Jones, Cassidy, and Shaver, 2015).

Psychologists recognize that personality measures cannot do full justice to the richness and individuality of human beings. However, relatively meaningful measurements can be made. Quantification is essential because it both permits comparison between people on given dimensions and also allows one to determine which factors are associated with these personality dimensions and how strong the associations are.

The measurement of personality traits is a major scientific challenge. There are no X rays available that will penetrate our psyche and reveal our innermost hopes, secrets, and passions. Useful measures have been developed for some facets of personality but not for others. No measure of personality is perfect; psychologists are engaged in an ongoing effort to improve and refine their measuring procedures and tests.

Reliability and Validity

There are two critical features of a measure that determine its quality: reliability and validity. *Reliability* refers to the consistency or measurement error of the measuring instrument. A test of introversion that yielded very different scores for a sample of individuals every time they were tested would have low reliability and would not be very useful. *Validity* refers to the degree to which a measure actually assesses what it is intended to assess. The measure of introversion could be highly reliable but would lack validity if it were precisely assessing anxiety or fatigue or nonconformity - attributes other than introversion. A major concern of personality investigators is the reliability and validity of the measures they use.

Reliability

Measurement error occurs in almost all forms of observation. It is assumed that for each quality we attempt to measure, there is a *true* score; the researcher's task is to make an observation that is used as the measure of this true quality. The *observed score* is usually not exactly the same as the true score. The deviation of the observed score from the true score is regarded as **measurement error**. In some fields of inquiry the measurement error may be quite small, whereas in other fields it tends to be great. An example of a situation in which measurement error might be minimal would be the measurement of height. In this case there is a standard measurement device such as a ruler or yardstick (see Figure 7.2). The true height of an object or a person might be the number of inches it stands above the

measurement error The degree to which the observed score on a measuring instrument deviates from the true score.

Height measured in centimeters and inches.

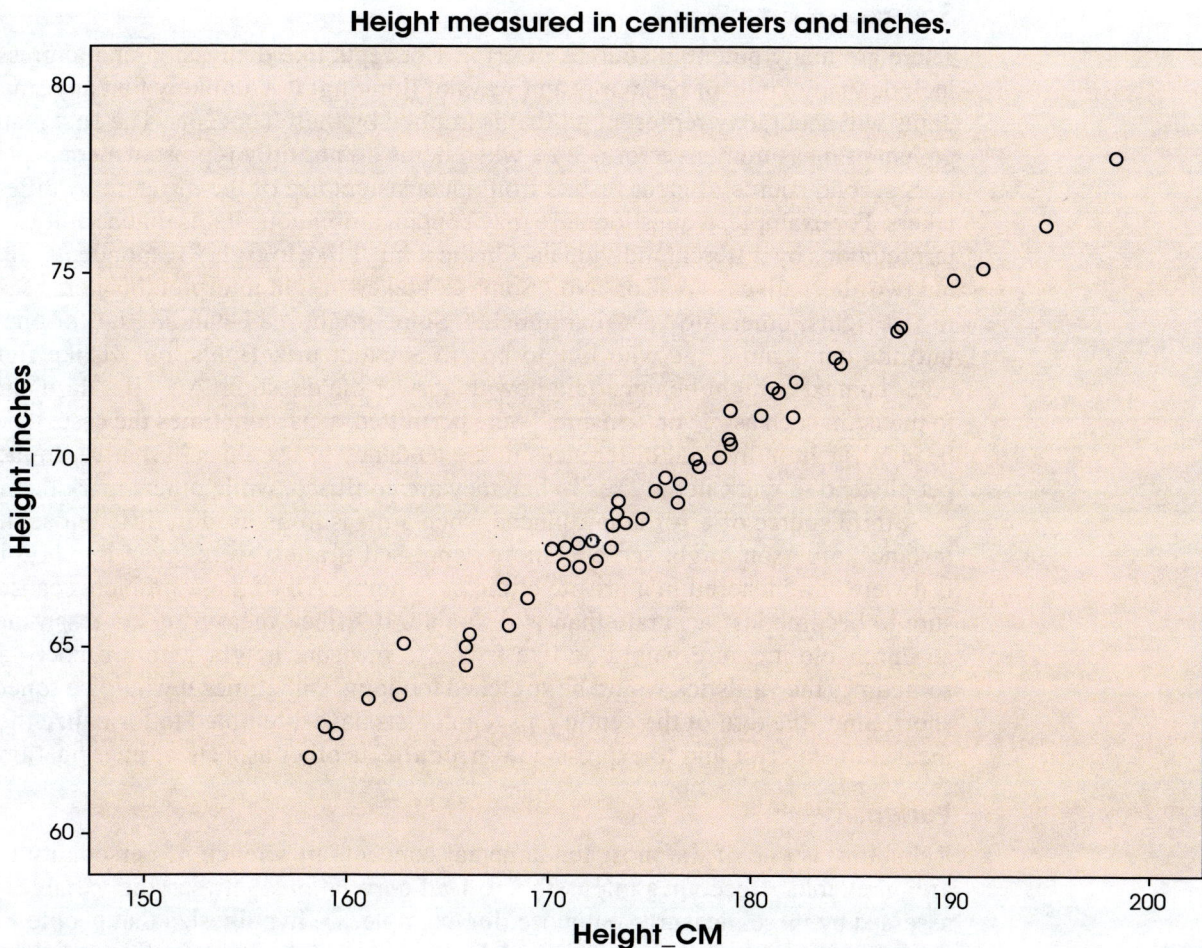

FIGURE 7.2

We would expect two measures of a person's height to be closely related, even if the measurement units are different. But even here we would expect to see some amount of measurement error.

floor. Using a yardstick, it is possible to obtain a measure of height which is close to, if not exactly the same as, the true score. Even in this example, however, there might still be some sources of error. For instance, the person using the yardstick might have made some small error in applying the stick to the second three feet after the first three feet had been marked. A second person could also measure, using a one-foot ruler to measure the person. This second person would have to move the ruler several times, increasing the possibility of error. The first person may have recorded, say, 70 inches even though the true measurement was 69 1/2 inches, or have made some clerical error in recording the measurement. The second person may have recorded 68 inches. All things considered, there is little error in the recording of height, but the quality of the tool used to do the measurement has an impact on the accuracy of the measurement.

Contrast this with some of the qualities that psychologists attempt to measure. Usually, the concept under consideration is not defined in terms of any single measure. There is no unambiguous yardstick to tell us how depressed or aggressive someone is, but we can attempt to build yardsticks to measure these characteristics. Developing a measure that correctly assesses what it is supposed to is a problem of *validity*. Assessing the error in application of the yardstick is a problem in *reliability*.

The scores yielded by a measure are of interest only if they vary between people. If they did not vary, then all people would be scored exactly the same. We are interested only in true variability, or real differences between people. Usually, some observed variability is unwanted, random variability, or *error variance*. The study of reliability can help determine how much of what is being measured is such unwanted error variance.

Sources of Error

There are many potential sources of error. Concepts like depression and aggressiveness include many kinds of behaviors and ways of thinking; it is unlikely that any small set of items will accurately represent all that is implied by these concepts. The first major component of measurement error occurs when items do not fully represent a concept.

A second source of error results from inconsistent use of the measure by different test takers. For example, a questionnaire may contain ambiguous items that permit varying interpretations by different individuals. On the item "I like to fight," respondents are permitted two alternatives: "Yes" or "No." Some test takers might interpret this item as referring to fist fights; others, to verbal arguments. Some might read standing up for one's rights into the item, and some who like to box in amateur prizefights, but dislike fighting in other contexts, might be uncertain how to answer the question. And, if a third alternative to the item, such as "?" or "Unsure," were permitted, as is sometimes the case, there might be significant individual differences in the tendency to use this alternative. In fact, some people tend to mark items "Yes" when they are confused, while others mark them "No."

A third source of error is introduced when a measure is used in different settings. For instance, a person might score as more depressed if a test were given in a hospital than if it were administered in a private clinic or at home. All of these problems cause a measure to become less accurate than is desirable. In effect, measuring aggressiveness with an unreliable measure would be like trying to measure height with a rubber yardstick: sometimes the yardstick would be stretched too long, sometimes it would be squeezed too short. Since the turn of the century, psychologists have attempted to formalize theories of measurement error and to express how error affects other aspects of investigations.

Variability

Reliability is one of the most fundamental concepts in science. If personality measures are unreliable, it becomes impossible to find correlations between the variables that are assessed by these measures. Suppose, for example, we hypothesize that people with high anxiety have a poorer memory of immediate events than people with low anxiety. Suppose further that every time we administer the measure, with repeated administrations only a few minutes apart, the scores vary so widely that the same person sometimes obtains the highest anxiety score, a middle-range anxiety score, or the lowest anxiety score. Since individual scores on the anxiety measure are so unstable, it would be impossible to establish a correlation between memory and anxiety, even if the hypothesis relating memory and anxiety were true.

Another way of describing our anxiety measure is in terms of the meaning of the different individual scores obtained on the measure. Let us suppose that some individuals obtain very high scores on the measure, others score in the middle range, and others fall into the lower range. These score differences can reflect the exact or true differences among individuals, if the measure is completely accurate, or they can reflect measurement error. The variability, which is based on individual differences, can therefore be divided into two components: *true variability* (representing real differences) and *error variability*. The reliability of a measure can be stated in terms of the relationship between these two components of variability; the greater the proportion of true variability relative to error variability, the more reliable the measure. This relationship can be expressed in simple quantitative form as follows:

$$\text{Reliability} = \frac{\text{True variability}}{\text{True variability} + \text{Error variability}} \quad \text{or}$$

$$= \frac{\text{True variability}}{\text{Observed variability}}$$

As can be seen in this formula, reliability expresses the proportion of the total variation that is true variability. The greater the error, the smaller the reliability ratio will be.

It is desirable to improve measures so that the proportion of total variability that is true variability increases, while the proportion that is error decreases. Unfortunately, it is no simple matter to find out which aspects of variability are true and which aspects are error.

Evaluating Reliability

There are many methods for evaluating reliability, with the choice of method depending on the potential source of measurement error. One source of error is time sampling. Errors arise from time sampling when a test is given at only one point in time and when a different score might be obtained if the test were given at some other time. Differences in an individual's responses might arise because of differences in mood, in interpersonal relationships, in physical condition, and in myriad other factors that can influence responses on a set of personality items. For example, consider the following items:

1. 1 like to spend a good deal of time by myself.
2. I feel uncomfortable in large social gatherings.
3. 1 have many friends.

Let us assume that, at time A, life is running fairly smoothly for a given extrovert. At time B, however, he or she has just experienced a very distressful break in a close relationship. At time A, the extrovert responds "No" to items 1 and 2 and "Yes" to item 3. But at time B, because of preoccupation with the disrupted relationship, he or she responds "Yes" to items 1 and 2 and, although hesitant, still responds "Yes" to item 3. Another extrovert, who might have responded in the direction of extroversion at time A, could have just moved to a new community at time B. He or she might have no friends in the community and might have just attended a social gathering that was cliquish and unresponsive to strangers. While still answering "No" to item 1, this person would answer "Yes" to item 2 and "No" to item 3. There are many other factors that can influence the consistency of responses from time A to time B: inattentiveness on one of the testing occasions; different interpretations of an ambiguous item (Does "friends" mean "close friends"? How many is "many friends"?); the sex of the tester; the degree of rapport with the tester; ad infinitum. One of the reasons for having many items on a test is to reduce the influence of changes on a few items on the overall test score.

For a measure to be reliable, there must be some individual stability in the responses given. If people changed their responses every time a test was administered, the measure would be highly unreliable. A quantitative determination of a test's degree of reliability can be made by giving the measure on two occasions to the same group of individuals. The correlation between scores obtained at two times is an estimate of **test-retest reliability**. Because many concepts in personality psychology are theorized to be stable over time, measures that show test-retest reliability are very useful. However, there are certain inherently unstable personality attributes for which the test-retest method of assessing reliability may be inappropriate. Emotions and moods such as joy, sadness, anger, fear, boredom, and fatigue are expected to fluctuate even though there may be individual differences in the basic tendency to be happy, angry, bored, or tired, thus we might see data like Figure 7.3.

A second method of determining reliability, which is applicable to measures of mood and emotional change, is evaluating the internal consistency of a test, using a variety of methods. One method is *split-half* reliability in which test items are divided into two groups (such as odd- and even-numbered items), and the correlation between scores for these halves is obtained. The higher the split-half correlation, the greater the reliability. Provided that the items on a measure are high-quality items, longer measures are more reliable. Ironically, when the measure is split in half, the reliability goes down. Fortunately, there are ways to correct for this artificial shortening of the measure.

test-retest reliability The correlation between scores obtained by administering a test on two occasions to the same group of individuals.

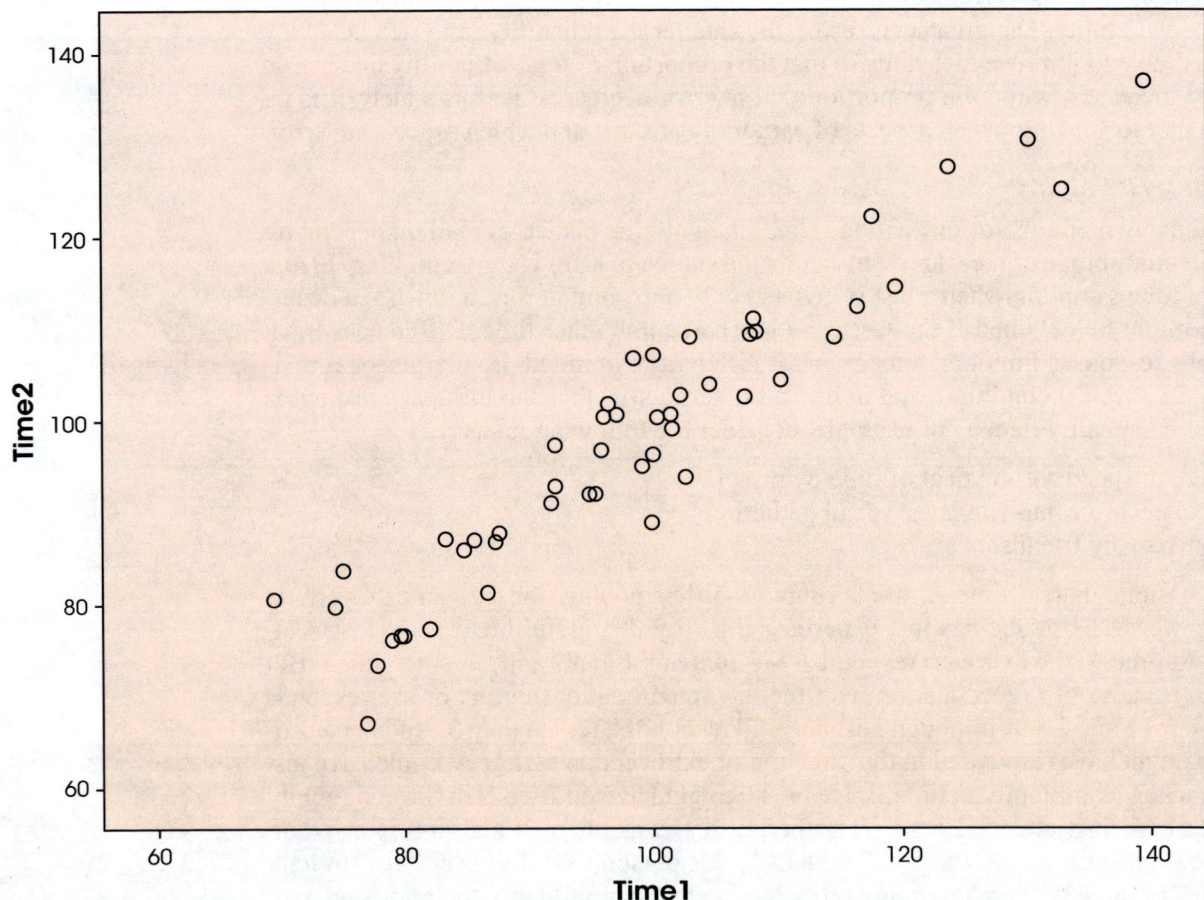

FIGURE 7.3 A Scatterplot of Scores Taken at Two Different Times

In test-retest reliability we would use the same measure at two different times. If the measure is reliable, we would expect to get approximately the same score on each administration of the measure.

Reliability of Observations

In addition to the reliability of tests, psychologists are also interested in the reliability of behavioral observations, which are used in many kinds of situations. Behavioral observations have the advantage of being closer to the actual behaviors of individuals than self-report questionnaires. However, if they are to be useful, they must meet the same criteria of reliability. Here the sources of error are associated with different observers' recording the same behavior and with time-sampling issues.

A psychologist who is studying the effects of a particular reinforcement program on attentive behaviors in a primary-grade classroom needs to define attention in terms of behaviors that can be reliably scored by classroom observers. The investigator who wishes to determine whether a questionnaire measure of aggression in hospitalized patients is related to the actual frequency of aggressive behaviors observed on the ward is confronted with a similar problem. If a single observer is used, it is important that the observer score the same behavior in the same way whenever it occurs. Inconsistency in observer scoring can become especially problematic when different observers are used. To ensure the reliability of observations, observers typically are required to take a training program in which they practice the observational scoring system and correct inconsistent scoring of the same behavior before the observational procedure is used in an actual experiment. Inter-rater reliability allows us to measure the agreement among those different observers.

In addition to minimizing potential observer error, it is also important to observe representative samples of behavior. If some preschool children are aggressive primarily before mealtime and others when they arrive each morning after being left by the parent who has brought them, it is important that both of these time periods are sampled in addition to other times.

Validity

It is not acceptable for scientific psychology to merely offer opinions about human behavior; psychologists must substantiate their claims, just as lawyers must provide evidence for the particular positions they advocate. There are many personality tests and it is important that psychologists become good consumers of these materials, which requires careful evaluation of the evidence used to support the claims of any given test.

Validity defines the meaning of a test or measure. Does it actually measure what it claims to measure? What does it mean to have a test that measures leadership potential, anxiety, moral values, manic-depressive psychosis, or the likelihood that one will fail a flight training program? The meaning, or validity, of a test of anxiety is determined by the behaviors considered to be indicative of anxiety that the test uncovers. Thus, high scorers on a test of anxiety might be more likely than low scorers to forget painful events, to manifest increased heart rate and trembling of the hands while taking an examination, and to be heavy smokers. If high scorers were no different from low scorers on these and other measures, our anxiety test would have no validity. Alternatively, if the anxiety test was found to be correlated with aggressive behaviors and not with anxiety indicators, we would then have to change its name and its claim.

Evidence for validity is derived from demonstrating clear associations between a test and other measures of behavior. These associations or correlations define the meaning of the test. The same principle applies to our test of leadership potential. Does our test predict success and failure in any kind of leadership context or only in one particular context—for instance, president of a sorority? The more behaviors and measures that are associated with a test, the more confident we can be and the more things we are willing to say about

Selecting an employee based on a measure of leadership depends on the quality of the measure, which includes both reliability and validity.

its connotations. There are several types of validity that give different types of evidence about the significance of tests: content, criterion, and construct validity.

To reiterate a point from earlier in the chapter, this measurement has real-life implications. Identifying who is truly suicidal is important. Accurately identifying who is likely to succeed in a flight training program can save millions of dollars in training and equipment costs. It can also save a company millions of dollars in litigation costs if it is sued because the measure is not a valid measure of what it claims to measure.

Content Validity

content validity The degree to which a test adequately represents the content it is designed to assess.

A test has **content validity** if it adequately covers the content area it is supposed to measure. For example, if you are being tested on what you learned in a personality course, the test is content valid to the extent that it represents all the material covered in the course. Traditionally, content validity has been of greatest concern in the area of educational testing. However, there are many instances in personality testing in which content validity is important. For example, if it is concluded that someone is compulsive solely on the basis of responses to a set of test questions, then, at the very least, there must be some assurance that the items on the test of compulsiveness adequately represent the behaviors encompassed by the diagnostic label "compulsive."

Content validity is the only type of validity for which the evidence is logical as well as statistical (Haynes, Richard, and Kubany, 1995). Establishing whether a test has content validity with regard to the inferences a test constructor wants to make requires good logic and intuitive skills. Establishing content validity for tests of knowledge, such as spelling competency, is more straightforward than for a test of a personality dimension like anxiety, where there is less agreement about the range of content that the test should sample. However, there can also be disagreement over the content validity of a test of knowledge. For instance, students may disagree with an instructor about whether the items on a particular examination adequately represented the material covered in lectures and readings. As will be shown in the following sections, other types of validity depend more on statistical methods, such as correlation, and less on intuition. Content validity is insufficient in itself to establish the validity of a test; other types of validity must also be used as the basis of making inferences about validity.

Criterion Validity

criterion validity The degree to which a test predicts, or correlates with, a subsequent factor **(predictive validity),** as well as the degree to which it is associated with other indexes that exist at the same point in time **(concurrent validity).**

Some psychological tests have a very specific purpose; many are used exclusively to make predictions. A good example of a test used for a predictive purpose is the Scholastic Aptitude Test (SAT). Most of you took either the SAT or the ACT to allow colleges and universities to evaluate your potential. To justify using SATs, the Educational Testing Service and the College Board, which are responsible for this instrument, had to provide some evidence that the test really was successful in forecasting future success in college. To do this they chose some index of success, such as grade-point average (GPA) during the first year of college, as the criterion against which the test was to be validated; thus the term **criterion validity**. The variables used to forecast the criterion are called *predictor variables*. The correlation between the predictor variables and the criterion defines the criterion validity of a test.

Tests should not be labeled as simply valid or invalid. Validity is not absolute; rather, it defines what can be inferred on the basis of a test or measure. Usually, tests have some validity for making certain specific statements. The SAT example in Figure 7.4 will help illustrate this point. At one large California university, it was shown that high school SAT scores correlated .40 with success in the first year of college. This means that the SAT can be expected to forecast about 16 percent of the variability in the first-year college GPA and that 84 percent of the variability cannot be explained by SAT scores.

Is the SAT valid for predicting who will do well in the first year of college? Yes, the test predicts performance better than just guessing. However, most of the variation in college performance is left unexplained. If the validity or the correlation between SAT score and first-year college GPA had been 1.0, then the SAT would be considered the perfect

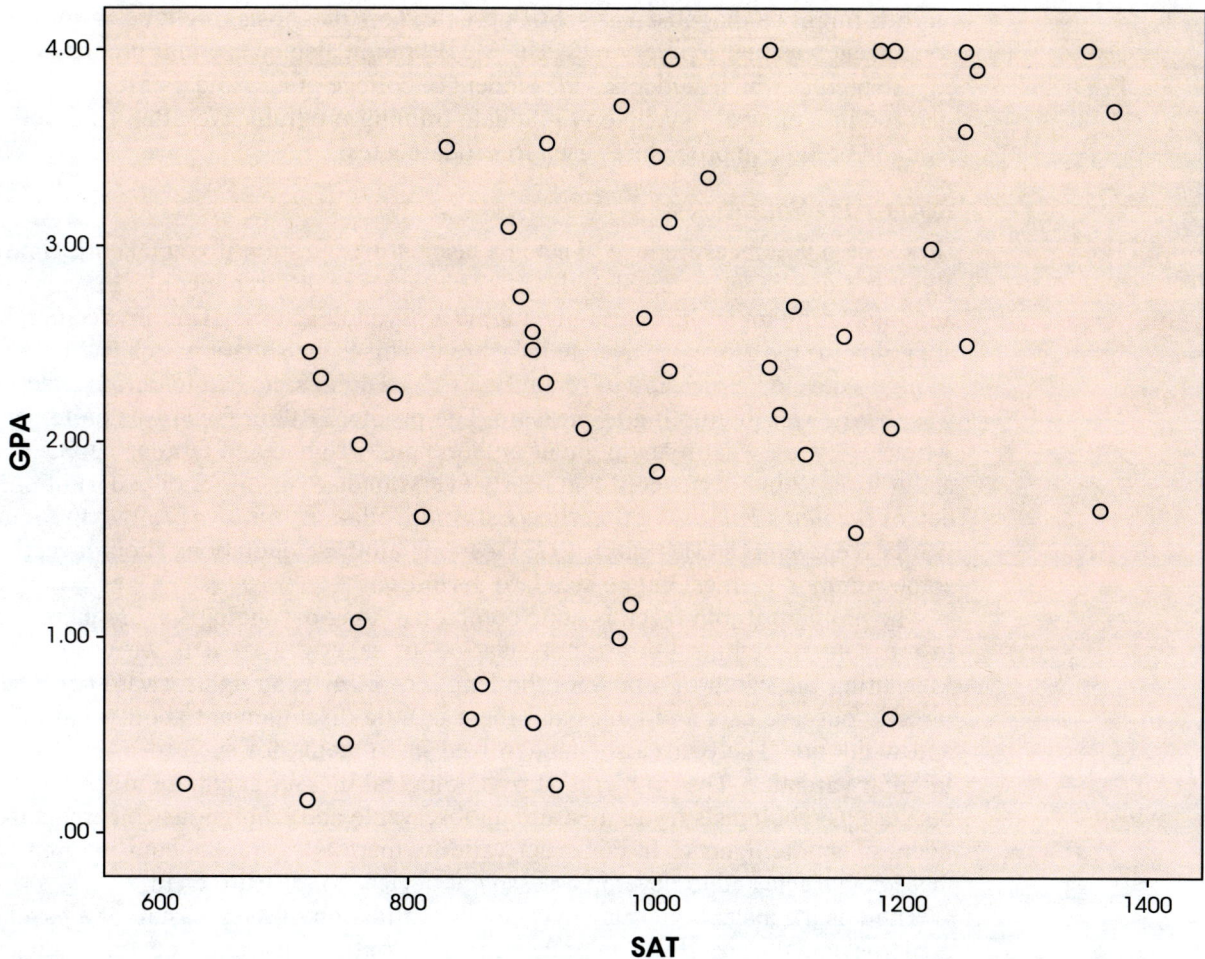

FIGURE 7.4

In this hypothetical example, SAT scores and first-year GPA show some relationship. The relationship is not perfect because many variables might influence first-year GPA, the SAT is not going to measure all of those, nor can it predict who is going to come down with an illness right before mid-term exams.

predictor of college success. Thus, a wise college might want to continue using the SAT because it gives them one significant predictor of college success, allowing admissions officers to make better predictions about who will do well in college than they would have been able to make without the test information. However, the Educational Testing Service also advises colleges that the evidence for validity suggests they consider other information about potential students in addition to SAT scores.

When a test is used to predict some criterion that will occur in the future, the problem is one of *predictive validity*. The SAT example is a problem of predictive validity because the test is given to high school students to predict how well they will do in college. Studies of predictive validity are also common in industry, where tests are given to potential employees to predict which people will have the most success on the job.

A related type of criterion validity does not attempt to forecast what will happen in the future. Instead, the criterion measurement and the assessment of the predictor may occur at the same point in time. This is called *concurrent validity*. The Minnesota Multiphasic Personality Inventory (MMPI), a measure discussed more extensively in the next chapter, is an example of a test based primarily on concurrent validity. The MMPI is used to diagnose specific forms of psychopathology and covers both the less severe forms of mental disturbance and more severe forms in which there is disruption in thought processes and contact with reality. For example, the test might be used to screen a large sample of military recruits. On the basis of scores on particular subscales of the test, some recruits might be diagnosed as schizophrenic. This diagnosis might be validated through concurrent psychiatric interviews. The MMPI might also be used for predictive purposes, e.g., to predict which students, independent of college grades and measures of ability, will succeed in a clinical psychology graduate training program. We often find both concurrent and predictive procedures used to validate a test.

Construct Validity

How would you measure love? That is a fascinating question if you take the time to think about it. Love likely means slightly different things to different people. Love is a complex and interesting topic. It is certainly a topic a psychologist may find interesting, but if we are going to study love, we need to measure it. This is the situation Zick Rubin faced when trying to develop a measure of romantic love. To do this, he had to define exactly what it was that he was attempting to measure. The problem Rubin faced was quite perplexing. After reviewing what many popular authors, playwrights, and famous people had to say about love, Rubin discovered that nearly everyone had his or her own definition. The index of *Bartlett's Familiar Quotations* lists more citations for *love* (769) than for any other word except *man* (843) (Rubin, 1973). Among all these quotations about love, there were some common themes, but no standard definition.

The problem Rubin faced is quite common among psychologists. Frequently, we want to measure something but are not clear about exactly what it is we want to measure. Measuring the width of a table or the length of a car is straightforward because we can directly observe cars and tables and there is little disagreement about what their length and width are. There are also standardized instruments for such measurement, like the familiar yardstick. The problems of psychological measurement are much more difficult because psychologists try to measure unobservable and ambiguous constructs like assertiveness or intelligence. In construct validity, there is a simultaneous attempt to define these constructs and to develop assessment devices to measure them.

There is a constant interplay between the validation of the measure of a psychological construct and the specification of the properties of the construct. Consider a questionnaire such as the Repression-Sensitization (R-S) scale, designed to differentiate individuals who tend to be repressors and those who tend to be sensitizers (Byrne, 1961) in their defenses against anxiety (see Chapter 3). Repressors are hypothesized as using a cluster of defense strategies characterized by avoidance of a threatening stimulus. Thus, they can be expected to deny threats; to forget painful, anxiety-evoking events; and to have difficulty verbalizing feelings of anxiety. Sensitizers, in contrast, are hypothesized as being especially wary of and attuned to possible threatening stimuli. They are likely to be overly preoccupied with threat, to be worriers, and to be obsessed with ideas and possibilities that evoke anxiety. They try to cope with threat, not by avoidance, but by preoccupation with the potential consequences of danger. They err on the side of alertness.

The measurement of this construct of repression-sensitization simultaneously poses two sets of issues. One set of issues has to do with the specification and demonstration of the properties of the construct. Does the concept apply to all threatening events or only to particular kinds of threats, such as threats to self-esteem? What are the specific ways in which avoidance and sensitization are manifested behaviorally? Do individuals consistently avoid or consistently behave in an oversensitized manner? Are some people repressors when faced with certain threatening stimuli and sensitizers when confronted with another type of threat? A second, related set of issues has to do with the validity of the Repression-Sensitization scale in differentiating between individuals who display the characteristics of repressors and those who manifest the characteristics of sensitizers. The two sets of issues are interconnected because, in order to study the construct of repression-sensitization, we must first have some way of determining the degree to which an individual is a repressor or a sensitizer. So we begin with one test that we have reason to believe might be a useful measure of this personality dimension. As we find out more about the correlates of the measure with other behaviors, we learn more about the properties of the construct. On the basis of a number of research studies (e.g., Bell and Byrne, 1978; Haley, 1974), it has been possible to gain a better understanding of the validity of both the R-S scale and the repression-sensitization construct.

It is evident that the construct validation of a test is a complex process with several steps. First, the concept of interest is carefully considered and items are generated that represent various aspects of the concept. At this point, the real work of construct validation begins. In a series of studies, scores on the test or measure are correlated with scores on other tests, measures, and behaviors. Each time a correlation is demonstrated, the meaning of the test is further defined and amplified. For example, if a measure of test anxiety is found to correlate −.40 with grade-point average and +.30 with number of illnesses experienced per year, then two new implications for the anxiety scale are found. The observed correlations define what the test measures; each time a new correlation is observed, the test takes on some new meaning. In this way, the test itself and the underlying theory or significance of the test develop together (Kaplan and Saccuzzo, 1981).

Construct validation is a never-ending process, in many ways similar to amassing evidence in support of a scientific theory. The researcher continually advances hypotheses, such as "If I am really measuring anxiety, then I would expect those scoring high on the anxiety scale to have more psychosomatic problems than those scoring low on the scale." This hypothesis is then evaluated in a systematic study, with each new study adding some meaning to the test.

In construct validation, two types of correlation are important to observe: convergent and discriminant. **Convergent validity** comes from demonstrating that a test measures the same thing as other tests that measure a similar construct. However, if the test correlates too well with other measures, then it might be unnecessary. If, for example, our anxiety scale correlated perfectly with one used for psychosomatic illness, then it might not be needed; the psychosomatic measure could be used in its place.

convergent validity The degree to which a test measures the same construct as that assessed by other tests.

Discriminant validity, on the other hand, establishes that a test is measuring a different construct than that assessed by other measures. For example, if the anxiety scale correlated highly with a well-established test of achievement, it could be measuring achievement motivation instead of test anxiety. But a moderate or low correlation would tell us that the tests are distinctive and thus that the anxiety scale is measuring something other than achievement motivation.

discriminant validity The degree to which a test measures a different construct than that assessed by other tests.

How Low Reliability Affects Validity

As previously indicated, a scientific investigator is working under a handicap when reliability is less than perfect. In most studies, one attempts to find relationships between variables. Finding these relationships is greatly hampered if one or more of the variables is measured unreliably. Over the years, psychologists have systematically defined the ways in which measurement error serves to hamper other aspects of research. To have validity, there must be a reasonably high correlation between two measures of a construct. An earlier example of the relation between a test of anxiety and a measure of immediate memory indicated that, when one of the measures is not reliable, the observed correlation will be lowered. This means that the correlation is less than would be expected if the quantities were measured without error.

Measurement theory allows one to estimate the maximum correlation between variables if one or both variables is assumed to have been measured with some error. For example, if television violence and viewer aggression were correlated perfectly in nature but the reliability of each measure were .60, then the observed correlation would be only .60. Thus, we could explain 36 percent of the variance, but 64 percent of the variance or predictability of one measure from the other would have been lost due to measurement error. A measure with a reliability of .50 on one variable would reveal only a moderate relationship with any other measure, even if the true association between them were perfect (+1.0). This tells us that, without reliability, it is impossible to obtain convincing evidence for validity. In other words, reliability is required in order to demonstrate that a measure has meaning.

Summary

1. The field of testing has a long history, dating back to early China. An especially important contributor was Sir Francis Galton.
2. The first questionnaire measure of personality arose out of a need during World War I to develop a test that could be used to screen soldiers for emotional disturbances.
3. *Reliability* refers to the degree of *measurement error*, or the degree to which the observed score deviates from the true score. Sources of error include inconsistent interpretation of items by test takers and the effects of the testing environment on test answers.
4. Types of reliability include *test-retest reliability*, in which the source of unreliability is differences in testing times, and *internal consistency*, which refers to the degree of consistency within a test at any given time period.
5. *Validity* defines the meaning of a test or measure; it indicates whether a test is in fact measuring what it is supposed to measure.
6. *Content validity* refers to whether a test adequately represents the content it is supposed to assess. The evidence for content validity is logical rather than statistical.
7. *Criterion validity* refers to the degree to which a test predicts (correlates with) a subsequent factor (*predictive validity*), as well as the degree to which a test is associated with other indexes that exist at the same point in time (*concurrent validity*).
8. A more complex type of validity is known as *construct validity*. In *construct validation* the meaning of a construct and the test measuring the construct are developed simultaneously. Test validation provides better understanding of the construct, while elaboration of the construct results in changes in the test.
9. Reliability places constraints on validity; for an instrument to have validity, measurement error must be minimized.

Key Terms

content validity (p. 136)
convergent validity (p. 139)
criterion validity (p. 136)
discriminant validity (p. 139)
measurement error (p. 131)

projective test (p. 127)
reliability (p. 127)
temperament (p. 129)
test-retest reliability (p. 134)
validity (p. 127)

Thought Questions

1. What advice would you give teachers who want to make their examinations more reliable and valid?
2. Describe a test that would have appropriate content validity as an instrument for selecting a good teacher or a good executive.
3. SAT scores predict subsequent grade-point averages, but leave much of the variation in grades unaccounted for. What factors might be responsible for this less-than-perfect validity? Could a test be constructed to assess these other factors?

Personality Assessment

CHAPTER 8

Source: Wichy/Shutterstock.com

Chapter Outline

Objective Personality Tests

Projective Personality Tests and Methods

Other Approaches to Personality Assessment

Psychologists frequently use tests to obtain information about clients and for research. There are now thousands of personality tests that attempt to measure every imaginable human characteristic. It would not be feasible to describe each of them, but we will focus on some of the best-known general approaches to testing and the most widely recognized tests.

With few exceptions, traditional approaches to assessment assume that human characteristics can be measured independently of the situation or environment. If, for example, someone scores high on a personality measure of outgoingness, it is assumed that this individual is outgoing in many different situations and that the tested characteristic is one that the person brings to any situation. Such environment-independent characteristics are typically referred to as **traits**, or enduring tendencies to respond in a particular manner.

Personality measures designed to assess traits also view these characteristics of personality as *stable over time*. Once characteristics are established, they are not expected to change significantly, though it is important to recognize that this is an important research question about personality. If, for example, a personality test reveals that Fred is aggressive, then it is expected that Fred will also be aggressive in the future. Fred will supposedly not display aggression for one month, followed by two months of passivity, followed by one week of aggression, and so on. The aggression should occur with some stability, or it will be concluded that Fred is unpredictable.

Most personality assessment techniques also assume that all humans possess the *same* characteristics but at different levels. People differ from one another

traits A distinguishing personal characteristic that is relatively stable and enduring.

only in the degree to which they possess these common traits, such as anxiety, aggression, or the need for achievement. On the other hand, there are some personality assessment techniques that allow for the possibility that, while certain characteristics exist to some degree in all humans, there are some specific characteristics that may occur in only a few. For example, perhaps only a few people display true altruism, the sacrifice of personal pleasure for the betterment of others. This assumption is consistent with the position that humans are at the same time like all other humans, like some other humans, and like no other humans. In addition to these assumptions, the predominant view is that an individual's personality represents the sum total of the variety and degrees of the relatively stable, consistent traits that he or she possesses.

Most personality assessment instruments are referred to more simply as personality tests. Traditionally, two major types of personality tests have evolved: objective and projective. In recent years, however, a number of newer approaches to human personality assessment have appeared. The two major types of personality tests, as well as the newer approaches (which are not really "tests" in the traditional sense) are discussed in this chapter.

Objective Personality Tests

You no doubt already have a good idea of what an objective test is; most college instructors give objective exams, with questions of the multiple-choice or true-false variety. This type of question requires that students recognize or remember items, rather than produce anything original, as in a term paper or essay test. In an objective test, one usually chooses from two or more designated alternatives. The response can be made on a standard answer sheet and can be machine- or computer-scored. The scoring is objective rather than subjective, with no judgments or evaluations required.

Like objective college exams, objective personality tests provide a written stimulus. The test taker is then asked to choose among two or more alternative responses, or to compare one written stimulus with one or more alternatives, selecting one or more of these choices according to a set of criteria. In some personality tests, people are asked to indicate which of two statements is more characteristic of them. For example, the following pair of alternatives appears in a test (the internal-external (I-E) locus of control scale) designed to assess individual differences in whether people believe that one can influence and control rewards and punishments or that they are externally controlled (see Chapter 17):

1. Many people can be described as victims of circumstances.
2. What happens to other people is pretty much of their own making.

The test taker is asked to select the alternative in which he or she more strongly believes.

Another test provides three statements and asks the individual to indicate which is most and which is least characteristic. In all objective personality tests, the stimulus is a word, phrase, or statement, and the response requires selection among provided alternatives. Unlike objective college exams, however, there are no right or wrong answers. Subjects simply recall or determine the responses they believe are the best according to the instructions given. The test usually contains a number of items related to each of several personality characteristics. All items related to a single personality characteristic are known collectively as a *scale*. Some objective personality tests contain only one scale; however, most consist of several. If a person marks a greater than average number of items in the appropriate or scored direction on a scale, then that person is assumed to possess a greater than average degree of the trait measured by that scale.

Although they are widely used, there are problems with objective personality tests. Early objective personality tests were particularly crude and inadequate by today's standards. But even the best of modern objective personality tests are not without recognized flaws. Psychologists continually strive to improve them, either through revision of existing scales or through development of new ones. Efforts to develop accurate objective personality tests have produced four major models or approaches to objective personality testing, each with its own unique assumptions.

Tests Based on Face Validity

Personality testing was used on a large scale in the United States during World War I. These early tests assumed that a person's response to an objective test item could be taken at face value. This assumption of **face validity** viewed the content of a test item as a straightforward indicator of a person's personality. If a person endorsed the item "I am outgoing," then it was assumed that this person was, indeed, outgoing. Linked to the assumption of face validity are the additional assumptions that people are honest, aware of their own characteristics, objective in evaluating these characteristics, and interpret the word *outgoing* in the same way as others taking the test and evaluating the test responses. This assumption about responses representing a particular personality dimension is assumed to be true but is not tested against any other criterion. Thus, it has face validity, but we know nothing about the construct or criterion validity. As a first step, it was acceptable, but it would no longer be considered useful in a scientific approach to personality psychology. However, many measures out in the world are based solely on the fact that the test looks good. Think of the tests you might find on a website: Some look as though they might be meaningful, whereas others are obviously not. For example, "Which Harry Potter character are you?" or "What city fits your personality?" Now that you are studying personality psychology, you will recognize that most of these tests don't even succeed on face validity.

The first objective personality test to assume face validity of test responses (see Chapter 7) was the Woodworth Personal Data Sheet (Woodworth, 1920). By the 1930s, however, many of the problems with the face validity approach had become apparent. Some of the problems were that people differ in their interpretations of an item's meaning and are limited in their ability to accurately observe and objectively report their own behavior. Other problems concern honesty. Tests based on face validity assume that a person is so open, flexible, and nondefensive that he or she responds as honestly as possible to each item. However, when tests are used to select people for jobs or, more dramatically, in criminal cases, honesty is not always in the test taker's best interests!

Closely related to the honesty of a test response is the notion of **social desirability**. A person might be honest but, without even being totally aware of it, might endorse the response believed to be the one the examiner wants to hear or the response that reflects most favorably on the subject. Edwards (1957, 1962, 1964) argued that the meaning of any response on an objective personality test is influenced by the number of acceptable, expected, flattering, and complimentary responses that are selected. When endorsing the socially desirable rather than the true or realistic alternative response, the test score simply reflects the individual's need to present desired and culturally valued qualities. If correct, Edwards's notion of social desirability suggests that objective personality tests measure the need to be accepted and approved, which tends to be confounded with the other behavioral tendencies that the tester wants to assess. There is considerable debate as to whether socially desirable responding is an artifact that should be acknowledged and eliminated, or is an important dimension of personality. From a measurement point of view, it is problem. From a personality psychology point of view, socially desirable responding is related to other behaviors that matter. If someone responds in a socially desirable way, that person is likely to be an employee who works in a socially desirable way (Ones, Viswesvaran, and Reiss, 1996).

Related to the concept of social desirability is the problem of response tendencies or biases. A **response bias** is the tendency to respond in a particular way, regardless of item content. Some individuals, for example, tend to agree or to say "Yes" regardless of the content of an item (see Jackson and Messick, 1962; Messick and Jackson, 1961). This tendency to agree with or mark "True" on an item regardless of the item's content is called *acquiescence*. There are many other biased response dispositions as well. For example, the corresponding negativistic response bias is the tendency to say "No," while the tendency to endorse the opposite of what a person believes to be true is known as *oppositional bias*. These response tendencies may in themselves reflect an individual's personality characteristics; e.g., acquiescence may reflect a tendency toward conformity

face validity The degree to which the items on a test appear to sample the content domain.

social desirability A factor, to be considered on personality tests, that connotes a person's tendency to respond in a socially approved or favorable manner.

response bias The tendency to respond to a test item in a particular way regardless of item content.

and compliance, while a negativistic response bias may indicate hostile, oppositional tendencies. However, the main implication of response bias is that objective personality tests may measure factors other than those the test constructor intended to measure; that is, the possibility always exists that these response patterns have influenced a person's test score to such an extent that the meaning of a test score is subject to some doubt.

Empirical Approaches

The psychologists who developed early personality tests were unaware of problems like social desirability and response bias. However, years of research gradually eroded faith in face validity approaches to personality testing. Twenty years of experience with these early tests gave way to the introduction of various *empirical* approaches, which began around 1940 (see Dahlstrom, 1969). Objective personality tests based on face validity were replaced by tests such as the Minnesota Multiphasic Personality Inventory (MMPI), Cattell's Sixteen Personality-Factor Questionnaire (16 P-F), and other personality measures whose validity was based on research procedures and findings.

Objective personality tests vary in the extent to which they are based on theoretical considerations as well as empirical findings. Some tests are almost completely empirically based, with the theoretical rationale for the content and structure of the test items irrelevant. The critical question is the relationship of test responses to some criterion; e.g., a test of depression should differentiate depressed and nondepressed populations, and a test of the successful salesperson's personality should differentiate known groups of good and poor salespeople.

The empirical approach to objective personality testing attempts to find the behavioral correlates of certain test responses. For example, a test constructor interested in developing a measure of aggressiveness might identify a group of people assumed to be aggressive because they have been in three or more fights during the past year. Then a second group of nonaggressive people might be selected from individuals who have never been in a fight. A set of items is given to both groups and the items or scales marked more often by the aggressive than by the nonaggressive individuals could be used as an indicator or "test" of aggressive tendencies. It need not matter what the actual content of the items is; perhaps aggressive individuals tend to endorse the item "I like carrots" more often than the nonaggressive. This nevertheless becomes a valid test indicator of aggressiveness under the empirical approach. In most instances, however, one can perceive the connection between items on empirically based tests and the criterion behavior.

The MMPI

The *Minnesota Multiphasic Personality Inventory (MMPI)* is perhaps the best-known and most widely used empirically based personality test. This test was introduced at a time when the problems facing objective personality tests seemed all but insurmountable. The MMPI not only came to the rescue, but actually kindled new interest in objective personality testing by providing solutions to the problems intrinsic to the earlier, face validity approach.

After use for several decades, a new version of the MMPI, the MMPI-2, was introduced. While the basic structure of the test remains the same, some offensive items have been deleted, sexist wording has been eliminated, and some new items have been added. Most importantly, the norms for the new version are based on a much broader and more representative sample of the population of the United States, one that takes ethnic diversity more into account.

The MMPI is a true-false questionnaire consisting of more than five hundred items. The subject is instructed to respond true or false to each item as it applies to him or her. The items vary widely in content, such as:

- I like to read news magazines.
- I never had trouble falling asleep.
- People are out to get me.

The test contains nine validity scales, ten standard scales, and fifteen content scales (Butcher, 1999). Consider that one of the most important personality measures is so concerned with validity that it has nine different ways to consider validity of the responses. That is also why Chapter 7 is so important to understanding the measurement of personality. The validity scales include careless responding (VRIN), defensive responding (K-scale), socially desirable responding (S-scale), and faking (F-scale). If someone has a pattern of responding on the validity scales that indicates that his or her responses are sufficiently different from either a general or psychiatric population, the clinical scales must be interpreted carefully or may not be interpretable at all.

The ten standard scales of the MMPI are used to measure specific disorders and related personality characteristics. It should be noted, however, that the MMPI was originally designed to measure *abnormal* or *disturbed personality*. Eight of the clinical scales of the MMPI were formed by the criterion-keying method, in which, as we mentioned, groups of people known to manifest a certain abnormal behavior, such as depression or schizophrenia, were given the items of the MMPI. Items that were more frequently endorsed in a certain direction by these groups than by a control group were then selected to form a scale that purportedly measured the characteristics (e.g., depression or schizophrenia) of the criterion groups. In other words, each scale consisted of those items discriminating the criterion groups from the normal group. In addition to depression and schizophrenia, there are scales to measure hypochondriasis, hysteria, psychopathic deviance, masculinity-femininity, paranoia, psychasthenia, mania, and social introversion-extraversion.

In spite of its apparent strengths and widespread use in clinical settings (Lubin, Wallis, and Paine, 1971), the MMPI also has a number of important limitations and problems. A detailed analysis of its limitations in terms of the various types of reliability reveals that test-retest reliability over short periods of time is acceptable, but often marginally so. And for longer time intervals, there is substantial unreliability. For most of the scales, individual scores are not stable (Dahlstrom and Welsh, 1960). The reasons for the poor long-term reliability of the MMPI have not been clearly established. One important factor that must be taken into consideration in interpreting the long-term unreliability of the MMPI is its dual use as a measure of psychopathology and as a measure of personality attributes. One would expect fluctuations over time in the degree of psychological disturbance as individuals seek treatment, as they mature and develop better skills in coping with their problems, as crises disappear, and as new stresses arise. There clearly are lower stabilities for measures of pathologies when compared with those measures of normal personality traits (Schuerger, Zarrella, and Hotz, 1989). These fluctuations in the individual's psychological state may obscure relative stabilities of the psychological traits that are also assessed by the MMPI.

Usage of the MMPI has extended far beyond its initial purpose. It is now being used for the screening of persons for sensitive occupations such as pilots or policemen, for the classification of prison inmates, and in cross-cultural studies of personality. Cross-cultural research with this instrument is possible because the MMPI has been translated into so many languages, including Chinese and Turkish (see Butcher, 1979). Newer investigations also attempt to find relationships between MMPI categories and personality types that were not included in the original scales. A study of *anhedonia* (a term used to describe the inability to experience pleasure) exemplifies this type of research. Although it is common to think of anhedonia as a form of depression, it has been suggested that groups experiencing this condition share many of the same characteristics as schizophrenics. Thus, it was hypothesized that anhedonia would be associated with an MMPI profile pattern that included a high score on the schizophrenia scale. Data have tended to confirm this pattern (Penk, Carpenter, and Rylee, 1979), thus defining a new meaning for a particular MMPI pattern. In addition, because the MMPI has a large number of items, it has become possible to derive new personality scales using subsets of these items. These new measures include several important research instruments such as the previously cited Repression-Sensitization scale (Byrne, 1961) and the Taylor Manifest Anxiety scale (Taylor, 1953).

Factor Analysis

factor analysis A statistical
method of reducing a large
amount of data from tests,
rating scales, or behavioral
observations to a smaller
and presumably more basic
number of dimensions of
personality factors.

Some approaches to the study of personality depend on sophisticated methods such as **factor analysis**, a statistical procedure taking large amounts of data from tests, rating scales, or behavioral observations and reducing them down into smaller, more manageable, chunks.

Factor analysis reduces the redundancy or overlap in a set of scores or data. If two variables are correlated, this means that the two overlap in measuring some common characteristic. For example, there is a correlation between how fast a person runs and how far he or she can jump. If we took a group of people and recorded their speeds in the hundred-yard dash and their distances in the broad jump, we would no doubt find a positive correlation. This correlation would mean that those who run faster also jump farther. The association or correlation between performance on these two track events suggests that some common process or ability, such as leg strength, underlies both running and jumping. Each event requires its own unique abilities, or the two would be perfectly correlated; however, a common factor, such as leg strength, is related to both. The correlation tells us the extent to which some common factor or factors underlie performance in both events; the higher the correlation, the more the two have in common.

It may be helpful to think of factor analysis as analogous to finding basic elements in chemistry. A chemist might use technical methods to find what elements or combinations of elements are parts of a given compound. In factor analysis, the "compounds" are large samples of behaviors or responses to tests and scales. Submitting such sets of data to factor analysis is like reducing a large array of information to its basic elements. Objective personality tests based on factor analysis assume that all the descriptive characteristics found in personality test scales can be reduced to just a few common factors that describe the underlying and fundamental aspects of human personality. Factor-analytic procedures are used to ascertain these fundamental aspects of human personality. The dimensions of personality obtained by a particular factor analyst can be viewed as a theory of personality; thus factor analysts often are considered to be personality theorists as well as investigators who use a particular technique to determine the structure of personality.

Early Factor Analytic Work

The pioneer in the factor analytic model of objective personality assessment was J. P. Guilford. Guilford's approach was to intercorrelate the results of a wide variety of existing personality tests to develop a single test that measured the essentials of all the other existing tests. Guilford's initial efforts were published in the early 1940s (Guilford, 1940; Guilford and Martin, 1943) and culminated in the Guilford-Zimmerman Temperament Survey (Guilford and Zimmerman, 1956). Presumably, the Guilford-Zimmerman scale reduced human personality to ten basic characteristics or dimensions: general activity, restraint, ascendance (leadership), sociability, emotional stability, objectivity, friendliness, thoughtfulness, personal relations, and masculinity. But despite the careful work and laborious effort that went into the Guilford-Zimmerman scale, the test failed to find widespread acceptance from either researchers or test users.

surface traits In Cattell's
factor analyses of personality
traits, clusters of responses or
overt behaviors that are related
or fit together.

source traits In Cattell's
factor analyses of personality
traits, basic organizing
structures that underlie and
determine surface traits.

Following Guilford's early work, R. B. Cattell also used the factor-analytic method to ascertain and measure the fundamental characteristics of human personality. Cattell's starting point consisted of an analysis by Allport and Odbert (1936) of over 4,500 adjectives applicable to human beings listed in an unabridged dictionary. Cattell first added to this list other descriptive adjectives taken from psychiatric and psychological literature and then reduced the list to approximately 170 items which he believed were relatively independent and captured the meaning of all the words on the original list. He then asked college students to describe their friends according to the terms on the reduced list and factor analyzed the results. Cattell reported that the items could be reduced to 36 dimensions that were labeled **surface traits** (see Cattell, 1957). Subsequent attempts to further reduce this list ultimately uncovered 16 dimensions, or factors, labeled **source traits**.

Presumably, Cattel's 16 source traits, including intelligence and ego strength, provided the same information that Guilford's ten dimensions of personality supposedly measured. In 1949, the items most strongly related to each of the 16 factors were identified and selected for inclusion in the 16 Personality-Factor Questionnaire, better known as the 16 P-F (see Cattell, 1949). However, even the factors of the 16 P-F intercorrelated, so that these 16 factors were themselves factor analyzed. The results of these additional factor analyses of the 16 P-F scale have yielded from 4 to 8 so-called second-order factors. Among the factors that were identified are introversion-extroversion, anxiety, affectivity, and free will versus resignation (Cattell, Eber, and Tatsuoka, 1970). Of these, the first two factors are best replicated, that is, most often found in other factor-analytic studies.

Later Factor Analytic Work

Since the work of Cattell, researchers have converged on a model of traits that have approximately five factors. This has been found so often that they are referred to as the **Big Five** or *Five Factor Model (FFM)*. These traits (and controversies) will be discussed in greater detail in Chapter 9. Because the traits are thought to describe a breadth of human experience, a measure of these dimensions is thought to capture much of the variability in human personality. Several personality measures have come from this approach. One of the most-used measures is called the Revised NEO Personality Inventory (NEO-PI-r; Costa and McRae, 1992). This measure assesses neuroticism, extraversion, openness to experience, agreeableness, and conscientiousness. There are facets within each of these dimensions as well. The NEO-PI-r appears to work across many different languages and cultures (McRae and Costa, 1997). Other researchers have developed measures of personality based on alternative factor analysis interpretations of personality. For instance, Lee and Ashton (2004) have developed the HEXACO-PI, which measures honesty/humility, emotionality, extraversion, agreeableness, conscientiousness, and openness to experience.

Big Five Many personality researchers now believe there are five basic personality traits. One popular classification system identifies them as: neuroticism versus emotional stability, extraversion, openness to experience, conscientiousness, and agreeableness.

The Theoretical Model

Another model of objective personality assessment uses theories of human personality in selecting test items. If, for example, a given theory divides human personality into three components—mood, thought, and behavior—then items would be selected to measure each of these components. A test that illustrates this approach, although not used as often as it once was, is the Edwards Personal Preference Schedule (EPPS; Edwards, 1954, 1959).

Murray (1938) theorized that a number of basic needs underlie human personality, including such motivations as the need to achieve, conform, affiliate, gain power, and be nurtured. Selecting from Murray's list of human needs, Edwards chose fifteen and constructed items to assess the extent to which each of these was present in any person. Like the MMPI and the 16 P-F, the resulting EPPS contained a number of validity items designed to detect response biases. Furthermore, to eliminate social desirability, the EPPS was constructed so that each person had to choose between two items in a pair, selecting the more characteristic one. Each item in the pair reflected a different need, and an effort was made to equate the items on social desirability in order to reduce the influence of this bias on the test results. An example of an item pair is:

1. I feel depressed when I fail at something.
2. I feel nervous when giving a talk before a group.

One difference between the EPPS and other objective tests is that the scores assessing each need are interdependent, reflecting each individual's own preference hierarchy. If some needs receive high scores, then others must receive low scores for a given person because of the forced-choice methodology that is used. For example, in pairing an achievement and an affiliation item, selection of the achievement item augments the achievement scale score while not adding to the affiliation scale score. In contrast, on other tests it is possible to obtain high scores on all the subscales. Although the EPPS is a well-designed instrument from a technical standpoint, it also does not have a good record for long-term stability. Thus, like the MMPI and the 16 P-F, it is subject to some of the same factors that limit the usefulness of these tests as measures of enduring personality traits.

There are hundreds of objective measures that are designed to assess just a few dimensions of personality. For instance, there are several different ways to measure self-esteem—the Rosenberg Self-Esteem Inventory (Rosenberg, 1965) and the Texas Social Behavior Inventory (Helmreich and Stapp, 1974) to name just two. The State-Trait Anxiety Inventory (Spielberger, 1983) differentiates between anxiety that is transient, and would show low test-retest reliability, and a stable trait like anxiety that does show high test-retest reliability.

Projective Personality Tests and Methods

Long before objective personality tests based on face validity were replaced by better objective instruments, an entirely new and different idea about personality assessment had emerged. This second major traditional approach is known as the *projective* method. In projective methods, the person's task is to produce something spontaneously, through such procedures as associating to test stimuli. Rather than selecting among written alternatives, the test taker has few guidelines for the type of response required; therefore, almost any response can be obtained. Given such a wide range of possible responses, it is difficult to formulate a set of rules for scoring purposes; subjective evaluation is often the most workable solution. As a result, agreement in scoring between testers and between responses is often far from perfect, even though some objective scoring techniques have been developed.

Projective tests begin by presenting a person with an ambiguous stimulus like an ink-blot or a picture with some indeterminate elements. The examiner might ask a question as simple as "Tell me what this might be," or the subject might be asked to make up a story about an ambiguous picture. In either case, the person must use his or her creative and analytical capacities in providing an answer; alternatives are not provided. In exchange for the loss of objectivity in scoring and evaluating a person's response, projective tests provide much more opportunity for the expression of individuality. They therefore are thought to be potentially capable of detecting more subtle and varied aspects of personality than is possible with objective tests.

All projective tests are based on the hypothesis that the person's response to an ambiguous or vague stimulus is a reflection (i.e., projection) of his or her own needs and feelings. That is, the person, in giving meaning to an ambiguous stimulus, "projects" onto that stimulus his or her needs, feelings, strivings, and thought processes. Moreover, the projection can take place without the individual's being aware that significant aspects of the personality are being revealed. Thus, it is assumed that projective tests provide more access to the kinds of unconscious impulses and attitudes with which psychoanalysis is concerned.

The Rorschach Inkblot Test

The *Rorschach Inkblot Test*, in which subjects are asked to respond to ambiguous ink-blots, maybe the first formal projective method. One of the earliest references to the possibility of using inkblots to assess individual differences dates back to the Civil War (Keiner, 1857). Keiner noted that, when asked to interpret the meaning of an inkblot, each individual tended to produce unique and idiosyncratic responses. Inasmuch as responses to inkblots were different for each individual, it seemed reasonable to conclude that different interpretations reflected differences between individual interpreters. If most subjects had provided the same or even similar responses to the same inkblot stimulus, then the obvious conclusion would have been that the interpretations were simply a reflection of the characteristics of the inkblot. For example, asking subjects to describe a table or a chair would not reveal much about the subjects because all responses would be relatively similar.

Objective personality tests attempt to measure individual differences in specific attributes. The Rorschach Inkblot Test, on the other hand, makes no assumptions concerning the characteristics that should or will be measured. Instead, the Rorschach is so flexible that it leaves open the possibility of assessing the most unique aspects of an individual. There are, however, certain broad dimensions of personality, including impulse control, sensitivity to internal thoughts and feelings, sensitivity to external inputs, and the tendency to distort reality, that the test attempts to assess in all individuals.

The Rorschach consists of ten cards, each displaying a meaningless, bilaterally symmetrical inkblot. To get an idea of what the cards look like, you can simply repeat the same method Hermann Rorschach used to construct the original test (Rorschach, 1921). Place a few drops of ink on a white card or piece of paper, carefully fold the card in half, open it, and then let it dry. What emerges is an apparently meaningless blob that is symmetrical on both sides of the crease, so that each half looks like the mirror image of the other half. A little inspection soon seems to reveal meaning, and all or parts of the inkblot will begin to resemble familiar shapes and objects.

The Rorschach test contains five black-and-gray inkblots; two that are black, gray, and red; and three cards consisting of a variety of pastel colors. The Rorschach is administered with minimal instructions since it is designed to be ambiguous and unstructured. Unlike objective personality tests, the Rorschach is typically administered individually, testing one person at a time. Throughout the sometimes-lengthy testing period, the examiner writes down each response, at the same time offering no clues to the type of response required. In the typical situation, the card is presented and the examiner asks, "What might this be?" The subject is then free to give one or several responses to each of the ten cards, responding to the entire inkblot, to some portion of it, or to both.

The person's scores, which can be summarized in terms of the frequency of each of the various dimensions, are referred to as the quantitative aspects of the test. Of equal significance, however, is an analysis of the actual content of the person's responses, which is referred to as the qualitative aspect of the test. Rorschach interpretation is based on an evaluation of each scoring category as well as the quality and specific content of each

Source: beloppoppa /Shutterstock.com

FIGURE 8.1 An Inkblot Similar to Those Used in the Rorschach Test

response and how this varies from card to card. Considering the scoring categories, the human movement response (for example, "A man dancing") is thought by some to reveal introversion, in that the perception of movement is believed to indicate inner-directedness. A response like "That is a bat, but not a good one" might lead to inferences about obsessiveness. According to a proponent of the Rorschach, an experienced examiner can make some rather detailed and specific descriptions of the person's personality and emotional functioning. The Rorschach, like the MMPI, finds its most extensive use in clinical settings in which there is a need to assess maladaptive thought processes, motivational conflicts, and problems in emotional and behavioral control.

The Rorschach is an extremely complex and subjective method of personality assessment. From the very start, it has been a highly controversial personality instrument. It has been extremely difficult to evaluate its reliability and validity, in part because there are no universally accepted methods of administration, scoring, and interpretation. In addition, because the number of responses can vary widely, it is difficult to be certain about the meaning of the frequency of particular response characteristics. For example, the number of human movement responses in a Rorschach record will vary with the total number of responses given as well as with the tendency to perceive human movement in the blots. Also, test-retest studies reflect considerable instability in Rorschach responses overtime. As a result of these and other problems, there is little consensus among psychologists concerning the soundness of the Rorschach and its validity as a measure of human personality. Beyond the problems that the Rorschach has with inter-rater reliability and criterion validity, there is evidence that use with non-Americans and American minorities is dubious (Lilienfeld, Wood, and Garb, 2000).

In the case of an instrument as flexible and complex as the Rorschach, one must address the questions about the test's validity. Validity for what? For each dimension of personality? For the assessment of psychopathology? For the prediction of reactions to the stress of pilot training? The evidence bearing on the utility of the Rorschach in various personnel selection programs has been largely negative, while evidence for its utility as a personality measure has been variable. For example, its validity is questionable as an indicator of self-concept and sensitivity to others, but the Rorschach has proved to be somewhat effective in assessing self-control and ego strength (Klopfer, 1954; Zubin, Eron, and Schumer, 1965). In addition, there are also data indicating that specified combinations of Rorschach scores can reliably distinguish schizophrenics from neurotics (Fisher, 1967), even though there are many negative findings concerning the assessment of psychopathology. As indicated earlier, there are multiple scoring systems devised to interpret Rorschach responses. A commonly used scoring methodology in current use is the Comprehensive System (Exner, 1974, 1986, 1991). Even this system has been critiqued for lack of inter-rater reliability and appropriate construct validity (Wood, Nezworski, and Stejskal, 1996). Other systems have been devised to focus on specific diagnoses or outcomes in clinical settings (e.g., Acklin, 1999; Jorgensen, Andersen, and Ham, 2000).

The Thematic Apperception Test (TAT)

The *Thematic Apperception Test (TAT)* was first published in 1935 by Christiana Morgan and Henry Murray of Harvard University. Like the objective EPPS, the TAT is based on Murray's (1938) theory of needs. Murray proposed that human beings have to deal with the expression, satisfaction, and frustration of a number of psychological needs such as aggression, nurturance, affiliation, achievement, dependency, power, and sex. The TAT was specifically developed as a vehicle that would permit individuals to express these needs. The TAT purports to be a measure of human personality functioning that can be used in the assessment of normal as well as abnormal personality. Unlike the Rorschach, the TAT is not widely used in determining the extent of emotional disturbances, although it is used to ascertain the content of an individual's conflict and the defenses employed in coping with psychological conflicts.

The TAT contains thirty cards, each showing a picture or scene. In addition, one blank card is included. Although vague, each picture contains a specific type of content in which the dominant feature is usually one or more humans; e.g., a picture of a seated boy and a violin resting on a table. Some pictures contain only a child and others, only adults. The ages and sexes of the characters are sometimes mixed, such as a middle-aged woman and an older girl, or a young man and an older woman. Although some of the cards can be used for any age group or either sex, others are specifically designed for men, women, boys, or girls. Inasmuch as the pictures of the TAT are more meaningful or structured than the Rorschach inkblots, each picture tends to elicit a certain type of response. Thus, for example, a picture of an older and a younger man together typically elicits stories about father-son relationships. However, there is sufficient variability between individuals' interpretations of the cards to yield information about personalities and problems. A card similar to some of the TAT stimulus cards is shown in Figure 8.2.

When administering the TAT, the examiner presents the cards one at a time. The subject is requested to make up a story about each picture, stating what led up to the story, what is happening, what the characters are thinking and feeling, and what the outcome will be. Responses are recorded word for word.

The TAT is similar to the Rorschach in several respects. Neither test has a universally accepted, standardized scoring or interpretation. However, both have a number of commonly accepted scoring techniques. Scoring of the TAT can be more difficult and complex than scoring of the Rorschach. Most scoring systems tend to require that the hero, needs, environmental forces or press, themes, and outcomes be identified. The hero is the central character in each picture; it is assumed that the storyteller will identify with the hero. Therefore, the needs and motives of the hero, particularly those that recur from story to story, are assumed to reflect the needs and motives of the storyteller. Press refers to the environmental forces or obstacles facing the hero. Again, as the same types of such obstacles recur in several stories, the likelihood increases that the storyteller perceives similar difficulties in his or her own life. Recurrent conflicts and outcomes also are believed to reflect characteristics of the storyteller. In sum, what the examiner looks for in the TAT are

Sources: (left) Sharpshutter/Shutterstock (right) ER_09/Shutterstock

FIGURE 8.2 Images Similar to Those Used in the TAT

A person would tell a story about the pictures, which then would be coded as revealing that person's needs.

themes concerning needs, motivations, obstacles, conflicts, or outcomes that recur in the individual's stories for different pictures. These repeated themes are interpreted as reflecting the basic underlying motivations and conflicts of the storyteller. When a well-defined scoring system is used, inter-rater reliability can be relatively high (Fineman, 1977; Cramer and Block, 1998).

As an example of how the TAT is used, consider the following story told by a person we will call Robert. The stimulus card to which his story was given depicts a young man with bowed head and an older woman looking into the distance.

The fellow has just told the woman some bad news. He is a friend of her son who was living in another town. I'm not sure why. Perhaps he was in the service or maybe he had taken a job in that town. The son has been in an accident. He was a passenger in the car that his friend was driving. His friend had been drinking, not heavily, but had taken a couple for the road, as it were. Anyway, he was driving pretty fast and didn't see the sign for an approaching S curve. When he tried to slow down, he skidded into a tree. He luckily had only a few scratches, but the woman's son was badly injured and is in a coma. The friend naturally feels guilty and it was very hard for him to tell the mother about the accident. (Q: What happens?) The mother is extremely upset but she manages to maintain her self-control. She rushes to the hospital where she keeps watch at his bedside. After 24 hours, he comes out of the coma and eventually recovers.

There are a number of themes and needs that can be inferred from this story. One might be the untrustworthiness of friends and frustration of the need for affiliation. Another theme bears on the relationship of a young man to a mother figure. The core sequence of events consists of a son separated from his mother; a very negative, painful experience; reunion with the mother; and then a positive outcome. One might infer from this sequence that separation from his mother is very painful for Robert. He cannot acknowledge the frustration of his dependency needs and can express it only indirectly, through physical injury and through the visit of his friend in the story. The guilt expressed by the friend, a central character in the TAT picture, may be a displaced expression of his own guilt about his anger over frustration of dependency needs. There are other features of the story that might also be revealing: drinking, self-destruction, displacement of responsibility (the accident was the friend's fault). In all cases, however, one looks for repeated expressions of a theme in a number of stories before drawing inferences about an individual's basic needs and conflicts.

In reviews of the TAT, Exner (1974) and Murstein (1963) noted that test-retest reliability can be quite high under the specific condition that only a particular variable is studied. But even under such a specific condition, data are still insufficient for drawing firm conclusions about the test's value. There is nevertheless extensive research bearing on the validity of the TAT. For example, several experimental studies have manipulated such needs as hunger, aggression, and sex in order to examine the effects of need arousal on stories elicited in response to a subset of TAT stimuli. In general, the results of these studies indicate that aroused subjects make more responses relating to the aroused need than do nonaroused subjects (McClelland and Atkinson, 1948). These findings contribute to the construct validity of the TAT. At the same time, though, they indicate that the TAT is subject to situational or temporary influences, a fact inconsistent with the traditional assessment goal of measuring enduring personality traits.

In general, as in the case of the Rorschach, validity studies have yielded variable findings. It is clear that there are circumstances under which the TAT and the Rorschach are predictive of significant aspects of personality. The problem lies in specifying those circumstances in order to tell in advance when the TAT and the Rorschach will provide valid pictures of a subject's personality.

Other Approaches to Personality Assessment

There are a multitude of ways in which we might get information about people's personality. We could ask them, we could ask their friends and family, we could observe them, we could look at data about their lives. A researcher or clinician may create a situation and observe the behavior. We may even want to measure biological functions. Each of these approaches has advantages and disadvantages.

The Interview

The *interview* is without doubt the oldest technique for assessing personality. The original objective personality test, the Woodworth Personality Data Sheet (1920), was actually an attempt to develop a standard psychiatric interview. Before the Woodworth, the only substantial tool available for assessing personality was the interview, which was most commonly employed by psychiatrists in determining an individual's emotional stability. The Woodworth attempted to specify a number of questions common to the psychiatric interview and to put these questions in paper-and-pencil form.

Interview techniques are commonly used in conjunction with objective and projective tests in the assessment of personality. Like the tests themselves, interview techniques have improved, and considerable data have accumulated in recent years concerning the nature of the interview (e.g., Marsden, 1971; Wiens, 1976). The evidence suggests that effective interviews are those in which the interviewer is able to display such attitudes as warmth, involvement, interest, and commitment (Orlinsky and Howard, 1967; Saccuzzo, 1975; Tyler, 1969). It is also important for the interviewer to communicate a feeling of empathy or understanding to the person being interviewed (e.g., Truax and Mitchell, 1971). The success of the interview has been shown to be related to the feelings, mood, nonverbal behavior, and even activity level of the interviewer (Bandura, 1971; Heller, Davis, and Myers, 1966). Good interviewers tend to remain calm, relaxed, and confident throughout the interview, while communicating interest, concern, and a sense of mutual sharing.

Although much is known about effective interviewing, there is no standard or universally accepted method for conducting an interview. As a result, interviewers have practically unlimited opportunity to explore any area they believe will aid in the assessment of personality. Interviews vary from the highly structured to the totally unstructured. In the most structured type of interview, the interviewer asks the same set of questions in a particular order. This type of interview is much like a test such as the Woodworth except that the examiner reads the questions and then records the responses. A totally unstructured interview, on the other hand, might begin anywhere, proceed in any direction, change topic at any time, and focus on whatever content the interviewer wishes.

There are little available data concerning the long-term reliability and validity of conclusions based solely on interview data. The variety of interview procedures, the wide differences among interviewers, and the unlimited focus of interviews have limited researchers' ability to produce convincing results concerning the interview's value. There is general consensus, however, that the less structured the interview, the less reliable the information it yields (Wiens, 1976). The less structured the interview, the greater the inconsistency between the information obtained by different interviewers. If different questions are asked with different goals in mind, then the results cannot help but be different. On the other hand, it is difficult to conceive how even the most structured interview can be any more reliable than the best-constructed personality test. At best, an interview might approach the reliability of personality tests, but no real evidence exists that this is the case.

Among the problems of assessing personality via interview is that the interviewer can and does affect the verbal (Greenspoon, 1962) as well as the nonverbal (Matarazzo, Wiens, Matarazzo, and Saslow, 1968) behavior of the person being interviewed (see also Matarazzo and Wiens, 1972). The interviewer can influence the interviewee through subtle expression of interest, approval, or disapproval conveyed by movements of the head and the body, and by voice intonation—without either interviewer or interviewee being aware of the interaction or its effects. Also, a specific explanation or theory held by the interviewer may create a set in which those beliefs are artificially confirmed. As a result, the validity of interview data is often suspect.

The interview is a valuable tool that will no doubt continue to play a role in efforts to assess human personality. However, in providing the most flexible method for assessing individuals, the interview is grossly limited in terms of the true meaning of its results. In its major strength also lies its most serious weakness. Consequently, even though our knowledge of it has grown rapidly in the last two decades, the interview, like traditional personality tests, leaves much to be desired in the area of personality assessment.

Self-Report

Earlier in this chapter we examined a few different scales in which people report on their own behavior. Various inventories make use of this technique. Let's also consider asking people about their own behaviors. For instance, "How many hours did you study for the last exam in this course?" A person may answer honestly, may distort his or her answer to look better (social desirability), or may simply have no real answer and just guess. An interesting example of this type of distortion is revealed in a study in which heterosexual men and women are asked how many sexual partners they have had. When there is a slight possibility of the answers being revealed, men report more partners than women, with means of 3.7 for men versus 2.6 for women. When participants are told they are hooked up to a fake lie detector, men and women report a nearly equal number of partners, 4.0 for men and 4.4 for women (Alexander and Fischer, 2003).

Many of the objective measures discussed earlier in the chapter are considered self-report inventories. Although these measures are still subject to problems of distortion or other errors, they are used frequently because they are reliable, cheap, fast, and easy. The person reporting probably has the best source of knowledge; no one has as much knowledge about himself or herself as that person. The person knows the last time he or she picked up a textbook and how confident he or she feels about the exam.

Observers

Having other people report on a person's behavior or traits allows us to avoid some of the distortion that is problematic in self-report data. We should consider two different types of observers: trained observers and informal, untrained observers who know the person. Trained observers will carefully observe the participant and code for each instance of the criterion behavior. For instance, if we want to know about a person's extraversion, coders may indicate each time a person talks to someone else. The coding may happen as the communication is happening, or the communication may be recorded and coded later. An advantage of the recording is that it can be slowed down if necessary, and it preserves a record of the behavior. Inter-rater reliability can vary, but with careful definitions of behaviors and observation, it can be quite high.

Informal observers are typically people who know the person well—for instance, parents, partners, or teachers. Again, consider assessing extraversion: a teacher would have a good sense of which children in his or her classroom are extraverted and which children are introverted. The teacher may be asked to rank order the children in the class from most extraverted to least extraverted. A person's roommate may be a good source of information about how much time that person spends studying. A person's spouse may be a good source of information about whether that person spends a lot of time worrying. In these cases there is less concern about the person presenting himself or herself well, but the observers may not know everything that is being asked. A roommate may assume that the time that person is in the library is spent studying, not socializing. This approach gains the advantage of removing some types of distortion, while introducing other types of errors.

Physiological Assessment

physiological assessment
Measurement of changes in bodily processes that presumably reflect changes in psychological states.

skin conductance
Measurement of relatively small changes in the electrical characteristics of the skin related to sweating and therefore is frequently used as an indicator of emotional arousal or anxiety.

The rationale for **physiological assessment** is that changes in bodily processes reflect changes in psychological, particularly emotional, states (Kallman and Feuerstein, 1977). The autonomic nervous system would be expected to change as a result of one's emotional state. Changes in heart rate, blood pressure, and **skin conductance** would likely be observed. Skin conductance measures relatively small changes in the electrical characteristics of the skin related to sweating and therefore is frequently used as an indicator of emotional arousal or anxiety. While self-descriptions of emotional states and even actions can be altered to disguise true feelings, it is extremely difficult to control one's skin conductance or other physiological responses.

Hormonal assays allow researchers to measure hormone levels that may be associated with aspects of personality. The hormones oxytocin, testosterone, progesterone, and estrogen would be expected to be correlated with a variety of behaviors. For instance, the hormone cortisol is strongly associated with stress reactions. It might be expected that people who score higher on measures of anxiety are also likely to show higher levels of cortisol (Schlotz, Schulz, Hellhammer, Stone, and Hellhammer, 2006). Hormones can be measured by drawing blood or even by having people spit into test tubes. The collected specimen then has to be carefully analyzed for the level of the hormone of interest. Assays of hormones have rapidly become cheaper and easier than in the past.

The study of the brain has advanced remarkably in the past few decades. The earliest brain technique was **electroencephalography** (EEG). EEG used small electrodes held against the skin of the head to measure the small electrical impulses caused by neuronal activity. Among the most popular of the recent developments in brain imaging is functional magnetic resonance imaging (fMRI). Blood flow changes in the brain are assumed to be associated with increased activity in that portion of the brain; this activity is then picked up by the fMRI. The fMRI is performed using a large, expensive machine, which has little space for the person to do much except to lie down. Despite those limitations, fMRI research is increasingly used in published research. At least one research team has reported good test-retest reliability in brain activity as measured by fMRI (Wu, Samanez-Larkin, Katovich, and Knutson, 2014).

Physiological measures require assessment of reliability and validity no less than any other measure. There can be a tendency to see these measures as more "scientific" and somehow more valid than other measures. That is a form of face validity, so it will be important for us as researchers and consumers of science to carefully examine whether the other important parts of reliability and validity are developed for these physiological measures.

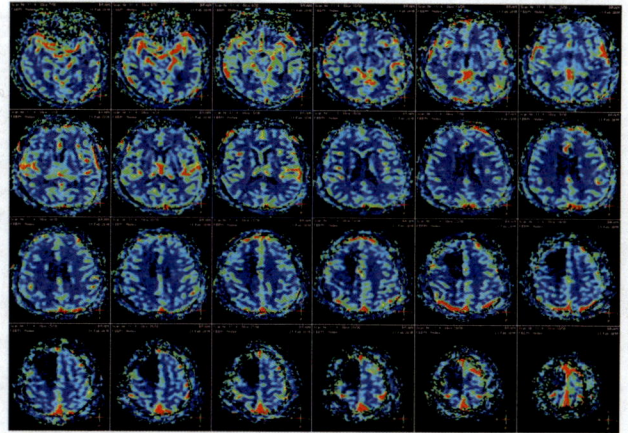

FIGURE 8.3 Brain Scans Using fMRI

As a region of the brain is more active, it lights up in the scan.

Source: AkeSak/Shutterstock.com

electroencephalography A measurement of brain activity conducted by measuring electrical impulses between neurons.

Summary

1. Psychologists measuring personality typically assume that personality traits are stable and general (exhibited regardless of situation).

2. *Objective* personality tests provide a set of responses to a particular item, to which the test taker responds by selecting the most appropriate alternative. The construction of the test may be guided by *face validity*, empirical evidence, or the search for underlying structure (*factor analytic* instruments).

3. Tests having face validity suffer from a number of problems because items may be interpreted differently or not honestly answered by the respondents.

There may be a tendency to answer in a way that reflects most favorably on the self (*social desirability*). In addition, response biases have been identified, such as *acquiescence* (agreeing with an item regardless of its content) and *oppositional bias* (disagreeing with an item regardless of its content).

4. Tests based on *empirical* approaches first identify groups that differ on a particular behavior or set of behaviors. Items given to both groups that are differentially endorsed are then included in the measuring instrument, regardless of the specific content or meaning of that item.

5. The *MMPI* is the most widely used of the empirically based questionnaires. In addition to ten clinical scales, the MMPI includes several validity scales. A new form, the *MMPI-2*, is now available.

6. *Factor analysis* is a statistical method that enables the investigator to identify the fundamental aspects of personality. Instruments by Cattell or based on the Five Factor Model are among the best-known factor-analytic batteries.

7. In *projective tests*, the test taker spontaneously produces a response, such as a story, for which scoring is often subjective. Projective tests are based on the assumption that a person's response to an ambiguous stimulus reflects his or her own needs and conflicts.

8. The *Rorschach Inkblot Test* was the first formal projective instrument. The validity of this test is questionable, although it appears to have validity for the assessment of personality characteristics like self-control and ego strength.

9. In the *Thematic Apperception Test (TAT)*, one of the most widely used projective instruments, the subject tells stories about a set of somewhat ambiguous pictures. As with the Rorschach, the validity of the TAT is unclear.

10. In *Self-report* a person reports on his or her own behaviors, feelings, or beliefs. Self-report is useful because a person knows himself or herself best, but the report may be subject to distortions.

11. *Observers* can report on a person's behavior and be less subject to social desirability distortions, but observers often have less information about the subject of the observation.

12. *Physiological measures* can measure physiological state, hormones, or brain activity. It is believed that these measures correlate with other measures of personality.

Key Terms

Big Five (p. 147)
electroencephalography (p. 155)
face validity (p. 143)
factor analysis (p. 146)
physiological assessment (p. 154)
response bias (p. 143)

skin conductance (p. 154)
social desirability (p. 143)
source traits (p. 146)
surface traits (p. 146)
traits (p. 141)

Thought Questions

1. Why do you think personality measures have low long-term reliability? Is personality unstable, or does the fault lie in the measures? If the latter, what might these faults be?

2. Can you think of a time when you were less than completely honest on a personality test, or when you answered in a socially desirable manner? Under what conditions are these types of responses most likely?

3. Different factor-analytic batteries tend to find different underlying personality structures. Do you think that there are certain basic aspects of personality that describe all individuals? What do you think they are?

4. Tell a story about the TAT picture shown in this chapter. Do you think that your response is meaningful and reveals your current needs and conflicts?

Traits, Situations, and Their Interaction

CHAPTER 9

Chapter Outline

Personality Types

Trait Theories

Trait and Situational Theories

Alternative Assessment Strategies

Trait Psychology Revisited

Source: mimagephotography/Shutterstock

Suppose that someone is about to introduce you to one of her best friends. A common inquiry in such circumstances is "What is she like?" In other words, what traits characterize her? Is she kind, aggressive, honest? Traits provide us with convenient methods of organizing information about others, of describing how they have behaved in the past, and of making predictions about how they will behave in the future (Jones and Nisbett, 1971; Kelley, 1967). Throughout the history of the study of personality, considerable effort has been devoted to building taxonomies of traits, developing methods for measuring traits, and finding the ways in which groups of traits cluster together. Indeed, the very concept of personality assumes that there are characteristics or traits that remain stable over time.

As described in Chapter 2, an important critique of trait psychology appeared with the publication of Mischel's (1968) book, *Personality and Assessment*. Mischel's review of the personality literature indicated that personality measures were very poor at predicting behavior in specific situations. Following the publication of Mischel's book, the field of personality had to rethink many of its most basic assumptions. This improved measurement and led to a better understanding of when traits predict behavior.

In this chapter, we first consider attempts to classify different kinds of human personalities in terms of types. We then consider some of the most influential attempts to classify personality in terms of *traits*, those of Cattell, Eysenck, and the Big Five model. From there, we move on to consider the debate over the, usefulness of trait notions.

Personality Types

The origins of theories of personality go back to Hippocrates and later Galen. Galen suggested there were four personality types associated with the four bodily fluids (humors) as well as with the four physical elements (see Table 9.1 and Highlight 9.1). The belief in a relationship between body type and personality has persisted into the present (see also Chapter 1). Toward the end of the nineteenth century, a German psychiatrist (Kretschmer, 1925) argued that people who were thin had a tendency to become schizophrenic, while those who were fat were more likely to develop manic depression. A more recent and better-known effort regarding body types was that of William Sheldon (1954; Sheldon and Stevens, 1942). Sheldon had people rated according to three physical structure types and then attempted to relate these body types to temperaments. Sheldon reported that people who had *mesomorphic* physiques (strong, athletic, and muscular) tended to have somatotonic temperaments (energetic, assertive, and courageous). *Endomorphic* body builds (soft, round, and with large stomachs) were associated with viscerotonic personalities (relaxed, gregarious, and food-loving). *Ectomorphic* physiques (tall, thin, and fragile) were common among cerebrotonic personality **types** (fearful, introverted, and restrained).

In Sheldon's investigations, individuals were photographed and rated on the extent to which they possessed each of the three body types. Untrained observers then rated the personality characteristics of these same people. Sheldon then found correlations between the physique and personality ratings. However, these findings have been questioned because the raters may have been biased by predominant contemporary stereotypes, such as that round body types are jolly and athletic body types are aggressive. In fact, studies

types Enduring individual differences in behavior disposition. These differences are thought to be arranged as a set of very few discrete categories.

TABLE 9.1 Relationship between Bodily Humors, Personality Types, and Elements, as Suggested by Galen

Bodily humor	Personality type	Characteristics	Elements
Yellow bile	Choleric	Irritable	Fire
Black bile	Melancholic	Depressed	Earth
Blood	Sanguine	Optimistic	Air
Phlegm	Phlegmatic	Calm; listless	Water

HIGHLIGHT 9.1

Elements and Temperament

The four physical elements identified by the Greeks—earth, air, fire, and water—were arranged according to the doctrine of opposites. Fire was perceived as the opposite of water, and earth as the opposite of air. As indicated in Table 9.1, each element was associated with a particular fluid and temperament. These associations were the basis of the prime theory of individual differences throughout the Middle Ages, and the distinctions are still persistent today. For example, literary critics have analyzed the elements predominant in the works of famous writers. It has been suggested that Nietzsche focused on air imagery, Flaubert on earth, and Poe on water.

Perhaps surprisingly, the associations postulated by Galen between elements and temperament have given rise to some research (Martindale and Martindale, 1988). These investigators asked subjects to combine adjective descriptions of the four temperaments (see Table 9.1) with words representing typical forms of the four elements. The college-aged subjects did combine the words by sorting them into piles in a manner consistent with the model proposed by Galen and the Greeks. For example, the pile containing words related to water (e.g., bath, ocean, rain) also included adjectives such as calm, controlled, and unemotional. It should not come as a surprise that someone who is choleric would be "full of piss and vinegar" and have a fiery temper.

in which individuals are rated on specific behaviors rather than on global traits tend not to show strong associations between body types and personality (Mischel, 1968).

Jung (see Chapter 4) believed that introversion and extroversion are both present in each individual, and he speculated that one of these dispositions would be dominant. Thus, he felt it appropriate to categorize individuals as primarily introverts or extroverts. Nevertheless, typologies like those proposed by Sheldon and Jung are used less frequently in current psychology. The complexity of human behavior makes it difficult to fit individuals neatly into a few simple categories. The description of someone as introverted or extroverted gives us too little information about the person. For most personality characteristics, people fit at some point on a **continuous distribution** of that characteristic rather than into the either-or categories provided by type concepts. A more scientific extension of the typology approach is represented in the work of trait-oriented psychologists.

Trait Theories

There have been many psychologists who have believed that personality is best understood by studying the organization of traits within an individual. Perhaps the most influential of the trait psychologists was Gordon Allport. Trait psychologists believe that there are characteristics of individuals that remain consistent over time and across situations. If you are an aggressive person, for example, trait theories imply that you will be aggressive in many different settings. In their study of behavior, trait psychologists use a trait as the unit of analysis or the basic focus of examination. Their task is to determine which traits occur together and how patterns of traits are organized within an individual. This taxonomic approach shares with the periodic table in chemistry the goal of identifying basic elements and expressing all compounds (traits) as elements or amalgams of the basic factors.

Cattell and Factor Analysis

To study the organization of traits, many psychologists have turned to complex statistical methods such as **factor analysis**, discussed in the previous chapter. The work of Raymond Cattell (1965) is among the best-known work of this type. In his search for the basic elements of personality, Cattell performed extensive factor analyses of three types of data: life records (ratings of behavior in everyday situations), self-ratings on personality scales, and scores on objective tests. To determine the nature and the organization of traits, Cattell first examined a list of 4,500 trait names and then reduced this list to less than 200 by grouping synonyms or near-synonyms. Then scores were obtained on the degree to which individuals possessed these traits, and the results were factor analyzed. This procedure yielded 36 *surface traits* (clusters of responses or overt behaviors that fit together) and a smaller number of *source traits* (more basic organizing structures that underlie and determine surface traits).

Various investigations by Cattell using life record and self-report data have produced a similar list of basic traits. Cattell had a fondness for coining words, to the extent that his technical titles needed to be translated into more popular labels. For example, the trait label *premsia* is short for "protected emotional sensitivity."

Most of Cattell's research was directed toward the identification of source traits, some of which he has called *environment mold traits*, or traits formed by the environment. Others, determined by factors within the individual, are called *constitutional source traits*. Another distinction Cattell made was between *specific* source traits, which describe how a person operates in a particular situation, and *general* source traits, which affect behavior in many different situations. Thus, in interpreting his factor analytic findings, the idea of trait consistency remains fundamental to Cattell's work and is reflected in the concept of a general source trait.

Eysenck's Hierarchy

Hans J. Eysenck is one of the more controversial figures in contemporary psychology. In his many active years as a psychologist, he took strong positions against traditional

continuous distribution There are many different gradations between the extremes of a scale. This is in contrast to discrete distributions that allow only a set number of possibilities. Traits are typically considered to have a continuous distribution; types are considered to have a discrete distribution.

factor analysis A statistical method of reducing a large amount of data from tests, rating scales, or behavioral observations to a smaller and presumably more basic number of dimensions of personality factors.

psychotherapy (Eysenck, 1952), was one of the earliest advocates of behavior therapy, and strongly supported the notion of intelligence as an inherited trait.

Eysenck's view of personality is in many ways similar to Cattell's, with behavior viewed hierarchically. At the bottom of the hierarchy are the *specific responses* that are actually observed. Just above these are *habitual responses*. *Traits*, at the next level of the pyramid, are analogous to Cattell's source traits, and at the top level are types. *Types* for Eysenck are basic behavior dimensions which are continuous rather than typological categories. Eysenck identified three types or dimensions that he regarded as the basic units of personality: neuroticism, extroversion-introversion, and psychoticism.

Using a variety of data sources, such as ratings, questionnaires, and physiological measures, Eysenck repeatedly identified the same dimensions in factor analytic studies. Most of his attention was devoted to classifying people along the dimensions of neuroticism and extroversion-introversion. Since neuroticism can be viewed as corresponding to emotional stability, individuals were classified along a continuum from stable to unstable. An unstable personality is seen as moody, touchy, anxious, and restless, while a stable person is characterized as calm, even-tempered, and carefree. With regard to extroversion and introversion, extroverts are seen as sociable, active, outgoing, and optimistic, while introverts are characterized as passive, quiet, careful, and unsociable. In many respects, the basic personality dimensions identified by Eysenck are similar to those described by Cattell. Eysenck acknowledged this but also contended that his approach was more dependable and more theoretically meaningful and parsimonious.

As mentioned in Chapter 1, Eysenck believed that the differences in introversion and extraversion were due to differences in the reactivity of a brain structure called the **ascending reticular activating system** (ARAS, or RAS). The ARAS is one of the systems responsible for alertness and arousal. Organisms (including humans) have a particular range of comfortable arousal. Too much or too little arousal is aversive, so humans seek out a comfortable level of arousal. Eysenck suggests that ARAS is chronically more aroused in introverts, and that stimuli are more arousing for introverts. Thus, for introverts, it does not take much environmental stimulation to reach a comfortable level of arousal. Extraverts, on the other hand, need more environmental stimulation to reach their comfortable state of arousal.

ascending reticular activating system A neuronal circuit responsible for wakefulness and associated with attention. Eysenck's model suggests that differences in introversion and extraversion are based on the underlying responsivity of this system. In this model, introverts have a more responsive system.

behavioral activation system A system that is sensitive to signals about the likelihood of reinforcement.

behavioral inhibition system A system that is sensitive to signals about the likelihood of punishment.

Gray and BAS and BIS

Gray, who was a student of Eysenck's, suggests a reorientation of Eysenck's dimensions of extraversion and neuroticism. Gray (1981) suggests that people differ in their sensitivity signals about reinforcements and punishments. In this model, there are two different systems: the **behavioral activation system** (BAS) and the **behavioral inhibition system** (BIS). The BAS is the system that is sensitive to signals about reinforcement. When the BAS notices signals about reinforcement, it activates behaviors in service of seeking that reinforcement. The BIS is the system that is sensitive to signals about punishment. When the BIS notices signals about punishment, behavior will be inhibited.

Consider a few college friends on a Thursday night who have been invited to a party but have exams on Friday. One friend may have a really strong behavioral activation and can sense all the positive things about going to the party, which is an extraverted behavior. That friend is not going to worry about the exam. This would be high extraversion and low neuroticism in the Eysenck model, and high BAS and low BIS in the Gray model. Another friend doesn't see any point in going to the party, since it will be loud, crowded, and she won't know anyone; plus, there is an exam. This would be

In Gray's model, people who have high behavioral activation and low behavioral inhibition are likely to choose rewarding activities even if there may be negative consequences by doing so. Even if there is an exam the next day, a party will seem like a good idea.

Source: View Apart/Shutterstock

low BAS and high BIS in the Gray model. Finally, there is the friend who can't wait to go to the party, excited that she will new meet people and dance, but then can't have any fun while she is there because she is so concerned about the exam the next day. This would be high BAS and high BIS in Gray's model.

Congruent with this model, Larsen and Kettelaar (1991) found that people high in extraversion, compared to people low in extraversion, react more strongly to a positive mood induction and people high in neuroticism, compared to low neuroticism, react more strongly to a negative mood induction. It also appears that people who measure as high on BAS (Carver and White, 1994) process anxiety-related tasks more efficiently in the anterior cingulate nucleus and left lateral prefrontal cortex according to fMRI measures (Gray and Burgess, 2004). Again, we have a suggestion of a brain structure associated with these personality traits.

The Big Five

More recently, a number of researchers have converged on the idea that there are five basic trait dimensions to personality. This concept is increasingly referred to as the **Big Five** model of personality. Sometimes this concept is known as the **Five Factor Model** (FFM). For our purposes, we will not differentiate between the two and will use the term Big Five.

The development of the Big Five model has its roots in the analysis of natural, everyday language (John, 1990). This is often known as the **lexical hypothesis**, the idea that important concepts will be represented within the language. A number of investigators over the years have collected words from the dictionary that represent personality traits (e.g., *strong-willed, assertive, introspective*) and then, using factor analysis, have sorted them into categories. Five factors have frequently appeared.

Others have arrived at a five-factor solution by factor analyses of personality tests. In a personality test, the subject rates the degree to which a statement describes someone. One of the most well known examples of this type of research is the work of McCrae and Costa (1990; 2008), who have developed their "NEO-PI-R" personality inventory to measure their version of the Big Five. McCrae and Costa's five factors are: Neuroticism, Extraversion, Openness to Experience, Agreeableness, and Conscientiousness. The factors are often labeled with one aspect of the trait, but recognize that there is also the other end of the dimension. The following list describes the basics of each of these five factors.

1. Neuroticism (versus emotional stability). People high on this scale may manifest anxiety, angry hostility, depression, self-consciousness, impulsivity, or vulnerability.
2. Extraversion (versus introversion). People high on this scale might be sociable, talkative, active, person-oriented, optimistic, or fun-loving. People low on this scale might be reserved, independent, quiet, or aloof.
3. Openness to experience (versus conventional). People high on this scale are imaginative, curious, and willing to entertain novel ideas. They experience a whole spectrum of emotions. People low on this scale tend to be conventional, conservative, and set in their ways.
4. Agreeableness (versus cold/hostile). People high on this scale tend to be good natured, altruistic, helpful, forgiving, and trusting. People low on this scale tend to be suspicious, uncooperative, irritable, cynical, or rude.
5. Conscientiousness (versus careless/unreliable). People high on this scale tend to be reliable, self-directed, punctual, scrupulous, ambitious, and hard-working. People low on this scale tend to be aimless, lazy, lax, negligent, and unreliable.

The identification of these five basic traits has come from two sources: analysis of the *words* and analysis of the *descriptions* that individuals make of themselves and of others. An immediate question that occurs is the degree to which the Big Five represent how the average English-speaking person views personality compared to how people in other cultures view personality. In other words: how universal are these Big Five traits? Past studies have found overall congruence for the Dutch and German languages (Hofstree et al., 1997), as

Big Five Many personality researchers now believe there are five basic personality traits. One popular classification system identifies them as neuroticism versus emotional stability, extraversion, openness to experience, conscientiousness, and agreeableness.

Five Factor Model One of the models that posits that there are five major personality traits: neuroticism, extraversion, openness to experience, conscientiousness, and agreeableness.

lexical hypothesis The idea that important concepts will be part of the language, and by examining language researchers will then be able to discover those important components.

A person who is conscientious is going to be hard-working and reliable. This is the kind of person you want working with you on a group project.

well as for Japan and China (John, 1990). Neuroticism and extraversion have been replicated for languages of the Solomon Islands and of India. De Raad (1992) found congruence between the Big Five and Dutch adjectives and nouns, but not as much support for Dutch verbs. In a subsequent analysis, De Raad and his colleagues (2010) found relatively strong support for three dimensions of personality across twelve different languages. These three dimensions were extraversion, agreeableness, and conscientiousness. John (1990) notes that the weakest evidence for universality is found for openness to experience. However, the overall results are encouraging for some degree of universality.

Big Five advocates view these traits as the basic structure of personality. However, if you look at the descriptions of the five factors, you will note that each broad factor includes a number of more specific traits. For instance, neuroticism includes such disparate emotional states as anxiety, hostility, and depression. Conscientiousness includes being reliable and punctual but also

facets Components that are subfactors that make up a factor in the Five Factor Model.

being ambitious and self-directed. This is because the five factors are conceived of as being *broad band* personality traits. That is, they are seen as forming the *general* underlying structure of personality, even though they encompass many more *specific* traits. For instance, the NEO PI-R (Costa & McCrae, 2008) has several **facets** for each of the five dimensions. John (1990) notes that the Big Five is similar to taxonomies in the natural world. The five factors are equivalent to terms such as *plant* and *animal*. Under *animal*, for instance, we have lions, tigers, dogs, and so on. In a similar manner, under *conscientiousness* we have *ambitious* and *reliable*. Advocates of the Big Five do not mean to imply that personality can be described *only* in terms of these five traits any more than the world of living beings can be described only in terms of plants and animals. In fact, many Big Five advocates have said that in order to actually predict an individual's behavior, the Big Five is too broad and general. One needs measures of the more specific traits within each factor.

Criticisms of the Big Five

While writers such as McCrae and John (1992) have argued that the field should now assume that the five-factor model is the correct representation of personality trait structure and move on to using it to explore other topics, there are those (e.g., Block, 1995; 2010) who believe that this conclusion is premature. Others, such as Eysenck and Cattell, whose personality tests are respectively based on three, and sixteen factors, respectively, would agree. We shall briefly note some of the criticisms Block has raised concerning the Big Five.

First, advocates of the Big Five have argued that one of the strongest sources of evidence for the existence of the Big Five is that it has been found *empirically*. That is, it was not based on someone's theoretical preconceptions, but simply found by factor analyzing words and sentences people use to describe other people. However, Block has noted that before these factor analyses were done, investigators had made numerous assumptions that may well have biased the outcome in favor of finding five factors.

Second, while many investigators have found five factors, they are not the *same* five factors. Block notes some important discrepancies among the various five-factor models. For instance, McCrae and Costa place *warmth* under *extraversion*, but Goldberg (another five-factor theorist) places it under *agreeableness*. They place *impulsivity* in *neuroticism*, but Goldberg places it in *extraversion*.

Third, while advocates of the Big Five claim that five factors consistently emerge, others have disagreed. We have already mentioned that Cattell bases his personality test on

Honesty

1. _____
2. _____
3. _____
4. _____
5. _____

Honesty is added to variations on the other five traits in the HEXACO model of personality traits.

sixteen factors and that Eysenck claims there are three main factors. Block's analysis of the personality assessment device he uses, the California Q Sort, finds eight factors. Hogan and Hogan (1992) have found that they must use six factors to describe their data adequately. Block argues that this suggests that there are important aspects of personality that are not being encompassed by the Big Five.

Despite criticisms, there is much enthusiasm for the Big Five model of personality. Only further research will clarify whether that enthusiasm is well founded.

Although trait and type classifications are commonly recognized by psychologist and layperson alike, their value has been a matter of serious debate. The next section of this chapter examines the attack on traditional trait psychology and introduces some new approaches to personality assessment that have arisen out of this debate.

Beyond Five Dimensions

When considering five dimensions to describe personality, it is certainly likely that particular facets or domains may be left out of the model. Consider a person's attitude about sexuality. There are individual differences about sexuality that are not well captured in the five dimensions (Shafer, 2001). Or, consider honesty. Is it a facet of conscientiousness? A really talented embezzler is likely to be very conscientious but dishonest.

One of the major alternatives to the Big Five is a model known as HEXACO (Lee & Ashton, 2004). The HEXACO model adds an honesty-humility factor that includes aspects of personality like trustworthiness, lack of greed, and modesty. The HEXACO model includes the usual extraversion, agreeableness, and conscientiousness. Their cross language data suggests that neuroticism is better interpreted as emotional vulnerability (Ashton et al., 2004). The last factor is a combination of intellect/imagination/unconventionality (Ashton et al., 2004; p. 363). The honesty-humility dimension is positively correlated with the proclivity to apologize (Dunlop et al., 2015) and negatively correlated with the use of impression management strategies in the workplace (Bourdage et al., 2015).

Trait and Situational Theories

Mischel's Argument

Mischel's (1968) book on the assessment of personality has often been interpreted as an all-out attack on the concept of traits. Mischel (2009), however, repeatedly denied this extreme position. Rather, he maintained that the evidence for the existence of traits is weak and that the methods for their assessment need reevaluation. Furthermore, he acknowledged the value of cognitive traits, such as intelligence and speed of processing and encoding information.

The essence of Mischel's argument is that trait measures are not valid predictors of behavior in specific situations. Although personality tests do well at predicting how people will score on similar personality tests, they do poorly at predicting how someone will actually behave in a given situation. One finds that questionnaire and projective measures of aggression are not very effective predictors of an individual's aggressive behavior on the athletic field, in confrontations with authority, in response to a friend's arriving late for an appointment, and in a myriad of other concrete situations in which variations in aggressive behavior can be observed. Moreover, observational measures of aggression are not very effective in predicting aggressive behaviors in situations other than the one in which aggression was initially assessed. Similar low predictability of behaviors in specific situations can be found for measures of impulsivity, achievement motivation, anxiety, and other personality characteristics. It can be maintained that if such tests are really meaningful, they should be able to forecast how people will behave in the specific tasks that psychologists create for laboratory studies.

Mischel reported that many investigations demonstrate that the correlation between test scores and behavior in specific situations is rarely greater than .30, or that around 91 percent of the variance in behavior is unexplained by the test score. Mischel called

Source: Borjaika/Shutterstock

Measured traits may not be good predictors of behavior from situation to situation.

these low correlations *personality coefficients* and suggested that knowledge of personal characteristics tells us little about how a person will actually behave. Mischel was more impressed with the amount of variation that would be explained by knowing about the situation in which the behavior is observed, rather than knowing about the person in that situation. Thus, he championed what is known as the **situational critique** of the concept of traits.

Mischel's original position led to many responses, some in support, others in contradiction. Below we consider other positions in response to his critique of traits.

situational critique The idea that the situation is a better predictor of an individual's behavior than personality.

Attribution Theory

Another perspective suggesting the need to modify traditional trait theories derives from **attribution theory**. Originally, attribution theory was primarily concerned with the judgments people make about others, particularly their inferences about others' intentions. However, research in this area now covers all aspects of how people attempt to understand the causes of events in their lives.

The basic ideas of attribution theory were first formulated in the mid-1940s and 1950s (Heider, 1944, 1958) but came to prominence decades later (Jones and Davis, 1965; Kelley, 1967). Kelley offered a model to capture how the layperson determines causation. He suggested that events are perceived as caused by three potential sources: persons, entities (aspects of the environment), or circumstances. To determine which of these, or which combination of sources, has caused an event, the person uses three criteria called distinctiveness, consensus, and consistency. If, for example, we wanted to explain why John enjoys the food at a particular restaurant so much, it would be helpful to ask if he always feels this way in restaurants (distinctiveness), whether others in the same restaurant also enjoy the food (consensus), and whether John enjoyed the food when he ate in this restaurant before (consistency). If all people enjoy the food in this eating establishment, then John's enjoyment would be attributed to the entity (it is a good restaurant); if John always enjoys food at restaurants, then the enjoyment would be attributed to him (he is a glutton); if John usually dislikes this restaurant, then his present enjoyment would be ascribed to special circumstances, such as unusual hunger, the presence of friends, or some special dish (Kelley, 1967; Orvis, Cunningham, and Kelley, 1975).

Jones and Nisbett (1971) have suggested that the selection of a trait or a situational explanation for behavior also depends on the role played by the person making the judgment. When people are observers and are making judgments about others, they tend to use dispositional or trait explanations. However, they use fewer trait concepts and more situational concepts to explain their own behavior. Thus, one might say, "You hit him because

attribution theory A theoretical approach based on the view that people attempt to explain and understand behavioral events through attributing the causes of those events to characteristics of the person or to factors in the environment; these causal ascriptions significantly influence goal expectancies and behavioral responses.

you are aggressive" (a trait explanation), but, "I hit him because he did something wrong" (a situation explanation). Thus, we are likely to use the traits to explain other people's behavior. Consequently, we see their behavior as due to that consistent trait.

Why should there be a difference between the attributions of actors and observers? Jones and Nisbett suggest that this is so because people know more about their own behavior than they know about the behavior of others. Searching through memories, a person can recall behaving differently in many different situations in the past. Information regarding the distinctiveness and inconsistency of behavior fosters situation attributions. Note, however, that this analysis assumes that individuals find little consistency in their behaviors across situations. Observers, on the other hand, are less likely to have the information available about others to rule out situational causes of behavior, and therefore make trait attributions for other people.

A classic demonstration of the actor-observer bias comes from Storms (1973). Participants were filmed, then shown that film of their own behavior from the perspective that other people would have. When a person views him- or herself from the viewpoint of other people, he or she tends to use trait explanations for his or her own behaviors, when typically this person would use a situational explanation.

Attribution Theory and Trait Psychology

Attribution theorists have not been concerned with the inadequacy of traditional trait tests for predicting behavior. Rather, traits are important because people use them to describe the behavior of others; they are part of the implicit or "naive" psychology that the layperson uses (see Chapter 6). Extensive research has demonstrated that both laypeople and experienced clinical psychologists favor explaining behavior in terms of enduring dispositions, instead of in terms of the situation. The tendency to overestimate the importance of traits and underestimate the importance of the situation in causing behavior has been labeled the **fundamental attributional error** (Ross, 1977).

Indeed, it appears that our first, relatively automatic reaction is to attribute what a person does to his or her traits. Only with conscious effort and thought do we take the situation into account (Gilbert, 1989). Gilbert has argued that when we are under cognitive load, we are more likely to ignore situational contributions to behavior and to overattribute the behavior to an individual's personality traits.

For instance, in a study by Gilbert, Pelham, and Krull (1988), subjects watched a silent videotape of a woman engaged in conversation with a stranger. The woman exhibited various visual signs of distress and anxiety: tapping her fingers, twirling her hair, biting her nails. In one condition, where subjects were told that the woman had been asked to talk about her sexual fantasies, it was assumed that the subjects would attribute her distress to the *situation*, that is, to having to talk about one's sexual fantasies to a stranger. In another condition, where subjects were told that the woman had been asked to talk about bland topics, it was assumed that the woman's distress would be attributed to her *personality*, that is, the woman acts anxious because she is an anxious person. These differences in behavior attribution were found as long as the subjects were not under stress themselves. However, when subjects had to engage in a memory task as they watched the video, all subjects tended to attribute the woman's anxiety to her personality, as if they had not bothered to take into account whether or not she was in an anxiety-producing situation (e.g., talking about sexual fantasies to a stranger).

Other research even suggests that the manner in which we make judgments about others is not strongly associated with either past experiences or our observations of these others. For example, one study examined peer ratings given by different groups of men (Norman, 1963). One group had lived together in the same fraternity for three years, while another group was less closely associated. Although the two groups had differing amounts of contact, they used very similar dimensions for making judgments about one another. Indeed, these same dimensions of judgment emerge when subjects rate complete strangers (Passini and Norman, 1966). These studies demonstrate that the same dimensions or traits are used to rate others whether or not the subjects are familiar with the people they

fundamental attribution error This is a tendency to attribute behavior of other people to their personality rather than to the situation.

are evaluating. These findings do not necessarily mean that the trait dimensions are being misapplied; rather, they suggest that trait ratings might tell us more about the raters than about the people being rated. But whether or not traits are valuable for understanding behavior, observers *believe* that they are and tend to perceive information in a manner that supports trait interpretations.

Alternative Assessment Strategies

Despite problems with the notion of traits, few psychologists have actually shelved their faith in personality dispositions. While the concept of traits may still have utility, it does appear that a complete reliance on traits is an oversimplification that can lead to incorrect predictions of behavior in a variety of situations. Although there is consistency and constancy in our lives, better measurement techniques are needed to predict future behavior. This requires methodologies that consider and include the evaluations of situations, the interaction of traits and situations, and other approaches to trait assessment.

The Interactionist Position

interactionist position The personality theory that views behavior as governed by both the properties of the person and the situation in which the person is acting.

It is meaningless to ask which is more important when it is evident that behavior is always a joint function of characteristics of the person and of the situation, as was discussed in Chapter 2. This **interactionist position** is a rapprochement between trait and situational approaches to personality assessment which acknowledges the importance of personality dispositions as well as the role of situations.

The interactionist position takes several multiple forms, each with different implications. One such form is the *transactional* approach (Magnusson, 1990). Whenever interaction is described in these terms, it refers to the reciprocal sequence of actions that take place between person and situation. Each situation poses its own demands and cues that tend to call for a particular set of behaviors. The relaxed setting of an informal gathering will elicit very different behaviors than a formal dinner party; the athletic field elicits different responses than the classroom. Each individual brings his or her own set of unique personality traits to each of these situations. These traits influence how the situation is perceived; different people will see different aspects of the situation as most important. Thus, at the dinner party, person A, who is characterized by anxiety over status and acceptance by others, will be oriented to the seating arrangement and to the amount of attention given by the host and hostess; person B, an outdoorsy extrovert, will find the stiffness and formality particularly frustrating.

Following the individual differences in perceptions of situations, people behave on the basis of these perceptions and their behaviors elicit reactions from others. The feedback from these behaviors and reactions will then influence subsequent behaviors. The behavioral outcome that is finally observed is a result of a sequence of reciprocal transactions between the individual, with his or her uniqueness, and the situation, with its uniqueness. This formulation of the trait-situation interaction is consonant with the views of situation-oriented theorists like Mischel, as well as with those of many trait-oriented theorists (Endler and Magnusson, 1976; Magnusson and Endler, 1977).

There is a common but more limited meaning of the term *interaction* that is also applicable to the trait-situation issue. In the statistical sense, interaction refers to a *differential* effect that the same situation may have on different people or the differential effect of the same disposition in response to different situations. For example, a highly insulting, frustrating situation will elicit more aggressive behavior than a nonfrustrating situation. However, the effects of the frustration are likely to be much more pronounced in individuals who have a strong disposition to respond with anger and aggression than in individuals who are low on this trait dimension. The difference in aggressive behavior between the high-aggressive and low-aggressive individuals under nonfrustrating conditions may be negligible; it is under conditions of frustration that the difference in personality traits becomes evident.

In comparison to the transactional model, the more limited interactional model is easier to investigate. Using this model, evidence for the interactionist position is obtained

Personality and the situation are going to interact to create behavior. The stress of the situation interacts with the woman's personality to create her behavior.

by comparing the proportion of variance in behavior that is explained by the person, by the situation, and by the interaction between person and situation. One might think of this by drawing a pie and dividing it to represent all of the different influences on human behavior. Figure 9.1 shows such a pie. One slice represents the proportion of variance attributable to personality traits; another slice represents the proportion of variance caused by situational influences; and a third slice is for the interaction between situational and dispositional influences. The interaction is due to unique combinations of traits and situations. Careful studies designed for application of the statistical method known as *analysis of variance* have separated the proportion of variance attributable to each of these factors. As shown in Fig. 9. 1, interaction accounts for a larger proportion of the variance in behavior than either person or situation (Magnusson and Endler, 1977).

Although it is revealing that unique combinations of persons and situations explain more of the variation than either influence by itself, the interaction position still explains only some of the behavior of some of the people some of the time (Bem and Allen, 1974). As Fig. 9.1 reveals, the largest slice of the pie is reserved for error variance: the proportion of the total that is not explained in terms of the three specified sources of influence. Although the interaction is a better predictor than either the trait or the situation, it is only slightly better. Thus, there is still a need for measurement methods that can be used to predict more of the people more of the time.

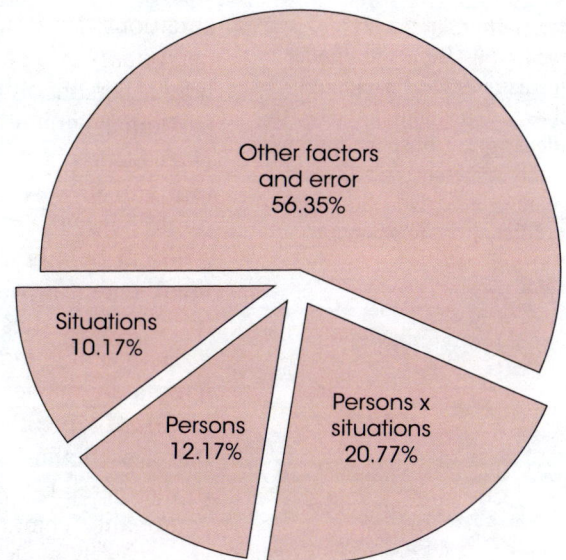

FIGURE 9.1 Factors Influencing Behavior

The Moderator Variable Approach

One solution to the dilemma of accounting for such little variance in predicting behavior from traits is to propose **moderator variables** (i.e., identify factors that are responsible for the lack of predictability of trait indexes) and then take them into account when attempting to predict behavior (see Cheek, 1982). One such moderator proposed by Bem and Allen (1974) is the reported *consistency* of each person's behavior in each domain

moderator variables These would be variables that will change the extent to which measured personality will be predictive of behavior. These could be things like the strength of the situation, or consistency of a particular individual's behavior overall.

of activity. Bem and Allen proposed that some individuals may be very consistent with regard to some personality characteristics, yet very inconsistent with regard to others. That is, some traits characterize some people while other traits characterize other people. And some people might not be characterized by any traits at all!

To demonstrate individual differences in consistency, college students rated whether their behavior would be consistent or inconsistent across different situations for the traits of friendliness and conscientiousness. They then examined the correlations among friendliness measures (self-reports, peers' and parents' reports, and objective behaviors) separately for subjects high and low in self-reported consistency. In accordance with predictions, intercorrelations of friendliness measures were higher for the high consistency group than for those declaring that they were low in consistency. That is, reported consistency moderated the relation between trait indexes and behavior. However, this procedure did not yield the predicted differences in intercorrelations for conscientiousness. In addition, the findings were not replicated by Chaplin and Goldberg (1985) or Paunonen and Jackson (1985).

Guided by this approach, Zuckerman et al. (1988) demonstrated that self-reported consistency as well as subjective trait importance moderates cross-situational consistency. If the individual reports that he or she is highly consistent and the trait has high relevance, then there is cross-situational consistency in behavior and a relation between trait measures and actions. These investigators recommend that psychologists search for an array of moderator variables; predictions of behavior from traits will then be enhanced.

The Template Matching Technique

Subsequently, Bem and Funder (1978) introduced a descriptive system of measurement that could be used to take advantage of the ability to predict our own behavior in particular situations. Their approach, termed the **template-matching technique**, attempts to match personality to a specific template of behavior. To employ the technique, one must specify how a person would behave in a particular situation without any information about the particular person. For example consider the question, "Should Cathy see the movie *The Hurt Locker*?" Perhaps the best way to guide Cathy would be to describe the movie in terms of how several hypothetical people might react to it. People who are squeamish might enjoy the movie but have bad dreams about it for a few nights. People with certain political beliefs might not like it because it presents a specific perspective about our involvement in wars. Cathy can now predict her own reaction to the movie by matching her characteristics with this set of "templates" that have been provided for her.

Bem and Funder (p. 486) proposed that situations can be characterized as sets of template-behavior pairs, with each template being a personality description of how an idealized type of person is specifically expected to behave in that setting. The probability that a particular person will behave in a particular way in a situation will be a function of the match between his or her characteristics and the template. For example, if Cathy's personality characteristics matched the template for those who would hate *War Correspondent*, then she might be best advised to avoid it.

The experiments by Bern and Funder indicated that by asking the appropriate question, it is possible to predict the behavior of more of the people more of the time. This research acknowledged that there are personality characteristics that aid in the prediction of behavior in particular situations and is consistent with the findings of Bem and Allen. The difficulty with this approach is that there are so many potential combinations of persons and situations.

Aggregation Techniques

The fact that behavior varies with situations suggests a strategy for reducing the variability contributed by the situation and maximizing the variability contributed by the person—namely, by averaging, or aggregating, behavior across different situations. This is essentially the strategy used in the development of objective personality tests, which typically have large numbers of items. In general, the larger the number of items, the more reliable the test. For example, each item of the MMPI scale of depression can be assumed to tap a generalized

template-matching technique Bem and Funder's measurement of personality that matches individuals with ideal types (those that are most likely to behave in a given manner in a given situation) to predict specific behaviors.

dimension of depression and also a reaction specific to that item. By using a large number of items, the influence of any single item relative to the general dimension of depression is reduced, and the reliability is thereby enhanced. Epstein (1979, 1980) has cogently argued that situations are analogous to questionnaire items, and that one can enhance the reliability of trait measures and their intercorrelations by averaging across situations.

There has been some controversy regarding the implications of this increased reliability for trait correlations when aggregated over many different situations, for aggregation seems to acknowledge that behavior in a specific situation cannot be predicted from a trait measure. However, a number of investigations have shown that aggregation procedures improve predictions and contribute to stronger trait relationships (Cheek, 1982; Rushton, Brainerd, and Pressley, 1983). For example, the correlation between self-ratings and ratings by fraternity peers on a number of personality dimensions increases as a function of the number of items being rated and the number of raters. When rated by one peer in one situation, the correlation tends to be about .29; when there are three raters for three items, the correlation tends to be about .44.

Measurement Error

Aggregation has been shown to make a difference in the implications of the classic series of studies conducted in the 1920s (Hartshorne and May, 1928, 1929; Hartshorne, May, and Shuttleworth, 1930). This large longitudinal study of honesty remains one of the most thorough and widely cited pieces of research in the field (see Chapter 12). Over the course of six years, a national sample of eight thousand children was repeatedly evaluated on a series of measures of honesty which included cheating during a game, cheating at school, cheating on a take-home exam, taking money, lying, and falsifying records. Epstein (1979) noted that this study is widely cited as evidence that personality is not general because honesty in any specific situation was not found to be a good predictor of honesty in any other specific situation. What is seldom mentioned, however, is that when several measures of honesty are combined into a single score, honesty at one point in time and across situations becomes a very good predictor of honesty at another time and across situations. In sum, the problems of inconsistency across situations and of instability over time may both result from measurement error. More reliable indicators can be created by averaging together behaviors in several situations.

Trait Psychology Revisited

It would now be worthwhile to review the various approaches that have already been examined in this chapter. First, we presented the work of traditional trait psychologists who felt that personality measures accurately assess personality traits. Next, Mischel's challenge to personality tests was presented. Although it appeared to many psychologists that personality was neither stable over time nor consistent across situations, it was also suggested that most people do perceive stable and general personality patterns. Bem and Allen, Bem and Funder, and Epstein have now forced us to reconsider whether the notion of traits was ever completely wrong in the first place.

Again there is a paradox. On the one hand, few people seriously deny the importance of personality characteristics. On the other hand, there is still little evidence that personality tests can predict behavior in particular situations. Nevertheless, many psychologists remain unconvinced by Mischel's critique of trait psychology and believe that personality dimensions can be demonstrated to be meaningful predictors of behavior. In a strong defense of traits and the personality tests used to measure them, it has been acknowledged that poor research does not support the existence of traits but that many well-conducted studies are supportive (Hogan, DeSoto, and Solano, 1977). For example, Gough (1965) demonstrated that the sociability scale of his inventory correlated .73 with delinquency in a study of over ten thousand youths. Other investigators have reported that the creativity of architects as assessed by other architects' ratings can be predicted very well on the basis of a few personality variables (Hall and MacKinnon, 1969).

There is also evidence that behavior patterns are stable. Some studies, in which people's self-reports are monitored over the years, have found that people's views of themselves remain constant. However, consistency in self-perception may not mean consistency in behavior. Without resorting to self-report studies, there are well-conducted longitudinal studies that demonstrate the stability of behavioral patterns (see also Chapter 13). Perhaps the most important of these used a set of data maintained at the University of California, Berkeley. Subjects in this study were first evaluated in junior high school, then again in senior high school, and once again when they were in their midthirties. In all, persons in the sample were rated on 114 personality variables by different observers at three different points in time. The results clearly demonstrated that many personality characteristics are stable. Indeed, between junior and senior high school, nearly 60 percent of the personality characteristics measured remained consistent.

A European study on aggressive behavior in boys produced even more convincing results with regard to personality stability. Over two hundred boys were rated on their tendency to start fights and other characteristics of aggressive behavior. The ratings were obtained when the boys were in the sixth grade and then again three years later. In each case, at least three raters were used. The results showed that aggressive tendencies were quite stable over the three-year period, with a correlation of .66 across the two time periods. When error of measurement was corrected, the correlation became even stronger, reaching a level of .80 (Olweus, 1973, 1974, 1977a, 1977b).

Finally, Funder (1989, 1991; Funder and Colvin, 1991) has forcefully defended the concept of traits. He has shown that if different people who know an individual well rate that individual's personality traits, there is considerable agreement among them. This is true even when the people doing the rating know the individual from different situations in his or her life. For instance, agreement on the item "enjoys aesthetic impressions" had a correlation of .64. In addition, Funder points out there are numerous correlations between trait ratings and specific behaviors. For instance, those individuals who took longest to complete the tests in his studies had been described by acquaintances as "tending to interpret basically simple situations in complex ways." Similarly, those who took the least time had been described by acquaintances as irritable, over-reactive, and prone to give up in the face of adversity.

states Transitory conditions of the organism such as emotions and moods that vary in intensity and fluctuate over time.

traits Enduring individual differences in behavior dispositions. These are typically thought to be arranged as a continuous scale.

State versus Trait

One factor that has been responsible in part for the low correlations between some trait measures and actual behavior is the failure to distinguish between states and traits. **States** refer to transitory conditions of the organism, to emotions and moods that vary in intensity and fluctuate over time, such as anger, panic, depression, and boredom. **Traits** refer to more enduring individual differences in behavior disposition, in the individual's *tendency* to be angry, afraid, depressed, or bored. A clearer understanding of the manifestations of a trait and of the relationship of the trait to behavior is obtained when a state measure is distinguished from a trait measure. This is best exemplified by the extensive amount of research that has been carried out on the distinction between state anxiety and trait anxiety (Spielberger, 1971a, 1971b; Spielberger, Gorsuch, and Lushene, 1970).

The difference between state and trait anxiety is made evident in the different ways in which they are assessed. Items on the state anxiety scale are answered in terms of the *intensity* of the individual's feelings and how the person feels at the moment. For instance, for the item "I am tense," the individual is given a choice among four alternatives ranging from "Not at all" to "Very much so." In contrast, items on the trait anxiety scale are answered in terms of the frequency of the feeling and how the individual generally feels. For example, for the item "I take disappointments

Everyone feels anxious some of the time; that is state anxiety. However, some people are anxious far more often than others; that is trait anxiety.

so keenly that I can't put them out of my mind," the individual's four choices range from "Almost never" to "Almost always."

Spielberger and his associates (1970, p. 3) defined trait anxiety in terms of "differences between people in a tendency to respond to situations perceived as threatening with elevations in state anxiety intensity." Whether anxiety will be elicited at any particular time and its manifestation in behavior depends on the strength of trait anxiety and the presence of situational stimuli that will evoke state anxiety. Furthermore, the influence of trait anxiety and of external stimulus stressors are mediated by the process of *cognitive appraisal*. If a stimulus is perceived as nonthreatening (e.g., "He wants to get back at me but he's powerless"), then no anxiety is elicited. If the stimulus is appraised as threatening, then the individual may respond with feelings of anxiety or automatically react with defensive behaviors that minimize the experience of anxiety. Extensive research has been carried out on the process of cognitive appraisal, and it has been shown that it is possible to reduce physiological and other anxiety indicators by manipulating the cognitive appraisal of an ordinarily highly threatening stimulus. For example, people exposed to a stressful film depicting the subincision rites of a preliterate culture were asked to perceive the film within an anthropological context. This introduces a method of coping with anxiety similar to that of intellectualization, which lets the viewers detach themselves from a threat that is otherwise reacted to in personal terms (Lazarus and Alfert, 1964; Lazarus and Averill, 1972). In Spielberger's terms, the cognitive appraisal that mediates state anxiety can be modified by situational, experimentally induced, defensive approaches or by variations in trait anxiety and accompanying defensive tendencies.

In accordance with the theoretical attributes of state and trait anxiety, there is a substantial amount of research indicating that trait anxiety is a stable measure, while state anxiety varies markedly with changes in situational stresses (Lamb, 1978). There is also evidence that individuals who differ in trait anxiety also differ, as expected, in the intensity of their state anxiety reactions to stressors, particularly to psychological rather than physical threats. These, along with other relationships indicating the value of the state-trait distinction for the study of anxiety, suggest that a similar distinction can be fruitfully applied in helping clarify the trait-situation interaction for other personality attributes. Eliminating state components from the trait measure and taking state changes into account results in more stable trait indicators and stronger relationships between traits and behaviors. Assessing both trait and state also helps reduce measurement error.

Attribution theory, introduced earlier in this chapter, also has implications for the trait-state distinction. Chaplin, John, and Goldberg (1988) asked subjects to rate a series of acknowledged traits and states on a variety of characteristics. They found that stability over time, consistency of behavior, and perceptions of internal or personal causality were linked with traits, whereas instability, inconsistency, and external causality were associated with states. Hence, an anxious person is perceived as always anxious in a variety of situations and that reaction is caused by the self. However, when a person reacts with anxiety in a specific situation, then that reaction is perceived to be temporary, different than in other situations, and is caused by something external to the person. Chaplin et al. (1988) suggest that trait perceptions enable people to predict behavior over time and situations and thus lead to social actions based on the person (e.g., seek out or avoid people with that characteristic). On the other hand, state reactions, being unstable over time, cannot be predicted from past experience with the person, but may be controlled by manipulating the situation.

Conceptualizing Traits

A person's behavior in a given situation can be thought of as a "final common pathway" resulting from the interaction of many factors, just as many other events in the world are the final product of many interacting causal contributors. (Consider, for example, that many diseases, such as cancer, arise from complex interactions of genetic predispositions, environmental pollutants, and aspects of a person's lifestyle—such as whether or not they smoke.) In sum, while personality traits may be imperfect for predicting behavior in a given situation, they are not meaningless psychological constructs.

Summary

1. Sheldon contended that three body types-labeled *mesomorphic*, *endomorphic*, and *ectomorphic*—are related, respectively, to energetic, relaxed, and introverted personality types. Typologies no longer play a central role in psychology because they fail to capture the complexity of personality.

2. Trait psychologists believe that characteristics of individuals are general over situations and endure over time. Cattell distinguished a number of different traits and sources of traits, while Eysenck suggested three higher-order types of traits: neuroticism, introversion-extroversion, and psychoticism.

3. The Big Five model of personality traits has come to be widely accepted as the basic structure of personality. These five traits include neuroticism versus emotional stability, extraversion, openness to experience, agreeableness, and conscientiousness. However, not all personality theorists believe there are only five basic personality traits. Some models use three traits, some use sixteen, and some use six basic personality traits.

4. *Attribution theorists* believe that observers tend to see the behavior of others as caused by trait characteristics and their own behavior as due to environmental conditions. This disparity may be due to the greater information held by actors about themselves or to the differential perceptual focuses of actors and observers.

5. *Interactionists* contend that behavior is governed by both the properties of the person and the situation in which that person is acting. The *transactional* approach emphasizes the reciprocal influence of the person and the environment on each other. Interactionism, however, typically refers to the fact that variation in behavior is best accounted for by considering both the person and the environment simultaneously.

6. Individuals differ in the consistency of their behavior across situations. In addition, within any individual there may be consistency in some characteristics and inconsistencies in others across different settings.

7. *The template-matching technique* identifies ideal types who would be most likely to behave in a given manner in a given setting. Individuals can then be matched with this ideal type to predict their behavior in that setting.

8. *Traits* are distinguished from *states* in that states are unstable, temporary conditions of the organism. Anxiety is considered to be both a trait and a state. As a state, anxiety is assessed with queries about current intensity of feeling; as a trait, it is measured with questions about frequency and generality across situations.

9. Behavior appears to be more consistent over time and across situations when many instances are sampled. Small samples of behavior, like tests with an insufficient number of items, result in error of measurement, which reduces correlations between the behaviors under study.

Key Terms

ascending reticular activating system (p. 160)
attribution theory (p. 164)
behavioral activation system (p. 160)
behavioral inhibition system (p. 160)
Big Five (p. 161)
continuous distribution (p. 159)
facets (p. 162)
factor analysis (p. 159)
Five Factor Model (p. 161)

fundamental attribution error (p. 165)
interactionist position (p. 166)
lexical hypothesis (p. 161)
moderator variables (p. 167)
situational critique (p. 164)
states (p. 170)
template-matching technique (p. 168)
traits (p. 170)
types (p. 158)

Thought Questions

1. Is your behavior consistent across different settings? Can you think of some behaviors that are consistent and others that are inconsistent?

2. Answer the above question about any friend. Why might the question be difficult to answer about another person, and what implications might this have for how you perceive that individual?

3. Create a personality template for a good teacher or businessperson. Now predict who among your friends best fits this description.

4. Consider where you are likely to place on each of the five major personality traits. Are you high, medium, or low on extraversion? Are you high, medium, or low on neuroticism? Are you high, medium, or low on agreeableness? Are you high, medium, or low on conscientiousness? Are you high, medium, or low on openness to experience?

5. Why would we expect to find a moderate positive correlation between state and trait anxiety?

Personality Development

CHAPTER 10
The Development and Functions of the Self

CHAPTER 11
Identify

CHAPTER 12
Social Development and Patterns of Childrearing

CHAPTER 13
Development Through the Lifespan

Source: Ollyy/Shutterstock

Part 4 is concerned with the genesis, or antecedents of personality, and changes in personality that occur during the course of life. The development of the self is presented as a key process for the development of personality because it contributes in different ways to almost all of the personality theories that have been reviewed. To understand personality, one should have some understanding of its developmental roots. There is a vast gap in behavior and personality between the newborn and the adult. Children must be socialized through the process of child-rearing and other influences so that they function effectively in a particular social and cultural setting. As children grow older, they are confronted with new requirements and new problems that must somehow be mastered. Personality development does not end in childhood or adolescence. The adult years also present unique demands and opportunities for personality growth and change.

The chapters in Part 4 examine the major changes in personality that take place over the developmental life span, and the various processes involved in bringing out these changes. Developmental changes are examined from the perspectives of (1) behavior changes that characterize most individuals in an age group and (2) individual differences in personality development.

Part 4 begins with Chapter 10 on the development of the self and its significance for personality. Chapter 11 addresses the development of identity in general and various aspects of identity, such as gender and ethnic identity, in particular. Chapter 12 begins with a discussion of attachment and its role in the beginning socialization of the child. It then continues with a discussion of topics such as moral development, the antecedents of other prosocial behaviors such as empathy and caring, and the influence of child-rearing practices on socialization. Chapter 13 considers development across the life span, beginning with a discussion of change and continuity in personality over time and then considering the developmental periods of adolescence, adulthood, and old age. Overall, these chapters are based on the ideas that personality undergoes constant change and development and that particular experiences are associated with particular ages. A principal objective of all four chapters is to convey the relevance of a developmental perspective for the understanding of personality.

The Development and Functions of the Self

CHAPTER 10

Source: oneinchpunch /Shutterstock

Chapter Outline

The Self

Development of the Self-Concept

Self-Processes

Self-Motives

Personality Theories and the Self

The self has an interesting history in psychology. William James devoted a chapter to the self in his *Principles of Psychology* (James 1890/1952). However, the rise of American behaviorism in the early part of the twentieth century caused the psychological study of the self to fall out of favor in the United States. The self has increasingly become a central topic of both theory and research in psychology. Before 1960, there were relatively few references to the self, although there were some theorists, such as Carl Rogers, who did emphasize the concept. Freud's theory did not specifically have a concept of self. Instead, it partitioned the mind into id, ego, and superego.

The concept of *self* has become a central focus of attention in many areas of psychology, including personality, social, developmental, and clinical psychology. An indication of this increased attention is that the number of topics that include the prefix *self* in the Psychological Abstracts has increased from eight in 1969 to thirty-three in 1989 (Hoare, 1990) to fifty-six in 2016.

However, the concept of self is anything but easy to define and study. The first part of this chapter will address the various meanings of the term *self*. We then proceed to discuss how the self develops, followed by the development of an experiential sense of self, self-boundaries, the self-concept, and self-esteem. We also consider various aspects of the self-concept. Next we study various self-processes, including self-monitoring, self-control, self-awareness, self-consciousness, self-enhancement, and self-consistency. We conclude by considering the role of the self in various theories of personality.

The Self

We all have an intuitive sense of the importance of the self for the understanding of human experience and behavior. To help make this intuitive sense more concrete, it is instructive to perform the following "thought" experiment. Imagine that you had no sense of self or self-concept. What difference would that make in your plans? You could not think meaningfully about getting a degree, or going to graduate school, or getting married, or becoming rich or famous, because planning for each of these objectives requires that you project *yourself* into the future. You would be different in a great many other ways as well. If you are religious, your worship would become rote and devoid of significance. Whatever is personal in the religious experience—grace, redemption, sin, guilt—would be lost. A basic element in the human tragic experience, the knowledge of one's mortality, would be gone.

Culture and the Self

In spite of the intuitive reasonableness of the idea of a "self" to those raised in Western culture, this concept is held with lesser degrees of strength and certainty in other cultures (Vignoles et al., 2016), and it has evolved and changed over time. We have already seen in Chapter 2 how different cultures have vastly different views of what the self is. Western culture sees the self as an inner entity, occupying an inner space, capable of controlling the body and of actualizing itself. It is bounded, separated from others, and should be autonomous, firmly defined, and stable. In contrast, many other cultures see the self as more inclusively defined in terms of one's connections with others.

In addition, the American emphasis on the importance of self-esteem may be culture-specific. Both Campbell (1993) and Markus and Kitayama (1993) have suggested that self-esteem may be a Western concept. Markus and Kitayama, for instance, have found that Japanese students did not exhibit the "false uniqueness" bias commonly found among Americans (Taylor and Brown, 1988). That is, when asked to compare themselves to others, most Americans tended to see themselves as "above average," whereas Japanese students did not. Self-effacement, rather than self-enhancement, seems to be more prevalent in Japanese society than in American society. Psychologists' emphasis on the importance of high self-esteem and on the tendency of individuals to strive to enhance and protect their self-esteem may be culture-specific (see the section later in this chapter on protection and enhancement of the self).

There have been efforts to trace the historical development in Western society of the concept of self and of self-related issues (Baumeister, 1987). The development of the individual, autonomous self is seen as beginning in the sixteenth century, with the emergence of the Renaissance. Changes that appear to have taken place between the medieval and modern eras in one's conception of the self and view of self-knowledge, and in the conception of self-fulfillment and means of attaining fulfillment, are outlined in Table 10.1. One notes that the notion of an "inner" self that is hidden and inaccessible to the conscious self is a relatively recent one, and that issues of self-deception do not emerge until the Puritan era. One also notes dramatic changes in how one seeks fulfillment—from being guided by religious and societal goals and standards to more personal, individualistic objectives. The sense that society can deter self-fulfillment, with consequent feelings of alienation and separation of work from self-fulfillment emerges after the Industrial Revolution. Although scholars may not necessarily agree with the self attributes and issues that are ascribed to particular time periods, there seems little doubt that self issues and attributes vary as a function of historical context and culture.

Definitions of Self

Two different meanings of the self have been used by psychologists. Sometimes the term *self* is used as an *object*, in which case an individual is depicted as having knowledge of and evaluating the self-as-object in much the same way one has knowledge of and evaluates another person. One can like or dislike another person; one can like and dislike oneself. We entertain beliefs about and concepts of other people, such as "She's bright,"

TABLE 10.1 Issues of Selfhood and Historical Stages

Historical era	Self-knowledge, self-conception	Fulfillment
Late medieval	Unproblematic Increased sense of unity of single life	Christian salvation (in heaven) (Possible) public acclaim
Early modern (16th to 18th century)	Unproblematic for own self; for others, question of inner *true* self vs. out *apparent* self Increased interest in individuality, uniqueness of self	Christian salvation Incipient secular fulfillment, as in creativity
Puritan	Self-consciousness Concern with self-deception (henceforth, self-knowledge uncertain)	Christian salvation: but individual is helpless Inner struggle to overcome sin and weakness
Romantic (late 18th, early 19th century)	Need to discover own destiny and fulfill it (duty)	Creativity Passion ("romantic" love) Thus, grope for secularized concept of fulfillment
Victorian (mid and late 19th century)	Repression, hypocrisy Involuntary self-disclosure	Seek fulfillment alone (transcendentalism) Private, family life is paramount
Early 20th century	Devaluation of self Impossibility of complete self-knowledge (Freud)	Society prevents fulfillment (alienation) Emotional fulfillment in family Work as unfulfilling
Recent 20th century	Belief in personal uniqueness Values of self-exploration	Quest for celebrity Quest for means of self-actualization

(Adapted from Baumeister, 1987.)

"He's ambitious," "The instructor is fair." Similarly, one has such beliefs about oneself. In this sense, the self becomes the object of one's attitudes, beliefs, and feelings. This set of attitudes, beliefs, and feelings about the self is referred to as the **self-concept**.

Is the self-concept always conscious, part of our phenomenal experience? The answer is no. We, of course, do have a conscious self-concept, but there may well be feelings about ourselves of which we are unaware. For example, we may have an unconscious perception of ourselves as physically unattractive, based on childhood experiences, even though we have physically changed and consciously judge ourselves, in accordance with the feedback from others, as attractive.

self-concept A description of who one is. It includes feelings, attitudes, desires, judgments, and behaviors that the individual considers to be characteristic of himself or herself.

The Self as a Concept

When considering the self as object, we are looking at the self as a concept like any other concept. The concept could be "personality psychology," or it could be "myself." As a concept in memory, we will use the tools of cognitive psychology to study the self-concept. Two of the most useful tools will be to look at storage and retrieval of information in memory, and the other will look at the speed of information processing.

One of the classic demonstrations of the self as a concept in memory comes from the self-reference effect (Rodgers, Kuiper, and Kirker, 1977). It is well known that connecting information to a memory structure leads to better encoding and retrieval of that information (Craik and Lockhart, 1972). In the general paradigm, people are presented with a list of words and then unexpectedly they are asked to recall the words later in the experiment. This is known as an implicit memory task. People are randomly assigned to experimental conditions in which they might be asked to answer whether the word presented "Means the same as shy?" or in a different experimental condition asked whether the word presented "Describes you?" or whether the word "Describes your personality professor?" The general effect is that people will remember the words far better if those words are connected to the self-concept (see Symons and Johnson, 1997, for an overview).

The *self-reference effect* is a powerful phenomenon; it turns out that in almost any variation attempted, words related to the self result in superior recall. This indicates that the self-concept is one of the most elaborated and well-developed concepts that we have. That should not come as a surprise, since the self is a concept that is activated in many different contexts, whereas other concepts are only occasionally activated.

Self as Agent

Another usage of the self is as an *agent* or *process*; that is, as a mechanism that does something. Thus, the self is said to influence perception and judgment, and to screen out threatening or inconsistent information. Related to this usage is the notion of the self as an organized structure or personality component. And, as we indicated in the chapters on personality theories, there are even broader usages of self—for example, in the motive for self-actualization and in the search for self-identity.

Sometimes the question is asked: "Why do we need a concept of self as agent? Isn't the whole person the agent?" In fact, however, sometimes we experience some of our behaviors as self-initiated, while we experience others as outside the self. For example, one maybe beset by an impulse or an idea that is experienced as "foreign" and that one cannot control. One may feel a loss of agency or responsibility for one's behavior, and even a loss of individuality. Hence, the organism does not always conceive of itself as an agent, and a concept of self is needed.

The terms "self" and "self-concept" are often used interchangeably. We believe it helpful to restrict the term self to its properties as an agent and organized structure of personality and the term self-concept to the attitudes, beliefs, and feelings about the self as object. From this perspective, the self-concept becomes one component, a very important one, of the self-system. It then becomes meaningful to refer to the self-concept of the self.

One major objective of personality theory and research is to provide a clearer, more precise definition of the self and the self-concept. We need to recognize, however, that there are ambiguities in how the self is defined and serious difficulties in our methods of assessment. In some overviews of the field of personality, very little attention is given to the self because of definitional ambiguities and measurement problems. It is our view that the concept of the self is critical to any comprehensive theory of personality development and function. The self provides a key to much of human motivation, social understanding, and personality disturbances. Basic to the personality development of both the child and the adult are changes in the self. Hence, this chapter examines the process of the development of the self and its significance in the understanding of personality.

Development of the Self-Concept

Self-Awareness

self-awareness A recognition of oneself, or the process of noticing the self and how others might view the self.

The development of the capacity for **self-awareness** appears to be crucial for the development of the self-concept (Lewis, 1990). This capacity, as we have said, seems to develop around eighteen months of age; and it appears to be unique to humans and higher primates. This conclusion is based on a series of clever research studies by Gallup (1970, 1975, 1979) in which animals and human infants observe themselves in mirrors.

Most of us have seen a dog staring at, sometimes snarling at, and approaching a reflection of itself. For most animals, seeing their own image in a mirror acts as a social stimulus. But does the dog recognize itself, or does the reflection simply signal a potential companion or threat? The evidence indicates that dogs and almost all other nonhumans do not recognize themselves. In his series of experiments, however, Gallup has shown that the chimpanzee does have this capacity. Gallup exposed chimpanzees in a

Source: GUDKOV ANDREY/Shutterstock

Humans and higher primates display recognition of the self in mirrors.

small cage to a full-length mirror for ten consecutive days. It was observed that over this period of time the number of self-directed responses increased. These behaviors included grooming parts of the body while watching the results, guiding fingers in the mirror, and picking at teeth with the aid of the mirror. Describing one chimp, Gallup (1975, p. 324) said, "Marge used the mirror to play with and inspect the bottom of her feet; she also looked at herself upside down in the mirror while suspended by her feet from the top of the cage; . . . she was also observed to stuff celery leaves up her nose using the mirror for purposes of visually guiding the stems into each nostril."

Two-year-old babies recognize their images in a mirror.

The researchers then devised a further test of self-recognition. The chimps were anesthetized and marks were placed over their eyebrows and behind their ears, areas the chimps could not directly observe. The mirror was temporarily removed from the cage, and baseline data regarding their attempts to touch these areas were recorded. The chimpanzees touched themselves in those spots very little (about once) without the mirror, but touched themselves over twenty-five times when the mirror was reintroduced. The data clearly suggest that chimps do recognize themselves, or are self-aware, for their attempts to touch the marks increased when they viewed themselves.

An analogous procedure incorporated in a study of human infants clearly reveals the role of developmental influences on this form of self-recognition (Lewis and Brooks-Gunn, 1979). Heavy rouge was applied to the noses of ninety-six infants, ranging in age from nine months to twenty-four months. The infants' actions when exposed to a mirror were observed prior to and after the application of rouge. While the nine- and twelve-month-old infants usually did not touch their noses when presented with a mirror, a dramatic change in responses indicative of self-recognition occurred during the latter half of the infants' second year, with an increase of over 50% in nose touching for twenty-one- and twenty-four-month-old infants.

Further Developments of the Self-Concept

The self-concept can be considered one's description of who one is. It includes feelings, attitudes, desires, judgments, and behaviors that the individual considers to be characteristic of himself or herself.

Developing a concept of who one is as a person is important. Consider what happens when one behaves in a way that is very different from one's typical patterns—for example, a sudden outburst of rage and profanity in a man who sees himself as calm, rational, and well-spoken. He might say, "This isn't like me," "Something must have come over me," or "I wasn't myself." If his behaviors persist, he may change his self-concept, integrating these new feelings and behaviors into his conception of his personality. However, this integration is not always easily accomplished, and the individual could feel that he is beset by strange, incomprehensible feelings, even that he is going crazy. What is important in terms of the development and dynamics of personality is that a developing image of who we are as people is a useful tool for helping us understand and predict our reactions to situations and experiences in our life. We learn to recognize and to count on our images of who we are, much in the same way we learn to recognize and count on our physical selves. Additionally, we work to maintain stability in these self-images.

The self-concept develops over time as the child has experiences that interact with its increasing cognitive understanding and development of language. There are changes in the content of the self-concept from childhood through adolescence (Harter, 1990). In childhood, the self-concept is primarily focused on the social exterior—what is observable from outside. Young children describe themselves primarily in terms of their behaviors, their achievements, their preferences, their possessions, and their physical attributes. Older children tend to emphasize traits such as "shy" and "outgoing."

Adolescence is a time when people are figuring out who they truly are.

In adolescence, when the ability to think abstractly increases, a number of changes in the self-concept occur. First, the psychological interior is emphasized. The self-concept includes an increasing emphasis on emotions, attitudes, beliefs, wishes, and motives.

Second, the self-concept becomes more complex and multidimensional. In early and middle childhood there are four general domains of the self-concept. By adolescence this has become differentiated into at least nine: scholastic competence, job competence, athletic competence, physical appearance, peer social acceptance, close friendship, romantic appeal, relationship to parents, and behavioral conduct (Harter, 1990).

Third, aspects of the self-concept become more abstract. For instance, a nine-year-old might describe herself as a girl with brown hair, who loves sports and has three brothers. A twelve-year-old would describe herself as a human, a girl, a truthful person, tall for my age. And as a seventeen-year-old, she would describe herself as indecisive, ambitious, an individual, lonely, liberal, conservative, and radical. The early descriptions are rather concrete, and at each stage become more complex and even contradictory, which leads to our next point.

Fourth, adolescents struggle to integrate their self-concept. Harter (1990) notes that children around the age of eleven do not detect conflicts in their personality. By ages fourteen through sixteen, however, adolescents are vividly aware of contradictions among various aspects of their self-concept and they are troubled by these contradictions. In fact, it is at this age that individuals experience the most conflict over contradictions. It is hard for them to reconcile, for instance, the fact that they are "cheerful" with their friends but "depressed" with their parents. In late adolescence they are able to begin to create abstract systems of self-descriptions that integrate the contradictions experienced at an earlier age. For instance, "cheerful" and "depressed" may be synthesized as "flexible" or "moody."

Finally, one other aspect of the development of the self-concept at adolescence is the increased importance of the distinction between the "true" and "false" self. Harter (1990) reports that sixth-graders have little insight into the true-false self distinction. However, by eighth grade virtually all adolescents find the distinction compelling. Harter found that most of her adolescents defined the true self as one who acts naturally, or is what one is inside, while a false self is one who acts primarily to please others.

Self-Schemata

Currently, the self-concept is thought of in cognitive terms in psychology. It is conceived of as a "knowledge structure" and consists of cognitive generalizations about the self. This is often referred to as a **self-schema** (see Markus, 1977). These schemata are believed to filter incoming information, organize new experiences, and guide subsequent action. For example, a person with a self-schema of independence is likely to interpret personal behaviors as indicative of being independent and is not likely to accept evidence from others that he or she is dependent. In addition, information will be readily available from memory to support the self-perception of independence. It has been demonstrated that people who regard themselves as masculine, or as feminine, can recall many instances in their lives when they acted in accordance with this self-perception. On the other hand, androgynous individuals (persons not sex-typed) or those without a schema with regards to gender (that is, gender is not a salient aspect of their self-concept) have few memories of instances in which they acted in a masculine or feminine manner (Markus, Crane, Bernstein, and Siladi, 1982).

There is a substantial body of research documenting the selective effects of the self-structure on the processing of information (Markus and Wurf, 1987). For example, in one study subjects were presented with a series of pairs of letters, each pair containing a letter from either their first or last name (Nuttin, Jr., 1985). The subjects' task was to choose which letter of the pair they preferred as quickly as they could. While the subjects

self-schema A knowledge structure that consists of cognitive generalizations about the self.

displayed no awareness of the relationship between their name and the letter pairs, they nevertheless selected more often letters from their own name. Because of this lack of awareness, this name-letter effect has become a common measure of implicit self-esteem (see Bosson, Swann, and Pennebaker, 2000; Krizan and Suls, 2008).

Other cognitive processes that have been shown to be selectively influenced by self-relevant stimuli include discrimination, memory, and judgment (Markus and Wurf, 1987). One also tends to more efficiently process information that is congruent with one's own personality. Thus individuals scoring higher on a personality scale measuring manipulative tendencies and given stories to read were significantly faster in reading a story depicting high manipulative tendencies than in reading one depicting low manipulative tendencies. The opposite difference was obtained for low manipulative individuals (cited in Markus and Wurf, 1987).

Pick your favorite letters in this image. Chances are good that you picked letters associated with your name.

Through the agency of the self, the self-concept acts as an important filter, selectively screening the information that we receive from the external and internal environment. The self selectively influences information processing, not only through a self-defense function, but also, as we have seen, through its sensitivity to self-relevant stimuli. At a later point in this chapter, some important self-processes will be discussed in greater detail.

Multiple Self-Concepts

In referring to a person's self-image, it is common practice to use the singular term: self-concept. However, current psychological perspectives suggest that the self-concept is multiple. Distinctions can be made between the unconscious and conscious aspects of the self-concept, between our perception of our past self, our perception of our current self, and our imagination of the future self. There is articulation between the different elements that constitute the psychological self. There are all the different roles that constitute vital parts of our self—our role as a student, as an offspring, as a male or female. One can also speak of our social self, our work self, our play self, and our athletic self. While these different aspects of the self may be interrelated and organized into a unitary self-structure, different features of the self become more salient and operative depending upon the particular context and circumstances.

A number of studies provide evidence that the self-concept is multiple. Research by Harter (1990) and Rosenberg (1985) shows that the self-concept appears to have multiple dimensions Rosenberg (1985) based on his study of 5,000 adolescents identifies the following components of the self-concept self-esteem a sense of "mattering" to others, a sense of certitude about who one is, feelings of control, "plane coordination" (the degree to which different aspects of the self are coordinated), how vulnerable one feels as a self, and the degree of anxiety or self-consciousness one feels.

A study by Smollar and Youness (1985) shows that we experience ourselves somewhat differently in different relationships in our lives. The authors asked adolescents to complete the statement "When I am with my (mother/father/close friend) I am. . . ." The adolescents showed much variability in who they experienced themselves to be in reference to different contexts. With fathers, for instance, adolescents typically reported being "capable, serious, and anxious." These aspects did not show up in reference to best friends, where they viewed themselves as "intimate and spontaneous," qualities that they did not typically experience with their parents.

Markus and Kunda (1986) have suggested that we have a whole set of self-concepts but that at any one time in any given context one self-concept is active and is the **working self-concept**. They use a computer metaphor: A computer may have many programs on its hard drive, but usually at a given moment only one is being used. An example from the Smollar and Youness study would be that with one's close friend one's concept of self as intimate and spontaneous is working that is it becomes active and guides one's behavior. With one's father, one's concept of self as serious is active and working.

working self-concept The version of the self-concept that is being used at that time.

To say that we have multiple self-concepts is not to say that there is no overlap among them. Physically, one will see oneself as a man or as a woman with both one's father and one's close friend, while psychologically, one may see oneself as reliable in both relationships. Therefore, while we may have multiple self-concepts, in most cases they are not completely distinct from one another, or exclusive.

The richness and complexity of the self-concept, or self-concepts, are further conveyed by the distinction that has been made between one's representation of: (a) one's actual self, (b) one's **ideal self**, the self one wants to be, and (c) one's **ought self**, the attributes and behaviors that we believe are our obligations or duty to possess (Higgins, 1987). Discrepancies between these self-concepts and the actual, ideal, and ought concepts that significant others (parents, close friends) may have of you can be a source of discomfort and distress. In one study, college students were administered these different self-concept measures. Six to eight weeks later, they completed a questionnaire in which they indicated the frequency with which they experienced various emotional-motivational states (Van Hook and Higgins, 1988). The students were divided into two groups depending upon whether there was a marked discrepancy between any pair of self-concept measures. The discrepancy-present group experienced more negative feelings than the discrepancy-absent group. This difference was especially marked for confusion-related items (i.e., unsure of self, uncertain about goals, confused about identity).

Possible Selves

Still another way to conceive of self-concepts that may function as important guides to behavior and sources of motivation and conflict is the notion of **possible selves** (Markus and Nurius, 1986). There are possible selves that we hope for and possible selves that we fear. Thus we may hope for a particular career, lifestyle, income level, and close interpersonal relations while we may fear loneliness, failure, or other life possibilities that we perceive as negative. Although there may be some overlap between these possible selves and the ideal self, there are sufficient differences to warrant a different label and, most importantly, a different measure. They found that one's perceptions of one's "now" self and of one's "possible" future selves correlated with one's current emotional and motivational state. However, images of possible future selves may sometimes predict a person's current behavior better than does the person's current self-concept. For instance, Oyserman and Markus (as referenced in Markus and Nurius, 1986) found that juvenile delinquents had positive current self-images (positive self-esteem) but were deficient in their images of positive possible future self-images. This is reminiscent of members of gangs, who may have positive self-concepts but act in an antisocial and dangerous manner because they believe that they will probably be dead by age twenty.

Complexity of the Self-Concept

We have seen that the self-concept includes a variety of aspects and dimensions. How a self-concept is organized in terms of its complexity, integration, and clarity is important in terms of how well it functions. Linville (1985) has found that those who have more complex self-concepts show greater emotional stability in the face of both emotionally positive and negative experiences. Linville measured self-complexity by having individuals sort cards, each of which had the name of a personality trait on it, into piles describing the self. The same trait could be placed in multiple piles. More piles indicated greater **self-complexity**. Subjects were then exposed to either a success or a failure experience and then rated their mood. Subjects whose self-complexity scores were low showed greater change in mood following success or failure than subjects who scored higher in self-complexity. She then replicated and extended this research in another study in which she had participants complete the self-complexity card sort along with measures of stressful events and illnesses at two different times, two weeks apart. People with high self-complexity who experienced stressful events were less likely to fall ill than people with low self-complexity who experienced stressful events (Linville, 1987). Another study combined the idea of possible selves and self-complexity, finding that when given false

---

ideal self The self one wants to be.

ought self The self one feels an obligation to be.

possible selves Positive and negative versions of the self that can be imagined for the future.

self-complexity The number and interconnectedness among different ways that a person thinks about the self.

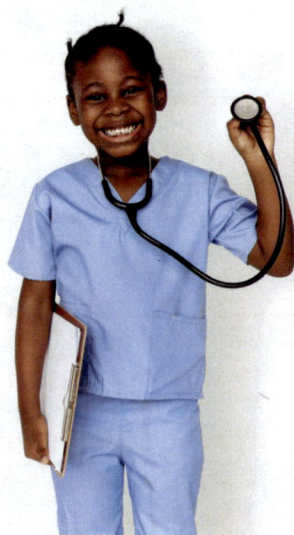

Source: Rawpixel.com/Shutterstock

Possible selves include things that a person can imagine in the future. These can include positive possibilities to pursue, as well as negative possibilities to avoid.

feedback about the present, a person's current self-complexity moderated the person's emotional reaction, while when the feedback is about the future, it is a person's possible self-complexity that predicts the person's emotional reaction (Niedenthal, Setterlund, and Wherry, 1992).

Other studies have found that individuals high in cognitive complexity in general are less likely to become depressed (Marsh and Weary, 1989) and that those with more integrated (Showers, 1992) and more clearly articulated (Campbell, 1993) self-concepts have higher self-esteem.

Self-Esteem

While self-concept refers to a complex, multifaceted organization of percepts regarding oneself, *self-esteem* usually connotes a generalized, overall attitude toward oneself. **Self-esteem** is usually thought of as the value that one places on oneself. Just as there are variations in the degree to which one values another person, whether we hold them in high or low regard and feel that they are worthy or unworthy, so there is variation in the degree to which one values oneself.

self-esteem A generalized evaluation of one's self.

Neither children nor adults feel neutral about all their self-characteristics. Positive and negative values are placed on particular attributes that we see in others and in ourselves. It is good to be tall (but not too tall), attractive, strong, intelligent, and socially skillful, and it is bad to be unathletic, shy, or poor. The evaluations we place on these self-attributes contribute to our feelings of self-esteem. It thus becomes evident that self-esteem is closely related to and depends on the self-concept, but self-esteem is not the same as self-concept. We can have beliefs about ourselves that are important elements in our self-concept but that do not affect the value we place on ourselves (self-esteem). For example, one may perceive oneself as introverted or emotionally expressive without feeling particularly good or bad about that self-perception. Whether success or failure at an activity will affect self-esteem is very much dependent on how important one perceives that activity to be (Crocker and Wolfe, 2001; Harter and Engstrom, cited in Harter, 1983).

The analysis of self-esteem must also reflect the complexity of the self. Epstein (1973) has proposed a hierarchical structure for self-esteem. At the summit of the hierarchy are feelings about the worthiness of the overall self-concept. Below this generalized attitude are more specific evaluations pertaining to four major areas of the self: general competence, moral self-approval, power, and love worthiness. Within each of these four areas, even more specific differentiations can be made. Thus, within the competence area, one can distinguish between the self-esteem associated with intellectual, artistic, and athletic competence, and make even further distinctions within these specifications—for example, between verbal and mathematical competence.

Crocker and her colleagues (Crocker and Wolfe, 2001) have suggested that there are seven different dimensions on which college students base their self-worth. These dimensions are things like academics, physical appearance, competition, family support, being virtuous, being loved by God, and receiving approval from others. Different individuals will value these dimensions in various ways. Some people will find academics to be crucial to self-worth, whereas others will emphasize physical appearance. They find that college students will allocate their time to the dimensions that person most values (Crocker, Luhtanen, Cooper, and Bouvrette, 2003).

The relationship between overall self-esteem (the degree of high or low regard in which one holds oneself) and the positive and negative values placed on specific components of the self-concept remains an interesting and unresolved issue. Some individuals' view of their academic skills might be the most important contributor to self-esteem, while for others it might be perceived popularity. However, there is a connection between one's appraisal of specific self-attributes and one's overall self-esteem. Studies have shown that the sum of an individual's evaluations of specific attributes—school performance, athletic skills, social interactions, physical attractiveness, and so on—is predictive of the person's overall sense of self-esteem (Coopersmith, 1967). Although people with high self-esteem rate

Many things can influence self-esteem, but social exclusion is one of the factors most associated with low self-esteem.

themselves as more attractive, thinner, and intelligent, objective measures yield correlations near zero on all those dimensions (see Baumeister, Campbell, Kruger, and Vohs, 2003, for a review). Though predictive of general self-esteem, it is important to recognize that the different dimensions of self-esteem are not the same as *general* self-esteem.

Many studies have found correlations between high self-esteem and positive outcomes, or low self-esteem and negative outcomes (Donnellan et al., 2005). It is important to recognize that this does not mean that self-esteem causes the positive outcome nor necessarily that the positive outcome raises a person's self-esteem. The state of California created a series of programs with the underlying idea that self-esteem is the cause of many social problems, and thus, raising self-esteem would reduce those problems. This has sometimes been termed "The Self-Esteem Movement." The problem with this approach is confusion of correlation with causation. If we used the Sociometer theory approach (Leary and Baumeister, 2000) that was discussed in Chapter 1, it would seem likely that violations of expectations of norms would lead to reduced feelings of belonging, and consequently lead to lower self-esteem. In this approach, the direction of causality is exactly the reverse of the Self-Esteem Movement model. Yet, we also know that low self-esteem in adolescence does seem to predict poorer outcomes in adulthood (Donnellan et al., 2005; Trzesniewski et al., 2006).

Since self-esteem will be based on a person's interactions with the world, we might expect that people who experience discrimination would experience low self-esteem. However, it appears that African Americans actually have higher self-esteem than white Americans (Crocker and Major, 1989). This appears to be due to people's ability to denigrate, or reduce the importance of particular aspects of the self. Further, it appears that a person's world view can interact with the experience of prejudice. Latin Americans experience reduced self-esteem if they hear about prejudice to their ethnicity, while they simultaneously believe that people who work hard will get ahead (Major, Kaiser, O'Brien, and McCoy, 2007). Interestingly, they also found that denigration of their group resulted in higher self-esteem if they believed that discrimination impacted the chances of a person's success.

Variability of Self-Esteem

People clearly differ in their level of self-esteem. Some people have high self-esteem, others have low self-esteem. People also differ in the stability of their self-esteem (Kernis, Cornell, Sun, Berry, and Harlow, 1993). Some people have stable high self-esteem; that is, they have high self-esteem all the time. But other people have unstable high self-esteem; their self-esteem is high but will vary considerably depending on what is going on in their lives. People with low self-esteem can also have stable or unstable self-esteem. Because people like to maintain positive feelings about themselves (we will discuss that in a few pages), this variability in stability has an impact on decisions people will make for themselves and how they react to criticism. People with unstable high self-esteem are more likely to act aggressively when their self-view is threatened (Baumeister, Smart, and Boden, 1996). Unstable self-esteem is associated with higher rates of depression (Kernis, Grannemann, and Mathis, 1993). People with unstable high self-esteem are more defensive when receiving negative feedback.

Self-Processes

The development of self-awareness leads not only to the development of a self-concept but also to the development of several other important personality processes. In Western culture in particular, the development of the ability to reflect upon oneself is seen as a useful skill (Landrine, 1992). It can be used to examine one's internal states and behavior and to enhance one's ability to control oneself. This ability can function in both positive and negative ways, though. Negatively, it can lead to painful self-awareness and self-consciousness. But, positively, it can lead to strivings to protect one's self-esteem and to maintain self-consistency. In this section, we consider each of these self-processes.

Self-Monitoring

One of the unique properties of humans to which we have already alluded is the capacity to observe and regulate our own behavior. When faced with temptation, young children can say to themselves, "Don't take a cookie; opening the cookie jar is naughty." For the older child and adult, these various prohibitions have been internalized in the form of a "conscience" which functions as a built-in self-monitor, as it were. Monitoring can also be a guide as well as a defense. Long distance runners observe when they need to slow down and pace themselves for the end of the race; dieters record their caloric intake and modify their eating behavior accordingly. **Self-monitoring** in varying degrees is an important part of our everyday activities and, as we have seen in the review of social learning theories, can be an important component of a cognitive behavior modification therapeutic approach.

self-monitoring The degree to which individuals regulate their social behavior in order to make a particular social impression.

Snyder and his associates (Gangestad and Snyder, 2000; Snyder, 1974; Snyder and Gangestad, 1986) have focused on a specific aspect of the general activity of self-monitoring. They have developed a scale assessing individual differences in self-monitoring tendencies. This scale has focused on the monitoring of the social presentation aspects of the self. It was designed to assess the degree to which individuals regulate their social behavior in order to make a particular social impression.

The items address the ability to control or manage expressive behavior, e.g., "I would probably make a good actor;" the tendency to perform in social situations and attract attention, e.g., "In a group of people I am rarely the center of attention" (scored in the reverse direction); and the tendency to behave as others expect, and contrary to the way one might feel, e.g., "I may deceive people by being friendly when I really dislike them."

High self-monitors would be expected to alter their behavior in response to specific situational demands, and therefore, display less consistency in their actions. While there are some exceptions, the data are generally consistent with this prediction (Snyder, 1987). There are numerous studies ranging from responsiveness to advertising, to dating behavior, to the degree of consistency between beliefs and actions, that verify the utility of this measure. However, there is considerable controversy as to the personality dimension or dimensions that are being assessed by the self-monitoring instrument (Briggs and Cheek 1988). There is debate as to whether the scale measures one personality dimension or is a combination of several different dimensions. For example, the self-monitoring scale is significantly correlated with such personality factors as extroversion and exhibitionism (Briggs and Cheek, 1988). These personality indicators would appear to relate more to temperament than to self-monitoring. The fact that there is a significantly greater correlation between identical twins on the self-monitoring measure than between fraternal twins suggests a genetic basis for this trait (Gangestad and Snyder, 1985), biological causation would be consistent with a personality temperament interpretation of what the self-monitoring instrument assesses.

Perhaps one of the most interesting parts of self-monitoring as a personality trait is that it has an impact on the consistency with which we see expression of other traits; for this reason, it is sometimes thought of as a meta-trait (see Chapter 8). Niedenthal and her colleagues (Niedenthal, Cantor, and Kihlstrom, 1985) found that people who are high self-monitors are less careful about choosing housing situations at college, which would be expected since they can adapt to many different situations. As such, there may be good reasons to believe that the ability to change to fit the situational demands can have positive outcomes, yet we are probably going to be worse at predicting the high self-monitor's behavior across situations.

Self-Control

There is a close relationship between self-monitoring and *self-control*. We have already alluded to the internal monitor or conscience. Self-monitoring refers primarily to the attention paid to one's behavior and feelings, while self-control refers to the ability to inhibit immediate gratification and alter one's behaviors appropriately. Self-control is also frequently used synonymously with self-regulation to connote future planning and the guiding of one's behavior in accordance with one's standards and situational demands. A number of theoretical explanations of self-control or self-regulation consider the monitoring of behavior as the first step in a three stage cycle (Bandura, 1978; Kanfer, 1970). For the second step, the observed behavior is then judged against a criterion based on one's own standards or the standards of significant others. The last step consists of the person reinforcing or criticizing the self for the behavior. Self-criticism then leads to efforts to modify the behavior so that it meets the standard.

Some theories consider the role of the third stage to be in its information rather than reward value (Carver and Sheier, 1982). A significant discrepancy between the observed behavior and the standard then elicits a motivation to reduce the discrepancy, resulting in efforts to modify the behavior.

Positive and Negative Effects of Self-Awareness

There are conditions under which individuals appear to function more effectively if they are not self-aware. For instance, athletes usually attempt to blot out awareness of the self. Baseball hitters cannot be conscious of every aspect of their batting techniques while swinging the bat and still be successful. There is a movement among athletic coaches to emphasize the Zen aspect of the sport; that is, to have players transcend any awareness of the self and to lose their identity by completely merging with the game. A best-selling tennis book stressed that the player should be aware of the seams on the tennis ball and nothing else. Self-statements after missing a shot, such as "I am a lousy player" or "I can't seem to hit a backhand today," are believed to impede performance.

There is a large body of research addressing the effects of self-awareness on personal functioning. One clear finding is that focusing awareness on the self produces more acceptance of oneself as the cause of events. For example, Duval and Wicklund (1973, p. 26) had subjects read several scenarios, such as:

1. Imagine that you have selected and purchased a race horse. You enter the horse in a major race and hire a good jockey to ride him. The horse wins first place. To what degree did your actions cause the victory and to what degree did the actions of the jockey cause the victory?
2. Imagine that a friend of yours wants to get you a date. You tell her what characteristics you like in a date and she selects one of her friends. You go out with him and have a very good time. To what degree did your actions cause the successful date and to what degree did the actions of your friend cause the successful date?

Half of the subjects read these stories under normal conditions; the remainder read the passages in front of a conspicuous mirror. The presence of a mirror was expected to shift the focus of attention to oneself. In accordance with their predictions, Duval and Wicklund found that individuals in the mirror condition made relatively more self-attributions than did subjects in the normal condition.

Duval and Wicklund (1972) also proposed that heightened self-awareness is an aversive state, as it makes us consciously aware of our shortcomings. In a related theoretical development, Wine (1971) and Sarason (1978) contended that when a stressful event arouses self-preoccupying thoughts, there will be performance decrements because task-relevant thoughts are diminished. Further, they stated that highly anxious people focus on the self during test performance, which may account for their relatively poor scores in test situations.

In this regard, Hamilton and colleagues (1993), Barlow (1988), and Baumeister (1990), among others, have argued that excessive self-awareness plays a role in depression, anxiety, suicide, substance abuse, and other psychological disorders (Mor and Winquist, 2002).

Among other things, self-awareness intensifies emotions. If one is feeling anxious or depressed, then excessive self-awareness will magnify those feelings. In addition, because self-awareness increases the tendency to see oneself as the cause of some event, if something goes wrong one is more likely to blame it on oneself. At the extreme, this can lead to excessive self-criticism and self-blame. Excessive self-focused attention can be so aversive under certain circumstances that one will strive to escape it, for instance by committing suicide (Baumeister, 1990) or by abusing substances.

However, the effects of self-awareness on behavior are far from settled. Carver, Scheier, and their colleagues (e.g., Carver, Blaney, and Scheier, 1979a, 1979b) have argued that if self-confidence and performance expectancy are high, then self-focus of attention will increase performance, whereas low confidence combined with self-focus will give rise to performance decrements. To test these ideas in an experimental investigation, people with snake phobias were asked to approach and pick up a snake. Some of these individuals were confident about their ability to overcome the phobia, while others were quite apprehensive and doubting. In one of the experimental conditions a mirror was present to heighten self-awareness. The data were as predicted: the mirror enhanced the likelihood of picking up the snake among the confident subjects but impeded snake handling among the non-confident subjects, relative to the behavior of persons without feedback from a mirror. Silvia and Phillips (2004) also found that self-awareness interacted with beliefs, such that those who believed that there was an opportunity to grow and improve did not see a decrement in performance caused by self-awareness.

In sum, common situations such as placement in front of a mirror, camera, or audience can heighten self-awareness. Changes in awareness or self-consciousness can have profound positive or negative behavioral effects. We next consider some of the negative aspects, of the related concept of self-consciousness.

Source: Milkovasa/Shutterstock

Heightened self-awareness can be an aversive state, as it can remind one of one's shortcomings.

Self-Consciousness

Self-awareness, in addition to its reflection in self-evaluation, is also manifested in *self-consciousness*—the extent to which awareness of self enters into one's thoughts and behaviors. For example, one is less likely to feel self-conscious joining a group of good friends who are having a party than joining a group of strangers. In the latter case, thoughts of the impression one is making are more likely to arise as one interacts with the group. Of course, one can be self-conscious with one's friends—e.g., wondering about their reaction to some new clothes one is wearing, or expecting congratulations from them regarding a recent award.

In addition to situational factors affecting self-consciousness, there are also personality differences in the tendency to be self-conscious. Some individuals are more insecure about the impression they make, constantly worrying what others think about them. A personality scale has been developed to assess these individual differences, distinguishing between differences in public self-consciousness and private self-consciousness (Fenigstein, 1987). Individuals who are highly conscious of the public aspects of one's self as contrasted to being conscious of private aspects, such as one's feelings and desires, display much more sensitivity to the behavior of others. For example, such individuals may react in a very personal and negative manner when ignored.

Self-Motives

Self-Protection and Self-Enhancement

One aspect of awareness of the self is that it can lead to a tendency to want to protect and enhance the self. We want to engage in behaviors and seek situations that will maximize

Sports fans will associate closely with a team when winning but distance themselves when the team is losing in order to maintain positive feelings about the self.

feelings of self-esteem and minimize threats to our self-esteem. There are many ways in which self-esteem can be enhanced or threatened, depending on the particular culture and on one's personal values and competencies. One can achieve self-esteem through financial success, through fame, through popularity, through mastery of a difficult task, through social dedication, and so on. How we maintain and enhance self-esteem is highly influenced by learning, but the need for self-esteem is a consequence of the emergent development of the self-concept.

Self-Evaluation Maintenance

We know that people are motivated to try to maintain positive self-evaluations. There are many ways in which people may attempt to do this. People may associate themselves with positive things. This is sometimes known as basking in reflected glory (Cialdini et al., 1976). A common example of this is how people will talk about athletic teams they support, using phrases like, "We won!" or "They lost." Notice how the phrasing connects the self to the win but distances the self from the loss. People will also shift the importance they place on aspects of the self following failure on those dimensions (Crocker and Wolf, 2003; James, 1890/1953).

People generally prefer and seek out positive feedback and attempt to reduce the impact of negative feedback (Snyder, et al, 1983). Studies of success and failure indicate that we tend to attribute success to our personal efforts and ability, while we are likely to attribute failure to the difficulty of the task or to bad luck (Weary, 1978). Research on what is called the "social comparison process" indicates that people make downward comparisons when they compare themselves to others in order to assess how well they are doing. That is, they compare themselves with others perceived as less able than, inferior to, or less fortunate than themselves, to enhance their own self-esteem (Gibbon, 1986).

By trying to maintain positive feelings about one's self, people may engage in maladaptive behaviors. People may perceive failure as reflecting on the self instead of an opportunity to improve. It may lead to people being more likely to cheat on academic work. The maintenance of self-esteem has costs that may actually stand in the way of success (Crocker and Park, 2004).

Taylor and Brown (1988), summarizing research evidence, have argued that humans show a tendency to have unrealistically positive views of the self. When negative aspects of the self are acknowledged, these aspects tend to be dismissed as inconsequential. A study by Lewinsohn, Mischel, Chaplin, and Barton (1980) is illustrative of people's tendency to have unrealistically positive self-views. In this study, observers watched subjects complete a group-interaction task. Each subject was then rated on a number of personality dimensions by the observers, as well as by the subjects themselves. Subjects' self-ratings were significantly more positive than the observers' ratings.

There is much controversy over what actually causes us to "self-servingly" interpret information in this fashion. While some have argued that we do it because of our self-serving desire to enhance or protect the self-image, others suggest that it has to do with how people process information. For instance, those who are used to success might logically attribute success at a particular task to their own efforts and failure to external factors. Numerous studies have tried to unravel which of these two explanations is correct. The conclusion drawn by most psychologists is that both factors are involved. People interpret evidence in a manner favorable to their self-concepts, both because they are acting logically based on the way they interpret experience and because they are trying to enhance their self-images. Once again we caution that the phenomenon of a self-serving bias may be culture-specific.

Even in our culture, not all individuals interpret evidence in a manner favorable to a positive self-image. Taylor and Brown (1988) point out that depressed individuals are actually often more "realistic" in their self-assessments than nondepressed individuals, who distort information positively. Swann and colleagues (1987), based on their view of self-consistency (see next section), have suggested that individuals with low self-esteem will actually reject positive information about themselves in order to preserve their negative self-image and, conversely, will accept negative information about themselves. Several decades ago, Lecky (1945) proposed that an important factor governing socially maladaptive behavioral symptoms in children was their tendency to act consistently with a negative self-image. Thus, children who see themselves as poor spellers or stutterers may spell poorly or stutter to maintain consistency with their self-images. Similarly, children who believe themselves to be "bad" may behave delinquently in accordance with their self-concepts, perhaps without being conscious at all of the process. Therapies based on Lecky's approach attempt to help the child become aware of these maladaptive efforts to maintain consistency and, in addition, to help the child modify a negative self-concept. The fact that some individuals appear to strive to maintain a *negative* self-image is compatible with the self-consistency motive, to which we now turn.

Self-Consistency

How we perceive ourselves shapes our judgments and behaviors through still another psychological mechanism: the motivation for **self-consistency**. Psychologists have found that inconsistencies in one's beliefs or between one's beliefs and behavior are a source of tension and discomfort (Heider, 1958). People are motivated to resolve such inconsistencies and to maintain consistency. For example, a miserly individual who sees himself as very generous can maintain consistency between his behavior and his self-image by perceiving himself as very poor, by exaggerating the significance of any pittance given to charity, by believing that people will be corrupted by gifts, by viewing others as exceptionally greedy and demanding of his resources, and so on. The motivation for cognitive consistency appears to be quite pervasive and is central to a number of personality and social psychological theories (Festinger, 1957; Heider, 1958). Inconsistencies need to be understood before one can be concerned about them. In addition, the motivation for consistency is probably influenced by social learning inasmuch as children are encouraged to be logical and consistent.

self-consistency A motivation to maintain consistent ways of thinking about the self.

The striving for consistency has been documented in a series of experiments by Swann and his colleagues (Swann, 2011; Swann et al., 1987; Swann and Hill, 1982; Swann and Read, 1981). For example, in one study (Swann and Hill, 1982) college students participating in an experiment were given feedback from an experimental confederate that they seemed either dominant or submissive. When the feedback confirmed the self-concept, the appraisal was accepted. However, if it was discrepant, the students resisted the feedback by exaggerating the behaviors indicative of the personality that they felt truly characterized them. Thus, subjects who saw themselves as dominant and were told they were submissive responded in an especially dominant manner while those with a submissive self-concept, who were labeled dominant, became especially submissive.

This research suggests that there are at least two motives relevant to the self-concept: the motive to enhance one's self-esteem and the motive to preserve the consistency of one's view of the self. The challenge is to determine, particularly for negative self-concept, low self-esteem individuals, the conditions under which each of these tendencies will be paramount. There has been some effort to address this problem. There is evidence that cognitive responses tend to be mediated by self-consistency and affective responses by self-enhancement (Swann, et al., 1987). Subjects, after their self-esteem was assessed, were asked to make a brief speech and then given positive or negative feedback regarding their self-confidence. Both the high and low self-esteem subjects felt happier and less hostile and anxious after positive rather than negative feedback, manifesting a preference for self-enhancing information. However, as one would predict from a consistency model, the cognitive reactions of the high and low self-esteem subjects differed. The high self-esteem subjects rated the favorable feedback as more accurate than the unfavorable feedback, and their evaluation of the feedback procedure was commensurate with this difference. The low self-esteem subjects, in contrast, considered the unfavorable feedback to be more accurate than the favorable feedback. They also viewed the evaluator providing the unfavorable feedback as more competent than the favorable evaluator.

Personality Theories and the Self

The *self* has become an increasingly important concept in the study of personality and social behavior. One will find the properties of the self-structure relevant to issues concerning personality development and personality dynamics that will be considered in the ensuing chapters. The self is also pertinent to personality measurement in that many measurement procedures require individuals to appraise themselves, and most of the personality traits that are measured are self attributes.

The Self in Personality Theories

We have seen that properties of the self are important in almost all of the personality theories that have been reviewed in the preceding chapters. The only theorist who does not employ any self-related concepts is Skinner. However, the other learning theorists all refer implicitly or explicitly to some aspect of the self in their theoretical models. For Dollard and Miller, self-references are largely implicit. However, the notion of self-based motivations and affects such as pride, achievement, dependency, insecurity, in addition to defenses that reduce threats to the self are quite compatible with their theoretical approach to personality. In the case of Rotter, we find more explicit references to self-based motivation such as needs for recognition, dominance, and dependency. In addition, Rotter introduces an important self-agency concept in his distinction between belief in internal versus external control of reinforcement. For Bandura, the self enters into his theory primarily through its agency functions. Self-efficacy beliefs and self-monitoring and self-regulation of one's behavior in terms of one's standards and goals have assumed an increasingly important place in his social learning theory (Bandura, 1989).

For the phenomenological theorists, the self is a central concept. However, the phenomenologists differ as well as share similarities in their treatment of the self. Whereas Rogers and Maslow both emphasize self-actualization and Kelly does not, both Rogers and Kelly place importance on one's self-concept and its function as a frame of reference.

Freud was well aware of self-based motives, but these were completely subordinated to instinctual, id motives, and hence self-based motives are not specified in the table. Adler was certainly aware of self-love, and both Freud and Adler recognized that personal attributes functioned as a frame of reference, but these were not central processes in their theories. In one instance, Freud's concept of narcissism was cited, although not previously introduced in the text, since Freud coined the term and since it has an important although not a central role in his theory.

It is apparent that almost every personality theorist addresses some aspect of the self. It is of interest that most of the differences between personality theorists lie in the particular function of the self that is emphasized rather than in different interpretations of the same function.

It is primarily in the category of specific self-based motives that we see differences between theorists in the motives that are deemed most important. Most of the theorists address only one or two functions of the self while none, including Freud, whose theory is the most comprehensive, addresses all of the self's properties.

Summary

1. An experiential sense of self as distinct from other objects, as an agent, and as an interpersonal organism, develops very early.

2. The self-concept, one's description or image of oneself, begins to develop at around eighteen months of age. It appears to begin to develop when human infants become self-aware, and it continues to develop into adulthood, becoming more complex and differentiated.

3. One of the most basic characteristics of the self-concept is the sharpness and permeability of its *boundaries*. If the boundaries are too permeable, the individual becomes excessively influenced by other people and other situations, with an accompanying loss of individuality. However, how boundaries are drawn around the self varies from culture to culture, and is even different for men and women.

4. *Self-schemata* are cognitive generalizations about the self that serve to filter incoming information, organize experience, and guide subsequent action.

5. Of the many components and features that make up the self-concept, only a small segment is germane to a particular situation and becomes accessible at any given moment. The self-concept that is operative is referred to as the *working self-concept*.

6. Discrepancies between the *actual self*, the *ideal self* and the *ought self*, and between *actual* and *possible* selves are an important source of motivation and of one's affective state.

7. *Self-esteem* is based on one's generalized positive and negative evaluation of the various features of the self-concept. Not all elements of the self-concept contribute to self-esteem inasmuch as many elements of the self are only descriptive.

8. Low self-esteem is not necessarily correlated with experiences of discrimination and minority status.

9. *Self-awareness* is a prerequisite for the development of self-monitoring and self-control. Self-awareness can function in positive and negative ways.

10. The *self-monitoring scale* is predictive of a wide range of behaviors bearing on the social presentation aspects of the self. High self-monitors are more responsive to situational demands and tend to display less consistency in their behavior. Because the self-monitoring scale is substantially correlated with extroversion and exhibitionism, there is some question as to whether it primarily measures temperament traits, both temperament and self-monitoring, or primarily self-monitoring.

11. The motivation for *self-consistency* can conflict with the motivation for *self-enhancement* in individuals with low self-esteem. There is some evidence that cognitive responses in situations in which these tendencies are operative are mediated by self-consistency while affective responses are mediated by self-enhancement.

12. The *self* is a key concept for almost all personality theories. However, the particular property of the self that has been addressed varies markedly with the personality theory.

Key Terms

ideal self (p. 182)
ought self (p. 182)
possible selves (p. 182)
self-awareness (p. 178)
self-complexity (p. 182)
self-concept (p. 177)

self-consistency (p. 189)
self-esteem (p. 183)
self-monitoring (p. 185)
self-schema (p. 180)
working self-concept (p. 181)

Thought Questions

1. Do you think chimpanzees may eventually be shown to have a psychological self? If not, why not?

2. Can you think of any character in fiction or drama, or television or movies, where there is a significant discrepancy between that individual's self-concept and others' concept of that person? What are the consequences of that discrepancy?

3. Which leads to more effective behavior and better psychological adjustment in individuals with actual minimal competencies—a self-concept that matches one's actual skills and behaviors or a self-concept that is more positive and over-estimates one's competencies? Justify your response.

4. What kind of society do you think is preferable—one that maximizes individuality and individual accomplishments or one that subordinates individual uniqueness, privacy, etc. to the practices and goals of the groups? Why?

5. Why might the idea of the self-concept as a cognitive structure lead to people being motivated to maintain a consistent view of the self?

Identity

CHAPTER 11

Source: FuzzBones/Shutterstock.com

Chapter Outline

Stages of Identity Formation: Erikson and Marcia

Racial and Ethnic Identity

Sexual Orientation Identity Development

Gender Identity, Gender Typing, and Gender Differences

Narrative and Identity

In the previous chapter we considered the development and functions of the self. In this chapter we consider aspects of the development of identity.

Identity deals with that which we consider to be most basic to our sense of self—the things that identify who we are, both to ourselves and to others. It includes our most basic values and goals and our ethnic and gender identifications. As fans of science-fiction movies or amnesia victims know, there is nothing more terrifying than the sense of losing one's identity. Identity involves the fundamental sense of *continuity* in one's life: I am who I was yesterday, and I am who I will be tomorrow. It provides a framework for taking action in the future.

Self-concept and identity are closely related ideas. Both can provide answers to the question "Who am I?" Yet they differ. *Self-concept* is one's *description* of who one is. *Identity* is one's *definition* of who one is (Baumeister, 1986); it consists of those things that most basically define who we are. Something can be part of one's self-concept ("I am sloppy") but not part of one's identity ("I don't consider sloppiness an integral part of who I am"). Identity is defined by our connection to various aspects of our life, and it helps us locate ourselves in terms of who we are and where we belong (Lewis, 1990).

Many psychologists believe that adolescence is the key developmental time period for the formation of identity. While individuals begin to develop an identity in early childhood and may continue to modify their identities throughout their lives, adolescence is thought to be the most crucial organizational period for forming an identity. This view characterizes the perspectives of Erik Erikson, James Marcia, Dan McAdams, and those who have developed models

identity The goals, values, and roles that are the key descriptors of who we are to ourselves.

of ethnic identity formation. However, gender identity, as we shall see, appears to develop considerably earlier.

Stages of Identity Formation: Erikson and Marcia

Erik Erikson has been the most influential theorist of identity (see Chapter 4). Erikson emphasized the ability to experience oneself as having continuity and sameness as an important aspect of identity. Identity includes one's bodily identity, the ability to sustain loyalties, and a sense of having a future. It also includes having a stable sense of self versus feeling self-conscious, being able to pursue a career versus feeling paralyzed in terms of work, being able to experiment with various roles versus rigidly locking oneself into a fixed role, feeling clear about one's sexual identity versus being confused about one's sexual identity, and having ideological commitments versus being confused about one's values.

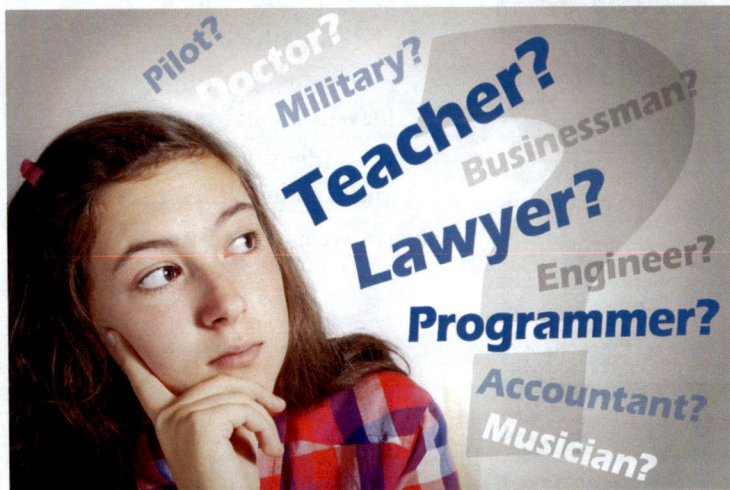

Determining an identity is a major task of adolescence. Choosing a career path is often a part of that identity.

Erikson believed that late adolescence was the time of identity achievement, although earlier developmental periods played a role. Identity achievement precedes the development of the capacity for intimacy, which occurs in early adulthood. However, Erikson theorized that this sequence is more characteristic of males than of females. For females, interpersonal aspects are at the core of their identity. Men therefore achieve identity first and intimacy second, while women achieve identity and intimacy concurrently, or intimacy first. Erikson also assumed that women do not complete an identity in adolescence because marriage and having children complete their identities.

James Marcia (1980), using an interview format, followed Erikson's ideas on the development of identity in adolescence. Others have subsequently developed objective measures based on Marcia's interview format (Grotevant and Adams, 1984). An example of items from one of these measures is given in Table 11.1.

TABLE 11.1 Sample Items from the Objective Measure of Ego-Identity Status

Status	Item
Diffusion	I haven't chosen the occupation I really want to get into, but I'm working toward becoming a ____ until something better comes along. When it comes to religion, I just haven't found any that I'm really into myself.
Foreclosure	I guess I'm pretty much like my folks when it comes to politics. I follow what they do in terms of voting and such. I've never really questioned my religion. If it's right for my parents, it must be right for me.
Moratorium	I just can't decide how capable I am as a person and what jobs I'll be right for. There are so many different political parties and ideals, I can't decide which to follow until I figure it all out.
Identity-achievement	A person's faith is unique to each individual. I've considered and reconsidered it myself and know what I can believe. It took me a while to figure it out, but now I really know what I want for a career.

Source: Adams, Gullota, and Markstrom-Adams, 1994, p. 274.

Marcia's original research involved interviewing adolescents about their vocational plans and goals, and their values and beliefs. They were asked about the degree to which they had explored each of these areas and the degree to which they had made a commitment in each area. In early versions, the identity interview focused on vocational achievement. Later, to correct for this bias, interpersonal elements were added to the interview. Currently the interview includes questions about vocational plans, avocations, religious beliefs, political ideologies, gender-role orientation, sexuality, values, friendships, dating, marriage, parenting, family and career, setting priorities, and ethnicity.

Marcia identifies four identity *statuses* during adolescence: diffusion, foreclosure, moratorium, and identity achievement. These four statuses vary along two dimensions: commitment and exploration. **Identity diffusion** is characterized by low levels of both commitment and exploration. The person neither has a set of commitments to goals or values nor is actively struggling with the process of forming such commitments. **Foreclosure** is characterized by a high level of commitment and a low level of exploration. Individuals in this stage are most likely those who have adopted an identity from their parents or culture without actively exploring and choosing. **Moratorium** is what we typically think of as an identity crisis and is characterized by high levels of exploration but a low level of commitment. The person is in the process of exploring who he or she is and what he or she wants to be but has not come to any stable set of commitments yet. **Identity achievement** is arrived at through exploration which results in a personally chosen commitment to a set of values and goals for one's life. The different combinations can be seen in Table 11.2.

In Marcia's scheme, identity achievement is the "highest" level, with moratorium the next, foreclosure third, and diffusion the lowest. However, a number of writers have noted that this order may be culturally biased. Only in Western society must one achieve an identity. In many other cultures, one attains one's identity from the culture and the role one plays in it (foreclosure). Therefore, for many cultures a foreclosed identity may be the healthiest. In fact, it has been found that for members of minority groups in the United States a foreclosed identity is more common than an achieved one. It has been argued that foreclosure may be a more functional identity for members of minority groups in a hostile society (Hauser and Kasendorf, 1983; Markstrom-Adams, Berman, and Brusch, 1993). Taking on an identity provided by one's group may be more adaptive than trying to individually achieve an identity in a society that blocks opportunities and conveys negative messages about one's minority status. This topic is discussed further in the section on ethnic identity.

Each of the four identity statuses can be thought of either as the state that a person is in or as a developmental stage. For some individuals, identity status remains relatively constant with time. In one study (Adams and Montemayor, 1988), constancy of identity status was found to occur for about 15 percent of the adolescents studied. For other individuals, the identity statuses form a kind of stage model, in which the individuals progress upwards through the four stages over time. About 50 percent of individuals were found to show steady progression over time. Still others showed an up and down pattern of progression and regression through the four statuses. A meta-analysis of 124 studies conducted

identity diffusion The status of a person who has low levels of both commitment and exploration to an identity.

foreclosure A person who has adopted an identity without consideration or exploration of alternative identities.

moratorium The status of a person who is in the process of exploring who he or she is but has not committed to an identity.

identity achievement Personally chosen commitment to a set of values and goals for one's life.

TABLE 11.2 The Two Dimensions of Marcia and the Four Alternative Identity Statuses

		Commitment	
		Yes	**No**
Exploration of alternatives	Yes	*Identity achievement*	*Moratorium*
	No	*Foreclosure*	*Identity diffusion*

by Kroger, Martinussen, and Marcia (2010) found that 49 percent of the adolescents in those studies remained stable in their identity, while 36 percent progressed to a higher identity status. Importantly, 15 percent regressed in their identity. Recognize that stability could be in any of the four identity statuses and that progress does not necessarily mean identity achievement.

Researchers have found a variety of correlates of the four identity statuses. Identity diffused individuals tend to show signs of poor psychological adjustment, such as feelings of inferiority and poorly articulated self-concepts. They are more likely to have parents who are rejecting or not affectionate and are more likely to have problems with substance abuse (Adams, Gullota, and Markstrom-Adams, 1994; Markstrom-Adams, 1992; Jones, 1992). Foreclosed individuals are more likely to be hardworking, quiet, obedient, respectful of authority, and industrious. They tend to come from families that are warm and supportive but that appear to stifle autonomous growth (Adams et al., 1994). Individuals in the moratorium status tend to be the most anxious, which is not surprising because they are in the midst of questioning their identity status. They appear to be high in self-directiveness while open to exploring alternative perspectives. They also tend to be introspective and emotionally responsive (Adams et al., 1994). Their families are likely to be democratically organized, but there is liable to be strain between the adolescent and the parents (Fuhrmann, 1986).

Identity achieved students have been found in many studies to have high levels of self-esteem, moral reasoning, self-confidence, psychological integration, emotional maturity, and social adeptness. They are also most likely to have established strong intimate relationships (Adams et al., 1994; Waterman, 1992). As with adolescents in the moratorium status, they are likely to have come from democratic homes (Fuhrmann, 1986). However, while the vast majority of the evidence indicates that identity achievement is associated with positive qualities, the findings are not entirely uniform. Kroger (1992) reports that some studies have found a high percentage of identity achieved participants to be excessively self-sufficient or detached.

Differences between men and women have been a major focus of investigation. As we have noted, Erikson assumed that interpersonal issues were at the core of women's identity, suggesting that their identities might not be completely formed until the intimacy stage in early adulthood. Research indeed supports the idea that identity and intimacy tend to merge for many women, while for men they are separated, that is, identity first and intimacy second (Patterson, Sochting, and Marcia, 1992). However, these researchers also conclude that the task of identity *begins* in adolescence both for women and for men. Further, for nontraditional women, late adolescence is the optimal time for resolution of the identity, as it is for men. For traditional women, whom Erikson expected would complete their identities when they married and had children, the evidence suggests that marriage and children do not complete their identities. Rather, these women put their identities "on hold" until their children have grown up, when they resume the task of identity completion. Josselson (1988) has studied identity formation in women by interviewing them in college and again when they were in their mid-thirties. She found that identity development for women does involve issues of interpersonal connection.

In early research on identity status it was found that for men, identity achievement and moratorium were the most "healthy" patterns (e.g., high self-esteem, etc.), while for women identity achievement and foreclosure were the healthiest (Patterson et al., 1992). At the time, Marcia (1980) suggested that the foreclosure status might be adaptive for women because society did not provide support for women, as it did for men, to explore and choose their identities. He predicted that if society changed, so would the pattern of these early research findings. Making Marcia look like a prophet, recent findings show that for women, as well as for men, identity achievement and moratorium are the more adaptive patterns. Patterson and colleagues (1992) note that this might be due to the fact that the identity status interview was changed over the years to take interpersonal issues more into account. However, they think this shift is more likely due to societal changes that now provide more support for women to choose careers.

Beyond Four Statuses

There is significant heuristic value in using Marcia's four identity statuses, but recent research has suggested a more nuanced view. Luyckx and colleagues have suggested that as a person commits to an identity, there is then a further exploration as to whether that identity is a truly workable identity (Luyckx, Goossens, and Soenens, 2006; Luyckx, Goossens, Soenens, and Beyers, 2006). A recognizable experience would be selecting a college major (Luyckx, Teppers, Klimstra, and Rassart, 2014). The first step is to identify the possible majors; this would be considered the moratorium stage. Then the person would decide on a major, which they termed exploration in breadth. Finally, the person deeply examines whether that is the right choice for who he or she is as a person, which they term exploration in depth (Meeus, 1996). For many people, that is the process. However, some people find the exploration to be very difficult and stressful. These people will continue to consider and reconsider *and reconsider* identities; this style is termed ruminative exploration (Luyckx et al., 2008).

It is also useful to consider different reactions to the diffusion stage as marked by concern over the lack of identity, or a relatively carefree diffusion in which the person is unconcerned about a lack of identity. The carefree diffusion is typically observed in the youngest adolescents and tends to be less common as the cohort ages (Verschueren, Rassart, Claes, Moons, and Luyckx, 2017).

There are several problems with the research done on identity statuses from Marcia's perspective. One problem is that most of the research has been done on college students, typically between the ages of eighteen and twenty-two. There is less research on adolescents not in college. In one study, Morash (1980) examined working-class youths and college students. It was found that working-class youths were more likely to be either identity achieved or diffused, while college students were more likely to be in moratorium or foreclosure. Working-class youths were also more likely to have experienced shorter, more concrete moratoriums. It may be that being in college allows one the luxury of a more leisurely moratorium period in which one can explore one's identity before making commitments. However, much more research is needed on adolescents not in college.

From a feminist perspective, Archer (1992) has criticized the research on identity statuses. She argues that focusing on differences between the genders is not fruitful. Individual men and women vary among themselves enormously, and the differences that have been found between men and women as groups are minimal. She believes it is more interesting to look at the question of how *individuals* pattern their identity achievement rather than at group comparison of genders. For instance, some of her research has found that reasoning about identity is "domain specific." This means that an individual's reasoning about identity in one area, such as vocation, is not necessarily the same as his or her reasoning in another area, such as relationships.

One criticism of identity status theory and research has previously been mentioned. That is that the whole concept of achieving an identity has a distinctly Western flavor. Myers, Speight, Highlen, Cox, Reynolds, Adams, and Hanley (1990), working from an Afro-centric paradigm, have noted that in Western culture one must establish one's worth through one's activities, while in other cultures one is valued just because one is. They believe that the Western idea is a product of our cultural assumptions, which separate self from others and separate the material from the spiritual. As previously noted, the foreclosure stage, therefore, may not necessarily be a less developed stage than the identity achieved stage in many cultures.

In conclusion, Marcia's theory of identity statuses has led to research that has helped clarify the process of identity development in adolescence. At the same time many issues remain to be clarified.

Racial and Ethnic Identity

We now turn to an important specific component of identity: **racial and ethnic identity**. Racial and ethnic identity has to do with those aspects of one's identity that relate to one's identification with one's ethnic group. Not everyone has specifically worked out an ethnic

racial and ethnic identity Those aspects of one's identity that relate to one's identification with one's ethnic group.

identity. However, it is a particularly important issue for minority group members in our culture. Because ethnicity and race are closely related, and at times fully mixed, many researchers use ethnicity to refer to both race and ethnicity (Schwartz et al., 2014). We will use that convention here, as the effects of discrimination seem to be the same whether it is based on race or ethnicity (Oyserman, Coon, and Kemmelmeier, 2006).

Individuals who are members of minority groups in our society face a particularly complicated task in forming an identity. First, they are often confronted with conflicting messages concerning important life values. For instance, the particular minority culture may hold the value that an individual's choice of careers should be influenced by the family, while the dominant culture in the United States emphasizes individual choice. Second, we have already seen that different cultural groups hold different views of what a self is: is it a "we" interconnected with others, or is it an "I," a separate, autonomous entity? Third, such individuals are often confronted with the social devaluation of their minority group status. In various implicit and explicit ways they are told that they are "less than" because they are members of a particular minority group. This message might be conveyed, for instance, through stereotypic television portrayals or through the relative invisibility of their group in television shows. Fourth, they face some objective limitations to their hopes and aspirations because of their minority group status and various concomitants, such as economic inequality.

There are two interrelated aspects to the formation of an identity for ethnic minority members. First is the issue of forming a positive, proactive identification with one's ethnic group. This is the issue that most models of ethnic identity formation have focused on. A second issue is that of acculturation—the degree to which the individual attempts to integrate with the dominant culture or chooses to remain separate and identify exclusively with the minority culture.

Ethnic identity, according to Phinney (1990), includes one's sense of self-identification as a group member, attitudes and values in relation to one's group, attitudes about oneself as a group member, the adoption of ethnic behaviors and practices, and the extent of one's ethnic knowledge and degree of commitment to one's group.

There is a commonality to many models of ethnic identity development. This commonality is shared by models of identity development for nonethnic minority groups as well, such as for gays and lesbians. The models tend to describe the process as proceeding in five stages (Umaña-Taylor et al., 2014):

1. Pre-encounter, in which one is unaware of or unconcerned about differences
2. Experiences with others leading to awareness of differences
3. A period of conflict between the old unawareness and the new awareness
4. Resolution and habituation
5. Commitment to the group and identity

Phinney (Phinney, 1990; 1991; Phinney and Rosenthal, 1992) has proposed a model of ethnic identity development that is synthesized from other models but is also based on the work of Erikson and Marcia. The first stage is that of an unexamined ethnic identity, which could be likened to Marcia's either foreclosed or diffused status. The adolescent either adopts an unexamined commitment to his or her ethnicity from the parents and is therefore foreclosed, or has no clear sense of commitment to ethnic identity but is not exploring it either and is therefore in a diffused state. In the second stage, some event—perhaps some act of discrimination (Quintana, 2007)—triggers the adolescent's awareness of his or her ethnic identity, and he or she begins to think about it. This stage is equivalent to the moratorium stage in Marcia's model. Indeed, during adolescence, exploration of ethnic identity tends to rise (French, Seidman, Allen, and Aber, 2006). In the third stage of ethnic identity development, some kind of commitment to an ethnic identity occurs. This follows a process of resolving conflicts and contradictions involved in being a minority in a majority culture where minorities have often experienced discrimination. Phinney and Chavira

(1992) studied the development of ethnic identity in minority youths between the ages of sixteen and nineteen and found movement from lower to higher stages, as predicted.

Using an ethnically diverse sample and statistical technique called cluster analysis, Yip (2014) found that the Marcia model fit her data well. Adolescents in the achieved category included ethnic identity across situations. The achieved adolescents showed higher levels of exploration and higher self-esteem. The achieved and moratorium adolescents reported being more aware of the ethnicity in their everyday life.

A fundamental question is whether ethnic identity status has a positive or negative impact on psychological adjustment. Phinney (1991) found that not all components of a positive ethnic identity correlated with high self-esteem, but the trend was that individuals with a strong ethnic identity were more likely to have high self-esteem. Having a developed ethnic identity appears to work as a defense against perceived discrimination, allowing healthier adaptation (Sellers, Copland-Linder, Martin, and Lewis, 2006).

With respect to acculturation, Berry and his colleagues (1989) have defined four modes of acculturation. Those who strongly identify only with their ethnic group are in a state of separation. Those who strongly identify only with the dominant culture are in a state of assimilation. Those who identify with both their own group and the dominant culture are considered to be bicultural. Finally, those who identify with neither are considered to be in a state of marginalization. In general, most theorists now hold that biculturation is the most adaptive mode. For instance, LaFromboise, Coleman, and Gerton (1993) have argued that biculturated individuals are those who have developed the competencies to function both in their culture of origin and in the larger majority culture. They are able to utilize the best of both cultures. Meta-analysis of 83 studies, which included 32,197 individuals, found that psychological and social adjustment tends to be higher in people who identify with two cultures (Nguyen and Benet-Martínez, 2013). In this sense, they will have also developed a more complex, differentiated, and integrated identity.

Source: LightField Studios/Shutterstock

Having a sense of identification with one's own culture can have a positive influence on one's own identity.

Sexual Orientation Identity Development

The process for forming identity for gay and lesbians has informed the models of race and ethnic identity, and been informed by those models as well. Unlike members of most race and ethnic groups, homosexuals are usually in the minority in their own families. Also, gays and lesbians can hide their identity, which members of many minority groups cannot do. There are two major theories of sexual orientation identity, and as we will see, they are similar, though not identical. Although both models were laid out to explain and understand the process for homosexuals, we can probably assume that the models work for other sexualities outside the mainstream.

Cass's model (1984) suggests that there are six stages to developing a sexual orientation identity that is different from the dominant model:

Stage 1: Identity confusion. A person starts to wonder if he or she may be homosexual. If that is accepted as a possibility, the person moves to the next stage.

Stage 2: Identity comparison. The person starts to compare himself or herself to homosexuals and nonhomosexuals.

Stage 3: Identity tolerance. The person starts to make more and more contacts with other homosexuals. The identity is tolerated, but not embraced.

Stage 4: Identity acceptance. A positive view of homosexuality starts to develop. However, disclosure of sexual orientation will be limited, and the person may often attempt to pass as heterosexual.

Stage 5: Identity pride. People will start to feel a great deal of pride about their sexual orientation. They will identify strongly with other homosexuals, and feel anger at the intolerance society directs toward homosexuals.

Stage 6: Identity synthesis. Roles models have typically helped the individual settle into the community and identity. The person feels comfortable in that identity, needing neither to hide nor flaunt the identity.

In this model, we see similarities to the moratorium and identity achievement stages that are key components of the Marcia model.

The other major model was laid out by Troiden (1988). This model includes typical ages at which the stage is experienced. He warns that the model is an ideal and simplified process. The real process is not linear and has many movements both forward and backward. Stages may overlap and be experienced more than once.

The first stage is sensitization. This is typically experienced before puberty. The child becomes aware that he or she is different from peers. Usually, this difference is not noted to be a sexual difference until after the onset of puberty.

The second stage is identity confusion. This stage is typically experienced in adolescence. The person realizes that he or she sexually different. Because most of the models to which the person is exposed are not homosexual, and because homosexuality is often stigmatized, this is often not a welcome recognition. Adding to the confusion is the general ease of arousal in adolescence that may lead to being aroused by either gender. At this point, the person can respond in several different ways. A person may deny or seek to change his or her sexual orientation. He or she may avoid situations that confirm desires. Among the forms of avoidance are the formation antihomosexual attitudes or escape via drugs or alcohol. A person may respond by redefining his or her desires—for instance, by claiming bisexuality, considering it a temporary stage, or describing it as a special case ("I'd only do this with you"). It is also possible that the person will accept the prospect and seek more information.

The third stage is identity assumption. This stage typically happens in the early twenties for men and somewhat later for women. At this point, the person will have included homosexuality into his or her self-concept. There is tolerance and acceptance of the identity, along with sexual experimentation and association with others in the community. Although a homosexual identity is developed, the identity is more tolerated than embraced.

The fourth stage is commitment. Homosexuality becomes a major part of the person's self-identity. The person usually enters into a same-sex love relationship. Typically, he or she finds it is much easier to live having adopted this identity than to continue to fight against it. As a result, personal happiness tends to increase.

Troiden's model has similarities to both Marcia's model of general identity development such as confusion and successful identity achievement. We also see aspects of the model of ethnic identity development with the experiences leading to awareness of differences, the resolution and habituation, and finally commitment to the group and identity.

Beyond the development of one's sexual orientation identity, members of the LGBTQ community must face another step: that is the process of coming out. The process of coming out can be a dangerous time, as there can often be an increase in prejudice and victimization directed at the person (Davison, 2005). Gay and lesbian youth show a suicide rate high above others of similar ages (Hottes, Bogaert, Rhodes, Brennan, and Gesink, 2016; Remafadi, French, Story, Resnick, and Blum, 1998), though legalizing same-sex marriage has been found to reduce the suicide rate in homosexual teens (Raifman, Moscoe, and Austin, 2017).

Legalization of same-sex marriage may reduce suicide rates for homosexual teens.

Gender Identity, Gender Typing, and Gender Differences

Some of the most active current research in developmental psychology concerns the development of gender identity and the related issues of gender differences and gender typing. While gender identity has to do with individuals' self-perceptions of who they are as males or as females, gender differences have to do with the question of whether there are objective differences in psychological functioning between the two genders. The issue of gender-typing has to do with how males and females develop their masculine or feminine identities, attributes, or behaviors. The issue of whether there are gender differences and how gender-typing occurs are intimately related to the development of gender identity. We first examine gender identity, then consider the issue of gender differences, and finally reflect upon how gender differences and gender identity develop, i.e., the issue of gender-typing.

The convention that we use when describing the differences between males and females is to use the term **gender** for anything that might be due to culture and socialization and sex to refer to differences that are due to biology (Frieze and Chrisler, 2011). We need to be very careful about the term sex, as it is easy to confuse biological influences with social and cultural influences. We might look at something such as running a foot race as a sex difference where anatomical differences mean that males are faster than females. However, the current world record time for women in the 200-meter race (21.34 seconds) would have won every men's 200-meter Olympic final from 1900 to 1928. It might be argued that the reason is changes in training, and that is likely correct. But, think of training as something that is cultural. So, even in something that seems obviously to be based on a sex difference, culture matters.

gender Aspects of oneself as male or female that may be due to culture and socialization.

Gender Identity

One of the most important components of identity is gender identity. In introducing his model of gender identity, Ashmore (1990), says that "it is assumed that sex and gender pervade most aspects of daily life and can shape many aspects of psychological structure and function" (p. 512).

gender identity One's
inclusion of his or her gender
as part of identity.

One's **gender identity** is defined by how one's perception of gender influences or plays a role in other aspects of identity. It could be said to be the answer to the issue of what it means to the individual to be a man or woman. It is how one's view of oneself as male or female is interwoven with all the various other aspects of one's identity. According to Ashmore (1990), gender identity consists of five general content areas. The first is the biological and physical attributes associated with gender, including aspects of appearance and dress. The second area is "symbolic and stylistic behaviors," including how one walks, one's body bearing, and how one communicates nonverbally. The third area consists of the interests and abilities that one sees as relevant to and characteristic of one's gender. The fourth area is "social relationships," which includes images of how one will differentially relate to men and women as well as how one's sense of masculinity or femininity are organized and expressed in relationship with others. The fifth area is perception of one's personal and social attributes—for instance, one's personality traits and how these relate to masculinity and femininity.

Gender Differences

Many differences can be observed between boys and girls and men and women in terms of "typical" behavior. More boys play with blocks and fire trucks than do girls, who tend to play with dolls and paper cutouts more than do boys; boys prefer football, while girls prefer dramatic play. Gender differences in toy and activity preference can be observed early in development, well before the age of three (Lewis, 1987). Later in life, more men than women study to be architects and engineers, while more women become nurses and school teachers than do men. There are many exceptions and, although changes are occurring in traditional gender roles, there are still gender differences in preferred activities and in such diverse domains as child-care responsibilities, work roles, and occupations. These differences are most likely a reflection of the contrasting social roles ascribed to men and women. Comparable kinds of gender differences in social roles are observed in other societies, both modern and preliterate.

We know that these gender differences exist at the social level. The intriguing question is what they are related to at the psychological level. To what extent do boys and girls differ in intellectual abilities motivation social skills and other personality attributes? There are many common stereotypes concerning gender differences in personality. For example, males have been regarded as aggressive, rational, and ambitious, while females have been described as passive, emotional, and nurturant. These stereotypes are opinions and are in part responsible for the differential occupational roles, income levels, and statuses of the genders. But to what extent do these gender stereotypes have a basis in fact?

Gender-typing begins early in life.

One task undertaken by psychologists has been to determine possible personality and cognitive attributes that distinguish the two genders and, in addition, to discern the age levels at which gender differences appear. This empirical task has proved to be far more complex than it initially seemed. First, one must assume that the samples of the genders studied are comparable on such variables as socioeconomic status and educational opportunity. It is also important to sample different ethnic and economic groups to establish that the findings are representative of boys and girls in general, rather than restricted to some particular segment of society. To add a further complication, as the culture undergoes economic and social change, there may be corresponding alterations in personality traits. For example, differences in dependency between the genders seem to have been greater in previous decades, indicating that gender differences reported at one time may not hold for another. Conversely, where there once were similarities, differences may suddenly appear. Finally, some of the psychological attributes distinguishing the genders are subtle and difficult to measure.

A second and even more challenging task for psychologists is determining how differences between the genders have come about, or how gender typing occurs. The role of biological versus social factors in determining behavioral differences between the genders is an especially interesting issue. It is evident from the extensive amount of research that has been conducted on gender differences that there is a great deal of overlap between the genders with regard to virtually any behavior. Because of individual variability within a gender and the overlap between genders, gender discrimination is psychologically, as well as legally, unjustified.

In the sections that follow, we consider research studies on gender differences and on the development of gender differences and gender identity.

Studies of Gender Differences

We are all aware that men and women are socialized to be different in a number of ways, such as in how they dress. However, are there basic *psychological* differences? A good deal of research has been done to determine whether there are such differences. In a classic review of the literature on human gender differences, Maccoby and Jacklin (1974) concluded that there were differences.

Research has indicated that men and women are now close to equal in the areas of both verbal and mathematical ability. In addition, even the finding that males are more aggressive appears to be just a moderate effect (Archer, 2004; Ashmore, 1990). Nonetheless, the data still indicate that men are more likely to be aggressive than women, although such a difference may depend on how aggression is measured (see the following discussion of how gender differences develop).

Ashmore's (1990) summary of research indicates that, overall, few psychological gender differences have been found that are of more than "small to moderate" size. There are differences between men and women in "social stylistic" behaviors, such as smiling and facial expressiveness. Women report themselves to be more empathic than men, although when empathy is objectively measured, only small differences are found. The largest differences found between men and women are in physical variables, such as in the distance to which they are able to throw a ball.

More recent findings have led to questions about some of these conclusions. For instance, early research on mathematical ability found differences between boys and girls; however, this difference has mostly disappeared in the United States (Hyde, Lindberg, Linn, Ellis, and Williams, 2008). Hyde (2014) reviewed the many meta-analyses that have examined the differences between the genders; many of the results of studies she reviewed are included in Table 11.3. A few of those meta-analyses she and her colleagues conducted, whereas others were conducted by other people as reported in her review.

Meta-analyses have been mentioned a few times so far in the text, and will be included several more times in the next chapters. **Meta-analysis** is a statistic process that allows an integration and analysis of multiple studies simultaneously. By doing this, the random variance that shows up in any one study is reduced, the impact of a single researcher's approach is reduced, and multiple methodologies can be combined. Meta-analysis is a uniquely powerful way of looking at research findings, and is one of the most trusted methods for confidently drawing conclusions about research. The product of a meta-analysis is the "effect size." In our table, the effect size indicates how much of a difference there is between males and females. By convention (Cohen, 1988), the absolute value of an effect size greater than .80 is considered large, near .50 is considered moderate, and near .20 is considered small.

It is worth noting that most gender differences are indeed quite small. Males report more interest in sex, but that is confounded with social demand characteristics (Fischer, 2007). Self-esteem differences build through adolescence, then become minimal in adulthood. Males do seem to be better at 3-D mental rotation, though even this may be due to practice effects in video games (Feng, 2007) and sports. The mental rotation effects do appear quite early (Quinn and Liben, 2008), which then might predispose boys to those activities.

meta-analysis A statistic process that allows an integration and analysis of multiple studies simultaneously.

TABLE 11.3 Gender Differences Effect Sizes from Various Meta-Analyses

Topic	Effect size	Topic	Effect size
Cognitive functions		Leadership effectiveness	−0.02
Mathematics	−0.05	*Temperament in childhood*	
Complex problem solving (HS students, 1990)	0.29	Inhibitory control	−0.41
Complex problem solving (HS students, 2008)	0.07	Negative affect	−0.06
3D mental rotation	0.56	Emotionality	0.01
Vocabulary	−0.02	*Personality traits*	
Reading comprehension	−0.03	Neuroticism facet anxiety	−0.27
Writing	−0.09	Extraversion facet assertiveness	0.49
Verbal fluency	−0.33	Agreeableness facet tender-mindedness	−1.07
Reading achievement U.S.	−0.26	Conscientiousness	−0.07
Math self-confidence	0.27	Sensation seeking	0.41
Math anxiety	−0.23	*Emotions*	
Interests		Guilt	−0.27
Engineering	1.11	Shame	−0.29
Science	0.36	Authentic pride	−0.01
Mathematics	0.34	*Aggression*	
Self-esteem		Physical	0.55
Elementary school	0.16	Relational	−0.19
Middle school	0.23	*Sexuality*	
High school	0.33	Masturbation	0.53
College	0.18	Use pornography	0.63
Post college adults	0.10	Number of sexual partners	0.36

Positive numbers mean males have larger scores; negative numbers mean females have larger scores. (Based on meta-analyses reported in Hyde, 2014.)

In general, most researchers believe that there are far fewer differences in basic psychological attributes between the genders than there are similarities. For instance, Hyde (1984) notes that gender accounts for about 5 percent of the variation in aggressive behavior in children, which means that about 95 percent of the variation in aggressive behavior is due to factors other than gender. As she points out, humans have 23 pairs chromosomes and only one is the sex chromosome, so we should expect more similarity than differences (Hyde, 2014, p. 378).

While there may be relatively few basic psychological differences between the genders, some differences in behaviors begin to develop very early. Boys between the ages of fourteen and twenty-two months already prefer trucks and cars to play with, while girls prefer dolls and soft toys (Smith and Daglish, 1977). Two-year-old girls prefer to play with other girls, and by age three boys prefer to play with boys (La Freniere, Strayer, and Gauthier, 1984).

Gender Typing: Development of Gender Differences and Gender Identity

There have been a number of different theories that try to account for differences that are observed between the genders. Biological theories hold that differences are based in biology and are observable as soon as children begin to interact and play with peers (around the age of two). Yet the role of biological factors is complex.

Evidence from primate studies indicates that male monkeys engage in more rough-and-tumble play than females do and that even male infants display more aggressive behavior when attacked than females do (Aldis, 1975; Devore, 1965). But whether these observations of monkey behavior are applicable to humans is uncertain. In humans in this culture, the process of treating males and females differently begins at birth, with pink and blue blankets. Girls and boys are not only differently identified through the use of different colors and clothing, but also reacted to with different expectations and behaviors. Thus, even these early differences in aggression may be attributed to social rather than biological factors.

Later in the book the question of gender differences in aggression and the role of biological and social factors are examined in more detail. At this point, it is useful to keep in mind that the greater aggressiveness noted in males is based on observations of direct physical and verbal aggression. Although the gender differences in direct aggression before the age of six have been questioned (Tieger, 1980), extensive evidence can be presented indicating that this difference is reliable (Maccoby and Jacklin, 1980) and can be observed in children as young as age three (Fagot, Leinbach, and Hagan, 1986). However, when one examines more indirect, subtle forms of aggressiveness, such as snubbing or ignoring peers or gossiping, there is some evidence that aggression is greater in females than in males (Feshbach, 1969; Lagerspetz, Björkqvist, and Peltorer, 1988). Indeed, the meta-analysis on relational aggression does indicate that girls use it more (Archer, 2004).

For the sake of completeness, we can include the psychoanalytic perspective. According to Freud, the process by which boys and girls develop sex differences and their gender identities is rooted in biology. For him, identification was the principal mechanism leading to sex typing. As a result of the process of identification, children acquire the attributes and orientations of their sex. The biological difference between boys and girls leads not only to their making a different choice of which parent to identify with, but also to a less satisfactory identification for females (see Chapter 3). Therefore, the process of identification has biological roots. Freud did recognize some influence of learning processes in the development of gender differences, however, and contemporary psychoanalysts acknowledge the importance of social variables to an even greater extent.

The social learning theorists stress the importance of the differential reinforcement boys and girls receive for "appropriately" imitating male and female models and for behaving in accordance with the norms and expectations of society. The behaviors that define the female and male roles are very much influenced by the culture in which a child is socialized. Gender role norms vary from society to society, but in each case children are rewarded for those behaviors that will help them fit the particular roles prescribed by society. This differential reinforcement begins very early. It is manifest in the disparate ways that males and females are handled by their parents, in the unequal rough-and-tumble play of fathers with boys versus girls, and in the reinforcements given for engaging in appropriate gender-typed activities. One of the earliest gender differences that is consistently observed is that a greater amount of physical stimulation and gross motor play is directed toward male infants than toward female infants (see Block, 1979; Parke and Suomi, 1980). Studies of child-rearing practices in this and other cultures (Antill, 1987; Block, 1973; Whiting, 1963) clearly indicate that parents have different expectations for boys and girls and respond differentially according to the gender of their child. It is inevitable that these socialization practices define and shape male and female behavior.

Children even act as enforcers of gender roles. Children will punish through statements or teasing of other children for playing with toys associated with the other gender (Langlois and Downs, 1980). Children know which other children act most often as the enforcers (McGuire, Martin, Fabes, and Hanish, 2007, as cited in Martin and Ruble, 2010). Thus, children learn to play only with gender "appropriate" toys or risk social sanctions. In adolescence, there is a continuation of this pattern, as adolescents report pressure from peers to act in gender-conforming ways (Kornienko, Santos, Martin, and Granger, 2016).

Source: LightField Studios/Shutterstock

Children often expect other children to not play with toys associated with the other gender.

It should be noted that in many instances of gender differences it is very difficult to disentangle the influence of biological and social variables. Parental practices may reinforce and enhance subtle biologically based sex differences or may obscure them. Application of the twin method to the analysis of individual differences in masculine and feminine personality attributes enables one to at least partially separate the independent roles of biological and environmental influence. In one study, monozygotic and dizygotic twins ranging in age from eight to fifteen years were administered several questionnaire measures of **masculinity** and **femininity** (Mitchell, Baker, and Jacklin, 1989). These self-report measures are based on attributes which men and women believe to be more typical of and appropriate to males and to females. An example of a masculine item is "I am often the leader among my friends," and a feminine item, "I am a kind and gentle person." The relationships between monozygotic twins proved to be much stronger than that for dizygotic twins for both femininity and, especially, masculinity scores, thus providing evidence of a genetic influence. Analysis of the data also reflected significant environmental influences.

It may be noted that masculinity and femininity are separate dimensions or traits rather than opposite ends of a single continuum. Thus, while boys tend to be higher in masculinity and girls higher in femininity, it is quite possible for a boy or a girl to obtain both high masculinity and high femininity scores. The original model of masculinity-femininity was unidimensional, meaning that as a person increased on one dimension, he or she

masculinity The extent to which a person manifests characteristics typically associated with men.

femininity The extent to which a person manifests characteristics typically associated with women.

necessarily decreased on the other dimension. The current conceptualization recognizes that individuals can have aspects of both dimensions as part of their personality.

The development of gender typing and gender-linked behaviors is a complex process in which maturational and cognitive factors are involved as well as gender and social influences. A study by Fagot and Leinbach (1989) illustrates the interaction of several of these factors. A sample of boys and girls and their parents were seen when the children were approximately eighteen months, twenty-seven months, and forty-eight months of age. At age twenty-seven months, half the children, designated as "early labelers," were able to successfully identify the gender of children and adults in photographs presented to them. The other half, who made several errors in identifying males and females, were designated as "late labelers." Differences between boys and girls, and between early and late labelers, in gender-linked behaviors at eighteen and at twenty-seven months are presented in Table 11.4. At eighteen months, there were no significant differences between the groups. However, at twenty-seven months, gender differences in male- and female-typed toy play and in aggressive behavior can be seen. In addition, these differences are strongly influenced by whether the child can successfully identify gender. The largest gender differences in gender-typed behaviors are between the boys and girls who can successfully identify gender (early labelers). Clearly, learning factors are entailed in the development of gender typing.

Kohlberg proposed that children pass through three stages as they acquire an understanding of what it means to be a male or female. The first stage is that of "basic gender identity," which consists of acquiring the basic label of oneself as a boy or girl, usually achieved by about age three. The second stage is that of "gender stability." A number of researchers have found that very young children, even when they understand that they are boys or girls, do not understand that gender is a stable attribute that does not change over time. This developmental achievement occurs somewhat later, around five or six. The third stage is "gender consistency," which is the understanding that one's gender is stable across situations. That is, one's gender is not changed by dressing in clothes of the opposite gender or by engaging in play activities preferred by the opposite gender. This is typically achieved by age six to seven. Some research has found that the gender concept does indeed develop sequentially, passing through the stages, and that this sequence has been observed across cultures (Munroe, Shimmin, and Munroe, 1984).

TABLE 11.4 Mean Percent of Time Children Spent in Gender-Stereotyped Behaviors

Child activity and child age	Boy		Girl	
	Early labeler	Late labeler	Early labeler	Late labeler
Male-typed toy play:				
18 months	4.1	6.8	.8	3.0
27 months	23.8	11.2	4.6	7.6
Female-typed toy play: ·				
18 months	2.7	4.7	4.5	4.1
27 months	1.9	5.1	20.8	10.2
Aggressive behavior:				
18 months	.8	2.5	1.1	.9
27 months	2.1	2.2	.4	1.9

Based on Fagot and Leinbach (1989).

An alternative to Kohlberg's view, Martin and Halverson (1981, 1987) have developed **gender schema theory**. They suggest that children develop a set of gender schemas, which are organized sets of concepts about males and females. Children begin very early to develop a basic gender identity based on a simple classification of toys and behaviors as "for males" or "for females." Using this basic categorization, they then begin to explore and gradually add more and more information to their gender schemas until they have developed a stable and consistent gender identity by about the age of seven. Of course, this does not signal the end of learning about gender, which continues throughout childhood and adolescence.

A study by Stangor and Ruble (1989) tested the gender schema model. One of the properties of a schema is that it selectively influences the kind of information one pays attention to and remembers. In this study, it was found that the proportion of pictures remembered by children that were consistent with their gender-role in contrast to pictures that were inconsistent with it, increased with age.

As we have mentioned, although gender-schema theory suggests that a stable and consistent basic gender identity is established by about age seven, new aspects of gender identity continue to develop as one grows older. Brown and Gilligan (1992) have showed that adolescence is an important time for socialization of certain aspects of the gender identity of girls. They studied how girls lose their "voice" during the transition from late childhood to adolescence. Nearly one hundred girls between the ages of seven and eighteen at a private girls' school were interviewed over a five-year period. It was found that as girls entered adolescence, they increasingly received pressure from their teachers and other adults to "be nice." They learned that in order to keep relationships, they had to lose an important part of relationships—authenticity. One of the girls says, "I do not want the image of a 'perfect girl' to hinder myself from being a truly effective human being, . . . yet, I still want to be nice, and I never want to cause any problems" (p. 41). In sum, girls' gender identity during adolescence comes to include "being nice" at the expense of being authentic.

Androgyny

Is there such a thing as a "healthy" gender identity? We have already seen how young girls making the transition from childhood to adolescence are socialized to lose a part of themselves that has traditionally been considered to be masculine—their assertiveness. At the same time it is likely that boys are being trained to lose a "feminine" part of themselves. Would it be better if children were able to retain both their masculine and feminine sides? Precisely this issue has been raised in the study of **androgyny**.

In early research, it was assumed that masculinity and femininity were two opposite ends of the same pole. If one was high in masculinity (that is, possessed traits characteristic of the male stereotype), one could not be high in femininity. Bem (1974), however, asserted that masculinity and femininity were two separate dimensions, and, therefore, a person could be high in both masculinity and femininity. As part of their gender identities, individuals could have traits characteristic of both the stereotypical male and the stereotypical female. Bem assumed that individuals who were high in both masculinity and femininity would be more flexible and adaptive. Using an inventory designed to measure both masculinity and femininity, it was found that such "androgynous" individuals did exist. Several research studies also found that individuals who were androgynous did appear to be more well-adjusted. However, there are a number of methodological problems that have made it difficult to conclude at this point that androgyny is indeed uniquely associated with better psychological adjustment (Ashmore, 1990).

Conclusions on the Development of Gender Identity and Gender Typing

Ashmore (1990) has pointed out that the development of gender identity is a product of a number of different factors, including general cultural factors, specific interactions with specific individuals (e.g., parents, teachers, etc.), and one's own self-guided activities. The result is that individuals' gender identities will vary from person to person, and it may be meaningless to talk about "masculinity" and "femininity" as if they were global traits that individuals simply have more or less of. Ashmore suggests that culture has often been treated as if it were homogeneous, when in fact different subcultures in the United States may have different beliefs and expectations about the behavior of males and females. Individuals socialized in these subcultures may therefore have different concepts of male and female gender identities than do individuals socialized in the dominant or mainstream culture.

It is quite likely that gender typing and gender identity are functions of all the mechanisms that have been discussed: identification, selective reinforcement, cognitive labeling, and gender schemas. In addition, one cannot ignore the contribution of biological factors, even if they may be overridden by social reinforcement. In sum, gender typing and gender identity are the result of the interaction between social and biological processes, leading to personality differences between the genders and variations within each gender.

Narrative and Identity

Dan McAdams (1989; 2001) has focused on the **narrative identity**. Narrative identity is a person's internalized and evolving life story, integrating the past and future (McAdams and McLean, 2013). This reflects a recent more general trend toward viewing individual experience in terms of narrative constructions (Howard, 1991; Singer, 2004; Smith, 1988). What these views all have in common is the idea that people's personal realities are "constructed." How we construct our experiences of self, others, and the world determines the world we inhabit. Our constructions are significantly influenced by the cultures or subcultures in which we live. As we have seen, the self is constructed differently by different cultures. Even our experience of gender is now being seen as a social construction (Ashmore, 1990).

narrative identity A person's version of his or her life story.

Mair, and others who adopt a narrative perspective, assumes that our constructions of reality take the form of stories:

> Stories are habitations. We live in and through stories. They conjure worlds. We do not know the world other than as story world. Stories inform life. They hold us together and keep us apart. We inhabit the great stories of our culture. We live through stories. We are *lived* by the stories of our race and place. It is this enveloping and constituting function of stories that is especially important to sense more fully. We are, each of us, locations where the stories of our place and time become partially tellable. (1988, p. 127)

Therefore, life experience is constructed along the lines of stories. Lives have plots and subplots, and main characters and minor characters. Paul Ricoeur, a French psychoanalyst, has argued that it is how we "emplot" our lives that provides meaning for the events in it. An event without being embedded in a "plot" has no meaning. He says:

> [A] story is made out of events to the extent that plot makes events into a story. An event, consequently, must be more than a singular occurrence, a unique happening. It receives its definition from its contribution to the development of a plot. A story, on the other hand, must be more than an enumeration of events in a serial order; it must make an intelligible whole of incidents. (1983, p. 152)

One's life can have a well-organized plot, a poorly organized plot, a plot that has few leads toward a productive future, or a plot poorly connected to the past.

The narrative perspective on personality is having an important influence on psychotherapy. Therapists representing psychodynamic, humanistic, and cognitive points of view have begun to view therapy as the "restorying" of an individual's life. Ricoeur (Smith, 1988) sees therapy as a process of reorganizing one's plot through sharing it with another. An important part of the healing process is the sharing of one's "untold" stories. What might be called "repressed experience" is really experience that has not previously been articulated and shared with another.

An example of how people can utilize narrative accounts to deal with a life problem is provided by Harvey, Orbuch, and Weber (1993). They studied hundreds of individuals dealing with traumatic experiences such as incest, armed combat, an airline crash, or the loss of a loved one. They argue that it is in developing an account of the incident that the victim learns how to cope with the event and to restore a sense of meaning to life. An *account* is a "story-like construction containing attributions, trait inferences, descriptions, emotional expressions, and related material regarding self and outside world" (pp. 1–2). Confiding in others as one develops the account appears also to be an essential part of the healing process. One study by Harvey and colleagues (1991) found that there was greater recovery if the individual engaged in account making through diary work, confiding in responsive, empathic others, or participating in support groups. Feelings of completion appear to be associated with accepting loss and appear to be crucial to recovery (Cox and McAdams, 2014).

Source: wavebreakmedia/Shutterstock

Psychotherapy can be seen as the process of restorying one's life.

As we have noted, the narrative perspective has been applied to the study of identity by Dan McAdams (1989, 2001, 2013), who argues that identity is a narrative construction based on one's "life story." Our sense of ourselves, how we interpret events and experiences in our lives, comes from the sense of the "stories" we see ourselves as living. Further, our goals and motives only take on meaning in terms of our life story.

McAdams (1988) has researched this theory by collecting life stories from individuals. He had students enrolled in his developmental psychology courses complete "identity journals" in which they had to write about issues relevant to the class material. For instance, when the issue of consistency in personality was being discussed, students were asked to think about it in terms of themselves by trying to remember an incident in which they had done something completely out of character. McAdams has also interviewed midlife adults (see the interview format in Table 11.5). McAdams's research is a good example of the personological tradition of research in personality. That is, his interest has been in studying the life paths of whole individuals rather than in studying one aspect of behavior (say, achievement motivation) across large groups of individuals.

McAdams, like Erikson, argues that adolescence is the major period of identity and life-story construction, although one continues this process for the rest of one's life. Infancy contributes the "feeling tone" of the story—such as fundamentally hopeful or frightening—based on early experiences with caretakers. Early childhood contributes a variety of images (see Highlight 11.1). In late childhood, children are able to work with

TABLE 11.5 McAdams's Life Story Interview Format

I.	Life Chapters
II.	Specific Scenes
	A. Peak Experience (High Point)
	B. Nadir Experience (Low Point)
	C. Turning Point
	D. Earliest Memory
	E. Significant Childhood Memory
	F. Significant Adolescent Memory
	G. Significant Adult Memory
	H. Significant Other Memory
III.	Important Persons
IV.	Future Script
V.	Stresses and Problems
VI.	Personal Ideology
VII.	Life Motif or Message
VIII.	Other

Source: McAdams, 1993.

Young children begin to develop their life stories by playing the role of fantasy characters.

Early Childhood Roots of the Life Story

A turning point in my daughter's life was the day she saw *Snow White*. It was almost a year ago; she was three years old. The original Walt Disney version of the fairy tale was playing at a local theater, so I took the opportunity to escort Ruth Megan to her first full-length movie.

Since that day, my family has lived with Snow White and the Seven Dwarfs. All seven of the dwarfs ride with us in the car to nursery school—Grumpy, Happy, Doc, Bashful, Sleepy, Sneezy, and Dopey. The Wicked Queen, the Peddler Woman (who is the Queen in disguise), the Queen's Huntsman, and the Handsome Prince frequently show up for dinner. When she first met a classmate named William, Ruth told him that she lived in a little cottage (like the Dwarfs') tucked far away in the woods. (Incredulous, William told her she was crazy, and then reported that he would be traveling to nursery school next week in his flying car.) When William comes over for lunch these days, Ruth pretends that she is the Wicked Queen and he is the Queen's Huntsman, and the two of them terrorize her little sister, Amanda, who is 1 1/2 and cast in the pitiful role of Snow White. They steal her stuffed animals and threaten to lock her up, even kill her (William's idea, I am sure); they hide poisoned apples under her pillow. On other days, Ruth herself is Snow White, organizing regular birthday parties for Grumpy, her favorite dwarf, taping pink crepe paper all over the dining room, making birthday cakes out of sugar, pepper, oregano, and water.

My daughter is obsessed with the story of Snow White! Yet it is not so much the integrated story—from beginning to end—that so fascinates her. Rather, it is various pieces of the story, easily divorced from their coherent narrative context, that she appropriates into her daily life of fantasy, play, and fun. One day she is the Wicked Queen. The next day she is Bashful. Her identification with each of these characters is ephemeral and idiosyncratic. Recently she was Grumpy, rescuing three of the "Little Ponies" who were stranded on a cliff. Yet in *Snow White*, Grumpy never rescues anybody. And there are no ponies in the movie—they originate from a popular television show.

Although Ruth seems to recognize that stories have a certain canonical form, she does not insist that her own renditions conform to the canon. Her make-believe world is inconsistent, illogical, and very fluid. It is populated by a rich and ever-expanding repertoire of *images*. It is the images in stories—not the stories themselves—that Ruth zeroes in on. This is not to say that she cannot follow a story's plot or that she fails to appreciate the dramatic building of tension in narrative, the climax, and the denouement. Ruth has a pretty good sense of the whole story, from beginning to end, of Snow White and the Seven Dwarfs. But it is not the whole story that captures her imagination, for it is too big and complex, too systematic and progressive, to find its way *in toto* into her daily world of imagination and play. Instead, Ruth dwells on the images, reworking them daily into her own fantastical plots.

Source: McAdams, 1990.

themes, and they begin to construct more truly story-like narratives about themselves and the events in their lives. During adolescence, individuals rearrange their past to develop a story of self that will help them face the future.

As adults face obstacles and setbacks, the story takes a turn toward redemption. People whose life stories include themes of personal agency and exploration tend to show better psychological adjustment (McAdams and McLean, 2013). As individuals progress into adulthood, they have a number of different *imagoes*, or self-images, of themselves inside. This set of self-images acts like a Greek chorus commenting on and guiding behavior. McAdams (1988) found in his study of midlife adults that, although they were relatively normal individuals, their life story accounts were described as if they were "multiple personalities." In particular, they often had two conflicting primary self-images.

Some of the polarities in self-images found were: adventurer/housewife, humanist/barbarian, good citizen/bum, and worker/escapist. One subject, for instance, struggled with his two conflicting images, one of himself as an artist (with all its bohemian connotations) and the other of himself as a "successful, worldly moneymaker." Ultimately individuals integrate the various imagoes into one.

Summary

1. *Identity*, in contrast to self-concept, consists of all the things one identifies with—the things one considers to define who one is. An important component of identity is the sense of continuity in one's life.

2. Erikson felt that continuity and experiencing oneself are important aspects of identity. He believed that late adolescence is the time of much identity achievement. Marcia, extending the work of Erik Erickson, postulates that there are four different *identity statuses* during adolescence: diffusion, foreclosure, moratorium, and identity achievement.

3. Research has shown different patterns on how individuals move through the four identity statuses.

4. Erickson predicted that identity development would be more closely tied to the development of intimacy for women than for men. While some research has supported this, the results are complex and there are no clear patterns that characterize all or most of one gender in contrast to the other.

5. Ethnic identity development appears to pass through stages, going from a diffused or unquestioned state to a clearly defined and worked-out state. Strong ethnic identity appears to be associated with higher levels of self-esteem.

6. Biculturated individuals, who are able to flexibly utilize the best from both the majority culture and from their own minority culture, appear to be the healthiest psychologically.

7. There appear to be relatively few basic psychological differences between the genders, although members of the two genders are socialized to behave in different ways.

8. Biological theories of sex differences assume that these differences have a genetic basis. Psychodynamic theories focus on identification with the parent. Social learning theories focus on the reinforcement of gender-typed behaviors. Cognitive labeling and gender schema theories assume that children develop concepts about what behaviors characterize being a member of a given gender. Children then assimilate information to these concepts.

9. Narrative approaches to personality assume that people's lives are bound together by the stories they tell about themselves. McAdams's narrative approach to identity assumes that identity is a *life story*.

Key Terms

androgyny (p. 208)
femininity (p. 206)
foreclosure (p. 195)
gender (p. 201)
gender identity (p. 202)
gender schema theory (p. 208)
identity (p. 193)

identity achievement (p. 195)
identity diffusion (p. 195)
masculinity (p. 206)
meta-analysis (p. 203)
moratorium (p. 195)
narrative identity (p. 209)
racial and ethnic identity (p. 197)

Thought Questions

1. Do you think your identity can be easily classified into one of the four major identity statuses: diffusion, foreclosure, moratorium, or achievement? Or do you think your identity may include components from more than one stage?

2. How have you struggled with the issue of your racial or ethnic identity, or sexual orientation identity?

3. What do you think accounts for differences between the genders?

4. In what way do you think you have constructed a "life story" that helps you make sense out of who you are?

Social Development and Patterns of Childrearing

CHAPTER 12

Source: XiXinXing/Shutterstock.com

Chapter Outline

Issues in Personality Development

Attachment Theory

Socialization and the Family

Moral Development

Prosocial Behaviors

The study of adult personality inevitably leads back to the study of personality development. One reason for this is the assumption, made by many personality theorists, that the roots of adult personality are laid in childhood. A second, related reason is that a number of issues and processes that are central to the understanding of adult personality are also encountered in the study of personality development. One such issue, the interaction of nature and nurture reviewed in Chapter 1, becomes immediately salient as one explores behavior among infants, young children, and adults. Another recurring issue throughout the life span is whether there are critical periods of development and developmental stages, characterized by relatively marked transitions from one level of development to another, as contrasted with a process of gradual, continuous change.

These issues will be considered in this chapter along with the processes basic to the development of social behavior. Particular attention is paid to the process of attachment, a key construct in personality development with implications for phenomena that will be discussed later in the text. Moral development and the development of prosocial behavior, is also considered. The development of a healthy, functional, moral, and prosocial adult has been a central concern of most personality theories.

Issues in Personality Development

Nature or Nurture?

Examining personality from a developmental perspective highlights certain issues in the emergence and development of personality. One familiar and significant issue is the question of nature versus nurture. Is personality primarily a process of biological maturation; or is it influenced by environmental factors? Forces of nature are involved in the child's progression from a state of helpless infancy to that of an autonomous individual with language, logic, familial attachments, and social involvements. But, as many of the points raised in Chapter 2 suggest, nature does not operate in a vacuum. Children in different cultures learn to speak very different languages and, if deprived of social contact, will develop only the most primitive of communication skills. Children raised outside a social milieu are not likely to develop ambition, conscience, and social concern. Tracing the interactions between biology and environment and determining each influence's role are among the primary scientific tasks of developmental psychologists.

The nature/nurture question is illustrated by the often striking individual differences among children. Some babies are highly active, others are calm and placid, and still others are sensitive and easily distressed (Belsky and Pleuss, 2009; Chess, Thomas, and Birch, 1965). What parents with a "different" child have not wondered what mistakes they made in bringing up the child? Other parents, whose children are quite unlike, wonder if they played any role at all in influencing the personality of each child. Developmental studies bear directly on the question of the causes or antecedents of individual differences and on the analogous question of group differences, such as those between males and females, which we considered in the previous chapter.

The observation of marked differences in temperament among children at infancy strongly suggests the influence of biological factors on personality. The calmness of some infants is reminiscent of the phlegmatic temperament described by the Roman physician Galen, while the irritability of other infants is suggestive of a choleric temperament. However, there are many features of infants' differences in temperament that do not correspond neatly to the ancient classification of temperaments. There are some babies—about one out of every ten (Thomas, Chess, and Birch, 1968)—who have been categorized as "difficult." These infants are characterized by extensive crying, unpredictable fluctuations in emotional state, intense reactions when aroused, and resistance to consolation and soothing. They are more likely than other infants to develop a subsequent behavior disturbance.

Although infants with difficult temperaments have a higher probability of manifesting later behavior problems, it would be misleading to conclude that these children display behavioral problems solely because "they were born that way." The data show a weak but consistent relationship between early infant disturbances and subsequent psychopathology (Chess and Thomas, 1984; De Pauw and Mervielde, 2010; Mervielde, De Clercq, De Fruyt, and Van Leeuwen, 2005; Sameroff and Chandler, 1975). Whether such infants will later develop behavior problems very much depends on the parents' response to an infant's behavior, on cultural resources and values, and on the particular experiences of the child with peers, in school, and in other contexts. This is not to say merely that a good environment will modify the effects of poor endowment or a birth injury; rather, there is a constant interaction over time between the child and its environment. The characteristics of a child may influence its environment; a difficult infant will evoke a range of responses from its caretakers different from those evoked by an infant with a more placid temperament. The responses from others will in turn modify the child. One mother's patient, warm, and consistent pattern of responding may, after time, foster positive changes in the child's emotional response, which in turn may modify the mother's behavior. Another mother's ambivalent response of oscillating between over solicitousness and avoidance may exacerbate the infant's difficult behaviors, which in turn may intensify the mother's ambivalence.

There are many other factors that influence the transactions between a child and its environment. A child with a biological handicap may develop a compensatory skill (see Adler, Chapter 4). Among a group of infants with difficult temperaments, one difficult child who initially had a very negative interaction with her father subsequently developed a strong interest in the piano. Her excellent skills as a pianist helped change her father's attitude from anger and rejection to pride and acceptance (cited in Sameroff, 1979). Nature and nurture form a continuous series of reciprocal interactions between the child and its environment.

Continuity or Stages?

A related developmental issue of importance to personality is whether the changes in behavior observed during childhood reflect a gradual, continuous process or are marked by discrete **stages** that introduce new patterns of behavior. The personality theories reviewed in Chapters 3 through 6 hold many different positions on the continuity/discontinuity controversy. Perhaps the two most opposing views are represented by the psychoanalytic and the learning theory schools. Psychoanalytic theory, which views the child as progressing through a series of transformations in the oral, anal, phallic, and genital stages, reflects the discontinuity position. Learning theories, on the other hand, portray development as a continuous process of change, determined by the particular behaviors that are reinforced or learned by the child. From a learning theory standpoint, personality development is not inherently "progressive"; rather, the direction that development takes is a function of the child's socialization experiences.

stages Discrete steps that are qualitatively different from the ones that precede or follow the current one.

For example, most children at the age of seven display a strong sense of conscience, internalized standards of conduct, and guilt feelings. In contrast, three-year-olds display only the barest rudiments of conscience, with few signs of guilt. Psychologists who perceive development as continuous explain this change in terms of the specific learning experiences to which a child has been exposed. Conversely, those who consider development as discrete developmental stages favor an interpretation based on changes in the child's psychological structure. Learning is not ignored, but the emphasis is on interactions of learning and biological maturation that produce new capacities and relationships that are *qualitatively* different from those that existed before. These newly developed stages make possible very different types of behavior than those the child could exhibit before entering the new stage of development.

Critical Periods

The concept of **critical periods** suggests another way of looking at the continuity-discontinuity issue or the question of stages. Experiences occurring during critical periods are believed to have greater impact than those occurring at other times during development. Psychoanalysts, for example, believe that the first five years of a child's life are critical for personality development. The basic features of one's personality are believed to be formed during this early period, with later experiences having only a secondary impact. A less extreme view held by most psychologists asserts that, while early childhood experiences are especially influential, significant changes in personality can occur throughout life.

critical periods Periods when something can be learned, and cannot be learned outside the period.

A second implication of conceptualizing critical periods as a significant factor in development is the view that certain skills and competencies can be acquired during these periods. If they are not, then the child may suffer a permanent deficit or one that is extremely difficult to remedy. These deficits may be emotional, social, or cognitive. For example, according to Erikson, a child who does not experience affection and nurturance during the oral-sensory stage will develop a basic mistrust of others and will have difficulty in responding to love and affection in later years.

For some behaviors and competencies, the critical period may cover a wide age range. Thus, it has been proposed that language, in general—not a specific language—must be acquired by early adolescence. If not, which may be the case if a child is raised in isolation, then language, according to this view, can never be taught to that child (Lennenberg, 1967). Exploration of this issue is one reason why feral children (children raised by packs of animals like wolves) are of such great psychological interest. Unfortunately, these children are typically brain damaged as well, limiting the clear testing of the critical period-language acquisition hypothesis. Nevertheless, there have been a number of documented instances of individuals acquiring some language after the supposed critical period (Snow, 1987).

Does this mean that there is no critical period in language development? The answer to that depends upon how we define critical. It is certainly easier to acquire language before adolescence than after it. Similarly, some personality patterns, such as aggressiveness and a basic feeling of security and self-confidence, appear to be particularly influenced by experiences in childhood, although later experiences also influence these behaviors. These early experiences are critical in that they exert a profound effect upon personality development which maybe, but are not necessarily, irreversible. A more recent and descriptive phrase referring to time periods during which particular experiences have an especially important influence on the organism's structure and future behavior is **Sensitive Periods** (Bornstein, 1989). While the term *critical* has an all or none implication, the term *sensitive* allows for more variation in the significance of a time period for the organism's development. Although the conception of sensitive or critical periods is in keeping with a good deal of animal and human data, many questions remain regarding the specification of sensitive periods and the kinds of behaviors and skills to which the sensitive period notion is relevant. These issues will become salient in the following discussion of attachment.

The question of whether personality develops in a continuous or stage-like fashion is currently unresolved, and, as with many psychological issues, the answer will probably involve both processes.

Attachment Theory

We turn now from an examination of the continuity of personality to a key process in the infant's early socialization and personality development: the formation of attachments to others. We will find evidence of continuity here as well; the kinds of attachments established in infancy are reflected at subsequent developmental periods.

Among the special characteristics of infancy are the infant's helplessness and prolonged dependency on its parents and other caretakers for food, protection, satisfaction of needs, and relief of discomforts. Prolonged dependency is one of the hallmarks of human as opposed to nonhuman development. There is evidence that the greater the cognitive ability of a species, the longer the period of dependency. A human infant could not survive for very long without the support and care provided by others. To facilitate survival in the first few months of life, an infant is equipped with a set of reflexive biological responses, such as crying, sucking in response to lip stimulation, head movements, thrashing about, babbling, and smiling. These behaviors directly modify the environment and function as signals to caretakers, informing them of distress and satisfaction. A caretaker must, of course, be able to interpret the signals correctly and to be appropriately motivated. Indeed, what sound is more compelling to parents than their baby's crying?

There are two broad implications of the infant's situation and behavior that warrant special notice. First, the human infant is thrust into a social situation from the moment of birth; social interaction is the normal state of affairs. Second, although dependent, the infant is not a passive creature totally subject to the whims of the environment. Through its cries and smiles the baby can significantly influence the behavior of its caretakers. While the mother's control of reinforcement contingencies is much greater than that of the infant, the baby's responses can also be said to shape the mother's behavior (Gewirtz and Boyd, 1977; Isabella, Belsky, and von Eye, 1989). While the mother has control over such reinforcements as food, attention, and relief of irritation, the infant can reinforce the mother and other caretakers through its responsiveness, the skills it acquires, and a pleasant versus an unhappy disposition. The amount of attention or even affection that parents give their infant will be influenced by the infant's reinforcing and aversive reactions. There is much evidence that the child-rearing practices of parents are to a great extent *determined* by the behavior of the child, as well as the more often discussed opposite sequence of child-rearing practices *determining* the behavior of the child. This is a point worth reiterating: the child evokes behavior from the caregiver (Stupica, Sherman, and Cassidy, 2011).

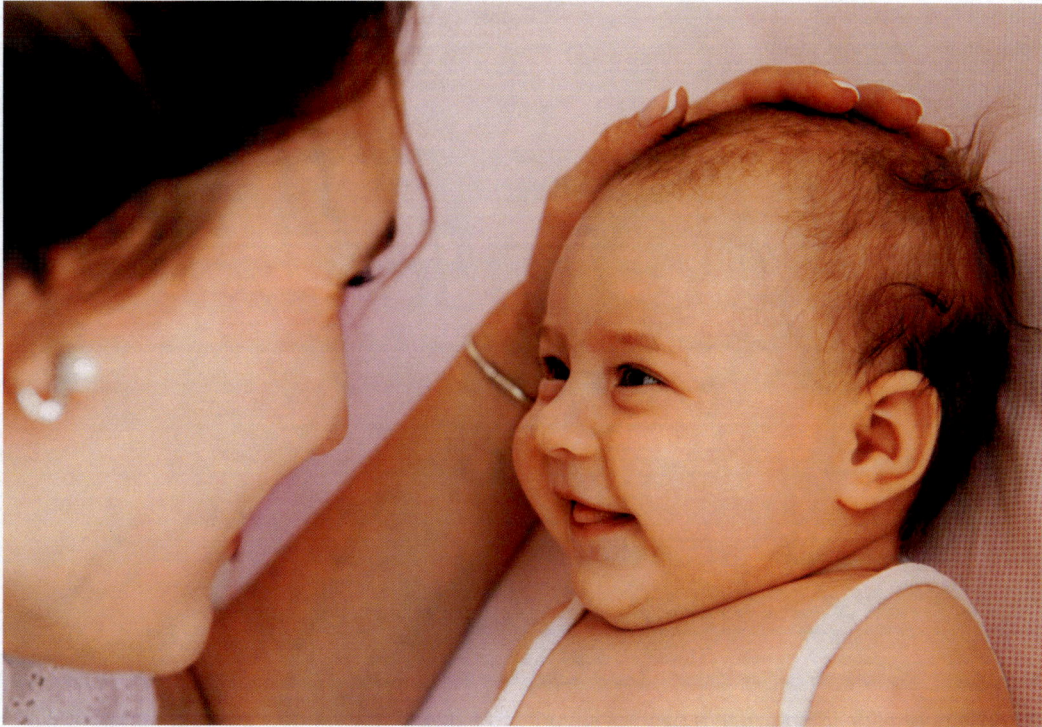

Source: Romanova Anna/Shutterstock

Infants' reactions of smiling and crying communicate states and need to those who care for them, and elicit attention and care.

During the first few months of development, the infant attends to the presence of people, observing them and perhaps smiling or becoming excited in their presence. But the infant does not yet discriminate between its mother or father or other people. There is no innate attachment by the infant to the mother, although this early period of social responding may be considered the first phase in the development of attachment to significant people in the infant's world (Bowlby, 1958, 1969). The formation of selective attachments to caregivers, or bonding, is usually manifested after three months of age. This bonding is considered to be of paramount importance for the infant's social development and, in the views of many personality theorists, is a prime determinant of the child's basic personality structure.

Characteristics of Attachment

How do we know when a child is attached to someone, and exactly what does it mean to say that a child has an attachment? These questions have been the subject of considerable theoretical debate and investigation, and there are no simple answers. The most comprehensive and influential analysis of attachment has been provided by British psychiatrist John Bowlby. The essence of attachment, according to Bowlby, is the maintenance of proximity to the caregiver, usually the mother. This proximity can be in terms of physical contact (e.g., touching the mother) or psychological contact (e.g., seeing the mother and knowing that she is close by). In addition to maintain proximity, the baby performs a set of attachment behaviors, including babbling, smiling, looking at the caretaker, and following or clinging to him or her.

One main characteristic of attachment to a person, then, is an effort to approach or maintain connection to that person. A second characteristic is distress and protest when the infant is separated from the individual to whom it is attached. The same person is able to soothe the child when it is upset. Finally, when the caretaker is present, the infant is able to explore new situations without displaying anxiety. The special caregiver provides the infant with a base of security that enables it to leave the safe and familiar and to explore new, potentially threatening environments.

Caregivers provide infants with a base of security to explore strange new environments.

The child's early attachments, although formed in infancy, are predicted to be evident in later periods of development as well. Theorists believe that early attachments provide the basis upon which children develop their basic **working model** of relationships. How early attachments are later manifested will depend on the age, the particular culture, and the idiosyncratic avenues of expression of the child.

working model A child's basic understanding of the world and social relationships.

The Universality of Attachment

Attachment behaviors are characteristic not only of infants in every culture, but also of many nonhuman species, especially mammals. The comparability between the attachment behaviors of primates and those of human infants has stimulated extensive primate investigations of the variables involved in the formation of attachments and the consequences of separation (Simonds, 1977; Suomi, 1977). The following description (Jensen and Tolman, 1962, pp. 132–33) of separation in rhesus monkeys conveys the flavor of attachment in a nonhuman primate species:

> Separation of mother and infant monkeys is an extremely stressful event for both mother and infant as well as for the attendants and for all other monkeys within sight or earshot of the experience. The mother becomes ferocious towards attendants and extremely protective of her infant. The infant's screams can be heard over almost the entire building. The mother struggles and attacks the separators. The baby clings tightly to the mother and to any object which it can grasp to avoid being held or removed by the attendant. With the baby gone, the mother paces the cage almost constantly, charges the cage occasionally, bites at it, and makes continual attempts to escape. She also lets out occasional mooing-like sounds. The infant emits high pitched screams intermittently and almost continuously for the period of separation.

The evidence of attachment behavior in nonhumans suggests that there are important biological factors influencing the human infant's attachment response. From an evolutionary standpoint, the attachment behaviors of both the mother and infant increase the likelihood of survival. From an ethological standpoint, the mother might be considered the stimulus that releases the innate smiling response from the infant while the smile, in turn, releases biologically programmed approach and loving responses. Thus, there is a complex chaining of events. In a similar manner, the baby's cry releases approach and comforting responses from the mother.

The foregoing discussion is not meant to imply, however, that learning does not affect attachment. Bowlby (1969) noted that the child has to *learn* to discriminate mother

---

HIGHLIGHT 12.1

Feeding and Attachment

Early explanations of attachment by learning theorists (Miller and Dollard, 1941) emphasized the primary reinforcement provided by nursing and bottle feeding. This reinforcement then generalizes to the caretaker, so that the mere presence or voice of the caretaker could serve to reduce the child's tensions and elicit positive reactions. However, there is much more taking place in the interaction between child and caregiver than feeding. The infant is typically held and soothed and its attention and motor responses are directed toward the caregiver, usually the mother. Thus, the child receives a great deal of stimulation from the mother, in addition to being fed.

The well-known cloth-versus-wire-mother experiments carried out by Harry Harlow of the University of Wisconsin provide compelling evidence that feeding is not central to the development of attachment. Harlow (1958, 1971) separated infant monkeys from their mothers immediately after birth. The infants were then fed through a bottle connected to a dummy that functioned as a substitute, or surrogate, mother. These "mother"

dummies were constructed of either wire mesh or wire mesh covered with terrycloth (see Fig. 12.1). If reduction of the infant's hunger drive is the primary basis for attachment, then the infant monkeys should have become attached to the mother surrogates associated with the giving of milk. But this was not the case. The animals fed by the wire mothers went to them only when they were hungry. But both wire-fed and terrycloth-fed infants preferred the terrycloth mothers and spent most of the day with them. When upset, both groups also were more readily comforted by the terrycloth mothers. Other research has indicated that the critical variable influencing monkey attachment is an opportunity to cling. Monkeys and chimpanzees have a strong tendency to cling, especially when upset, and the terrycloth surrogates were much better than the wire mother substitutes for this response. The monkeys fed by the cloth mothers later manifested severe social problems, demonstrating that a real monkey mother is best.

FIGURE 12.1 The Clinging Response of Harlow's Monkeys to a Cloth "Mother" and of a Human Infant to an Adult

from other adults and stressed the importance of the quality and pattern of the child's interaction with the mother in determining the nature of the attachment bond between them. If the mother, for example, is depressed or for some other reason unresponsive to the infant's smile, then the attachment relationship will take an atypical course. Some theorists thought that the biological explanation and the notion of an emotional bond is superfluous and have attempted to account for attachment behavior on the basis of Skinner's principles of reinforcement and operant conditioning (Gewirtz and Boyd, 1977). However, as we examine variations in attachment, it will become clear that although operant conditioning principles are pertinent, they cannot easily account for many attachment phenomena.

Physiological studies also indicate that the lack of tactile stimulation, rather than food deprivation, is the critical factor mediating the adverse effects of separation from the mother (Shanberg and Kuhn, 1980). These studies demonstrate that tactile stimulation of rat pups can counteract the negative biochemical effects of maternal deprivation. Similarly, other studies have shown that tactile stimulation of premature human infants significantly increases their weight gain (White and LaBarba, 1976). Touch and breast-feeding even seem to reduce the experience of pain in newborn humans (Gray, Miller, Philipp, and Blass, 2002; Gray, Watt, and Blass, 2000).

Mary Ainsworth and The Strange Situation

Mary Ainsworth is one of the key figures in the development of attachment styles. Using naturalistic observations of mother-child interactions among a group of East African Ganda living in the bush, she noted that the child actively sought contact with the caregiver when hurt or scared, and would use the mother as a safe base from which to explore the world (Ainsworth, 1967; Ainsworth and Bowlby, 1991). While in Uganda, she identified three different styles of attachment. After accepting a position at Johns Hopkins University, she with her students and colleagues developed a research paradigm known as **The Strange Situation** that would allow for the study of attachment behavior in a laboratory setting (Ainsworth, Bell, and Stayton, 1971).

In The Strange Situation, a caregiver (nearly always the mother) and infant enter an unfamiliar room; the infant plays while the mother is present; a stranger enters and the stranger and mother are both present for a while; the mother leaves and the infant is left with the stranger; the mother returns and the stranger leaves; the infant is then left alone in the room for a few minutes; the stranger returns; and finally, the mother also returns. The infant is observed for (1) the ease with which he or she recovers from the distress of separation upon reunion with the mother; (2) how comforting contact with the mother is; and (3) the degree to which the mother serves as a secure base for the infant's explorations. Infant crying on separation from the mother is *not* a critical factor in assessing **attachment style**.

Observation of one-year-old infants' behavior during this sequence of events led to classifying the babies into three groups: **secure attachment**, **avoidant attachment**, and **anxious/resistant attachment**. These last two are considered to be insecure but organized attachment in that the theme is consistent patterns of insecure attachment. Later researchers found a group that could not be classified. This group is often given the term **disorganized/disoriented attachment** (Main and Solomon, 1986; 1990).

The infants in these categories seemed not only quantitatively, but also qualitatively, different in their attachment to their mothers (Sroufe and Waters, 1977a). Avoidant infants differ from others in that they are the only babies to avoid proximity with the mother in the reunion situation. But this does not mean that avoidant infants are indifferent to their mothers. Recordings of infants' heart rates in laboratory situations indicate relatively-long-lasting heart rate acceleration in avoidant infants when the mother returns, suggesting emotional arousal rather than indifference (Sroufe and Waters, 1977b). In comparison, the heart rates of most attached infants recover to a normal level more rapidly.

The Strange Situation A research paradigm developed by Ainsworth to measure attachment.

attachment style A pattern of attachment behavior between a child and caregiver.

secure attachment An attachment style that is marked by using the caregiver as a base of security, nurturance, and caring.

avoidant attachment An attachment style marked by low demands for attachment by the child.

anxious/resistant attachment An attachment style marked by wanting and also avoiding attachment to the caregiver.

disorganized/disoriented attachment A child attachment style that is not predictable or doesn't fit in the other styles.

Caregiving and Attachment

Because infants are incapable of taking care of themselves, they must engage in attachment behaviors to solicit the help that they need. In this process, the infant discovers which behaviors lead to care and will continue to use those behaviors. It is important to emphasize that these behaviors are adaptive, and in that sense, none of the organized patterns are necessarily better than the others (Howe, 2011). The caregiver is often the mother but may be either or both parents, grandparents, siblings, or anyone who acts as the major caregiver. It is also possible for there to be different attachment styles to different caregivers.

The caregiver provides safety in two ways: either by removing the danger or by responding to the distress of the infant (Goldberg, 2000). The way that the caregiver responds to the distress will lead to the development of an internal working model of how interactions with caregivers work. Each attachment style is associated with a working model that has been formed based on the caregivers' responses, which may be responsive, sensitive, and predictable. Alternatively, the caregiver might be unresponsive, insensitive, or unpredictable.

Secure Attachment

The caregiver of a securely attached child is consistently responsive to the child's needs. She tends to be attentive to the child's environment and have some understanding of how the child is experiencing the world. The caregiving does not have to be perfect but is usually good enough (Howe, 2011). Because of this, the child is able to use the caregiver as a guide for dealing with emotional upset (Beebe, 2004). In this situation, children can predict the responses of others and consequently have confidence in how others will respond. This leads to the secure attachment style. The development of this working model allows the child to have the confidence to explore the world and predict the response of the caregiver. The working model that the child develops is that others can be counted upon and trusted.

Researchers have found that the quality of attachment is related to the behavior of the caregiver. Mothers of securely attached children were observed to respond more readily to their infants' crying than mothers of insecure and avoidant children (Ainsworth et al., 1978). Furthermore, securely attached infants do not cry as much as the others. This finding is difficult for learning theorists to explain, inasmuch as greater responsiveness to crying should reinforce and increase the frequency and duration of crying.

Studies of maternal responsiveness to their infant indicates that mothers of secure infants are sensitive to a variety of cues provided by their infant besides crying (Smith and Pederson, 1988). In addition, relationships have been demonstrated between behaviors of the mother toward a three-month-old infant, prior to the manifestation of the attachment relationship, and the infant's attachment behaviors when one year old (Lewis and Feisking, 1989). It is even found that children are more physically competent when the caregiver is paying attention to the child and less physically competent when that caregiver is paying attention to a cellphone (Stupica, 2016).

Avoidant Attachment

Sometimes the child's need for comforting distresses the caregiver. Because of the caregiver's distress, he or she is unable to provide the comforting that the child needs or desires. The child, however, discovers that the caregiver is attentive and supportive when the child is not distressed. The child, therefore, learns that being needy causes distress in others, but being self-sufficient results in positive attention. The child learns the best strategy is to avoid displaying negative emotion and needing attachment.

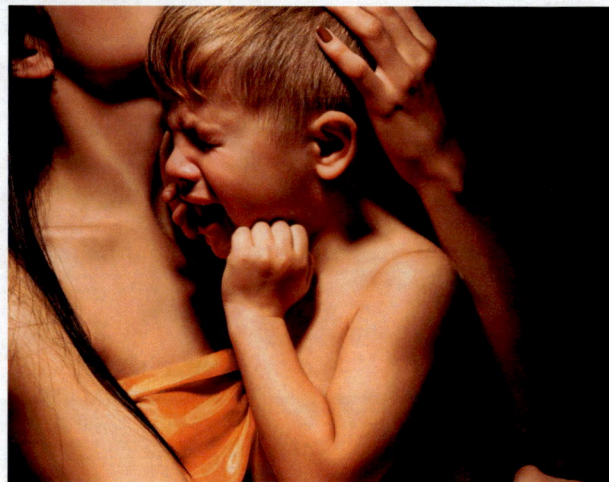

Source: Sonsedska Yuliia/Shutterstock

Caregivers who are responsive and soothing to the needs of the child will usually raise securely attached children.

This leads to the avoidant style of attachment. The working model that the child develops is that others are unloving and undependable. It is important to be self-sufficient, as the child cannot expect that others will love and support him or her. Despite this early emphasis on independence, by early elementary school it is observed that the avoidant children are more dependent on teachers than the securely attached children (Sroufe, Egeland, Carlson, and Collins, 2005).

Ambivalent/Resistant Attachment

When caregivers ignore or do not pay close attention to the child's needs, the child will learn that he or she must express the need with more intense displays. This lack of attention to a child's needs may include not intervening in instances of emotional upset, or unwanted intervention when the child is competently exploring the environment alone (Cassidy and Berlin, 1994). This will lead to the ambivalent/resistant style of attachment. By making an extreme display, the child increases the likelihood that the caregiver will respond as needed. The child then learns to overreact to distress to get attention (Main, 1990). The child is likely to learn that he or she is unworthy or undeserving of attention. The working model is that other people are insensitive, unreliable, and unpredictable.

Disorganized Attachment

Finally, a caregiver may physically abuse, ignore, or be emotionally unavailable to the infant; or do things to the infant for which the infant is unprepared. This is likely to lead to the disorganized style of attachment (Carlson, 1998). These caregivers create a problem for the child inasmuch as they are both the only source of comfort while simultaneously being an unpredictable source of fear (van IJzendoorn, Schuengel, and Bakermans-Kranenburg, 1999). This type of parenting is often associated with additional stressors in the parent's environment. These stressors may be money problems, psychiatric and additional problems, or relationship difficulties. It is also suggested that a caregiver's unresolved childhood trauma may have an impact on his or her ability to provide care. Fortunately, interventions that focus on training caregivers to be more sensitive to the child's needs appear to reduce disorganized attachment (Bakermans-Kranenburg, Van IJzendoorn, and Juffer, 2003; 2005).

Childhood Outcomes

Under most circumstances, a child is likely to develop a secure attachment to the caregiver, as can be seen in Table 12.1. This is true for children in the United States, Western Europe, and in non-Western countries. Even in high stress situations, secure attachment is the most common form of attachment. The exception is maternal maltreatment (Van IJzendoorn, Schuengel, and Bakermans–Kranenburg, 1999).

A securely attached child develops a positive self-reliance. These children are more likely to use positive emotions when approaching or when approached by peers. They use better coping strategies and are less likely to use aggression. Securely attached children and adults typically show higher levels of social competence (Sroufe, Egeland, Carlson, and Collins, 2005).

In a longitudinal study by Sroufe and colleagues, they observed children in school and even were able to send them to a specially designed summer camp. They found middle-school-age children classified as resistant initiated more contact with camp counselors, while the counselors initiated more contact with the avoidant children. The secure children had good relationships with camp counselors and tended to be focused on their relationships with peers (Sroufe, 2005). Resistant children tended to have few friends at summer camp despite seeming to want to be friends. The avoidant children tended to not have many friends, and tended to try to maintain exclusive friendships with those friends (Shulman, Elicker, and Sroufe, 1994).

The quality of attachment appears to affect the child's cognitive development. The securely attached child, for instance, tends to be more developmentally advanced (Belsky,

TABLE 12.1 Percent Distribution of Attachment Patterns in Children

	A Avoidant	B Secure	C Ambivalent/ Resistant	D Disorganized/ Disoriented
U.S. infants under 24 months	15	62	9	15
U.S. children over 24 months	19	56	10	15
European sample	20	53	10	17
Non-Western European/U.S.	8	53	18	21
Low SES infants U.S. under 24 months	17	48	10	25
Low SES children U.S. over 24 months	19	41	29	11
Maternal maltreatment	28	9	15	48
Teen mothers	33	40	4	23
Maternal depression	21	41	17	21

Source: Adapted from van IJzendoorn, Schuengel, and Bakermans–Kranenburg, 1999.

Garduque, and Hrncir, 1984). For example, children at around age two who had been classified as secure infants engage in more advanced symbolic play activity than children who had been classified as insecure or avoidant (Slade, 1987). Children who are rated as securely attached at age seven performed better as adolescents on a variety of cognitive tasks, such as deductive reasoning, compared to those rated as insecurely attached at age seven (Jacobsen, Edelstein, and Hofmann, 1994). Children who measure as secure at fifteen or thirty-six months show higher levels of social self-control in first grade, which then predicts school engagement in fifth grade (Drake, Blelsky, and Fearon, 2013). Resistant children in preschool more often solicit help and contact from their teachers. The teachers in turn responded to the children by giving more help and being more tolerant of rule breaking. The resistant children often seemed younger than their same-age peers (Sroufe, 2005).

Cultural Variations

Attachment is believed to be a universal phenomenon. While much attachment research has been carried out in the United States, there have been a substantial number of studies carried out in other countries. The data indicate that the majority of infants in other countries are classified as secure. The predominant cultural difference that emerges is in the proportions of ambivalent/resistant versus avoidant infants. For West European nations, a much higher proportion of infants display ambivalent/resistant as compared to avoidant patterns, while the reverse holds for Japan and Israel. The proportions for United States' infants fall in between, with more infants classified as ambivalent than avoidant, and with the proportional difference being much smaller than that for the West European nations.

The implications of this difference for the development of children in these different cultural contexts have yet to be determined. In addition, it remains for future research to determine the specific features of the culture, and possibly the specific temperamental attributes of infants in that culture, that bring about these differences in attachment patterns.

From the perspective of those who see attachment as a key organizing dimension of behavior, attachment bonds not only protect the child and maintain its security, but also form an integral part of subsequent love relationships. "When people are attached to another, they want to be with their loved one. They maybe content for a while to be apart in the pursuit of other interests and activities, but the attachment is not worthy of the name if they do not want to spend a substantial amount of time with their attachment figures—that is to say, in proximity and interaction with them" (Ainsworth et al., 1978, p. 14). Indeed, attachment is hypothesized to be a key element in the formation of stable, affectionate bonds with siblings and friends, as well as in marital relationships (Ainsworth, 1989).

Measurement in Adults

Findings from longitudinal studies indicate substantial consistency between attachment patterns assessed at age six and the attachment behaviors in The Strange Situation at infancy (Main, Kaplan, and Cassidy, 1985). Indeed, studies of attachment patterns in adult love relationships indicate that these adult patterns are significantly related to reports of early attachment relationships (Hazan and Shaver, 1987)

As we consider attachment styles in adults, we must consider how to measure attachment. We are probably not going to have a thirty-year-old and her mother come to a room filled with toys, and have the mother leave for a short while like The Strange Situation. Consequently, researchers have developed two different traditions to measure attachment in adults. One style uses self-report, the other major style is a semi-structured interview.

The self-report measures have people respond to a Likert scale about their current views of relationships and attachments. For instance, the Relationship Scales Questionnaire (RSQ, Griffin and Bartholomew, 1984) has items like: *I find it easy to get emotionally close to others; It is very important to me to feel self-sufficient; I know that others will be there when I need them.* The self-report measures are usually measuring two dimensions: anxiety and avoidance. The items on this scale can be used to sort people into the traditional secure, avoidant, and anxious/ambivalent categories, with a fourth category of fearful avoidant added to the model. Many different self-report scales are available (see Ravitz, Maunder, Hunter, Sthankiya, and Lancee, 2010, for a review). It is important to note that the self-report measures and the Adult Attachment Interview (AAI, which is described in the next paragraphs) are only slightly correlated with each other (Roisman et al., 2007). Consequently, the findings based on the AAI or RSQ potentially differ.

In the AAI, the interviewer asks a series of questions about the interviewee's interaction with caregivers while growing up (Main, Goldwyn, and Hesse, 2003; Main, Kaplan, and Cassidy, 1985). The transcript is then evaluated for instances in which the person idealizes the parent; describes being loved by or being rejected by the parent; where the child had to parent the parent; where the child was neglected; where the parent is idealized or derogated; or there is unresolved loss or trauma. Finally, the transcript is evaluated for coherence.

As with children, there are four different styles, although the labels are slightly different. The secure style is called the secure/**autonomous style**. These people are comfortable with both intimacy and independence. The avoidant style in children appears to be very similar to the **dismissing style** in adults. These adults value autonomy but are uncomfortable with intimacy. The ambivalent/resistant style in children becomes the **preoccupied style** in adults. These adults are preoccupied with intimacy and relationships, to the point of feeling anxiety without those. As in children, we would consider dismissing and preoccupied to be insecure attachments. Finally, there is the unresolved and cannot classify, which would be similar to disorganized attachment in children.

We see in Table 12.2 that the proportions in each category are similar to the proportions observed in children using The Strange Situation. Notice that trauma and high stress do similar things to adults as they do to the children.

A review by van IJzendoorn (1995) found that a mother's attachment style appears to be related to her infant's attachment style. Securely attached mothers almost always have securely attached children (82 percent). Mothers coded as having the dismissive style tend to have avoidant children (65 percent). Preoccupied mothers tend to have securely attached children (41 percent) or resistant children (35 percent).

autonomous style An adult attachment style that is similar to secure attachment.

dismissing style An adult attachment style similar to the avoidant style in children.

preoccupied style An adult attachment style that is marked by excessive worry about relationships.

TABLE 12.2 Percent Distribution of Attachment Patterns in Adults

Sample	D Dismissing	F Secure	E Preoccupied	Unresolved cannot classify
Mothers	16	56	9	18
Fathers	24	50	11	15
Adolescents	34	44	11	11
Student (university age)	28	48	7	17
European	25	52	11	12
Japan/Israel	18	66	4	12
Nonclinical overall	24	50	9	16
At-risk sample	32	30	7	32
Combined clinical	23	21	13	43
Violence within the family	19	19	25	38
Clinical and at-risk groups overall	27	25	10	38

Source: Adapted from Bakermans-Kranenburg and van IJzendoorn (2009).

As we have seen in many places in this book, genetics can have a major impact on aspects of personality. We know that parents are likely to reiterate their attachment style with their children, securely attached parents tend to have securely attached children. Interestingly, there appears to be no genetic contribution to attachment style (Frearon et al., 2006; Roisman and Fraley, 2008).

Adult Outcomes

In adulthood, we see most attachment being with children and romantic partners. We have already seen the effects of attachment style on parenting, and will examine relationships in Chapter 18, where we will see that the attachment styles have important impacts on romantic relationships.

Priming feelings of secure attachment appears to lead people to being more accepting of those who are different (Mikulincer and Shaver, 2001). Secure attachment, whether naturally occurring or experimentally induced, increased the likelihood of helping someone in distress, and avoidant attachment was associated with a decrease in willingness to help (Mikulincer, Shaver, Gillath, and Nitzberg, 2005). Secure attachment allows people to deal constructively with negative affect and creatively use positive affect (Mikulincer, Shaver, and Pereg, 2003). It appears that attachment even influences the way that people perceive emotion. Participants with insecure attachment styles perceive happy and angry faces in others as persisting longer than people with secure attachment styles. Interestingly, this is not true of sad faces (Niedenthal, Brauer, Robin, and Innes-Ker, 2002).

Although the relationship is small, there is a connection between insecure attachment and depression (Simpson and Rholes, 2004; Sroufe, 2005). The insecure styles are associated with depression in adulthood. The disorganized style is associated with higher rates of psychopathologies in adulthood, especially Borderline Personality Disorder (Critchfield, Levy, Clarkin, and Kernberg, 2008; Fonagy and Bateman, 2007; Levy, 2005).

When people reach old age, often their children have developed lives of their own, and often a spouse or partner has died. An examination of attachment in older adults found that the main attachment figures were to living spouses and children, but it was also found that attachments included figures like clergy, dead spouses, and pets (Cicirelli, 2010).

Socialization and the Family

The families in which children are reared are very complex social systems, varying in size, stability, economic status, stress, misfortune, the personalities of and relationships between parents, openness of communication, and the practices used to train children. Since we cannot do justice to this complexity here, we will focus on one major source of family influence: child-rearing procedures.

It is useful to distinguish two related categories of child-rearing or socialization practices. The first refers to the specific practices used to train certain behaviors—for example, the methods used to wean or toilet train the child, control aggression, inhibit sexuality, and so on. The second encompasses broad characteristics or overall patterns of child-rearing activities, such as degree of warmth, control, or punitiveness. The broader patterns are obviously reflected in the more specific training practices, but to varying degrees and with varying relevance to the behavior being trained. It is this second category that will be our focus.

Child-Rearing Patterns

There are many differences between parents' approaches to the task of child rearing. Some are warm and affectionate, others are cold and aloof; some are strict, others are permissive; some believe that the child should participate in decisions, others favor a more authoritarian style; some are anxious, others are assured; many are gentle, a few are cruel. Parents bring to their child-rearing role completely different personalities, values, and expectations. A basic theoretical and empirical question for the psychologist concerns the influence of all these factors on the personality development of the child.

In our review of attachment, we find that if a child does not experience the warmth and security of attachment, there can be negative effects on development and adjustment. But there are significant variations within the less extreme, more normal range of child-rearing practices that also warrant attention. In assessing these child-rearing practices by interviewing parents or directly observing parent-child interactions, it has been found that many aspects of child rearing are interrelated and tend to cluster together. Thus, it is possible to describe the differences in child-rearing practices between families with reference to just a few basic characteristics. One such characteristic is degree of *permissiveness versus strictness*; another is degree of *warmth and nurturance versus coldness and hostility* (Becker, 1964). With just these two dimensions, a given child-rearing pattern could be described as permissive and warm, strict and warm, permissive and cold, or strict and cold.

Is it better for the child's development if parents are strict in their demands and discipline, or will the child have better psychological adjustment if parents are more permissive and less authoritarian in their behavior? It is known that the effects of both permissiveness and strictness are negative if the family environment tends to be cold and hostile. A hostile and permissive environment is likely to produce an aggressive and delinquent child, while a hostile-suppressive or restrictive family environment fosters children who are anxious and inhibited. In warm and nurturing family environments, the effects of permissiveness versus strictness are less clear. Several early studies (e.g., Baldwin, 1949; Watson, 1957) revealed that children raised in warm and reasonably permissive, democratic families that allowed the child freedom of choice tended to be friendly, assertive, and creative, whereas children raised in warm but strict and controlling homes tended to be conforming, low in curiosity, and well behaved.

Parenting Styles

Work by Diana Baumrind (1971, 1972, 1978, 1991, 2012, 2013) and by other investigators (Dornbusch et al., 1987; Steinberg, Elmen, and Mounts, 1989) suggest that the exercise of strong parental controls may have more positive developmental consequences than a permissive approach. Baumrind divided a sample of nursery school children into three personality groups on the basis of observations of their behavior. Children in one group were described as competent, self-reliant, content, inquiring, and assertive. A second group of children was described as moderately competent and mature, but also somewhat fearful, disoriented, and withdrawn. Finally, the least mature children formed a third group. They were highly dependent, fearful of novel situations, and displayed little self-control. Baumrind then assessed the child-rearing practices of the parents through interviews, home visits, and controlled laboratory observations. She found striking differences in the child-rearing procedures used by the parents in the three groups of children. Child-rearing practices among the mature, competent children were characterized by high levels of control and maturity demands (parental pressures to behave at intellectual and social levels congruent with the children's capacities). But control and demands were accompanied by a high degree of communication clarity; explanations and reasons were used to influence the children's behavior and feelings. The communication dimension most differentiated the parents of this mature group of children from the parents of children in the two other groups. The parents of the highly mature children were also the most nurturing, displaying warmth and involvement with their children. Baumrind's description of the parents of well-adjusted children is partially inconsistent with earlier data on the effects of permissiveness. Consistent with prior evidence, the "better" parents used reason and communicated openly with their children, but were higher in control than the **permissive** parents described in earlier studies. These data suggest that control is not necessarily associated with arbitrary or highly punitive discipline; one can be **authoritative** without being **authoritarian**.

These and related findings suggest a two-by-two classification of **parenting styles** that include four main classifications. Table 12.3 describes the patterns resulting from the different combinations of the two dimensions of accepting-rejecting and behaviorally demanding-undemanding. A third dimension of psychological control (Aunola and Nurmi, 2005) adds explanatory power. Psychological control is control of a child's emotions, or use of emotions like guilt or withdrawal of love to exert control over the child (Barber, 1996). In later work, Baumrind and colleagues (2010) have suggested seven classifications, very close to the eight that would show up in a warmth by behavioral control by psychological control configuration. Theory might predict eight combinations; however, that doesn't mean that all eight will be observed in the real world. Finally, like many classification schemes, the underlying dimensions are continuous with one shifting into the other.

The child-rearing pattern that is the most conducive to the child's development is the combination of high behavioral demands and high warmth and acceptance. Additional evidence for the adaptive effects of a parental authoritative approach to child rearing is provided in studies of adolescent school performance. An extensive survey of a large socioeconomically and ethnically diverse group of adolescents reflected a consistent positive relationship between authoritative parenting and school success in adolescents, whereas authoritarian and permissive parenting were negatively related to the offspring's school success (Dornbusch et al., 1987; Spera, 2005). A longitudinal approach to adolescent school performance confirmed this finding and, in addition, strongly suggested that the mediating factor between authoritative parenting and school success was psychosocial maturity; that is, authoritative parenting fostered greater psychosocial maturity

permissive A parenting style with low behavioral demands.

authoritative A parenting style marked by high behavioral demands and high warmth.

authoritarian A parenting style marked by high behavioral demands and low warmth.

parenting styles The ways in which parents treat their children that are a combination of behavioral demand and interpersonal warmth. Typically, there are thought to be four styles.

TABLE 12.3 A Two-Dimensional Classification of Parenting Patterns

	High warmth and affection	Rejecting, cold, unresponsive
High behavioral control, Demanding of age-appropriate maturity	Authoritative	Authoritarian
Undemanding, low in behavioral control attempts	Permissive	Neglecting or Laissez-Faire

Authoritative parents make demands on their children but typically also communicate well and show love and caring to the children.

(as assessed by a Psychosocial Maturity Inventory), and the latter, in turn, contributed to the adolescent's success in school.

The advantage of authoritative parenting over other styles has been shown in studies ranging from preschool (Baumrind, 1989) to high school (Steinberg. Lamborn, Dornbusch, and Darling, 1992) to grades in first-year college students (Turner, Chandler, and Heffer, 2009). A study of adolescents in Sweden found that children from authoritative families used less task-irrelevant behavior and lower levels of failure expectations, while children from neglectful families reported more task-irrelevant behaviors (Aunola, Stattin, and Nurmi, 2000). A similar pattern was observed for children from the permissive families, but less so. Children from authoritarian families reported more failure expectations and task-irrelevant behaviors than children of authoritative but less than the permissive and neglectful groups.

Parenting styles appear to have effects beyond academics. Mothers with a parenting style of authoritative have children with higher self-esteem and life satisfaction. Fathers with neglectful and permissive styles have children with higher measured depression (Milevsky, Schlechter, Netter, and Keehn, 2007). Meta-analysis revealed that positive parenting is associated with less relational aggression in the child (Kawabata, Alink, Tseng, IJzendroorn, and Crick, 2011). Relational aggression includes things like spreading rumors, excluding from friend group, or giving the cold shoulder. Negative and harsh parenting was associated with more relational aggression. Again, we can see that on some dimensions, fathers and mothers appear to have different effects. Mothers have an effect when the neglectful style is used. Psychological controlling fathers have the larger effect on relational aggression than psychologically controlling mothers. A different meta-analysis (Hoeve et al., 2009) found negative aspects of parenting such as neglect, hostility, rejection, and poor supervision were associated with delinquency. The effect was stronger for the effects of a parent on the same gender child (i.e., mothers for daughters, and fathers for sons).

Despite these findings, one must be cautious in directly extending them to other cultures. The same parental behavior may be interpreted differently, and as a consequence, have different effects in a different culture. Thus, cross-cultural studies have indicated that in cultures where strict parental discipline is the norm, children perceive the discipline as an expression of parental concern rather than arbitrariness or rejection. The same behavior in more child autonomy and communication-oriented cultures is perceived as unfair and rejecting (Kagitcibasi and Berry, 1989; Rohner, 1986).

A critique has been raised that the advantages of authoritative parenting are true only for some groups. Although this is a fair criticism, there is evidence that the authoritarian style is associated with better academic and social adjustment in mainland China (Chen, Dong, and Zhou, 1997). However, the differentiation between authoritative and authoritarian may not be substantial or useful in that culture (Xua et al., 2005).

Problem behaviors in African American children decrease when mothers report an authoritative parenting style and tend to increase when she reports using the authoritarian or permissive style (Querido, Warner, and Eyberg, 2002). Counter to a common stereotype, working-class and middle-class African American mothers tended to use reasoning as their main mode of parenting (Bluestone and Tamis-LeMonda, 1999), which would typically be indicative of the authoritative style. A laboratory investigation (Tamis-LeMonda, Briggs, McClowry, and Snow, 2009) revealed that African American mothers were coded primarily as responsive during a cooking and cleaning-up task with their child. However, higher rates of controlling behavior were observed when interacting with sons compared to daughters. The controlling behavior was associated with higher rates of negative behaviors on the tasks.

Finally, let's consider Baumrind's recent thoughts on parenting. She contends that it is important for parents to be controlling of the child, but in very specific ways. The authoritative parent uses what she terms confrontive power. The authoritative parent confronts a disobedient child and is not coerced by the child (Baumrind, 2012). This differs from the authoritarian parent, who uses coercive power. She defines this as the use of arbitrary discipline, use of severe physical and verbal punishment, and psychological control (Baumrind, 2013). The stance of the authoritarian is "Do as I say because I am the parent." The authoritative parent often has a give-and-take discussion with the child, especially as the child gets older, about the rules and why those are the rules.

Moral Development

In the previous sections, we saw how the infant develops significant attachments to adult figures, usually its parents. Attachment theorists believe that a secure attachment to a parent provides a secure base for the child to develop in a prosocial manner. Further, the model of a good relationship with a parent provides a basis for having a fundamentally positive and trusting attitude towards others. We now consider in more detail how infants are socialized into being moral and prosocial adults.

How does the infant develop from a creature dominated by biological urges, seeking immediate satisfaction, to an individual with a sense of right and wrong? How does a child become a moral being? Major theoretical approaches to personality—psychoanalytic, cognitive, and social learning theory—offer very different explanations of the process of moral development. In part, these different theoretical explanations arise from their emphases on different aspects of morality. The psychoanalysts have been concerned with the emotional and motivational aspects of morality, particularly the acquisition of guilt and conscience. Cognitive theorists have focused on the development of understanding of moral conduct or rules, or changes in the child's perception of right and wrong. Social learning approaches have been more concerned with the child's moral behaviors and good or bad actions, as well as with mechanisms for the acquisition of these behaviors.

The Superego and Moral Development

The key element in the psychoanalytic theory of moral development is the superego. As noted earlier (see Chapter 3), the superego refers to an internalized set of prohibitions and standards acquired by the child in the resolution of the Oedipal conflict through identification with the same-sex parent.

The theory implies that boys display a more integrated set of moral standards and behaviors than girls do, but the evidence suggests the contrary: girls tend to be more consistent in their moral attitudes and behavior than are boys (Maccoby and Jacklin, 1974). Psychoanalytic theory indicates that superego formation does not occur until the age of four or five; however, it is evident that children show indications of conscience well before those ages. Younger children use self-monitoring to resist forbidden acts and often "confess" when the resistance was insufficient to inhibit the act (Sears, Rau, and Alpert, 1965).

Given the available evidence, one can conclude that the classic Freudian explanation of the acquisition of conscience or superego is seriously inadequate and, in important respects, incorrect. Moreover, the concept of the superego as an unconscious, unrelenting internal censor that blocks and punishes the expression of id and egoistic impulses requires modification. More generally, however, psychoanalysis offers an inconsistent and ambiguous picture of the neurotic versus healthy implications of guilt, conscience, and responsibility. There is the suggestion in psychoanalytic writings, as well as in the writings of some self-actualization and cognitive theorists, that rigidly held "ought" and "should" rules of behavior have no place in a truly healthy personality.

Stages of Moral Development: The Cognitive Approach

In addition to feeling guilty, confessing wrongdoings, telling the truth, and not cheating, conscience involves an understanding of moral issues, including what it means to be good or bad.

Kohlberg's Contribution

preconventional A style of morality typical of small children that is based on pleasure or punishment.

conventional A style of morality marked by a social approval and law and order.

postconventional A style of morality based on maximizing good, or based on one's own dedicated value.

One of the most influential cognitive models of how people think and reason about moral issues is that of Lawrence Kohlberg (1969b), who based his work on an earlier cognitive model of moral development developed by the Swiss developmental psychologist Jean Piaget (Cowan, 1978). Kohlberg postulated six stages of moral development, each characterized by qualitatively distinctive modes of thinking. In the course of development, which extends into adolescence, more advanced stages supersede earlier, more immature stages. The six developmental stages, described in the following paragraphs, are grouped into three moral levels: the **preconventional**, or premoral; the **conventional**; and the **postconventional**, or principled.

At level 1, rules and expectations are perceived as external to the self. The child does make a distinction between right and wrong, but defines right first on the basis of what authorities such as parents and the law demand (stage 1) and subsequently on the basis of concrete reciprocal *hedonism*, characterized by the phrase, "If I do something for you, then it's right that you do something for me" (stage 2). Level 2 begins at approximately age nine and, according to Kohlberg, is the level of most adolescents and adults. Morality here is based on good intentions and obtaining social approval (stage 3) and on a recognition of the importance of laws and rules as means of maintaining the social order (stage 4). The minority of individuals achieving level 3 do so in late adolescence, supposedly around the age of twenty. At this highest level, morality is perceived in terms of contractual obligations and laws based on democratic participation (stage 5). Ultimately, morality is a matter of individual conscience and universal ethics (stage 6). Stage 6 morality is characterized by reasoning from a set of principles that both are universally acceptable and stem from the individual's formulation of moral standards. These stages of moral development are summarized in Table 12.4.

Kohlberg derived these stages from an analysis of responses to a series of stories that posed moral dilemmas. Children of different ages and cultures had to arrive at moral judgments based on the content of these stories. For example, in one story a man's wife is desperately in need of a drug recently discovered by a local druggist. The druggist, however, has priced the drug very high in order to make a substantial profit. The husband cannot

TABLE 12.4 Kohlberg's Stages of Moral Development

Level I (Preconventional Morality)
Stage 1. Moral judgments based on conformity to authority figures.
Stage 2. Moral judgments based on concrete reciprocal hedonism.
Level II (Conventional Morality)
Stage 3. Moral judgments based on desire for social approval.
Stage 4. Moral judgments based on law and order orientation.
Level III (Postconventional Morality)
Stage 5. Moral judgments based on achieving the good of all.
Stage 6. Moral judgments based on the development of one's own set of ethical principles.

pay the price and breaks into the man's store to steal the drug for his wife. The question posed is whether the husband should have stolen the drug. Some children argue that the man is justified in stealing the drugs. Others say he is not. However, what is important is the *reasoning* the child uses to arrive at a conclusion.

Kohlberg and his associates have found that the stages observed in samples of American children also characterize the developmental pattern of moral understanding in children from other cultures, including those of Mexico, Taiwan, and Turkey. There is some question as to whether the superiority of the highest stage is a function of social and cognitive development or is largely a matter of an arbitrarily imposed cultural value. In addition, there is evidence that people use different rules for different situations and that the stages are not sequential (Kurtines and Greif, 1974). Finally, the stage approach is limited in that it focuses on moral *thought* and does not consider the motivational and affective aspects of moral *actions*.

Gender Differences

A major critique of Kohlberg's stage theory has been voiced by Gilligan (1982) in her book *In a Different Voice*. Gilligan asserts that males and females differ fundamentally in their orientation to moral issues; that males approach issues of morality in terms of justice and rights, while females see moral issues more in interpersonal terms of degree of helping and caring for others. As a consequence, females are more likely to be found at stage 3 in Kohlberg's scheme in which concern for others is preeminent, and fewer females than males win be at the "higher" stages.

While Gilligan's arguments seem cogent and she reports on research findings that appear supportive of her views, considerable controversy has arisen regarding the evidence for gender differences and its interpretation (Baumrind, 1986; Walker, 1984, 1989). Relatively few gender differences in cognitive moral stage attainment have been reported, and these become minimal when education is controlled (Walker, 1984). If instead of using the standardized Kohlberg hypothetical dilemma, participants are asked to recall and discuss a recent real-life moral dilemma from their own experience, then differences in moral orientation are found between adult females and males that are consistent with Gilligan's view (Walker, 1989). However, these differences reflect differences in the kinds of moral dilemmas that females and males are concerned with rather than gender differences in moral reasoning or level of cognitive moral stage attainment. Sara Jaffe and Janet Shibley Hyde (2000) conducted a meta-analysis of moral orientation and found very small differences between men and women on the justice orientation Kohlberg espouses and the care orientation that Gilligan espouses.

The Social Learning Approach

For social learning theorists, moral behavior is not fundamentally different from any other class of social behavior. It is acquired through punishment for deviation from social rules and through reinforcement for conforming to these standards. Through a process of conditioning, in which rule breaking is first followed by punishment, the child learns to experience discomfort and fear even when thinking about or anticipating breaking a rule. This discomfort inhibits the deviant action even in the absence of likely discovery and punishment. Furthermore, the child comes to feel guilty following a transgression and learns to reduce that guilt through self-punitive remarks and confession (Aronfreed, 1964). Finally, the child also learns to covertly verbalize statements that help control and inhibit socially disapproved actions. These statements, such as "Don't hit the baby" or "Don't take the candy" are often initially voiced aloud. But they eventually become silent and provide the basis for the voice of conscience.

There are a number of studies indicating that moral behaviors and judgments in children can be influenced through the observation and imitation of models (Bandura and McDonald, 1963). From a social learning standpoint, each society's norms and models form the primary source of moral behavior, but social influence is insufficient to account

"Here, have some of mine!" This photograph shows an example of prosocial behavior.

prosocial behavior Positive social behavior, often socially prescribed and viewed as moral action, that is enacted to help others.

for all aspects of morality. Social learning theorists point out that the child must develop the cognitive competence required to understand moral rules, as well as the behavioral competence, such as self-control, required to comply with those rules (Mischel and Mischel, 1976). Efforts to relate Kohlberg's all-encompassing stages of moral development to specific moral behaviors have yielded similarly small but significant and consistent correlations (Blasi, 1980).

Prosocial Behaviors

The discussion of moral behavior focused on prohibitions, conformity to social rules, and developmental changes in children's concepts of what constitutes good and evil. We now turn to positive social behaviors, such as generosity, caring, and helping, which frequently are socially prescribed and viewed as moral kinds of actions. The four-year-old preschooler sharing her lunch with a peer is engaging in prosocial behavior, as are the young opponents of an injured football player who pat him on the back as he is helped from the field. There are, of course, many other behaviors that are included in the prosocial category, such as dedication to improving the lot of the poor, efforts to overcome social injustice, and struggles to eliminate brutality. More generally, "**prosocial behavior** covers a board range of actions intended to benefit one or more people other than one's self—behaviors such as helping, comforting, sharing, and cooperating" (Batson and Powell, 2003, p. 463).

Evolution of Positive Social Behaviors

Whenever the question of what human beings have inherited from their animal ancestors arises, characteristics such as aggression, sex drive, and territorial competition are typically cited. Rarely does one think of such positive social behaviors as cooperation, generosity, and altruism as part of our animal heritage. Yet there is no doubt that many animal species display cooperative social patterns; even instances of self-sacrifice are not uncommon. However, whether the same biological factors that govern nonhuman prosocial behaviors are relevant to human prosocial behaviors is debatable.

The complex cooperative societies of social insects like the ant and the bee have been described in countless popular articles, and the interaction of genetic programming with environmental influences in these insects has been extensively studied. But cooperation and sharing are by no means restricted to social insects. Chimpanzees display cooperation in multiple ways (Muller and Mitani, 2005; Teleki, 1973; Wilson, 1975). And bonobos are even more cooperative (Hare, Melis, Woods, Hastings, and Wrangham, 2007). Positive social behaviors are common even among African elephants. "Young calves of both sexes are treated equally and each is permitted to suckle from any nursing mother in the group. Adolescent cows serve as 'aunts', restraining the calves from running about and nudging others awake from their naps" (Wilson, 1975, p. 494). When a young bull elephant was felled with an anesthetic dart, "the adult cows rushed to his aid and tried to raise him to his feet" (p. 494). The African wild dog provides a striking contrast between savage behavior displayed when attacking prey and gentle, nurturing behavior extended to others in its pack. When the pack has eaten their prey, they return to the den and regurgitate, making it possible for the young and other adults who remained behind to share in the bounty. The sick and the crippled, unable to participate in the hunt, are thus maintained by the pack. As the incident described in Highlight 12.2 illustrates, a similar kind of cooperative behavior can be observed in dolphins.

Prosocial Behavior in Dolphins

A school of approximately 50 *Delphinus delphis* was sighted. As soon as the Zodiac (our boat) approached, they increased speed, dived and changed direction under water. The school reassembled behind the Zodiac. The yacht took over the chase and an animal was wounded by the harpoon. We saw quite clearly how other dolphins came immediately to the help of the wounded animal on the starboard side of the yacht.

They supported the wounded dolphin with their flippers and bodies and carried it to the surface. It blew 2–3 times and then dived. The whole incident lasted about 30 seconds and was repeated twice when the animal appeared unable to surface alone. All the animals including the wounded dolphin then dived and swam quickly out of sight.

Source: Pileri and Knuckey, 1969, from Wilson, 1975, p. 475.

Many of these behaviors can be considered instances of altruism, since, in an effort to save members of their own species, these animals risk their own wellbeing. But perhaps the most striking examples of altruism are provided by the social insects. Honeybee workers that embed their barbed stings in an intruder threatening the hive will die as a result but, in the process, perhaps save the rest of the hive. Similarly, termite soldiers spray predators with a glandular secretion fatal to both themselves and their enemies. The colony's king and queen are thereby protected and remain able to preserve and expand the colony through breeding. The insects sacrificing themselves are relatives of and share common genes with the surviving insects. The altruistic organism is therefore contributing to the survival of its own gene pool (see also Chapter 1). Evolutionary theorists argue that such acts of altruism are built into organisms because of **kin selection**, where helping those who share genes (those that are closely related) increases the probability of those genes surviving and being reproduced.

Evolutionary psychologists have extended this argument to suggest that there is a genetic basis for altruism and other prosocial behaviors among humans. However, while one can draw a crude analogy between altruism in nonhumans and humans, it is pure speculation to propose that the same mechanisms are operative in both species (Langergraber et al., 2011). Human altruism takes many different forms and is affected by a great range of social influences. Rather, the importance of animal studies lies in their demonstration that prosocial behaviors are as natural to many animal species as are the more often cited examples of destructive behaviors. Human tenderness, caring, attachment, and self-sacrifice are, then, just as "animalistic" as are human competitiveness, selfishness, and brutality.

kin selection The hypothesis that helping related individuals increases the amount of shared genes in subsequent generations.

Cooperation

Describing behavior as "natural" does not necessarily mean that it is inborn; rather, it implies that the organism has the potential for developing this pattern of behavior and will do so under normal environmental circumstances. Infants are not cooperative, but preschool children display sharing, reciprocity, and other forms of cooperation in their play behavior. In an observational study of a twenty-minute interaction between children and parents on a cooperative game, one of eight one-year-olds and seven of eight two-year-olds participated in at least one cooperative interchange (Hay, 1979). By two years of age, children verbalize sympathy to individuals in distress and make efforts to assist them (Zahn-Waxler and Radke-Yarrow, 1982).

These positive social behaviors are related to the child's general mental development (Emmerich, Cocking, and Sigel, 1979) and personal adjustment (Block and Block, 1980). An extensive longitudinal study of nursery school children indicated that children rated by their teachers as high in such characteristics as helpfulness and cooperativeness obtained low scores on measures of impulsiveness and high scores on an index of their capacity to recover to a state of normalcy after a stressful experience (Block and Block, 1980). Moreover, four-year-old children described as dependable, calm, and cooperative tended to behave generously at age five on a measure of sharing and distributing rewards. However, four-year-old children described as overreactive and not competent in handling stress tended to be low in generosity at age five.

Cross-Cultural Cooperative Behaviors

Cooperative behaviors are strongly influenced by the larger culture as well as by individual traits of the child. Whiting and Whiting (1975) gathered detailed, naturalistic, observational data of children between the ages of three and eleven in six different cultures: Kenya, Mexico, the Philippines, Okinawa, India, and a New England community. The majority of the children observed in Kenya, Mexico, and the Philippines were above average on such behaviors as "offers help" and "offers support." The children in the other three cultures scored low on this constellation of prosocial responses. Children from Okinawa, India, and the New England community were more self-seeking and dominance oriented in their social interactions.

Laboratory studies of cooperation and competition by Madsen and his colleagues (Kagan and Madsen, 1971; Madsen and Shapira, 1970) have helped sharpen our understanding of the nature of some of these cultural differences. In several experimental studies of Mexican and American children, in which a child must choose either to cooperate or to compete with a peer, Mexican children were found to be much more cooperative than Americans (Knight and Kagan, 1977). These laboratory findings therefore are consistent with the cultural differences reported by the Whitings, using naturalistic observations, and illustrate how both laboratory and field research methodologies can mutually contribute to understanding. However, it is still unclear whether the greater cooperativeness of the Mexican children was due to the fact that they were less competitive or was an indication of a stronger tendency to be cooperative. In one study bearing on this issue, children were given a task in which they could prevent their partner from receiving a toy. This was done twice as often by American as by Mexican children. In another investigation it was revealed that, in an effort to avoid conflict, Mexican children would give their toys up to their partner when only one could receive a toy, while this was not the case with the American children. Hence, the Mexican and the American children apparently differed in competitiveness. But why these Mexican and American children differed in their behavior—whether the critical factors were cultural norms, family structure, or rural-urban background—remains an unresolved question.

Source: Jack Jelly/Shutterstock

Children often cooperate on tasks.

Generosity and Caring

People who are cooperative also tend to be more generous in their willingness to come to the aid of others in distress. In addition, many of the variables that influence cooperation, such as personal adjustment, cognitive level, imitation, and cultural background, also influence generosity and caring behavior. However, generosity toward others and responsiveness to distress are sufficiently different from cooperation to warrant separate discussion.

A common experimental procedure in the study of generosity is to have children win a prize or earn some reward, such as crayons, pennies, or candy. Then the children are asked to make a donation from their earnings to help needy children. The amount that each child donates serves as a measure of generosity. This procedure has the advantage of providing an objective, quantitative measure that can be readily used in experimental settings, but it also has the disadvantage of a lack of naturalism, for children are not usually called on to make donations to charity. Their generosity is more typically expressed in interactions with playmates and siblings. Nonetheless, this methodology has yielded some interesting findings. For example, relatively brief exposure to an adult model who donates generously has been shown to have a surprisingly strong positive effect on children's generosity. This increased generosity has been reported even months after the observation of the model (Midlarsky and Bryan, 1972; Rushton, 1976). It therefore seems reasonable that children with a generous parent or parents, who identify with that parent, will be high in generosity. In support of this, it has been found that when parents place a high value on prosocial behaviors, their children are more generous and caring (Feshbach, 1975; Hoffman, 1975). A very different and dramatic source of data reflecting parental influence on prosocial behavior is provided by a study of Christians who rescued Jews from the Nazis (London, 1970; Oliner and Oliner, 1988). In their interviews, the rescuers conveyed a strong identification with moral, principled parents.

Empathy

One can be generous, supportive, and cooperative because these responses are encouraged and reinforced by the culture. But one can also engage in these same prosocial behaviors because of an understanding of other people's needs and feelings and because one shares in those feelings. The term *empathy* has been used to describe the process of social understanding and common emotional responses. In some theoretical treatments of empathy, the cognitive or social-comprehension aspect of empathy is stressed, while in other treatments the emotional aspect receives greater emphasis. But it appears that empathic responses involve the ability (1) to discriminate and label feelings in others; (2) to assume the perspective and role of another person; and (3) to experience and respond with feeling (N. Feshbach, 1978).

Evidence of the emotional component of empathy, particularly the response to distress, can be discerned rather early in the child's development (Hoffman, 1981, 2000; Sagi and Hoffman, 1976). Although before twelve-months general agitation is the principal response to another infant's cries, by twenty-four months one can observe more differential and more frequent empathic-like responses, such as patting and bringing objects to the distressed child (Zahn-Waxler and Radke-Yarrow, 1982). Many theories of empathy have suggested that it is necessary to understand what someone else is experiencing. This is known as a **theory of mind**. It is typically believed that a theory of mind is developed by age 10, but empathy develops before the theory of mind is complete (Pfeifer and Dapretto, 2009; Rochat 2001). Infants understand where others are focused (Reddy, 2003) and imitate facial expressions at a young age (Meltzoff and Decety, 2003).

theory of mind An understanding that other individuals have a mind, and it probably works similarly to other minds.

To study empathy in older children, a test has been developed that involves presenting the children with a series of slides depicting happiness, sadness, fear, or anger (N. Feshbach, 1978). After each sequence, the child was asked how he or she felt. The number of times the child's reported affect matched the depicted emotion was the measure of empathy. Children scoring high on this measure of empathy were rated by their teachers as high in cooperation, and children scoring low in this measure were rated as high in competitiveness

Altruistic Persons

The movie *Schindler's List* presented a portrait of a man who becomes altruistic and bankrupts his business to save Jews from extermination in Nazi Germany.

A unique study of prosocial, altruistic individuals entailed a comparison of other individuals in Nazi-controlled countries during World War 11 who rescued Jews with individuals from these same countries who remained bystanders (Oliner and Oliner, 1988). These acts of rescue took various forms—hiding Jewish children and adults, transporting them to a safer place, falsification of records, deceiving friends as well as authorities, but all constituted truly altruistic acts in that they entailed risk of imprisonment and a very real risk of being condemned to death. Following the destruction of the entire Jewish community in his town, the senior author, then a 12-year-old boy, was able to escape and obtain refuge in the home of a Polish peasant woman.

The difficult task of identifying rescuers had already been made by an Israeli commission using the following criteria: (1) the rescuer had to be motivated by humanitarian considerations only; (2) risked his or her own life; (3) received no remuneration of any kind. Some 6,000 such rescuers have been formally identified, although the actual number is considerably larger. A sample of several hundred rescuers from eight different countries and a smaller group of bystanders were interviewed.

The focus of the study was to determine whether one could identify an "altruistic personality," although recognizing that opportunity and other situational factors were also relevant. On the one standard personality scale that was administered, the Internal/External locus of control scale (see Chapter 5), the rescuers obtained significantly higher "internal" scores than the bystanders, reflecting a stronger sense in the rescuers that one's own efforts affect the rewards one receives. Also, in their self-descriptions, rescuers perceived themselves as being more honest and helpful than did bystanders. Questions regarding family influences were particularly revealing. Rescuers were three times as likely as bystanders to report that their parents taught them to care for other people while a significantly higher proportion of bystanders indicated that their parents placed importance on self-oriented values such as economic achievement. Differences in degree of attachment to the family and others were particularly striking. Seventy-eight percent of the rescuers in comparison to 52 percent of the bystanders report being very close to their family, while 76 percent of rescuers in contrast to only 44 percent of the bystanders indicate a close relationship with an influential person other than their parents.

These findings reflect a much stronger association between emotional relationships and altruistic behavior than between stages of cognitive moral development and altruistic behavior. Being able to conceptualize moral issues at Kohlberg's higher stages may contribute to moral behavior but is insufficient. More important appears to be the degree to which one is concerned about other people, the kind of moral orientation that Gilligan has emphasized.

(Barnett, Matthews, and Howard, 1979; Marcus, Telleen, and Poke, 1979). Empathic children tend to be low in aggressiveness (N. Feshbach, 1978; Feshbach and Feshbach, 1969). Higher levels of empathy are associated with lower levels of cyberbullying (Ang and Goh, 2010). However, the relationship between empathy and prosocial behaviors is variable and appears to depend on a number of factors (Radke-Yarrow, Zahn-Waxler, and Chapman, 1983). With older children and using other measures of empathy, fairly consistent positive relationships have been found between empathy and prosocial behaviors and inverse relationships with aggressiveness (Eisenberg and Miller, 1987; Miller and Eisenberg, 1988). Empathy, in addition, has been shown to be associated with higher levels of moral reasoning (Eisenberg et al., 1987), consistent with the view that empathy in older children and adults has an important cognitive component as well as an emotional component (N. Feshbach, 1978).

There have been a number of attempts at empathy training which demonstrate that this approach holds considerable promise for the development of prosocial behavior (Feshbach and Feshbach, 2009; Feshbach, Feshbach, Fauvre, and Ballard-Campbell, 1983). For example, Staub (1971) had children participate in training sessions in which they played the role of helper to an individual in need of aid. Girls with role-taking experience subsequently responded more frequently to cries of distress on a recording in an adjacent room than did girls without such experience, while boys with experimental training displayed more subsequent sharing than did boys with no role-playing experience.

Summary

1. While many developmental psychologists believe that early childhood experiences are critical for the child's subsequent cognitive, emotional, and social development, there is still considerable debate over the usefulness of the concept of *critical periods*.

2. The evidence of *attachment* behavior in nonhumans suggests that there are important biological factors influencing attachment in human infants. From a biological standpoint, the infant's attachment to a caregiver increases the likelihood of receiving nourishment and protection and therefore increases the infant's chances of survival.

3. Research indicates that there are significant differences among infants in the quality of their attachment behavior and that the classification of infants into *securely attached*, *insecurely attached*, and *avoidant* categories is predictive of subsequent attachment behavior and adjustment.

4. The effects of parental control depend on the degree of parental acceptance and the clarity of parental communication to the child.

5. Authoritative parenting, consisting of a combination of parental acceptance and understanding of the child and of guidance, communication, and appropriate controls, fosters psychosocial maturity and effective school performance in the child, whereas authoritarian and permissive parenting tend to have negative developmental effects.

6. Cross-cultural studies based on Kohlberg's moral-dilemmas test reflect a developmental pattern that is consistent with Kohlberg's postulated six stages of moral development.

7. Reward and punishment, exposure to models, and verbalization of moral rules and prohibitions are processes that social learning theorists suggest are relevant to moral behavior.

8. Evolutionary psychologists, citing evidence of altruistic behavior among nonhuman species, have suggested that there is a genetic basis for human altruism. They argue that acts of altruism have evolved because, despite the individual sacrifices involved, the survival of genes among related organisms is facilitated.

9. Cooperative behavior in children varies significantly with cultural background and situational factors.

10. Children's generosity is markedly enhanced by exposure to models displaying generosity. Advocacy of generosity by the model is less effective than an actual display of generous behavior.

11. Empathy is facilitated by situational factors such as similarity between people. Empathy also has some of the characteristics of a personality trait, in that children high in empathy tend to be more cooperative and less competitive than children low in empathy.

Key Terms

anxious/resistant attachment (p. 222)
attachment style (p. 222)
authoritarian (p. 229)
authoritative (p. 229)
autonomous style (p. 226)
avoidant attachment (p. 222)
conventional (p. 232)
critical periods (p. 217)
dismissing style (p. 226)
disorganized/disoriented attachment (p. 222)
kin selection (p. 235)
parenting styles (p. 229)

permissive (p. 229)
postconventional (p. 232)
prosocial behavior (p. 234)
preconventional (p. 232)
preoccupied style (p. 226)
secure attachment (p. 222)
sensitive periods (p. 218)
stages (p. 217)
theory of mind (p. 237)
The Strange Situation (p. 222)
working model (p. 220)

Thought Questions

1. There are some philosophies, mostly Eastern, that argue that we must unlearn attachments and that attachments limit our freedom of choice. How do you feel about this position?

2. Why aren't moral beliefs and moral understanding more closely related to actual moral behaviors?

3. Is teaching children to be cooperative and generous likely to handicap them if the culture at large is highly competitive and self-oriented?

4. Is there a "best way" to raise children, a set of socialization practices that all parents should use? What variations from these child-rearing practices would you allow?

Development Through the Life Span

Source: Monkey Business Images/Shutterstock

Chapter Outline

Personality Continuity and Change

Adolescence and Emerging
    Adulthood

Adult Development

Old Age

This chapter begins with a consideration of the issue of the degree to which personality stays the same or changes overtime. It then extends the discussion of developmental changes germane to personality into the adolescent period, adulthood, and old age. Adolescence is a period marked by substantial changes in the self. Issues of self-definition and self-integration also emerge in adulthood and old age. Attention is directed to the particular problems and issues that confront most people during maturity and old age and to how resolving these problems and issues can contribute to personality change and growth. The chapter concludes with a discussion of psychobiography, which is an effort to analyze the development of particular individuals over time.

Personality Continuity and Change

In the previous chapter, we considered the issue of whether personality developed in a continuous or in a stage-like fashion. The term *continuity* has another meaning besides that of gradual change. It also refers to the constancy, or stability, of behavior overtime. Are traits displayed by children during the early years predictive of similar behaviors during later periods of development? Is a fearful and timid child likely to develop into an anxious adult? Similarly, are aggressive children likely to remain aggressive adolescents and adults? Are other traits such as intelligence and dependency relatively enduring over the life span?

The answers to these questions, like those for most psychological questions, depend on a number of factors. First, answers depend on *what* aspects of personality are measured and how. For instance, McCrae and Costa (2003) define personality as the individual's underlying set of personality traits. Using measures of traits, they argue that personality stabilizes in early adulthood and then does not change very much thereafter. On the other hand, Helson (1993) defines personality as "the relatively enduring organization of motivations and resources" (p. 97) and uses different measures than do McCrae and Costa. She finds evidence of change in certain aspects of personality during the adult years. For instance, women show drops in "succorance" (the degree to which they are motivated to help others) from the time they are new parents to the time when their children have grown up.

Second, answers depend on *when* measures of personality are made. Block (1993), for instance, found significant correlations between childhood and adulthood for his measures of ego-resiliency and ego-control in males, but not in females. Ego-resiliency refers to the degree of flexibility in coping. Ego-control refers to the degree of impulse control exhibited by individuals. For females, there was consistency through the childhood years, but that consistency did not extend into adolescence. From adolescence on, there was again consistency, but there was no relation between consistency in the two time periods of childhood and adolescence/adulthood. These findings also suggest that gender can make a difference in whether or not there is continuity.

Third, answers depend on what is meant by stability and change. For instance, while Block (1993) found significant correlations between measures of male ego-resiliency in early childhood and in adulthood, suggesting continuity, there was nonetheless change. Individuals tended to maintain their relative rankings with respect to one another in the degree of ego-resiliency. However, all individuals showed increases in this capacity from childhood to adulthood. Thus, it is useful to differentiate **rank order stability** from **mean level stability**. Rank order stability examines the extent that people maintain their relative rank over time. Are the most extroverted in elementary school still among the most extroverted forty years later? Mean level stability addresses whether there has been a change in the actual scores over time. Do people have the same score on extraversion at twelve as at fifty-two?

Roberts and his colleagues have conducted large-scale reviews of the literature on both rank order stability and mean level stability. They found that rank order stability of personality traits tends to become stronger as a person ages (Roberts and Del Veccio, 2000). Rank order stability is lower for teenagers than for people in their thirties. They find the highest rank order stability for people in their fifties. Although there is a great deal of stability, there is also plenty of change. Because temperament is typically believed to have a genetic component, it is interesting to examine that stability. They found high stability for negative emotionality, task persistence, and adaptability. Interestingly, activity level had low stability.

In examining mean level stability, it was found that the level of agreeableness and conscientiousness increased across the life span (Roberts, Walton, and Viechtbauer, 2006). The social dominance facet of extroversion continued to increase into a person's forties and then flattened out. Openness to experience tended to have a large increase from eighteen to twenty-two, then stay at the same level for several decades, before declining in a person's sixties and seventies.

Furthermore, psychologists distinguish between **absolute stability** and **personality coherence** (Caspi and Bem, 1990). If a person throws temper tantrums both as a child and as an adult, that is an illustration of absolute stability—the behavior in childhood is closely related to or similar to the behavior in adulthood. Personality coherence refers to the idea that the adult will exhibit behaviors that are *conceptually* similar to those in childhood but different in form, thus suggesting that there is some degree of change in the manifestation of an underlying trait. For instance, a child who throws temper tantrums may grow up to be an irritable, uncooperative adult, but the adult does not throw temper tantrums. As an example of coherence, Caspi, Bem, and Elder (1989) found that men who

rank order stability The extent that people maintain their relative rank over time.

mean level stability The change in actual scores over time.

absolute stability The behavior in childhood is closely related to or similar to the behavior in adulthood.

personality coherence Behaviors that the adult will exhibit are conceptually similar to those in childhood but different in form.

were rated as acting dependent in childhood tended to be more nurturant and more stable marital partners as adults. Girls who had frequent temper tantrums were more likely to be divorced and be worse mothers as adults. These are not the same behaviors, yet they fit with the behaviors observed in childhood. One could argue that dependent individuals are invested in maintaining relationships and develop more mature ways of doing this with age. For the girls, there is probably a tendency to be impulsive. In general, psychologists believe it is more likely that personality coherence, and not absolute stability, between childhood and adulthood characterizes the development of personality. Personality coherence is a concept that encompasses both continuity and change.

Source: Veronica Louro/Shutterstock

In cross-sectional research, all these students might be tested at about the same time.

Finally, whether personality changes or is stable from childhood to adulthood may vary among individuals (Ozer and Gjerde, 1989). For instance, Sampson and Laub (1990) studied 500 delinquent children and compared them to 500 controls. As adults, the former delinquents were more likely to have had unstable employment histories, to have been arrested, and to drink excessively. However, there were considerable differences among the subjects studied. That is, while many exhibited consistency, many were found to have undergone considerable positive change, becoming reliable adults. Similarly, women who worked were found to exhibit increases in independence between the ages of twenty-one and forty-three, while women who were homemakers did not (Helson and Stewart, 1994).

Other factors that influence continuity include the time intervals at which change is measured, what statistical procedures are used (Weinberger, 1994), and the methods of measurement (Edmonds, Goldberg, Hampson, and Barckley, 2013). The sheer numbers of factors that can influence the stability of a behavior pattern over time make it difficult to interpret the relationship between the childhood manifestation of a trait and later displays of that trait. It is known that certain traits, such as intelligence and aggression, are stable over time; that is, a child who is aggressive at age five also tends to be aggressive at age ten and age sixteen (see also Chapters 9 and 18). This finding of continuity in aggression is particularly true for boys. Similarly, children having high IQs at the age of five tend to score high on IQ tests during the rest of their lives, as well. This continuity can be accounted for by genetic factors.

Psychoanalytic theory also argues that the early formation of personality accounts for similar manifestations of personality in later life. Subsequent experiences are of secondary importance compared to the overwhelming influence of those early experiences. One might also assume a less extreme position, acknowledging the importance of experiences later in life, while maintaining that early influences are much more powerful than later ones.

A contrasting position, and one held by many social learning theorists, asserts that behavior is continuously shaped by the reinforcements in our environment, by the models to whom we are exposed, and by the cognitive feedback they provide. From this perspective, personality is largely environmentally determined (see Chapter 5) and therefore subject to major changes throughout life. Hence, whereas psychoanalytically or genetically oriented theorists expect stability in personality over time, social learning theorists anticipate situational influences. But even if personality stability in social behavior is uncovered, social learning theorists still may contend that, in these instances, there has been constancy in environmental reinforcers and external stimuli. There are some family environmental factors that influence aggression, for example, and it may be that the continuity of these family influences is responsible for the continuity observed in this personality disposition. Thus, the stability observed in aggressive behavior over long periods could be due to consistency of the deprivation and frustration experienced by the child or to the family's consistent reinforcement of aggressive responses.

Humanistic theory (see Chapter 6) also holds that personality should change over time. For Carl Rogers, the person is an "open system," continually learning and integrating new experience into the personality. Personality will therefore evolve, although this does not mean that earlier forms of coping will be abandoned. Rather, as documented in the Caspi et al., study of men who were dependent as children, earlier forms of coping will develop into more mature forms.

Genetic theory seems to hold that if personality is genetically based, it will be fixed and unchanging from early childhood on. This implication, however, is incorrect. In fact, behavior geneticists argue that the tendency to change is itself heritable, and changes in personality over the childhood years are genetically based (Brody, 1994).

longitudinal study Measures are taken in the child's early years and again at subsequent periods of development.

The research strategy most often used to address the question of stability is the **longitudinal study**. Measures of personality are taken in the child's early years and again at subsequent periods of development. For instance, the children might be tested at one, seven, twelve, and eighteen years of age. This allows us to see the change in the children across time. A potential confound is something known as a cohort effect. The children all would be the same age when particular things are happening—for instance, an economic downturn resulting in mass unemployment of their parents, a terrorist attack provoking cultural anxiety, or the election of the first African American president. An alternative research strategy is called a **cross-sectional research design**. In this type of research, different age children are measured at the same time. For instance, a research group may go to a school and measure seven-year-old second graders, twelve-year-old seventh graders, and eighteen-year-old high school seniors. The children are not tracked across time. This approach avoids a few of the cohort effects, but not all, nor does it provide the ability to see how an individual changes over time. The **cross-lagged design** combines aspects of both longitudinal and cross-sectional designs. In this research, children of different ages are measured and then followed through time. Our seven-, twelve-, and eighteen-year-olds are measured, then measured again five to six years later, and then also another five to six years after that.

cross-sectional research design A type of research in which children of different ages are measured at the same time.

cross-lagged design Children of different ages are measured and then followed through time.

A classic major longitudinal project at the Institute of Human Development of the University of California, Berkeley, has been able to provide data for a number of investigators interested in the continuity issue. One of these studies (Block, 1971) compared personality ratings obtained at three different times: when the subjects were in junior high school, in senior high school, and thirty to forty years old. The data provided evidence of consistency. About 60 percent of the personality items on which the subjects were assessed in junior high school were substantially correlated with the senior high school ratings, and about 30 percent of the senior high school ratings were comparable to the ratings obtained during adulthood. For males, substantial consistencies emerged on ratings of such items as, "Is a genuinely dependable and responsible person," "Tends toward undercontrol of needs and impulses, unable to delay gratification," and "Enjoys aesthetic impressions, is aesthetically reactive." Examples of items on which stable ratings were obtained for females include "Basically submissive," "Emphasizes being with others, gregarious," and "Rebellious and nonconforming."

While Block's (1971) findings are often taken as evidence of consistency, the finding that only 30 percent of the traits showed substantial correlations from adolescence to adulthood suggests the presence of change as well. Other studies have found evidence of changes in personality from childhood into adulthood (Chess and Thomas, 1984), and most researchers now agree that personality does not stabilize until sometime between the ages of twenty and thirty. Even after age thirty, as we shall consider in a later section of this chapter, there is evidence of further personality change. With regard to other data on stability, Caspi and Bem (1990) conclude, "In general, differences in aggression, dominance, dependency, sociability, and shyness are preserved from middle and late childhood through adolescence and adulthood" (p. 558).

The study of the consistency of personality over time indicates both stability and change. But what are the mechanisms that underlie stability over time? One possibility is that early childhood experiences form personality traits that persist. Many current psychologists, however, favor more complex explanations involving the series of transactions between the person and his or her environment over time (Caspi, 1993; Caspi, Roberts, and Shiner, 2005; Sroufe, Carlson, and Shulman, 1993). For instance, children who show early antisocial, aggressive behaviors tend to interpret others as treating them negatively. They may then react aggressively to these other people, thus provoking negative reactions that sustain and reinforce the child's antisocial, aggressive tendencies. As the child gets older he or she may gravitate to a peer group of like others, who further reinforce and support the antisocial behavior. It is now believed that while there are chains of continuity between childhood and adulthood, these chains are complexly forged out of a whole series of interacting experiences.

The question becomes what are the actual patterns of personality stability and change, and what are the underlying processes (Roberts and Caspi, 2005). It is important to remember that as time passes more life events are likely to occur: births of children, marriage, death of spouse, or employment changes. It is often those life events that are the impetus of change. For instance, conscientiousness increases with having the first job and decreases with retirement. It also tends to increase for men upon the death of a spouse (Specht, Egloff, and Schukle, 2011).

In sum, the question—Is there continuity and stability in personality from childhood to adulthood?—needs to be rephrased. A more productive question is: What are the factors that make for stability or change? Some attitudes and behaviors are likely to be more stable than others. For example, child behaviors that are closely related to physiology, such as activity level and emotionality or what is commonly called temperament, are personality characteristics that are likely to remain relatively stable over time (Chess, Thomas, and Birch, 1965). Because so much of the research focuses on the continuity of personality traits, we are less certain about changes on other variables like goals and motives (Fraley and Roberts, 2005).

Adolescence and Emerging Adulthood

We now turn to a consideration of developmental aspects of personality in adolescence. There are those who believe that adolescence, as much as or perhaps even more than early childhood, is a key developmental period for personality. Measures of personality in early adolescence predict adult personality more accurately than do measures in early childhood (Livson and Peskin, 1980). Caspi (1993) says, "It may be no coincidence that studies grappling with the puzzle of life-course change have pointed to experiences in late adolescence and young adulthood that appear to deflect life trajectories" (p. 364).

Adolescence is a period of transition; the adolescent is in the process of moving from the status of child to the status of adult. It is a period of development marked by profound physical, psychological, and social changes. Physical changes in sexuality and body size are often rapid and dramatic. Though often welcome, these changes can nevertheless be disquieting until they are fully incorporated in the adolescent's altered body image. At the same time, adolescence brings with it new social roles, with increased independence, choice, and responsibilities. These new roles are in fact a reflection of society's recognition of: (1) the psychological development that has taken place when the individual enters adolescence; (2) the adolescent's increased physical and cognitive powers; and (3) the fact that the adolescent has entered a higher level of cognitive and moral development, and can see situations in their full complexity (Elkind, 1970; Kohlberg, 1969b).

These changes in the physical, social, and psychological spheres affect and upset the self-concept and tend to produce a state of uncertainty in the adolescent as to his or her true self. "Who am I?" "What can I do?" "What do I really want?" are questions with which the adolescent is suddenly confronted. Much of adolescent behavior can be understood as efforts to resolve these questions. However, it must be emphasized that the degree of disruption entailed by the changing self-concept, the amount of emotional turmoil experienced by the adolescent, and the extremeness of behaviors are strongly influenced by cultural and familial factors. While adolescence is frequently described as a period of *Sturm and Drang* (the German equivalent of "storm and stress"), this often is not the case. Social and biological variables interact in determining the pattern of behavior displayed in adolescence (Petersen, 1988).

Biological Changes

Adolescence begins with the onset of puberty, the period of maturation of the sex organs and other sexual characteristics. Actually, two closely related changes in physical development are occurring, both stimulated by an increase in a particular hormonal secretion. The gonadotropic hormones, secreted by the pituitary gland, stimulate and enlarge the gonads—the ovary in females and the testes in males—which then release larger amounts of sex hormones. These hormones, in turn, regulate the changes taking place in masculine and feminine bodily characteristics: the enlargement of breasts, the rounded contours and, most dramatically, the menstrual flow in females and the growth of body hair, the deepening of voice, and ejaculation in males. Testosterone (the masculinizing hormone) and estrogen (the feminizing hormone) are necessary for normal sexual development in both males and females. The proportions differ, however, with more testosterone secreted in boys and more estrogen in girls.

At the same time, working in conjunction with the sex hormones, growth hormones secreted by the pituitary initiate a growth spurt. The increase in muscle tissue is greater in boys than in girls so that males, on the average, become biologically stronger than females. Augmenting these biological differences in strength are greater heart and lung size in males than females and corresponding differences in other capacities. These changes culminate in the maximum physical size the individual will achieve (excluding weight) during the course of his or her development. While it may be an exaggeration to say that one's decline begins as one enters the twenties and adulthood, we certainly cannot look forward to an increase in height at that point. However, in contrast to the pattern for physical development, one can grow psychologically throughout one's lifetime.

Hormonal Changes and Behavior

There is little doubt that the hormonal changes that occur in connection with puberty exert a significant influence on sexual interest and activities. However, the relation between

Sexual maturation and sexual interest characterize adolescence.

these hormonal changes and other aspects of the adolescent's behavior, such as aggressiveness and psychological adjustment, remains very much at issue. While there is some evidence of a correlation between testosterone level and aggressive attributes (Olweus et al., 1980), it is at best a very weak relationship (Book, Starzyk, and Quinsey, 2001); other studies have reported only a complex, indirect relationship for males and a negligible relationship for females (Susman et al., 1987). Consider, though, the interaction between hormones and the social environment. Testosterone is influenced by social hierarchies. For instance, bullied girls produce less testosterone, while bullied boys produce more testosterone than their nonbullied peers (Vaillancourt, deCatanzaro, Duku, and Muir, 2009).

Individual Variations

Pubertal change entails the most extensive and rapid change in postnatal life. The responses of the self and others to these physical changes may be more important than the physical changes themselves (Petersen, 1988).

Having experienced the changes of puberty and observed them in our peers, most of us are quite aware of the marked individual variations in the onset and termination of sexual growth. Early-maturing girls may begin to menstruate at age ten while, for some late-maturing girls, menstruation may not begin until age seventeen. Similar variations occur in the initiation and completion of other physical changes. Boys show corresponding variations in their sexual maturation and growth spurts, although as a group they reach puberty about two years later than girls. These differences in rate of physical maturation have consequences for the adolescent's changing self-concept. Early pubertal onset in boys has been found to be related to enhanced body image, higher self-esteem, and improved moods (Blyth et al., 1981; Petersen, 1988). There are, of course, many individual exceptions to these generalizations. The early maturer who is physically awkward or suffers excessively from blackheads and acne will not see himself as highly attractive. For girls, early pubertal development is associated with decreased feeling of attractiveness, while later maturation is associated with positive psychological outcomes such as higher self-esteem (Simmons and Blyth, 1987). Also, girls who are very early or unprepared for their menarche report more negative reactions and symptoms than average maturers (Ruble and Brooks-Gunn, 1982).

Autonomy and Conformity

Over a relatively short period of time, the adolescent acquires new physical powers, matching those of the adults who are the controlling forces in society. The adolescent is beset with intense sexual feelings that motivate sexual interests and behaviors that remain largely prohibited by adult society. The drive toward assertion of one's powers and self-definition as an independent decision maker, and toward autonomy from parents and from social rules that are seen as controlling and repressive, is therefore strong. The adolescent may express this drive in a number of different ways: through career choice, political action, sexual experimentation, defiance of speed limits, cigarette smoking, or experimenting with alcohol or drugs. How an adolescent manages his or her independence striving, whether in a socially acceptable or a socially deviant manner, whether with rebelliousness and parental conflict or in the context of maintenance of strong family ties, depends on (1) the stresses and transition structures that exist in the culture, (2) the family atmosphere and response to the adolescent's efforts at independence, and (3) the personality of the individual adolescent.

But the adolescent's search for independence is only half the struggle; the adolescent also needs a support system and a place in society. The adolescent needs feedback on the new self that is in the process of definition (Hamachek, 1976), including answers to questions of self-uncertainty, such as "Am I attractive?" "Am I as powerful as I think I am?" "Can I make intelligent decisions on my own?" "Am I capable of assuming the responsibility of an adult?" In addition, the process of separation from family controls and protection can be painful and isolating. To reduce pain and loneliness, the adolescent is often motivated to seek out some group with which to affiliate. This group can be one's immediate peers, a political organization, a new religious movement, or the military. Paradoxically, in some cases it can even be one's immediate family. There is evidence that adolescents with a cohesive family to whom they have a secure attachment (cf. Chapter 12) have a more favorable self-concept than adolescents who are insecurely attached or emotionally detached, and are better prepared for independence and autonomy (Ryan and Lynch, 1989). The emotionally detached adolescent appears to be less self-reliant and more dependent on peers for self-expression (Steinberg and Silverberg, 1986).

Thus, the adolescent who is on the one hand striving for independence, on the other hand needs a group that can provide feedback, validation of the self, and emotional support. Under these circumstances, strong attachments to the group can develop, with the group exercising powerful conformity pressures on its individual members. The adolescent asserting his or her independence from adult norms and prohibitions may also adopt every new style of dress, in music, and in slang (Eckert, 2003; Remmers and Radler, 1957). In a real sense, the adolescent is dependent on a social group in order to achieve independence.

Trait Level Changes

During adolescence, and especially into the transition to early adulthood, we observe personality traits maturing as well. This has been termed the maturity principle (Roberts, Wood, and Caspi, 2008). There are strong increases in conscientiousness and emotional stability. These increases were observed to occur earlier for girls than for boys (Klimstra et al., 2009), just as we observe earlier puberty in general for girls than for boys. When we examine the process of this maturation, it appears that societal demands impact the development of particular traits. For instance, at the end of high school, students in Germany take final exams, which also function as entrance exams into university. During this last year of high school, levels of conscientiousness rise. The increase tends to be greatest for the students who care about how they do on those exams (Bleidoorn, 2012). In cultures in which adolescents transition to adulthood earlier, we see the development of these traits happening sooner (Bleidoorn, 2015).

Continuity Between Adolescents and Parents

We have focused on the adolescent's efforts to separate from the parents and to establish his or her own identity. However, adolescents also have attachments to their parents and, in most societies, the parents have been the most influential adults in the adolescent's life. Consequently, one might expect some similarities between adolescent and parent in attitudes, values, and preferences. In a major study of adolescents, in which fourteen-year-olds were followed through school and, in most cases, through age twenty-two, Offer (1969; Offer and Offer, 1975) found that the values and social orientation expressed by most teenagers were fundamentally similar to their parents'. There were value conflicts, of course, and occasionally severe disagreements and discord, but, on the whole, the teenagers shared their parents' value structures. "The goals they were striving toward were very appropriate in the sense that they fitted very nicely into the cultural milieu in which they were living, and were almost always in accordance with the parents' expectations" (Offer, 1969, pp. 60-61). The similarities between adolescents and their parents has been found in Italian adolescents and emerging adults (Barni, Alfieri, Marta, and Rosnati, 2013), and Jewish and Arab mothers with their children in Israel (Barni, Knafo, Ben-Arieh, and Haj-Yahia, 2014).

Source: pixelheadphoto digitalskillet/Shutterstock

Discord between parents and teenagers is more rare than common. Teenagers and young adults usually share similar values.

We must remember that adolescents share their parents' socioeconomic status, religious affiliation, and residential area—all sociological, demographic factors that exert a powerful influence on social values. In this regard, teenage children of a southern farmer who is a member of an evangelical church are likely to have more in common with their parents than with upper-middle-class, urban adolescents on the East and West coasts. But even when adolescents are matched on demographic factors, one still finds evidence of similarity between parental values and those of their offspring (Troll, Neugarten, and Kraines, 1969).

Adult Development

Concern with personality development throughout the life span is relatively recent in psychology. Adolescence was recognized as a period of self-uncertainty and self-change that finally culminated in the crystallization of the self upon entrance into young adulthood. There were some studies of personality and attitude change during the college years (Newcomb, 1943), but it was implicitly assumed that by the time one graduated from college, if not before then, personality was more or less "set" until one reached old age. Research on even this latter period remained quite limited until the increase in elderly people in the population gave special social and economic significance to the physical and psychological changes that occur with aging. Brim (1992) described the period between adolescence and old age as the last uncharted territory.

What does a developmental approach to personality in the adult years contribute to our understanding, beyond simply studying the changes and continuities in personality over time? Certainly, we can expect that the personalities of adults will be affected by repeated experiences of success versus failure, by prolonged unemployment, by tragedies and serious illness, by positions of prestige and responsibility, and so on. What, then, does it mean to talk about personality *development* in the adult years?

There are three kinds, or levels, of answers that have been given to this question, depending on how closely the personality change is linked to a particular age period and how regular or inevitable the change is seen as being:

1. One can examine the effects on adult personality of unusual life events such as a prisoner-of-war experience (Hunter, 1976), an untimely death in the family (Weisman, 1973), or exposure to severe persecution (Ostwald and Bittner, 1968). Developmental considerations become relevant to the extent that one takes into account age-related variations in the social, emotional, and cognitive status of individuals; for example, the fact that these severely stressful events may have occurred to recently married couples, or to men and women with well-established positions and growing families, or to elderly residents of a nursing home.

2. One can focus on the implications for personality change of experiences that occur only or primarily to all those of adult status or to particular age groups within the adult category. Marriage, divorce, becoming a parent, job dissatisfaction, career achievement, and retirement are examples of such experiences. Of course, there is no simple, one-to-one relationship between these experiences and their effects on personality. The personality consequences of marriage, divorce, or a new job depend in part on other personality attributes of the individual. Nevertheless, these events have powerful meanings for adults; they satisfy or frustrate significant needs and may enlarge or narrow one's self-understanding and sensitivity to others.

3. From the most explicitly developmental viewpoint, one can conceive of adult personality as a series of age periods in which specific aspects of personality are acquired, enhanced, or modified. Some investigators maintain that there is a regular sequence in the patterning and fluctuations of personality over time (Buhler, 1962; Erikson, 1950; Gould, 1972; Levinson, 1978). Just as adolescence and the preceding developmental periods have special significance for the formation of personality, so are the periods of early adulthood, middle adulthood, and old age characterized by their own growth-related issues of marriage, parenthood, career, and retirement. In this section, we will focus to a large extent on research that approaches the adult personality from this perspective.

Adult Developmental Stages

In *As You Like It*, Shakespeare described seven ages of man (see Highlight 13.1). You will recall, too, that Erikson (Chapter 4) proposed a sequence of three psychosocial tasks and corresponding age periods with which the developing adult must deal: intimacy-early adulthood (20–40); generativity-middle adulthood (40–65); and integrity-later adulthood (65–). According to Erikson, the principal problem faced by young adults, in their twenties and thirties, is the achievement and maintenance of a close personal relationship or, alternatively, the living of one's life as an independent but emotionally isolated individual. On entering the forties, the individual's problems shift. Will one cling to established routines, to old patterns and old habits, or will one look forward to and pursue different satisfactions and future opportunities? Old age presents both the most difficult challenge and possibly the highest level of self-realization: recognizing one's limitations and the ultimate finality of life. At the same time experiencing life as meaningful and integrating the mosaic of tragedies and joys that life presents is equally fulfilling.

Erikson, then, saw adulthood as a series of age-related stages, each presenting its own developmental task. The successful resolution of these tasks results in the individual's progressive attainment of higher levels of self-realization. Despite the value that Erikson placed on the greater maturity that aging offers, however, adults over thirty in this culture generally prefer to be somewhat younger (Kastenbaum, Derbin, Sabatini, and Ant, 1972). Young adults, the middle aged, and the aged have nevertheless been shown to report the same degree of life satisfaction (Cameron, 1972). Furthermore, in that same study, the middle aged were considered by the other groups to be the happiest. Middle-aged Swiss adults prefer their own age, and older adults report middle age being their preferred age as well (Freund and Ritter, 2009).

Many people report midlife to be the happiest time in their life.

HIGHLIGHT 13.1

The Seven Ages of Man

William Shakespeare

All the world's a stage,
And all the men and women merely players.
They have their exits and their entrances,
And one man in his time plays many parts,
His acts being seven ages. At first the infant,
Mewling and puking in the nurse's arms.
Then the whining schoolboy, with his satchel
And shining morning face, creeping like snail
Unwillingly to school. And then the lover,
Sighing like furnace, with a woeful ballad
Made to his mistress' eyebrow. Then a soldier,
Full of strange oaths and bearded like the pard,
Jealous in honor, sudden and quick in quarrel,
Seeking the bubble reputation

Even in the cannon's mouth. And then the justice,
In fair round belly with good capon lined,
With eyes severe and beard of formal cut,
Full of wise saws and modern instances,
And so he plays his part. The sixth age shifts
Into the lean and slippered Pantaloon,
With spectacles on nose and pouch on side,
His youthful hose, well saved, a world too wide
For his shrunk shank, and his big manly voice,
Turning again toward childish treble, pipes
And whistles in his sound. Last scene of all,
That ends this 'strange eventful history,
Is second childishness and mere oblivion,
Sans teeth, sans eyes, sans taste, sans everything.

Source: *As You Like It*, Act 2, Sc. 7, lines 139–166.

The degree of life satisfaction that one attributes to different stages in life is one component of the way in which different age periods are perceived. Another component is the changes that are believed to occur at different life stages. A study of the perception of age changes in a sample of young (20–36), middle-aged (40–55), and older adults (60–85) indicated that these adults do not see personality as fixed (Heckhauser, Dixon and Baltes, 1989). Rather, they believe that substantial personality changes take place during the course of adult development, and that most of these changes are positive. While the percentage of "gains" in comparison to "losses" is seen to decline with increasing age, developmental *gains* were perceived to outnumber losses throughout adulthood, with the exception of very advanced age (beyond 80). In addition, the middle aged and older adults perceived more and varied changes occurring during adulthood than did the young adults.

These studies of satisfaction, age perception, and preferences tell us that people do find meaning in such a division of adult life into different age periods. However, we have to look to other kinds of data to determine whether there are stages of personality development associated with these different age periods. One source of data has been the study of individual biographies. Charlotte Bühler (1962) initiated the collection of life histories from elderly people in Vienna in the early 1930s and continued working on life-span development after emigrating to the United States. Her approach in inferring personality patterns from these life histories was essentially clinical and impressionistic, and her theoretical orientation was in the humanistic tradition. She postulated five basic life tendencies: need satisfaction, adaptive self-limitation or adjustment, creative expansion, establishment of inner order, and self-fulfillment. These life tendencies were assumed to emerge and become dominant at different age periods, and the way in which they were reflected in behavior also varied with age period. For instance, need satisfaction is assumed to be dominant in the first year and a half of life, again during the adolescent years, and once again in very old age. Adaptation and adjustment are assumed to be dominant in early childhood (ages 1.5–4) and again in the early adult years. Creative expansion is assumed to be dominant in late childhood, and between the ages of twenty-five and fifty. Research findings that are consistent with Bühler's analysis (Ryff, 1982) reflect changes in values and in the needs for achievement, dominance, and social recognition as one moves from middle age to old age.

Midlife "Crisis"

Imagine a man who is making good money but is unhappy at work and thinking about changing his career. His marriage isn't going well, and he is interested in a twenty-five-year-old neighbor. Of course, he just bought himself a new red sports car. If we imagine him as twenty-nine, it sounds as if he is still trying to figure out his life. If we imagine him as forty-nine, he would often be labeled as having a midlife crisis.

Midlife crisis is a concept that has truly escaped from clinical use to the general population. A Google search of news articles including the term "midlife crisis" revealed dozens upon dozens of articles published in just month previous to when this book was being written. It is doubtful that this particular month is an anomaly. Research has found that 90 percent of the people contacted for research on midlife had heard of the term, despite many researchers doubting the concept (Chirigoba, 1997; Reid and Willis, 1999; Wethington, 2000).

The work of Daniel Levinson and his collaborators (Levinson, 1978) was influential in laying out the concept. In this study, adult males between the ages of thirty-five and forty-five were interviewed. (Due to limited resources, the investigators reluctantly limited their sample to men). The sample of forty individuals was equally divided among four occupational groups: executives, biologists, novelists, and factory workers.

The most significant conclusion of this study is the finding of an orderly sequence of development, of an evolution of life structure during the adult years, and further that "the essential character of the sequence is the same for all the men in our study and for the other men whose biographies we examined" (Levinson, 1978, p. 49). It is reasonable to question whether these investigators' findings are as universal as they claimed. They saw development as marked by stable periods in which the individual copes with particular developmental tasks and by transition periods, or stressful times when one must change from one level of adult development to the next.

At about age forty to forty-five, he enters the midlife transition period, characterized by a review and questioning of basic life structure. "What have I accomplished?" "Does my work matter?" "What do I really get from and give to my wife and children?" "Am I getting what I want out of life?" "What happened to my dreams?" This is the period of the so-called *midlife crisis*, a theme popularized in films and books in the 1970s (Sheehy, 1976). The crisis is normal and, if successfully resolved, healthy. Some men emerge from this crisis defeated and resigned to a life of decline. In this conceptualization, we see the influence of the stage theorists, especially Freud and Erikson.

Freund and Ritter (2009) lay out three different versions of the concept of midlife crisis. The strict version is that everyone experiences the re-evaluation of goals, that this happens in a bounded time frame (i.e., Levinson's forty to forty-five time frame) and that a midlife crisis is uniquely different from other periods of resetting goals. To begin to address this, we have to establish what middle age means. Researchers have found that people's definition of middle age might be described as anywhere from thirty to seventy depending on a person's age (Lachman, Lewkowicz, Marcus, and Peng, 1994), with a few people listing even slightly higher values as the exit age. Wethington (2000) found that many people report having a "midlife" crisis, but the majority of those who report having this experience are outside the forty to fifty age range. Some report as early as seventeen, and others as late as seventy-five. Further, most divorces happen earlier than forty, as do job changes. People constantly adjust their goals depending on circumstances (Brandtstadter and Greve, 1994). Goal setting is considered to be a dynamic process that happens throughout the life span (Carver and Scheier, 1998). The goals to be adjusted may differ at different ages, but the process is considered to be consistent.

We should also reexamine the assumption that there is a single path through adulthood. There is enormous variability in when people do things in their lives. Some are just fully getting into their careers when they are in their mid-fifties, whereas others headed into retirement. At age forty, some women are having their first baby, whereas others are grandmothers. This variability is influenced by ethnicity and socioeconomic status.

The lenient version (Freund and Ritter, 2000) is that *some* people experience a crisis, and that there are unique challenges in middle age. As we saw in Wetherington (2000), some people do report having a crisis. Women and men are just as likely to report having had a crisis. Interestingly, people are most likely to report a crisis near the turning of a decade. Turning forty or fifty increases the likelihood of reporting having had a crisis, but turning forty-seven doesn't. Middle adulthood does have challenges. At this age, many people are simultaneously raising their own children while taking care of their aging parents. It is in this time span that many will experience the death of those parents, which is likely to raise issues of mortality. The lenient version probably does work.

Continuity and Change in Adulthood

The theoretical debate as to whether development in childhood is best characterized by discrete stages has its counterpart in competing views of adult development. Erikson's and Charlotte Bühler's stage models assert that adult development is marked by age periods that pose particular developmental issues, and that the resolution of these issues are steps in a sequential path of increasing self-fulfillment. Levinson (1986) agrees with the view that certain age periods are critical in that personality changes are most likely to occur during these periods.

Others, on the basis of data indicating continuity in personality and the failure to find evidence of systematic transformations in adult personality, have argued against the notion of age-linked developmental stages (McCrae and Costa, 1984). McCrae and Costa (1990) have argued that there is little change in personality at all during the adult years. Tests-retests six years apart on the NEO-PI found rank order stability ranging from r = .76 for neuroticism to r = .84 for openness to experience. When all five traits were considered simultaneously, the profiles showed a coefficient of .66. The Roberts and Del Vecchio (2000) meta-analysis of longitudinal studies finds correlations above .50 for all age groups after adolescence. When the big five traits were considered, neuroticism showed the lowest at r = .50, and extraversion and agreeableness both had r = .54. Clearly, there is stability, yet there is still a great deal of variability that is not captured in those measures.

However, we have already mentioned data from Helson (1993) suggesting change in some characteristics overtime. Helson and Stewart (1994) cite a variety of studies showing changes in impulsiveness and flexibility (Dudek and Hall, 1991), ambition and autonomy (Howard and Bray, 1988), and the need to achieve (Franz, 1994) during the adult years. Franz (1994) found a change towards being more relationship oriented between the ages of thirty-one and forty-one, and McAdams, de St. Aubin, and Logan (1993) found that individuals became more concerned with "generativity"—the desire to take care of others, as they aged (see Highlight 13.2 for other evidence of adult personality change).

In addition, the fact that personality *traits* may not generally change over the adult years does not mean *personality* does not change. It depends on what we define personality to be (Heatherton and Nichols, 1994; McAdams, 2001). We could conceive of personality as the overall organization of one's traits, values, and motivations. Changes can occur in goals, values, and motivations, as well as in the overall organization of personality, while trait structures remain relatively constant. The kinds of changes Bühler and Levinson describe have more to do with the overall goals and organization of the person's personality at different times in the life sequence than they do with changes in particular traits.

As an example of how personality can change, Elder (1986) has shown that the opportunity for military service provided by the Korean War tended to have a positive effect on the personality development of men who joined military service before the age of twenty-one. These were young men whose parents had been particularly hard hit by the Great Depression of the 1930s. Most of them as high school adolescents had below average grades and were less assertive and less self-confident than either late joiners or non-veterans. But military service helped reshape the life course for many of these veterans. Full-time employment, marriage, and children all started later in life: the early veteran also changed his educational aspirations. Although almost a third had entered the service before completing high school, all of the early joiner sample earned their

HIGHLIGHT 13.2

Psychological Resilience

In recent years, there has been a great deal of research interest in the topic of psychological resilience. Is a child permanently scarred and inevitably doomed by having a dysfunctional early childhood? Apparently not. A number of researchers have found that many children appear to thrive despite highly unfavorable early childhood experiences. George Vaillant (1993) has studied a sample of 456 individuals who were followed from age fifteen into their sixties. Eleven men were identified as having the poorest risk histories, including low self-esteem, low socioeconomic status as children, and a dysfunctional family life. At age twenty-five all appeared to be "broken beyond repair" (Vaillant, 1993, p. 287). However, by their sixties, eight of the eleven had "self-righted" themselves, and all but one were in the top 25 percent in terms of mental health. In general, researchers who have studied resilience have identified a number of factors that seem to "buffer" children against unfavorable circumstances. These include the temperament and disposition of the child, the presence of an adult (not necessarily a parent) who provides support and encouragement, the attributional style of the child (see Chapter 17), and good physical health.

high school diploma. In addition, a quarter went on to enroll in a university, while almost one-half continued through junior college or vocational school. This change in educational goals is accompanied by evidence of marital stability and also by dramatic gains in psychological competence when assessed around age forty. The early joiners had increased significantly on measures of self-confidence and goal-orientation, while showing a decrease in submissiveness and feelings of inadequacy. If one excludes the role of combat, these data indicate that military service fostered the personal growth of men who had little to look forward to as adolescents.

More broadly, the findings of Elder and other investigators are supportive of the view that personality change in adulthood does occur and that these changes are related to the interaction of significant social events with the personality and age-related stage of the individual.

Old Age

The miracles of modern medicine and public health programs have made possible the extension of the life cycle into old age for increasing numbers of people, a change that in the United States is sometimes referred to as the "graying of America" (Datan, Rodeheaver, and Hughes, 1987). Sheer numbers have posed enormous medical, economic, and social problems for Western society, which places such a premium on productivity and youth. In addition, the urbanization and mobility of the American family make it difficult for the family to accommodate an elderly parent in the household. To further complicate the role and status of the elderly, the larger society's vision of older people is distorted by myths, half-truths, and stereotypes. The elderly themselves may accept these commonly held half-truths about their own intellectual functioning and emotional life.

Thus, in examining the question of personality change in old age, we do so within a particular social context in which attributes such as the wisdom of the elderly are not highly valued, in which old age is a time of economic hardship for many, and in which large numbers of the elderly live in nursing homes and retirement communities, segregated from younger age groups in society. We have the very difficult task of determining the extent to which behavioral changes in the elderly are due to the process of aging and the extent to which they are attributable to the particular social conditions experienced by the elderly in this society. Not surprisingly, even thinking about the elderly changes people's behavior (Bargh, Chen, and Burrows, 1996).

Many changes take place simultaneously during old age. There is a noticeable slow-down in reactivity and movement (Hicks and Birren, 1970); the skin is wrinkled and spotted; there is typically a decline in visual acuity and hearing. The aged are very vulnerable to illness and to such chronic diseases as diabetes, arthritis, and heart impairments. Mental illness also increases after the age of sixty-five. Much of this increase is due to biological disorders such as *cerebral arteriosclerosis*, in which the blood vessels thicken and blood flow to the brain is reduced. In disorders such as Alzheimer's, there is a decrement in brain cell function. But there are also mental disorders among the aged that are reversible: anxiety, depressive reactions to the loss of loved ones, and disturbances brought on by alcohol or drugs.

Trait Stability into Old Age

As we have seen in other ages, traits tend to show rank order stability into old age. In a study of Harvard alumni (Soldz and Vaillant, 1999), personality traits measured at age twenty-two were correlated with those traits at about age sixty-seven. After that length of time, correlations were lower than observed in samples reported earlier in the chapter. Correlations ranged from .19 on extraversion to .38 on openness to experience.

Probably the study with the longest interval between measurements was one conducted on children born in Scotland in 1936. They were originally tested in 1947. A subsample of that group, who happened to be born on six particular days in that year, was then given further testing when they were fourteen years old. There were 1,208 children in that subsample. In 2012 (sixty-five years after the first measures, sixty-two years after the second) the researchers were able to find 635 still alive and living in Great Britain. Of that group, 174 agreed to take part in further research. Those who agreed to participate further were one standard deviation above the mean on IQ as children. Those who refused or did not reply were at the mean. Those who agreed to participate were rated by teachers as more dependable than the population as a whole (Harris, Brett, Johnson, and Deary, 2016). They did find stability on their versions of conscientiousness and stability of moods. Cognitive ability did show stability across that time span (Deary and Brett, 2015), and was confounded with conscientiousness. Otherwise, researchers did not find much stability from adolescence to old age. Based on this data, they suggest that personality is consistent over shorter periods of time, but those small changes become large over very long periods of time.

We can see interesting change showing up in old age. A study investigating the impact of cognitive training revealed an interesting effect on openness to experience (Jackson et al., 2012). In this study were people between the ages of sixty and ninety-four. Some were randomly assigned to participate in the cognitive training, and others were assigned to a group termed waitlist control. A waitlist control group is a group that is interested in participating, but for the time being serves as the control group to test the impact of the intervention. If both groups improve (or decline) together, we would conclude that there is no impact of the intervention. Those who were in the training group were given increasingly difficult Sudoku and crossword puzzles. They were also given inductive reasoning exercises along with inductive reasoning training. At the end of the study, these participants did show improved inductive reasoning. More interesting for our purposes is that this group also showed increased scores on openness to experience. Again, we see evidence that personality traits do have the potential to change.

Aging and Health

The biological and behavioral changes that occur in the aged are closely related (Fillenbaum, 1977), supporting a holistic approach to the problems of aging. The field of **gerontology**, which addresses the phenomena associated with old age, draws its experts from various biological and behavioral disciplines. A pioneering study carried out by James E. Birren and his colleagues (1963) illustrates the value of a multidisciplinary, gerontological approach to aging. A major objective of the study was to separate the effects of aging from the effects of the illnesses from which old people frequently suffer. Volunteer males, at least sixty-five years old, were screened for evidence of medical disorders, and only the healthier men were retained for inclusion in the study. The mean age of the final group of forty-seven "healthy" individuals was 71.5 and all were living independently in the community, in most instances in households with their wives. Detailed physiological and psychological evaluations of the men were carried out. The results were quite striking. These old men constituted a vigorous, alert, even optimistic group of individuals who were very much involved in their daily lives. The image of rigid, confused oldsters certainly did not apply to this sample. There was evidence of depression and distress in some of the men, but these reactions seemed appropriately linked to personal losses. More intensive analyses and comparisons with a sample of young men reflected differences on some physiological measures but similarities on many others. For example, elevations in blood pressure did not discriminate

gerontology An interdisciplinary approach to studying aging that draws its experts from various biological and behavioral disciplines.

Source: Rawpixel.com/Shutterstock

Many senior citizens stay active. Illness, rather than aging per se, accounts for many of the differences observed between younger and older people.

between healthy old men and healthy young men and therefore can be taken as a sign of pathology rather than a result of a process of aging. The Birren findings point to the importance of separating the effects of illness from the effects of aging. What does seem to be true about the process of aging is that the organism becomes increasingly *vulnerable* to disease, accident, and life's hazards.

Participants from the cohort study in Scotland mentioned earlier have also been participating in a long-term health study. Conscientiousness and openness were associated with lower levels of biological markers of inflammation (Mõttus et al., 2013). Because it is correlational, we don't know the direct relationship, but either stress or healthful behaviors are likely candidates. A different study in Scotland of men and women between fifty-five and seventy-four years of age found that increasing levels of conscientiousness and openness were associated with a reduced rate of death (Taylor et al., 2009).

Competence and Survival

An intriguing experimental study by Judith Rodin and Ellen J. Langer (1977) also bears on psychological factors in the aged that may be associated with survival. A group of elderly nursing home residents were given a talk by the hospital administrator which emphasized the responsibility the residents had for themselves. A contrasting talk was given to a control group of residents in the same institution which stressed the staff's responsibility to the residents as patients of a nursing home. In addition, the experimental group that received the communication emphasizing self-responsibility was offered plants to care for, while the comparison group was given plants that were watered by the staff. There were a number of significant immediate effects of the experimental manipulation of responsibility on the attitudes and behavior of the elderly patients. The elderly residents in the responsibility-induced group became more active, displayed greater alertness, and reported feeling happier than the control group. Patients in the responsibility-induced group also showed an increase in involvement in different kinds of social activities such as movie attendance, social interaction with friends and with staff, and participation in contests (Langer and Rodin, 1976).

Eighteen months later, a follow-up evaluation indicated that the experimental effects still persisted. The survivors who had been in the responsibility-induced group were judged to be more self-initiating, sociable, involved, and vigorous than those survivors who had been in the control group. The most striking result was the finding that a significantly smaller proportion of patients in the responsibility-induced group (seven out of forty-seven) had died in the eighteen-month period than in the comparison group (thirteen out of forty-four). The findings indicate that it is possible to improve the psychological status and physical well-being of the elderly; programs designed to encourage the assumption of greater self-responsibility are a promising avenue for accomplishing these goals.

Changes in attitudes toward the elderly, particularly the labels used to describe them, constitute another important avenue for enhancing the way older age groups in our society function. In other experiments that have been carried out Langer and Rodin (1980) have shown that labels such as "senile" foster negative stereotypes and expectations of the elderly, and may, in turn, influence their self-concept and behavior. In contrast, positive expectations of the elderly motivate them to increase their cognitive activity and can lead to significant improvements in memory functioning and in feelings of well-being.

To Disengage or Not to Disengage

For many years, the prevailing view of how to grow old most effectively was a *disengagement* model (Cumming and Henry, 1961). The disengagement theory held that, since slowing down was a natural aspect of aging, the psychologically healthy response for the aging individual was to gradually reduce his or her activities and social involvements.

The theory stimulated a good deal of research which nevertheless failed to support the disengagement model. Old people, for example, regret the reduction in their level of activity (Havighurst, Neugarten and Tobin, 1968) and, in fact, the degree of activity and social engagement is positively related to reports of satisfaction with life.

Brandstädter and Greve (1994) have pointed out that while many believe that aging will bring with it reduced well-being, self-esteem problems, and a sense of loss of control, research has generally failed to support these beliefs. These authors suggest that aging individuals utilize three processes to maintain a positive attitude towards life and thus cope with developmental losses and changes. First, they utilize instrumental and compensatory actions to prevent or alleviate losses in functioning. These actions might include, for instance, changes in diet and exercise. Second, they modify their goals and aspirations to more realistically reflect what they can hope to accomplish. Third, they utilize psychological self-protective mechanisms, such as interpreting evidence in self-protective ways, to minimize experiences of loss.

From the perspective of Bühler's and Erikson's conceptions of adult stages of development, old age offers an opportunity to attain a higher level of self-development than is usually possible at younger ages. It entails a level of maturity and wisdom that Erikson refers to as *ego integrity*. Individuals who have achieved this stage have accepted their fate in life, see the inevitability and meaning of their life's course, and realize the inescapability of their triumphs and defeats. They do not engage in fantasies of "If only I had done _____ rather than _____." They experience order in their lives. They find satisfaction in life but are also prepared to accept the inevitable finality of life. Young and middle-aged adults may try to approximate some of these attitudes toward life through the adoption of non-Western philosophies such as Zen Buddhism and training in disciplines such as yoga. However, according to Erikson, there is no substitute for the experiences of the life cycle and the review and acceptance of that span of experience if one is to realize this highest stage of self-development.

Demography

The process and problems of aging have been described as if they were uniform for the elderly, with the exception only of personality differences in how individuals cope with the psychological and social role changes. However, the problems and consequences of aging undoubtedly vary with cultural factors that influence the social role, status, and economic welfare of the elderly. Thus, the problems of aging that confront women, while sharing similarities with those confronting men, may also differ in important respects.

Women aged sixty-five and above experience significantly greater distress than men in this age group (Levy, 1981). Women, in fact, tend to report greater distress than males throughout the adult life span. However, the factors responsible for greater female distress may differ at different stages of adult life. For middle-aged women, anxieties concerning separation and divorce, feelings of loss over the departure of children from the home (the "empty nest" syndrome), and concerns over the lack of economic skills are among the major sources of distress. For the elderly female, problems of poverty, loneliness, and isolation emerge as significant issues. The elderly female is three times as likely as her male peer to live in a nursing home. Because the life span of women is longer than that for men, the elderly female is more likely than the elderly male to have to cope with the loss of her partner. Also, while there are relatively few studies of the effects of retirement on women compared to the more extensive literature on male retirement, available data indicate that women are less likely to look forward to retirement than men. Women are more likely to express dissatisfaction with their lives as a whole, and to express wishes that they had done something differently, such as completing their education or marrying later (Levy, 1981). At the same time, elderly women also tend to display greater coping strength than elderly males, appearing to have a greater capacity than males to overcome the limitations of body illness.

Summary

1. The issue of whether personality remains stable or changes from early childhood to adulthood is complex. The answer depends on what is meant by change and stability and on when one measures personality. However, evidence indicates that personality both changes and remains stable.
2. The physical changes of puberty are brought about by an increase in the pituitary gland's secretion of growth hormones and gonadotropic hormone. The latter, in turn, stimulate the gonads to secrete masculinizing and feminizing hormones in differing proportions for males and females.
3. The psychological changes in puberty are only weakly linked to direct effects of hormonal changes and are more closely linked to the responses of self and others to the hormonal and accompanying physical changes. The timing of puberty affects the response to puberty, early pubertal onset having favorable effects for boys and tending to have negative effects for girls.
4. The adolescent is confronted with a conflict between the need to express sexual feelings and establish and assert autonomy on the one hand and the need for support and conformity to social rules on the other. The intensity and mode of resolution of the conflict will vary with cultural, familial, and personality factors.
5. Despite the conflict and discord that may occur in adolescence, there is considerable continuity or similarity between the values of parents and those of their adolescent offspring.
6. There is some empirical evidence for the hypothesis proposed by several theorists that adulthood can be divided into a sequence of periods or stages, each posing a particular set of problems and issues. Coping with these issues can stimulate personality change and growth in adults.
7. The *midlife crisis* is reported by some adults. It should be considered as a normal experience for that age group that can result in positive personality development.
8. There are suggestive findings indicating that many of the so-called "effects of aging" are actually a manifestation of the effects of illness to which old people happen to be vulnerable. Relatively healthy elderly individuals do not display the rigidity and mental confusion that often accompanies aging.

Key Terms

absolute stability (p. 242)
cross-lagged design (p. 244)
cross-sectional research design (p. 244)
gerontology (p. 255)

longitudinal study (p. 244)
mean level stability (p. 242)
personality coherence (p. 242)
rank order stability (p. 242)

Thought Questions

1. Do you think personality is stable or changeable from childhood to adulthood?
2. Is it better for an adolescent's personality development if the adolescent period is marked by "storm and stress" rather than by relative calm?
3. How might cultural factors influence the stages of adult development observed among samples of adults studied in the United States?
4. Do you think it is wise for society to organize separate residential communities for the elderly? Why or why not?

PART 5

Personality Dynamics

Source: Ollyy/Shutterstock

CHAPTER 14
The Dynamics of Behavior

CHAPTER 15
Emotion and Stress

CHAPTER 16
Consciousness

So far, we have examined the determinants of behavior that individuals encounter as soon as they enter the world: their genetic predispositions and the physical and social context in which they are placed. Then, after reviewing some of the major theories of personality, we turned to the structure and development of behavior and its measurement. Now we ask: how are these structures expressed in action? What is the dynamic interaction between an individual, attempting to adapt, satisfy needs, and survive, and the environment, which provides the need satisfiers? Here we encounter themes of conflict, impulse control, substitute gratification, emotion, and stress.

In addition, in this section of the book we deal with questions of consciousness and awareness. Although we must adapt to the environment, often we are not consciously aware of the information that it provides or, for that matter, of the informational signals that our own body sends us. There are multiple levels of awareness. Furthermore, it is often apparent that we are operating within different realms of consciousness, as during dream, and hypnotic states. In these latter instances, environmental information is almost totally blocked or, on the other hand, there may be a heightened focus of attention.

Dynamics is defined in the dictionary as forces that produce motion. In this Part, we are concerned with the forces acting on the individual that produce psychological "motion": the expression and inhibition of needs and feelings, the entering or leaving of a particular state of consciousness, and the goals and functions of behavior.

The Dynamics of Behavior

CHAPTER 14

Source: lassedesignen/Shutterstock

Chapter Outline

A Historical Introduction

Topics in the Study of Personality Dynamics

Conflict

Impulse Control and Delay of Gratification

Substitution

Frustration

Goals and Life Tasks

A Historical Introduction

There is an intimate relationship between the structure and the dynamics of personality, although the terms refer to different aspects of the study of personality. The *structure* or "anatomy" of personality concerns basic dispositions and interrelationships of the different elements of personality. **Personality dynamics**, on the other hand, is concerned with the meaning and function of behavior. In considering personality dynamics, one looks for the purpose or the objective of an act—why the individual behaves the way he or she does. Questions of dynamics are also typically addressed to the immediate situation in which the action occurs, whereas questions about the structure of personality generally deal with relatively enduring and stable aspects of behavior. Three research traditions are linked with the study of psychodynamics: behaviorism, Gestalt psychology, and psychoanalytic psychology.

personality dynamics The concern with the meaning and function of behavior.

Psychodynamics from a Psychoanalytic Perspective

The influence of the French upon Freud already has been discussed. The French interest in hypnosis and hysteria continued with more detailed studies of *dissociation*, or the split between behavior and awareness that occurs under these conditions. The American Morton Prince reported a number of intriguing cases of multiple or split personalities. Prince also studied patients exhibiting amnesias, automatic writing, sleepwalking, and related dissociation symptoms. Particularly significant for the emerging field of personality was Prince's founding of the Harvard Psychological Clinic in 1927. Here, Henry

Murray, Prince's successor, demonstrated how the ideas and observations of Charcot, Prince, and Freud could be studied experimentally.

Henry Murray developed a theory of personality that emphasized the full range of human motivation. He also pioneered in the measurement of human motivation and developed the well-known Thematic Apperception Test (TAT). In Murray, one can see again that the various areas in personality do overlap, because Murray was a personality theorist who developed an instrument to assess individual differences to further the experimental study of conflict and related areas.

Researchers following the psychoanalytic tradition in the study of psychodynamics have been particularly guided by the idea of unconscious motivation. Thus, they have examined subliminal perception, repression, and other phenomena that often demonstrate an individual's lack of awareness of the determinants of his or her behavior. Many of these phenomena are examined in this text.

Behaviorism

The fields of clinical psychology and personality assessment were born in Europe, particularly France, Austria, and England. But in the early 1900s America began to develop its own special brand of psychology, known as *behaviorism*. Whereas psychoanalysis envisioned the mind as filled with unconscious fantasies and early childhood residues, the behaviorists emptied the mind of its contents, even rejecting the very concept of mind. (It is sometimes said that psychology first lost its soul and then its mind!) In a famous article that appeared in 1913, John B. Watson criticized prevailing psychology as subjective and unreliable; he argued for a *science* of psychology based on objective measures of observable behaviors and of the external, stimulus situation. The task of psychology, he contended, was to (1) predict the response, given the stimulus; (2) identify the stimulus, given the response; and (3) predict the change in the response, given a change in the stimulus. Watson's views on psychoanalysis were especially severe. He predicted that "twenty years from now an analyst using Freudian concepts and Freudian terminology will be placed upon the same plane as a phrenologist" (1930, p. 27). Watson, like Freud, was willing to pursue the implications of his theory and observations wherever they might lead. And, also like Freud, he had a profound influence on the psychology of personality.

Behaviorism was also strongly influenced by the ideas of Darwin. Prior to the Darwinian period, humans were perceived as intelligent and "good," while non-humans were considered "evil" and merely governed by instinctive urges. The behaviorists believed in Darwin's proposal of a human-nonhuman continuum. Thus lower organisms, just as humans, were thought to have some degree of intelligence. Behaviorists, therefore, paid much attention to learning and the ability of nonhumans to adapt to their environment. When studying lower organisms, such as rats and pigeons, it was assumed that something was being learned about human behavior and its causes.

The behaviorists also differed from the early personality theorists and assessment psychologists in their methodological approach. Rats or pigeons cannot report on their wishes, desires, or values; these must be inferred from their behavior. Thus, the method of gathering data shifted, with increased ingenuity demanded of the experimenter to obtain the kind of evidence that was desired.

Efforts to translate psychoanalytic concepts into a form that could be empirically tested were undertaken by psychologists,

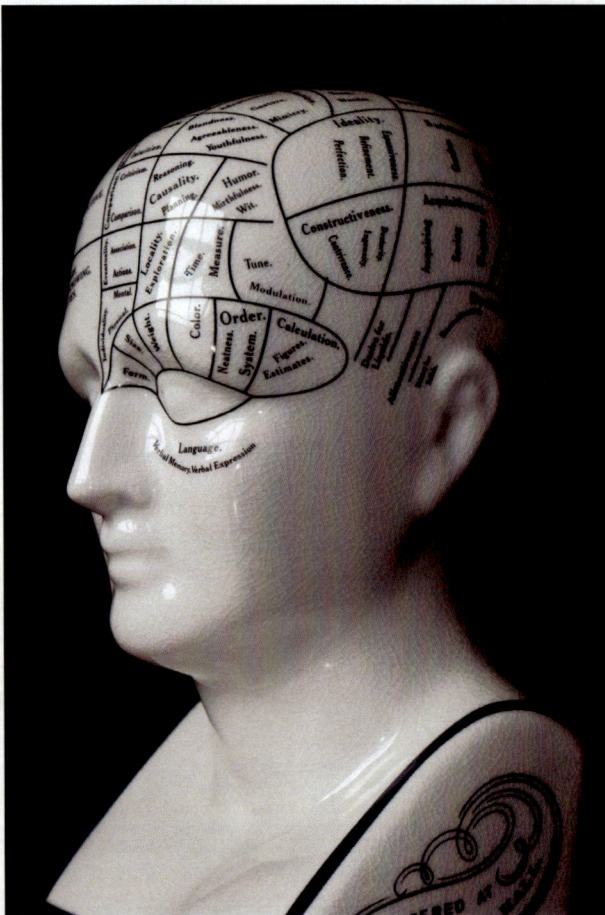

Phrenology was a pseudo-scientific idea developed by German physician Joseph Gall who said that bumps on the skull were indications of skills and personality traits. Phrenologists would charge people to have their skulls read, much like palm reading today. It was very popular in the 1800s. It was also wrong.

including John Dollard and Neal Miller (see Chapter 5), influenced by Watson but advocating a more elaborate theoretical perspective. This group stressed the importance of a laboratory-based learning theory. Learning theory places great emphasis on the significance of situational factors, postulates few mental processes, and attempts to deal with personality processes within a rigorous and objective experimental framework. Psychologists conducted a number of laboratory experiments linking aggression to the occurrence of frustration (see Chapter 18). The hypothesis of a relation between frustration and aggression was a significant advance over the Freudian position, which postulated an instinctive aggressive drive. Conflict, fixation, and other complex behaviors and processes also were studied by the behaviorists.

Gestalt Psychology

Gestalt psychology primarily developed in Berlin after the start of the 1900s and reached its heights in the 1920s and 1930s. In opposition to the behaviorists, the Gestaltists did not want to empty the mind; rather, they asserted behavior is influenced by how a person interprets the world. A horseback rider might ride over a snow-covered, frozen lake without worry, they contended, if he or she thought they were merely crossing a field. Thus, they embraced the idea that a person acts on the basis of his or her perception of reality. This position challenged the contention of the behaviorists that behavior could be predicted from knowing the objective, external situation.

Another essential aspect of Gestalt psychology was its assumption that the determinants of behavior are interrelated. For example, the near simultaneous flashing of two lights in close proximity, as on a movie marquee, gives the illusion of movement. Analysis of each light independently would not explain the phenomenon of perceived movement. The whole, Gestaltists argued, cannot be neglected and is different than the sum of the parts. Personality theorists with a Gestalt orientation thus consider the "whole person," and consider specific problems in relation to an integrated personality.

Kurt Lewin (1890–1947) brought the principles of Gestalt psychology to bear upon the study of psychodynamics. He was the first psychologist to experimentally test some of Freud's ideas. Lewin initially examined the Freudian notion that a wish, once aroused, persists until it is either directly satisfied or is indirectly fulfilled by the attainment of substitute gratifications. In his exploration of this area, as well as in the study of such topics as frustration and conflict, Lewin always considered the total "field of forces" acting on an individual and how a change in one force affects other aspects of the situation.

Gestalt psychology, as elaborated by Lewin, subsequently influenced the study of personal aspirations, achievement strivings, and other topics considered in some detail later in this text. Unlike behaviorism, Gestalt psychology did not create a dramatic following and then largely fade from the center of psychology. Rather, it has remained in the background as a subtle yet persistent influence.

Topics in the Study of Personality Dynamics

Why are people motivated to think and behave as they do? One widely accepted and broad answer to this question is that thoughts and actions serve to maximize pleasure and minimize pain, a position most explicitly assumed by Freud (1920, p. 1), who stated: "The impressions that underlie the hypothesis of the pleasure principle are so obvious that they cannot be overlooked." We can think of this as the hedonic position on human nature.

There are two components of the pleasure principle that dictate the directions of our behavior. One indicates that we want to approach and get more of desirable objects and feelings; the second is that we want to avoid or withdraw from undesirable objects and negative emotions. But, to complicate matters, it is often not in our best interests to attain pleasurable goals or to avoid unwanted events *immediately*. That is, it may be functional and adaptive to forgo immediate pleasure in the pursuit of more sustained happiness. Thus, we study to attain a distant career rather than putting down our books and going to a good movie; we do not hit someone when we are angry, because it may lead to retaliation; and so on. In other words, we develop controls over our pleasure-seeking impulses; our defenses inhibit immediate goal attainment but enhance the likelihood of reaching long-term satisfactions. And to further aid in the pursuit of pleasure, if a desired goal is not attained, alternative goals may be established that partially or perhaps entirely satisfy unfulfilled needs. However, it is also often the case that neither desired goals nor satisfactory substitutes are reached, and frustration is experienced.

Each step in this chain of events—from the arousal of feelings and desires to their frustration and gratification—raises a host of interrelated theoretical and empirical questions. Consider a student who must choose between studying for an exam and going out on a date. Each behavior satisfies a different set of goals related to achievement and academic success versus affiliation and social satisfaction. The student is in conflict between which behavior to choose and which motivation to pursue. What are the properties of such psychological conflict? What kinds of conflict are there? What determines how conflict is resolved? How is the student able to delay the impulse toward being with his girlfriend? The choice the student makes also has important consequences. When a decision is made, some goals are temporarily, or perhaps more permanently, frustrated. Does the desire for the unselected alternative persist? What are the possible responses to frustration? How do these responses influence our student's effectiveness? And how is the unsatisfied desire finally gratified? Through substitute behavior, or even just fantasizing about the postponed desire?

Although a great many questions about the dynamics of behavior have been raised here, the analysis of the situation is still not complete. Given a particular choice, how will the student feel after taking action? Happy? Sad? Angry? Guilty? What determines his or her emotional response? And, beyond the specific context of choice and the feelings involved, there are further questions about the effects of the tension and stress generated by the experience of conflict. Such stress can accompany the decision and become even more intense following the choice. Of course, in this example the stress might have been minimal, but consider the stress associated with a decision between maintaining a close relationship versus accepting a distant job opportunity.

This chapter is concerned with the topics of conflict, impulse control, substitution, and frustration. In the following chapter we examine emotion and stress. All of these topics are subsumed under the general heading of the dynamics of personality, or *psychodynamics*.

Conflict

We live in a world of conflict. Should we marry or remain single? Whom should we marry? What career should we pursue? Should we lie about a wrongdoing or honestly take our punishment? At any given moment in time there are many possible alternatives from which to choose, even in everyday activities. For example, you might be deciding now whether to stay in and study or to go join some friends. If your decision is to study, should you continue with psychology or move on to some other subject? These are conscious conflicts that do not involve any violation of social standards or norms. Other conflicts, however, involve unconscious desires and inhibitions and are of fundamental importance to personality.

Conflicts vary in strength. Some are serious and difficult to resolve, while others are relatively meaningless and easy to settle. The magnitude of a conflict is determined by a number of factors. Assume, for example, that you want to go to a movie, that there is only one movie playing that you have not seen, and that it is precisely the movie you have been waiting for. It is intuitively clear that little conflict exists in this situation. But if two movies are showing that you haven't seen, then more conflict is generated. In general, we can state that *the greater the number of alternatives available, the greater the degree of conflict* (Berlyne, 1960; Markus and Schwartz, 2010). It would seem that having many options would be good, but it makes it harder to choose, thus the paradox of choice (Schwartz, 2004).

There are other determinants of conflict magnitude in addition to number of alternatives. For example, contrast the situation in which none of the movies except one is considered good with the situation in which many of the movies have been favorably reviewed. Again, there is intuitively more conflict in the latter instance. A second law determining the magnitude of conflict therefore is: *the greater the equality in the attractiveness of the alternatives, the greater the degree of conflict.*

Now suppose you are deciding which college to attend, which job to accept, or which person to marry, as opposed to which movie to attend. Much greater conflict will be aroused in the former instances. Thus, *the greater the importance of a decision, the greater the degree of conflict.*

Temporal, Spatial, and Discriminative Conflict

There are many types of conflicts and different schemes have been proposed that group them into categories. This is an essential scientific step, for it points out the underlying similarities and differences between the various conflict types. One interesting classification scheme distinguishes temporal, spatial, and discriminative conflict (Brown, 1957).

Temporal conflict exists when the attractiveness of alternative choices. changes over time. For example, an engaged couple might become more and more uncertain about their decision to marry as the date of the wedding draws near. Job shifts and moving also tend to be perceived with increasing or decreasing favorableness as the time of change approaches.

Because of the potential importance, choice of a career may create a great deal of conflict.

Source: Maridav/Shutterstock

Spatial conflict varies as a function of physical distance. A teenager might decide to fight the neighborhood bully, for example, but as he approaches him begins to doubt the wisdom of his decision.

Discriminative conflict is best illustrated by an experiment conducted by Ivan Pavlov. Pavlov presented dogs with food following a 600-cycle-frequency tone. A second, 800-cycle-frequency tone was also presented to the animals, but was not followed by any reward. Then, on the conflict trials, a tone of 700 cycles was presented. The dogs had to decide if this was a "food" or a "no-food" tone. Pavlov reported that this conflict gave rise to emotionality and disturbance in his laboratory dogs. He compared these behaviors to the neurotic actions of humans and suggested that certain forms of mental illness might be a result of insoluble discriminative conflicts.

Lewin's Classification System

A more complete taxonomy of **conflict** has been proposed by Kurt Lewin. Lewin (1935) differentiated three types of conflict: approach-approach, avoidance-avoidance, and approach-avoidance. *Approach-approach conflicts* occur when there are two or more positive alternatives from which to choose: for example, the proverbial donkey choosing between two bundles of hay or someone deciding which of two award-winning movies to see. *Avoidance-avoidance conflicts* are created when a choice is confined to two or more unattractive alternatives, such as a command to either wash the dishes or vacuum the rug.

Lewin contended that approach-approach conflicts are easy to resolve and labeled them **unstable conflicts**, whereas avoidance-avoidance conflicts are difficult-to-resolve, **stable conflicts**. Lewin reasoned that, in approach-approach conflicts, as one comes closer to one of the goals, the attractiveness of that goal increases. For example, as one drives to a restaurant, enters the door, reads the menu, and finally sees the food, that food is more and more desired. Thus, in an approach-approach conflict, when an alternative is selected, its attractiveness increases, while the attractiveness of the unselected alternative decreases because one is psychologically further from it. The conflict therefore is readily resolved, as illustrated in Figure 14.1, which shows that the difference in the relative attractiveness of alternatives increases as one comes closer to either of the goals.

conflict The difficulty in making a choice usually because the options are both good or both bad.

unstable conflicts Conflicts that tend to be resolved quickly—for instance, approach-approach conflicts.

stable conflicts Conflicts that take longer to resolve—for instance, avoidance-avoidance conflict.

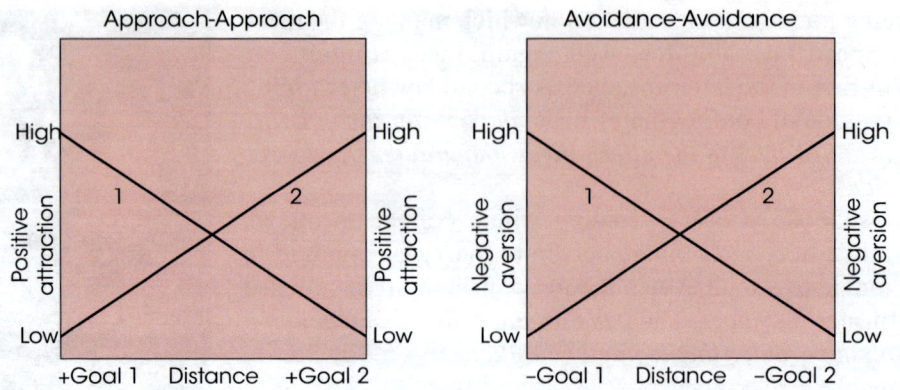

FIGURE 14.1 The Attractiveness of Alternatives, According to Lewin

On the other hand, given an avoidance-avoidance conflict (see Fig. 14. 1), as one of the aversive alternatives is approached, it becomes increasingly negative. For example, anxiety increases dramatically as one gets closer and closer to the edge of a cliff; less dramatically, washing the dishes will appear increasingly unattractive as the soap and hot water are experienced. In addition, the aversiveness of the unselected alternative decreases, for one is getting psychologically further from it. This change in the perceived aversiveness of the alternatives will cause one to oscillate and repeatedly shift choices. This analysis assumes that escape from both negative alternatives is impossible. Lewin argued that one of the great disadvantages of using negative alternatives and punishments is that energy must be expended to ensure that the individual does not attempt to leave the situation, thereby avoiding both alternatives.

To test the idea that approach-approach conflicts are easier to resolve than avoidance-avoidance conflicts, Arkoff (1957) presented participants with a number of hypothetical choices representing both types of conflict, such as "Would you rather be more attractive or more intelligent?" and "Would you rather be less attractive *or* less intelligent?" The time taken to make a choice or resolve the hypothetical conflicts was much less in approach-approach than in avoidance-avoidance situations.

The third type of conflict identified by Lewin, *approach-avoidance conflict*, was the basis for a well-known theory presented by Neal Miller (1944, 1959). Miller, previously discussed in Chapter 5 on learning theory approaches to personality, used learning theory terminology to explain complex conflicts.

The way a question is framed shows up in modern decision science (Kahneman, 2011). To oversimplify an example: If there was a disease that is rather deadly, would you want to use a treatment for the disease that would save eighty out of one hundred people, or a treatment in which twenty out of one hundred die? The outcome is the same, but when the question is framed in the negative, we try to avoid that negative outcome (Kahneman and Tversky, 1979; Tversky and Kahneman, 1981).

Choosing a car can have multiple conflicts—from which one to choose, to deciding whether to get one at all.

Source: Zoriana Zaitseva/Shutterstock

Miller's Conflict Model

The most prevalent type of conflict is *approach-avoidance conflict*, which occurs when both positive and negative consequences are associated with the same action. For example, we like to buy new clothes, but they are expensive; we want to eat a candy bar, but it is fattening; we would like to hit people we are angry at, but this is likely to be punished. Observation of approach-avoidance conflicts often reveals ambivalent behavior; the organism approaches the desired object, only to turn away, reapproach, and so on. The behavior oscillates from approach to withdrawal and hence is labeled **ambivalent**. Miller's model is able to account for this behavior.

ambivalent Behavior that changes back and forth from approach to avoidance.

In accordance with Figure 14.1, Miller assumed that the tendency to approach a positive goal, as well as the tendency to avoid a negative goal, is stronger the nearer the organism is to those goals. However, he asserted that the strength of avoidance increases more rapidly with nearness to the goal than does the strength of approach. This process is depicted in Figure 14.2. The differential steepness of the slopes in Figure 14.2 is based on the fact that avoidance behavior is determined, in part, by one's level of fear. Fear is a learned drive which varies as a function of one's nearness to the feared situation. For example, fear is great when one is at the edge of a cliff, or perhaps in a dark room, but decreases rapidly when one steps a few feet from the edge of the cliff or turns on alight. On the other hand, approach behavior is typically based on internal drives, such as hunger, which remain relatively constant even though the external environment may change. For these reasons, Miller posited that the avoidance tendency would be steeper than that of approach. Further inspection of the approach-avoidance conflict gradients shown in Figure 14.2 reveals that the organism should approach the goal until reaching point X, the place where the strengths of both tendencies are equal. Beyond that point, the strength of avoidance exceeds that of approach and the organism should begin to withdraw, thus producing oscillation and the appearance of ambivalence.

Miller, Brown, and others have conducted a number of experiments to test this model. Often rats have been used as the experimental participants, so that rather severe hours of deprivation as well as the strength of a shock could be varied. In one of the original investigations, Brown (1948) developed a technique for measuring the strength of the approach and avoidance tendencies in rats. The rats were fitted with a harness that allowed the experimenter to test how hard they pulled. Animals had been trained in separate goal boxes either to approach food or to avoid shock and were then placed at various distances from the food or shock. As hypothesized, the strength of pull varied as a function of distance from the goal, and the distance from the shocked compartment influenced the intensity of pull more than distance from the rewarded compartment.

Other tests and derivations of the model have concerned the effects of the degree of hunger or strength of shock on conflict resolution. Figure 14.3 repeats Figure 14.2, except that a second approach gradient has been added. The two approach gradients differ in magnitude, showing the difference in intensity of motivation caused by, for example, unequal levels of hunger. The distance between points A and A' represents the differential distance of approach to the goal. As the figure shows, the intersection of the approach and avoidance gradients occurs at a point closer to the goal when the approach desire is heightened.

The situation depicted in Figure 14.3 has some interesting behavioral implications. Suppose, for example, that the figure represents strength differences in the aggressive

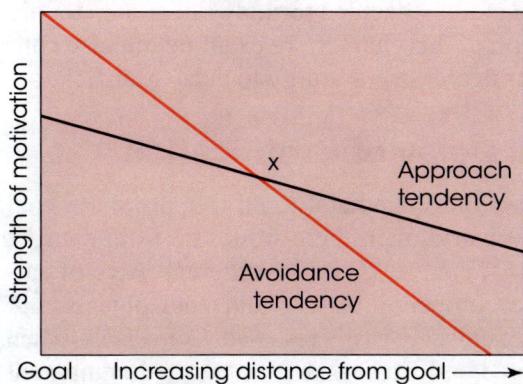

FIGURE 14.2 Goal Strengths in Approach-Avoidance Conflicts

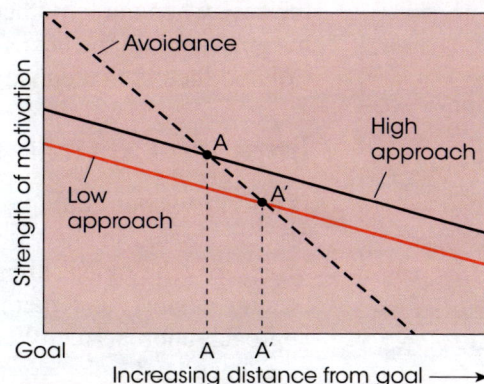

FIGURE 14.3 Differences in Approach Gradients

Choosing between healthy and unhealthy foods can be an ambivalent conflict. The unhealthy food tastes so good but is unhealthy. The healthy food is healthy but doesn't taste quite as good.

displacement Changing from a dangerous focus to a safer focus.

approach tendencies of two individuals. Because the avoidance gradient at the goal is greater than either of the approach gradients, neither individual will engage in overt hostile actions. However, because the individual with the stronger drive comes closer to the goal, he or she experiences more fear and more conflict. Thus, the amount of fear and conflict displayed by an individual can be an index of his or her attraction to that situation. The Miller conflict model therefore can account for Freud's paradoxical observation that the intensity of avoidance behavior is often a direct reflection of the intensity of temptation.

Conflict and Displacement

The term **displacement** refers to the observation that one's goals may change, even though the desire to reach the original goal has not subsided (see Chapter 3). Freud contended that there are "vicissitudes of the instincts"; in other words, there are a variety of objects that may satisfy an underlying wish. The most frequently cited example of such displacement activity is in the study of aggression, where it is often pointed out that someone who cannot express anger at his or her boss comes home to take it out on an unsuspecting spouse. Freud (1915, pp. 174–175) used a more humorous example to illustrate displacement:

> There was a blacksmith in the village who had committed a capital offense. The Court decided that the crime must be punished; but as the blacksmith was the only one in the village and was indispensable, and as on the other hand there were three tailors living there, one of them was hanged instead.

Taking it out on one's spouse is the equivalent of taking it out on the tailor—unfair—but there are often greater consequences of expressing the anger to one's boss. Displacement activity, or the shifting of goal objects, has been incorporated into Miller's conflict model. Consider the employee angry at the boss but not directly expressing this hostility. Miller would reason that the aggressive tendency directed toward the boss is inhibited by a stronger avoidance tendency. Thus, the person responds aggressively to someone other than the boss, as depicted in Figure 14.4. In Figure 14.4, the horizontal or X axis, which represented physical (spatial) distance in previous figures, now depicts "psychological" distance or "similarity" to the figure eliciting hostility. Of course, Figure 14.4 is a simplified analysis of what can be a very complex process, inasmuch as displacement is affected by a number of psychological factors such as previous experience with the displaced object, the availability of alternative goal satisfiers, and the like.

In situations of conflict, one often must forego a desired goal, as was the case when our hypothetical student decided to study rather than to join his girlfriend. In the next section of this chapter, we examine impulse control and factors that enhance or decrease our ability to delay gratification.

Impulse Control and Delay of Gratification

If all our wishes could be acted on immediately, and if appropriate goal objects existed in the external world, then there would be little conflict of any psychological import. Of course, there are different ways of satisfying desires, and there are competing wishes and goal objects, but approach-approach conflicts typically are easily resolved. Conversely, when avoidance tendencies are elicited and barriers preventing goal attainment are imposed, as is the case when there are social norms prohibiting desired actions, then the potential for severe psychological consequences exists.

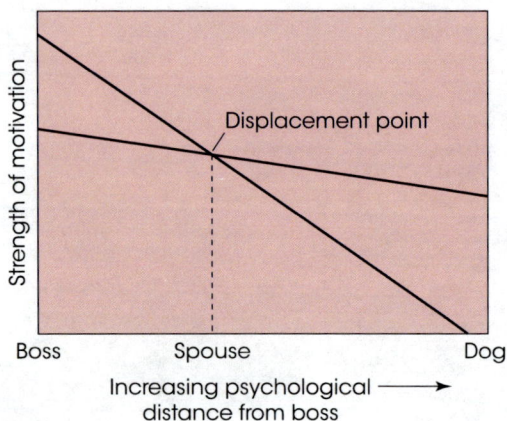

FIGURE 14.4 Displacement

On the one hand, wishes may be left unfulfilled, while on the other hand, goal satisfaction might entail such great personal cost as retribution, punishment, and loss.

From the perspective of psychoanalytic theory, ego mechanisms recognize the demands of the social world and impose restraints on behavior. Ego constraints postpone goal-directed actions until external conditions are more suitable for the expression of one's drives. Repression, which was discussed in detail in Chapter 3, is the main mechanism responsible for preventing the immediate gratification of wishes. Recall that the defenses often intervene so that a wish does not enter consciousness and thus is not directly acted upon.

Ego controls are necessary if the organism is to function in society and avoid the punishment that might accompany immediate sexual or aggressive gratification. With the individual's increasing cognitive development and maturity, such controls become a virtue as well as a necessity, for the ability to delay enables one to attain highly desirable long-term goals that require the abandonment of immediate gratification. For example, studying to do well on an exam might require foregoing a pleasant social encounter, and enrollment in graduate or medical school necessitates giving up immediate monetary gain for a better position in the future. Thus, ego functions include not only the recognition of appropriate external conditions for drive expression, but also more general self-imposed constraints, or everyday "will power" (Loevinger, 1976). Even researchers without a psychoanalytic orientation will sometimes use the term *ego strength* to refer to this process.

Imaginary Images

Freud (1911) argued that in the absence of satisfying external objects, images of these objects are called forth and pleasure is attained through hallucinations or fantasy activity. Hallucinations, therefore, are one way to cope temporarily with lack of gratification; they bridge the delay between one's desires and their expression—a function frequently referred to as *time binding*.

The effects of mental representations of rewards on the ability to delay gratification have been examined experimentally by Mischel and his colleagues (Mischel, 1974*a*, 1974*b*; Mischel and Ebbesen, 1970). In these studies, children were placed in a choice dilemma in which they might have received either a smaller, immediate reward (a candy bar) or a larger reward (two candy bars) at a later time, in exchange for their cooperation at a task. A variety of factors then were manipulated to assess their effects on the choices the children made.

To examine the influence of the visual presence of the reward on **delay of gratification**, Mischel and Ebbesen (1970) created situations in which the delayed reward, the immediate reward, both rewards, or neither reward was in the participant's visual field during the delay period. In this study, the child could wait for the experimenter to return with the larger reward or signal for him to return and immediately receive the smaller reward. The results of this investigation clearly reveal that waiting time was maximal when neither of the rewards was visible, and minimal when both rewards could be seen. In a subsequent investigation of the effects of mental representation of a reward, the researchers devised two experimental conditions in which the rewards were not visible and the participants were instructed to either think about the rewards or think "fun" (Mischel, Ebbesen, and Zeiss, 1972). In this study, they found that thinking about a reward impedes the ability to delay gratification.

On the basis of these and other data, Mischel contended that one consequence of the mental representation of a reward object during the delay interval is frustration. The additional frustration then decreases the ability to delay gratification. Any activity that distracts the person from thinking about the reward should, therefore, lessen frustration and increase delay behavior. Perhaps we intuitively realize this; when we want something that is unobtainable, we may distract ourselves to forget about it. Furthermore, even given the visual appearance of the desired reward, the individual may engage in coping activities that help delay gratification. For example, when children had a potential reward of

delay of gratification The ability to wait to receive a reward.

pretzels, and thought about them as logs or other objects, delay ability was enhanced. However, it can be contended that a choice between candy bars does not reflect any strong internalized desires and does not quite capture the problems that Freud addressed. Thus, one must be careful in the generalization of these data to more intense need situations.

Years later, Mischel, Shoda, and Peake (1988) contacted some of the children who participated in the first delay of gratification experiments. The children were now in their early adolescence. It was found that the participants who were able to wait longer at the age of four or five were rated by their parents as more academically competent, verbally fluent, rational, attentive, and planful when in their teens. Mischel et al. (1988) suggest that the ingredients necessary for effective delay—ability to divert and control attention and to purposefully distract oneself from frustration—influence long-term development.

Learning Theory Approaches

It is evident from the previous discussion that, according to psychoanalytic theory, delay is an ego function determined by intrapsychic factors. Mischel (1968, p. 153) contrasted this position with that of the social learning theorists:

> According to the psychoanalytic theory of delay behavior, aroused impulses press for immediate discharge of tension through overt motoric activity. . . . The psychoanalytic approach . . . leads one to seek determinants of delay behavior in such hypothetical internal events as ego organizations and energy-binding ideations [hallucinations]. In contrast, social behavior theory . . . views manipulable social-stimulus events as the critical determinants of self-controlling behavior.

In the tradition of social learning (see Chapter 5), Bandura and Mischel (1965) examined the role of a model in altering delay of gratification. These investigators first identified children who were willing to delay reward and others who sought immediate gratification. The children then observed a model displaying behavior inconsistent with their own delay preferences. For example, the high-delay children observed a model choosing cheaper, plastic chess figures without delay rather than waiting one week for a more attractive chess set. In one condition the model was "live," while in a second condition the model's responses were read rather than actually observed. Both before and immediately after the model's performance, and one month later, delay of gratification was assessed. The high-delay children's preference for immediate, less valuable rewards increased dramatically in the model conditions. Furthermore, the influence of the live model remained effective at the one-month retest period, or post exposure, and at a related choice task (a "generalization" condition). As is usual for the social learning perspective, role models matter.

In addition to observational learning, there are other procedures and contingencies that can establish self-control. For example, guided by Skinnerian principles, one woman who had problems controlling her "cussing" fined herself a dollar every time she swore. This money was immediately put aside for charity. Other control techniques that manipulate the environment, like putting a lock on the refrigerator, have been used to prevent impulsive expression. And cognitive behavior modification techniques such as covert self-statements (see Chapter 5) have been used effectively to control motoric discharge ("If I miss this shot, I will not throw my racquet").

Expectancy and Delay of Gratification

Rotter's social learning theory (see Chapter 5) also has been applied to the study of delay behavior. Mahrer (1956) demonstrated that delay behavior is in part determined by the expectation of reinforcement. Children seven to nine years old were offered a choice between a smaller immediate reward and a

Source: Chubykin Arkady/Shutterstock

What strategies can children use to delay gratification?

TABLE 14.1 Choices of Immediate and Delayed Reinforcement

Reinforcement choice	Expectancy					
	High		Moderate		Low	
	Same experimenter	Different experimenter	Same experimenter	Different experimenter	Same experimenter	Different experimenter
Immediate	6*	6	15	5	18	7
Delayed	19	14	11	15	6	15

Source: Adapted from Mahrer, 1956, p. 104. * Number of participants making that choice.

more attractive delayed reward. Before the choice dilemma, they induced three levels of expectancy for the receipt of a promised reward. On each of five consecutive days the experimenter told the children that for performing an activity they would receive a small balloon on the following day. To develop groups of high, moderate, and low expectancy for delayed reward, this promise was kept variously 100 percent, 50 percent, or none of the time. Three days later, the same participants were offered a choice between the immediate and the delayed reward. Furthermore, the experimenter offering the choices was either the same one who conducted the training session or a person differing from the first experimenter in sex and age. The results of this study are shown in Table 14.1. The table shows that the groups of participants tested by the different experimenter all exhibited the same delay behavior, regardless of prior training. On the other hand, responses to same experimenter were consistent with the expectancies based on prior experiences, with higher expectancies leading to greater delay behavior.

Substitution

If one's wishes are not attained, either because of conflict and impulse control or because the goal object is not available, then psychological processes are elicited to help one cope with the situation. One such process, considered in the previous section, is hallucination. Freud contended that hallucinations about goal objects serve to gratify one's wishes (although the experiments by Mischel and his associates might be considered as evidence contradicting this notion). Other fantasy activity such as dreaming (which is examined in detail in a later chapter) has also been considered to have wish-fulfillment functions. And, as discussed in the chapter on psychoanalytic theory, even such diverse behaviors as slips of the tongue and jokes were thought to reduce aggressive and sexual urges.

But perhaps the most prevalent, most adaptive way of coping with goal frustration is to establish alternative goals. Freudian theory, as has been pointed out, posits that the object of a desire may change. A forbidden, unfulfilled wish can, for example, become directed toward objects that have some similarity to the desired object yet permit expression of the original wish. Freud stated that ultimately a libidinal tendency might even be expressed in cultural activities such as painting or composing. In his analyses of Michelangelo and da Vinci, Freud contended that these great artists had strong unfulfilled sexual urges that were deflected into socially acceptable channels. Freud labeled this defense mechanism (see Chapter 3) *sublimation*.

Displacement activity, examined in the section on conflict, and also one of the defense mechanisms, concerns desires that are deflected from a primary goal because of conflict. Displacement refers to the direction of behavior, or the goals that one selects. The study of alternative goal gratification, or **substitution**, concerns a related, yet different problem; namely, does the attainment of substitute goals satisfy one's desires? That is, is the original wish partially or completely satisfied? More specifically, assume that you want to aggress against an authority figure like your father, but are prevented from doing so by conflict. Aggression is now displaced toward your brother. Is this displacement

substitution Replacing a problematic goal with a different goal.

activity of motivational value; that is, are your aggressive tendencies satisfied through the substitute goal gratification? The latter question is the focus of the study of substitution.

Kurt Lewin and his students conducted a series of experiments that examined the properties and functions of substitute goals. Lewin (1935, pp. 180–181) believed that substitution is manifested in many different ways.

> There is, for instance, the man who dreams of a palace and brings a few pieces of marble into his kitchen. There is the man who cannot buy a piano, but who collects piano catalogs. Again, we find the delinquent boy who knows that he will not be allowed to leave his reform school but who asks for a traveling bag as a birthday present. . . . These and a hundred other examples make us realize how important and far-reaching the problem of substitution is in regard to psychological needs as well as with reference to bodily needs such as hunger and sex.

To examine the value of substitution in a laboratory experiment, Lewin and his students first allowed their participants, typically children, to engage in an attractive, gamelike task, such as a building activity, and then interrupted the children before the task was completed. Earlier research had established that there is a strong motivational force to return and complete such interrupted tasks; this is called the Zeigarnik effect. Then, before allowing the children to finish their task, the experimenters permitted them to engage in some other activity. After this, the children had the opportunity to resume the interrupted activity. If the children resumed the previously unfinished task, then the intervening activity did not serve as a substitute. But if the originally unfinished activity was not undertaken, then the intervening activity had substitute value. Thus, resumption became the behavioral indicator identifying substitute goals and their effects.

One of the first experimental studies of substitution was conducted by Lissner (1933). In her experiment, children were interrupted while making a figure from clay. Then, after they had made a different figure, they were tested for resumption. Lissner identified two factors that influence the substitute value of an activity: its similarity to the first activity and its level of difficulty. The more similar and difficult the intervening task, the greater its substitute value and the less likely the resumption of the unfinished task. Mahler (1933) gave participants an intervening activity that could be completed in ways that differed in how closely they resembled the original, overt behavior. Participants could think about doing the task, talk through its completion, or actually do it. In general, substitute value varied directly with the degree of reality of the substitute action, with the least substitution value provided by the imaginative task. This implies that daydreams and other fantasy activity may have little (yet *some*) value for the reduction of persisting desires.

In sum, these studies demonstrate that goals can substitute for one another. Further, some of the relevant dimensions and determinants of substitute value have been identified. There clearly are interrelationships between psychological needs, as Freud and Lewin argued. Unfortunately, while there has been some followup of the work of Lewin and his students, there has been very little recent research on the problem of substitution. One exception has been investigations of the catharsis or discharge of aggression through fantasy, particularly studies that examine the effects of violence on television. This will be discussed in detail in Chapter 18.

One should not conclude from the dearth of research on substitution that it is a minor element in the dynamics of personality. The research techniques developed by Lewin's research team were appropriate to rather minor, experimentally induced motivations and goals, such as cutting out paper dolls, making clay figures, and so on. However, making substitute choices is intrinsic to human experience; questions of the factors determining the value of substitutions are fundamental for human motivation. If we fail to make the football team but play on the baseball team, is our desire to play on the football team thereby less intense? If we aspire to be a novelist but, after a series of rejection slips, shift to a successful career in business, will the desire to write abate? Clearly there are many fundamental unanswered questions concerning the value of substitute choices, and this should be a fertile area of study for future personality psychologists.

Frustration

So far we have examined the dynamics of conflict and how coping with conflict is aided by means of impulse control and the establishment of substitute goals. However, goals must frequently be forsaken. In those cases, there is likely to be frustration as well as a number of more well-defined emotions, including anger, disappointment, and guilt.

Frustration has diverse meanings for psychologists. It may refer to an independent variable, or experimental manipulation. Often this involves blocking the attainment of a goal, inducing failure, or delivering a personal insult. Hence, the definition refers to the situation. Performance of a "frustrated" group is then compared to the performance of a "nonfrustrated" control group. Frustration may also refer to a dependent variable, in which case the researcher measures the amount of frustrated behavior. For example, one might examine whether individuals high in anxiety display more frustrated behavior than persons low in anxiety. This definition therefore refers to the condition of the organism. Finally, frustration frequently pertains to an intervening variable, or a complex process inferred from certain observable responses. For example, on the basis of observed aggressive behavior, one might conclude that an individual is frustrated.

Toward the tail end of the behaviorist era, a good deal of research was done on frustration. In laboratory situations the association of frustration to other variables such as aggression, fixation, enhanced goal strivings, and regression was studied. The relationship of frustration to aggression was found to be a complex one, and it is documented more thoroughly in Chapter 18.

Fixation is the tendency of an organism to persist in responding the same way even when those responses are ineffectual in achieving a goal. Fixated behavior is maladaptive, in that it does not flexibly respond to the demands of the situation or task and it can often be seen in people experiencing psychological problems. In Maier's (1949) early research with animals, frustration was induced by giving rewards and punishments to animals in a completely random fashion, no matter what they did. Maier found that frustration increased the probability of animals responding in a persistently maladaptive manner.

Enhanced goal strivings refers to the tendency of some individuals to respond to frustrating obstacles by enhancing their efforts and by being more creative. Both fixation and enhanced goal strivings now appear to be a function of whether an individual feels helpless or competent when he or she encounters frustration (see Chapter 17). They do not appear to be a function of frustration per se.

Regression is the tendency to repeat earlier, more primitive modes of behavior when under stress. An example might be running home to mother when one experiences difficult circumstances. Studies by Lewin and his colleagues (e.g., Barker, Dembo, and Lewin, 1943) found that children's play became more primitive when they were under stress. More up-to-date research (see Chapter 15) has found that stress can lead to lower levels of thinking—thinking in more concrete rather than abstract terms.

Goals and Life Tasks

Up to this point, we have been considering how people deal with goals. We have examined some of the dynamics of conflict, and we have examined frustration and goal replacement. Let's take a closer look at goals themselves. Goals can exist at multiple levels of abstraction. For instance, a person may have a goal to finish reading this chapter, or to do well in this course, or to graduate, or to get a good job, or to have a happy life. These goals can all work together with one goal serving to facilitate another goal. Alternatively, the goals may be in conflict; "I want to study for this exam" and "I want to go to the party."

In the late 1980s, many psychologists became concerned with the study of goals in personality (Pervin, 1989), and a number of researchers began to study goals and goal behavior at an individual level. Unfortunately, they all seemed to name these goals different things. For instance, Klinger (1987) studied the *current concerns* that influence a person's moment-to-moment behavior by sampling what the person is thinking about from moment

Being on one's own away from one's family is an important task for many college students.

life tasks Current problems and goals that a person is motivated to try to solve.

to moment. Emmons (1989) studied individuals' *personal strivings*, the chronic enduring goals or concerns that underlie individuals' everyday behavior. Emmons and King (1988) found that the more conflict and ambivalence people had associated with their personal strivings, the more likely they were to score high on measures of neuroticism, depression, negative affect, and psychosomatic complaints. Little (1989) examined the *personal projects* of individuals by asking them to list their current personal projects. These might include projects such as watching baseball games, making new friends, or developing a philosophy of life. Little's research found that personal well-being is enhanced to the degree that individuals are engaged in personal projects that are meaningful, well structured, supported by others, not excessively stressful, and that lead to a sense of personal efficacy. Next, we consider one other concept, that of life tasks, in greater detail.

The concept of life tasks has been influenced by Erikson's model of identity development (Cantor, 1994). **Life tasks** are "self-articulated problems that individuals are motivated to try to solve, to which they devote energy and time, and that they see as organizing their current daily life activity" (Cantor and Zirkel, 1990, p. 150). For instance, for college students, life tasks include "being on my own away from my family" and "setting career goals." Cantor (1990) sees life tasks as goals and issues that become particularly important at specific life transitions. They are embedded in the agendas of cultures and social groups at particular developmental times. For instance, "becoming independent" means something different and is worked on in different ways during different life transitions, such as leaving home to go to college or getting a first full-time job.

Cantor (1994) reports research conducted by herself and her colleagues in which the "life task" of achieving intimacy was studied in college students. Cantor suggests that how individuals frame the goals involved in the life task will determine how they go about achieving it. For achieving intimacy, some may adopt a more "communal" view, in which the goal is to learn how to share thoughts and feelings. Others may adopt a more "agentic" view, in which the goal is to learn how to maintain one's independence while in relationships. Depending on how one defines the goal, one's behavior differs. Those who define the task more communally are more likely to engage in more serious relationships of longer duration. Those who identify the task more agentically are more likely to have a greater number of casual partners. These differences in orientation are also associated with safe sex practices. Those who adopt a communal orientation are *less likely* to engage in safe sex activity than those who adopt an agentic orientation. Consider that again, those who are interested in developing intimacy, sharing thoughts and feelings, are less likely to use safer sex practices. Those who just want to have sex, use condoms. Cantor and her graduate students used this information to design an HIV/AIDS intervention program. For more communally oriented individuals, the program focused on skills of negotiation and communication about condom use, while for agentically oriented individuals, the program focused on technical skills designed to make a person feel more efficacious about the use of condoms. It was found that when the intervention corresponded to the student's definition of the life task, the student was more likely to report greater favorable attitudes toward condom use at a three-month follow-up (Cantor, 1994).

In contrast to a focus on global themes of life goals and tasks, researchers such as Cantor and her colleagues have been more interested in the day-to-day business of how individuals weave goals into their everyday life. Their studies provide a more complete picture of how individuals function than do the studies that focus on more global, general issues and values.

Safer sex practices are influenced by a person's life tasks.

Summary

1. Three historical movements in psychology: behaviorism, Gestalt psychology, and psychoanalysis have influenced the study of psychodynamics.
2. The strength of a *conflict* is in part determined by the number of available alternatives, the relative attractiveness of those alternatives, and the importance of the decision involved.
3. *Approach-approach conflicts* involve a choice between two or more attractive alternatives; *avoidance-avoidance conflicts* involve a choice between two or more aversive alternatives. The latter are especially difficult to resolve.
4. *Approach-avoidance conflicts* occur in situations where an alternative has both positive and negative characteristics; they tend to produce ambivalent behavior. According to Miller, the observed ambivalence can be accounted for by postulating that the gradient of avoidance, or the change in motivational strength as a function of distance from the goal, is steeper than the gradient of approach.
5. Evidence suggests that the visual presence of desired goals increases frustration and reduces the ability to delay gratification. Hallucinatory images, the behavior of models, social engineering techniques, and expectancy of future goal attainment all influence delay of gratification.
6. *Substitution* refers to the gratification provided by goals attained in place of the original one. Substitution is greatest when the substitute goal is similar to the original goal and is actually attained, rather than imagined.
7. *Frustration* can refer to an independent (manipulated), an intervening (inferred), or a dependent (measured) variable. It produces behaviors as disparate as aggression, fixation, regression, and enhanced goal striving.
8. *Life tasks* are the goals and problems that a person is currently trying to solve. Life tasks are likely to be different at different stages of life, even if the goal appears to be the same.

Key Terms

ambivalent (p. 267)
conflict (p. 265)
delay of gratification (p. 269)
displacement (p. 268)
life tasks (p. 274)

personality dynamics (p. 261)
stable conflicts (p. 265)
substitution (p. 271)
unstable conflicts (p. 265)

Thought Questions

1. Think of some conflicts you have had recently. Can you classify them according to any of the types of conflict discussed in this chapter? If so, does your classification help you to understand the dynamics of your conflict better?
2. Individuals trapped in an approach-avoidance conflict sometimes resolve the conflict after a few drinks. How does the ingestion of alcohol make conflict resolution possible?
3. In what ways are the concepts of conflict, frustration, displacement, and substitution interrelated?
4. What are your current life tasks? How are you trying to solve them?

Emotion and Stress

CHAPTER 15

Source: lassedesignen/Shutterstock

Chapter Outline

Emotion
The Body as the Source
Two Factor Model
Cognitive Theories
The Structure of Emotion
Mood
Stress

The topics examined in the prior chapter, particularly conflict, delay of gratification, and frustration, are all intimately related to the study of emotion and stress. Certainly, these are negative states—they are experiences we generally would prefer not to undergo, and they create stress. In addition, as will be seen, actions are guided by either current emotional states, such as guilt and shame, or by the anticipation of positive and negative emotional outcomes. Hence, emotions are a central topic in the study of personality and psychodynamics, as are the stresses that we all face in everyday life.

In this chapter we first consider the definition of emotion. We then consider different theoretical perspectives on emotion, including arousal theories, cognitive theories, and recent developments in theories of emotion. We next consider the structure of emotion, including individual differences in emotional reactivity, and move on to consider mood. We conclude with an examination of stress and methods of coping with stress.

Emotion

For many years emotion was seen primarily in terms of its capacity to cause problems and disrupt conscious rational self-control. Much was written about ways to overcome the passion of emotion in order to achieve that rational self-control. Emotion was seen as a relatively peripheral or secondary aspect of behavior, something to be overcome. Current views of emotion, however, stress its often central role in the organization and activation of behavior. Even fields such as economics that formerly considered humans to be entirely "rational actors" have started to include the role of emotion in some of their models (Rick and Lowenstein, 2008). As the study of emotion has continued to develop and spread to related fields, an entire field of "emotion science" has developed (Lerner, Li, Valdesolo, and Kassam, 2015; Niedenthal and Ric, 2017).

Definition

emotion An intense, shorter duration form of affect, usually having a distinct cause.

mood A longer duration and lower intensity form of affect.

affect Overarching term encompassing mood, emotion, and evaluation.

The word **emotion** is derived from the Latin *emovere* ("to move out"). It is further cognate with the term *motivation*. All of these suggest the idea of motion and movement. Tomkins (1980) further suggests that emotions serve to amplify motivations.

There is an array of emotion-related terms distinguished by psychologists, including affect, feeling, evaluation, mood, and, of course, emotion. Each of these terms tends to imply slight differences in the intensity and duration of the form of affect. **Mood** is considered of longer duration than an emotion, and it is often not centered around a particular object or event. Thus, moods may be thought of as diffuse background experiences. Emotion is often thought of as being more intense, of shorter duration, and usually having a distinct cause. **Affect** tends to be used in clinical settings or as the overarching term encompassing all of these. But psychologists tend to use the terms somewhat interchangeably (Plutchik, 1994).

Averill (1982) points out that emotions are interpreted as passions, rather than actions. An action is something a person does deliberately. A passion, however, is something the person suffers. Thus, a disease is a "passion," and it is of interest to note that the words passion, patient, and passivity all stem from the same root. Hence, a person is "gripped" by fear, "falls" in love, is "torn" by jealousy, is "dragged down" by grief, and so on. In these examples, something happens to the person that does not appear to be subject to volitional control and also suggests movement.

A number of distinguishing characteristics are also associated with emotions. Not all emotions are described by all the characteristics, but if all the characteristics are evident, then an emotional state can be inferred with some certainty.

1. Emotions have a positive or negative experiential quality. That is, they are something the person likes and wants to get more of (joy, love, pride) or something the person dislikes and wants to be rid of (sadness, hatred, guilt).
2. The positive and negative characteristics vary in magnitude. Thus, one can feel a little or a great deal of happiness, somewhat sad or very sad, and so on.
3. The feelings might be accompanied by certain facial expressions and body postures. Smiling often accompanies positive emotions; curled lips and tightened facial muscles are linked with anger; and pride maybe displayed with an upright posture.
4. The emotions signal certain types of behavior. Thus, for example, one strikes out in order to "eliminate" the object of anger; gratitude gives rise to a reciprocal favor; and so on. Tomkins (1970; 1980) has proposed that emotions, not drives or desires, are the chief movers of behavior.
5. Emotions often follow particular thoughts. For example, if you fail an exam because you believe that others hindered you, anger is a likely reaction; success ascribed to help from others elicits gratitude; both success and failure believed to be due to luck bring about surprise; and so on. Thus, one's feelings are determined in part by one's thoughts. The subjective interpretation, not the objective facts, determines emotions. For example, one may fail because of insufficient studying, yet anger (rather than, say, guilt and self-blame) is experienced if the failure is believed to be due to the teacher's bias.

The emotion itself is an amalgam; it represents the entire system and way in which the components are organized. This complexity in the definition and determination of an emotion reminds one of a story about a new student first visiting a university. The student is given a tour and told "This is the administration building; this is the student union; this is the gymnasium. . . ." After the tour is over, the student asks: "But where is the university?" In a similar manner, the antecedent thoughts, the facial expression, the behavioral consequence, and so on of an emotion can be pointed out. But where is the emotion? The emotion is all the combined elements.

One final definitional issue should be addressed, namely, the distinction between a "cold" cognition ("This is a table" or "I *should* feel angry") and a "hot" emotion ("I stubbed my %$#@ toe!" or "I feel angry"). There is sometimes value in differentiating between cognition and emotion, though the interplay between cognition and emotion is very close. Some researchers would go so far as to say that because of the organization of the brain, we are unlikely to ever successfully fully differentiate cognition and emotion (Storbeck and Clore, 2007).

Areas of Study

The study of emotion, like the study of the entire field of personality, is quite diverse and mirrors the subdivisions of the field of personality. Some researchers have been interested in the evolutionary and biological determinants of emotional states and expression, as previously reviewed in Chapter 1. There it was indicated that some emotional expressions appear to be universal, hence implicating genetic or inborn influences. Others have examined the cultural determinants of emotions and emotional expression. It is known, for example, that overt expressions of joy are often masked in Thailand, consistent with their tendency to be very controlled, as discussed in Chapter 2. Different cultures have different "display rules," including, for example, what amount of grief is appropriate at funerals depending on the genetic closeness with the person who has died. Even within the United States, different occupational subcultures are in part paid to feel, or at least pretend to feel, certain emotions such as cheerfulness. This has been termed emotional labor (Hochschild, 1983; Judge, Wolf, and Hurst, 2011).

Still other schools of emotional thought examine the structure of emotions. One approach is to consider emotions via a dimensional approach, with emotions varying among dimensions such as negativity, intensity, and approach/withdrawal. Other taxonomies consider discrete emotions, such that although anger, fear, and sadness are all negative, they are fundamentally different from each other. These underlying questions are quite similar to the search for the basic dimensions of personality structure and the fundamental trait dimensions. Yet others study the function of emotions and their role as instigators of behavior. And finally, there are general emotion theorists who consider what emotions "are" and attempt to describe all emotional states with a few general principles.

The Body as the Source

Perhaps the oldest psychological theory of emotion comes from William James (1890/1952). James's model is a bit counterintuitive. In his model, "the bodily changes follow directly the perception of the exciting fact, and that our feeling of the same changes as they occur is the emotion" (p. 743). In this model, we are afraid because we run; we are sad because we cry. It is the body that is the cause of emotion, and we understand it only after the body has changed. (Danish physician Carl Lange independently developed this theory at about the same time, so both are given credit—consequently, the term James–Lange theory of emotion.)

facial feedback model The theory that we understand emotions through the facial display of that emotion.

Following from a body-based model is the idea that we know and experience our emotions because of the expressions on the face. In this theory, we know that we are sad because we cry; we know that we are happy because we are smiling. One of the most famous demonstrations of the **facial feedback model** is a study conducted by Strack, Martin, and Stepper (1988). In this study, participants were randomly assigned to hold a pen in their nondominant hand; between their teeth, thus mimicking a smile; or with their lips pursed, thus not allowing a smile. The participants

In the James–Lange and facial feedback theories, we know we are happy because we are smiling.

Source: mimagephotography/Shutterstock

then rated the humorousness of a cartoon. The pursed lip condition rated the cartoon as least funny, the teeth/smile condition rated the cartoon as funniest. This suggests that the expression on a person's face influences his or her experience of emotion.

This effect has been well replicated (c.f., Wagenmakers et al., 2016) with seventy articles listed by Strack (2016) supporting this model in various ways. Preventing frowning through the injection of Botox reduced clinical depression in several studies (e.g., Alves, Sobreira, Aleixo, and Oliveira, 2016; Wollmer et al., 2012). Further, people who were blocked from mimicking other people's faces had greater difficulty recognizing emotion in other faces (Wood, Lupyan, Sherrin, and Niedenthal, 2016). This particular finding may indicate that facial mimicry is an important part of understanding other people's emotions.

Two Factor Model

The concept of arousal has been one of the most dominant themes in the study of emotion and is the basis for various theories of emotion. Arousal refers to the intensity, state of activation, or general drive level characterizing an individual.

An early theory of emotion specified that too high of an activation level would result in overexcitement, while too low a level would produce depression. Furthermore, emotions were believed to lead to either behavioral organization or disorganization, depending on the intensity of the emotion or the person's level of arousal.

This conception of emotions, however, proved to be inadequate. First of all, emotions do not necessarily disrupt behavior. Emotions of great intensity may be quite adaptive and survival relevant. Equally important, given the same level of arousal, there are different emotional reactions. For example, high arousal might be accompanied by intense hate, intense love, or excitement. Arousal is therefore not a sufficient explanation of experienced emotions; it does not provide the conceptual tools to distinguish between emotions.

Schachter (1964) and Schachter and Singer (1962) supplemented arousal theory so that it could differentiate between emotions. They proposed that emotions are a function of two factors: level of arousal and cognitions about the arousing situation. In real-life situations, the situational cues that arouse an organism also provide the information necessary for understanding the event. For example, the appearance of a birthday cake may heighten arousal and act as a stimulus for positive affect (joy); the sight of a gun is likely to cause heightened arousal and act as a cue for fear. However, in laboratory settings, Schachter and his colleagues manipulated arousal and cognitive factors independently to study their joint effect on emotional expression.

In the best-known of their studies, Schachter and Singer (1962) injected participants with epinephrine (an activating agent that often produces autonomic arousal), under the guise of studying "how vitamin supplements affect the visual skills" (p. 382). Some participants were told of the effects of the drug and could thus appropriately label the source of their feelings. But other participants were either misinformed or uninformed about the drug's effects, and control participants were injected with a placebo. The participants then awaited their "visual test" in the presence of another participant, who was in fact working for the experimenter. The person working for the experimenters either acted in a very happy manner or feigned anger at some of the personal inquiries that were part of a questionnaire administered during the waiting period. During this interval, the participants' behaviors were observed and rated for happiness or anger. The main findings were that uninformed, epinephrine-injected participants (aroused, but "unlabeled") were relatively angrier in the anger-inducing situation and relatively more euphoric when with the person acting happily compared to control participants. Thus, emotion is a function of arousal level, and individuals in an aroused state may experience disparate emotions as a function of the social (cognitive) situation in which they find themselves.

Schachter's theory suggests that emotional experience results from the following sequence:

1. There is a bodily reaction (arousal).
2. The individual becomes aware of this reaction.

3. There is a need to seek a reason or explanation of the reaction.
4. An external cue is identified and the internal reaction is labeled. This labeling provides the quality or the naming of the emotional feeling and is thus a key determinant of experienced emotions.

This has led to other so-called "misattribution" paradigms to study emotional experience. Nisbett and Schachter (1966) gave participants a placebo after being told that they were about to receive a series of electric shocks. The participants who were told they had taken a pill that would cause effects like a pounding heart, shaky hands, and other effects that we would recognize as arousal were able to tolerate higher levels of shock than those who were given other information about the effects of the pill. The pill was actually a placebo. The misattribution of the fear symptoms (which were objectively due only to the shock) to the pill resulted in a reduction of fear itself.

Studies in the aggression area have shown the influence of misattribution on hostile responding and feelings of anger (see Rule and Neasdale, 1976). In these studies, a participant is treated badly by another (typically, a confederate). In addition, there is heightened arousal from an extraneous source, such as loud noise, erotic stimuli, or physical exercise. Under the heightened arousal conditions, angered participants acted more aggressively than participants who lacked additional arousal. However, the additional arousal did not have this effect if it was attributed to its true source (see Zillman, 1978).

The arousal-plus-cognition theory of emotions proposed by Schachter has been severely challenged (see Marshall and Zimbardo, 1979; Maslach, 1979, and Reisenzein, 1983). Among the objections to the model are the following issues:

1. Unexplained arousal is akin to free-floating anxiety and has a negative quality, rather than being a neutral state to which any emotional label can be applied.
2. When individuals seek to explain a state of arousal, they do not use merely the behavior of others in their environment. Rather, many other sources of information are called on, particularly their own personal histories. That is, they search for prior occasions on which they felt this negative arousal state to explain its occurrence now. The behavior of others may dictate or suggest how one should behave in the situation, but it does not provide information for why one feels as one does. For example, if a confederate were behaving in a completely inappropriate manner, the subject would not use this action to infer something about his or her own emotional state. In this instance, the attribution for the confederate's behavior may not be at all applicable to the subject.

A number of other investigations contradict Schachter's position and suggest that cognitions are sufficient to produce emotional behavior. To demonstrate that the energizing, physiological effects of arousal do not influence emotional expression, Valins (1966) presented fake information to his subjects. At times the subjects overheard bogus heart-rate information indicating that they were in a heightened state of arousal while viewing slides of female models in various states of undress. After viewing the stimuli, the subjects rated the attractiveness of the women. It was found that the women associated with a perceived change in heart rate were rated more attractive than the pictures of women not linked with this bogus information. Valins therefore concluded that internal events such as arousal act only as a source of information to the actor; actual arousal is not necessary for emotional experience.

Further evidence that arousal is not necessary for the experience of emotion comes from recent studies of spinal cord injured patients (Chwalisz, Diener, and Gallagher, 1988). This injury prevents autonomic feedback to the brain, depending on the degree of the injury. According to Schachter's theory of emotion, these individuals should not experience emotion, or should experience it in greatly reduced intensity. However, Chwalisz et al. (1988) report intense emotional feelings, thus contradicting the Schachter theory and some earlier studies that were not well-controlled.

The data from Valins (1966), Chwalisz et al. (1988), and others suggest that cognitions are sufficient to produce emotional behavior. Thus, we turn to the cognitive approach to emotional experience.

Cognitive Theories

The cognitive position concerning emotions is relatively straightforward-emotions depend on the interpretation or meaning of an event. Thus, "cold" knowledge, or "hot" appraisal (which includes an interpretation of the personal significance of an event) determine feelings (Lazarus and Smith, 1988).

Consider, for example, a simple classification of emotions proposed by Mowrer (1960). Mowrer distinguished between situations connoting increases or decreases in the likelihood of undergoing positive or negative experiences. Increases in the perceived likelihood of experiencing positive events gives rise to hope, while decreases in this estimate produce disappointment. Considering negative events, increased likelihood promotes fear, while decreases in their anticipated appearance produces relief (see Fig. 15.1). Note, then, that the only determinants of emotion are cognitions about the change in probability of an event and the perception of the positivity of that event. Arousal is not discussed as a determinant of these emotions.

The scheme proposed by Mowrer is obviously limited in that it addresses only four among the many, many emotions. In a similar manner, Higgins, Strauman, and Klein (1986) have developed a classification scheme that examines four emotions, but the emotions are quite different from those addressed by Mowrer.

Like Mowrer, Higgins and colleagues first differentiate two cognitive determinants of emotion. As we saw earlier in the book, they differentiate the self according to an "ideal" self (how one would ideally like to be) and an "ought" self (a representation of the attributes that someone should possess; see Chapter 10). They also distinguish between the frames of reference according to which one is judged—from the perspective of the self or from the perspective of others. This again results in a 2 X 2 classification scheme, as shown in Figure 15.2. Figure 15.2 reveals that if there is a discrepancy between an ideal and a perceived actual self when judged from one's personal point of view, then dissatisfaction is experienced. Thus, for example, if one would like to be smarter than he or she is, then the affect is to feel dissatisfied. However, when this shortcoming is considered from the viewpoint of others, then one experiences shame. Turning next to the ought self, if one thinks he or she is less honest than should be, then guilt is felt. However, if judged from the perspective of others, then the emotional experience is insecurity. Note again that a simple division of thinking is brought creatively to bear on a small subset of feelings.

When comparing the disparate emotions addressed by these two theories, one becomes aware of the difficulties of a cognitive approach to emotion: one must be able to specify which cognitions are linked to which emotions. Inasmuch as there are myriads of pertinent thoughts, there also must be classification systems that reduce the number of thoughts to underlying dimensions, yet this classification system must remain rich and diverse enough to account for a wide range of emotions. Mowrer and Higgins and colleagues had rather sparse classification systems, based respectively on dimensions of changes in probability of an event as well as perceived valence of the event, and types of self and perspective of evaluation.

	Positive event	Negative event
Signaled increase	Hope	Fear
Signaled decrease	Disappointment	Relief

FIGURE 15.1 Mowrer's Analysis of Four Emotions

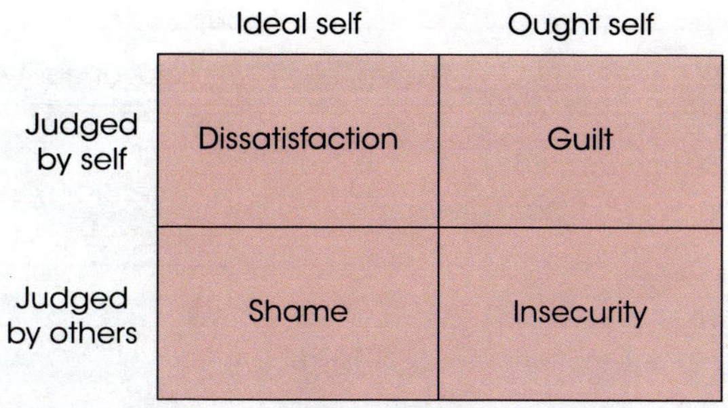

	Ideal self	Ought self
Judged by self	Dissatisfaction	Guilt
Judged by others	Shame	Insecurity

FIGURE 15.2 Four Emotions as Interpreted by Higgins et al. (1986)

An Attributional Approach to Emotions

Attribution theory was previously introduced in this text when traits and the trait-state distinction were discussed. Here, we want to consider how attribution theorists relate their ideas to emotion (see Weiner, 1985, 1986).

Attribution theory is concerned with perceptions of causality. This approach embraces two basic questions: First, how are causal beliefs reached? For example, how does one "know" that failure was due to lack of ability, as opposed to insufficient effort? The second question relates to the function of attributions. For example, what difference does it make, or what are the consequences, of an attribution to low ability as opposed to lack of effort?

Attribution theorists have argued that causes such as ability and effort can be compared and contrasted on three dimensions of thought: locus (is the cause inside or outside of the person?); stability (is the cause temporary or stable?); and controllability (is the cause something the person can volitionally change?). Ability (or aptitude) typically is construed as inside the person, stable, and uncontrollable, while effort also is thought of as internal to the person, but unstable and controllable. Each of the causal dimensions has been related to particular emotions and actions.

1. *Locus of causality.* It has been argued that internal attributions for success are necessary for the experience of pride. Thus, for example, one feels proud if high performance on an exam is attributed to ability or effort. However, if that high performance was because the exam was very easy (all the other students also did well), then pride will not be felt. Pride, in turn, is a reinforcer that increases the likelihood that similar actions will be undertaken again. Hence, attribution of success in achievement domains to ability and/or effort will raise the likelihood that the individual will engage in future achievement actions.

   The relation between internal attributions and self-esteem is part of common knowledge and is used in everyday interactions. Thus, when rejecting a person for a date, the rejector does not say: "You are too (tall, short, fat, thin, dumb, etc.)." It is known that these internal attributions will hurt the feelings of the rejected other. Instead, an external attribution (and perhaps a lie) is communicated that does not result in a loss of self-esteem for the other (e.g., "My parents are in town; I have an exam tomorrow") (see Folkes, 1982).

2. *Causal stability.* The stability of a cause connotes whether the cause might change in the future. Failure at math attributed to low math aptitude, for example, implies that the cause will not change so that there will be future failures. On the other hand, failure perceived as due to lack of effort gives rise to the belief that the future might produce a better outcome, inasmuch as effort can be increased. It therefore follows that hope (failure ascribed to something unstable) and hopelessness (failure ascribed to something unchanging) are related to perceived causal stability.

3. *Causal controllability.* Some causes, such as effort and strategy, can be personally changed. On the other hand, causes such as aptitude, the weather conditions, luck, etc. cannot be willfully altered. Perceived controllability relates to a variety of affects (see Figure 15.3) including:

	Attribution	
	Lack of effort	Lack of ability
Self-generated emotion	Guilt	Shame
Other-generated emotion	Anger	Pity

FIGURE 15.3 Self- and Other-Affected Consequences of Failure Due to Lack of Effort Versus Lack of Ability

a. *Anger*. If negative self-related outcomes are controllably caused by others, then anger is experienced. One is angry at a roommate who has not cleaned the house, at others for lying, and so on. Anger gives rise to the desire to "eliminate" the other. This association also is part of common knowledge. Hence, if one has broken a social contract by, for example, arriving late for an appointment, an uncontrollable reason is communicated (e.g., "The traffic was heavy"). One would not reveal "I took my time because it was a nice day," for this would arouse anger.

b. *Pity*. Pity is experienced when a victim has no control over his or her fate. Thus, we pity the elderly, the sick, those struck by natural disasters, etc. Pity (sympathy) gives rise to desires to help others, to put the situation back into a state of balance.

c. *Guilt*. Guilt is linked to self-blame regarding the violation of moral codes and values. Thus, one is guilty for lying, or cheating, or other situations in which there was personal controllability. Guilt gives rise to the desire to make amends; under usual conditions, therefore, it is a positive motivator.

A different approach to the emotions of shame and guilt is suggested by Tagney (1991) and her colleagues. In her model, shame tends to be associated with the self, while guilt tends to be associated with the behavior (Covert, Tangney, Maddux, and Heleno, 2003). An interesting demonstration comes from a study that looked at what a person would undo following either shame- or guilt-inducing experiences (Niedenthal, Tangney, and Gavanski, 1994). People in the guilt-inducing situations tended to want to undo the behavior. People in the shame-inducing situations wanted to change something about themselves. Because guilt is associated with behavior, it may be possible to repair the outcome of the behavior. Shame, on the other hand, being so closely tied to the self, may make a person withdraw from others.

Source: Andrey_Popov/Shutterstock

What emotion would you feel if your roommate broke your television? What emotion would you feel if you broke your roommate's television?

Appraisal Approach to Emotions

appraisal The meaning a person imposes on the current situation.

Attributions are one type of **appraisal**—they refer to the meaning a person imposes on the environment (see Lazarus, 1982; 1991). But attributions are only one among many possible types of appraisal, each with emotional significance. Smith and Ellsworth (1985, 1987) have proposed eight dimensions of appraisal in differentiating emotional responses. The dimensions are:

1. pleasantness: the extent to which a situation is perceived positively
2. anticipated effort: the extent to which the person feels effort is needed

3. attentional activity: the extent to which the person wants to attend
4. certainty: the extent to which the person understands what will happen
5. responsibility: who brought about the situation
6. control: who the person perceives is controlling the situation
7. legitimacy: the extent to which the situation is perceived as fair or unfair
8. perceived obstacles: the extent to which the person perceives problems that hamper goal attainment

These dimensions have been found to be associated with (produce) a wide variety of emotional experience. For example, it has been reported that hope is associated with appraisals of personal control, certainty, and anticipated effort. Surprise, on the other hand, is associated with uncertainty and external control. It is evident that the appraisal approach, by including many dimensions of thinking, is the most complex of the cognitive approaches presented thus far.

The Structure of Emotion

Basic Emotions

Emotions are also seen by many as being a product of evolution and therefore as having a biological basis (Izard, 1992). This implies that emotions are not merely distracting annoyances but rather biologically adaptive; and several theorists hold that emotions organize and activate the organism to take adaptive action. Frijda and Swagerman (1987) feel that "emotions are parts of a provision for ensuring the safeguarding and satisfaction of the [organism's] goals" (p. 237).

Rather than asking about the dimensions of emotions, some have suggested that there are "basic" or **primary emotions**, with the other emotions derived from these. Based on his study of facial expressions and observations of children, Izard (1977) suggested ten primary emotions: interest, enjoyment, surprise, distress, anger, disgust, contempt, fear, shame/shyness, and guilt. Quite similarly, as discussed briefly in Chapter 1, Ekman and Friesen (1975) isolated six primary emotions—fear, surprise, disgust, anger, happiness, and sadness (see Highlight 15.1 on the emotion of disgust). Notice in nearly every list of primary emotions, the number of positive emotions is fewer than the number of negative emotions.

Plutchik (1980) also suggests a small number of primary emotions based on his Psychoevolutionary theory. He believes that emotions are communication and survival mechanisms and are evolutionary adaptations. Consequently, emotions have a genetic basis. In this model, situations are evaluated, and if relevant to the organism, they will lead to

primary emotions The basic, irreducible emotions.

HIGHLIGHT 15.1

Experiences of Disgust

Rozin and Fallon (1987) have recently reported research on the emotion of disgust. In a series of studies they and their colleagues have found that individuals: prefer not to drink a glass of juice in which a sterilized cockroach has been placed and then removed; prefer not to consume chocolate fudge shaped as dog feces; prefer not to wear a clean, laundered shirt of someone whom they dislike, such as Hitler; prefer not to drink from a bowl of soup that they have spit in with their own saliva; prefer not to lick their own blood from a bandage (though they will lick fresh blood from a pricked finger); prefer to hold a rubber drain mat in their lips rather than a piece of rubber imitation vomit from a novelty store; and prefer not to eat soup out of a brand-new bed pan nor to eat soup stirred by a brand-new fly swatter.

Rozin and Fallon believe that the emotion of disgust is ultimately based on the eating of food and includes as an important part the avoidance of contamination. They claim that virtually all the above reactions are based on a kind of superstitious avoidance of contamination, and they note that individuals tend to base such reactions more on the laws of magical thinking than on strict rationality.

physiological changes and impulses associated with the emotion and stimulus. The emotions can be arranged in a circle of similarities similar to a color wheel. A small set of emotions are primary emotions, and other emotions are a blend of the primary emotions. Plutchik (1994) suggests that emotions can vary in terms of intensity and duration. At low intensity, we would consider it a mood. At high intensity, we would tend to label it as an emotion. If a person tends to experience a particular emotion frequently, we might even consider it a personality trait. We might describe someone as quarrelsome or gloomy or timid. If the emotion tends to be extreme often or for an especially long duration, we would consider it to be a form of psychopathology. Prolonged sadness is labeled depression. Fear is associated with post-traumatic stress disorder, or other anxiety disorders.

There are those who question whether there are any emotions that could be considered primary or basic (Ortony and Turner, 1990). For instance, Ortony and Turner note that different theorists produce different lists of primary emotions. Even the evidence that various facial expressions are associated with discrete emotional states (see Chapter 1) is being challenged by research that does not find such clear relationships in young children (Thompson, 1993). Instead of experiencing discrete, separable emotions, some suggest that we experience subtly nuanced blends of emotional states (Thompson, 1993).

A study that sheds some light on these issues was conducted by Zelenski and Larson (2000). The participants were from a personality psychology course, like many of you reading this text. The participants filled out an emotion scale three times a day for twenty-eight days. In this study, people tended to report more frequent positive emotions than negative emotions, and the positive emotions were rated as more intense than the negative emotions. The experience of state emotions revealed that positive emotions tended to blend together, but negative emotions tended to be experienced as discrete emotions. When considering emotions at a trait level, it appears that a dimensional model works best, with the dimensions being positive affect and negative affect.

Therefore, while it is probably safe to say that most theorists still believe that there are basic emotions, the issue may be more complex than previously thought. If there are basic emotions, there does appear to be some convergence that fear, anger, surprise, and a positive general emotion such as happiness are among them.

Individual Differences in Emotional Reactivity

The implication of models like Plutchik's is that people differ in the content of their emotional life. People also differ consistently in the intensity of their emotional responses (see Larson and Diener, 1985, 1987). We all know of individuals who seem to be highly emotional and react to each situation as though it were a matter of life and death, while others are quite "cool" in the face of either great adversity or great gain. Research has shown that the same individuals who react so strongly to positive events also react strongly to negative events. Furthermore, individual differences in affective intensity are stable over time and across situations. We can think of this as a person's **emotional style**.

emotional style The size of emotional reactions that a person typically experiences.

What might account for this emotional style difference? Larson, Diener, and Cropanzano (1987) suggested that particular cognitions augment the intensity of emotionality. They contend that tendencies to personalize events (overestimate the degree that events are related to themselves and be excessively absorbed in personal meanings), to selectively attend to the most emotional aspects of events, and to see the event as quite general (or "blowing the situation out of proportion") increase the level of emotional responding. Research has supported these hypotheses, thus documenting that not only do cognitions determine the direction or kind of feeling that is experienced, but also the intensity of that experience.

Mood

As indicated earlier in this chapter, mood differs from emotion in that it is of greater duration and not tied to any specific object. Hence, surprise and pity are not considered mood states, since they have a short time span and a specific elicitor. However, happy, sad, and even angry are terms that can refer to mood states.

To study the effects of mood on cognition and behavior, psychologists have devised a number of ways to induce positive and negative moods in the laboratory. One method is to have participants read a series of positive or negative statements to themselves, such as "things will get better and better today" or "everything seems empty and futile." They might also be told to then think about the most positive or negative of these statements. A second methodology is to play music that elicits positive or negative states (Niedenthal, Setterlund, and Jones, 1994). When using instrumental music, this approach has the advantage of not being confounded with the words used to induce the mood. Still a third procedure used in field investigations is to have participants find money in a phone booth, be handed a gift by a "survey taker," or have some other small but positive event take place. In all these situations, the experimenter then examines the effect of the positive or negative mood induction on other variables of psychological interest.

It has been well-documented that background mood states exert profound influences over a wide variety of thoughts and behaviors. For example, individuals in depressed mood states exhibit less interest in social, leisure, intimate, and strenuous activities than those exposed to a positive mood induction (Cunningham, 1988). In addition, and perhaps unexpectedly, persons in positive mood states take less risk than those in negative states (Isen, Nygren, and Ashby, 1988). It appears that people feeling happy are cautious optimists: they report higher probabilities of gains and lower probabilities of losses, yet they avoid risk. They are especially sensitive to loss, so that taking a chance seems not to be worth the risk.

People appear to be faster at recognizing emotion congruent information, so happy people put into a happy mood recognize happy related information faster than people in the sad condition (Niedenthal and Setterlund, 1994). One of the best-documented effects of mood is on memory and judgments of others. When in a happy mood, people make more positive judgments about others and recall more positive facts about them than when they are in a sad mood (Forgas and Bower, 1987). This also is the case with one's self—individuals in depressed moods tend to retrieve negative past events and negative characteristics about themselves to a greater extent than those in a positive mood. Thus, mood tends to be self-perpetuating, which obviously has implications for mental health, coping, and emotional well-being.

We now turn from the topic of emotion to that of stress, which obviously also has emotional significance. Just as in the study of emotion, the way one appraises a stressful situation has important implication for the consequences of that stress, and individual differences also influence this process.

The idiom "rose-colored glasses" refers to seeing the world in an artificially positive way, but it is possible that people in a positive mood really do see more positive things.

Source: XiXinXing/Shutterstock

Stress

In physics, **stress** is a force that acts on a body, producing some kind of strain. In the social world, it also is the case that stressors such as war, fire, and impoverished conditions put a "strain" on the organism. In addition, there is accumulating evidence that any circumstances requiring a change in life pattern, such as marriage, a new job, or the birth of a child, are stressors.

stress Any circumstance requiring a change in life pattern.

Stress connotes an organism's response to stressful conditions. Stress reactions are determined by many factors, including the characteristics of the stressor, such as its intensity and duration; the availability of social support systems, such as the family and the church; and characteristics of the person, such as prior experience and the ability to use coping defenses.

Life-Event Stress

The role of stressful life events in the etiology of various illnesses has been a prominent field of investigation in the last decade, although the possibility of a connection between stress and illness has long been suspected (see Kobasa, 1979). This research has focused on the relationship between recent life events that require personal change and the onset of an illness. It has been contended that the more such events have occurred in the recent past, the greater the likelihood that one will become seriously ill.

Many of these investigations have used some version of a scale constructed by Holmes and Rahe (1967); see Table 15.1. The items on the scale represent typical incidents of stressful change; the respondent reports which of these events happened within the last six to twenty-four months, depending on the study. Each stressor is given a value, usually determined by judges' ratings, indicating the necessary readjustment that the event requires. Note from Table 15.1 that death of spouse (Highlight 15.2 discusses grief in more detail) and divorce were judged to require great readjustment, whereas a vacation or a minor law violation were believed to involve little change in one's normal routine. Also note that $10,000 was the dividing point for large versus small mortgages in 1967.

TABLE 15.1 The Holmes-Rahe Schedule of Recent Life Events

Life event	Scale value
Death of spouse	100
Divorce	73
Marital separation	65
Jail term	63
Death of close family member	63
Personal injury or illness	53
Marriage	50
Fired from work	47
Marital reconciliation	45
Retirement	45
Change in family member's health	44
Pregnancy	40
Sex difficulties	39
Gain of new family member	39
Business readjustment	39
Change in financial state	38
Death of close friend	37
Career change	36
Change in number of arguments with spouse	35
Mortgage over $10,000	31
Foreclosure of mortgage or loan	30
Change in responsibilities at work	29
Son or daughter leaving home	29
Trouble with in-laws	29

Outstanding personal achievement	28
Spouse begins or stops work	26
Starting or finishing school	26
Change in living conditions	25
Revision of personal habits	24
Trouble with boss	23
Change in work hours or conditions	20
Change in residence	20
Change in schools	20
Change in recreation habits	19
Change in church activities	19
Change in social activities	18
Mortgage or loan less than $10,000	17
Change in sleeping habits	16
Change in number of family gatherings	15
Change in eating habits	15
Vacation	13
Christmas season	12
Minor violations of the law	11

Source: Reprinted with permission from *Journal of Psychosomatic Research, II,* T. H. Holmes and R. H. Rahe, "The Social Readjustment Rating Scale," copyright © 1967, Pergamon Press, Ltd.

A great deal of research has demonstrated that scores on the scale shown in Table 15.1 relate significantly to the onset of illness. For example, Rahe (1974) found that sailors who began a cruise with a high score on the scale suffered more illnesses at sea than sailors who started the voyage with low stress scores. This general finding has been replicated many times, using procedures that are both retrospective (data concerning participants' remembrance of stressful events and illness in the past are collected at the same time) and prospective (stressful events are assessed before illness) (see reviews in Maddi, Bartone, and Puccetti, 1987; Rabkin and Streuning, 1976). It also has been found that at times a severe stressor, such as the unexpected loss of a spouse or child, can result in long-term distress. In one study interviewing people who had lost their spouse in an automobile accident, depression and lack of resolution of the event were evident among some respondents four to seven years after the loss (Lehman, Wortman, and Williams, 1987).

Although the reported research findings have been quite consistent, the investigations are not without their critics. The Holmes and Rahe scale includes positive, negative, controllable and uncontrollable, events. Many investigators have argued that these should be separated, and that uncontrollable negative events are the important precursors to illness. In addition, respondents often do not answer the questions in the same way at a second testing session (low test-retest reliability), and it has been found that the correlation between a wife's responses about her husband and a husband's responses about himself are lower than desired (low interrater reliability). That is, there is likely to be inaccuracy of

The Myths of Coping with Loss

There are a number of assumptions that people maintain about how others respond to serious loss, such as death of a loved one. It is expected that there will be a period of intense distress and that failure to experience such distress indicates a psychological problem. Further, it is assumed that successful adjustment to loss requires that persons "work through" their feelings of grief and not deny them. However, it also is anticipated that within a reasonable period of time people recover from their loss and return to their typical level of functioning (see Wortman and Silver, 1989). In contrast to these naive beliefs, it has been found that: (a) there is not invariably intense distress after a major loss or after a severe disabling injury; (b) those who fail to experience distress do not necessarily have difficulties later; to the contrary, those most depressed following a loss also are most depressed one or two years later; (c) a substantial minority of individuals continue to exhibit distress for a much longer time period than is normally assumed; and (d) individuals are not always able to achieve some resolution to the loss. In sum, contrary to universal stage theories of distress, some persons do not show distress initially or even following a period of time, while others continue to remain in a state of high distress. There are some individuals who follow the predicted course from high to low stress, but other patterns are quite prevalent.

Grief is a common initial reaction to the stress of loss. (Michael Grecco/Stock, Boston)

Source: Syda Productions /Shutterstock

reporting. Another problem is that both a life event and an illness could be due to a third cause. For example, both being fired from work and subsequent illness might be brought about by fatigue, in which case job change does not *cause* illness, even though the two factors vary together. Finally, some of the question items, such as mortgage payment and pregnancy, may be irrelevant to particular classes or groups.

The model relating life stress to health thus far has been relatively simple:

$$\text{Stressful life events} \rightarrow \text{Adverse health change}$$

To increase the predictability of adverse health change, some investigators (e.g., Lazarus, 1985) have in fact shifted focus from major stressful events to the ongoing stresses and strains of daily living. Daily **hassles** with family, work, physical abilities, money, and even weather are considered proximal or immediate determinants of stress, whereas major life events are more distal influences.

hassles The stresses and strains of everyday living.

Investigations of daily hassles typically ask participants to complete a daily hassle scale each night before going to bed. In addition, a daily health record also is kept which asks about a number of health-related symptoms such as headaches, digestive system complaints, etc. Alternatively, phone interviews can be used to probe for the experience of daily hassles (Almeida, Wethington, and Kessler, 2002). It has often been reported that there are significant relations between daily stress and the occurrence of both concurrent and subsequent health problems (e.g., DeLongis, Folkman, and Lazarus, 1988).

Rather than focusing on external psychosocial factors that might increase health problems, others have been concerned with factors within the person that augment health risk. Foremost among these has been the so-called Type A personality and its relation to coronary heart disease. Clinical observations of cardiac patients led two cardiologists to suggest a coronary-prone behavioral pattern that might explain the association between high-pressure job environments and coronary heart disease (thus, the alternative term, coronary prone behavior). The early observations indicated that a type of person who engages in a continuous struggle to do more and more in less and less time is prone to a coronary heart attack. This behavioral pattern includes time urgency, competitiveness, and aggression and hostility that are aroused when obstacles are encountered (Matthews, 1988).

Since its original postulation, there has been a huge literature regarding the Type A personality and its relation to heart disease. Recently, most of the evidence is against the hypothesis that Type A behavior is a reliable predictor of death (i.e., Šmigelskas, Žemaitienė, Julkunen, and Kauhanen, 2015) and coronary heart disease (Siegman, Townsend, Civelek, and Blumenthal, 2000). Meta-analyses are revealing a lack of relation between Type A personality and either coronary heart disease (Myrtek, 2001) or cardiac related mortality (Mathews et al., 2004). However, both of those meta-analyses did show a relationship with hostility. People who show higher rates of dispositional hostility have higher rates of heart-related problems. However, Myrtek (2001) did point out that the effect size was so small as to be nearly meaningless.

Effects of Stress on Thinking

Stress can have negative impacts on other aspects of functioning such as thinking and problem solving. Under stress, individuals often make mistakes, become obsessed with detail, and are easily distracted from the task at hand. Pennebaker (1989) argued that there are different levels of thought ranging from more abstract and complex levels to more concrete and specific levels, and he has suggested that stress affects the level of one's thinking. He assesses level of thinking by having participants write their thoughts out in a "stream of consciousness" manner. In one research study, participants heard a loud noise as they wrote out their thoughts. Half of the participants were told that they had control over the noise—they could turn it off if it became unbearable—and the other half believed they had no control over the noise. While no participants turned the noise off, those who believed they had control wrote thoughts at a higher level of thinking than participants who believed they had no control.

Coping with Stress

Thus far, the factors that contribute to stress and, in turn, illness have been examined. But we have failed to consider how individuals deal with stress and how that process influences the onset of illness. As Folkman and Lazarus (1988) state:

> There is a long-standing and widely held conviction among researchers and practitioners in the fields of mental health and behavioral medicine that the ways people cope with the demands of stressful events make a difference in how they feel emotionally (p. 466).

The addition of such coping processes complicates both Models A and B, for additional mediating processes are proposed that act as buffers to stress, as shown in Model C, which builds on Model A.

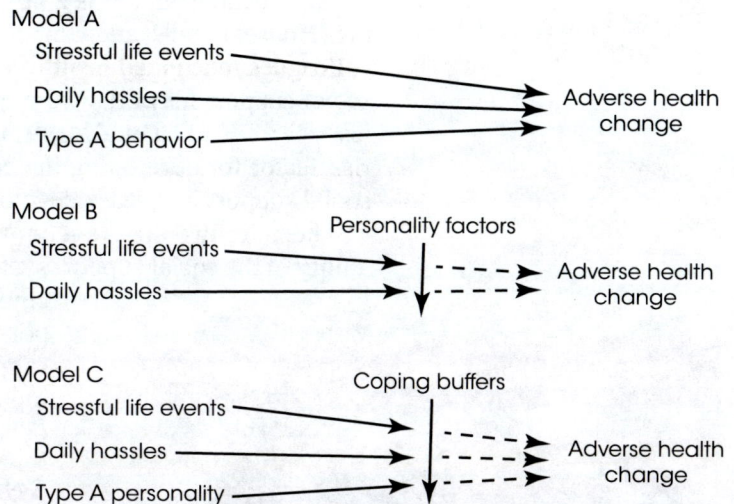

Model A
Stressful life events
Daily hassles
Type A behavior
Adverse health change

Model B
Stressful life events
Daily hassles
Personality factors
Adverse health change

Model C
Stressful life events
Daily hassles
Type A personality
Coping buffers
Adverse health change

A number of **coping** strategies to deal with stress have been identified, including confrontation (standing one's ground), distancing (acting as if nothing happened), self-control (keeping feelings to oneself), seeking social support from others, accepting responsibility, escaping and avoiding (eating, taking drugs, etc.), planful problem solving, and reappraisal (growing as a person as a result of the action) (see Folkman, Lazarus, Dunkel-Shetter, DeLongis, and Gruen, 1986).

coping The process by which a person deals with stress.

Of the ways to cope with stress, two components have the greatest impact. The first is how a person perceives the stress and one's ability to respond. The second is the impact of social support.

Appraisal and Problem-Focused Coping

primary appraisal The evaluation of what is happening and determining that impact on one's well-being.

Appraisal is described earlier in the chapter, but we return to it here. The first step in the appraisal process requires and understanding of what is happening and determining the impact on well-being (Lazarus, 1991; Smith and Lazarus, 1990). This is typically known as **primary appraisal**. The second step is determining whether a person has the skills to deal with the situation. This is known as **secondary appraisal**.

secondary appraisal The evaluation of whether one has the skills to deal with a stressor.

This second step can lead to planful problem solving, where the person focuses on solving the problem. This step requires dealing with the problem straight on and can actually solve the problem that is causing the stress. For instance, talking to a spouse who is not doing his or her fair share of the housework is more likely to lead to the person sharing the work than ignoring the problem. Some situations cannot actually be solved—for instance, caring for a loved one suffering from a terminal illness. The illness, of course, cannot be cured, but the caregiver can focus on the things that can be controlled, such as picking up medicines and scheduling medical appointments.

In field research, Folkman and Lazarus (1988) assessed how various types of coping affect emotions of worried/fearful, disgusted/angry, confident, and pleased/happy. Both coping and affect were assessed with retrospective reports. It was found, for example, that planful problem-solving was positively associated with confidence and their pleased/happy scale, while confrontive coping and distancing were positively associated with a disgust/anger scale and negatively related to confidence and happiness among younger married couples.

Social Support

social support The friends, family, and groups that a person can rely on.

The other major influence on successful coping with stress is **social support**. Social support is so widely understood to be important that there are over 1,100 articles published on the topic per year (Taylor, 2011). This research has been in vogue because it appears to buffer the effects of life stress on health and well-being (Cohen and Wills, 1985) and because it suggests interventions for stressed individuals that will facilitate adjustment.

The impact of social support impacts both psychological adjustment and physical health. Social isolation is a larger risk factor for all-cause mortality than cigarette smoking (House, Landis, and Umberson, 1988). In an interesting set of research, Cohen and his colleagues inoculated healthy volunteers with a cold virus. People with better developed social support networks were less likely to develop colds, or their cold symptoms were less severe (Cohen et al., 1997). They also found that severe chronic stress was a greater risk factor for developing the cold than acute stress (Cohen et al., 1998). The impact on social support in disease development and recovery is extensive (see Taylor, 2011).

There are two different components to social support. The first is the perceived availability of the social support system—for instance, friends, family, and support groups. We could consider this to be a breadth component on social support. The second part is the quality of support received. Social support may provide assistance with tasks or with reinterpreting the situation and provide reassurance and encouragement (Thoits, 1995). Often, simply talking about it helps.

Having a group of friends who can provide support is one of the best predictors of coping well with stress.

Self-Disclosure and Expression

One of the major values of a social support network is that it may provide the opportunity for the expression of emotion and the sharing of traumatic experiences. It has long been held by both lay people and professional therapists that "confession is good for the soul." Individuals who come to therapy are encouraged to "get it out" and "get it off their chests." (See Highlight 15.3 for a brief discussion of differences in the effects of crying, depending on type of social support.) To what degree is the expression of one's emotions and the sharing of one's traumatic experiences helpful in coping with stress?

Why Do People Cry?

Although the eyes of all mammals are moistened and soothed by tears, only human beings shed tears in response to emotional stress; yet we know nothing about this uniquely human behavior. A recent theory suggests that tears help to relieve stress by ridding the body of potentially harmful stress-induced chemicals. Thus far, it has been demonstrated that emotionally induced tears have a higher protein content than tears produced in response to eye irritation, such as that caused by a cut onion. However, stress-related chemical differences have yet to be identified.

Other provocative evidence supports this idea. For example, one report found that people with stress-related illnesses cry less than their healthy counterparts. Who a person cries with and the setting influence whether a person feels better or worse (Blysma, Croon, Vingerhoets, and Rottenburg, 2011) after "a good cry." Though, it does matter who a person cries with. In our society, it has been documented that men cry much less frequently than women, and they appear more susceptible to ulcers and some other stress-related problems.

Attachment style appears to have an impact as well. People with the preoccupied style cry more and people with the dismissing style cry less than people with a secure attachment style (Laan, van Assen, and Vingerhoets, 2012).

Pennebaker (1990) has reported an extensive series of studies documenting the positive effects of "letting it out." Pennebaker reports that studies of those who suffer traumatic experiences in childhood have found that those who do not talk about their experiences have more health problems as adults than those who do talk about their experiences. Similarly, those who have experienced recent traumas, such as the suicide or accidental death of a loved one, are more likely to have coped well with the loss if they have disclosed it than if they have not.

However, expression and disclosure need not be through discussion with another person. Pennebaker has found that even extensive writing about one's traumatic experiences is beneficial (Pennebaker and Smyth, 2016). In one study, Pennebaker (1990) and his colleagues had undergraduate participants write about the most significant traumatic experience in their lives. Pennebaker discovered that those who were asked to write extensively about their thoughts and feelings showed a subsequent 50 percent reduction in visits to the student health center, compared to those who did not write about their thoughts and feelings.

A question concerning expression of traumatic experiences is whether the benefits of expression come primarily from the catharsis and discharge of the emotions involved or whether it is also important that some cognitive process of reworking the meaning in one's life also take place. In Pennebaker's study, those who were instructed to express only their emotions, as well as those instructed to express only their thoughts, showed less benefits than those who expressed both their emotions and thoughts. This is consistent with research on the expression of anger, in which Bohart (1980) concluded that sheer anger expression by itself does not appear to be beneficial, while anger expression accompanied by cognitive insight does, thus showing the interaction of emotion and cognition.

Multicultural Aspects of Stress

Several writers have pointed out that our dominant models of stress need to be modified to take into account the experience of diverse groups (Cervantes and Castro, 1985; Slavin, Ranier, McCreary, and Gowda, 1990). For instance, issues of acculturation (see Chapter 11) appear to be important as causes of stress for members of ethnic minority groups. Studies show that those who have not successfully resolved issues of acculturation experience more stress (Cervantes and Castro, 1985; Slavin et al., 1990). As expected, though, Mexican American college students who have strong parental support and used problem-focused coping experienced less anxiety and depression (Crockett et al., 2007). Similarly, on the Holmes-Rahe scale it is events that occur to oneself or to one's spouse or children that are most influential sources of stress. However, in one study of Mexican participants (Hough, McGarvey, Graham, and Timbers, 1982), it was found that illness symptoms were most associated with events that occurred to important others in one's environment (other than oneself, one's spouse, or one's children). This study illustrates how the meaning of *stressor* depends on how one's culture construes events. Social support can also take different forms. Kim, Taylor, and Sherman (2008) report that east Asians and Asian Americans are less likely to explicitly seek support from their support network, but perceiving the existence of the network helped.

Individual Differences in Stress Reactions and Hardiness

Inasmuch as there are individual differences in the preference and use of defenses, it might be expected that some persons are better able to cope with stress than others. There is accumulating evidence that the *manner* in which one copes with stress is as important as the *amount* of objective stress encountered. Kobasa (1979) examined the impact of stressful life events on the onset of illness among two groups of executives: those reporting high stress followed by illness and those who did not became ill after stressful encounters. There appeared to be something trait-like in the executives who coped well with the stress, which was labeled "**hardiness**." Hardiness appears to buffer stress because it is associated with the use of effective coping strategies. Three components contribute to hardiness (Kobasa, Maddi, and Kahn, 1982; Maddi, 2002):

hardiness An individual difference that helps a person cope with stress.

1. Commitment (they have a sense of values and goals and are personally important, rather than feeling alienated and isolated)
2. Control (they believe they are capable of having an effect on the outcomes rather than feeling powerless and passive)
3. Challenge (they believe that change and stress are a normal part of life and change and stress provide occasions to grow rather than believing things are always easy and comfortable)

Like the Type A behavior pattern, this individual difference approach has received not only a great deal of attention, but also a great deal of criticism. First, of the components of hardiness, only control and challenge are predictive of health (Hull, Treuren, and Vernelli, 1987). In addition, the "nonhardy" person who reports experiencing no control and who has no commitments also scores high on trait neuroticism. It is known that neurotic individuals also report high levels of physical complaints (Allred and Smith, 1989). This suggests that hardiness not be a buffer to stress, but rather that the lack of control and commitment covaries with poor adjustment and therefore is associated with illness, or tendency to report more illness.

Hardiness appears to be developed in some people by childhood experiences of stress. These children successfully deal with stress through parents or other adults encouraging them to believe that it is important, that they can achieve it, and that they can grow through what is learned (Khoshbasa, 1999). It also appears that it is possible to develop the habits of hardiness through training programs (Maddi, Kahn, and Maddi, 1998). College-age students who received hardiness training early in college had higher hardiness scores, as well as a higher GPA over the following two years (Maddi, Harvey, Khoshbasa, Fazel, and Resureccion, 2009).

Conclusion

In conclusion, it is very clear that stress is associated with health and psychological adjustment. Coping with stress is best accomplished by planful problem solving, appraising the stressor as a challenge that can be overcome, and having a supportive social network. (Go make some friends as soon as you get done studying.)

Summary

1. Emotions are "passions" as opposed to actions; their onset does not appear to be subject to volitional control.
2. Emotions have a number of distinguishing characteristics, including positive or negative quality, intensity, facial expressions and bodily postures, antecedent thoughts, and consequent actions. Not all emotions have all these characteristics.
3. Schachter and Singer contend that the process of emotion begins with a state of arousal. The individual then labels this arousal according to the cues in the social situation. This conception is now doubted.
4. Cognitive emotion theorists identify those characteristics of thought, such as increased or decreased likelihood of an event, perceived ideal vs. real self, and causal attributions, that give rise to specific emotions.
5. New models of emotion integrate cognitive, arousal, and other bodily aspects. Emotion is seen as resulting from a network of interrelationships. Further, emotion is seen as adaptive, mobilizing the organism for action.
6. People characteristically differ in their intensity of responding. This might be due to the tendency to personalize experience or the relative complexity of one's goals and thoughts.
7. Moods differ from emotions in that they are long-lasting and not tied to a specific object. Moods can be manipulated experimentally in a variety of ways, and influence memory retrieval.
8. Life event stress produces susceptibility to illness, as do daily hassles in living.
9. Self-disclosure seems to help individuals deal with stress and appears to reduce subsequent psychological and physical symptoms.
10. A variety of coping mechanisms decrease the adverse effects of life stress. Both individual differences in "hardiness" and social support also may serve as buffers to adverse health reactions following stressors, although this remains to be established with certainty.

Key Terms

affect (p. 278)
appraisal (p. 284)
coping (p. 291)
emotion (p. 278)
emotional style (p. 286)
facial feedback model (p. 279)
hardiness (p. 294)

hassles (p. 290)
mood (p. 278)
primary appraisal (p. 292)
primary emotions (p. 285)
secondary appraisal (p. 292)
social support (p. 292)
stress (p. 287)

Thought Questions

1. Can you think of some situations where your emotions were determined by the rules and norms of the culture? Do you think your emotions were influenced or merely the outward expression of these emotions?
2. Recall some situations where you felt the emotions of anger, pity, and guilt. Did the concept of controllability and responsibility play a role in this experience?
3. Might we expect that someone who is depressed will see more sad things in the world? Why or why not?
4. Think about recent times in your life when you or someone else became physically ill. Were these times preceded by any stressful circumstances, and do you think that the stress might have brought about the illness?
5. How might a psychologist focusing on emotion and stress explain depression?

Consciousness

CHAPTER 16

Source: pathdoc/Shutterstock

Chapter Outline

The Relationship of Consciousness to Nonconscious Information Processing

Altered States of Consciousness

The Divided Self: Split-Brain Experiments and Consciousness

Fantasy and Consciousness

At any given moment, we are bombarded with a variety of external and internal stimulation. Although humans can process much information, there are limits to our capacities. It therefore follows that some information from the environment, or even from our own bodies, will be overlooked or will not attract our attention. Conversely, other information will be the focus of attention and we will be well aware of it. What is selected depends on our own biological receiving mechanisms, our needs, our past histories, and stimulus characteristics. For example, a number of voices are likely to be heard at any given moment at a party, but only one or two of them will be of concern and will be the focus of attention; other sounds will be ignored. Yet, if someone says your name, your attention is drawn to that. There must be some **nonconscious** part of the mind that was scanning for that important information. Similarly, when we view a landscape, much will be "seen" or registered, but we will be aware of only a limited portion of the scene and only a small part of what meets the eye will be retained or recognized later. On other occasions, as when auditioning for a part in a play or posing for a picture, we might be acutely aware of ourselves and even fewer external factors will be noticed. Thus, our personal consciousness represents only a small portion of reality.

When psychologists speak of *consciousness*, they are often referring to awareness, or what one knows about his or her experience and how reality is constructed. Consistent with this approach, John Locke defined consciousness as "the perception of what passes in a man's own mind" or, as Ornstein (1972) put it, "subjective life." As just indicated, we are frequently unaware of

nonconscious Another term for the unconscious, the part of the mind about which we do not have awareness.

many aspects of our environment and, as Freud so clearly pointed out, individuals are also unaware of many of the important internal determinants of behavior. These inner causes are considered to be "unconscious," or "nonconscious." There are those who say that our experience of conscious will is actually just an illusion, an epiphenomenon, and it is the nonconscious part of our mind that is in control (e.g., Wegner, 2002, 2004). Others can point to good evidence that conscious will does have an impact on behavior (e.g., Baumeister, Musicampo, and Vohs, 2001).

On other occasions our consciousness may be "expanded"; that is, there is heightened sensitivity to external sounds and colors or increased awareness of our own feelings, past experiences, and thoughts. Repeated exposure to new musical artists may make us conscious of variations in the music of which we were not initially aware. Introspection about a problem in an important personal relationship can lead to the recognition of feelings toward the person that we never knew we had. One of the goals of psychoanalytic and Rogerian therapies is to expand consciousness of our inner life. Eastern philosophies of Yoga and Zen Buddhism share this same goal and also place great emphasis on enhancing our experience of the physical world.

Instances of heightened inner awareness, as might be experienced when under the influence of a drug or during deep meditation, are examples of *altered states of consciousness*. Altered states are clearly evident in physical objects, as when liquid water changes to solid (ice) or gas (steam). But whether the human mind can be "altered" to a state qualitatively different from the normal waking state is less clear. It is evident, however, that modifications in awareness are often accompanied by a number of profound physiological and psychological changes. For example, there are changes in the clarity and organization of thought, sense of control, and attention. It is also clear that individuals can readily pass from one level of consciousness to another, as from waking to daydreaming or reverie and then back to alert consciousness again. We thus move through different levels of consciousness during the normal course of our lives.

The issue of the nature of conscious and of its relationship to nonconscious functioning has been important to the study of personality since Freud first postulated that many aspects of personality were based in the unconscious. In this chapter we first examine the relationship of consciousness to nonconscious functioning, and we look at their relationship to such behavioral phenomena as acting mindlessly, engaging in ruminative thought, and biases in how we perceive people. We also consider the relationship of the self to consciousness, and whether nonconscious processes are "smart" or "dumb." From there we go on to consider other aspects of conscious and nonconscious functioning that are of relevance to personality, such as altered states of consciousness—including dreams, hypnosis, and drugs—the right brain-left brain dichotomy, and fantasy.

The Relationship of Consciousness to Nonconscious Information Processing

In our discussion of the relation of consciousness to nonconsciousness, we adopt the term *nonconscious information* processing instead of the term *the unconscious* because when people see the *unconscious* they most often think of Freud's unconscious—full of primitive repressed thoughts, feelings, and motivations. Much modern work, while converging on a belief that *nonconscious* processes—processes that lie outside of conscious awareness—can influence conscious functioning, still leaves unresolved the question of whether nonconscious processing has the motivational properties that Freud attributed to it. Therefore, we have chosen to use the term *nonconscious* over the better-known term *unconscious*.

If mental functioning can be conceived of as including both conscious and nonconscious elements, what is their relationship? First, we might ask "What is the purpose of consciousness?" A number of theoreticians and researchers have suggested that a major function of consciousness is to correct or reprogram behavior when behavior is not succeeding (Hofstader, 1979; Langer, 1989; Gilbert, 1989; Wegner, 1994; Carver and Scheier, 1981). Many theorists hold that there are two systems controlling behavior—a conscious, relatively voluntary or controlled system and a relatively more **automatic** system that usually functions outside of awareness (Kahneman, 2016). Many aspects of behavior are under relatively automatic control.

Control theories (Carver and Scheier, 1981, 1990, 2002; Powers, 1973) provide models that view behavior as a function of both conscious, or controlled, and relatively nonconscious or automatic processes. These theories view the human being as a *cybernetic system*—a system in which feedback from the environment is being continually monitored and then used to correct the behavior of the system. Individuals are seen as comparing their current states to their desired goal states and as assessing the progress they are making toward those desired goal states. If no difference is found then individuals continue as they have been or exit the loop and begin to pursue other goals. However, if a difference is noted (i.e., the individuals notice that there is a discrepancy between their desired goal state and the progress they are making towards it) then individuals alter their behavior in order to bring the current state closer to the one that is desired. It is when we are confronted with problems that we devote conscious attention to efforts of controlling various aspects of behavior. To quote Martin and Tesser (1989, p. 311), one major function of consciousness is that it is a "troubleshooting process."

automatic A cognitive version of the "unconscious." It is assumed that many of the schemas that guide our behavior operate outside of awareness.

"May I use the copy machine, because I need to make copies?"

Mindlessness

An example of the idea that consciousness is primarily utilized to alter automatic processes when necessary is provided by Langer's work on **mindlessness**. Consider the experiment by Langer, Blank, and Chanowitz (1978), in which a person about to use a copy machine was approached by an experimental confederate who asked for permission to

mindlessness A tendency to respond automatically in many situations, thus not really thinking about it.

use the machine first. The requestor stated that she had either a small or a large number of copies to make and made the request in one of three ways (Langer et al., 1978, p. 635):

1. Request only: *Excuse me, I have 5(20) pages. May I use the Xerox[1] machine?*
2. Placebic information: *Excuse me, I have 5(20) pages. May I use the Xerox machine because I have to make copies?*
3. Real information: *Excuse me, I have 5(20) pages. May I use the Xerox machine because I'm in a rush?*

Condition 2 is called "placebic information" because the reason offered is entirely redundant of the request. After all, "What else would one do with a copying machine except make copies of something?" (Langer et al., 1978, p. 48). The point is that condition 2 offers essentially the same information as condition 1. If participants were really conscious of the information given, then the rate of compliance with the request should have been the same in the "placebic information" and "request only" conditions. The results show that when the request to use the copier was small, five pages, 60 percent complied. However, if a reason was added, even if the reason was redundant with the request, compliance rose to 93 percent for the placebic condition and 94 percent for the hurry condition. When the request was large, the no reason condition and the "because I have to make copies" condition each resulted in 24 percent compliance, while the "I'm in a rush" condition led to 42 percent compliance. When the favor is small, people are not going to think much and just process "because" as a legitimate reason. However, when the request is large, people will be motivated to fully consider the situation and reject the redundant "because I need to make copies." In general, mindlessness is most evident when outcomes are not personally relevant, when no accountability is involved, and when the decision is unimportant (see the review in Langer, 1989).

Automaticity

Langer's work suggests that we can alter some of our automatic processes when necessary. However, other researchers have argued that automatic scripts and schemata often function outside of conscious control (Kihlstrom, 2002, 2013). Most of us have experienced unwanted thoughts or feelings (perhaps something so simple as a melody) that we can't get out of our minds no matter how hard we try. Many of us have had the experience of "choking" in a situation—of trying so hard to avoid making an error that the error occurs. Psychotherapy largely exists because simply having a conscious, intellectual conception of "how I should be" or "how I want to be" frequently does not affect or effect behavior (Todd and Bohart, 1994) as many would-be dieters know. Finally, many individuals, especially after experiencing trauma or loss, have had ruminative thoughts, which they go over and over but cannot banish from their minds (Martin and Tesser, 1989; Tait and Silver, 1989).

We introduced Wegner's (1994) Ironic Process model in Chapter 3, but here let's focus on the automatic part of the process. As you recall, Wegner and his colleagues asked participants to "NOT think of a white bear" (you can try this yourself). No matter how hard they tried, most participants kept finding the image of a white bear reappearing in their thoughts even when it had temporarily been banished. Wegner notes that when we try to control ourselves not only do we not always succeed, but sometimes we end up doing the diametric opposite of what we want to do. The more we try to make ourselves go to sleep, the wider awake we become. The more we try to diet, the more we think about food.

Wegner holds that these ironic effects of attempted mental control occur because there is a conscious, controlled process that is trying to achieve our goal, and an automatic, nonconsciously controlled process that is monitoring or keeping a look out for the very thing we don't want to happen. Sometimes, especially under stress, the conscious part of

---

[1]A Xerox machine was the most common type of copier at the time of the research; consequently, this term was used as a synonym. The Xerox corporation was opposed to usage as a synonym because it was concerned about losing the trademark.

the process gets disrupted, and then what pops into awareness is the part of ourselves that is keeping an eye out for the thing we don't want to happen. The undesirable thing then floods into consciousness.

In one study, Wegner and Erber (1992) asked participants to think or to not think about a target word (e.g., *house*) and then to give their associations to a variety of other words. Some of the other words they were given were related to the word they were to suppress (e.g., *home*) and some were unrelated (e.g., *adult*). Participants who were to suppress a word and who were put under time pressure to respond, frequently blurted out the very word they were supposed to not think about, more so than participants who were not under time pressure to respond.

What expression is displayed on this man's face? If you have been primed with the term *hostile,* you would be more likely to interpret the face as hostile.

Priming

There are other ways nonconscious processes may influence our conscious activities. One of these can be demonstrated by the many studies of priming and accessibility. The idea of **priming** is based on the idea that we have many *schemata*—cognitive plans or structures for organizing our experience and guiding our actions—that are latent in the mind. If the schemata are primed, they become active and form the basis for how we interpret our experience in a given moment. In a typical priming study, a word or a phrase—say, the word *hostile*—is presented to the participant. Sometimes these words are presented subliminally, sometimes not. In another part of the study, which the participant is led to believe is unrelated to the first part, the participant is asked to read an ambiguous description of a person and to give a characterization of that person's personality. Typically, the participant "sees" the person in terms of the primed word. In our example, the participant would see the person as somewhat hostile. This effect appears to be stronger if the participant is unaware of having been primed (Higgins, 1989).

In an even more complex priming study, Lewicki (1986) had participants respond to brief flashes on a screen by pressing a button. In actuality, the flashes were words presented so rapidly that participants were unable to report seeing them. In one condition the

priming A process that aids accessibility to a concept by suggesting the concept or related items prior to the need to use the concept.

Source: fizkes/Shutterstock

words presented were *harm*, *rape*, *attack*, and *pain* (negative words). In another condition the words were neutral words, such as *chair* or *button*. In a second phase of the experiment, participants were presented with a short essay describing a woman named Jane. The description was ambiguous, and participants were asked to rate Jane on a series of traits, such as *resistant to threat*, *not fearful*, or *relaxed*. Men who had been exposed subliminally to the negative words saw Jane as feeling threatened and as vulnerable to threat. In contrast, women who had been exposed subliminally to the negative words saw Jane as not threatened and as resistant to threat. It is not clear why this occurred, but Lewicki speculates that nonconscious activation of a sense of physical threat in men influenced them to see Jane as a potential victim. In contrast, nonconscious activation of a sense of threat in women led them to perceive Jane as unlikely to be victimized. Lewicki believes this may be based on cultural stereotypes. Men may tend to underestimate threat and see it as something that pertains to others rather than to themselves, while women may see themselves as more likely to be victimized and therefore as needing to protect themselves from threat. The important point, however, is that whatever the mechanisms operating, they appear to have operated at a nonconscious level.

An interesting demonstration of priming below conscious awareness comes from a study by Dijksterhuis, Preston, Wegner, and Aarts (2008). One of the questions they were addressing is perceptions of who or what is responsible for an action—oneself or others? In this study, participants were to decide as quickly as possible whether a string of letters made a word. This is called a lexical decision task. For instance, provided the string of letters ROFG, the person would indicate no, while if given FROG, the participant would indicate yes. As soon as the participant hit the button to indicate yes or no, the word would disappear from the computer screen. Additionally, the computer would sometimes remove the word before the person could answer. Prior to the lexical decision task, the person would be presented with XXXXXX, which would be replaced with a priming word for fifteen to seventeen milliseconds (depending on the study) and then immediately replaced with the XXXXXX again. The target word would be presented and the participant would attempt to make the lexical decision before the computer made the word disappear. The person was then asked to decide whether the target word was removed because of the button pressing to make the lexical decision or because of the computer. In study 1, the priming words were related to the self (*Ik* and *mij*—I and me in Dutch). Compared to the control condition, primes related to the self resulted in people rating themselves as more responsible for removing the word. In study 2, the primes were computer-related terms. In this case, people rated the computer as more responsible for removing the word. In study 3, the primes were related to God. In this study, when people believed in God, they rated less control of removing the word and indicated the computer was more responsible. If they did not believe in God, the rated control of removing the word was not different than the control conditions. There are two important things to consider about this research: the first is that priming below conscious awareness changes the way we view the cause of our own behaviors (see also Wenke, Fleming, and Haggard, 2010). The second is that a person's existing belief structures matter in that interpretation.

Some schemata may be *chronically accessible* (Higgins, 1989), guiding our experience but at a level of which we are unaware. For instance, many studies have suggested that negative schemata for construing experience are chronically accessible in people who are depressed; thus, they quickly perceive events in a negative fashion.

The Relationship of the Self to Consciousness

Kihlstrom (1987, 1990) has speculated that the complex relationship between conscious and nonconscious processes is mediated by the existence of the self. He has argued that consciousness requires that a mental representation of an event be linked to a mental representation of the self. Consciousness takes the form of "*I see* (or *hear*, *smell*, *taste*, etc.) this, now" (Kihlstrom, 1990, p. 458). In other words, there would be no conscious experience if there were no sense of self linked to that experience. This fits with our discussion of the development of the self in Chapter 10, in which we noted that the development of a self-concept appears to begin around the time that individuals develop self-awareness.

Kihlstrom goes on to suggest that amnesia and other instances in which individuals cannot consciously remember experiences they have had occur either because the experience was not associated with the self in the first place, or because that association to the self was subsequently lost. This is congruent with many approaches to therapy, in which efforts are made to help clients integrate their experiences into their sense of self. If Kihlstrom's speculation is correct, then the nature of consciousness is intimately linked to the nature of the self, and disturbances in the association of self to experience leads to amnesia, dissociation, and other aspects of memory loss.

Are Nonconscious Processes "Smart" or "Dumb?"

While most psychologists now agree to the existence of nonconscious processes, there is still considerable controversy over their nature. Many of the great personality theorists, such as Freud, Rogers, and Jung, believed that processes that lay outside of awareness could involve the operation of complex mental processes. For instance, for Freud, the unconscious part of the ego organized the defenses that protected the individual from conscious awareness of repressed material. In that sense, the unconscious could operate in a "smart" fashion, although it consisted mainly of "primary process" material (see Chapter 3) and such processes were not necessarily "rational" in their operation. However, some modern psychologists (e.g., Greenwald, 1992) argue that there is no evidence for a "smart" unconscious that involves complex mental operations. Rather, nonconscious processes are seen as relatively simple and automatic, consisting of the automatic operation of simple well-learned routine procedures, such as that involved in driving.

Others, such as Erdelyi (1992) and Lewicki, Hill, and Czyzewska, (1992) disagree. They hold that information can be processed in complex and sophisticated ways at a nonconscious level. In other words, nonconscious processes involve more than simple routinized procedures, and in some sense, they can be said to involve "thinking."

Complicating the resolution of this issue are methodological problems—it is difficult to assess whether or not an individual is really unaware of the information being processed (see Highlight 16.1). In studies demonstrating complex nonconscious information

---

HIGHLIGHT 16.1

Learning Without Awareness

A controversy in psychology that generated much attention in the late 1950s and 1960s involved the examination of whether verbal behavior can be directly manipulated with reinforcement techniques. In a typical experiment, participants were given a series of cards, each containing a verb and six personal pronouns (Taffel, 1955). The participants were asked to make up a sentence using the verb and any pronoun: The experimenter then rewarded each sentence starting with *I* or *we* by saying "good" when the sentence was completed. It was found that during the reinforcement phase of this experiment the use of *I* and *we* greatly increased, but when reinforcement was later withheld, the use of these pronouns decreased. The participants in the initial investigations reported that they were unaware of the contingency between their response and the reinforcement: It appeared that the learning took place because of the automatic strengthening property of the reinforcer. These research studies were interpreted as supporting both the Skinnerian position and, surprisingly, the Freudian notion, of the unconscious.

Subsequent research, however, using more sophisticated, post-experimental interview techniques and indirect assessment procedures, found that only participants who were aware of the contingency between the response and the reinforcement increased their rate of "correct" responding (see Spielberger, 1962). Participants who remained unaware of the experimental linkage between *I* or *we* and *good* responded in a random manner. Cognitive psychologists contend that these findings refute the behaviorist belief in mechanical, stimulus-response connections.

processing, questions have been raised as to the participants' degree of lack of awareness. In many ways, the answer depends on the particular focus and definition of nonconscious (Bargh and Morsella, 2008), and at this point the question becomes what the capabilities of the nonconscious system happen to be. This is an issue that continues to be researched. The answers will have important implications for some of our theories about personality.

Altered States of Consciousness

Our normal waking state is but one form of consciousness. In this state, knowledge is communal, or consensual; that is, we share information with others and are mutually aware of the stimuli in the environment. In addition, the passage and constraints of time are recognized. Normal waking states are considered the primary condition of the mind; other types of consciousness are thought of as "unreal" or as "imaginary."

There are a number of states of mind that fall within the rubric of the "unreal." These include sleep and dream states, delirium, hypnotic trances, and drug and meditational experiences. In these conditions, new mental functions and capabilities are experienced that may not have counterparts in normal experience. Time is distorted, illogical events are perceived as real or possible, and there may be a loss of self-awareness. These altered states may be externally induced, as in drug conditions, or part of our natural lives, as in sleep, dreaming, and daydreaming. They may be of long or short duration. They may be passive experiences, with increased awareness of, openness/to, and preoccupation with the environment, or active and creative states with preoccupation with inner sensations. They may give rise to positive or negative emotions. And they can be produced by under- or overstimulation. But in all such cases consciousness is perceived as somehow different.

Sleep

All mammals sleep, although there is great variety in the amount of sleeping activity. Among humans, there is also a wide range of individual differences in sleep habits, with the amount of sleep for college students averaging 7.4 hours during the week and 8.5 hours on the weekend (White, 1975). Indeed, there appears to be great stability in the sleeping process. Contrary to popular belief, research has not substantiated the hypotheses

Source: Milkovasa/Shutterstock

Sleep quality may be affected by the light of a television.

that sleep is affected by viewing violent television programs or studying before bedtime, though there is gathering evidence that blue light emitted by laptops and LED televisions may decrease quality of sleep (Holzman, 2010). See Highlight 16.2 for suggestions for dealing with difficulty sleeping.

One of the main characteristics of sleep is that the sleeper is relatively unresponsive to the external world. However, there is not complete unawareness of environmental stimulation. For example, it has been found that important names are more likely to awaken the sleeper than irrelevant ones. A second characteristic of the sleeper is a great reduction in activity. The decreased behavior that accompanies sleep is thought by some to be the key to sleep's function (Webb, 1975). Such nonresponding could be instrumental to survival if it kept one protected from a hostile world and occurred when responding would be unlikely to result in goal attainment. Among humans, hunting was extremely hazardous at night because of our primary dependence on vision. Thus, it may have been survival relevant to "keep the curious quiet and the frightened still" (Webb and Bonnet, 1979, p. 465) until daylight. But of course, being unaware of the environment is a dangerous situation. A rather typical pattern across cultures is adolescents and early adults tend to stay up late, while older people tend to wake up early. Based on the sleep cycles of a hunter-gatherer tribe, researchers have suggested that this is an evolutionary adaptation so that someone in the group is awake nearly all the time (Samson, Crittenden, Mabulla, Mabulla, and Nunn, 2017).

An alternative to this explanation of the function of sleep is that sleep enables the organism to restore body chemicals and repair damage that has occurred during the day. Part of the sleep cycle is associated with release of growth hormone (Sassin et al., 1969). This hypothesis has received some substantiation. Furthermore, it takes as much energy to sleep as it does merely to lie quietly awake.

A number of sleep disorders have been identified. These disorders vary in intensity and frequency of occurrence for any given individual. Night terrors apparently do not originate in bad dreams, as is often thought, but result from abrupt awakening from deep sleep. Similarly, sleepwalking is also not dream related and is typically outgrown by adolescence; it is now considered a developmental disorder rather than a psychological disturbance. A small percentage of the population are victims of narcolepsy, or sudden "sleep attacks" that often occur without warning, particularly during times of heightened excitement, and last from a few to fifteen minutes. Narcolepsy is likely to be a genetic disorder; dogs bred from narcoleptic parents show exacerbation of this sleep tendency. A large percentage of the population suffers from a perceived lack of sufficient sleep. However, this figure is probably inflated because the elderly seem to need less sleep and indeed do sleep less, yet are more likely to report sleep problems. Studies have been unable to uncover any personality differences between long- and short-duration sleepers.

HIGHLIGHT 16.2

If You Can't Sleep

Various suggestions have been offered to those experiencing difficulties in sleeping. They include:

1. Never oversleep because of a poor night's sleep. Get up at the same time each morning, for this establishes the body's internal sleep/wake mechanism.
2. Try to establish a relatively regular bedtime.
3. If you wake at night, relax in bed for a while. If that does not work, get out of bed and try some quiet activity until you are sleepy again.
4. Cut down on alcohol, smoking, chocolate, coffee, tea, and caffeinated soft drinks.

5. Schedule some time to write down worries or concerns about what you will do the next day.
6. Avoid heavy meals too close to bedtime.
7. Experiment with your bedroom's noise level and temperature until you find what is best for you.
8. Keep physically active, even after a bad night's sleep.
9. Try relaxation techniques such as visualizing peaceful scenes.
10. Find out if medical conditions or prescription drugs are keeping you awake.

In addition, sleep-disorder clinics located throughout the United States are available for consultation.

Dreams

Sleep is also characterized by dream activity. Dreams exemplify primary process thinking (see Chapter 3). They may be illogical, are not bound by the constraints of time, there is fusion of objects into one, and they may include symbolic representations of thoughts and objects.

Freud contended that sleep is preserved by dreams. According to Freud, the antecedent for all fantasy behavior, including dreaming, is deprivation (unfulfilled wishes); the consequence of fantasy behavior is need reduction. By providing the opportunity for substitute or hallucinatory wish fulfillment, dreams "drain off" internal stimulation and preserve sleep. A simple illustration can clarify this idea. Assume that you go to bed without dinner. After some period of time, hunger cramps are felt that might cause awakening. During sleep, however, you dream about eating food. The content of the dream might be disguised with the food appearing in symbolic form (e.g., string rather than spaghetti). Such a wish-fulfilling dream produces a diminution in subjective hunger, thereby reducing stomach cramps and preserving sleep. As you might expect, it is extremely difficult to gather scientific evidence that dreams are wish fulfillments and that they preserve sleep by reducing internal stimulation.

The Study of Dreams

Useful scientific research on dreaming was initiated about sixty years ago. One reason for this relatively late start was that, prior to this time, only the dreamer had direct access to the dream. Therefore, it was not possible to assess the reliability of dream reports (that is, whether or not a dream had occurred, as opposed to the content of the dream). There was a need for a witness to the dream in addition to the dreamer.

REM Rapid eye movement sleep. This is the part of sleep that is primarily associated with dreaming.

An objective technique for the detection of dreams was discovered in the early 1950s (see Dement and Kleitman, 1957). During sleep, *rapid eye movements* (**REM**) were discovered, with the eyes exhibiting quick, side-to-side motions under the lids. Individuals awakened during these REM periods reported dreams more frequently than people awakened at other times. Some mental and cognitive activities do occur during non-REM (NREM) periods, but reports of visual and hallucinatory experiences occur only during REM sleep. NREM reports are more like thinking, being less visual and less unusual.

Research has also revealed that there are cyclical patterns of brain activity during the course of sleep (see Dement, 1965). This activity can be monitored with the recording of brain waves (EEG readings). Four different patterns of brain waves have been detected during sleep (see Fig. 16.1). Stage 1 sleep, in which there is a lack of long and narrow waves, as well as *delta*, or large, waves, is highly associated with REM periods and dream reports. It is now quite clear that REM observations and particular patterns of brain waves provide reliable, observable criteria for identifying internal dream processes.

During the course of an eight-hour sleep period, an individual has five or six sleep cycles. On average the sleep cycles last eighty to ninety minutes. Each cycle will include a period devoted to dreaming. In general, the longer one sleeps, the greater the total dream activity, with more time devoted to dreaming in each subsequent sleep cycle. The average dream lasts around fifteen minutes, with the length of the dream increasing as the night progresses. The initial dream episode lasts between five and ten minutes, while final dreams may continue for as long as fifty or sixty minutes. Individuals also progress through a regular nondream-dream sequence during the course of the evening. To enter a REM stage, there first is passage through stage 2 of the sleep cycle.

The percentages of both sleep and dream time are systematically related to maturation. Infants sleep more than half the time and that nearly half of this sleeping time, or around eight hours, is spent in REM activity. However, this percentage drops off rapidly; by early adolescence, the percentage of time spent dreaming begins to stabilize at around 20 percent. However, the total amount of sleep continues to decline very gradually. Foulkes (1990) has suggested that dreams mature along the same lines as does waking consciousness. As conscious mental processing expands in organization, range, and flexibility, so do dreams.

HUMAN BRAIN WAVES

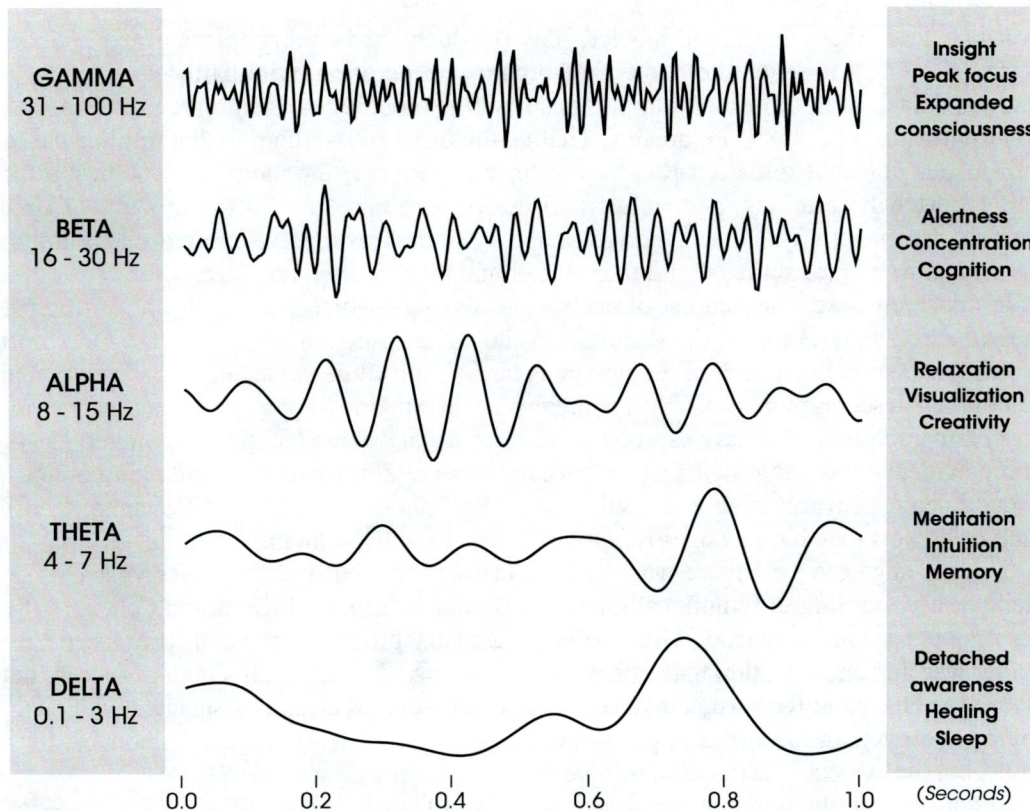

FIGURE 16.1. Sample EEG Patterns for the Waking State and the Four Stages of Sleep

Source: artellia/Shutterstock

The Function of Dreams

Freud believed that through dream analysis we could learn about unfulfilled wishes and desires, as well as about the symbolic manifestations of needs. Given an objective dream index, one might expect that the "royal road to the unconscious" (which is how Freud characterized dreams) would become a superhighway and that Freud's speculations would be either confirmed or discarded. Although this has not been the case, inferential data have been gathered that bear on some of the issues raised by Freud.

First, it appears that all individuals dream. The universality of the dream experience was anticipated by Freud. Indeed, many nonhuman species exhibit dream-state sleep. But if it is inferred from REM observations that lower organisms also dream, then it is difficult to contend that the function of dreams is to fulfill wishes and deficits. It seems unlikely that dreams preserve sleep, but rather that the presence of sleep ensures dreams.

Dement (1960) found that if the sleeper is awakened every time a REM period is entered, then the REM periods are more frequent on subsequent evenings, and it subsequently takes more vigor to awaken the sleeper. The organism seems to be making up for a REM deficit.

But if there is a need to dream, then dream deprivation should affect psychological functioning. At present, it is uncertain whether this is the case. Some investigators do report that individuals become more emotional and less psychologically balanced after losing REM sleep, but other investigators find no such disturbing psychological effects. Furthermore, there are perfectly well-adjusted individuals who sleep less than one hour a night! Whether REM deprivation has adverse psychological effects may be dependent on the personality of the individual. A number of studies suggest that repressors (individuals prone to forget conflictual material) are more disturbed by REM interruption than non-repressors (Cohen, 1977).

It is evident that what Freud labeled "day residues," or memory traces of experiences during the day, influence the content of dreams. In addition, stimulation during sleep, such as a flash of light or tactile input, is sometimes incorporated into dreams. But such stimulation does not instigate dreams. That is, the onset of stimulation that might awaken the sleeper does not initiate a REM episode. Furthermore, emotional upsets during the day, reported frustrations, and unfulfilled desires are unrelated to the amount of time spent in dream activity. Indeed, the vast majority of dreams involve commonplace activities in commonplace settings, and their emotional tone is often negative.

In sum, there is a cyclical course of sleep during the night which is relatively uniform across individuals. The question of the dream's psychological function remains moot. One must certainly question the notion of the dream as having substitute value and reducing internal stimulation. It seems more probable that dreams aid in thinking through problems and providing creative solutions that have escaped us during normal waking thought (see Singer, 1974). Some evidence has suggested that dream contents are similar to the daydream contents. A good deal of daydreaming is related to everyday concerns (Singer and Bonanno, 1990). That is, dreams may have a cognitive rather than a stimulus-reducing function.

There is suggestive evidence from both animal and human studies that REM sleep may facilitate new learning and emotionally adaptive waking behavior (McGrath and Cohen, 1978). For example, a number of studies have demonstrated that groups deprived of REM sleep have poorer learning and retention than control groups deprived of an equal amount of sleep, but allowed to engage in REM (dream) sleep. The idea that REM sleep is associated with either storing or forgetting memories (e.g., Walker and Stickgold, 2004) became fashionable for a while, but the evidence seems to be turning against that particular model (Vertes, 2004).

In addition, it appears that the dream state is not qualitatively different from waking thought, with factors such as sex, age, race, and social class all reflected in dream content. For example, women report more emotions in their dreams than do men, who report more aggressive content (Winget, Kramer, and Whitman, 1972). It seems that dream characteristics correctly reflect the concerns and styles of waking life (Webb and Cartwright, 1978; Hermans, 1987).

Source: Elena Schweitzer/Shutterstock

Threat simulation theory suggests dreams are a safe place to practice for anxiety-provoking things.

A theory has been laid out that dreams function as a simulation for real life, particularly threatening situations (Revonsuo, 2000). He calls this model the Threat Simulation Theory (TST). Proceeding from an evolutionary perspective, he suggests that it is in dreams that the organism is able to experience threatening situations and then practice ways of dealing with those situations. Valli and colleagues (2005) found that children who experienced traumatic war-related events had more dreams about dangerous events and responses than nontraumatized Finnish children. In other research, they found that recurrent dreams were more likely to have threatening themes (Valli and Revonsuo, 2009). Other researchers found similar rates of threat in recurrent dreams, but unlike the strict TST model, the dreams often were not realistic (Zadra, Desjardins, and Marcotte, 2005). Still others find that realistic threat-related situations or escapes make up only a small percentage of dreams (Malcolm-Smith and Solms, 2004). No matter which model of dreaming is used, current worries are noted as a frequent source for dream material. This model has a good explanation for why that would be true, as those would be the threats that are on a person's mind.

Hypnosis

The word *hypnosis* Greek for "sleep." For a long time, hypnotic trances were thought to be akin to sleep, but this similarity is more apparent than real. Brain recordings and a variety of other indicators taken during hypnotic states are the same as those recorded in waking conditions, and both differ from the responses of a sleeping person (see Kihlstrom, 2007, for an overview). Furthermore, during hypnosis an individual can acquire and retain new information and be normally active or even hyperactive. Thus, the two main characteristics of sleep, non-responsiveness to stimulation and lack of activity, do not describe the hypnotic participant.

hypnosis A trancelike state in which the cooperative subject is highly responsive to suggestions made by the hypnotist.

Hypnotic trances have rather unique features:

1. The person ceases to make plans. There is a loss of initiative and the individual is generally passive, giving himself or herself over to the care of the hypnotist.
2. There is selective attention. Although this also is true in waking states, hypnotic participants exhibit an even narrower range of focus.
3. Reality testing is reduced, and distortions and inconsistencies are accepted. This is sometimes called *trance logic*.
4. There is increased suggestibility and a compulsion to please and to follow the biddings of the hypnotist.
5. The participant readily enacts unusual roles, such as rowing a boat while in a room. Antisocial behavior may also be undertaken if it is not construed as antisocial by the person under hypnosis.
6. Subjective experience is altered in accordance with the hypnotist's suggestions.
7. There is increased control over bodily functions, such as the capacity to hear, see, and not feel pain. This will be elaborated on in the subsequent discussion.
8. There can be post-hypnotic amnesia if suggested by the hypnotist. The extent of memory loss varies among individuals and according to the depth of the trance. This blockage is unique to hypnotic states.

There are differences in the extent to which these characteristics describe the state of any given individual during hypnosis. Around 10 percent of the population does not respond to hypnotic induction and, at the opposite pole, about 5 to 12 percent can enter deep trances in which even the commands of the hypnotist are no longer processed. A wide array of humans, including children, can be hypnotized. Furthermore, a single attempt is usually sufficient to determine if a person is susceptible to hypnosis and susceptibility has been found to be stable over a twenty-five-year period (Piccione, Hilgard, and Zimbardo, 1989). Performance scales have been developed to indicate the susceptibility of an individual to hypnosis. Such scales require individuals to attempt experiences ranging, for example, from simple falling forward without stiffening to blockage of smells and voices (Weitzenhoffer and Hilgard, 1962).

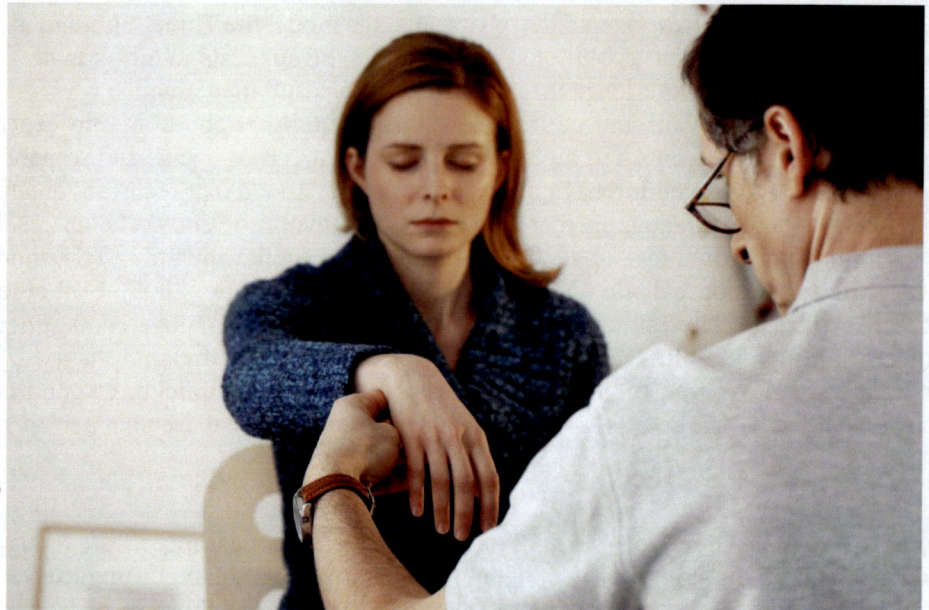

People differ in their susceptibility to hypnosis.

One question that immediately comes to mind is whether there are traits that distinguish good hypnotic participants from poor ones. J. R. Hilgard has suggested that a good participant must have the capacity to become deeply involved in imaginative experiences. For example, one highly susceptible participant described herself as follows (Hilgard, 1970, p. 24):

> When I get really involved in reading, I'm not aware of what is going on around me. I concentrate on the people in the book or the movie or in imagination as it is in hypnosis. Reading a book can hypnotize you.
>
> After each book, I'm completely washed out. After hypnosis, it was the same. I was completely washed out and couldn't keep my eyes open. I lacked the ability to communicate.

Although traits that clearly distinguish good from poor hypnotic participants have not been convincingly demonstrated thus far, a capacity for total absorption and losing oneself does seem to correlate with level of hypnotic susceptibility (Nadon, Laurence, and Perry, 1987; Tellegen and Atkinson, 1974). In addition, there is increasing evidence that skill-training can enhance responsiveness to hypnotic induction (see Spanos, Lush, and Gwynn, 1989). The training procedures include instilling positive attitudes and motivation, exposure to videotaped models, and information about misconceptions regarding hypnosis (e.g., hypnosis does not involve total loss of personal control).

Control of Bodily Functions

The most dramatic reports concerning hypnosis involve control over basic sensory and cognitive functions. For example, in an experiment by Blum (1961), participants were instructed not to see a particular design on a card. This design, which had elicited great anxiety, gave rise to no physiological reactivity whatsoever after the hypnotic instructions.

However, hypnotic participants do not become literally blind at the moment blindness is suggested; they will blink at a bright light. In a similar manner, apparent deafness can be easily induced in a hypnotic participant, but it can be demonstrated that the individual does process sound. In one such demonstration, individuals were tested in a delayed auditory feedback context, in which personal voice feedback is delayed by about one second, a delay that typically causes speech impairment. The adverse effects of auditory speech delay were not erased under hypnotic "deaf" instructions (Barber and Calverley, 1964).

As previously indicated, there is also apparent hypnotic influence on memory, for hypnosis is perhaps most often identified with amnesia for events during hypnosis. Yet even this aspect of hypnosis is not without ambiguity. For example, although participants are unable to consciously recall events during hypnosis that they have been instructed to forget, traditional measures of recognition and relearning are not affected by suggested amnesia (see Williamsen, Johnson, and Eriksen, 1965). Further, other research has demonstrated that individuals *can* remember, under the right conditions, when not hypnotized (Spanos, 1986). Indeed, it has even been suggested that posthypnotic amnesia is not real, but is "pretended" by participants (Coe, 1978). However, even if hypnotic amnesia is real, it is unclear whether the individual cannot retrieve the memories or whether the memories are not "stored" (Evans and Kihlstrom, 1973).

Most of the research on sensory blocking during hypnosis has examined pain reactions. In these experiments, participants may be shocked or have their arms placed in very cold water. Control groups are hypnotized and either told nothing about pain or allowed to remain in a normal state. If normal, awake participants are highly paid for this experience, they may tolerate a great deal of pain, like the hypnotic participants. But, unlike the hypnotic participants, they are aware of and remember the feeling. The hypnotic participants appear neither to be consciously aware of nor to recall the pain. In one quite dramatic experiment, J. R. Hilgard (1970) told hypnotic participants that they had lost their hands; when shock was administered to either hand, pain was not reported. However, in these experiments brain activity in response to pain was not altered.

Other research has demonstrated the positive effects of hypnosis on various other bodily functions. For instance, Klein and Spiegel (1989) have shown that hypnosis can be used to either stimulate or inhibit gastric acid secretion. For example, hypnotized participants showed a 39 percent reduction in basal acid output. Other studies have found hypnosis beneficial in the treatment of duodenal ulcers (Colgan, Faragher, and Whorwell, 1988) and irritable bowel syndrome (Hammond, 1990).

Another attempt to demonstrate the apparently powerful effects of hypnosis concerns age regression. During hypnotic trance, participants are told to return to an earlier period in their lives. This suggestion does produce experiential change, in that participants might act and feel like children. But there are important differences between hypnotic regression and participants' actual behavior as children. For example, age-regressed participants' reports of what happened at particular birthday parties differ from reports by adults who attended those parties. Similarly, results of tests administered to age-regressed participants and of actual tests taken at the earlier age do not correspond (see Orne, 1975).

What Is Hypnosis?

Given this array of observation, it is now reasonable to ask, "What is hypnosis?" First of all, many aspects of the hypnotic state seem also to be part of the basic equipment of waking consciousness. These aspects include the capacity to become completely absorbed in an activity and to follow the suggestions of another. Second, it is evident that some role playing is involved in hypnosis. For example, in one investigation participants were falsely told that the arms stiffen under hypnosis (Orne, 1959); more than half the participants exhibited this reaction when hypnotized. In sum, hypnosis seems to be a complex phenomenon involving interpersonal relationships, the relinquishing of personal control, some role playing, and the ability to imagine and hallucinate.

Any substance that affects the structure or function of the body can be considered a drug, including nicotine in tobacco and caffeine in coffee.

Drugs

Consciousness may be changed by natural occurrences like sleep or by external sources like hypnotic induction. One frequent and controversial method of consciousness alteration through artificial induction is the ingestion of chemical substances. Any substance that affects the structure or function of the body can be considered a drug, including tobacco and caffeine. But here our attention is restricted to drugs that might alter consciousness by causing some combination of:

1. Change in thought.
2. Change in the sense of time.
3. Alteration of emotional responses.
4. Change in perception.

The effects of drugs on any particular person, of course, are dependent on many factors, including the personality of the drug taker, the amount of previous drug experience, the purity of the drug, the social climate during the drug experience, whether the drug is taken singly or in combination with other drugs, and so on.

The use of a number of drugs for nonmedicinal purposes has increased enormously over the past three decades. How drugs work, who takes them, the mechanisms behind addiction, and the effects of drugs on behavior have become topics of great interest to the public and the scientist alike. In terms of the major focus of this chapter, the aspect of drugs that is of special interest to us is their influence on consciousness. It is claimed that certain drugs "expand" consciousness; facilitate clearer, sharper perceptions of the physical world; help provide deeper insights into the psyche; expose hidden, repressed materials; and under some circumstances, enable the individual to achieve a more integrated self and sense of spiritual unity. These claims all require careful scientific scrutiny.

Not all drugs are alleged to have positive, consciousness-altering effects. Alcohol may produce a pleasant euphoric state and relax inhibitions, but it predominantly fosters inner confusion, perceptual distortions, and a narrowing rather than an expansion of consciousness. Narcotics like heroin also tend to produce changes in mood and self-confidence, with little else in the way of desirable psychological consequences. The class of drugs called the hallucinogens is most likely to give rise to unusual visual experiences and inner feelings. There is no doubt that the hallucinogens can dramatically alter consciousness. The problematic question is whether, in this alteration, any raising or expanding of consciousness takes place.

Many hallucinogens have been known for many centuries, with the exception of lysergic acid diethylamide (LSD), which was first synthesized in 1938. The American Indians used peyote, whose active ingredient is mescaline, to induce states of ecstasy and mystical experience. In his book *The Doors of Perception*, Aldous Huxley (1954, pp. 16–18) helped popularize the consciousness-altering effects of mescaline.

> I took my pill at eleven. An hour and a half later, I was sitting in my study, looking intently at a small glass vase. The vase contained only three flowers. . . . I continued to look at the flowers, and in their living light I seemed to detect the qualitative equivalent of breathing—but of a breathing without return to a starting point, with no recurrent ebbs but only a repeated flow from beauty to heightened beauty, from deeper to even deeper meaning; words like "grace" and "transfiguration" came to my mind, and this, of course, was what, among other things, they stood for.

The possibility that hallucinogens could help individuals break through the ordinary barriers of consciousness and achieve a deeper level of self-understanding was explored by some psychotherapists (Caldwell, 1968). One patient, following a therapeutic session in which she had taken LSD, described her experience (Aaronson and Osmond, 1970, p. 330):

> After I had felt that hours must have gone by and then learned that it was only five minutes; after I had seen flowers open and close their petals and held in my hand a peeled grape that became, before my eyes, a tiny brain; and after I had closed my eyes and seen one beautiful vision right after another; well, then I decided that *anything* must be possible, including the transformations of character and personality I had heard about, and to some extent believed, but which only now I really felt confident could happen.

Although there were very occasional clinical reports of insights achieved through hallucinogenic drugs, the evidence is uncertain whether they are actually helpful. One reason for the lack of evidence is that the research was stopped in the early 1970s. Research has started up again, and there are hints of benefits in treatment of addictions (Bogenschutz and Pommy, 2012).

In addition, hallucinogens can produce very unpleasant experiences. "Bad trips" are not uncommon and experts (Caldwell, 1968) emphasize the necessity for careful supervision of the individual who takes hallucinogens, particularly LSD or mescaline. Huxley also stresses the need for monitoring, portraying mescaline as opening the door to either heaven or hell.

To evaluate the hallucinogens, their immediate effects on consciousness must be separated from their long-term effects. A vivid, dramatic, or ecstatic experience is not the equivalent of personality growth, of a new insight into oneself and the world. Thorough evaluation studies of the effects of LSD have not supported the hypothesis that taking LSD facilitates creativity, produces self-insight or enhances one's perceptions of the surrounding environment (McGlothlin and Arnold, 1971; McGlothlin, Cohen, and McGlothlin, 1967). A similar conclusion applies to marijuana. The principal scientific uncertainty concerning the effects of repeated use of marijuana and other hallucinogens is over the likelihood of such negative personality effects as decreased energy and goal striving and subtle disturbances in thinking. Moreover, whatever the subjective experiences provided by marijuana, at the objective level marijuana intoxication interferes with motor coordination, visual perception, and reaction time (*Marijuana and Health*, 1977). In brief, aside from the temporary alterations in mood and perception that hallucinogens produce, their consciousness-expanding effects have yet to be scientifically demonstrated

The Divided Self: Split-Brain Experiments and Consciousness

The human brain is divided into two halves. The left side (or *hemisphere*) controls the right side of the body, while the right hemisphere controls the left side of the body. In humans, these halves of the brain are functionally different, with the left side specialized in language functions such as speaking and writing, and the right half more limited in terms of language abilities. It has also been found by researchers that the right hemisphere is superior at visual-spatial tasks such as spatial orientation.

Under normal circumstances, information is relayed between the two halves of the brain. However, the connections can be severed experimentally, so that there is disruption of the knowledge flow and each half of the brain may be independently examined. Split-brain operations are typically performed on laboratory animals such as cats or monkeys. But very occasionally this operation is performed on humans, for it has been found that splitting the brain reduces the severity of epileptic seizures. Some individuals suffer such extreme forms of this illness, with as many as twelve seizures daily, that the operation is of great benefit in spite of negative side effects. In addition, through accidents some individuals have greatly damaged one side of their brains, thus permitting the experimental study of half the brain.

Split-brain experiments have revealed that each half of the brain can process information outside the realm of the other half's consciousness. For example, if a word is flashed to a split-brain patient's left (typically major) hemisphere, the patient is able to say the word and write it with his or her right hand. But if the right (typically minor) hemisphere receives this information, then the word cannot be verbalized or written with the left hand (see Sperry, 1968).

On the basis of these data, some individuals have argued that there are two independent spheres or modes of consciousness; that there is a duality in human consciousness, with the "conscious" left side of the brain specializing in verbalization capacities, and the "unconscious" right side not having this function. One might *experience* with the right hemisphere, but that experience would not be part of conscious (verbalizable) awareness. For example, in one experiment a patient was shown a picture of a nude. When the nude was presented to the left hemisphere, there was affect along with verbalization about the picture. But when it was viewed by the right hemisphere, there was affect without any apparent understanding of why. Indeed, the patient appeared to search for a reason to justify and make sense of his feelings. These data led not only to speculation about the independent modes of consciousness, but also to the belief that there is a duality in human nature, with each aspect of a person having independent representation in the brain.

It now appears, however, that there has been an over dramatization of the uniqueness of the two sides of the brain (Gazzaniga and LeDoux, 1978). First of all, the hemispheres are typically intact and there is mental unity. If there really were two independent brains, where and how would they be integrated and synthesized? Furthermore, the right hemisphere can perform logical operations. For example, if the left hemisphere is damaged early in life, the right develops linguistic capabilities. In addition, although the right hemisphere cannot verbally label objects, if the left hand is allowed to feel an object,

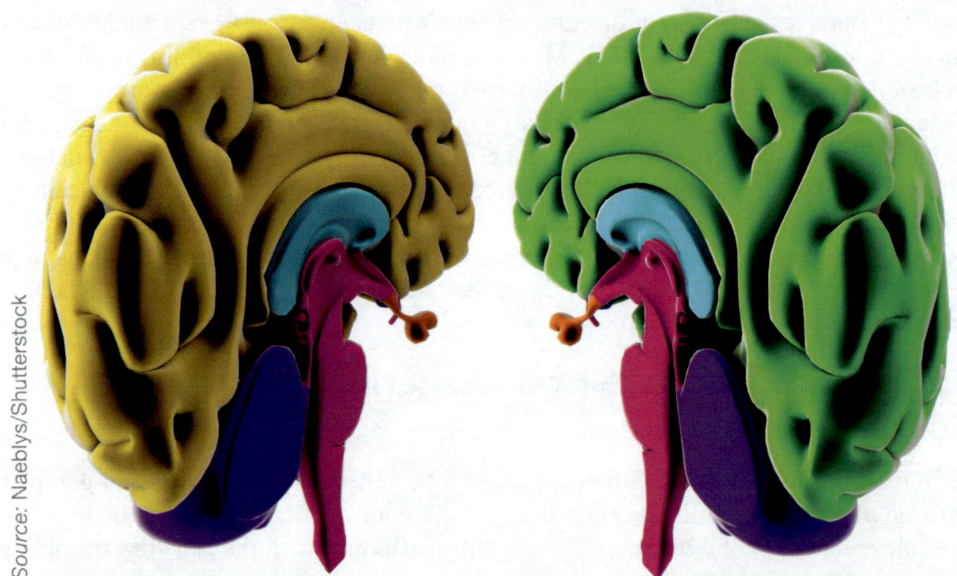

Source: Naeblys/Shutterstock

The two hemispheres of the brain may have some different functions, but remember that unless there has been damage, the two halves communicate.

a correct match to an object flashed on a screen can be made. Thus, although response production through the linguistic mode is not possible by the right hemisphere, it is not without consciousness.

In sum, there are localized differences and specialization of brain functions, primarily due to linguistic development that is typically localized in the left hemisphere. But there is unity and integration in mental functioning, the two hemispheres do not oppose one another, and the differences between the hemispheres are quantitative rather than qualitative. The romance associated with split-brain research maybe waning. For example, claims that the right brain is the seat of creativity and that artists are more oriented toward this hemisphere *have not been* substantiated. But it is evident from this research that there can be experience without verbalization, which is consistent with the theme presented throughout this chapter.

Fantasy and Consciousness

Most of you have had the experience of finding yourself on the same page of a book after a half-hour supposedly spent studying. You wonder where the time went and what happened during the interval. You then realize that your mind has "wandered." Perhaps you were thinking about an upcoming date or a recent party, or imagined yourself reaching a goal or occupying a position of power and status. Our thought processes are engaged in this kind of fantasy activity a surprising amount of the time; our minds are rarely blank or idle. Engaging in such fantasies or daydreams does not entail as radical an alteration of consciousness as that produced by drugs or dreaming. However, there is a relation between these altered states of consciousness and fantasy activity. In all these experiences attention is directed toward or dominated by the inner, rather than the outer world. In reality-directed activity, we attend to real physical stimuli—sounds, odors, visual displays, and the like—while in fantasy or imaginary activity, we attend to internal representations of physical stimuli—thoughts and ideas. Hence, in fantasy our inner life plays the important role in determining the contents of consciousness.

One of the most common forms of inner fantasy is daydreaming. Research has found that most people are aware of daydreaming to some extent every day. The content of daydreaming varies considerably from individual to individual and from time to time. In general, research has identified three styles of daydreaming. One style is "positive-constructive" daydreaming, in which individuals use daydreaming to solve problems, both everyday concerns and long-range problems. A second style is "guilty-dysphoric" daydreaming, in which individuals tend to ruminate over failings and transgressions. The third style is a "poor attentional control" pattern, in which the individual is unable to focus on extended fantasy (Singer and Bonanno, 1990).

One important element of daydreams and related fantasy experience is the notion of *imagery*, or "pictures in the mind." Vivid imagery is readily induced by hypnosis, is one of the consequences of hallucinogens, and is a common characteristic of dreams. Thinking in images has been shown to have different properties than thinking in words. For example, images facilitate memory and appear to be understood and stored differently than words (Paivio, 1971).

There is evidence among both children and adults that individuals who engage in fantasy experience are less impulsive and display more positive adjustment patterns than individuals who engage in very little fantasy activity (Singer, 1966, 1973). But the term *fantasy* is a broad construct embracing many different kinds of activity such as imagery, constructing stories, engaging in play, and even reading fiction and watching theatrical productions. It is not unlikely that the effects of these disparate types of fantasy may be quite different.

In terms of the issues with which we have been concerned in this chapter, it is of interest that the effects of an event portrayed on television differ dramatically, depending on whether children viewing the event perceive it as real or as a fantasy. In one experiment (Feshbach, 1972), children nine to eleven years old were individually shown a six-minute segment of a campus riot, made up by combining shots of a real campus riot with parts of a movie about a campus riot. Before seeing the television program, children assigned to a reality-set condition were told that the program was taken from a television newscast, while children assigned to a fantasy-set condition were told that the program was part of a film made in Hollywood. A control group was not shown a program. Each child was then given the opportunity to aggress against the experimenter by administering an aversive noise that varied in its loudness and severity. The data revealed that children in the fantasy-set condition were less aggressive, while children in the reality-set condition were more aggressive than the no-television control group. The importance of this finding lies in its demonstration that the same event has a different impact when experienced as a fantasy than when experienced as reality.

Summary

1. *Consciousness* refers to awareness, or what is known, about one's experiences. We are not consciously aware of all the internal and external sensations that impinge upon us.
2. In this chapter, instead of the term the *unconscious*, we use the term *nonconscious* to differentiate modern views of nonconscious information processing from Freud's view of the unconscious. Research generally supports the proposition that much information processing occurs at a nonconscious level.
3. *Automaticity* refers to the idea that many nonconscious properties operate automatically.
4. *Priming* refers to the idea that inactive nonconscious processes can be activated by a stimulus in the environment.
5. Trying not to think of something often increases the probability of thinking about it.
6. Dreams are one of a number of *altered states of consciousness*. The presence of a dream is inferred by *rapid eye movements* (REM) and a particular pattern of brain activity. Humans and many nonhuman species pass through a typical dream cycle during the night.
7. Freud's speculations about dreams are not confirmed by dream research. Dream deprivation does not necessarily impede psychological functioning; the onset of external stimulation during sleep does not initiate a dream; and most dreams appear quite commonplace and somewhat unpleasant. Dreams may have a biological or problem-solving, rather than a wish-fulfilling, function.
8. Physiological activity during a hypnotic state corresponds to that in a normal waking condition. However, the individual is highly suggestible, reality testing is reduced, there may be heightened control over bodily functions, and there is posthypnotic amnesia. The hypnotic influence over seeing and hearing is not evident in subtle tasks related to these processes, such as delayed auditory feedback.
9. There are a variety of drugs. Hallucinogens have vivid and immediate effects on consciousness, but there is no evidence that they produce any long-term positive effects.
10. The brain has two hemispheres: the left specializing in language function and the right specializing in spatial orientation. Research has shown that presentation of visual material to the right side of the brain results in an experience that cannot be verbalized.
11. In fantasy, as in altered states of consciousness, attention is directed toward or dominated by the inner, rather than the outer, world.

Key Terms

automatic (p. 299)
hypnosis (p. 309)
mindlessness (p. 299)

nonconscious (p. 297)
priming (p. 301)
REM (p. 306)

Thought Questions

1. There are times, as during sporting events, when we are under great pain, but are able to "forget" that pain and continue striving. How might this be explained?
2. In what ways are dreams, hypnotically induced images, and daydreams similar? How do they differ?
3. Are your dreams often scary? If so, why?
4. What do you think of the proposition that we often act mindlessly?

Complex Personality Processes

PART 6

Source: Ollyy/Shutterstock

CHAPTER 17
Perceived Causality and Control

CHAPTER 18
Love and Hate

CHAPTER 19
Summing Up

Chapters 17 and 18 focus on complex personality processes and behaviors. In Chapter 17, we consider a set of topics that relate to an individual's being in charge of his or her life and being able to take effective, proactive action, especially in the face of failure experiences. In Chapter 18, we consider the theoretical and empirical literature on love and aggression. These topics are fundamental to human personality and represent active research areas. Other significant personality processes and behaviors, such as anxiety, have been considered at various other points in the text.

Chapters 17 and 18 also illustrate different aspects of personality research. Chapter 17 illustrates how concepts that are central to humanistic views of personality, such as feeling in control of oneself, taking responsibility for oneself, and feeling free, can be systematically investigated using objective, quantitative procedures. In addition, the study of achievement motivation illustrates how a personality construct can be used to investigate socioeconomic change and development in the larger culture. Chapter 18, on love and aggression, illustrates the multidetermined basis of personality and the interplay of diverse biological and social factors.

Attempts to explain complex personality processes and behaviors in terms of single causes are simplistic and misleading. There are many antecedents to major personality dimensions, and an adequate understanding of personal responsibility, achievement, and love and aggression requires analysis of the roles of each of them.

Perceived Causality and Control

CHAPTER 17

Source: Jacob Lund/Shutterstock

Chapter Outline

Perceived Control

Achievement Motivation

Competence

Attributions of Responsibility

In Chapter 2, we discussed Western culture's emphasis on an individualistic self that must be able to direct and control its own activities. Further, this self must be responsible for itself, must be able to mobilize itself to take action to achieve its goals, and must be able to cope with adversity and failure. This emphasis appears in most of the major theories of personality. For Freud (see Chapter 3), the goal of psychotherapy was to put the ego in charge so that the individual could consciously make choices rather than be the victim of forces outside of his or her control. Kohut (see Chapter 4) believed that a fundamental component of a healthy self-structure was the ability to mobilize the self and work to achieve goals. Rogers (see Chapter 6) saw therapy as helping individuals grow towards autonomy, self-direction, and the ability to take responsibility for themselves. Finally, both cognitive and behavioral therapists (see Chapter 5) have devoted a great deal of effort to developing individuals' skills and perceptions related to effective self-management and self-control.

The belief in an individual self goes hand in hand with an emphasis on freedom and self-determination. Philosophically, there is much controversy in psychology concerning the degree to which individuals are "free" to direct their own behavior. While humanistic theorists such as Rogers have assumed freedom and self-direction, other theorists, such as Skinner, do not believe humans are free.

In his provocative book *Beyond Freedom and Dignity*, Skinner (1971) contended that we must give up the illusion of freedom and admit that behavior is controlled by reinforcements (see Chapter 5). According to the principles of operant reinforcement, *external* stimuli paired with rewards are responsible for behavior. For example, if food follows the pressing of a lever, then the appearance of that lever initiates a particular chain of behaviors. If we give up the illusion of freedom, Skinner argued, then our knowledge of behavioral engineering can be used to control human behavior for the betterment of society. But, Skinner went on to state, people refuse to give up this illusion and the false belief that we are autonomous actors, possessing free will and deserving credit for our actions. He concluded that, in order for society to survive, this conviction must be replaced with the acceptance of external control.

The issue of free will versus determinism is an old and persistent philosophical problem which neither philosophers nor psychologists have been able to solve satisfactorily. Consideration of the different ways with which this complex problem has been dealt would take us beyond the scope of this chapter. However, what is directly pertinent are the psychological effects of people's *perceptions* of their freedom of choice.

There is much research to suggest that the belief that one has some personal control over what happens is important to effective functioning. In this chapter we first consider the effects of perceiving oneself to have control in one's life and the opposite effects of feeling helpless. Next we consider efforts to preserve a belief that one has control over one's self and one's life. After this we consider some limitations to the belief that one has personal control.

Believing that one has some control over one's fate is related to how one perceives the causes of success and failure in one's life. In turn, how one perceives the causes of success and failure is related to how competently one copes with achievement situations and with failure experiences. So, we move from perceptions of control to a consideration of perceptions of causality and their relation to achievement motivation and competence. Following this we apply ideas from previous sections to perceptions of responsibility.

Perceived Control

A number of psychologists and philosophers have contended that personal control is integral to self-concept and self-esteem and constitutes a fundamental psychological need. Moreover, control appears to be especially important given stressful circumstances and helps reduce experiences of stress and aids with coping. For example, laboratory research has shown that when participants are faced with shock, loud noise, a test, etc., and have no information about the timing or onset of those events and have no actions they can take to alter the events, then their reactions are especially negative. They experience "jitters," have reduced concentration, and report great discomfort (see, for example, Glass and Singer, 1972).

Locus of Control

locus of control A perception of the influence that one has on the attainment of reinforcement.

In the field of personality, much of the current concern with the notions of freedom and self-responsibility grew from the concept of **locus of control** (Rotter, 1966) and a distinction between *internal* and *external* control (see Chapter 5). Locus of control refers to the perceived influence that one has on the attainment of reinforcement. This concept has its roots in social learning theory and is related to schedules of reinforcement. Reinforcement theorists have distinguished between two kinds of reinforcement schedules: ratio versus interval. Given a ratio schedule, the responder gets rewarded after a certain number of responses. That is, there is covariation between personal responding and the reward. On the other hand, given an interval schedule, the respondent receives a reward after a certain time interval. For the most part, the reward is independent of responding and is under the control of the experimenter. These types of schedules respectively capture the notions of internal versus external control.

There is a further distinction, in part generated by learning theorists, that also represents the difference between internal versus external control, namely, the differentiation between skill-determined versus luck-determined tasks. Given a skill-related activity, such as athletic games or general school performance, outcomes depend in part on effort and work input. These are under personal control. On the other hand, at luck-determined games, such as the toss of a coin, the outcome is not under personal control. Chance or fate is not subject to volitional change.

It has been postulated that internal versus external control is a dimension of personality; some persons perceive greater personal (internal) control, while others perceive the situation (external control) as more salient. Rotter (1966, p. 1) defined such internality and externality as follows:

> When a reinforcement is perceived . . . as . . . not being entirely contingent upon his action, then, in our culture, it is typically perceived as the result of luck, chance, fate, as under the control of powerful others, or as unpredictable because of the great complexity of forces surrounding him. When the event is interpreted in this way by an individual, we have labeled this a belief in *external control*. If the person perceives that the event is contingent upon his own behavior or his own relatively permanent characteristics, we have termed this a belief in *internal control*.

A number of psychologists have asked whether there are individual differences in beliefs about internal versus external control.

Assessment Procedure

There are many scales designed to assess the perception of events as internally versus externally controlled, for both children and adults. However, the most frequently used instrument is a 29-item self-report inventory (see Rotter, 1966). This test, called the *Internal-External Control Scale* (*I-E scale*), has a forced-choice format with an internal belief pitted directly against an external belief for each item. The items on the scale are classified in six general subcategories on the basis of type of need portrayed and characteristics of described goals. The six categories are academic recognition, social recognition, love and affection, dominance, social-political beliefs, and life philosophy. Some sample items and their keyed responses (italic letters represent externality choices) are:

1. a. Many of the unhappy things in people's lives are partly due to bad luck.
   b. People's misfortunes result from the mistakes they make.
2. a. The idea that teachers are unfair to students is nonsense.
   b. Most students don't realize the extent to which grades are influenced by accidental happenings.

It is evident that the questions on the scale are very broad. As Rotter (1975, p. 62) indicated, "[The scale] was developed not as an instrument . . . to allow for a very high prediction of some specific situation, such as achievement or political behavior, but rather to allow for a low degree of prediction of behavior across a wide variety of potential

Source: Antonio Guillem/Shutterstock

Is the cause of the bad grade something that the student can control, or is it outside of the student's control? The student's own belief is likely to reflect locus of control.

situations." Typically, the situational cues in a setting most influence beliefs and behavior. However, generalized beliefs about control are also presumed, to a lesser extent, to influence a person's specific beliefs and actions.

Personality Correlates

Phares (1976, p. 60) has stated that

> The best single validity of the I-E scale would undoubtedly be evidence showing that internals are more active, alert, or directive in attempting to control and manipulate their environment than are externals. Since locus of control refers to expectancies for control over one's surroundings, a higher level of coping activity would be anticipated from internals.

There is some evidence supporting this position. In one early series of studies, Seeman and Evans (1962) and Seeman (1963) reported, respectively, on information seeking and retention of personally relevant information among institutionalized individuals. It was found that, among hospitalized tuberculosis patients, individuals classified as internals knew more about their illness and asked doctors more questions than patients who were external in locus of control. In addition, prisoners who were internals retained more information pertinent to parole than did externals. In sum, among both patients and prisoners, the behavior displayed by those high in internal control was instrumental to improving their life situations. On the other hand, it appeared that among those low in personal control, the acquisition of information was seen as less likely to serve any useful function.

Other investigators have studied the differential cognitive activity of internals and externals. For example, Wolk and DuCette (1974) presented participants with protocols to be scanned for errors. It was found that internals were better at incidental learning (remembering the material that had been scanned) and at finding errors. In general, theorists in this area have contended that "the cognitive functioning of internals should enhance their personal effectiveness as compared to externals. And it apparently does" (Phares, 1976, p. 65). It is not at all clear, however, how these disparate dispositions come about, inasmuch as there is little pertinent developmental data.

One of the difficulties faced by researchers in this area is related to the trait-situation controversy examined in Chapter 9. It is quite evident that beliefs about personal control may vary from situation to situation. For example, one might perceive oneself to be personally responsible for positive outcomes in affiliative contexts, yet believe that success in academic affairs is a matter of good luck or help from others. These issues have been relatively neglected by researchers in locus of control (see Lefcourt et al., 1979).

Learned Helplessness

The previous section has shown that perceiving oneself as having some control has psychological consequences. Perceiving oneself as not having control, i.e., as being helpless, may often be quite harmful. Two experimental investigations with rats as participants dramatically illustrate some of these adverse effects. In fact, the procedures used and the consequences observed were so injurious in these particular investigations that lower organisms had to be the experimental participants.

In one of the investigations, Mowrer and Viek (1948) gave hungry rats the opportunity to eat ten seconds before the onset of a shock. For half the animals, the shock could be terminated by jumping into the air. The second group of rats could not terminate the shock through their own actions. Rather, each was paired with a "controlling" rat and received the same amount of shock that the partner had received before the partner jumped to terminate its own shock.

Since it was known from prior experimental research that fear inhibits eating, the experimenters measured the eating behavior of both groups to examine the effects of the helplessness experience. The data revealed that the noncontrolling, or helpless, rats were inhibited in their eating, whereas the behavior of the controlling rats was not greatly affected. This difference existed even though the two groups received identical amounts of shock.

In the course of subsequent research, Richter (1958) observed cases of sudden death among rats during experimentation. For example, in a study of swimming endurance, many unexplained drownings occurred after the rats swam for only a short period of time. Richter speculated that (pp. 308–309) "the situation of these rats is not one that can be resolved by either fight or flight—it is rather one of hopelessness: Being restrained . . . in the swimming jar with no chance of escape is a situation against which the rat has no defense. . . . They seem literally to give up." In sum, a loss of control has dramatic and aversive effects on the well-being of an organism (see Lefcourt, 1973).

Further research investigations of helplessness were conducted with researchers administering inescapable shock to dogs for a period of time. The dogs were placed in a harness and shock was administered to one of their hind legs. Then these animals, as well as other dogs not given prior inescapable training, were placed in a two-compartment box. When a tone signaling that shock would follow was sounded, the dogs could move from the shock side to the no-shock side of the box. Seligman and Maier (1967) reported that many of the dogs given prior inescapable shocks did not attempt to escape in this situation. Rather, they passively accepted their supposed fate; they appeared to have **learned helplessness**. The untrained dogs, on the other hand, engaged in a variety of responses until the escape response was learned. Seligman and Beagley (1975) found learned helplessness in rats, as well. Similar differences in behavior have been reported in experiments using fish, rats, cats, and other nonhuman species. It must be noted, however, that not all animals exposed to inescapable shock exhibit helplessness, and deficits are displayed on some subsequent tasks but not on others. Furthermore, in some cases helplessness is exhibited if testing immediately follows training, while a waiting period erases helplessness effects (see critique by Levis, 1976). In sum, there are many questions yet unanswered about the existence of this psychological state.

learned helplessness The acquired expectation that one's actions will exert little control over outcomes.

The most systematic and influential analysis of loss of control is that reported by Seligman (1975), who contended that organisms are helpless when their actions are perceived as not influencing their outcomes. If a response does not increase the likelihood of receiving a reinforcement, then conditions for helplessness have been established. For example, assume that a baby goes to sleep after crying for one hour. The harried parents try to shorten this aversive period by rocking, feeding, or even playing music to the baby. Despite all these actions, however, the baby still doesn't fall asleep until an hour of crying has gone by. Thus, the reinforcer (the end of crying and the onset of sleep) is independent of the parents' behavior. The parents, therefore, are helpless in this situation.

Source: Amma Shams/Shutterstock

A dog that has learned that its behavior cannot control a shock will display learned helplessness.

To explain observations of learned helplessness, Seligman proposed a three-stage theory:

1. Information is gained about the contingency between outcomes and responding. In the case of helplessness training, this information reveals that there is no contingency or association between actions and reward.
2. This information results in the development of the expectation that responses and outcomes will remain independent in the future.
3. The low expectation causes deficits in future learning as well as motivational and emotional disturbance.

Learned-helplessness research then expanded to include human participants. In one exemplary research investigation, Hiroto and Seligman (1975) exposed participants to either an escapable or an inescapable aversive tone. Participants were then given a different task in which they could escape the noise by making a particular hand movement. It was found that individuals previously exposed to the inescapable tone performed poorly as compared to groups without prior inescapable-tone training.

A person who has learned that behavior does not control outcomes may experience depression.

Learned Helplessness and Depression

The research of Seligman and others has called attention to a parallel between helplessness learning in the laboratory and human depression. Both learned helplessness and depression are marked by passivity, weight loss, appetite loss, and social and sexual deficits (Seligman, 1975). It certainly appears fruitful to think of some kinds of depression as akin to learned helplessness, but it must also be remembered that clinical depression is not a unitary illness; many kinds of depression have been identified, and there are many determinants of depression.

More recently, attributional analyses of learned helplessness and depression have been formulated (Abramson, Seligman, and Teasdale, 1978; Miller and Norman, 1979). Recall from Chapter 9 that attribution theorists are concerned with the perceived causes of an event. It has been contended that how one perceives the causes of prior outcomes determines the type and course of depression. Specifically, if one experiences a *negative event* and attributes its cause to *internal, stable, and global* or relatively general factors, one is more likely to become depressed (Abramson, Metalsky, and Alloy, 1988). For example, one is more likely to become depressed after failing a test if one believes "I failed the test because I am stupid" rather than "I failed the test because I didn't study hard enough."

Abramson and her co-workers (1978) distinguished between personal helplessness and universal helplessness. *Universal helplessness* is experienced when responses and outcomes are not contingent for any person in that situation. For example, if a child develops leukemia, despite all efforts of the parents and doctors, the child's life may not be saved. The parents and doctors would probably not perceive themselves as personally responsible, although they would experience helplessness. Conversely, *personal helplessness* connotes a situation in which a person feels helpless but in which others might be able to attain the desired goal. For example, a person unable to receive passing grades in school in spite of effort will experience personal helplessness, for others obviously can receive passing grades. Although in both cases low expectancies and helplessness are experienced, low self-esteem is likely to be a consequence only of personal helplessness. Depressed patients may fail to make this distinction and may perceive situations of universal helplessness as indicative of personal helplessness and their own shortcomings.

Individual Differences

The merging of ideas about learned helplessness with perceptions of causality gave rise to a rich literature concerned with what has been called **attributional style**, or the disposition to perceive or judge particular causes as most salient across a variety of situations. Some causal perceptions might be particularly dysfunctional and predispose one toward depression. Abramson et al. (1978) suggested that attributing failure to the self is particularly perilous because this would lower self-esteem. In addition, this might lead individuals to believe that change is not possible and that failure was out of their control. Hence, this attribution was anticipated to lead to the onset of depression; if combined with negative life events, this attribution makes individuals vulnerable to symptoms of helplessness (see Brewin, 1985).

This thinking resulted in the development of an Attributional Style questionnaire (Peterson et al., 1982). Scores on this measure were then related to depressive symptoms. The scale presents individuals with hypothetical positive or negative outcomes (e.g., "You go to a party and do not meet new friends."). The respondents then provide a reason for this outcome and rate that cause on the dimension of locus, stability, and cross-situational generality. There have been issues related to the psychometrics of the Attributional Style questionnaire (see Carver, 1989; Cutrona, Russell, and Jones, 1985), with the very typical problem related to a lack of cross-situational consistency.

And what about the relationship of helplessness to depression? There is a great deal of inconsistency in the literature, with some individual investigators and general reviews supporting the helplessness position, while others fail to find such support. The most recent summary articles present evidence that attributional style does weakly to moderately correlate with depression, and that scores on the locus subscale are particularly predictive (see Robbins, 1988). There is also some evidence that attributional style precedes depression onset (rather than depression causing alterations in perceived causality). However, the causation issue remains uncertain.

Optimism

Seligman (1990; 2011) shifted his focus from helplessness to optimism. He argues that those who feel optimistic generally function more effectively and are both physically and psychologically more healthy. For Seligman an optimistic explanatory style is one in which individuals tend to attribute success to themselves, and failure to external circumstances. In a variety of research studies, Seligman and colleagues have developed a system to score public speeches, personal reports, and other verbal material for optimism. They have found, among other things, that baseball teams whose public statements contain more optimistic imagery are more likely to win, and presidential candidates whose speeches contain more optimism are more likely to win.

Peterson, Seligman, and Vaillant (1988) report that explanatory style at age 25 (assessed by means of content analysis of available protocols of wartime experience) predicted health status at ages 45–60 (but not between the ages of 30–40). Seligman cites several studies suggesting that optimism is correlated with positive physical and mental health. In one study, individuals with cancer were trained to think in an optimistic manner. Compared to those who did not receive such training, the trained individuals showed an increase in immune system functioning.

Seligman paints an optimistic portrait of optimism. However, there is some evidence that pessimism is not always dysfunctional, depending on what kind of pessimism one is talking about. Norem (1989) has studied **defensive pessimism**. Defensive pessimists are individuals who predict catastrophe for themselves but then use that prediction to mobilize themselves for action. When they come to prepare for a midterm exam, they predict catastrophe, believing that they don't know the material well enough, they'll never pass, and so on. In effect, they scare themselves into studying harder and typically proceed to do well on their exam. Defensive pessimism, which leads to positive action, contrasts with dysfunctional pessimism, which leads to helplessness and inaction. Norem's research has

attributional style A predisposition to evaluate the cause of outcomes to a particular locus of control, stability, and generalizability.

defensive pessimism A technique used by individuals who predict catastrophe for themselves but then use that prediction to mobilize themselves for action.

suggested that defensive pessimism can be an adaptive style. She points out that there are roles—such as director of a nuclear power plant—in which most of us would prefer to have a defensive pessimist.

Efforts to Preserve a Sense of Personal Control

Because of the evidence that individuals who are optimistic and who perceive themselves to have an internal sense of control function better than those who feel helpless, it is no wonder that some researchers have found evidence that individuals strive to maintain a sense of personal freedom and control. In the following discussion, we consider three examples of this behavior. First, when individuals perceive their sense of freedom to be threatened, they react against this threat and act in ways to maintain that sense of freedom. Second, they strive to maintain an illusion that they have a sense of control over their fate. Third, when individuals believe themselves to be intrinsically motivated to do something, they are more likely to continue to do it than when they believe that their motivation comes from external sources.

Reactance

Fights for political freedom have occurred throughout history, often involving acts of extreme heroism that dramatically illustrate the motivational effects of loss of freedom. Similarly, we may engage in daily battles to preserve our psychological freedom. Being confined to one's room as a child, being forced to accept a decision, hearing a message that one prefers not to listen to, being pressured by others, and having censorship imposed are some examples of loss of personal, psychological freedom.

According to Brehm (1966, 1972), when a person's freedom to engage in a behavior is threatened or taken away, the motivation to perform that behavior, and therefore to reinstate freedom, increases. As Brehm (1972, p. 1) stated, "A person is motivationally aroused any time he thinks one of his freedoms has been threatened or eliminated. This motivational arousal, or 'psychological reactance,' moves a person to try to restore his freedoms."

psychological reactance An aversive state experienced when freedom is perceived to have been taken away.

Many experimental investigations have demonstrated the motivational effects of **psychological reactance**. In the majority of these research studies, individuals find themselves unable to engage in behaviors that they thought were available. For example, an alternative is eliminated or an expected message is censored. The experimenter then typically measures the perceived attractiveness of the available and unavailable options. It is believed that a change in the desirability of the alternatives, so that the unavailable alternative increases in attractiveness, is one indication of an attempt to restore freedom.

In one of the first such experiments, children were asked to rank-order the desirability of nine different candy bars (Hammock and Brehm, 1966). As a reward for this task, some children were told that they would have *a choice* between two candy bars, while others in a control condition were told that they would be *given* one of two different kinds of candy bars. The children were then shown their third- and fourth-ranked candies, and all were given the more attractive of the two. Thus, reactance was created in the decision condition by telling the children who thought they would have a free choice that they were denied this opportunity. But notice, in every condition the children received their third-ranked candy bar. Following the giving of the candy (but before it was eaten), the experimenter had the children re-rate their candy preferences.

If the hypotheses about reactance and perceived attractiveness (attitude) are correct, then the preference for the denied (eliminated) alternative should increase in the choice condition. They found that in the condition designed to provoke reactance the ranking of the candy bar they were given (third-ranked) decreased, and the ranking of the fourth-ranked candy bar slightly increased. In the control condition, there was no impact on the candy bar they were given. Even though the children got an objectively good outcome, when the perception of choice was taken away the outcome was viewed as less good, and the removed option becomes better.

Reactance notions have also been tested in field, rather than laboratory, settings. In Miami, Florida, an antipollution law was imposed that prohibited the use of cleaning materials containing phosphates. Reactance theory suggests that shoppers should have had an increased desire for these banned products. To test this idea, purchaser attitudes in Miami were compared with those in Tampa, where the antipollution law was not in effect (Mazis, 1975). The investigator had the experimental participants (housewives) rate the effectiveness of the various detergents they had used during the six months prior to the survey. The ratings of the phosphate detergents were significantly higher in Miami, where the products were unavailable, than in Tampa. In addition, in Miami there was a strong negative attitude toward the quality of the alternative detergents (for related research, see Brehm and Brehm, 1981).

The Illusion of Control

Another way individuals have of maintaining a sense of control is to have an illusion of control in which individuals often perceive themselves as having control in situations when they do not. For instance, several studies have found that individuals believe they can influence the outcome of thrown dice if they throw the dice themselves (Fleming and Darley, 1990; Langer, 1975). However, Taylor and Brown (1988) report that depressed individuals do not exhibit this illusion. Paradoxically they are more realistic than nondepressed individuals in assessing how much control they have.

Issues of Personal Control

While there is evidence that people strive to maintain a sense of control, a number of writers have raised some issues with the idea of personal control. The first issue comes from Bandura (1986), who has distinguished his conception of **self-efficacy** from personal control. Bandura notes that having a sense of efficacy, or a sense of "ableness" to do something, does not necessarily mean one has control in that area. For instance, a baseball player may have a high sense of self-efficacy as a hitter yet succeed only one-third of the time. Clearly it would be dysfunctional for that person to believe that he or she has complete control over getting a hit. Yet it is functional to feel efficacious as a batter. This same batter may have a feeling of high self-efficacy about baseball but feel incapable of fixing a car, thus having low self-efficacy in that domain.

self-efficacy A person's expectation that he or she can effectively cope with and master situations and bring about desired outcomes through personal efforts.

A second issue is whether it is always desirable to believe that one has control. There are instances in which trying to control things that are not controllable can cause problems. An example is sexual dysfunction. When an individual has problems getting aroused, trying to get aroused is counterproductive. Paradoxically, the way to get aroused is to stop trying to control one's arousal and to focus on other aspects of the situation. Mahoney (1985) has argued that Western culture's heavy emphasis on control may lead to certain kinds of psychiatric disorders. In contrast, in some Eastern cultures, acceptance of one's fate is more valued.

In recent formulations of models of effective control, the idea that active attempts at control are not always good has been included in the form of the idea of secondary control (Fiske and Taylor, 1984), that is, gaining some kind of control by giving up control in other areas. For example, an individual who is paralyzed in an auto accident may have to relinquish control over walking again and shift efforts to things he or she can control, such as activities that he or she will be able to engage in.

Intrinsic versus Extrinsic Motivation

Belief in an internal locus of control goes with the idea that when individuals perceive themselves to be the source of their actions there are different psychological effects than when they believe their actions are being controlled from outside. This, in turn, relates to the issue of intrinsic versus extrinsic motivation. Teachers often feel that students study not because of *intrinsic* interest in the material, but rather because of the course grade, or the *extrinsic* motivator that is contingent on their efforts.

Deci (1975) contended that when someone receives extrinsic rewards for engaging in intrinsically motivating activities, there may be a change in beliefs about why one is engaging in the activity. Using the language of locus of control theory, perceived causation may change from internal (intrinsic interest) to external (the extrinsic reward initiates the activity).

An experiment by Lepper, Greene, and Nisbett (1973) demonstrated this phenomenon in the laboratory. In this study, nursery school children interested in a drawing task were selected as the participants. The children were asked to perform the drawing task under one of three experimental conditions. In an *expected-reward* condition, the participants were told beforehand that they would receive a Good Player Certificate if they played with the experimental materials. In an *unexpected-reward* condition, the participants received the same reward but had no knowledge that they were going to receive the certificate until the drawing activity was completed. Finally, in a control condition, the reward was neither expected nor received.

One or two weeks later, the children were given the opportunity to perform the drawing task again during one of their regular classroom hours. The participants were free to engage in the drawing activity or in other games that were available. No rewards were mentioned, and the teachers did not encourage play with any particular material. To assess the dependent variable (time spent with the drawing task), researchers secretly observed the children in their free-time activities through a one-way mirror. The data revealed that the children in the expected-reward condition exhibited less interest in the task during the free-time period than did the children in the other two conditions (see Condry, 1977).

Source: ESB Professional/Shutterstock

Children who expected to get a reward for drawing were more likely to choose to not draw later. Their intrinsic motivation became controlled by extrinsic rewards.

It seems intuitively unreasonable to contend that reward always decreases interest. One useful distinction in this regard differentiates between the controlling and the informational aspects of a reward. Deci believed that every reward has both controlling and informational aspects. If the controlling aspect is made salient, then there will be a change in perceived locus of causality. But if the informational aspect is salient, then changes in feelings of competence and self-determination are initiated. Hence, rewards indicating that an individual is competent at a task often enhance, rather than undermine, intrinsic motivation. For example, a medal for the best performance, an indication of superiority,

The Flow of Experience

Intrinsically motivated activities are often associated with leisure time—one is doing what one wants for its own sake. On the other hand, extrinsically motivated activities often are associated with work. One is engaged in the activity because of monetary reward and would not choose that activity as a way of spending time if there were no monetary rewards. In their research, Csikszentmihalyi and his colleagues (e.g., Csikszentmihalyi and LeFevre, 1989) examined differential reactions and affects when in work and leisure activities. They were especially concerned with the quality of those experiences and the notion of "flow," or optimal experiences of high challenge along with high skills that are associated with feeling active, alert, and creative. They used a method called experience sampling. In this procedure, the participants wear a "beeper" and at certain intervals are "buzzed" and asked to report on their activities as well as their feelings. Perhaps surprisingly, the vast majority of flow experiences are reported when working, not when in leisure activity. However, most intrinsic motivation was reported during leisure activity. But whether in leisure or in work activity, experience was most positive when demands were high in the face of high skills.

would not be expected to undermine interest. More generally speaking, when reward is not contingent on good performance, but is merely contingent on doing the task, then undermining is likely. In these latter instances, the individual merely goes through the task as fast as possible in order to receive the reward.

The so-called undermining effect of extrinsic reward appears to be a robust and powerful phenomenon, given a tangible reward. The implication of such a finding for the practices of teachers in the classroom, or even for business managers, is enormous. But, in order for teachers, managers, and parents to effectively apply the principles of extrinsic versus intrinsic motivation, conditions must be specified in which undermining will occur as well as those in which reward will enhance intrinsic interest.

Self-Determination Theory

Based on these types of findings, Deci and Ryan (1985) laid out a model they called **Self-Determination Theory**. In Self-Determination Theory, Deci and Ryan connect needs, motivations, and goals. They suggest that all people experience three major needs. They are need for competence, need for relatedness, and need for autonomy (Deci and Ryan, 2000). In this model, these needs are universal. However, one's experience in achieving these needs leads to differences in causality orientation. This concept is similar to the internal versus external locus of control that we see in Rotter, and one of the three dimensions in attributional style. How those needs have been achieved will also influence the development of life goals (see Chapter 14). We have seen the need for relatedness in topics like social support for coping (Chapter 15) and the need for autonomy (see the earlier "Reactance" section).

An interesting test of the needs component comes from an investigation of enjoyment of video games (Ryan, Rigby, and Przybylski, 2006). These researchers found that enjoyment of video games was highest in games that allowed players to have competence and autonomy. In an additional test study, they examined multiplayer games that allowed communication among players. In these games, competence, autonomy, and relatedness all independently predicted enjoyment of the game.

The two different types of motivation in this theory are autonomous motivation and controlled motivation. **Autonomous motivation** is based on intrinsic motivations and the types of extrinsic motivation in which a person has found the activity so valuable to have integrated it into the self. **Controlled motivation** is controlled by extrinsic factors such as punishment or rewards. The reward can be the typical types of rewards: money and prizes. The extrinsic control can also be approval from others, avoidance of shame or guilt, and

Self-Determination Theory An integrated theory that proposes three needs and two motivations.

autonomous motivation A motive based on intrinsic motivations and the types of extrinsic motivation that are integrated into the self.

controlled motivation A motive that is controlled by extrinsic factors such as punishment or rewards.

contingent self-esteem (Deci and Ryan, 2008). When motivations are from within, people will be more excited and have more interest and greater confidence (Deci and Ryan, 2000). Notice here the many similarities to the humanistic theories from Chapter 6.

The development of life goals will be influenced by a variety of factors, but the goals will have impacts on well-being. If the goals are motivated by extrinsic factors, people will tend to experience greater depression and anxiety, whereas goals related to the intrinsic factors tend to be associated with higher self-esteem and self-actualization, and lower anxiety and depression (Kasser and Ryan, 1996).

Many of the theories that we have examined posit a fundamentally hedonic approach to understanding behavior, implying that people are motivated to behave and achieve goals because it feels good. Self-Determination Theory proceeds from a eudaimonic approach, suggesting that it is the process rather than the outcome that is fulfilling (Ryan, Huta, and Deci, 2006).

Achievement Motivation

We have seen that believing oneself to have some control appears to be adaptive, at least in Western culture. The issue of control becomes most critical when we confront failure and adversity. Most important aspects of life—work, relationships, and family—involve periodic experiences with failure and adversity (Dweck and Leggett, 1988). How do we react to failure in a proactive, competent way? Do we simply give up or do we creatively and proactively strive to find new solutions? How we react to failure and adversity appears to have a great deal to do with how we perceive ourselves in relationship to the failure experience. If we see ourselves as able to cope, we will be more likely to persist and look for creative solutions. If we see ourselves as unable or helpless, we will be more likely to give up.

The study of achievement motivation was one of the first systematic efforts to look at how individuals cope with success and failure. We first consider this topic and then examine other research relevant to the topic of ways of coping with adversity.

Even Freud contended that there are two main avenues of satisfaction in life: *Arbeit und Liebe*, work and love. If the meanings of these terms are somewhat broadened to include what is called achievement and affiliation motivation, then Freud's statement seems to be correct. A count of our day's activities would reveal that, in general, most of the time is spent in accomplishing tasks and goals and in maintaining or expanding friendships or intimacy. Of course, humans also strive for power, seek entertainment, engage in acts of aggression, attempt to satisfy curiosity, and so on. But achievement and affiliation motivation appear to be dominant concerns within our culture. Thus, it is not surprising that the study of achievement strivings has played a major role in the psychology of personality.

The motivation to achieve takes many different forms. The college student working late into the night to prepare for the next day's examination, the teenager practicing each day in the schoolyard to perfect a basketball shot, the aspiring executive investing funds in a promising venture, and the scientist persisting in the effort to solve a difficult theoretical problem despite repeated frustration and failure are all displaying achievement motivation. What are the roots of achievement motivation? Why do some individuals strive to reach as high as their abilities will permit, while others are satisfied with much lower levels of accomplishment? What is the relationship between the culture or the economic structure of a society and achievement motivation? Why are some people so unrealistic in the goals they set for themselves? How do perceptions of the causes of success and failure alter our behavior?

The starting point for the systematic psychological study of achievement motivation was in the work of Henry Murray (1938), although other psychologists like Freud and Lewin also played significant roles. Murray was the head of the influential Harvard clinic and one of the founders of the experimental approach to the study of personality. He devised a taxonomy that included twenty basic human needs. These needs were thought of as stable dispositions of the person. Individuals were assumed to vary along these personality dimensions, so that some people had "more of" or stronger dispositions than others. One of these he called **need for achievement**, which was conceived as the desire (Murray, 1938, p. 164):

> To accomplish something difficult. To master, manipulate or organize physical objects, human beings, or ideas. To do this as rapidly and as independently as possible. To overcome obstacles and attain a high standard. To excel one's self. To rival and surpass others. To increase self-regard by the successful exercise of talent.

These desires, Murray said, are accompanied by the following actions (p. 164):

> To make intense, prolonged and repeated efforts to accomplish something difficult. To work with singleness of purpose towards a high and distant goal. To have the determination to win. To try to do everything well. To be stimulated to excel by the presence of others, to enjoy competition.

need for achievement One of Murray's needs, that pertains to a desire to do something difficult and outstanding.

The Measurement of Achievement Needs

For scientific progress, it is not sufficient merely to indicate that there is a predisposition to strive for achievement. Rather, a measure must be constructed to assess this characteristic accurately, so that individuals can be assigned a score indicating the *magnitude* of their need or motivation. Murray (1943) developed an instrument, called the Thematic Apperception Test (TAT), to assess need states (see Chapter 8); it was readily adapted for the assessment of achievement needs. One of the main reasons for its widespread use was that early influential investigators were guided by the Freudian belief that a good place to find indications of motivation is in the fantasy life of individuals. In free responses to ambiguous situations, like those portrayed in Rorschach cards or the TAT, just as in dreams and daydreams, it was believed that individuals revealed their underlying desires and true wishes.

The Procedure

The general TAT methodology used to assess achievement needs has remained virtually unchanged since its inception. Four to six pictures are projected on a screen, typically in a group setting, with participants responding to four directing questions (What is happening? What led up to this situation? What is being thought? What will happen?) The pictures vary in content, portraying one or two individuals engaging in tasks, having an apparently serious or a casual discussion, and so forth. Four minutes of writing time are allowed for each story, and a total achievement need score is obtained for each person by summing the scores of the individual stories.

To score for achievement needs, it is decided whether a story contains achievement-related imagery. Examples of such story imagery include unique accomplishments, such as inventions or novels; long-term achievement concerns, such as wanting to be a success in life or a doctor; and competition with some standard of excellence, such as building the best model.

While the TAT has led to many useful results, it's methodology not without problems. First, a number of issues have been raised concerning internal consistency and test-retest reliability (see Chapter 7). Second, the test is cumbersome; it takes a great deal of time to properly code for the needs.

Achievement Needs as a Personality Structure

It has been indicated that Murray conceived of an achievement need as a trait or an enduring personality disposition. Therefore, two issues are of immediate relevance: (1) what is the generality (or extensiveness, or breadth) of the need for achievement? and (2) is this disposition stable, or at least relatively enduring? Unfortunately, neither question has been adequately answered. It is not known, for example, whether a person who strives for success in a particular occupation also exhibits such achievement drives on the tennis court, in night-school accounting class, or in other situations. It certainly seems reasonable to believe that there are circumscribed avenues or outlets for achievement expression in a given individual. For example, we might expect the driven athlete to exhibit competition on the playing field, but not in the classroom; on the football field, but not in a less central sport such as bowling or ping-pong.

The stability of achievement needs has been the subject of more research than the issue of generality. This is perhaps surprising, inasmuch as longitudinal studies are difficult to conduct. An overview of this research suggests significant but weak correlations between scores on need achievement scales when the measures are taken as many as six years apart (Feld, 1967; Kagan and Moss, 1959; Moss and Kagan, 1961). Research of this type is hampered because of the uncertain test-retest reliability of the TAT. That is, it is impossible to determine if achievement needs are stable if the test-retest reliability of the measure employed is low. Note how closely related the fields of personality structure, measurement, and development are. For example, the demonstration of stable structures and antecedents of development requires valid and reliable measurement instruments.

The question of motive stability is beset with other difficulties as well. For example, it has been found that some parents of low-achievement-orientation adolescents react to their children's lack of achievement concern by stressing independence and achievement. These reactions then influence subsequent achievement concerns and alter the stability of the need system, so that retesting will indicate low trait stability. Therefore, stability is in part dependent on the type and the consistency of socialization experiences.

The essential questions of generality and stability are unanswered. The next question is: what is known about people who are labeled as high in need for achievement, or high in the desire to achieve success? The clearest, most understandable correlates of achievement needs have been derived from the various theories of achievement motivation that are examined later in this chapter. However, there are several personality characteristics associated with achievement motivation that can be noted at this point. For example, there is some evidence that, given a choice among tasks of high, intermediate, or low difficulty, tasks of intermediate difficulty are more attractive to individuals highly motivated to succeed than to those lower in achievement needs.

In a similar vein, individuals high in achievement needs have been characterized as realistic and have occupational goals that are congruent with their abilities (Mahone, 1960; Morris, 1966). The desire for intermediate risk may indicate a preference for personal feedback or knowledge about oneself. This informational explanation is consistent with the high achiever's reported preference for business occupations, where feedback (profit) is immediately evident (McClelland, 1961; Meyer, Walker, and Litwin, 1961). In addition, individuals high in need for achievement apparently are better able to delay gratification (Mischel, 1961) and get higher grades in school than individuals low in achievement needs, if the grades are instrumental to long-term success (Raynor, 1970). Furthermore, they are thought of as hope rather than fear oriented. For example, there is some evidence that they are especially optimistic about their chances of success (Feather, 1965). Finally, individuals high in achievement needs take personal responsibility for success and generally perceive themselves as high in ability (Kukla, 1972). This self-attribution for success increases their feelings of worth and may account, in part, for their high self-concept as reported by some investigators (Mukherjee and Sinha, 1970).

Achievement Motivation and Economic Development

Numerous sociological and anthropological investigations of achievement motivation have gone on outside the laboratory. Foremost among these was an attempt by McClelland (1961) to relate achievement motivation to economic growth.

The initial influences on McClelland's analysis of economic growth were Winterbottom's (1953) data relating early independence training to the growth of achievement needs and the speculations of Max Weber (1904) concerning the Protestant reformation. Weber noted that the Protestant revolt emphasized the importance of self-reliance and productivity. Furthermore, because of religious beliefs, the results of one's labors could not be spent self-indulgently. Thus, profits were reinvested, resulting in further prosperity.

McClelland perceived a relationship between these notions and the work on achievement motivation. He suggested that Protestant values produced early independence training that, in turn, promoted need for achievement and economic development. This hypothesized sequence is shown in Figure 17.1, which indicates four relationships: (1) Protestantism and

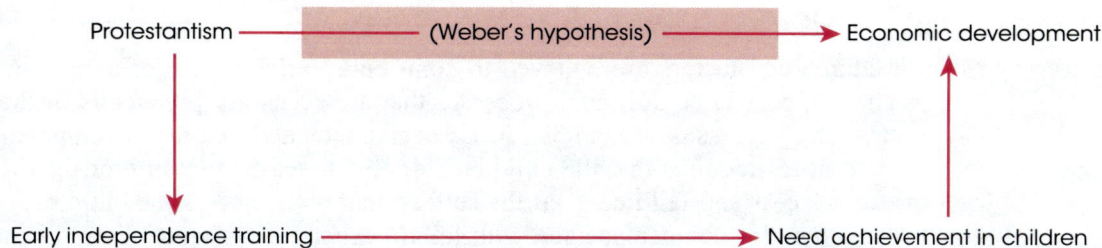

FIGURE 17.1 Hypothetical Relationship between Self-Reliance Values and Economic Development

early independence training; (2) early independence training and need for achievement; (3) need for achievement and economic development; and (4) Protestantism and economic development. Of these, the alleged relationship between achievement need and economic development has produced the most extensive, novel, and controversial findings.

The TAT assessment procedure originated by Murray has a unique advantage in that it is applicable to any prose material. Thus, to examine the relationship between achievement needs and economic growth, McClelland scored prose material, such as children's readers, speeches, folktales, and songs, for achievement needs. These scores were then related to available indexes of economic activity, such as consumption of electrical power, quantity of imports, and number of independent artisans within a society. Data from a wide array of cultures and times, including Tudor England and ancient Greece, provided evidence that increments in need for achievement, inferred from the scoring of the various prose material, precedes economic development, while decreases in need for achievement are predictive of economic decline.

You might be wondering, by this time, about the achievement motivation in U.S. culture. Figure 17.2 indicates that people's achievement needs in America, ascertained from children's readers, increased from 1800 to 1910. Since 1910, the indicators of achievement concerns have steadily decreased. Does this hint that our economy is also going to decline? Figure 17.2 also reveals that the patent index, one indicator of unique accomplishment and achievement needs, and an economic stimulant, is declining as well.

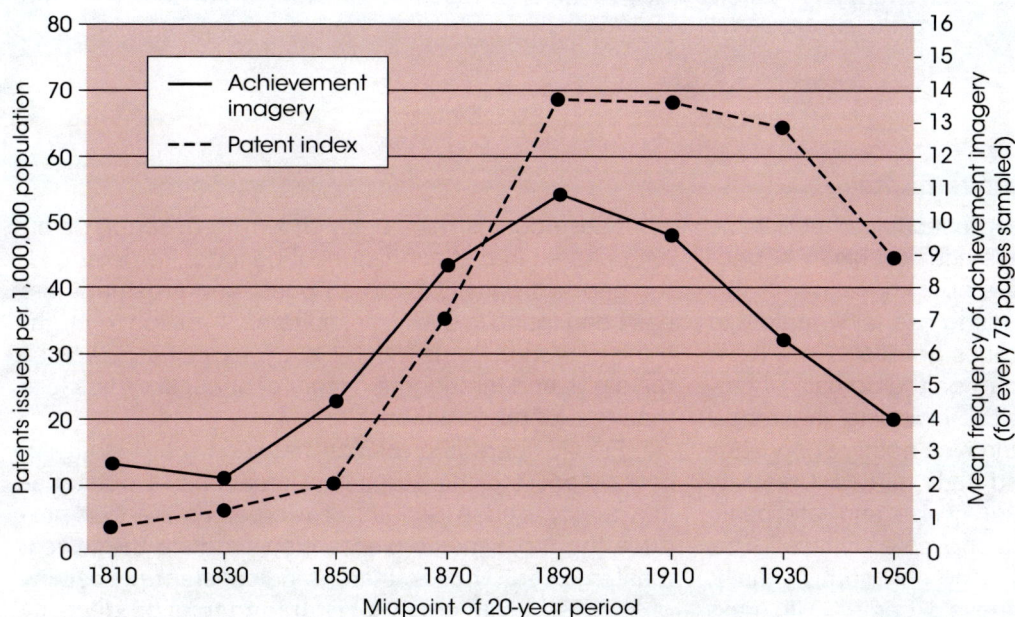

FIGURE 17.2 Mean Frequency of Achievement Imagery in Children's Readers and the Patent Index in WEE the United States, 1800–1950

Source: (Based on de Charms and Moeller, 1962, p. 139)

The Development of Achievement Needs

Maturational factors are believed to contribute to the growth of achievement strivings. There appear to be universal processes that are necessary precursors of the tendency to strive for success. For example, it has been contended that the development of achievement needs requires that the child be able to "direct the pleasure or the disappointment after success and failure . . . at the self, so that with success the child experiences pleasure about his competence and with failure experiences shame about his incompetence" (Heckhausen and Roelofsen, 1962, p. 378). This suggests that developing self-attribution is a necessary antecedent to achievement striving. A different cognitive analysis of achievement proposes three stages in the development of achievement strivings: (1) an intrapersonal competition, or autonomous, stage in which the child competes with itself; (2) an interpersonal competition, or social comparison, stage in which competition is with others rather than with the self; and (3) an integration of the two previous stages (Veroff, 1969). Passage from stage 1 to stage 2 typically takes place when the child enters school and acquires the ability to use social norm information in making comparative judgments.

Atkinson's Theory of Achievement Motivation

A very prominent theory of achievement motivation was formulated by John Atkinson (1957, 1964). This theory was influenced by Miller's conflict model (introduced in Chapter 14). Achievement-oriented behavior was viewed by Atkinson as a conflict between approach and avoidance tendencies. Associated with every achievement-related action is the possibility of success (with the consequent emotion of pride) and the possibility of failure (with the consequent emotion of shame). The strengths of these anticipated emotions determine whether an individual will approach or avoid achievement-oriented activities. That is, achievement behavior involves an emotional conflict between hopes for success and fears of failure.

Let us consider some hypotheses derived from Atkinson's conception and some empirical studies testing those hypotheses. Take the situation in which a person is confronted with a number of alternative choices varying in difficulty. For example, at an athletic event, a tennis player might choose to play against a competitor of equal skill, one who would be very difficult to beat, or one who should be fairly easy to beat. Or a student might have to decide among three sections of a course that vary in difficulty, such that

---

HIGHLIGHT 17.2

Age and Outstanding Achievements

For a long time there has been speculation about the association between a person's age and his or her accomplishments. A few facts are now known about this relation. First, productivity tends to rise fairly rapidly to a definite peak, and then declines gradually. The location of this peak depends in part on the domain of creative achievement. Some fields, including theoretical physics, pure mathematics, and lyric poetry show early peaks in the late twenties and early thirties. Creativity in other fields displays a leisurely rise and late peak, with the peak in the late forties or even early fifties. This holds for novel writing, history, and philosophy. Finally, other disciplines fall between these extremes, with maximum output rate around the age of forty. Psychology is among the fields exhibiting this productivity curve.

These curves have been shown to describe different cultures in distinct historical periods. For example, the gap in creativity between poets and prose authors has been found in every major literary tradition throughout the world. Poets exhibit a life expectancy across the globe and throughout history of about six years less than that of prose writers.

Finally, there is a relation between the quantity of one's work and the number of creations of outstanding quality. Those periods of a creator's life that produce the most masterpieces also produce the fewest masterpieces! That is, there is a "constant probability of success," with creativity related to total productivity (see Lehrman, 1953; Simonton, 1988a, 1988b).

the chances of getting an A or a B are very low in one section, intermediate in a second section, and almost a sure thing in the third section. Although some cynics might feel that most people would choose the easy section or the easy competitor, there are significant individual differences in the extent to which people select tasks of high, moderate, or low difficulty, that is, there are differences in their *level of aspiration* (Frank, 1935; Lewin, Dembo, Festinger, and Sears, 1944). The Atkinson model enables us to predict the choices that different people make.

Most importantly, according to the Atkinson model, attraction to a sure thing, to a long shot, or to a moderate challenge depends on the relationship between the levels of success motive and the difficulty of the task. Based on this model, motivation is highest for all individuals at tasks of intermediate difficulty. Thus, the intuitively reasonable observation is captured by the theory that athletic teams and spectators are most motivated when the score is even. However, this is more so for those with high achievement needs than for those with low achievement needs. The theory predicts that the higher the achievement needs, the greater the attraction toward tasks whose probability of success equals .50.

The Atkinson model predicts that high-achievement individuals will prefer tasks of intermediate difficulty more than low-achievement individuals will. How do these predictions measure up when compared with empirical data? An experiment by Atkinson and Litwin (1960) bears directly on this question. In this investigation, participants attempted to toss rings over a peg. They were allowed to stand at varying distances from the peg and could change position (increase or decrease aspirations) following each toss. It was assumed that a position close to the target corresponded to a high probability of success and that probability of success decreased as the distance from the peg increased. Thus, distance from the peg was the observable indicator of choice and of task difficulty. The participants were classified into motive groups on the basis of individual differences measures, including the TAT. The data on choice behavior indicated that intermediate task preference was greatest for the high-motive group, least for participants low in achievement needs, and neither high nor low for participants at the middle in achievement needs.

An Informational View Alternative Explanation

Atkinson's prediction of disparate personality-group preferences is based on the belief that choice among achievement tasks follows the principle of maximization of positive affect. That is, anticipatory emotions and hedonistic concerns determine which tasks one will attempt to perform. As indicated in Chapter 14, most psychologists consider hedonism to be the main source of motivation and behavior.

An alternative interpretation of risk-preference appeals more to informational and self-concept principles than to hedonism, reflecting the trend toward cognitive explanations of action that is now prevalent in psychology. Research has demonstrated that outcomes at tasks of intermediate difficulty provide performers with the most information about their efforts and capabilities. There are logical reasons why this is the case. Selection of easy tasks typically results in success and the outcome is ascribed to the ease of the task. In a similar manner, selection of very difficult tasks generally results in failure, with blame placed on the characteristics of the task. Thus, selection of very easy or very difficult tasks usually confirms our knowledge about the external world. Success on tasks at which almost everyone succeeds and failure on tasks at which almost everyone does poorly tell very little about the skills of the individual engaged in those tasks. However, tasks of intermediate difficulty are just as likely to produce success as failure, and performance at such tasks provides information about the efforts and abilities of the person undertaking them. From this perspective, differential preference for tasks of varying difficulty between groups differing in achievement needs indicates disparate desires for personal feedback and self-evaluation. Of course, it is quite functional and adaptive to have a realistic view of oneself and one's capabilities. A research study by Trope (1975) supports the informational view that high achievers seek situations that are diagnostic of their relative level of ability.

Attribution Theory and Achievement Strivings

The discussion of choice behavior called attention to the informational or self-evaluative aspects of task selection. It is now apparent that other aspects of achievement motivation are also influenced by cognitive or inferential processes. Foremost among the mental events that affect achievement-related behaviors are causal attributions. This concept was examined earlier when perceived responsibility and helplessness were discussed.

Causal Attributions

Causal attributions in achievement-related contexts refer to beliefs about the reasons for one's success or failure. There are, of course, many possible reasons for a positive or a negative achievement outcome, but research has shown that a few factors are perceived as most responsible for success and failure. These factors include ability, effort, task ease or difficulty, luck, and help or hindrance from others. That is, if one succeeds, then the outcome is ascribed to high ability, hard work, the ease of the task, etc. In a similar manner, failure is generally ascribed to low ability, lack of effort, a difficult task, etc. Of these causes, ability and effort are particularly salient. That is, outcomes typically depend on what we *can* do and how hard we *try*. Other, less-used attributions for success and failure include the bias of a supervisor or teacher, mood, illness, fatigue, and home environment.

As revealed earlier, the perceived causes of success and failure have been incorporated within a few basic causal dimensions which describe the underlying properties of causes (Weiner, 1979, 1986). One dimension, which has been examined in some detail in the prior chapter, is labeled **locus of causality**. Causes are perceived as either internal (within the person) or external (in the environment). For example, ability and effort are person causes, whereas task difficulty, help from others, and luck are among the environmental determinants of an outcome. A second dimension of causality has been identified as the *stability* or constancy of a cause. Some causes, such as aptitude, the ease of a task, and conditions in the home, are typically perceived as relatively enduring or stable. On the other hand, causes such as effort expenditure, luck, mood, and illness are generally perceived as subject to momentary or periodic fluctuation. Still a third dimension of causality is the *controllability* of the cause. For example, how much effort we expend is subject to personal influence, whereas luck and illness generally are not. In sum, classifications of causes have been developed that allow each causal factor to be placed within a multidimensional framework.

The Consequences of Causal Attributions

It has been demonstrated that causal attributions are linked to specific psychological consequences. The *locus* of a causal attribution influences affective reactions to success and failure. If, for example, one attributes success to such internal causes as ability or effort, then more pride and self-enhancement are experienced than if that success is attributed to external factors like task ease or good luck. The *stability* of a cause influences the subjective expectancy of success at the task, or how likely the person feels that future success is within reach. For example, if a previous failure is ascribed to lack of effort or bad luck, then future success might be anticipated. But if failure is attributed to a fixed cause such as "no mathematical aptitude," then future failure will be anticipated. The dimension of control is particularly important in interpersonal evaluations. For example, if you are a member of a team and you do poorly for reasons within your control, like lack of effort, then your teammates will be angry with you. On the other hand, poor performance due to an uncontrollable cause, like illness, often elicits sympathy from others. In addition, when one fails because of lack of effort, guilt is often experienced, whereas failure because of lack of ability tends to produce shame and humiliation.

Suppose, for example, that a student gets a low grade in a class and then decides to drop out of school (see Fig. 17.3). How might an attribution theorist explain this behavior? First, when the student receives this grade, he or she asks: "Why have I done so poorly?" If the student has failed in the past, while others have performed well, then the likely attribution for the current performance is to the self. The student might conclude: "I am dumb or unable."

locus of causality A determination of whether the cause of the behavior or outcome is internal, that is within the person, or external, that is luck or something about the situation.

Causal ascriptions	Causal dimensions	Consequences	Behavior
Ability			
Effort	Locus →	Esteem-related affect	Choice
Task difficulty	Stability →	Expectancy	Intensity
Luck	Control →	Social affects (guilt, shame, pity, anger)	Persistence
Others			

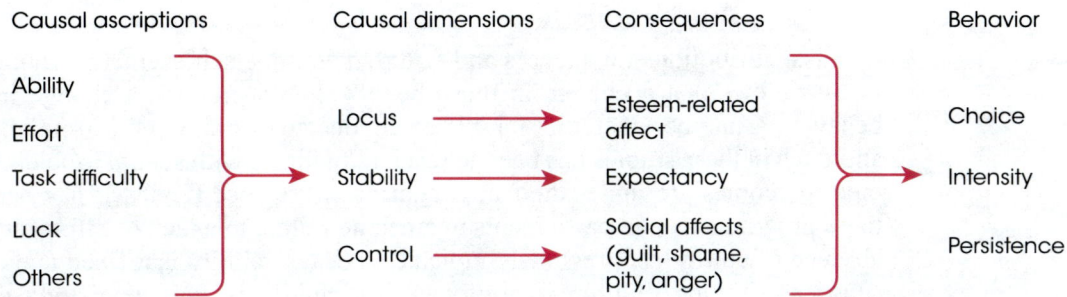

FIGURE 17.3 An Attributional Model of Achievement Strivings

Pity, Anger, and Achievement Performance

It is generally thought that pity and sympathy are "good" emotions and that anger is a "bad" emotion. However, attribution theorists have pointed out that the consequences of these emotional expressions are complex. In one investigation, Graham (1984) gave participants (twelve-year-old children) false failure feedback during an achievement task. For some children, this was accompanied by the remark: "I feel sorry for you" as well as body postures and facial gestures that accompany sympathy (head down, hands folded, etc.). To other students, the experimenter said: "I am angry with you." Students receiving the pity feedback tended to blame the failure on themselves (low ability) and their performance declined. On the other hand, students receiving anger feedback attributed their failure to lack of effort and their performance subsequently increased. This is not to advocate that sympathy is always detrimental and anger always facilitative. Rather, the consequences of feedback depend on how that feedback is construed and what it means to the recipient of the communication. Other kinds of feedback, such as praise for success at an easy task and excessive and unsolicited helping, also tend to convey that the student is "unable" and therefore have some negative consequences.

This attribution is internal to the student, so that self-esteem is decreased. In addition, the attribution is stable; ability is not anticipated to be changeable. Furthermore, attributions of failure to low ability produce humiliation, while others express pity. This feedback further enhances the belief that "I cannot" (see Highlight 17.3). Low self-esteem, humiliation, and low expectancy of success then result in the student's decision to drop out of school.

In sum, individuals who react to failure by attributing its cause to something fixed and uncontrollable about themselves are unlikely to be able to cope productively with challenges. They are more likely to be pessimistic about their chances of future success, and as we have previously noted, more likely to react in a helpless manner.

Explanatory Style and Achievement Strivings

Earlier in this chapter, we saw that individuals have biases or dispositions to attribute outcomes to particular causes. This attributional style has especially been related to depression. In addition, attributional or explanatory style has also been associated with achievement strivings. Peterson and Barrett (1987) reported that students who generally tend to explain bad academic events with stable causes internal to themselves, such as low aptitude, receive lower grades as freshman than students who tend to ascribe failure to external and unstable causes, such as bad luck. This pattern held even when ability was constant between the groups.

Pride in accomplishment is one of the indicators of high achievement strivings.

Source: El Nariz/Shutterstock

Changing Attributions

If causal attributions for success and failure determine achievement strivings, then it logically follows that a change in these beliefs should produce a change in achievement behavior. A number of studies have been conducted examining this principle. The general approach in these studies has been to teach individuals with school problems that achievement outcomes are under their own control. More specifically, it has been the goal of these programs to lead participants to attribute failure to a lack of effort rather than to the absence of ability. As previously indicated, because ability is a fixed and uncontrollable cause, ascriptions of failure to ability are particularly dysfunctional and debilitating.

One exemplary investigation in this area was conducted by Dweck (1975). Her participants were eight- to thirteen-year-olds who had been independently identified by their teacher, school psychologist, and principal as having a high expectancy of failure and as displaying performance decrements in failure situations. Dweck's method was to verbalize to participants that failure during a series of training sessions was due to lack of effort. During these training trials, 20 percent of the responses resulted in failure. The attributional training procedure was compared to a program of inducing 100 percent success (without any causal attributions) and, in so doing, supposedly increase self-confidence. Dweck's data, shown in Figure 17.4, revealed the efficacy and value of attributional training and its superiority over the success-only treatment. Following training, only the attributional treatment group did not show decrements in responding in the face of failure. However, the interpretation of these findings is somewhat complicated by the fact that the attributional group received partial reinforcement, which might have contributed to their relatively better performance (see Chapter 5). These types of findings were influential in the development of a theory that we will discuss shortly.

Other change programs have been successful with less complex treatments. For example, Wilson and Linneville (1982, 1985) demonstrated that merely informing students that the policy of the university was to "ease up" on grading following the first year of

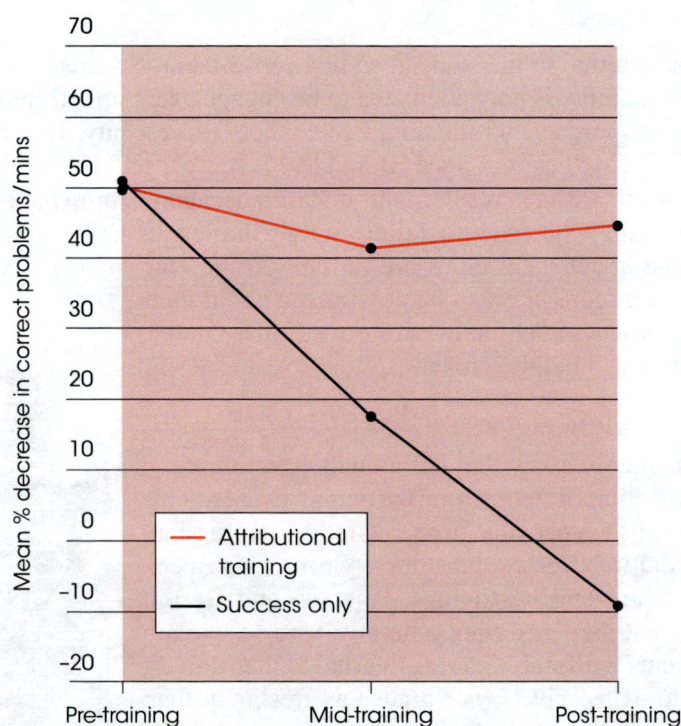

FIGURE 17.4 Mean Percentage Decrease in Correct Problems

Source: (Based on Dweck, 1975, p. 82. Copyright 1975 by the American Psychological Association)

study increased achievement strivings among students dissatisfied with their first-year performance. Information that the poor performance was due to an unstable cause (rather than, say, low ability) resulted in maintaining expectancy of future success and, in turn, increased motivation (see Foersterling, 1985).

Competence

The study of achievement motivation has shown that high achievers approach tasks in such a way that they are more likely to achieve success because they are not paralyzed by attributing failure to stable, internal, uncontrollable causes. This finding is in keeping with other findings from the study of competence.

As we consider it here, *competence* is the ability to perform as capably as one can on a task, regardless of one's level of ability or skill. Primarily, competence has to do with how one perceives oneself, the task, and obstacles encountered as one works on the task. Findings from a wide variety of sources—such as research on Bandura's concept of self-efficacy (Bandura, 1986; see Chapter 5), Dweck and Leggett's (1988) research on a mastery-oriented versus helpless stance towards problems in children, and others (Sternberg and Kolligian, 1990)—converge on the following conclusions. First, a competent performance on a task involves keeping one's eye on the immediate aspects of the task itself rather than focusing' on whether or not one is ultimately going to succeed. A good football team must take it "one play at a time" even if they are behind by twenty-one points. Second, one's attention must be focused outward on the task demands themselves rather than inward on what success or failure means about the self.

Mindset

An interesting model developed by Carol Dweck (1999) and her colleagues helps explain these kinds of differences. This model has been known as self-theories (Dweck, 1999) and as mindset (Dweck, 2006). As has been explained a few times in this book, people act as naïve scientists developing theories about people. One of these theories is about stability and change in personality and ability (Erdley and Dweck, 1993). Some people believe that people change and grow, whereas others believe that people do not change much. Those that believe that change happens are typically labeled **incremental theorists**. Change happens little by little, i.e., in small increments. Those who believe that personality, skills, and intelligence are fixed are usually labeled **entity theorists**. The belief of entity theorists is that people either have it or they don't. They have the entity of intelligence or they do not. They are good at soccer or they are not. This implicit theory has implications for the meaning of effort and failure.

If an ability is fixed, it also means that success or failure is diagnostic about the amount of ability. This has the consequences of engaging the person, but if failure is encountered, it means that the person must not be good at it and may as well move on to other activities. Consider the implications of someone trying to learn mathematics. If that person fails, he or she clearly isn't "good at math." This will lead to feelings of helplessness in that domain. Contrast this with someone who believes that skills are incremental. Failure is feedback that the skills are not fully developed and more effort is needed (Dweck and Leggett, 1988). Finally, consider the implications of a teacher who holds these different implicit theories. An entity theorist teacher would focus on the best students, since they have what it takes, and an incremental theorist teacher would focus on the struggling students to allow those students to gain the skills they are missing.

There are going to be different goal orientations as a result of these implicit theories. The entity theorist will be oriented toward a performance goal. By performing well, there is the goal of positive attention, and avoidance of negative judgements. The incremental theorist will have learning goals, with the goal of increasing ability and competence. In one study (Farrell and Dweck, 1985), students were assessed for performance goals versus learning goals. There was no difference in ability on a pretest of a science concept, and

incremental theorists People who have the implicit theory that ability can change with effort.

entity theorists People who have the implicit theory that a person has a set amount of ability.

Beliefs about whether abilities change or are fixed impact student goals and effort.

there was no difference on the knowledge gained while students studied the concepts. The difference was in applying the concepts to a new problem. The students who had the learning goals were able to apply the concept to the new problem better than the students who had performance goals. You have probably noticed these types of differences in your peers. There are those who focus entirely on doing well on the test, and others who are focused on learning the material.

The *meaning* of effort is also different for the two different mindsets. For someone who has an entity perspective, working hard implies that the person "doesn't have it." While for someone who holds the incremental mindset, working hard is how you get it. This model has become very popular in education and coaching. For instance, U.S. Youth Soccer is recommending all coaches read *Mindset* (2006). In these contexts, the concepts have typically been renamed "Growth" and "Fixed" mindsets.

Integrating Perceived Control with Achievement Motivation and Competence

There is a general trend underlying most of the topics considered in this chapter. Under the general umbrella of approaching life in an effective and proactive manner, we suggest that people who are more likely to approach challenges in a proactive, mastery-oriented manner are individuals: (1) who believe that they have some degree of control over the outcomes in their life, (2) who attribute success to themselves in such a way as to reward themselves for their efforts and who attribute failure to factors that do not cause them to paralyze themselves, (3) who feel optimistic and not helpless (4) who believe that ability is changeable with effort and (5) who as they perform focus on the immediate demands of the task rather than on the ultimate outcome of success or failure or on what success and failure mean about the self. Generally, people who are less likely to perform proactively are individuals: (1) who do not feel they have control, (2) who are pessimistic (especially if their pessimism leads them to believe they have no control), (3) who attribute success in such a manner that they get no reward for their efforts and who experience failure in such a manner that they feel hopeless to ever achieve success by their own efforts, (4) who believe their ability or its lack is fixed and unchangeable, and (5) who focus on success or failure rather than on immediate task mastery.

There may appear to be a contradiction between research suggesting that competent performance involves a focus on the task and not on the self and research suggesting that competence is enhanced by attributing success to oneself. This apparent contradiction can be resolved if we break task performance into two segments: the performance itself, and reflecting on the performance after it is over. While performing, it appears to be more functional to be not thinking about the self. (We have previously discussed the negative effects of excessive self-focused attention in Chapter 10.) However, after the performance is over and one reflects on why one has succeeded or failed, it appears to be effective to attribute success to oneself and failure to either oneself in the form of something controllable, such as a lack of effort, or to external factors, such as luck or task difficulty. Another implication of this is that not all kinds of internal attributions are beneficial. This becomes important as we shall see in the following discussion of attributions of responsibility.

Attributions of Responsibility

When something positive or negative happens, we become concerned with the question of whether or not we can hold a person responsible for the outcome. Attribution of responsibility involves many of the same issues we have already considered in this chapter. Basically, in attributing responsibility for an outcome we ask ourselves: did this outcome arise or not arise from factors over which the person had control? Attributions of responsibility for the outcome of an event often determine how we subsequently respond to an individual.

Evaluation

As we have seen, achievement evaluation is affected by the responsibility that is assigned for success and failure. In one experimental demonstration (Weiner and Kukla, 1970), participants were asked to pretend that they were teachers and were to provide evaluative feedback to their students. The pupils were described as having just completed an exam with one of five possible outcomes: excellent, fair, borderline, failure, and clear failure. In addition, the pupils were described jointly in terms of ability (high or low) and effort (high or low). For example, one pupil was characterized as high in ability, low in effort, and having a borderline test performance. Evaluation was indicated by giving each pupil a score from + 5 (highest reward) to –5 (highest punishment).

The results are depicted in Figure 17.5, which reveals that test outcome, a factor commonly known to affect evaluation, indeed influences feedback in the expected manner: the greater the success, the more favorable the feedback. But pupil characteristics and perceived personal responsibility also affect evaluation. First, high effort motivation results in a more positive evaluation than does low effort, at all outcome levels. And, perhaps

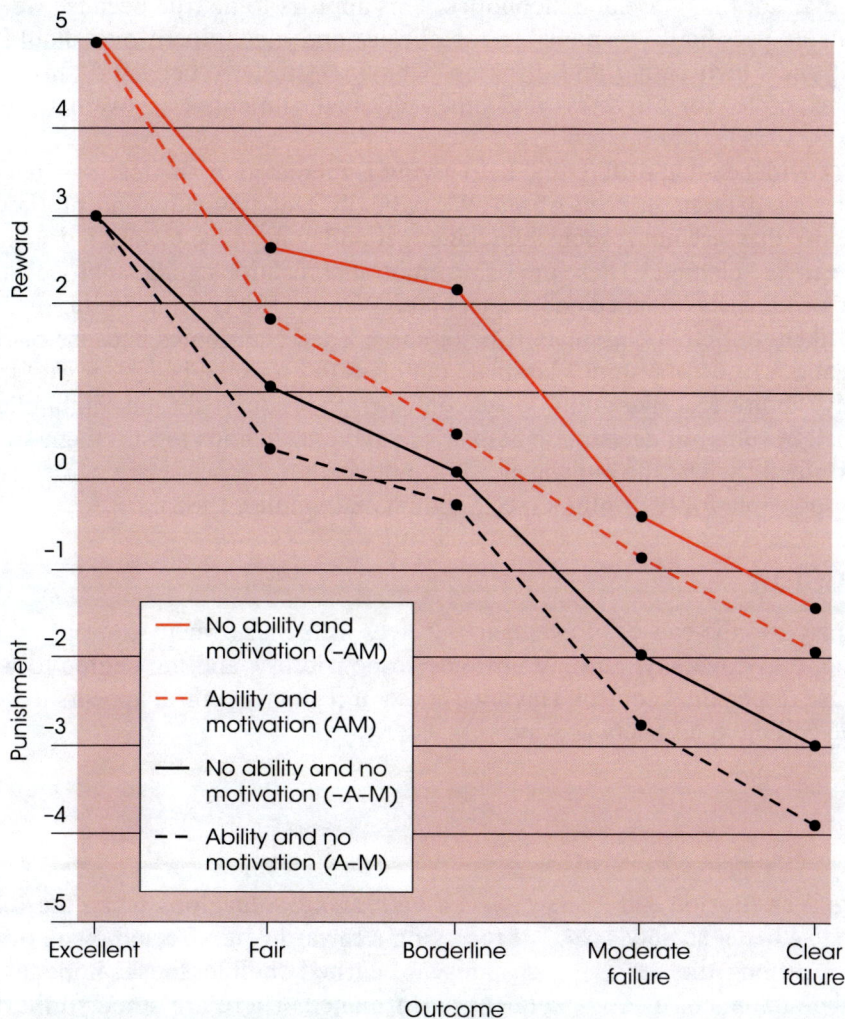

FIGURE 17.5 Evaluation (Reward and Punishment) as a Function of Pupil Ability, Motivation, and Examination Outcome

Source: (Weiner and Kukula, 1970, p. 3)

surprisingly, low ability produces a higher evaluation than does high ability. This is because low ability coupled with high effort and success is especially rewarded. For example, the handicapped person who completes a marathon or the cognitively impaired child who persists in completing a task elicits great social approval because each is considered personally responsible for success. On the other hand, high ability coupled with low effort and failure is maximally punished. For example, the bright dropout or the gifted athlete who refuses to practice and performs poorly generates great social disapproval. Again this is because each is perceived as personally responsible for failure. These individuals did not have to fail; they had freedom of choice and could have chosen a different outcome. Because low ability coupled with high effort and success is so strongly rewarded, while high ability linked with low effort and failure is correspondingly punished, lack of ability emerges as a beneficial attribute in this particular kind of experiment.

Helping Behavior

It is also evident that whether we help others and the kind of aid we are willing to give are in part dependent on whether we perceive the person in need of aid as responsible for his or her plight. For example, it has been clearly demonstrated that people are more likely to help a disabled person than a drunk (Piliavin, Rodin, and Piliavin, 1969). In a similar manner, it is much easier for a charity to raise money for battered children or the blind than for the obese and alcoholics. This appears to be true because we perceive individuals as personally responsible for obesity and alcoholism; one should be able to control one's own eating and drinking behavior. On the other hand, this is not the case, for example, for blindness and other physical ailments (see Weiner, Perry, and Magnusson, 1988).

There is evidence that differential help giving is mediated by the feelings that are elicited by various persons in need of aid. We typically feel sympathy and pity toward the blind because they are not responsible, but anger and annoyance toward a drunk because she or he can be "blamed." These opposing emotional reactions guide approach and helping behavior versus avoidance and neglect (see Weiner, 1980). In a similar manner, you might be likely to help a classmate if he or she needed class notes because of illness or hospitalization. But if the same classmate cut class to go to the beach, or said that he or she merely "didn't feel like going to school," then the request for aid might elicit anger and neglect. In sum, our decision to help others and our feelings toward them are in good part determined by why the aid was needed and whether the needy are perceived as personally responsible for their plight (see Schmidt and Weiner, 1988).

Conclusion

How we perceive the causes of events in our lives influences whether or not we successfully respond to adversity, how we attribute responsibility, and the degree to which we have a sense of personal control. Having a sense of personal control appears to be related to positive coping in a variety of ways.

Summary

1. Skinner has contended that freedom is an illusion and that acceptance of this fact will lead to a better society.
2. *Locus of control* refers to beliefs regarding the perceived influence that one has on the attainment of a reinforcement. Questionnaires have been devised to classify individuals as *internal* versus *external* in locus of control. There is some evidence that persons labeled as internal function more effectively.
3. *Learned helplessness* develops when the likelihood of receiving a reward is unaffected by an organism's response. Learned helplessness impedes subsequent performance. There are some similarities between laboratory-induced helplessness and the state of depression.
4. An Attributional Style questionnaire has been developed to assess individual differences in causal

perceptions. The disposition to attribute failure to the self may be a precursor for the onset of depression.

5. *Intrinsic* motivation indicates that behavior is undertaken for its own sake; *extrinsic* motivation connotes that the action is undertaken because of an extrinsic reward. Use of an extrinsic reward to motivate behavior may undermine or decrease intrinsic interest in the activity. Undermining occurs when the controlling, rather than the informational, aspects of the reward are salient.

6. Individuals attempt to restore freedom if it is taken away, a reaction termed *psychological reactance*. One manifestation of this attempt is demonstrated in attitudes: increased liking of a "forbidden" choice and decreased liking of available alternatives.

7. There is evidence that individuals maintain an illusion that they have control over their fates.

8. Henry Murray played an important role in the study of achievement needs by defining the achievement motive and specifying the actions that it instigates.

9. Need for achievement is typically assessed with a projective technique, the Thematic Apperception Test (TAT). However, this measure has a number of shortcomings, such as low internal consistency.

10. The generality of need for achievement as a trait remains uncertain, and there is only scattered evidence that the trait is relatively enduring.

11. Among the personality correlates of the need for achievement is the tendency for individuals high in achievement needs to (a) prefer intermediate-difficulty tasks, (b) be realistic in their aspirations, and (c) desire performance feedback.

12. Cognitive maturational factors, including self-attribution of success and integration of competitive stages, appear to be necessary precursors for the development of achievement strivings.

13. The effects of early socialization practices, such as early independence training and stress on good performance, have not been convincingly demonstrated as necessary antecedents for the development of high achievement needs.

14. Atkinson proposed a mathematical model of achievement motivation in which achievement tendencies are determined by the difference between hope for success and fear of failure. Atkinson's mathematical model leads to the prediction that individuals high in achievement needs prefer tasks of intermediate difficulty.

15. Studies on *diagnosticity*, or the information gained about one's ability following task performance, have shown that individuals highly motivated to succeed are especially desirous of feedback about their abilities.

16. Causal attributions for success or failure are important determinants of achievement striving. Three basic properties of causes—locus, stability, and controllability—influence, respectively, esteem-related affective reactions, expectancy of success, and social emotions.

17. There is some evidence that increments in need for achievement precede the positive economic growth of a society.

18. A variety of achievement-change programs focus attention on changing attributions for failure from lack of ability to insufficient effort.

19. Children who behave in a mastery-oriented manner keep attention focused on the task when they fail. They do not give up prematurely and they try new strategies. Helpless children when confronted with failure give up prematurely. Or, if they persist, they repeat the same dysfunctional strategy over and over. Further they focus their attention on what failure means about them rather than keeping attention focused on the task.

20. Evaluations of others are affected and the likelihood of help giving is minimized when others are perceived as personally responsible for their plight.

Key Terms

attributional style (p. 325)
autonomous motivation (p. 329)
controlled motivation (p. 329)
defensive pessimism (p. 325)
entity theorists (p. 339)
incremental theorists (p. 339)
learned helplessness (p. 323)

locus of causality (p. 336)
locus of control (p. 320)
need for achievement (p. 331)
psychological reactance (p. 326)
Self-Determination Theory (p. 329)
self-efficacy (p. 327)

Thought Questions

1. What do you think of Skinner's position that we have only an illusion of control?

2. What situations in your present environment give rise to feelings of control and feelings of helplessness?

3. Can you recall a situation in which your freedom was restricted? What were your feelings and subsequent actions at the time? Did you make an attempt to restore freedom?

4. Do grades in school undermine your intrinsic interest in the subject matter? If grading were eliminated, would you have more or less interest in studying the material?

5. Are your goals based on extrinsic motivations or needs like competence, relatedness and autonomy?

6. Do you think that achievement strivings tend to be expressed across a variety of situations or are specifically channeled into a few activities? Can you think of individuals who meet each of these descriptions?

7. When you do well on a test, what attributions do you generally make? How about when you do poorly? Do these influence your feelings and your expectations?

8. How would you teach an eighth grader about implicit theories about ability so that they will work harder following failure, rather than giving up.

Love and Hate

Source: g-stockstudio/Shutterstock

Chapter Outline

Love's Infinite Variety

Research on Love

A Triangular Model of Love

Passionate Love

Companionate Love

Intimacy

Choosing a Partner

Love and Sex

Love and Hate

Aggression

Cultural Influences

The Physical Environment

Personality Theories and the
    Antecedents of Aggression

Developmental Influences

Aggression as a Personality Trait

Catharsis and the Regulation of
    Aggression

Literature, movies, television, and clinical experiences all convey the presence and power of love and hate in human relationships. They are polar opposites: one fostering caretaking, giving, and growth, the other fostering discord, conflict, and destruction. However, they are often intimately connected. Love can give way to hate, as reflected in the number of homicides that take place between family members and lovers. In addition, some sexual behaviors have components of both love and hostility. Indeed, although mutually consenting sex is a loving act, there are some theorists who have suggested that hostility can nevertheless be a major source of sexual excitement (Stoller, 1979).

It is evident that love and hate are manifested in diverse ways and that they are complex terms. Each refers to a broad domain of feelings and behaviors. In this chapter, we shall distinguish between different meanings of love and caring, and of hate and aggression. We shall also review the empirical exploration of these rather complex but fundamental dimensions of human experience. Aggression, in particular, has been extensively studied, whereas the empirical examination of love has been relatively recent. However, the research on love, like the research on aggression and hostility, demonstrates that despite the vagueness and ambiguity of the concept, a scientific approach can increase our understanding of the phenomenon.

Are humans fundamentally aggressive or loving? Is hatred learned? What is the relationship of the love of a parent for a child to the love between adult partners? What does it mean "to be in love"? Is it possible for society to control hatred and aggression effectively? Do sports and the entertainment media serve as outlets for aggression? Unfortunately, there are no simple answers to these questions and, in some instances, it is not yet possible to give any answer. However, theoretical analyses and empirical studies have at the very least provided a framework that enables us to discuss these issues sensibly and systematically.

Love's Infinite Variety

The ancients distinguished between at least three kinds of love. The *eros* of Plato, the *philia* of Aristotle and the agape of St. Paul and the Gospels are all types of love. They differ in their purpose, yet are often indistinguishable in their manifestations. Plato's eros, which Freud used as a label for libidinal strivings, has both a sexual and nonsexual connotation. In its earliest stage, eros, according to Plato, entails the love of the physical beauty of another's body. At later stages, eros becomes the love of virtue and knowledge. Thus Plato, in the *Symposium*, defines eros as the "desire for the perpetual possession of the good" (1972, p. 86).

Aristotle's *philia* refers to the reciprocal love in a friendship. This love is transitory when based upon the instrumental utility of the partners for each other the economic help, the emotional support, the amusement, and so forth—that the partners may provide each other. As these qualities wane, the basis of the friendship is lost and the friendship fails. However, philia is enduring when it is based on "the friendship of men who are good and alike in virtue" (Aristotle, 1947, p. 475). Whereas philia and eros are directly linked to and affected by the attributes of the beloved, agape is independent of the merits of the loved object. Agape is a more generalized feeling—a love of God and of all mankind.

These three categories—eros, philia, and agape—by no means exhaust the different meanings of the concept of love (for example, love of an activity such as music or sports, love of one's country, love of one's children). However, they convey important differences in the qualities of love, differences that are reflected in contemporary theoretical and empirical analyses of love. We have already reviewed in some detail one form of love, namely, the attachment of an infant to a caregiver (see Chapter 12). One might speculate that the formation of these early attachments is essential for the development of different forms of love manifested later in life. We do know from the data on early separation that disruption of these attachments in young children can produce emotional disturbances and persistent adjustment difficulties. However, these data, though indicating that early attachments are important to later development, do not tell us whether these early attachments provide the basis for subsequent love relationships. Psychoanalytic theory suggests that the individuals chosen as partners in a love relationship are very similar to individuals to whom one was attached as a child—not unlike the message of the opening lines of a song from over one hundred years ago, "I want a girl just like the girl that married dear old Dad." But songs and theory do not provide adequate support for the proposition that adult love relationships are rooted in early childhood love relationships.

HIGHLIGHT 18.1

The Varieties of Love

Elizabeth Barrett Browning's *Sonnets from the Portuguese* (1888) offers some extraordinarily beautiful and vivid descriptions of love. The following is a well-known sonnet from that volume:

How do I love thee? Let me count the ways.
I love thee to the depth and breadth and height
My soul can reach, when feeling out of sight
For the ends of Being and ideal Grace.
I love thee to the level of everyday's

Most quiet need, by sun and candlelight.
I love thee freely, as men strive for Right;
I love thee purely, as they turn from Praise.
I love thee with the passion put to use
In my old griefs, and with my childhood's faith.
I love thee with a love I seemed to lose
With my lost saints,—I love thee with the breath,
Smiles, tears, of all my life!—and, if God choose,
I shall but love thee better after death.

Research on Love

The many meanings of love posed difficult obstacles for psychological study (Berscheid, 2010; Rubin, 1988), and for many years love remained a topic for psychological speculation rather than systematic research. A pioneering contribution was made by Rubin (1970), who introduced a scale for measuring romantic love. By distinguishing between responses to an item when it referred to a partner with whom one was romantically involved as opposed to referring to a platonic friend, he was able to develop a Love Scale that was factorially independent from a Liking Scale (see Chapter 7). Rubin then administered the Love Scale to a sample of dating (but nonengaged) college-student couples who completed the instrument with respect to their dating partner and later with respect to a close friend of the same sex as the partner. As anticipated, the findings indicated that although loving and liking are related, they are only moderately correlated, though more for men than for women. Since that early work, there have been a number of different scales developed to measure love, each informed by the theory from which it sprang (e.g., Hendrick and Hendrick, 1990; Sternberg, 1997).

The construct validity of the Rubin's Love Scale is supported by the finding that although both men and women loved their dating partner much more than their friend, there was very little difference in their liking of their dating partners and friends. Also, the love scores were more highly correlated with self-reports of being "in love" and with perception of the probability of marriage than the liking scores. In addition, observations of the couples in a laboratory situation revealed that couples who were strongly in love spent significantly more time gazing into one another's eyes than did couples who were only weakly in love.

An examination of the Love Scale items suggests that there are four different components contributing to the love score: needing, caring, trust, and tolerance (Kelley, 1983). Needing is the desire to be in the other's presence and to be cared for by that person. Caring entails a different set of attitudes and behaviors—the desire to help, to take care of the partner. Trust involves the exchange of confidences of intimate personal matters whereas tolerance pertains to the willingness to accept another's faults. Are each of these components equivalent indicators of love? A study distinguishing care, needs, and trust indicates that this is not the case (Steck, Levitan, McLane, and Kelley, 1982). Hypothetical situations in which the care, need, and trust components were systematically varied were rated by college student samples for love, liking, attraction, and friendship. Situations depicting a high degree of caring for another were judged to display greater love than those depicting high need or high trust, although the latter did influence judgments of love. Although trust is more strongly related to ratings of friendship than to ratings of love, it is still a significant component of love. A study of self-disclosure between couples who were dating indicated that the amount of disclosure of personal intimacies between partners was significantly related to the measure of loving but unrelated to a measure of liking (Critelli and Dupre, 1978).

The finding that caring is more important to love than needing the other, must be interpreted with caution. What these data say is that caring is a necessary component of romantic love. To indicate that you would be miserable without your partner but are not greatly concerned for their welfare implies a selfish need or attraction. However, caring without need, especially the needs entailed in strong attraction, implies love without great romance or passion. The Rubin Love Scale, which yields a single score, does not discriminate between these different combinations of care, need, and trust and the different types of love they might reflect. A multidimensional approach would better capture the variations of love.

A Triangular Model of Love

The **triangular model of love**, proposed by Sternberg (1986), is an example of a multidimensional approach. Sternberg proposes that there are three essential components of love: **intimacy**, **passion**, and **decision/commitment**. These components can be visualized as forming the vertices of a triangle as in Figure 18.1. Intimacy refers to the degree of

triangular model of love A model of love that suggests there are three components: intimacy, passion, and decision/commitment.

intimacy A feeling of psychological closeness with another person.

passion A component of love that is a combination of romantic feelings and sexual desire.

decision/commitment A component of love that is about staying together.

closeness and warmth between two individuals. Sternberg and Grajek (1984) indicate that intimacy entails mutual understanding and communication, the desire to promote the welfare of the loved one, and feeling able to count on the loved one when in need. It also involves sharing, emotional support, and experiencing happiness when with the loved one.

To intimacy, Sternberg adds a passion component that connotes the romance and excitement that may be involved in a love relationship. While sexual feelings and needs usually constitute the principal contributors to passion, Sternberg suggests that other needs such as self-esteem, affiliation and dominance can also contribute to the experience of passion. Finally, to complete the model of love, Sternberg believes there is an important cognitive decision component that must be considered. He suggests that there is a short-term decision that one is in love and also a longer term commitment to maintain that love. The commitment dimension is clearly important. However, the significance of the short-term decision, independent of the feelings of love, remains unclear.

One of the properties of the triangular model is that it provides a framework or map for designating the components of different types of love, as in Figure 18.2. The vertices signify the type of love represented by each component alone. Thus intimacy, without

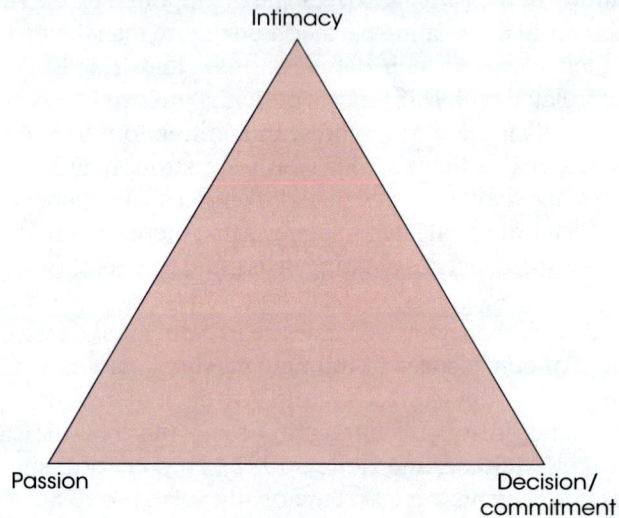

FIGURE 18.1 The Three Components of Love

Source: (From Sternberg, 1986, p. 119)

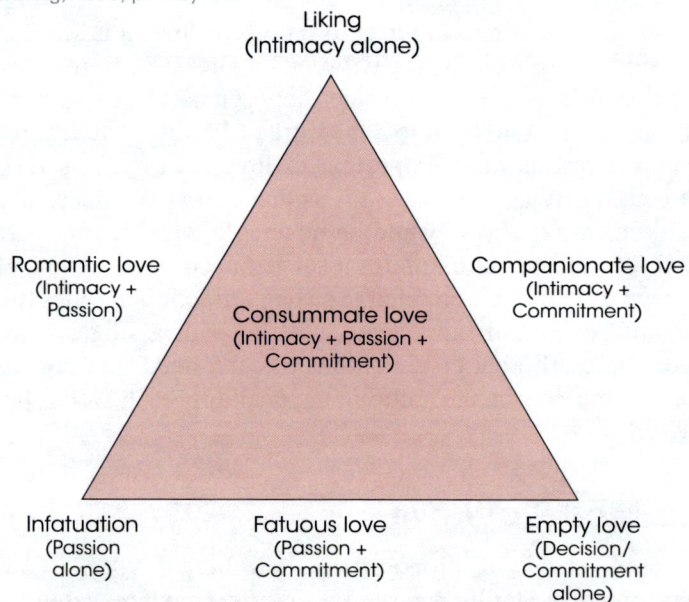

FIGURE 18.2 The Kinds of Loving as Different Combinations of the Three Components of Love

Source: (From Sternberg, 1986, p. 123)

passion or decision/commitment, is essentially liking, while passion without intimacy or decision/commitment constitutes infatuation, and decision/commitment without intimacy or passion is merely hollow or Empty Love. Other forms of love are represented by different combinations of the components. Thus intimacy plus passion constitute Romantic Love, while intimacy plus decision/commitment make for Companionate Love in which the partners feel close and committed to each other but passion is absent. The presence of all three components constitutes Consummate Love, or the type of love that most individuals in this culture strive for in a marital relationship.

It may be noted that other relationships such as parental love for their children and closeness between friends can be mapped onto the triangular model of love, as well as the sexually oriented romantic relationships. Sternberg (1997) has created a scale designed to measure the three components independently.

Source: Click and Photo/Shutterstock

The triangular theory of love posits three components: intimacy, passion, and commitment.

Passionate Love

Romantic love is clearly complex in nature, and its characteristics may change over time. More detailed analyses of one component of romantic love, **passionate love**, highlight the need component and the intensity of accompanying emotional responses. Passionate love is characterized by preoccupation with thoughts of the love object, with the desire to spend as much time as possible with him or her, with sharp variations in feeling— from the heights of elation to the depths of despair, and with strong sexual arousal (Hatfield, 1983; Hatfield and Walster, 1981). Why does one "fall in love"? What are the determinants of passionate love? Behavioral studies have not yet emerged with satisfactory, scientifically-based responses to these questions, which have preoccupied poets and youth for centuries. An influential theory of passionate love proposes three conditions as necessary (Berscheid and Walster, 1974; Hatfield and Walster, 1981):

passionate love A type of love characterized by preoccupation with thoughts of the love object, with the desire to spend as much time as possible with him or her, and with strong sexual arousal

1. *One must be raised in a culture that believes in the idea of romantic love, and reinforces that idea in young people.* Romantic love is considered so important in our culture that approximately 85 percent of men and women said they would not marry someone even if they had all the other qualities desired (Simpson, Campbell, and Berscheid, 1986). Romantic love has been seen as largely a Western concept that arose in Europe in the Middle Ages. Only many centuries later did it become viewed as the appropriate basis for marriage. There is little doubt that cultural factors exert a strong influence on conceptions of love and on such practices as arranged marriages in contrast to marriages predicated on the partners being "in love." For instance, even in modern India, about 90 percent of the marriages are still arranged by families, a practice as common among educated professionals as among the less educated (Rosenbaum, 1992). Rosenbaum notes, "The general notion is that marriage is too important an economic and social arrangement to be left to the whim of personal impulse and attraction, and that love will grow from continued association and companionship" (p. 67). In cultures that believe in romantic love as a basis for marriage, cultural factors probably reinforce the idea of falling in love and increase its likelihood through expectancy. Moreover, cultures that reinforce the belief in love may also reduce inhibition and constraints that block passionate love and make available to the individual emotional relationships that are less accessible to someone in another culture. However, it should be noted that the idea that romantic love is only a Western concept has recently been challenged by several writers.
2. *The presence of an appropriate love object.* Here, the principal question is, what makes an appropriate love object? There is a good deal of evidence that physical attractiveness is an important variable (Folkes, 1982; Walster et al., 1966). However,

other factors are also important, particularly the degree to which the couple shares similar interests and the extent to which there is mutual reinforcement and gratification of needs (Berscheid and Walster, 1978).

3. Perhaps the most controversial is the requirement for *intense emotional arousal that is interpreted by the individual as love*. This condition is consonant with Schachter's (1964) theory of emotion, which maintains that specific emotional experiences are a consequence of one's cognitive interpretation of a nonspecific emotional arousal (see Chapter 15).

Passionate love is of sufficient interest in its own right that a scale has been developed to assess it specifically, thereby facilitating its investigation (Hatfield and Sprecher, 1986). The following are examples of items on the Passionate Love scale:

Sometimes my body trembles with excitement at the sight of _____.

I would feel despair if _____ left me.

_____ always seems to be on my mind. I eagerly look for signs indicating _____'s desire for me.

Although there is some overlap in the content of the Passionate Love Scale and the Rubin Love Scale, the items on the Passionate Love Scale generally reflect more intense feeling. Nevertheless, the two scales are very highly correlated, Hatfield and Sprecher (1986) finding correlations greater than .80. These data reflect a very close relationship between the emotional excitement and romantic passion associated with "being in love," and the attitudes and feelings of needing, caring, trust, and tolerance for one's partner. Whether these attitudes and feelings are simply consequences or manifestations of passionate love or whether they exist prior to and contribute to "falling in love" remains an open question. Probably both processes occur.

Companionate Love

companionate love A type of love and affection we feel for people with whom our lives are deeply intertwined.

Although there is disagreement about the conditions that are essential to the manifestation of passionate love, the evidence is clear that passionate love typically declines in intensity the longer a couple has been together (Hatfield and Walster, 1981). What becomes essential in long-term relationships between partners are the factors that contribute to **companionate love**, which is defined as "the affection we feel for those with whom our lives are deeply intertwined" (Berscheid and Walster, 1978). Here, the caring component (Steck et al., 1982) becomes more salient and critical. Shared experiences and interests and mutual trust contribute to the relationship. In addition, although sexual gratification may remain important, even if the intensity of the passion has declined, gratification of other needs that the relationship provides becomes more central. The factor of commitment is of particular importance.

In a test of changes of types of love over time (Hatfield, Pillemer, O'Brien, and Le, 2008), it was found that the levels of passionate love *and* companionate love decrease the year after marriage. In long marriages, the trend continues, with those who have been married less than thirty-three years reporting higher companionate love than women married longer than thirty-three years. The same pattern is repeated for passionate love. This is counter to many expectations that companionate love would increase and passionate love would decrease. The good news is that the levels of both types of love are still relatively high—there is still passion in long-term marriages.

The factors that foster commitment to a relationship overlap with those that foster other dimensions of love. However, there can be love without commitment, as in the case of the

Companionate love and passionate love tend to decline over time but still remain at relatively high levels.

Source: Lucian Coman/Shutterstock

partner who refuses to make a commitment to a relationship because of personality, economic issues, or other reasons, despite his or her feelings of love. There can also be commitment without love as exemplified by couples who no longer love each other but remain married "because of the children," for fear of social rejection, or for financial or religious reasons. There are likely to be both stable and unstable factors in a relationship. Examples of positive stable factors that might promote an interaction (close relationship) between two individuals are shared interests and attitudes and personality attributes such as intelligence, warmth, and assertiveness. Physical attractiveness, although relatively stable, may well change during the course of the relationship. Examples of unstable positive factors are sexual arousal and a fun evening together. Both unstable and stable positive factors contribute to love; only stable factors are assumed to promote commitment. Examples of nonpositive stable factors that foster commitment, but not love, are feelings of obligation to a contract and shared economic interests that make termination of the relationship costly. In terms of this analysis, the most enduring and satisfying relationships are ones based on positive stable factors that foster both love and commitment.

Intimacy

As we know, even relationships that appear to begin with stable positive factors of shared interests and attitudes may end in conflict and dissolution. One problem area is difficulty in maintaining intimacy. The study of intimacy and close relationships has emerged as a major research area for psychologists (Hendrick, 1989; Penman and Duck, 1987). Research on intimacy indicates that the establishment of intimacy will vary with situation and partners, but there is also evidence of personality differences in the ease or difficulty with which an individual establishes intimate relationships.

One such personality difference influencing the maintenance of intimacy is in the degree of self-monitoring (see Chapter 10). It will be recalled that the high self-monitoring individual is predominantly situationally oriented, whereas the low self-monitoring person tends to be more directed by inner attitudes and dispositions. One might conjecture that an intimate relationship requires some consistency of behavior and of interest in the partner in different situations. "Out of sight, out of mind" is unlikely to foster a close, intimate relationship. Thus, one would expect high self-monitoring individuals to form more superficial relationships than the low self-monitors. And there are data to support this expectation (Snyder and Simpson, 1987). High self-monitors were found to be more willing than low self-monitors to change their current dating partner, to take longer to develop an intimate relationship, and to tend to prefer less close, less exclusive romantic relationships.

Another factor that discriminates individuals who have difficulty in maintaining intimacy is communication skills. Training programs have been developed to improve communication skills in partners who experience conflict and lack of intimacy in their relationship (Hatfield, 1988). The partners are encouraged to express their feelings, even where some risk may be involved. At the same time, they learn skills in how best to convey their feelings and how best to respond to the reactions of their partners.

Attachment style predicts emotional reactions to separation at the airport (Fraley and Shaver, 1998).

Attachment Styles

Still another variable shown to be related to the establishment of intimate relationships are individual differences in modes of attachment (Hazan and Shaver, 1987). Shaver and his co-workers have proposed that a critical component of romantic love is the attachment process that is first manifested by the infant in the interaction with his/her caretaker (Shaver, Hazan, and Bradshaw, 1988). They point out there are striking parallels between features of adult love and characteristics of infant attachment. Some of these parallels are enumerated in Table 18.1 (Shaver and Hazen, 1988). To explore more specifically the relationship between variations in attachment and qualities of the love experience, brief one-paragraph versions appropriate for adults were prepared of Ainsworth's descriptions of Secure, Insecure (or Anxious, Ambivalent) and Avoidant attachment types (Chapter 12; also note that assignment to category is based on questionnaires). The Secure paragraph states that the individual finds it relatively easy to get close to others and isn't especially worried about being abandoned by the partner; the Insecure description focuses on concern about the love and commitment of the partner; and the Avoidant paragraph reflects discomfort at getting too close to others. Adult respondents chose which of the three descriptions best fit them and were categorized accordingly.

Significant differences in features of the love experience were found for several samples of adult respondents, depending upon their attachment style (Hazan and Shaver, 1987). Those in the Secure attached group were more likely to describe love as especially happy, friendly, and trusting, and they were able to accept the partner despite the partner's faults. Moreover, the mean duration of their relationships was impressively longer than those reported by the other two groups—10.0 years in comparison to 4.9 years for the Insecure and 6.0 years for the Avoidant groups. The Insecure respondents were more likely to describe love as involving obsession, emotional highs and lows, and extreme sexual attraction and jealousy. The Avoidant group descriptions also tended to convey emotional highs and lows and jealousy, plus a fear of intimacy.

TABLE 18.1 Some Features of Attachment and Adult Romantic Love

Attachment	Romantic love
Formation and quality of the attachment bond depend on the attachment figure's perceived sensitivity and responsiveness.	Romantic love includes an intense desire for the partner's (real or imagined) interest and reciprocation.
Infant's feelings of joy and distress depend on the attachment figure's perceived availability and responsiveness.	Adult lover's moods depend on his or her current perceptions of the partner's reciprocation or rejection.
When the infant's attachment relationship is secure, she or he is happier, has a higher threshold for distress, is more willing to explore unfamiliar environments and interact with strangers.	When adults are in love, they often report feeling more relaxed, less worried, less defensive, more creative and spontaneous and more courageous.
Attachment behaviors include: maintenance of proximity and contact—holding, touching, caressing, kissing, rocking, smiling, making eye-contact, following, etc.	Adult romantic love is indicated by: holding, touching, caressing, kissing, rocking, smiling, making eye contact, following, etc.
Separation from the attachment figure causes intense distress, initiates vigorous, attention-consuming reunion efforts, and results in despair if reunion proves impossible.	Unchosen separation from the partner causes intense distress, initiates attention-consuming reunion efforts, and results in grief if reunion is impossible.
Intense desire to share discoveries and reactions with the attachment figure.	Intense desire to share discoveries, feelings, opinions, etc., and to give gifts to one's love partner.
Infants coo, 'sing', talk baby talk, etc., and attachment figures talk baby talk.	Adult lovers coo, sing, talk baby talk, use affectionate baby-like names for each other.

Taken from Shaver and Hazen, 1988, p. 48.

Although the primary research focus has been on the role of the attachment system in adult love, it has been proposed that biologically-bound behavioral systems are also involved in varying degrees in adult love—caregiving and sexuality (Shaver, Hazan, and Bradshaw, 1988). Caregiving is especially evident in parental love, but it is also believed to be an important element in maintaining enduring romantic relationships. Under stress, the anxious style is associated with less care seeking, and it appears that those with the anxious style of attachment are less good at caregiving (Collins and Feeny, 2000).

Choosing a Partner

To skip right to the bottom line, birds of a feather flock together and opposites don't attract. As Buss (1985, p. 47) says, "we are likely to marry someone who is similar to us in almost every variable." People who marry tend to be similar in age, especially among the young married. Usually, there is similarity in personality traits. There is a statistically reliable correlation with years of education, highest degree earned, and high school and college GPA (Botwin, Buss, and Shackelford, 1997). People tend to marry others with similar faces (Little, Burt, and Perret, 2006). Among newlyweds, there is strong similarity in religiousness and political orientation (Watson et al., 2004). People even seem to find partners with similar levels of antisocial behavior (Kruger, Moffitt, Caspi, Bleske, and Silva, 1998). Meta-analysis has indicated that four of the five factors are predictive of relationship satisfaction. Those factors are low neuroticism, high agreeableness, high conscientiousness, and high extroversion (Malouff, Thorsteinsson, Schutte, Bhullar, and Rooke, 2010).

Although romantic partners tend to match up, there are similarities across people. Buss and Barnes (1986) found that the most commonly listed attributes people wanted was someone who is honest, affectionate, dependable, considerate, and kind. They did find gender differences such that women wanted someone who was ambitious, career oriented, and tall, more than men did. Men placed more emphasis on finding someone physically attractive and a good cook. Although there is similarity in age, there has been a general finding that men tend to look for someone younger, while women tend to look for someone older. Some have explained this as an evolutionary adaptation (e.g., Buss, 1989; Kenrick and Keefe, 1992), whereas others explain this as caused by differential access to resources and wealth and social roles (Eagley and Wood, 1999).

Source: Karan Bunjean/Shutterstock

People tend to have relationship partners who are similar on most dimensions.

Love and Sex

What is the relationship between sexual desire and love? We have already indicated that with the passage of time, the erotic or passionate component of love tends to decline. Does it mean that the sexual element is irrelevant to the experience of love in later phases of the relationship? Although sexual intimacy may not be necessary to a loving relationship between partners, it probably is the case that sexual contact helps maintain and enhance the partners' love for each other.

However, clinical evidence and theory are not consistent on this point. Most clinicians, including psychoanalysts, feel that given physically healthy partners, continuing sexual contact is both an expression of and helps maintain the love relationship. Yet, according to psychoanalytic theory "love is aim-inhibited sexuality" (Sigmund Freud, 1955, p. 142), suggesting that love is a form of modified sexual feeling. It would then follow that given a fixed level of sexual energy, the more energy that is invested in sex, the less energy that is available for love! The solution to this paradox is suggested by the high level of sexual passion that the partners direct to each other in the initial phases of a romantic relationship. Given this initial level, even if sexual energies are diverted, or "converted," as it were, into love, there still would be sufficient libido available for sexual intimacy. At the same time, Freud's conjecture implies that a close, caring, loving relationship will not develop if the couple attempts to maintain sexual passion at the high level of intensity that characterized their early relationship.

Sexual feelings can be a significant component of love. However, a relationship based on sexual attraction alone is a very different from one based on love. According to Erich Fromm (1956),

> Sexual desire can be stimulated by the anxiety of aloneness, by the wish to conquer, or be conquered, by vanity, by the wish to hurt and even to destroy, as much as it can be stimulated by love. . . . Sexual attraction creates, for the moment, the illusion of union, yet without love this "union" leaves strangers as far apart as they were before—sometimes it makes them feel ashamed of each other, or even makes them hate each other, because when the illusion has gone they feel their estrangement even more markedly than before (pp. 54–55).

Yet sex without love does not necessarily lead to the kinds of negative feelings between partners described by Fromm. For some individuals and couples, love is a prerequisite for sex, whereas others are quite clear that their sexual intimacy has no implications beyond physical attraction and sexual satisfaction. In a two-year longitudinal study bearing on this issue (Peplau, Rubin and Hill, 1977), college-age dating couples were divided into three groups:

1. *Sexually traditional* couples who felt that the commitment of marriage as well as love is a necessary prerequisite for sexual intercourse.
2. *Sexually moderate* couples for whom sex is permissible if the partners love each other.
3. *Sexually liberal* couples who may feel that sex with love is desirable, but do not view love as a prerequisite for sexual intercourse.

These three orientations were, as to be expected, related to the timing of the first intercourse—abstention characterizing the first group, later sex the second group, and early sex describing the third group. Most germane to the question of the influence of sex on the relationship was the finding that couples in all three groups reported similar satisfaction with their relationship. Moreover, there was no difference two years later in the dating status of each group. About 46 percent of the couples had broken up, 34 percent were still dating, and 20 percent had gotten married. These percentages were similar, regardless of the amount of sexual intimacy. Apparently, neither early or late sex nor abstention had a consistent effect on the development of a lasting commitment. But also remember, these were college-age couples.

Nor does sexual exclusiveness have a clear impact on a love relationship. In a study comparing gay male couples who had agreed on sexually-open relationships with gay male couples who had agreed on a closed relationship of sexual exclusivity, no differences were found between the groups in degree of love and liking for partner, and degree of satisfaction with and commitment to the relationship (Blasband and Peplau, 1985). Whether a similar finding would obtain for heterosexual couples with sexually-open and sexually-exclusive relationships would be of interest to determine. In this regard, it may be noted that a number of similarities have been observed in heterosexual and gay or lesbian relationships (Peplau, 1988). Homosexuals, like heterosexuals, typically desire enduring relationships and frequently are able to achieve them. The same models of love—the triangular model, the attachment model, passionate and companionate love, in all likelihood apply with equal cogency to both homosexual and heterosexual relationships. Interestingly, the male preference for partners slightly younger than themselves is evident among gay men too (Hays, 1995).

Love and Hate

Love and hate are typically conceived of as polar opposites and, indeed, for the most part they are. They pertain to fundamentally different ways in which organisms can interact. A key question is the extent to which interactions are dominated by love-related tendencies, such as cooperation, mutual assistance, and self-sacrifice, versus hate-related tendencies, such as threats, attack, and killing (Eibl-Eibesfeldt, 1974).

At the human level, scholars over centuries have argued about whether humans are fundamentally governed by love-based impulses or hostile, aggressive urges (compare the views of the different theorists discussed in Chapters 3–6). For Freud, Eros (love) and Thanatos (hostility, anger, aggression) constituted two basic, biologically rooted drives from which all other significant human motivations emerged. Eros and Thanatos are not necessarily in conflict, as in the case of sadistic and masochistic behaviors, which are characterized by erotic pleasure being associated with aggressive acts—whether inflicting pain or being the recipient of pain.

It has been suggested that the uncertainty associated with someone about whom one feels ambivalent may heighten one's attraction to them, and that jealousy, frustration, and anger as well as reward, intimacy, and joy may enhance one's passion (Hatfield and Walster, 1981). Nevertheless, although there are circumstances in which the love-passion motivational system and the hate-anger-aggression motivational system may be mutually facilitating, on the whole they lead to incompatible behaviors and attitudes. Love diminishes the likelihood of hostile, aggressive acts toward the love object, and hate diminishes caring, loving acts toward the individual eliciting hostile feelings.

Love and hate maybe connected to each other in another way. One of the sad ironies of close relationships is that the love on which they were based frequently gives way to hostility. In addition, in many instances, the more intense the love when the relationship was harmonious, the more intense the hostility when the relationship becomes discordant. Why should a relationship in which loving feelings initially are predominant become vulnerable to negative, hostile interaction? There appear to be three basic reasons for this:

1. *In any relationship in which there is close, frequent interactions over an extended period of time*—between husband and wife, parent and child, sisters and brothers, or roommates—*conflicts are likely to arise.* Each individual in the pair has his or her own needs, interests, and habits, and these have to be coordinated and sometimes reconciled. Studies of young heterosexual couples reflect an extremely wide variety of issues over which conflict may arise (Gottman, 1979; Peterson, 1983). Conflicts arise over money, household chores, in-laws, personal habits, frequency of sexual intercourse, jealousies, child-rearing, and a host of other issues. More harmonious couples deal with conflicts more effectively by focusing on issues that they perceive differently and by keeping the boundary of the discussion specific to the issues in question (Raush et al., 1974). The more distressed couples tend to extend the discussion beyond the behaviors or views at issue, and attack the partner in general terms with negative aspersions about their personality. An example of the difference between harmonious and discordant couples in their approach to conflicts would be discussing a conflict over expenditure of money in terms of each partner's views regarding freedom of choice and economic priorities versus discussing the partner's stinginess, selfishness, immature, spendthrift nature, or other personality aspersions.
2. *The risk and vulnerability entailed in love itself.* If one does not love, one cannot feel rejected. The greater the love, the greater the pain of rejection, and the greater the pain, the greater the likelihood of anger and hostility. Individuals who feel inadequate and whose self-concept is very much dependent upon the approval of the partner are particularly prone to react to possible rejection with anger. Because they tend to be readily threatened, such individuals can be beset by feelings of jealousy, with its attendant problems of conflict and hostility (White, 1981).
3. *The unrealistic perceptions that one typically has of one's partner* (Hatfield and Walster, 1981). Romantic love, as the popular saying goes, is blind. One tends to idealize the partner's virtues and to be oblivious to failings; but as relationships continue, reality begins to intrude, and the unrealistic perceptions culminate in

profound disappointment. One might feel frustrated, misled, or even bitter, attributing the initial erroneous impression of the partner to his or her deceptiveness rather than to one's own love-clouded vision.

Love need not be as fragile as suggested by these problems of conflict, jealousy, and misperceptions with which it is often associated. Love is also associated with understanding, acceptance, forgiveness, and compromise. Although some relationships that begin in romantic love end in discord and hostility, others develop into deeply intimate, supportive, and caring partnerships. Some of the reasons love may turn into hostility rather than a companionate relationship have been suggested. A more thorough and systematic understanding requires an examination of the dynamics of aggression.

Aggression

It is within a topic like aggression that we can see many of our themes come together. We see the influence of heritability (Chapter 1). We see the impact of culture (Chapter 2). We see ways in which aggression may be part of our instincts (Chapters 1 and 3) and the ways in which aggression is learned (Chapter 5). We see the interaction of the person and situation in the way that the situation influences the person, how a person chooses the situation to enter (Chapter 9), and in how the person construes the situation (Chapter 6). We see the way in which a person thinks about the self impacts aggression (Chapter 10). We see the impact of gender differences (Chapter 11) and parenting (Chapter 12). We see the ways in which goal (Chapter 14) frustration leads to aggression. We also see the way that emotion (Chapter 15) can increase or decrease aggression.

What Is Aggression?

The term *aggression*, as used by both layperson and scientist, covers many different behaviors. It includes murder, physical attack, verbal insults, and outbursts of rage. To these we might add destruction of property, menacing gestures, social humiliation, prejudice, playful jostling, and violent dreams and fantasies. While the behaviors embraced by the term aggression may have important elements in common, their diversity makes it difficult to establish general laws or principles that apply to all forms of aggression. It also leads to confusion in communication, so that different investigators might mean different things when they refer to aggressive behavior. In addition, people may differ in their perceptions of what is aggressive so that the same act may be viewed as non-aggressive by one person and aggressive by another (Tedeschi, 1983). A fairly

aggression A behavior directed toward a person with the intention of harming that person, and the person is motivated to avoid that harm.

typical definition would be that **aggression** is a behavior directed toward a person with the intension of harming that person, and the person is motivated to avoid that harm (Anderson and Bushman, 2002).

There are certain theoretical distinctions that are helpful in understanding some of the controversies and experimental findings concerning the causes and functions of aggression. First, it is important to distinguish between the behavior and the motive or reason for that behavior. For example, an attack by a mugger is a clear instance of an aggressive act. However, there may be important psychological differences in the reasons for such an attack. The mugger's primary motive might be to steal the victim's wallet. If the wallet falls or can be successfully picked out of the victim's pocket, the mugger will be equally satisfied. In this instance, the aggressive attack is one of a number of possible *instrumental* behaviors that may or may not involve aggression for achieving a basically nonaggressive goal. Suppose, however, that the mugger is angry at his victim and that his primary goal is to humiliate and physically hurt the victim, with theft being incidental. Here, the aggressive behavior is no longer instrumental to a nonaggressive goal (i.e., money) but is motivated by *aggressive drive*, or *drive-instigated* hostility. What is critical to the mugger is that the victim be injured or publicly disgraced. He would be equally satisfied if he witnessed someone else carrying out the attack or if a member of the victim's family were injured. Other factors also influence the nature of the aggressive action, and sometimes instrumental aggression and aggressive drive-motivated behavior may overlap (e.g., the mugger may both hate his victim and want his money). But, as we will try to show, the distinction between instrumental and drive-instigated aggression helps clarify some of the theoretical confusion and debate concerning the causes of human aggression. For example, social learning theorists have been largely concerned with the acquisition and performance of **instrumental aggression**, while psychoanalytic theorists have focused on the dynamics of aggressive *drive*. In addition, not all aggressive acts are necessarily instrumental or motivated by aggressive drive. Some aggressive acts may be responses that are elicited innately or through conditioning by aggressive *cues*. For example, the perception of a weapon might stimulate aggressive thoughts and other aggressive responses. Some researchers use alternate terms for aggression, preferring to use the term *proactive aggression*, which would be very much like instrumental aggression, and *reactive aggression*, which is aggression as a result of some sort of provocation.

instrumental aggression
Aggression that functions to get something.

Two young boys engaging in aggressive behavior, which may not be motivated by aggressive drives if they are only "playing."

Source: Rawpixel.com/Shutterstock

Biological Aspects of Aggression

Do humans have an innate propensity to use instrumental aggressive responses? Do they have an innate aggressive drive that, like hunger and thirst, must somehow be satisfied? There are three areas of biological study that relate to these questions:

1. Ethology, which entails systematic observations of animals in their natural settings.
2. Physiological research on hormones, brain structures, and brain chemistry involved in aggression.
3. Genetic research, with both animals and humans, on the inheritance of aggression.

Ethological Research

The investigation of the bases for aggression in animals has been and continues to be of major interest to ethologists. A substantial part of the research for which two pioneering ethologists, Konrad Lorenz (1966) and Nikita Tinbergen (1953, 1968), received Nobel prizes involved contributions to our knowledge of aggression. Among these contributions was the discovery that there are stimuli that act as innate *releasers* of aggressive responses. For example, male robins, on perceiving the red patch on the breast of a rival, will respond by attacking him. Removal of the red patch eliminates the aggressive response (Lack, 1943). Another well-known instance is the aggressive response of a male stickleback fish to the red belly of another stickleback who enters his territory (Tinbergen, 1951).

However, ethologists have also discovered that, in most species, fighting between members of the same species rarely escalates to killing or to severe injury. Much of the fighting is ritualistic and, often involves only threat displays, with little or no physical contact. For example, a study of aggression among elephant seals indicated that for every actual fight, there were sixty-seven aggressive encounters that consisted solely of aggressive threat displays (LeBoeuf and Peterson, 1969). These displays vary according to the species under study. In a cat, the back arches, the hackles rise, the teeth bare, and the claws extend, all of which serve to make the cat appear larger. Birds commonly fluff their feathers and spread their wings for the same effect. And wild chimpanzees engage in a variety of rituals, including staring an opponent into submission, stomping the ground, and hooting and screaming (Van Lawick-Goodall, 1968b).

These aggressive displays serve to inhibit the behavior of the target animal that provoked the aggressive display. Such provoking behaviors include intrusion on territory, approach to another's female partner or cache of food, and efforts at dominance. If threat gestures do not suffice and an actual fight takes place, in many species ritualized behaviors come into play that act as *inhibitory* rather than releasing stimuli, so that a victorious animal will cease its aggressive attack before the vanquished animal is seriously injured. For example, a dog who is the loser of a fight may present its unprotected neck to the mouth of the victor or roll over on its back exposing its vulnerable underside (Lorenz, 1966). Thus, for most animal species a sequence of interactions has evolved to act as a brake on intraspecies fighting and killing. Severe fighting does occur and intraspecies killing does take place; lions of one group have been observed to attack and kill lions of another group (Eibl-Eibesfeldt, 1977, p. 130). Also, occurrences of infanticide by adult males have been observed in a number of mammalian species, including primates (Struhsaker and Leland, 1987).

In addition, contrary to earlier impressions of the great apes, extensive observations of chimpanzees in their natural settings have revealed instances of invasions by groups of males of the territory of a branch community of chimpanzees and the killing of several members of that community (Goodall, 1986).

Even the "peaceful" chimpanzee, the Bonobo, will fight on occasion. Within-species nonhuman aggression rarely results in death. Usually, threat displays suffice, and an actual fight does not take place.

However, these incidents are infrequent, and the behaviors of the chimpanzee groups can hardly be characterized as "warlike" (Huntingford, 1987). Ethological studies of aggression in nonhuman species do not support the notion that it is biologically "natural" for people to kill each other or, as some maintain (Ardrey, 1967), that we humans have an inborn killer instinct.

What these studies do suggest is that it is possible that some instrumental aggressive responses are innately "wired into" our neuromuscular system. Observations of children born deaf and blind indicate that a number of patterns of aggressive behavior, such as stamping the feet, clenching the teeth, and making fists are present in these children despite lack of opportunity to observe these behaviors (Eibl-Eibesfeldt, 1977). It is also possible that these aggressive reactions are wired to releasing stimuli. However, there are no good examples in humans of simple stimuli that automatically release an aggressive response. The possible counterparts of releasing stimuli—restraint of infant movement, intense discomfort, exposure to deliberate frustration, or malicious attack on a loved family member—are complex affective-cognitive situations rather than relatively simple physical stimuli. And, if there are innate aggression inhibitors in humans—for example, tears, pleading, and submissive gestures—they are unfortunately quite weak and all too frequently do not work. The human capacity to experience empathy, the sharing of another's perspective and feelings (Chapter 12), may be one mechanism that helps restrain an aggressor from continuing an attack, but empathy is not automatic and requires experience and training (N. Feshbach, 1979).

Anger and Aggressive Drive

Several of the innate aggressive reactions that have been described resemble the emotions of anger or rage. Anger, like other emotions, has an important adaptive value: the organism becomes fiercer and more capable of defending itself when angry. Anger adds to one's strength and to the intensity of one's behaviors. Anger, like the other emotions, is also a form of social communication; the facial expressions, sounds, and postures displayed by an angry organism tell another animal or individual to stay away or desist from whatever it is doing. This threat property, noted by Charles Darwin (1872), has probably evolved to ensure adequate territorial spacing of the species, with distributed access to food, and, in primates, to foster the maintenance of a socially stable group with an effective dominance hierarchy (Bernstein and Gordon, 1974).

Intrinsic Aggression

There is evidence that some animals will seek opportunities for aggression. We will call this motivation toward aggressive response *intrinsic aggression* (Reykowski, 1979) to distinguish it from aggressive *drive*, which traditionally implies the motive to inflict injury. Intrinsic aggression refers to the motivation to perform an aggressive act: to fight, rather than to hurt or inflict damage. When intrinsic aggression is observed, it is usually the result of blocking an aggressive response after exposure to an aggression-releasing stimulus or after interruption of a fight sequence.

A word of caution is necessary at this point. In reviewing the animal literature, the focus has been on innate mechanisms that influence the occurrence and inhibition of aggression. However, it must be emphasized that these patterns of aggressive behavior are strongly affected by learning and social experience. While it can be shown that genetic, physiological, and other biological factors influence aggression in mammals, even within nonhumans patterns of aggression are sharply affected by learning experiences. For example, victory and defeat are naturally occurring experiences that have a major effect on aggressive response tendencies. In rodents or in primates, these outcomes determine dominance hierarchies and patterns of aggression in social groups. A mouse, rewarded by his apparent success, substantially increases the frequency of attack on other mice, including mice with which he would not ordinarily fight (Scott, 1958). On the other hand, punishment decreases the frequency of attack. If learning experiences are important in influencing the aggressive behavior of mice, how much more significant their influence is likely to be on human aggression!

Physiological Influences

Before we dive into human research, it would be best to understand how a great deal of the research is conducted; after all, we wouldn't want anyone to get hurt while studying aggression. Aggression is often studied in the laboratory using a device that makes it seem like a shock is given to someone in a different room, although no one is actually getting a shock—except sometimes the participant in the study. The key dependent variables are the choice of level of shock or the duration of the shock. Verbal aggression is often measured either by coding negative statements to a target or in negative evaluations of the target. To create aggression, the participant usually needs to be provoked in some way. The provocations can be things like insults and unfairness (which also tells us something about aggression). Laboratory measures of aggression tend to have external validity, but occasionally laboratory and real-world studies find different results (Anderson and Bushman, 1997).

Alcohol, Drugs, and Aggression

In a famous novel by Robert Louis Stevenson, the hero, a friendly, gracious, civil English doctor, becomes transformed into a hostile, cruel, sadistic monster by simply swallowing a potion. We are all familiar with the Jekyll-and-Hyde story. While there are no chemicals that have this dramatic an effect, a number of chemicals have been identified that significantly influence aggressive behavior. The relationship between alcohol and aggression is one obvious example. Drinking is a major contributor to violent incidents.

The mechanism by which alcohol influences aggression is complex and involves more than internal physiological effects. Although the occurrence of aggression is related to the amount of alcohol that is consumed (Taylor and Gammon, 1975), it is also strongly influenced by features of the social context in which the drinking takes place. Keep in mind that the use of alcohol strongly covaries with the social setting, economics, and mental health issues (Roizen, 2002).

Intoxicated individuals are not automatically aggressive. It depends upon whether there are frustrating events or other aggression-instigating cues in the situation (Bushman, 2002). Alcohol interacts with thought in the creation of aggression (Gallegher, Lisco, Parrott, and Giancola, 2014). In addition, because alcohol appears to affect judgment and attention (Hull and VanTreuren, 1986; Steele and Josephs, 1988), alcoholics may be responsive to clear "messages" but miss less obvious but no less important cues.

One of the ways in which we see the impact of alcohol on aggression is in executive functioning. Executive function is typically thought of as things such as planning, initiating, maintaining, or altering goals. People differ in their executive function. Some are good at it, others are not. A number of studies have demonstrated that people with low levels of executive function prior to the administration of alcohol respond with higher levels of aggression following administration of alcohol (Ginacola, 2004; Pihl, Assaad, and Hoaken, 2003).

Hormones and Aggression

Still other well-known chemical influences on aggression, familiar even in ancient times, are the male sex hormones, the androgens. The symbol of violence, the bull, is rendered a docile ox through castration. In general, removal of androgens tends to lower aggression, whereas the administration of androgens tends to increase it. Also female hormones, the estrogens, tend to reduce aggressivity (Moyer, 1971). However, the relationships among hormones, sexuality, and aggression are quite complex for both lower animals and humans (Herbert, 1970).

The species and the age at which administration or removal of the hormone takes place are particularly critical variables. Hormonal manipulation during the very early stages of development is believed to have a critical influence upon the organization of the brain and is generally more effective than at later periods. Nevertheless, the relationship between sex hormones and level of aggression in humans has not been well established and remains a matter of debate. Dabbs and Morris (1990) studied testosterone levels in 4,462 men and found that high levels tended to correlate with a variety of antisocial behaviors such as adult delinquency and substance abuse. This relationship, however, was moderated by socioeconomic status—the relationship was weaker among men higher in socioeconomic status. We also have to be careful about the direction of causation: does testosterone cause antisocial behavior, or does antisocial behavior increase testosterone? Another study of young male prisoners indicated higher levels of testosterone in prisoners who had engaged in more aggressive crimes such as armed robbery, assault, and murder during adolescence. The testosterone levels in prisoners whose offenses had been restricted to more routine offenses of burglary and larceny were, on the other hand, relatively low (Kreuz and Rose, 1972). However, the meaning of this finding is unclear since there was no relationship between testosterone levels and the amount of fighting and other aggressive behaviors displayed in prison. A study of male adolescents, carried out in Sweden, indicated a significant positive relationship between the boys' aggressive responses to frustration or threat and their testosterone levels. But, complicating the interpretation of this finding, testosterone level was not associated with unprovoked aggressive behavior (Olweus, 1986; Schaal, Tremblay, Soussignan, and Susman, 1996).

Genetics and Aggression

Infants display striking differences in temperament. Longitudinal studies suggest that these temperamental differences interact in time with environmental experiences to form the child's personality (Thomas and Chess, 1976). Some of these temperamental traits appear closely related to aggression. For example, the pattern of unpleasant moods, unfriendly social responses, and intense motor reactions may be a precursor to aggressiveness. There are a number of possible prenatal factors that may be the principal causes of these aggression-related temperamental differences: mother's diet, activity level, smoking, and ingestion of alcohol or other drugs. But perhaps the most likely places to look for the cause of temperamental differences are genetic disparities.

The examination of the genetics of aggression has revealed hints of a genetic influence, though the results are not extremely clear (see DiLalla, 2002). Several studies have used ratings of twins by parents or teachers. When this method is used, there appears to be a heritable component (Baker, Raine, Liu, and Jacobson, 2008; Brendgen, Vitaro, Boivin, Dionne, and Pérusse, 2002). That is, monozygotic (identical) twins are rated more similarly on aggression than dizygotic (fraternal) twins. However, it turns out that parent ratings of most traits show heritability, which may indicate more about how parents perceive twins than the actual heritability of those traits (Plomin, 1981). The same issue may arise with teacher ratings. The alternative is for researchers to directly observe behavior. These types of studies have tended to show very little heritability (see Miles and Carey, 1997, for a meta-analysis).

Although aggression and antisocial behavior are not the same, we can use research on antisocial behavior to explore the concept further. Antisocial behavior includes aggressive behaviors such as assault, but it will also capture behaviors like burglary and vandalism. Antisocial behavior will not capture concepts like rumor spreading or social exclusion. However, the literature on antisocial behavior is well developed and is perhaps even more "real" than a questionnaire asking how aggressive a child is.

A meta-analysis by Rhee and Waldman (2002) found that heritability accounted for about 38 percent of the variance in antisocial behavior. Shared environment (which would be things like parenting) accounted for 18 percent, and nonshared environment accounted for 44 percent of the variability in antisocial behavior. As with many aspects of behavior, there is a genetic component, but the environment clearly matters. But here it gets interesting and complicated. Genes and the environment interact; consequently, we may be overestimating the effect of the genetics because of that interaction (Moffitt, 2005). Remember that the parent and child share genes; as a result, the environment that the parents create to fit their own interests and dispositions will be the environment that the child experiences. In that, we see a gene environment interaction. There is evidence that parenting is influenced by the parent's own genes (Towers, Spotts, and Neiderhiser, 2001; Wade and Kendler, 2000). Adoption studies allow us to look at this by removing the shared parent-child genes. Here, it appears that the child's genes influence adoptive parents' parenting style, such that children genetically at risk for being aggressive are parented with more discipline and control (Riggins-Caspers, Cadoret, Knutson, and Langbehn, 2003). The methodologies and data are being developed, but that interaction of gene and environment may be where a lot of the behavior is created (Moffitt, 2005).

Cultural Influences

Many critics now argue that the United States is a violent culture. But is the United States unique in this, or are all cultures violent? In fact, it appears that some cultural groups are peaceful; others are warlike. In some cultures, violent solutions to conflict are common; in others, they are rare. For some groups, killing is a sin; for others, it is a virtue. The enormous variations in the level of violence between societies underline the importance of social influences on human aggression. Biological factors, as we have seen, exert a significant influence on aggressive behavior. But the influence of biological factors is very much dependent on the social context and the organism's past experiences.

The importance of cultural influences on aggressive behavior is readily illustrated by a simple inspection of national differences in homicide rates. In Table 18.2, mean homicide rates per 100,000 people for selected countries are presented for the 1990s, the first decade of the 2000s, and 2010 to 2014. It is noteworthy that the United States was consistently among those countries with the highest homicide rates. When the United States is compared with other English-speaking nations, it can be seen to have had about four to six times that of Australia, Canada, or the United Kingdom. The United States usually

TABLE 18.2 Average Intentional Homicide Rates per 100,000 People by Selected Country and Decade

Country	1990s	2000s	2010s
United States	6.76	5.66	4.53
Australia	1.71	1.51	1.08
Canada	1.76	1.69	1.48
New Zealand	1.29	1.28	0.94
United Kingdom	1.43	1.54	1.03
Denmark	1.21	0.91	0.80
Finland	2.70	2.49	1.80
France	1.85	1.62	1.26
Germany	1.48	0.88	0.70
Israel	2.38	2.61	1.90
Italy	1.59	1.12	0.86
Japan	0.54	0.51	0.32
Netherlands	1.41	1.06	0.85
Norway	0.90	0.81	0.96
Spain	1.15	1.19	0.76
Sweden	1.05	0.83	0.70
Switzerland	1.18	0.94	0.62
India	4.36	3.77	3.36
Burkina Faso	NA	0.72	0.63
Ghana	NA	1.97	1.70
South Africa	58.27	40.74	31.30

Source: Based on the UN Office on Drugs and Crime's International Homicide Statistics database.

has about five times the number of murders per 100,000 people as western European countries. The United States is higher than the rates for India plus the African countries of Birkina Faso and Ghana. Many countries have higher rates. South Africa is included, but Brazil and much of Central America are higher as well. One note of optimism is that for the most part, each of those countries (and most of the countries not reported here) is seeing a reduction in the number of homicides.

The Physical Environment

As we saw in Chapter 2, the physical environment in which people live may exert a significant impact on their personality and social behavior. Aggressiveness is commonly cited as an example of a significant personality component that is strongly affected by features of the physical environment—for example, by heat, crowded living conditions, urban noise, and so on. However, research indicates that many factors influence the effects of these environmental stimuli. For example, in one study of crowding, males in a crowded room displayed more aggression than males in a room less densely populated, whereas an opposite effect was observed for females (Freedman, Levy, Buchanan, and Price, 1972). Males do not consistently show a crowding effect; for example, four- to five-year-olds were found to display significantly less aggression when they played in a small area than when they played in a much larger one (Loo, 1972).

Noise is another factor that has an impact on aggression. Consider the following experiment by Donnerstein and Wilson (1976). Male college students were either angered or treated positively by an experimental assistant. They were subsequently given the opportunity to administer electric shocks of varying intensities to the assistant while wearing earphones through which low-intensity or high-intensity noise was transmitted. Noise enhanced aggression only for the participants who had been angered, that is, for whom aggressive responses were more dominant. The same effect occurs when physical exercise rather than noise is the source of physiological arousal. Two and one-half minutes of strenuous physical exercise significantly heightened the level of aggression toward an assistant among those participants who had previously been angered by the assistant, while having no effect on the non-angered participants (Zillman, Katcher, and Milarsky, 1972). Of course, the experimental effects of noise manipulation may differ from those of real noise. Real-life noises can be either more or less grating, annoying, louder, and painful than those used in experimental investigations. In addition, the effects of persistent, long-lasting noise may be different from those of the sporadic, short-duration noise used in most research. All of these effects must be evaluated in order to determine whether noise pollution in our urban environments is a significant contributor to urban violence.

Heat has been consistently linked to aggression. Using data up to 1997, hotter summers have been associated with higher rates of murder and assault (Anderson and Anderson, 1998). Cohn and Rotten (1997; Rotten and Cohn, 2001) find that as the temperature goes up, so do assaults. This was true in England and in Minneapolis. Some of the effect may be due to people's beliefs about the effects of heat (Anderson, Anderson, Dorr, DeNeve, and Flanagan, 2000). They further suggest an interesting phenomenon that the relationship between temperature and aggression is M-shaped. Near comfortable temperatures, lower rates are observed. As the temperature moves to an uncomfortable range, aggression increases, but as it moves further, it drops again. When people are too cold or too hot, aggression decreases.

There is even heat-related research from baseball. Baseball pitchers occasionally hit batters on purpose as a retaliation for things that have happened during the game. Researchers have found that batters are more likely to be hit by a pitch as the temperature goes up (Timmerman, 2007); this is especially likely as temperatures rise and there have been teammates hit by pitches earlier in the game (Larrick, Timmerman, Carton, and Abrevaya, 2011).

Baseball pitchers are more likely to retaliate by hitting a batter when the temperature is high.

Source: Jon Osumi/Shutterstock

Evidence is starting to accumulate that the natural environment that surrounds us can have an effect on health and stress (Donovan et al., 2013; Lohr, 2011; Ulrich, 1984). People living near green space with grass and trees reported lower levels of aggression and violence (Kuo and Sullivan, 2001).

Finally, let's return to the idea of Cohen and Nisbett (1997) that environment influences the development of cultures and those cultures impact stable personality traits (Chapter 2). In their model, climate leads to particular types of agriculture, which then gives rise to a "culture of honor." They then claim that a culture of honor leads to more aggressive behavior in defense of one's honor.

Personality Theories and the Antecedents of Aggression

We have seen that human aggression is influenced by biological and social variables, neurological mechanisms, cultural differences, individual learning experiences, and the physical and social environment. How do the facts on aggression relate to theories of personality? We will find that the personality theories that have given special attention to the problem of aggression differ in the relative emphasis placed on biological versus social variables, and in the particular social influences believed to be of primary importance. A discussion of theoretical views and research on the principal mechanisms causing aggression provides a basis for integrating the diverse data on aggression with other personality issues and for understanding the controversies concerning the development of aggression and its control.

Psychoanalytic Theory

Freud's views on aggression, like his views on other issues, underwent substantial modification during the course of his long career. In his early writings, Freud believed aggression to be primarily an innate reaction to frustration and pain: "the ego hates, abhors and pursues with intent to destroy all objects which are for it a source of painful feelings" (Freud, 1925, p. 81). This view persisted but was made subordinate to a subsequent formulation of aggression as arising from a biological drive. He proposed a new dichotomy in which the libidinal instinct, Eros, was enlarged to embrace all of the positive, constructive, life-enhancing tendencies and was contrasted with the death instinct, Thanatos, which encompassed the organism's tendencies toward aggression, self-destruction, and ultimately death (Freud, 1920). By the late 1920s, partly in response to the destruction of World War I, Freud had elevated aggression urges to a status equivalent to that of libidinal urges.

The death instinct is one of Freud's more speculative concepts and is not an integral part of psychoanalytic theory (see Chapter 3). However, while the concept of a death instinct has gained little acceptance, many psychologists support the assumption of an innate, biologically-rooted aggressive drive. This view of aggression has important social consequences. It leads one to emphasize social controls and power as a means of checking human aggression rather than to modify social conditions and relationships that might foster aggression. Concerning the necessity of strong social controls, Freud stated: "Civilized society is perpetually mirrored with disintegration through this primary hostility of men toward one another. . . . Culture has to call up every possible reinforcement in order to erect barriers against the aggressive instincts of men" (Freud, 1930, p. 86).

Broad assumptions about human behavior, such as the view that humans have innate aggressive urges, are difficult to test or disprove. The work of ethologists like Lorenz and Tinbergen is sometimes cited as support for the innate aggressive drive hypothesis. However, as has been noted earlier, there are fundamental differences between the observations of ethologists and the psychoanalysts' conception of innate aggression. These differences may be summarized as follows:

1. Nonhuman aggression is primarily reactive rather than internally generated. Aggression is elicited by specific stimuli, referred to as *releasers*.
2. Innate aggressive responses by animals are primarily instrumental. If the object of aggression ceases the aggression-eliciting behaviors (e.g., intruding on territory, competing for food), then the aggressive attack usually ceases.
3. Withdrawal by or a submissive signal (an inhibitor) from the opponent is usually sufficient to terminate a conflict. Injury to a same-species opponent is not required for an animal to terminate aggression.
4. Consistent with the psychoanalytic hypothesis, aggressive displacement has been observed in some animals. There is also evidence that some animals are motivated to continue or initiate a fight and will cross an electrified grid to do so. However, an animal's drive to complete an aggressive response, to express anger, or even to

initiate a fight must be distinguished from the psychoanalytic conception of an innate drive to inflict injury.

5. The desire to hurt, to inflict injury, and to seek revenge is observed primarily in humans, not in animals. It seems quite likely that an aggressive drive in this sense is an acquired or learned motivation (Feshbach, 1974).

We have noted that, in psychoanalytic theory, the theme of reactive aggression coexists but is theoretically subordinate to the theme of innate aggressive drive. Nevertheless, in their writings, and especially in their practice, psychoanalysts also make extensive use of the idea that aggression is a reaction to particular experiences. Thus, in exploring the basis for a particular patient's anger and hostility, the analyst will look for situations in early childhood that might be responsible for the patient's aggression; for example, rivalry with a sibling may be exacerbated by parental favoritism toward that sibling. Psychoanalysts have also believed that frustration of biologically based oral or anal impulses (Chapter 3) is a significant cause of aggression. However, studies investigating the relationship of aggression to the severity of weaning or toilet training have yielded negative or inconsistent findings (Feshbach, 1970). Modern psychoanalytic theory, with its emphasis on object relations and ego development, is more likely to look for the causes of aggression in the child's relationship with its parents and in the factors that promote the ineffective development of self-control, rather than to focus on the biology of the organism.

Learning Theory Models of Aggression

Learning theory models of aggression have in common the effort to establish systematic relationships between antecedent events and aggressive behavior. They differ in the particular antecedents or mechanisms thought to be most important. Adherents of Hullian and the Dollard-Miller theory have focused on frustration as an antecedent to aggressive drive. The elaboration of the relationship between frustration and aggression eventually led to a reformulation of the frustration-aggression hypothesis through the incorporation of significant elements from cognitive theory. In contrast, adherents of Bandura's learning theory have addressed their attention to the acquisition of instrumental aggressive responses and to the role of imitation in the development of aggression. Investigators favoring a Skinnerian model of learning have stressed the role of direct and subtle reinforcements in the acquisition of instrumental aggressive behaviors. These reinforcements could be getting the other kids' lunch money or the attention of teachers. In addition, several other theoretical positions will be considered that have incorporated aspects of learning theories but also have some unique features and emphases (Berkowitz, 1989, Feshbach, 1974).

The Frustration-Aggression Hypothesis

The formulation of the **frustration-aggression hypothesis** and the publication in 1939 of the Dollard et al. volume *Frustration and Aggression* marked the first systematic treatment by psychologists of aggressive behaviors. In addition, it provided a significant link between psychoanalytic theory and experimental psychology. And finally, the frustration-aggression hypothesis helped integrate a very diverse set of observations, ranging from violent dreams reported during psychotherapy to the frequency of lynchings, by linking these events to frustrations experienced by the individual and by members of a group. Although psychologists have significantly revised the hypothesis, it is still extensively used by social scientists and considered to be a landmark theoretical proposition.

The frustration-aggression hypothesis asserts very simply that the frustration (interference, blocking) of an ongoing activity produces an instigation (drive, motivation) whose goal response is injury to some person or object. No assumption is made regarding how the connection between frustration and aggression comes about, whether it is innate or learned, although it is acknowledged that reactions to frustration can be altered through

frustration-aggression hypothesis Interference with achieving a goal leads to frustration, which results in a goal of aggression.

learning. The initial statement of the hypothesis, namely that "aggression is always a consequence of frustration" has two implications: (1) aggression is always due to frustration and (2) frustration always leads to aggression. These statements are not equivalent; one can be false and the other true. For example, it might be that frustration always produces an impetus to aggression but that there are other factors besides frustration that also instigate aggression. It was immediately recognized by critics and also by the authors that, in using such exclusive terms as always, these propositions were too strongly phrased. The authors then acknowledged that there are other causes of aggression besides frustration and maintained that frustration produces a tendency to aggress as well as other response tendencies (Miller, 1941). Consequently, overt aggression, while likely, is not an inevitable response to frustration, and the relationship between frustration and aggression can be modified through learning. But the hypothesis, even if less strongly stated, still had a number of important properties. The amount of aggression was hypothesized to be quantitatively related to the amount of frustration experienced by the organism. In addition, the authors also proposed that when the instigation to aggression was blocked through, for example, fear of punishment, there would still remain a drive to aggress toward available targets. Thus, the formulation provided a model for the analysis of the displacement of aggression.

The frustration-aggression hypothesis has stimulated a good deal of research. A very early study, which reflects its potential utility as an explanatory tool, used as the measure of aggression the number of lynchings that took place yearly in the United States, largely in fourteen southern states, during the period from 1882 to 1930. Since cotton was the basic commodity in these states, the value of the cotton yield each year during this period was also determined. It was hypothesized that the lower the cotton yield, the greater the economic frustration experienced by the community, and the greater the likelihood of displaced aggression resulting in lynchings. An analysis of the data revealed a sizable and significant negative correlation consistent with the hypothesis: the lower the yearly cotton yield, the higher the frequency of lynchings that year. Recent reanalyses of these data, using more sophisticated statistical procedures, have confirmed the original results, although the correlation is not as high as initially reported (Hepworth and West, 1988).

A more direct test of the effects of the magnitude of frustration employed a simple but clever experimental procedure in a natural setting (Harris, 1974). The experimenter had an assistant cut into a line of individuals who were waiting their turn at places like ticket windows, restaurants, and grocery stores. The critical dependent variable was the amount of aggression displayed by the individual whose place in line the assistant had displaced. Hypothesizing that the amount of frustration would be greater the closer that individual was to the beginning of the line, the assistant cut in front of either the second or the twelfth person in line. The person who had been closer indeed displayed much more aggression (fortunately, mostly verbal) toward the assistant than the person who had been farther along in line.

While these findings point to the usefulness of the frustration-aggression hypothesis, it is also the case that many investigators have failed to find an increase in aggression following frustration (Feshbach, 1970). The difficulty in evaluating these negative findings is that the level of frustration experimentally induced in the laboratory may often be too weak to evoke aggression. However, apart from the question of the adequacy of experimental tests, it is clear that the frustration-aggression hypothesis has serious limitations. First, the concept of frustration is vague. Insults and physical pain have been shown to be powerful elicitors of aggression. But are they frustrations? Failure would seem to be an obvious frustration, yet the frustrating effects of failure are dependent on expectancy. Your reaction to failing an examination would greatly depend on whether you had expected to pass. Second, in addition to the need to establish explicit criteria for what constitutes a frustration, the particular motivations that are frustrated must also be taken into account. Experiences that threaten an individual's self-esteem and sense of security appear to be much more likely to elicit hostility than experiences that interfere with satisfactions of a physiological drive like hunger (Maslow, 1941).

Although the frustration-aggression hypothesis has some validity, it is too broadly stated. What is required is a determination of the particular properties of interfering events that tend to foster aggressive reactions. Cognitive theories have proved to be very helpful in this regard. Cognitive attributes both determine the meaning of the frustration and strongly influence the likelihood of an aggressive response to the frustration. At least four cognitive attributes of frustration can be specified. While these are related to one another, it is helpful to separate them:

1. *Expectancy*. As has been noted, the degree to which a negative experience is frustrating depends on the degree of expectation of that experience. We expect some amount of discomfort in a crowded subway car and consequently react with less anger to jostling than if the car were half-empty. Expectancy also has significant implications for predicting the response to economic deprivation. Individuals from middle-class backgrounds who are unable to attain the standard of living they experienced when living in their parents' home are likely to feel more frustrated than individuals at the same income level but from poorer backgrounds. The aggression that sometimes accompanies small improvements in economic level in economically disadvantaged groups is also understandable in terms of expectancy, in that the small economic advance may have led to increased expectancies for substantial economic improvement that are subsequently frustrated.

2. *Arbitrariness or inequity*. A frustration is more likely to evoke aggression if it is perceived as arbitrary rather than justified. You are much more likely to get angry at a poor grade if you feel the instructor assigned the grade at random or was otherwise unfair, than if you feel the grade was deserved. The roles of both arbitrariness and expectancy are nicely illustrated in an experiment in which participants were promised a prize and given their first, second, or third choice under one of three anticipatory conditions: (a) they might or might not receive their first choice (no-expectancy); (b) they would receive their first choice (expectancy); or (c) they would be able to select any prize they wished (choice). The participants were not given a reason when they did not receive their expected choice. This lack of explanation increased the likelihood that they would perceive the frustration as arbitrary. The participants then received either their first choice, second choice, or third choice prize. When there were no expectations of getting one's choice, the type of prize didn't have much of an impact on verbal aggression. When they were led to believe they had some choice, verbal aggression increased when they got their third choice. When they thought they would get their first choice, the aggression was higher when they got their second choice and higher still when they got their third choice (Worchel, 1974).

3. *Intentionality*. We are much less likely to be angered by the same frustrating or painful event (e.g., being tripped while walking down, an aisle) if we perceive it as accidental rather than intentional. This effect is clearly demonstrated in an experiment in which participants received either strong or weak electric shocks administered at the presumed option of a fellow participant (Nickel, 1974). Half the participants in each of these two groups were then informed that a switch had been placed in the wrong position and that the shock level actually intended was directly opposite to the one received. The amount of aggression subsequently expressed by the participants toward the fellow participant was much more closely linked to the fellow participant's intended shock than to the actual level of shock inflicted. Intentionality also has been shown to contribute to individual differences in aggressive tendencies: Aggressive boys display a consistent tendency to overattribute hostile intentions to their peers as compared to nonaggressive boys (Dodge, 1980; Dodge and Frame, 1982).

4. *Responsibility*. Related to intentionality is the attribution of responsibility. The greater the perceived responsibility of the frustrating agent, the greater the likelihood of an aggressive response. Given the same frustration, one does not react with equal aggression or punishment when the agent is a two-year-old as when the agent

is a twelve-year-old. The role of responsibility is explicitly recognized in our legal code. If a person is forced to commit a criminal aggressive act, then he or she is not held "responsible" and the penalty is much less severe (see Chapter 17).

A full understanding of the relationship between frustration and aggression must consider the cognitive attributes or meaning of the frustration. There is naturalistic and experimental evidence that sometimes people become angry and aggressive even when a frustration is perceived as accidental or justified (Averill, 1982; Berkowitz, 1989). However, cognitive attributes are important determinants of the amount of aggression that is elicited by frustration (Averill, 1982; Ferguson and Rule, 1983; Weiner, 1985). Learning also influences the response to frustration. Children can, for instance, be trained to respond less aggressively to frustrating events (Davitz, 1952). As we will see, learning is a powerful determinant of aggressive behavior.

A further change has been introduced in the frustration-aggression hypothesis by Berkowitz (1989) who proposes that frustrations elicit aggression only to the extent that they produce negative affect. The hypothesis would then be broadened to read "negative affect–frustration." This formulation integrates findings demonstrating that physical pain (Monteith, Berkowitz, Kruglanski, and Blair, 1989), disgust (Zillmann, Bryant, Comiskey, and Medoff, 1981), unpleasantly high room temperatures (Rule, Taylor and Dobbs, 1987), and depressed affect (Berkowitz, 1983) as well as frustrating, goal-interfering events can evoke angry feelings and aggression. Notice how this tends to cohere with the information about the physical environment from earlier in the chapter.

Social Learning and the Modeling of Aggression

Several of the basic experiments by Bandura and his coworkers, which provided the foundation for his theory of observational learning, involved the modeling of aggression (Bandura, 1962; Bandura, Ross, and Ross, 1963a; see Chapter 5). Preschool children who had observed an adult model carry out a series of discrete aggressive responses toward a Bobo doll (an inflated plastic clown, weighted with sand so it will come back to upright when hit) subsequently displayed a striking degree of imitation of the adult aggressive behavior in interacting with the Bobo doll. The adults performed rather idiosyncratic behaviors with the doll, such as hitting it with a hammer while sitting on it. As Figure 18.3 indicates, the children imitated the adult whether the model was live, on film, or dressed as a cartoon cat. The finding that children imitated filmed adult aggression and cartoon aggression suggested that similar effects might occur as a result of children observing

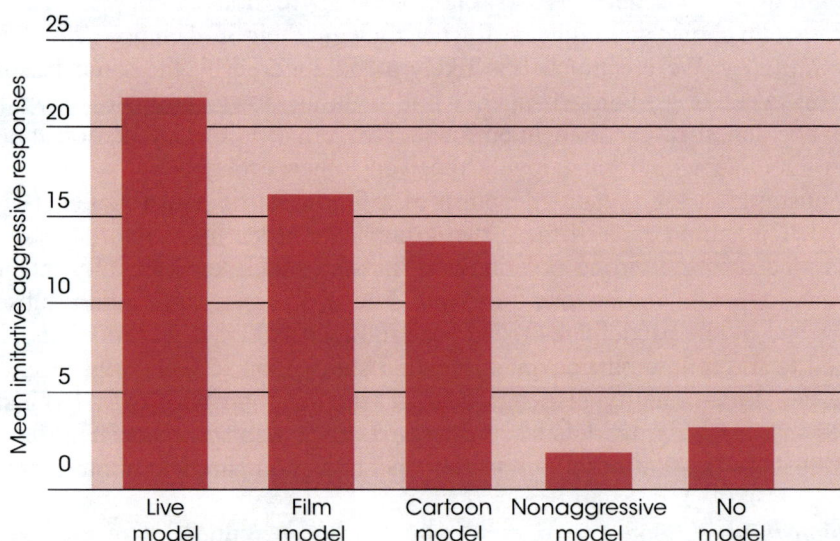

FIGURE 18.3 Mean Imitative Aggressive Responses Performed by Children

Source: (Plotted from data by Bandura, Ross, and Ross, 1963a, pp. 3–11)

televised aggression and has stimulated research and theorizing on the possible modeling influence of television on the aggressive behavior of child and adult viewers.

Although imitation is undoubtedly one process by which children acquire aggressive and other social behaviors, children obviously do not imitate every aggressive act they observe. We need to know the conditions under which they are likely to imitate an aggressive model. There have been a number of studies addressed to this issue. For example, verbalization of aggressive actions increases the amount and persistence of imitation (Bandura, Grusec, and Menlove, 1966). In addition, children are more likely to imitate an aggressive model if they have had a prior frustrating experience as, for example, when losing in competitive play (Nelson, Gelfand, and Hartmann, 1969). And witnessing a model being rewarded for aggression tends to increase imitation, while punishment of the model's behavior tends to reduce imitation. Importantly, there is evidence that children learn the punished behavior and will perform it when likelihood of punishment is reduced (Hicks, 1968).

The concept of modeling has been applied to the spread of violent actions. An event can be modeled through verbal description, without visual representation, as in a newspaper report. It has been argued that media publicity given to airline hijackings, random shootings on highways, suicide, and other violent acts has increased the frequency of such acts through the process of modeling. However, in view of the enormous variability in imitation of observed behaviors, we need to know much more about the situational and individual factors that determine when a model is imitated.

Reinforcement

Why have some people learned to be aggressive? One reason may be that they have been exposed to models of aggressive parents, peers, and perhaps favorite television characters. Another, probably more potent, reason is that they have found that aggression "pays off," that it gets them the rewards of money, sex, status, and power over others that they seek. There is a good deal of evidence that aggressive behavior is governed by the same principles that govern other instrumental responses. Aggression increases when reinforced, and declines when not reinforced or when it results in punishment (Brown and Elliot, 1965; Walters and Brown, 1963). We have seen, in our discussion of nonhuman aggression, that victory and defeat play a powerful role in determining the level of aggressive behavior.

A naturalistic study in which preschool children were observed over a nine-month period indicated similar effects at the human level (Patterson, Littman, and Bricker, 1967). The effects of reinforcement and punishment were especially noticeable in passive children who entered nursery school with weak aggressive tendencies. The passive children who were attacked by other children and whose counterattacks were unsuccessful remained submissive in their behaviors. However, the initially passive children whose counterattacks were successful showed a significant increase in aggressive tendencies.

There has been a great deal of interest in the use of reinforcement procedures for the modification of aggression in highly aggressive youngsters. These reinforcement programs have been carried out in institutional settings, in classrooms, and in the home. The programs are characterized by the careful monitoring of the child's behavior, the administration of positive rewards (e.g., prizes and privileges) for prosocial behaviors, and either ignoring of or mild punishment (e.g., brief isolation periods, loss of privileges) for aggression and related negative behaviors. Patterson and his colleagues have pioneered in the development of methods for training parents to cope more effectively with aggressive problem children through the appropriate utilization of reinforcement procedures (Patterson, 1979, Patterson and Bank, 1989). Their findings indicate that after twenty-five to thirty treatment hours with parents and children, over a period of several months, significant reductions occur in the level of the children's aggression and other aversive behaviors (e.g., whining). In addition, positive changes in parental behaviors, such as monitoring of the child, are significantly related to decreases in antisocial behaviors.

One of the contributions of the behavioral method developed by Patterson and others on the basis of Skinnerian principles is that it requires close attention to the behavior that

Aggression can be reinforcing!

is to be discouraged or rewarded. The parent, teacher, and other authority figures thus become more conscious of the subtle ways in which they may be reinforcing an undesired behavior: for example, they may reinforce aggression by paying attention to a child whenever he is difficult or by finally yielding to demands after an escalating sequence of aggression and punishment.

Aggressive Cues

aggressive cues Cues in the environment that function as releasing stimuli for aggression.

Even when individuals are frustrated, have strong aggressive tendencies due to reinforcement, or are otherwise aggressively disposed, they still are not aggressive all the time. An *aggressive cue* is usually required in order for the aggressive tendency to be expressed in behavior. Leonard Berkowitz (1978) proposed that these **aggressive cues** have acquired the property of eliciting aggression through conditioning. It is assumed that aggressive words and aggressive instruments have accompanied frustration and other stimulus events that evoke aggressive responses and, through this pairing, become conditioned stimuli or cues for aggression. Berkowitz and his students have carried out an extensive series of ingenious experiments demonstrating the importance of such cues in the regulation of aggressive behavior (Berkowitz, 1965b; Berkowitz and Geen, 1966). For example, participants who had seen a film depicting a brutal prize fight and who had previously been angered by a research assistant administered a greater number of shocks to that assistant when he was described as a college boxer than when he was described as a speech major. Several control conditions that were included indicated that this difference in cue labeling was not effective unless the participant had seen the fight film and was also angry. A similar effect was obtained when the assistant was introduced to the participant merely with the same first name as the major character in the boxing film (Berkowitz and Geen, 1966).

In another provocative demonstration of the role of aggressive cues, angered or non-angered participants were given the opportunity to shock a fellow participant either while observing a .38-caliber revolver and a 12-gauge shotgun placed in the vicinity of the shock button or with these objects absent (Berkowitz and LePage, 1967). The amount of shock delivered by the participants who had been angered was significantly greater when the weapon cues were present than with the weapons absent. Subsequent efforts to repeat these findings have yielded mixed results. Some investigators have obtained the "weapons effect," while others have not. Nevertheless, there is little doubt concerning the role of aggressive cues in the facilitation of aggressive behavior.

Social Influence

Social norms and social influences can be considered aggressive cues that may directly encourage aggressive behavior. Even non-aggressive individuals may participate in aggressive actions because of conformity to social expectations and social pressure. A dramatic demonstration of the power of an authority figure to elicit conformity and obedience to rather extreme demands and expectations is provided in a famous experiment by Stanley Milgram (1963). Adult volunteers were requested and then commanded to use increasing levels of shock whenever a fellow participant made an error on a learning task. The switches controlling shock levels were clearly labeled, with the indicator ranging from 15 to 450 volts. Protesting participants increased the shock levels under pressure from the experimenter, even when the presumed "victim" pounded on the wall that separated himself from the participant, as if in great pain. Whenever the participant wanted to stop the proceedings, the experimenter would tell the participant that he or she had to continue. Under these circumstances, 65 percent of the participants proceeded to the final 450-volt shock. The Milgram study suggests that conformity pressures can induce individuals to carry out extreme aggressive acts. Many individuals who participated in implementing the atrocities ordered by the Nazis were probably doing so out of such obedience and fear.

It is evident from this review of the diverse explanations that have been offered for human aggression that there are many different processes mediating aggressive behavior. There is no single mechanism that one can point to as *the* cause of aggression. The various personality theories have tended to focus on different processes rather than offering rival interpretations of aggression. Thus, frustration, particularly when perceived as intentional or arbitrary; rewards and punishments; modeling; the presence of aggressive cues; and conformity to social norms are all determinants of aggression. The least satisfactory hypothesis is the psychoanalytic assumption of an instinctive aggressive drive, or innate hostility. However, there are undoubtedly biological factors involved in some forms of aggression. In other respects, as in its focus on the family's role in the development of aggression, the psychoanalytic contribution to our understanding of aggression has been substantial.

Developmental Influences

Child-Rearing Practices

On the basis of the antecedents of aggression that have been discussed, we might expect that a history of frustration and parental rejection, or of parental permissiveness and reinforcement of aggression, would be associated with the development of aggression in offspring. This is indeed the case (Feshbach, 1970; Parke and Slaby, 1983). Parents who are permissive about aggression or encourage some forms of aggression; parents who make few demands of their children with regard to positive social behaviors and who are lax in their supervision; and parents who essentially reject the child through their coldness or actual hostility are likely to have highly aggressive children. What about the effects of parental punitiveness, particularly the use of physical punishment? There is some disagreement among investigators on this issue. From a theoretical standpoint, physical punishment can affect aggression in several different ways. First, because of its aversive features, it has an inhibitory function for the disapproved behavior. However, physical punishment is painful, frustrating, and frequently humiliating—all of which are likely to stimulate aggression. In addition, the parent, while physically punishing the child, is serving as a model to the child. Imitation of the parent's behavior would enhance aggression. And, in this connection, the parent may be teaching the child a social norm that essentially states that if you are injured or frustrated by someone, you respond by physically punishing them.

With few exceptions, studies of child-rearing practices have indicated that the frequency of parental use of physical punishment is one of the best predictors of aggression in children (Feshbach, 1970; Olweus, 1980). Differences arise in the interpretation of this relationship since these studies as a rule do not clearly distinguish between physical punishment that is limited and restrained and punishment that is brutal. In addition, it may be that more aggressive children elicit more severe and more frequent punishment from their parents.

Even harsh parenting that does not use physical punishment is associated with higher rates of aggression by the child at school (Change, Schwartz, Dodge, and McBride-Chang, 2003). Controlling parenting by mothers increases aggression in children who are already at risk for aggression (Joussemet et al., 2008). Care and supervisory neglect combined with harsh and punitive parenting are also associated with higher rates of aggression. This research suggests that the child does not learn to regulate his or her own behavior and consequently does not learn to regulate aggression. We can contrast this with the extensive evidence (see Chapter 12) that warmth and positive attention have positive effects on the child's behavior. There is evidence that these parenting skills can be taught and that these skills will result in lower levels of aggression (e.g., Brotman et al., 2008).

Child Abuse

Child abuse is a form of aggression that is particularly distressing in that young children are the objects of physical abuse and adults, most often parents, are the abusers. It is a problem that unfortunately is not rare. Personality studies of child abusers have reported some differences between this group and nonabusing parents, but the differences are not great and are outnumbered by the similarities (Parke and Collmer, 1975).

There is some evidence that the same factors associated with aggression in general also are involved in child abuse. Observations of child-abusing parents reveal that they are more irritable and engage in other negative interactions more frequently with their children than nonabusing parents (Reid, 1986). Frustrations, such as job dissatisfaction, are also more common among abusive parents. In addition, abusive parents tend to expect more of their children than is age appropriate. They are more likely to see the child as a fully responsible agent and perceive the child's failure to conform to parental requests as intentionally motivated. In addition, one of the personality characteristics of abusive parents that does distinguish them from other parents is low self-esteem; threats to self-esteem are generally considered to be among the most powerful instigators of anger and hostility (see the later discussion of narcissism).

Most people abused as children do not grow up to abuse children. Most child abusers were not abused.

However, it should be pointed out that those who have been abused as children are not doomed to become abusers. While being abused increases the likelihood of becoming an abuser, only about 30 percent of those who were abused go on to become abusers (Widom, 1989). Also it is interesting to note that the majority of adults who abuse children were *not* abused as children (Widom, 1989). Therefore, while child abuse certainly contributes to an increased likelihood of being aggressive, many other factors are involved in whether an adult will be an abuser.

Aggression as a Personality Trait

The literature that has been reviewed provides substantial evidence of situational factors influencing aggression. But data have also been cited reflecting individual differences in aggressivity. Evidence for the stability of aggressive behavior over long periods of time provides strong support for viewing aggression as a personality dimension in which individuals differ. Relational aggression tends to be stable for girls from early childhood (Crick et al., 2006). In a detailed review of sixteen studies on the stability of aggressive behavior patterns, an impressive degree of consistency in aggressive characteristics was observed over periods ranging from six months to as much as twenty-one years (Olweus, 1979). In a very ambitious longitudinal study, aggression at age eight proved to be predictive of antisocial behavior at age thirty, including criminal behavior and spouse abuse (Huesmann et al., 1984).

Data from these and other studies indicate that aggression is not only relatively stable over time but that there are also consistencies among different indicators of aggression. Self-report questionnaires have been shown to be related to peer ratings of aggression, while these measures in turn are related to aggressive choices and to aggressive behaviors (Carlson, Marcus-Newhall, and Miller, 1989; Lefkowitz et al., 1977; Olweus, 1978). Although there is evidence for the consistency of aggressive behavior, the role of situational factors should not be minimized. A very aggressive person at home and among peers may be unaggressive in a work situation because the job is particularly satisfying or because of fear of losing the job.

Fear of punishment and guilt or anxiety over aggression complicate the findings on the consistency of aggressive behavior. Aggression-anxious persons would appear, at a superficial level, to be inconsistent in their aggressive behavior, displaying very little aggression in some situations and exaggerated aggression in other contexts (Eron et al., 1971; Feshbach, Stiles, and Bitter, 1967). But by taking into account both their conflict over aggressive impulses and the presence of situational cues that elicit anxiety, one can find order and consistency in their behavior (see Miller's conflict model, Chapter 14). Thus, a more indirect, subtle indicator of aggression—withholding rewards—was shown in one study to be more discriminating of aggressive attitudes than the administration of electric shock (Caprara et al., 1986).

Hostile Attribution Bias

Some research has shown that children who exhibit antisocial aggressive behavior exhibit characteristic differences in how they process information compared to children who are not aggressive (Dodge and Crick, 1990; Dodge and Newman, 1981). First, they interpret the behavior of others in ways that make them feel more hostile toward those others. For instance, they are more likely to attribute hostile intentions to others when others act in ways that provoke them. Second, they seem to have access to fewer alternative strategies when they are provoked; they tend to think only of aggressive options. Third, they evaluate the usefulness and effectiveness of aggressive behavior differently than do nonaggressive children. For instance, they are more likely to believe that aggressive behavior will lead to more favorable interpersonal outcomes (e.g., peer approval). Children who have this **hostile attribution bias** appear to have lower verbal intelligence and are later in developing a theory of mind (Choe, Lane, Grabell, and Olson, 2013).

Aggressive adolescent boys in a mental health facility were more likely to interpret ambiguous faces as hostile (Nasby, Hayden, and dePaulo, 1980). In a study of adolescent boys in a maximum security juvenile prison, it was found that the hostile attribution bias was associated with committing violent interpersonal crimes, while there was no relationship to nonviolent crimes (Dodge, Price, Bachorowski, and Newman, 1990). As we saw earlier, alcohol can have an impact on aggression, and it appears to interact with the hostile bias. Alcohol-related aggression was associated with having the hostile attribution bias, while there was no effect of alcohol for those husbands and wives who did not hold that bias (Kachadourian, Homish, Quigley, and Leonard, 2012).

hostile attribution bias A tendency to see others in the world as having aggressive intentions.

Narcissism

Often men who commit violent acts will have strong beliefs about their own superiority, and when those beliefs are challenged, they are likely to react with aggression. Consequently, it is suggested that threatened egotism is a risk factor for aggression (Baumeister, Smart, and Boden, 1996). Like many relatively new ideas, the true dimensions are being worked out, for instance, what exactly is egotism. There is some good evidence that it is likely to be some combination of unstable self-esteem and **narcissism** (Baumeister, Bushman, and Campbell, 2000).

Stücke and Sporer (2002) conducted a study in which participants were given negative information about their intelligence. Participants who scored high on narcissism and

narcissism A belief about one's unique superiority to others.

had an uncertain self-concept tended to react with more verbal aggression. Another study found that narcissism was positively correlated with aggression, especially verbal aggression, and self-esteem was negatively correlated with aggression, anger, and hostility (Donnellan, Trzesniewski, Robins, Moffitt, and Caspi, 2005). Yet, other studies have indicated that after one is provoked, it is high self-esteem and high narcissism that is associated with aggression (Bushman et al., 2009). The research on self-esteem is ongoing, and it appears too early to draw conclusions. However, multiple studies and clinical observations have found relationships between narcissism and threats to one's self-views (Lambe, Hamilton-Giachritsis, Garner, and Walker, 2016).

In summary, the response to the question of the personality characteristics of aggressive individuals depends on the degree and type of aggression. Instrumental aggression, reactive aggression, aggressive drive, and repressed hostility are interwoven in various combinations and shades; each pattern of aggression seems to have a different constellation of personality factors.

Catharsis and the Regulation of Aggression

There are a number of methods for modifying anger and the response to aggressive provocation. It would be misleading if the presentation of these alternatives suggested that it is a relatively simple matter to modify aggression. The methods are intended only as guides. They offer a basis for designing procedures to cope with and hopefully mitigate destructive social behaviors.

Catharsis

catharsis The reduction of emotional tension through expressive release activity; sometimes restricted to release through vicarious activity, such as watching a play or film.

Aristotle believed that witnessing a dramatic play would result in a discharge of feelings, which was termed *catharsis*. Currently, catharsis is used to refer to the reduction of aggression through any aggressive activity, whether shouting epithets, witnessing the depiction of violence on the stage or in film, inflicting injury on an innocent target, or directly aggressing against the instigating source. There are a number of studies indicating that, in order for a reduction in aggression to occur, the individual must be angry at the time of the aggressive act (Doob and Wood, 1972; Feshbach, 1964; Konecni, 1975). Hitting a punching bag will not reduce aggression toward an irritating supervisor unless one is angry at the supervisor while punching the bag. The evidence for catharsis is also stronger when fantasy aggression is expressed directly toward the instigating target rather than toward a displaced target. While there are several studies indicating that the expression of aggression in fantasy or imagination can be cathartic (Feshbach, 1956; Manning and Taylor, 1975), there are others that question this effect and suggest that only direct, overt expressions of aggression are cathartic (Hokanson and Burgess, 1962).

It is significant that an aggressive act in which too much or too little pain is inflicted will not provide drive reduction (Fromkin, Goldstein, and Brock, 1977). This finding is in keeping with the proposition that aggressive drive is based on social norms or rules that regulate retaliation; these rules state essentially that if you have been injured by someone, you are supposed to reciprocate by inflicting an equivalent injury on that person (Feshbach, 1974).

Finally, it is widely believed that expressing anger will reduce the anger, that feelings are discharged through expression. However, a good deal of research has suggested that while expressing anger can be beneficial and can lead to anger reduction, it does not always do so (Bohart, 1980). Furthermore, the idea that anger—or any emotion, for that matter—can be discharged simply through expression appears to be at least partially wrong because emotional discharge alone is not always helpful (Bohart, 1980; Nichols and Efran, 1985). Other factors that appear to be important in determining whether expression relieves one's feelings include gaining new understanding through the expression (Bohart, 1980), sharing one's feelings with an empathic other (Bohart, 1980), gaining a sense of acceptance of the emotion (Greenberg and Safran, 1987), restructuring one's dysfunctional cognitions as a result of emotional expression (Greenberg, Rice, and Elliott, 1993), or dealing with the frustrating events that instigated the feeling (Lewis and Bucher, 1992).

Cognitive Control Mediators and Prosocial Expression of Anger

Experienced anger can be controlled through the participant's empathy with the frustrating agent and through the capacity to delay expression of anger and contemplate alternatives. If one can take the perspective of those with whom one is in conflict and understand their feelings, their behavior is less likely to seem frustrating and arbitrary and therefore is less likely to evoke aggression. The ability to think before acting, to consider a range of possible responses to a provocative situation, is also likely to increase the probability of nonaggressive, prosocial alternatives. Several promising programs designed to enhance prosocial behavior and reduce aggression through empathy training (N. Feshbach, 1979), social understanding (Pitkänen-Pulkkinnen, 1979), and problem-solving skills (Goldstein, 1981; Spivack and Shure, 1974) have been developed.

Altering Stimulus Meaning

Aggression and anger can also be modified by changing the meaning of a stimulus. For example, an individual may be perceived as not being responsible for or not having intended some injurious act. An example of this procedure is provided by a study in which an experimenter acted in a rude and obnoxious manner. The participants were informed that the experimenter was very "uptight" about a forthcoming midterm examination. This information resulted in a sharp reduction in participants' verbal aggression and blood pressure. The latter finding suggests that the participants were not simply inhibiting their anger (Zillman and Cantor, 1976).

Summary

1. The concept of love has many different connotations. Two connotations that have been distinguished and measured are romantic love and liking.
2. There are data indicating that caring is a more critical component of love than need. This is especially likely to be the case for companionate love, as compared to passionate love.
3. The triangular model of love asserts that there are different types of love in accordance with different combinations of Passion, Intimacy, and Decision/Commitment.
4. It has been proposed that passionate love is a function of cultural beliefs, the presence of an appropriate love object, and the labeling of aroused emotion.
5. There are striking similarities between patterns of adult love and patterns of early attachment, suggesting that the attachment process may be basic to love.
6. Studies indicate that the degree of sexual intimacy prior to marriage is unrelated to the development of a lasting commitment.
7. The term *aggression* includes a great many behaviors that may have different functions and causes. Distinctions should be made between the emotion of anger and the motivation to inflict injury, or *aggressive drive*, and the *instrumental* use of aggression to obtain nonaggressive goals.
8. For many nonhuman species, intraspecies aggression is regulated by stimuli called releasers that elicit innate aggressive responses and inhibitory stimuli that serve to terminate an aggressive interaction.
9. Although there is evidence that male sex hormones will, under certain conditions, increase aggressive behavior for several nonhuman species, no clear relationship between male sex hormones and aggression has been established for humans.
10. There is some evidence that genetic factors influence criminality and aggressive behavior. However, in either case environmental factors have been shown to exert powerful effects.
11. Crowding, noise, and heat have been shown to both increase and decrease aggressive behavior. These factors apparently intensify whatever behavior, aggressive or nonaggressive, is prepotent at the time.
12. The extent to which frustration elicits aggression depends on the nature of the motivation that is frustrated and on such cognitive factors as expectancy of frustration and whether the frustration is perceived as arbitrary, intentional, and caused by a responsible agent.
13. People who hold a hostile attribution bias tend to perceive others as having more hostile intentions and often respond more aggressively.
14. Narcissism appears to increase aggression when that person's ego is threatened.
15. Catharsis sometimes reduces aggression and sometimes increases aggression.

Key Terms

aggression (p. 356)
aggressive cues (p. 370)
catharsis (p. 374)
companionate love (p. 350)
decision/commitment (p. 347)
frustration-aggression hypothesis (p. 365)
hostile attribution bias (p. 373)

instrumental aggression (p. 357)
intimacy (p. 347)
narcissism (p. 373)
passion (p. 347)
passionate love (p. 349)
triangular model of love (p. 347)

Thought Questions

1. Why should marriages be based on romantic love rather than on friendship?
2. Is love an innate biological motive, need, or emotion? What influence, if any, does learning have on love?
3. To what extent is modern warfare a result of biologically based aggressive tendencies?
4. If a drug were discovered that practically eliminated violent behavior through chemical action on brain sites, would you favor its administration to violent criminals?
5. What types of frustrations is a person likely to experience that would lead to aggression? Is the threat to the ego of someone high in narcissism a form of frustration?

Summing Up

CHAPTER 19

Source: Rawpixel.com/Shutterstock

Chapter Outline

Interactionism

The Multidimensionality of the
  Person

The Self

Personality as a Science

The Future

As we noted in our introduction, we have adopted an integrative philosophy in writing this text. For instance, rather than favoring any one of the major theoretical perspectives (see Chapters 3 through 6), we have attempted to show the contribution that each makes to the understanding of various topics such as personality continuity or change, aggression, or consciousness. In this chapter we consider some broadly integrative themes in the current study of human personality that have recurred throughout the text. Four major themes recur: interactionism, the multidimensionality of the person, the self, and personality as a science. After identifying these recurrent themes and reaching some general conclusions about them, we look to the future. Using a combination of a crystal ball and our own sense of current trends, we will suggest the directions in which the field of personality is moving and which problems we think should be addressed in the years to come.

Interactionism

Human behavior and personality are a function of the interaction between the person and the environment. The important theme of interaction is present throughout this text. It appears in the early chapters on the biological versus the physical, social, and cultural determinants of personality. These chapters make it evident that both nature and nurture exert significant influences on personality. For example, how can one possibly argue that all the determinants of behavior reside in the environment, given the similarities between the traits of monozygotic twins, or given the differential concordance rates for schizophrenia among monozygotic versus dizygotic twins? On the other hand, how can one logically believe that genetic determinants of behavior account for cultural and social class differences? Individuals strictly committed to either an environmental or a genetic approach cannot give satisfactory answers to these questions.

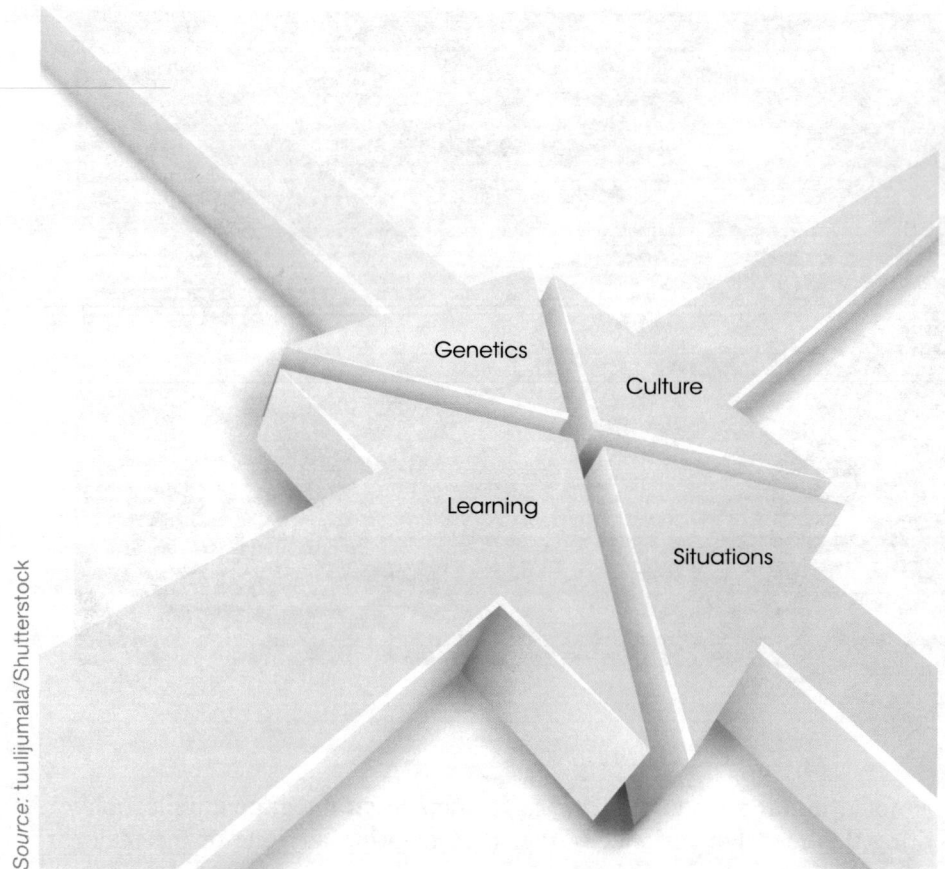

Personality is going to be the result of interactions among factors such as genetics, culture, situations, and learning.

But the concept of interaction implies even more; it indicates that the influences of nature and nurture do not work in isolation, but rather are interdependent. For example, both nonhuman and human data indicate that a predisposition to alcoholism can be inherited. But the genetic predisposition alone cannot produce alcoholism. An environment in which alcohol is available is also necessary. In certain cultures, such as Islam or Mormon communities where alcohol consumption is forbidden, an inherited vulnerability to alcoholism is not likely to develop into alcoholism. Aside from the availability of alcohol, the development of alcoholism may also depend on the interaction of a genetic predisposition with other environmental factors such as repeated situational stress.

Another example of the interaction between biological and environmental factors is the relationship between physique and personality. A child's physique is influenced by environmental as well as genetic factors. He or she must have the appropriate diet and exercise if a genetic predisposition toward athletic (mesomorphic) body build is to be manifested. Because of muscularity, there may in turn be increased likelihood of the child's experiencing success in aggressive encounters or sports. The culture may also share certain stereotypes about mesomorphic individuals, like the belief that they are dominant, courageous, and aggressive. The child may then acquire these behaviors in the process of living up to stereotyped expectations. Thus, it would be just as wrong to say that a child's assertiveness is due to his or her inherited physique as to view the attribute as solely determined by environmental experiences. Both biological and environmental factors contribute to personality traits. In this example, the interaction between the child's body structure and subsequent experiences is critical.

The theme of interaction extends beyond nature and nurture. It is also intrinsic to the dynamics of behavior. For example, different periods of life pose special problems for adaptation and development. By knowing that someone is an adolescent or in midlife, we glean some information about the kinds of problem situations that person will confront. Clearly, the situations encountered by a teenager are very different from those of an adult dealing with that teenager, aging parents, and career demands. But there are also significant individual differences between and among adolescents and adults in approaching problem situations, in the intensity of developmental crises, and in how the situations are resolved.

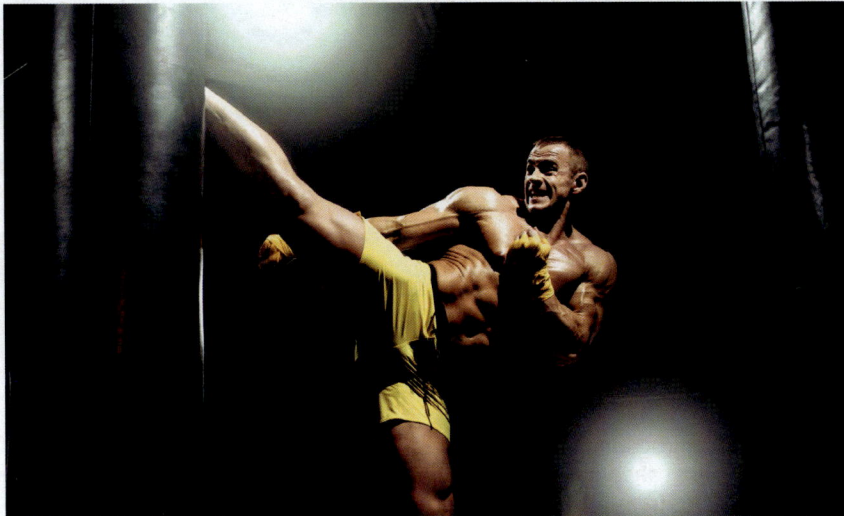

Body shape will be influenced by genetics, exercise, and diet. This could influence success in sports or aggressive encounters.

Numerous other instances of the person-situation interaction can be found in the text. Many reactions to frustration have been identified. For example, frustration may increase the probability of aggression. But this effect is more marked in children who are "undercontrolled" than in children who are labeled as "over-controlled." In addition, while some individuals react to frustration with hostility, childishness, and disruptiveness, others may withdraw and become apathetic, while still others respond with increased problem-solving activity that can lead to new, creative solutions for overcoming the source of frustration. You are encouraged to look for other experimental examples of person-situation interactions that are cited or implicit in the text.

At one level, it may appear that the interaction notion is so obvious that it hardly requires special emphasis. However, it is all too easy to view behavior as determined by either situational or person factors. Indeed, the procedures used in investigating personality frequently lend themselves to a one-sided perspective. To make research possible, it is often necessary for researchers to simplify their studies; consequently researchers may concentrate on the effects of the situation and ignore differences in personal attributes or, conversely, they may focus on individual differences while ignoring the properties of the situation that are relevant to those individual differences. For example, consider the following experiments which have demonstrated a situational focus: exposure to a television episode depicting altruism or to a nurturant caretaker increases prosocial behavior in young children; the visual presence of a prospective reward reduces delay of gratification; frustration decreases the constructiveness of play; and precise instructions for completing a task lead to decreased satisfaction. In these and many more studies, the investigators manipulated some situational property and determined its effects on behavior, but the attributes of the person that were essential to these situational effects were ignored. Because subjects are not equally affected by experimental manipulations, psychologists conduct experiments with many subjects, rather than simply generalizing from the responses of one particular individual. A few subjects, in fact, may respond in a manner opposite to the general trend. For some, very precise instructions and a high degree of structure may result in heightened, rather than decreased, satisfaction. This does not mean that the experiments are flawed or uninformative, or that the experimenters were unaware of the importance and possible interactions of subject attributes. Rather, it is easy to forget that one is really dealing with interactions even when an investigation has focused on situational variables.

A comparable problem arises when experimenters center on person variables. In these instances, the situational component of the interaction is neglected. You may recall that there is a tendency to overestimate the importance of personal traits and to underestimate the importance of the situation as a determinant of others' behavior. We tend to characterize people in trait terms that are independent of situations, such as introversion-extroversion or high achievement need-low achievement need. The situations in which introversion or high achievement strivings are evoked are typically unspecified. This is also the case in experimental studies. For example, reports that high achievement-oriented persons are more realistic than those low in achievement needs ignore the fact that this finding was obtained under particular circumstances, in a specific situation.

Very precise instructions may lead to increased satisfaction for some people, but decreased satisfaction for others. This illustrates the interaction of the person and the situation.

Although traits are often considered properties of the person, they may be better conceptualized as predispositions to respond to particular types of situations in certain ways Thus when an individual is labeled high in anxiety, this should not be taken to mean that that person is always anxious; rather, he or she is predisposed to become anxious in certain situations. The range of situations can be quite broad, such as becoming anxious when competing, or more narrow, such as becoming anxious when taking a test in a classroom. But whether the range of situations in which a trait is manifested is broad or narrow, trait effects like situational effects, usually imply an interaction.

In phenomenological theory, the interaction between person and situation is exhibited in the subjective perceptions and meanings that individuals impose. Theorists in the phenomenological tradition tend not to be concerned with traits or with external physical events, but assume instead that the individual's subjective experience is of fundamental interest. This experience reflects an interaction between the objective stimulus situation, or what is really out there, and the attributes of the person that filter that external environment and provide meaning to the world. Thus, phenomenological theorists are concerned with interactions at the level of subjective perception and personal understanding.

The Multidimensionality of the Person

Human beings are thinking, feeling, motivated, behaving organisms. Some theoretical approaches, notably the learning theories, have placed primary emphasis on overt behavioral responses, largely because these are observable and subject to direct verification. Psychoanalytic theorists, on the other hand, stress the feelings and motivations of the organism, while the phenomenological, cognitive theorists are particularly interested in the individual's thoughts and perceptions. In the approach to personality that has been followed in this text, all these dimensions of human functioning are considered significant.

Some theorists might argue that, while all components—thoughts, feelings, desires, and response tendencies—are necessary to understanding human personality, one component is primary and the others are secondary. For example, it could be argued that cognitions determine feelings, motivations, and behavior. Thus, if you believe that someone deliberately humiliated you (cognition), then you are likely to become angry (emotion) and wish to retaliate (desire). If you believe that you have a good chance of retaliating without punishment (cognition), then you might act aggressively toward the person who injured you (behavior). In this example, cognitions are primary, producing certain feelings, motivations, and behaviors. But motivations are sometimes primary. For example, an extremely ambitious person might perceive other people as obstacles and threats, in which case motivations determine cognitions. And overt responses or behaviors can also be primary: a boy may act aggressively because he has been repeatedly reinforced for aggressive acts. When acting aggressively, he may rationalize his behavior, perceiving other children as initiators of the hostile exchange.

Under certain circumstances, each component might be of central importance and determine the other processes. At a more fundamental level, the cognitive, affective, motivational, and behavioral aspects of human personality are interrelated. For example, a highly aggressive person not only has a low threshold for responding with aggressive behaviors, but also tends to perceive others as threatening. Thus, the disparate aspects of personality form an organized whole; each aspect has a significant role and none can be considered sufficient to account for the complexity of human action.

There is an apparent contradiction in human behavior that also highlights the necessity of being willing to draw on insights from each of the major approaches. On the one hand, humans are quite rational. They can

Aggressive behavior can be understood as being caused in multiple ways.

consciously employ coping strategies to handle threat and anxiety; goal expectancies are calculated and logical decisions are made; information is sought out and processed; causal inferences are made; and self-insight can be attained. On the other hand, it is also evident that we are sometimes irrational. Motivations may be outside awareness, and we defend ourselves in ways unknown to us; in times of stress and frustration, distinctions may be blurred and fixated behavior is displayed; overgeneralizations are made when there have been negative outcomes and perceived lack of control; information is not properly processed; illogical decisions are reached; and there is personal delusion.

A list of the contradictions in human behavior could go on and on. Because logical and rational or illogical and irrational behavior might be exhibited in any given situation, the creation of a general theory of personality is indeed a difficult undertaking. And, given this diversity, one must accept that many equally important components or processes play an active role in human personality and behavior.

The Self

The self and related ideas of self-concept and self-esteem were discussed in some depth in Chapter 10. However, research and theories about the self are by no means restricted to the contents of that chapter; in virtually all the other chapters of this text, issues involving some aspect of the self have been addressed.

Consider first the place of the self in the various theories of personality. Clearly, the self is a central construct for phenomenological theorists, with their concentration on self-worth, self-perception, the ego ideal, and self-actualization. But the other theoretical approaches also place considerable importance on the self. Psychoanalytic defenses such as regression, reaction formation, and projection are mechanisms for maintaining self-esteem and preventing the individual from awareness of painful attributes of the self

(Hilgard, 1949). And social learning theory gives considerable attention to self-monitoring processes. Another attribute of the self that has assumed central importance in social learning theory is the sense of self-competence or self-efficacy.

In a very general way, phenomenological theorists have focused on the cognitive, experiential aspects of the self (who am I?); psychoanalytic theorists have been oriented toward the motivational properties of the self (how can I protect myself?); and the social learning theorists have stressed the response properties of the self (what are the response consequences of high or low self-efficacy?). Remember, though, that these differences are a matter of emphasis, as all the theoretical approaches recognize the cognitive, motivational, and behavioral components of the self.

The self is important for many different approaches in personality psychology.

The various aspects of the self have assumed a significant role in personality research. For example, we have reviewed studies in this text that concern self-control, self-esteem, self-focus, discrepancies between perceived and ideal self, and the relations between self-attributions and affect. Furthermore, how we believe we appear to others and the avoidance of guilt and shame are among the most powerful of human motivations and determinants of human striving. But the importance of the concept of the self has perhaps been best revealed in the discussion of perceived freedom and personal responsibility. An impressive amount of data indicates that self-determination and the perception that one has choice and control over life events have profound behavioral consequences.

In addition, the very nature of what a self is has become a focal point for the increasingly important discussion of how factors of cultural and other kinds of diversity need to be included in a truly comprehensive view of personality. The fact that many cultures view the self in sociocentric, inclusive terms rather than in egocentric, exclusive terms (as most influential Western theories have done) may significantly challenge much of the research and many of the current models of the self. Similarly, increased awareness of ethnicity, gender, sexual orientation, and other factors have led us to an awareness that development of a coherent self and identity may intimately involve sociocultural and group factors and may not be just a matter of individual achievement.

The role of the self in the analysis of personality often goes unrecognized. But close inspection reveals that it is one of the unifying themes in the study of personality. It stands alongside interactionism and the multidimensionality of the person as a strong motif in this text.

Personality as a Science

At the outset, we indicated that the study of personality must be guided by empirical evidence and scientific principles. Certainly, many of the complex issues in personality are difficult to investigate. Manipulation of antecedent conditions thought to influence personality development, such as parental warmth, are neither ethical nor feasible, and precise measurement of constructs such as parental warmth is exceedingly difficult. Despite the difficulties, the study of personality is not exempt from the scientific method.

Throughout this book we have asked if assumptions or conclusions are supported by appropriate evidence. For example:

1. Psychoanalytic theory postulates a death instinct and conceptualizes humans as closed energy systems. It was pointed out that these presumptions are not supported by empirical evidence, but rather are theoretical assumptions not subject to proof or disproof. On the other hand, there is some empirical support for the existence and function of psychoanalytic defenses, such as repression, denial, and intellectualization.

2. Social learning theorists hypothesize that exposure to a model influences learning and behavior. This has been well established. In addition, other social learning theorists accept the belief that rewards and punishments alter behavior. This is certainly true, but there are exceptions or contradictions to this fundamental principle. For example, rewards and punishments do not appear to influence frustration-induced fixation, and an extrinsic reward might actually undermine an intrinsic interest.

3. The humanistic principle of self-actualization has not been subject to scientific proof or disproof, although studies of the resiliency of human beings are compatible with some aspects of the self-actualization hypothesis. Similarly, in support of humanistic hypotheses, there is evidence that the discrepancy between the ideal self and the perceived self does change during the course of psychotherapy.

The number of known and established facts about personality is truly enormous. At the same time, our ignorance is all too apparent. We have tried to indicate what the facts are and when we are ignorant, what is speculation and what is established. One must constantly try to remain aware of this distinction. A major theme of this book is that appropriate data should always be brought to bear on statements concerning personality.

Source: racorn/Shutterstock

Social learning theory has established empirically that exposure to a model influences learning and behavior.

The Future

The field of personality is constantly changing. New theoretical approaches are developing, new content areas are being explored, new methodologies are evolving, and new empirical findings are being reported every year. It is extremely difficult to predict future developments in the field, given this constant ferment and change. What we can do, however, is suggest some future directions that the study of personality may take, as well as indicate the topics that we would like to see pursued.

It is evident from the text that many issues remain to be resolved. Some broad and fundamental empirical questions still at issue include the role of nature and nurture and their interaction in human personality; the degree of trait consistency and generality; the extent to which personality is crystallized in childhood; and the modifiability of basic personality attributes in later life. There is also disagreement on many quite specific issues. Psychologists are not in agreement on the extent of sex differences in personality, the validity of self-report personality scales, the major antecedents of aggression, and the effects of factors such as anxiety, stress, meditation, and self-esteem on performance quality and intensity. Clearly, many more disagreements can be added to this short list of examples.

The fact that so many issues remain unresolved does not mean that there has not been significant progress in the investigation and understanding of personality. In the study of personality, it is true that similar questions have been examined again and again. But when the questions do reappear, they are often in improved forms that make more meaningful answers possible. As one looks at the history of inquiry into personality issues, it can be seen that there have been profound changes in the sophistication of the questions asked and the methods of research employed.

Personality often asks similar questions again and again, often reappearing in improved forms that allow for better answers.

These positive trends are illustrated in the study of aggressive instincts. Questions regarding the instinctiveness of aggressive behavior have been addressed for many years by philosophers and early psychologists. In previous eras it was believed that aggression was a product of an aggressive instinct and that one either had or did not have such an instinctive tendency. Research first revealed that aggressive behavior is not an either-or matter, but involves degrees or amounts of aggression; that is, there is variability in the extent of aggressive actions. It was later determined that environmental variables, such as aggressive models, frustration, and the presence of weapons in the environment, may contribute to aggressive actions. The investigation of the contribution of learning and situational factors to aggressive behavior caused still further revision of thought on the matter. It became clear that, for a genetic predisposition to be manifested, particular environmental conditions were required. Thus, regardless of the relative contributions of personal and situational determinants of hostility, aggression is always determined by both innate qualities and the environment. In addition, more precise analyses of aggressive phenomena revealed that the phrase *aggressive instinct* is far too vague and undifferentiated. The internal determinants of aggressive responses that appear to be instinctive, like those studied by ethologists, must be distinguished from aggressive drives, and these drives must, in turn, be distinguished from simple expressions of anger.

There is no fully satisfactory answer to the question of the instinctive nature of human aggression. But the systematic study of personality has enabled us to provide a more sophisticated answer than was possible in the prescientific era. A similar statement can be made about virtually any of the topics reviewed in this text. In accordance with this analysis, we do not expect that developments in the immediate future of personality will provide final answers to the difficult and unresolved issues. However, we do believe that they will help provide better, more sophisticated answers.

Personality Structure

A *structure* refers to something made up of interdependent elements or parts, with a fixed pattern of organization. Thus, when we discuss the structure of personality, we mean the relatively fixed and interdependent components of the person. There have been many references in this text to various aspects of personality structure. *Introversion*, *need for achievement*, and *aggressive inclination* are structural terms; id, ego, and superego are also structural concepts, as is the self. In some cases, the meaning of these terms is clear and procedures are available for measuring and studying them. However, in other instances the concepts are unclear and difficult to assess.

But an even greater shortcoming is the absence of a coherent system that specifies the interrelationships among the many structural terms. Part of the difficulty here is that psychological structure is analogous to physical structure; it is easy to equate and confuse the two. But psychological structures are not the same as physical structures, and psychological distance cannot be measured in physical dimensions of inches or feet. Indeed, psychological direction may be opposite to physical direction, as when one runs toward a fire in order to escape from it. Furthermore, passing an examination or getting married involves psychological movement, even though there may be no change in physical location.

In spite of these difficulties, there is some utility in thinking of personality in terms of structural concepts derived from the physical sciences. The chapters on the development of the self, traits, and consciousness all have to do with the structure and organization of personality. The issue, then, is not one of establishing that there is a structure to personality. Rather, the task is to formulate a logical set of constructs relating to personality and to develop a clear set of procedures for measuring and making inferences about these constructs.

Individual Differences and Their Development

Psychologists have devoted a great deal of attention to the study of individual differences in personality. Measures have been developed for traits like introversion, aggression, achievement, and the belief in internal versus external control, to cite a few. After establishing a trait category or dimension of individual difference, a logical next step is to identify the antecedents of a trait. There have been some investigations of the effects of differences in socialization practices on personality development. And, especially in recent years, there has been considerable interest in the role of biological variables in personality development. But, in general, insufficient attention has been paid to the causes of individual differences, and much more research has been directed toward establishing trait categories and trait measures than toward sources of individual differences. The next step will be connecting the biological variables to those trait categories in ways going beyond simply saying that they go together.

We can anticipate that there will be more extensive and coordinated efforts in this area. In particular, what is needed in addition to more research on social and biological variables is an integration of these two research traditions. Much of the biologically oriented research has been devoted to the demonstration that there are genetic and physiological factors influencing personality. In a similar manner, socialization research has focused on demonstrating the role of child rearing and cultural variables. But more attention must be given to the interplay of both sets of variables. We anticipate that there will be an increasing number of investigations tracing the interaction over time between a child's biologically based inclinations and the behaviors encouraged by parents, peers, and other socializing agents.

An additional source of personality influence that contributes to this interaction is the character of the physical environment, both natural and artificial, in which the child is reared. Because of the complexity of the interactions among these influences, we can expect new research methods to be formulated to facilitate investigations of personality development.

Expect to see a focus on the study of individual differences being developed by those interested in variables such as identity, life tasks, personal strivings, and personal projects (see Chapter 11). The study of these kinds of variables represents an opportunity in personality research such that these variables can be studied both by looking at differences between individuals (i.e., we can study the unique organization of how a given individual's personal projects affect his or her life) and by looking at general trends across all individuals (i.e., we can study the general kinds of personal projects people typically set for themselves).

Personality Dynamics

A close inspection of the studies in Chapter 14 concerned with psychodynamics will reveal that they were conducted earlier than the

The influence of goals on personality continues to develop as an important research area.

experiments discussed in other chapters of this text. The investigations of substitution undertaken by Kurt Lewin and his students took place, for the most part, in the 1920s and 1930s; and studies of conflict were conducted primarily in the 1940s and 1950s. We find it unfortunate that the experimental study of these topics is only weakly represented in contemporary psychology, inasmuch as behavioral dynamics encompasses extremely important and interesting issues for the field of personality.

There are many understandable reasons why investigators do not continue to pursue a particular phenomenon. First, there are diminishing payoffs for the study of any given problem or theory. Second, there are many other interesting ideas and issues competing for attention. Third, scientists quite naturally want to establish their own reputations in uncharted areas. Finally, the problems of psychodynamics are especially difficult to solve, discouraging investigators who then seek more fruitful fields elsewhere. These are valid reasons and the goals of the investigators are laudable. But as a result of premature diminution of research in an area, problems are left behind before sufficient scientific progress has been made.

There is beginning to be a return to the study of basic psychodynamic phenomena, such as substitution and displacement. Lewin and Freud both pointed out the importance of the interrelationships of need systems and the fact that attainment of one goal can serve to satisfy other unfulfilled needs. Goals, as a topic of study, are gaining momentum. This and related problems in psychodynamics are key issues for the field of personality and are in need of systematic investigation.

An Integrated Theory of Personality

The current state of personality theory is unsatisfactory. Chapters 3 through 6 presented a number of alternative conceptions of human behavior. In some reviews of personality, as many as twenty-five different theories are presented, one chapter after the other, with little or no theoretical integration or connection. Inasmuch as one of the tasks of science is to provide a general theory with as few constructs as possible, one could hope that there will be a significant reduction in the number of theories of personality that are offered. Of course, for this to be true there must first be an increase in the availability of pertinent data that permit one to reject certain theories and accept others.

There are some who argue that we shouldn't be spending as much time as we do teaching the old "grand theories of personality" (e.g., Freud, Rogers, Kelly). Mendelsohn (1993) argues that these are not even theories in the scientific sense because many aspects of them are untestable. Further, he notes that these theories were largely developed in the early 1900s and are of questionable contemporary relevance. At the same time, most of the major research questions explored by personality psychologists have been derived, in one way or the other, from these grand theories. Therefore, while they may not be proper scientific theories, they have been fruitful sources of ideas concerning human behavior.

As we have already indicated, these grand theories have some aspects that are primarily philosophical. If they are not proper scientific theories, they are general philosophical perspectives on the nature of human beings, from which more testable theories can be derived. Therefore, while we agree with Mendelsohn that too much emphasis is sometimes placed on these grand theories, we nonetheless believe that they still have a role to play in the study of personality.

There are several possible directions theory development in personality may take. First, many personality researchers are developing theories that are specific to some aspect of functioning rather than attempting to develop a grand theory that would explain all of human personality. Throughout this text, we have considered a number of examples of this approach such as the use of attribution theory to help understand achievement behavior, personal control, and competence. One advantage of starting with the development of a solid theory in a specific area of study, such as achievement motivation, is that such theory, after having been solidly tested in one domain, can sometimes be extended into new domains. Ideas based on attribution theory in the study of achievement behavior, for instance, are now being generalized to help us understand stigma and perceptions of responsibility in general (e.g., Weiner, 1993). We are beginning to see the solid theories of attribution, emotion, cognition, and social learning being combined under an umbrella of a social-cognitive approach to personality.

A second direction that theory development may take is toward integration. We have previously noted that personality is multidimensional and that aspects emphasized by each of the major theories are important. This suggests the possibility of building an integrative theory to take all of these aspects into account. For instance, there could be a theory developed that somehow balanced both conscious and unconscious factors and cognition and feeling, viewed humans as both exhibiting continuity and change, and took into account both internal psychological factors as well as environmental and reinforcement factors. It would seem that this will ultimately be what will evolve. However, at the present time this will not be easy to achieve because, as we have discussed earlier, different theories consider different aspects to be primary.

In a field related to personality theory, the area of psychotherapy, there have been numerous attempts to integrate psychoanalytic, cognitive, behavioral, and humanistic perspectives (see Arkowitz, 1992, for an overview of the field of psychotherapy integration). Each attempt, however, has tended to consider as primary one or the other of the major orientations and, for that reason, none have been successful at capturing the allegiance of those who hold a different primary orientation.

Therefore, for the foreseeable future, it is unrealistic to expect that the field of personality will be able to settle on one theory that is acceptable to all. Although one can anticipate that competing theories will be with us for a longtime, it is both possible and valuable to begin to formulate a comprehensive theory of personality based on an integration of compatible elements drawn from extant theories. Each theory—Freudian, Rogerian, behaviorist, social learning, and so on—has important statements to make that are consistent with the available data about personality. These propositions about personality can begin to be incorporated within a common framework and a common terminology.

The matter of language is not a simple obstacle to overcome, since the theories employ such different concepts or use the same term to refer to different concepts. However, for a number of reasons we feel that a common theoretical language can be formulated.

Contemporary personality psychology thinking is more flexible and broader than was the case a few decades ago; cognitive psychology has achieved respectability; there is a general interest in affects and their relation to motivation and behavior; the concept of self is widely used; and both the mind and the emotions have been readmitted to formal, scientific psychology. With increasing agreement about the appropriateness of structural, cognitive, emotional, motivational, and behavioral terms, it may well be possible to start the task of a more integrated and comprehensive theory of personality.

Summary

Four themes that are represented throughout this text have been pointed out: interactionism, multidimensionality, the self, and personality as a science. In addition, future directions in the areas of structure, development, dynamics, and theory have been suggested. The field of personality is vital and growing; this growth is evident in the increasing sophistication of the questions asked and in the increasing refinement of the answers provided.

Thought Questions

1. Which personality areas do you feel are most in need of study?
2. In which personality areas do you feel that the most progress has been made and the most knowledge has been generated?
3. Which personality areas discussed in the text most interested you and motivated you to find out more about them? Why?
4. Do you think that any one of the personality theories discussed in the text will be dominant in the future? Defend your answer.

Glossary

absolute stability The behavior in childhood is closely related to or similar to the behavior in adulthood.

adolescence The transitional period of human development between childhood and adulthood, from the onset of puberty to the early twenties.

affect Overarching term encompassing mood, emotion, and evaluation.

aggression A behavior directed toward a person with the intention of harming that person, and the person is motivated to avoid that harm.

aggressive cues Cues in the environment that function as releasing stimuli for aggression.

agonistic behavior Offensive and defensive fighting and competitive activity; a term used by biologists to define aggression.

allocentric A person's focus on sociability, family, and the importance of in-groups, as opposed to individuality, independence, and uniqueness. This is at the individual level, not the cultural level.

altered states of consciousness Instances of heightened inner awareness, as might be experienced when under the influence of a drug or during deep meditation.

altruism Concern for the welfare of another without regard for oneself.

ambivalent behavior Behavior that oscillates from approach to withdrawal.

amnesia A loss of both identity and recall of the past.

analytic psychology Jung's personality theory that deviates from psychoanalysis in its emphasis on the collective unconscious and on the human striving toward self-fulfillment.

androgyny A combination of high levels of both femininity and masculinity.

anxiety A state of unrealistic fear.

anxiety hierarchy An ordered list of anxiety-provoking things and situations, used in systematic desensitization.

anxious/resistant attachment An attachment style marked by wanting and also avoiding attachment to the caregiver.

appraisal The meaning a person imposes on the current situation.

approach-approach conflict Lewin's classification for conflict in which there are two or more positive alternatives to choose from.

approach-avoidance conflict Lewin's classification for conflict that occurs when both positive and negative consequences are associated with the same action.

archetypes In Jungian theory, the primeval contents of the collective unconscious.

arousal The intensity, state of activation, or drive characterizing an individual.

ascending reticular activating system A neuronal circuit responsible for wakefulness and associated with attention. Eysenck's model suggests that differences in introversion and extraversion are based on the underlying responsivity of this system. In this model, introverts have a more responsive system.

associationist learning theory A learning theory that views humans in terms of stimulus-response variables and as essentially creatures of habit.

attachment style A pattern of attachment behavior between a child and caregiver.

attributional style A predisposition to evaluate the cause of outcomes to a particular locus of control, stability, and generalizability.

attribution theory A theoretical approach based on the view that people attempt to explain and understand behavioral events through attributing the causes of those events to characteristics of the person or to factors in the environment; these causal ascriptions significantly influence goal expectancies and behavioral responses.

authoritarian A parenting style marked by high behavioral demands and low warmth.

authoritative A parenting style marked by high behavioral demands and high warmth.

autism A disorder marked by deficits in social communication and interactions, and/or restricted repetitive patterns of behavior.

automatic A cognitive version of the "unconscious." It is assumed that many of the schemas that guide our behavior operate outside of awareness.

autonomous motivation A motive based on intrinsic motivations and the types of extrinsic motivation that are integrated into the self.

autonomous style An adult attachment style that is similar to secure attachment.

autonomy The ability to act for and by oneself.

avoidance-avoidance conflict Lewin's classification for conflict in which a choice is confined to two or more unattractive alternatives.

avoidance learning A form of negative reinforcement, in which the organism has learned to avoid punishment by avoiding particular situations, people, or behaviors.

avoidant attachment An attachment style marked by low demands for attachment by the child.

balancing selection An intermediate version of a trait of behavior may be preferred in some instances of natural selection.

behavior Any activity, covert or overt, of an organism.

behavior modification Therapeutic techniques that use Skinnerian methods of changing behavior to modify disturbed behaviors.

behavior therapy Psychotherapeutic techniques based on learning principles.

behavioral activation system A system that is sensitive to signals about the likelihood of reinforcement.

behavioral inhibition system A system that is sensitive to signals about the likelihood of punishment.

the "Big Five" Many personality researchers believe there are five basic personality traits. One popular classification system identifies them as neuroticism versus emotional stability, extraversion, openness to experience, conscientiousness, and agreeableness.

biofeedback The process of monitoring and providing information to the person about involuntary body functioning, usually as a therapeutic method for learning how to control maladaptive physiological responses.

body image The organized perception of one's physical structure.

bonding (attachment behavior) The formation of stable attachments to particular caregivers.

catharsis The reduction of emotional tension through expressive release activity; sometimes restricted to release through vicarious activity, such as watching a play or film.

cathexis The psychic energy that has been invested in a desired object.

causal attributions A term used in achievement-related contexts to connote beliefs about the reasons for one's success or failure—for example, ability, effort, task ease or difficulty, or luck.

classical conditioning A type of learning in which an organism learns to pair a stimulus with a response.

client-centered therapy The psychotherapeutic approach used by Rogers, which employs trust, acceptance, and empathy to help clients realize their goals.

cognitive behavior modification A modified Skinnerian approach to human behavior, derived from modified Skinnerian principles, that stresses the role of cognitive factors in mediating behavior and attempts to bring about change through alteration of these cognitions.

cognitive conceit A defensive belief in one's own greater intelligence and insight.

cognitive style A person's consistent ways of perceiving in relation to himself or herself and the surrounding world.

cognitive theory The theory of personality that focuses on human thought processes and levels of understanding as a major determinant of behavior.

collective unconscious In Jungian theory, the site of inherited primitive, universal attitudes and ideals (archetypes) of which we are not conscious.

collectivistic A cultural focus on sociability, family, and the importance of in-groups.

companionate love A type of love and affection we feel for people with whom our lives are deeply intertwined.

complex In Jung's theory, a group of feelings, ideas, memories, and behaviors organized around a significant object.

concordance The rate at which pairs of individuals share a trait, status, or diagnosis. Usually used in the context of twin research, thus the rate at which one twin is schizophrenic, if the co-twin is schizophrenic.

concrete reciprocal hedonism The view that if one person does something for another, it is right for the other to do something in return.

conditions of worth The conditional positive regard—the "do's" or "don'ts," "shoulds" and "shouldn'ts"—that people live by in order to feel appreciated and accepted by others.

conflict The difficulty in making a choice usually because the options are both good or both bad.

consciousness Awareness, or self-knowledge, of one's experiences.

construct validity The degree to which a test represents the meaning of the construct it is designed to measure.

constructive alternativism Kelly's basic tenet that "meaning" and "reality" are dependent on the person's interpretation and therefore are subject to change.

content validity The degree to which a test adequately represents the content it is designed to assess.

continuous distribution There are many different gradations between the extremes of a scale. This is in contrast to discrete distributions that allow only a set number of possibilities. Traits are typically considered to have a continuous distribution; types are considered to have a discrete distribution.

controlled motivation A motive that is controlled by extrinsic factors such as punishment or rewards.

conventional A style of morality marked by a social approval and law and order.

convergent validity The degree to which a test measures the same construct as that assessed by other tests.

coping The process by which a person deals with stress.

correlation A mathematical index used to express the degree of association between two variables.

criterion validity The degree to which a test predicts, or correlates with, a subsequent factor (predictive validity), as well as the degree to which it is associated with other indexes that exist at the same point in time (concurrent validity).

critical periods Periods when something can be learned, and cannot be learned outside the period.

cross-lagged design Children of different ages are measured and then followed through time.

cross-sectional research design A type of research in which children of different ages are measured at the same time.

cue Any stimulus, often a subtle one, that directs behavior.

culture The shared beliefs, traditions, expectations, and norms of a particular group of people at a particular point in time.

decentration The cognitive capacity to assume the point of view of another.

decision/commitment A component of love that is about staying together.

defense mechanisms In psychoanalytic theory, unconscious strategies that enable a person to avoid awareness of unpleasant or anxiety-arousing experiences.

defensive pessimism A technique used by individuals who predict catastrophe for themselves but then use that prediction to mobilize themselves for action.

delay of gratification The ability to wait to receive a reward.

denial A defense mechanism in which a person refuses to acknowledge the truth, or the implications of that truth.

depression A disorder marked by sad mood, or irritability, or the loss of interest and pleasure in nearly all activities.

diagnosticity The information gained about one's ability following task performance.

directional selection An extreme version of a trait or behavior may be preferred in some instances of natural selection.

discordance The rate at which pairs of individuals do not share a trait, status, or diagnosis.

discriminant validity The degree to which a test measures a different construct than that assessed by other tests.

discriminative conflict As noted in Pavlov's studies, a conflict in which similar stimuli are associated with different consequences so that it is difficult to distinguish whether the outcome of a choice will be favorable or unfavorable.

discriminative stimuli A stimulus that indicates the probability of punishment or reinforcement.

dismissing style An adult attachment style similar to the avoidant style in children.

disorganized/disoriented attachment A child attachment style that is not predictable or doesn't fit in the other styles.

displacement A defense mechanism in which a person shifts a reaction from an original target person or situation to some other person or situation.

dissociation An altered state of consciousness in which a person lacks awareness of significant segments of his or her behavior or identity.

dizygotic twins Twins that develop from two fertilized eggs.

drive Any motive or need that impels action.

drive reduction A decrease in the intensity of a motive or need force, which, according to associationist learning theory, also strengthens the stimulus-response connection.

ectomorph A person with a tall, thin physique, whom Sheldon observed as also tending to have an introverted temperament.

ego In Freudian theory, the part of the personality that mediates between the demands of id impulses, superego, and external reality.

ego ideal In Freudian theory, standards that guide behavior because they are believed to constitute worthy goals to strive toward.

egocentricity A self-centered frame of reference in which one assumes that others perceive the world from the same perspective as oneself.

Electra complex A psychoanalytic conflict that happens to girls during the phallic stage, during which the girl develops the superego.

electroencephalography A measurement of brain activity conducted by measuring electrical impulses between neurons.

emotion An intense, shorter duration form of affect, usually having a distinct cause.

emotional style The size of emotional reactions that a person typically experiences.

empathy The ability to discriminate and label feelings in others, to assume the perspective and role of another person, and to experience and respond with feelings similar to another.

endomorph A person with a rounded physique, whom Sheldon observed as also tending to have a relaxed and gregarious temperament.

entity theorists People who have the implicit theory that a person has a set amount of ability.

environmental psychology The study of the role of environment in regulating behavior.

escape learning A form of negative reinforcement in which the organism learns to escape ongoing punishment by particular behaviors.

existential humanism A personality theory that views the individual as responsible for his or her own actions and as having to cope with guilt and anxiety.

expectancy A belief that a particular behavior will lead to a reward or goal.

expectancy-value theory A motivational theory emphasizing that behavior depends on the probability that an act will lead to a goal and upon the value of that goal.

extinction A behavior decreasing in likelihood due to no longer being reinforced.

extrinsic motivation The undertaking of an activity for an expected external reward.

extroversion From Jung, the tendency to be strongly oriented toward other people and social situations.

facets Components that are subfactors that make up a factor in the Five Factor Model.

face validity The degree to which the items on a test appear to sample the content domain.

facial feedback model The theory that we understand emotions through the facial display of that emotion.

factor analysis A statistical method of reducing a large amount of data from tests, rating scales, or behavioral observations to a smaller and presumably more basic number of dimensions of personality factors.

femininity The extent to which a person manifests characteristics typically associated with women.

Five Factor Model One of the models that posits that there are five major personality traits: neuroticism, extraversion, openness to experience, conscientiousness, and agreeableness.

fixation (learning) The persistence of responses that apparently result in repeated failure and nonreward.

fixation (psychoanalytic) A disturbed focus of libidinal energy at a particular psychosexual stage preventing full maturation through other stages.

foreclosure A person who has adopted an identity without consideration or exploration of alternative identities.

frustration A state of arousal that occurs when a person is unable to reach his or her goal and produces behaviors as disparate as aggression, fixation, regression, and enhanced goal striving.

frustration-aggression hypothesis Interference with achieving a goal leads to frustration, which results in a goal of aggression.

fundamental attributional error A tendency to attribute behavior of other people to their personality rather than to the situation.

gender Aspects of oneself as male or female that may be due to culture and socialization.

gender identity One's inclusion of his or her gender as part of identity.

gender schema theory The idea that once a child has developed the idea that there are different genders, the world is then perceived through the lens of gender and what is appropriate for each gender becomes relatively fixed, thus changing behavior.

genome The organized set of DNA that every living thing has.

genotype A person's set of inherited characteristics, as determined by genetic makeup.

gerontology An interdisciplinary approach to studying aging that draws its experts from various biological and behavioral disciplines.

habits Stable stimulus-response connections.

hallucination Perception of visual images or audible sounds that are not actually present in the environment.

hallucinogen Any drug that produces hallucinations.

hardiness An individual difference that helps a person cope with stress.

hassles The stresses and strains of everyday living.

heritability The degree to which genetics plays a role in the development of a particular aspect of a trait or behavior.

homeostasis A tendency towards equilibrium or balance among internal processes; the maintenance of a relatively stable internal environment.

hostile attribution bias A tendency to see others in the world as having aggressive intentions.

humanistic psychology The system of psychology that focuses not only on what a person is, but also on what a person has the potential to become.

hypnosis A trancelike state in which the cooperative subject is highly responsive to suggestions made by the hypnotist.

hysteria A psychological reaction state (for example, dissociation) characterized by high excitability and anxiety, incapacitating bodily symptoms, and altered states of consciousness.

Id In Freudian theory, the most primitive and inaccessible part of the personality, made up of sexual and aggressive instincts, which strive continually for gratification.

idealism A dissatisfaction with the state of the world, a desire to improve it and to make life more fulfilling.

ideal self The self one wants to be.

identification The process by which the child imitates and subsequently internalizes the perceived attitudes and values of the parent while still maintaining a distinction between its own and the parent's identities.

identity The goals, values, and roles that are the key descriptors of who we are to ourselves.

identity achievement Personally chosen commitment to a set of values and goals for one's life.

identity diffusion The status of a person who has low levels of both commitment and exploration to an identity.

ideocentric A person's focus on individuality, independence, and uniqueness, as opposed to sociability, family, and the importance of in-groups. This is at the individual level, not the cultural level.

imagery Pictures one visualizes or imagines, which can facilitate memory and alter feelings and behaviors.

implicit psychology The perceived laws of behavior held by naive observers, or the personality theories of individuals who are untrained psychologists.

imprinting The process of establishing an attachment of first exposure to an object (noted in Lorenz's studies of newborn nonhumans).

incremental theorists People who have the implicit theory that ability can change with effort.

individualistic A culture that focus on the unique and independent aspects of the self and members of a group.

instinct An innate, biologically based mode of response to certain stimuli.

instrumental aggression Aggression that functions to get something.

interactionism The personality theory that views behavior as governed by both the properties of the person and the situation in which the person is acting.

interactionist position The personality theory that views behavior as governed by both the properties of the person and the situation in which the person is acting.

internal consistency A measure of test reliability; the degree of consistency within a test during any given time period.

Inter-rater reliability The extent to which independent raters arrived at the same rating. This is important in assessing whether there is high-quality measurement.

intimacy A feeling of psychological closeness with another person.

intrinsic aggression Aggressive behavior motivated by the satisfaction of engaging in aggressive activity, as contrasted with behavior motivated by the desire to inflict injury.

intrinsic motivation The undertaking of an activity for its own sake without expectation of external reward.

introversion In Jung's theory, the tendency to be attentive and interested in one's own thoughts and feelings.

isolation paradigm The experimental procedure used to study innate behaviors in which infant nonhumans are isolated so that they cannot observe others' responses and hence exhibit only innate responses.

kin selection The hypothesis that helping related individuals increases the amount of shared genes in subsequent generations.

learned helplessness The acquired expectation that one's actions will exert little control over outcomes.

learning theory As applied to the area of personality, a set of assumptions that the development and functioning of the personality is based on experimentally derived principles of learning.

lexical hypothesis The idea that important concepts will be part of the language, and by examining language researchers will then be able to discover those important components.

libido Freud's term of psychic energy, derived primarily from the sexual, pleasure-seeking instincts of the id.

life structure Levinson's term for the basic pattern governing a person's adult life stages.

life tasks Current problems and goals that a person is motivated to try to solve.

locus of causality A determination of whether the cause of the behavior or outcome is internal, that is within the person, or external, that is luck or something about the situation.

locus of control A perception of the influence that one has on the attainment of reinforcement.

longitudinal study Measures are taken in the child's early years and again at subsequent periods of development.

masculinity The extent to which a person manifests characteristics typically associated with men.

mean level stability The change in actual scores over time.

measurement error The degree to which the observed score on a measuring instrument deviates from the true score.

mediated generalization An unobservable association process by which dissimilar situations elicit the same mediating response.

mediating response Any unobservable internal response that intervenes between the observable stimulus and the overt response.

meditation Any attempt to alter consciousness by means of systematic concentration and sustained self-regulation of attention.

mesomorph A person with an athletic physique, whom Sheldon observed as also tending to have an energetic and assertive temperament.

meta-analysis A statistic process that allows an integration and analysis of multiple studies simultaneously.

midlife crisis In Levinson's theory, a transitional period in adult development (the forties) during which one assesses his or her basic life structure.

mindlessness A tendency to respond automatically in many situations, thus not really thinking about it.

modeling (imitation) (observational learning) The process of acquiring new behaviors through observation of another person performing them.

moderator variables Variables that will change the extent to which measured personality will be predictive of behavior. They could be things like the strength of the situation, or consistency of a particular individual's behavior overall.

monozygotic twins Twins who develop from a single fertilized egg.

mood A longer duration and lower intensity form of affect.

moratorium The status of a person who is in the process of exploring who he or she is but has not committed to an identity.

narcissism A belief about one's unique superiority to others.

narcolepsy Sudden "sleep attacks" that often occur without warning, particularly during times of heightened excitement, lasting from a few to fifteen minutes.

narrative identity A person's version of his or her life story.

natural behavior Patterns of behavior that one has the potential for developing and that will develop under normal environmental circumstances.

need for achievement One of Murray's needs that pertains to a desire to do something difficult and outstanding.

negative reinforcement Having something aversive or undesirable removed as a result of behavior, leading to a greater probability of the same behavior in the future.

neurosis An emotional, nonpsychotic disorder characterized by anxiety and other symptoms and resulting in partial impairment of functioning.

nonconscious Another term for the unconscious, the part of the mind about which we do not have awareness.

nonshared environment effect Findings from genetic research have indicated that siblings growing up in the same family appear to share little in common in terms of their personalities. This suggests that while individuals are growing up in the same general family environment, they do not share the same "subenvironments" within the family.

object relations theory In psychoanalytic ego psychology, the theory that ego development and subsequent interpersonal relationships are based on the infant's attachment to the mother and other figures.

object representation A person's internalized image of a significant object.

Oedipal conflict (Oedipus complex for boys; Electra complex for girls) In Freud's psychosexual theory of development, sexual attraction to the opposite-sex parent, and jealousy and hostility toward and fear of punishment from the rival, same-sex parent.

operant conditioning A type of learning that a behavior leads to reinforcement or punishment.

operants Behaviors that "operate" on and change the environment—for example, releasing a latch that opens a door.

organismic humanism Maslow's theory of personality and human motivation describing a hierarchical human needs system, from strong physiological needs to self-actualization needs.

ought self The self one feels an obligation to be.

outcome expectancies The beliefs about whether a particular behavior will accomplish a particular goal.

ovulatory shift A woman's preference for attractive healthy partners who may not invest in offspring during ovulation.

parenting styles The ways in which parents treat their children that are a combination of behavioral demand and interpersonal warmth. Typically, there are thought to be four styles.

partial reinforcement An intermittent reward schedule that strengthens a response.

passion A component of love that is a combination of romantic feelings and sexual desire.

passionate love A type of love characterized by preoccupation with thoughts of the love object, with the desire to spend as much time as possible with him or her, and with strong sexual arousal.

peak experience A moment of great ecstasy or awe that is experienced without the use of drugs or other stimulants.

permissive A parenting style with low behavioral demands.

personal construct theory Kelly's personality theory that focuses on how a person, as perceiver, organizes his or her world and interprets, or construes, events.

personal space A small, invisible area surrounding a person, within which an intrusion by another person causes discomfort and annoyance.

personality Relatively enduring behavior patterns and traits that distinguish people, groups, and cultures; the overall organization and structure of these enduring patterns and traits; and the interactions among these patterns and the interactions of these patterns with fluctuations in the internal state and with changing external stimuli.

personality coherence Behaviors that the adult will exhibit are conceptually similar to those in childhood but different in form.

personality continuity The stability of personality traits and behavior over time.

personality dynamics The concern with the meaning and function of behavior.

personality measurement A system of assessing the extent of specific personality traits and other characteristics.

personality structure The organization of the basic components of the personality.

personification The image of oneself or another based on one's personal feelings and attitudes.

phenomenology The study of subjective experience, or the "meaning" that a person gives to events.

phenotype The totality of observed characteristics or behaviors of an organism that result from the interaction between genotype and environmental influences.

physiological assessment Measurement of changes in bodily processes that presumably reflect changes in psychological states.

polygraph An instrument used to monitor various physiological indicators.

polymorphism Different versions of a gene.

positive reinforcement Receiving a positive reward for behavior, leading to a greater probability of that behavior in the future.

possible selves Positive and negative versions of the self that can be imagined for the future.

postconventional A style of morality based on maximizing good, or based on one's own dedicated value.

preconventional A style of morality typical of small children that is based on pleasure or punishment.

preoccupied style An adult attachment style that is marked by excessive worry about relationships.

pride A sense of self-satisfaction typically arising from the attribution of success to one's own efforts and abilities.

primary appraisal The evaluation of what is happening and determining that impact on one's well-being.

primary drive An innate, biologically based motivational force, such as hunger or thirst.

primary emotions The basic, irreducible emotions.

priming A process that aids accessibility to a concept by suggesting the concept or related items prior to the need to use the concept.

projection In Freud's theory, a defense mechanism involving the unconscious attribution of one's own unacceptable feelings or motives to others.

projective test A test consisting of ambiguous stimuli, to which an individual produces spontaneous responses; scoring is often subjective.

prosocial behavior Positive social behavior, often socially prescribed and viewed as moral action, that is enacted to help others.

psychoanalysis A system of psychology and psychotherapy, founded on Freud's theory of conflict in relation to unconscious libidinal impulses.

psychodynamics (personality dynamics) The psychological "motion" of the personality produced by forces acting on the individual: the expression and inhibition of needs, the entering or leaving of a particular state of consciousness, and the functions or goals of behavior.

psychological reactance An aversive state experienced when freedom is perceived to have been taken away.

psychopathology The science of the study of mental disorders.

psychosexual stages Periods of life that are oriented toward particular sources of pleasure that children pass through during development according to psychoanalytic theory.

psychosis Severe mental disorder involving personality disorganization and impairment of contact with reality.

psychosocial stages In Erikson's theory of personality, the periods from birth to maturity posing particular developmental tasks and providing the basis for specific personality characteristics.

puberty The period of maturation of the sex organs and other sexual characteristics.

punishment An outcome to behavior that can be either adding something aversive or removing something positive.

Q-sort A rating technique in which a set of adjectives or statements is categorized into piles according to the degree to which they are descriptive of an individual.

racial and ethnic identity Those aspects of one's identity that relate to one's identification with one's ethnic group.

radical behaviorism The approach to psychology that views human behavior as controlled by external stimulus situations.

rank order stability The extent that people maintain their relative rank over time.

reaction formation In Freud's theory, a defense mechanism in which a person behaves in a way directly opposite from some underlying anxiety-provoking impulse.

reciprocal determination Mutual interactions between the person, situation, and behavior.

regression In Freudian theory, a return to some earlier stage of psychosexual development in the face of some current frustration.

reinforcement Stimulation following a response, which increases the probability that the same response will occur again in the same situation.

reliability The consistency, or degree of accuracy, of a measuring instrument.

REM Rapid eye movement sleep. This is the part of sleep that is primarily associated with dreaming.

REP test Kelly's way of measuring and eliciting the role constructs that people use to predict and understand their world.

repression A defense mechanism in which an anxiety-arousing memory or impulse is prevented from becoming conscious.

repression-sensitization continuum An approach-avoidance stylistic dimension of individual differences in defense reactions.

response bias The tendency to respond to a test item in a particular way regardless of item content.

schizophrenia A severe psychosis characterized by major disturbances in thought, emotion, and behavior, often reflected in withdrawal and a fantasy life of delusions and hallucinations.

secondary appraisal The evaluation of whether one has the skills to deal with a stressor.

secure attachment An attachment style that is marked by using the caregiver as a base of security, nurturance, and caring.

selective breeding Choosing organisms with positive characteristics to reproduce.

self A person's fundamental sense of identity.

self-actualization A principle of human behavior stating that individuals strive to develop their capacities and talents to the fullest—that is, growing and enhancing the basic self.

self-awareness A recognition of oneself, or the process of noticing the self and how others might view the self.

self-complexity The number and interconnectedness among different ways that a person thinks about the self.

self-concept A description of who one is. It includes feelings, attitudes, desires, judgments, and behaviors that the individual considers to be characteristic of himself or herself.

self-consistency A motivation to maintain consistent ways of thinking about the self.

self-determination theory An integrated theory that proposes three needs and two motivations.

self-efficacy A person's expectation that he or she can effectively cope with and master situations and bring about desired outcomes through personal efforts.

self-esteem A generalized evaluation of one's self.

self-ideal discrepancy The difference between how one perceives oneself and how one would like to be.

self-insight Increased awareness of one's feelings, drives, and attitudes.

self-monitoring The degree to which individuals regulate their social behavior in order to make a particular social impression.

self-schema A knowledge structure that consists of cognitive generalizations about the self.

sensitive periods Periods when it is easier to learn things.

shame A sense of devaluation, dishonor, or loss of respect based on the attribution of misbehavior to the self.

shaping The process of establishing a behavior by rewarding successively closer approximations of that behavior.

situational critique The idea that the situation is a better predictor of an individual's behavior than personality.

situational selection The environments and situations people choose to fit their personalities.

situational theory The personality theory that emphasizes the impact of situations over the impact of personality characteristics in determining behavior.

skin conductance Measurement of relatively small changes in the electrical characteristics of the skin related to sweating and therefore is frequently used as an indicator of emotional arousal or anxiety.

social desirability A factor, to be considered on personality tests, that connotes a person's tendency to respond in a socially approved or favorable manner.

social deviance Nonconforming, socially unapproved behavior(s).

social learning theory Several related personality approaches that emphasize an individual's expectancy that certain behaviors will be rewarded by parents and society.

social stratification The ranking of individuals into groups within a culture.

social support The friends, family, and groups that a person can rely on.

socialization The process of developing the motivations and behaviors that are appropriate in one's culture.

sociometer A theory that suggests the function of self-esteem is to measure the extent to which people fit in their social environment.

somnambulism Walking or carrying out acts while apparently in a sleeping state.

source traits In Cattell's factor analyses of personality traits, basic organizing structures that underlie and determine surface traits.

species-spacing Spreading members of the same species across environment to enhance survival.

stable conflicts Conflicts that take longer to resolve—for instance, avoidance-avoidance conflict.

stages Discrete steps that are qualitatively different from the ones that precede or follow the current one.

state anxiety Temporary anxiety that varies in intensity, fluctuates over time, and is strongly influenced by situational factors.

states Transitory conditions of the organism such as emotions and moods that vary in intensity and fluctuate over time.

states of mind Mardi Horowitz's modern psychodynamic idea that individuals at different moments experience different states of mind in which they see themselves differently, have different emotional experiences, and see others differently.

(The) Strange Situation A research paradigm developed by Ainsworth to measure attachment.

stress Any force acting on a person that produces psychological or physiological strain.

sublimation In Freudian theory, a defense mechanism in which libidinal (sexual) energy is redirected from an unacceptable to a socially approved mode of expression.

substitution Replacing a problematic goal with a different goal.

superego In Freudian theory, the part of the personality representing the morals, values, and ideals of one's society.

suppression The process of keeping uncomfortable thoughts and feelings out of conscious awareness.

surface traits In Cattell's factor analyses of personality traits, clusters of responses or overt behaviors that are related or fit together.

symbiosis A state of a rewarding attachment and interdependence between two organisms.

systematic desensitization A process in which a person unlearns previous associations between stimuli and reactions. Usually, this is used with phobias, unlearning the association between the fear-inducing stimuli and the fear reaction.

temperament Behavioral characteristics that are present at an early age and that are believed to have some basis in biological processes partly determined by heredity.

template-matching technique Bem and Funder's measurement of personality that matches individuals with ideal types (those that are most likely to behave in a given manner in a given situation) to predict specific behaviors.

test-retest reliability The correlation between scores obtained by administering a test on two occasions to the same group of individuals.

theory of mind An understanding that other individuals have a mind, and it probably works similarly to other minds.

time-binding A process that helps delay the immediate gratification of a need.

token economy A behavior modification technique in which desired behaviors are reinforced with tokens that can be exchanged for desired objects and activities.

trait anxiety An enduring tendency to be anxious.

trait psychology The system of psychology based on the study of personality characteristics that are believed to be general over situations and enduring over time.

traits Enduring individual differences in behavior dispositions. These are typically thought to be arranged as a continuous scale.

transactional model An approach to human development that views the interaction between the child and its environment as a reciprocal and continuous process.

triangular model of love A model of love that suggests there are three components: intimacy, passion, and decision/commitment.

types Enduring individual differences in behavior disposition. These differences are thought to be arranged as a set of very few discrete categories.

unconditional positive regard Rogers's term for the accepting and valuing of a person per se, regardless of the degree to which he or she exhibits specific behaviors that are approved or disapproved.

unstable conflicts Conflicts that tend to be resolved quickly—for instance, approach-approach conflicts.

validity The degree to which a test actually measures what it is intended to measure.

variability In personality testing, individual differences reflecting both true differences and error.

variable In personality testing, an individual characteristic that can be measured.

working model A child's basic understanding of the world and social relationships.

working self-concept The version of the self-concept that is being used at that time.

References

Aaronson, B., & Osmond, H. (1970). *Psychedelics: The use and implications of hallucinogenic drugs*. Garden City, NY: Anchor Books/Doubleday.

Abramson, L. Y., Metalsky, G. I., & Alloy, L. B. (1988). The hopeless theory of depression: Does the research test the theory? In L. Y. Abramson (Ed.), *Social cognition and clinical psychology*. New York, NY: Guilford, 33–65.

Abramson, L. Y., Seligman, M. E. P., & Teasdale, J. D. (1978). Learned helplessness in humans: Critique and reformulation. *Journal of Abnormal Psychology*, *87*, 49–74.

Acklin, M. W. (1999). Behavior science foundations of the Rorschach test: Research and clinical applications. *Assessment*, *6*, 319–326.

Adams, G. R., Gullota, T. P., & Markstrom-Adams, C. (1994). *Adolescent life experiences*. Pacific Grove, CA: Brooks/Cole.

Adams, G. R., & Montemayer, R. (1992). *Patterns of identity development during late adolescence: A descriptive study of stability, progression, and regression*, 1988. Manuscript submitted for publication, as referenced in Adams, G. R., Gullota, T. P., & Markstrom-Adams, C. *Adolescent life experiences*. Pacific Grove, CA: Brooks/Cole.

Adams, H. E., Wright, L. W., & Lohr, B. A. (1996). Is homophobia associated with homosexual arousal? *Journal of Abnormal Psychology*, *105*, 440–445.

Adler, A. (1927). *Practice and theory of individual psychology*. New York, NY: Harcourt, Brace & World.

Adorno, I. W., Frenkel-Brunswick, E., Levinson, D. J., & Sanford, R. N. (1950). *The authoritarian personality*. New York, NY: Harper & Row.

Agros, W. S., Schneider, J. A., Arnow, B., Rachurn, S. D., & Teilch, C. F. (1989). Cognitive-behavioral and response-prevention treatments for Bulimia Nervosa. *Journal of Consulting and Clinical Psychology*, *57*, 215–221.

Ahadi, S., & Diener, E. (1989). Multiple determinants and effect size. *Journal of Personality and Social Psychology*, *56*, 398–406.

Ainsworth, M. D. S. (1967). *Infancy in Uganda*. Baltimore, MD: Johns Hopkins.

Ainsworth, M. D. S. (1989). Attachments beyond infancy. *American Psychologist*, 709–716.

Ainsworth, M. D. S., Bell, S. M., & Stayton, D. J. (1972). Individual differences in the development of some attachment behaviors. *Merrill-Palmer Quarterly of Behavior and Development*, *18*(2), 123–143.

Ainsworth, M. D. S., Blehar, M. C., Waters, E., & Wall, S. (1978). *Patterns of attachment*. Hillsdale, NJ: Lawrence Erlbaum, 1978.

Ainsworth, M. D. S., Blehar, M. C., Waters, E., & Wall, S. N. (2015). *Patterns of Attachment: A Psychology of the Strange Situation*. New York, NY: Psychology Press.

Ainsworth, M. D. S., & Bowlby, J. (1991). An ethological approach to personality development. *American Psychologist*, *46*, 333–341.

Ainsworth, M. D. S., & Stayton, D. (1971). Individual differences in strange situation behavior of one-year-olds. In H. R. Schaffer (Ed.), *The origins of human social relations*. London, UK: Academic Press.

Alden, L. E. (1988). Behavioral self-management controlled-drinking strategies in a context of secondary prevention. *Journal of Consulting and Clinical Psychology*, *56*, 280–286.

Aldis, O. (1975). *Play fighting*. New York, NY: Academic Press.

Alexander, I. E. (1982). The Freud-Jung relationship—The other side of Oedipus and countertransference. *American Psychologist*, *37*, 1009–1018.

Alexander, I. E. (1988). Personality, psychological assessment, and psychobiography. *Journal of Personality*, *56*, 265–294.

Alexander, M. G., & Fisher, T. D. (2003). Truth and consequences: Using the bogus pipeline to examine sex differences in self-reported sexuality. *Journal of Sex Research*, *40*(1), 27–35.

Allen, K. E., & Harris, F. R. (1966). Elimination of a child's excessive scratching by training the mother in reinforcement procedures. *Behavior Research and Therapy*, *4*, 79–84.

Allen, M. J., & Yen, W. M. (1979). *Introduction to measurement theory*. Belmont, CA: Brooks/Cole.

Allport, G. W. (1937). *Personality: A psychological interpretation*. New York, NY: Henry Holt.

Allport, G. W. (1955). *Becoming: Basic consideration for a psychology of personality*. New Haven, CT: Yale University Press.

Allport, G. W. (1961). *Pattern and growth in personality*. New York, NY: Holt.

Allport, G. W., & Odbert, H. S. (1936). Trait-names: A psycho-lexical study. *Psychological Monographs*, *47*(1, Whole No. 211).

Allport, G. W., & Vernon, P. E. (1933). *Studies in expressive movement*. New York, NY: Macmillan.

Allred, K. D., & Smith, T. W. (1989). The hardy personality: Cognitive and physiological responses to evaluative threat. *Journal of Personality and Social Psychology*, *56*, 257–266.

Almeida, D. M., Wethington, E., & Kessler, R. C. (2002). The daily inventory of stressful events: An interview-based approach for measuring daily stressors. *Assessment*, *9*(1), 41–55.

Altman, I. (1975). *The environment and social behavior*. Belmont, CA: Brooks/Cole.

Altman, I. (1976). Environmental psychology and social psychology. *Personality and Social Psychology Bulletin, 2*, 96–113.

Alves, M. C., Sobreira, G., Aleixo, M. A., & Oliveira, J. M. (2016). Facing depression with botulinum toxin: Literature review. *European Psychiatry, 33*, S407–S408.

American Psychiatric Association. (1994). *Diagnostic and statistical manual of mental disorders*. Washington, DC: American Psychiatric Association.

American Psychologist. (1965). *20*, 990.

Ames, C. (1984). Competitive, cooperative, and individualistic goal structures: A cognitive-motivational analysis. In R. E. Ames & C. Ames (Eds.), *Motivation in education* (Vol. 1, pp. 177–207). San Francisco, CA: Academic Press.

Ames, L. B. (1952). The sense of self of nursery school children as manifested by their verbal behavior. *Journal of Genetic Psychology, 81*, 193–232.

Amsterdam, B. (1972). Mirror self-image reactions before age two. *Developmental Psychobiology, 5*, 297–305.

Anastasi, A. (1976). *Psychological testing* (4th ed.). New York, NY: Macmillan.

Anderson, C. A. (1987). Temperature and aggression: Effects on quarterly, yearly, and city rates of violent and nonviolent crime. *Journal of Personality and Social Psychology, 52*, 1161–1173.

Anderson, C. A (1989). Temperature and aggression: The ubiquitous effect of heat on the occurrence of human violence. *Psychological Bulletin, 106*, 74–96.

Anderson, C. A., & Anderson, K. B. (1998). Temperature and aggression: Paradox, controversy, and a (fairly) clear picture. In R. Geen & E. Donnerstein (Eds.), *Human aggression: Theories, research and implications for social policy* (pp. 247–298). San Diego, CA: Academic Press.

Anderson, C. A., Anderson, K. B., Dorr, N., DeNeve, K. M., & Flanagan, M. (2000). Temperature and aggression. *Advances in experimental social psychology, 32*, 63–133.

Anderson, C. A., & Bushman, B. J. (1997). External validity of "trivial" experiments: The case of laboratory aggression. *Review of General Psychology, 1*(1), 19–41.

Anderson, C. A., & Bushman, B. J. (2002). Human aggression. *Annual Review of Psychology, 53*, 27–55.

Anderson, C. A., Jennings, D. L., & Arnoult, L. H. (1988). Validity and utility of the attributional style construct at a moderate level of specificity. *Journal of Personality and Social Psychology, 55*, 979–990.

Anderson, M. C., & Green, C. (2001). Suppressing unwanted memories by executive control. *Science, 410*, 366–369.

Ang, R. P., & Goh, D. H. (2010). Cyberbullying among adolescents: The role of affective and cognitive empathy, and gender. *Child psychiatry & human development, 41*(4), 387–397.

Ansbacher, H. L., & Ansbacher, R. R. (Eds.). (1956). *The individual psychology of Alfred Adler*. New York, NY: Basic Books.

Ansbacher, H. L., & Ansbacher, R. R. (Eds.). (1964). *Superiority and social interest by Alfred Adler*. Evanston, IL: Northwestern University Press.

Anspach, M. S. (1991). Is a change in the theory of the person necessary? *Theoretical and Philosophical Psychology, 11*, 111–115.

Antill, J. K. (1987). Parents' beliefs and values about sex roles, sex differences and sexuality: Their sources and implications. In P. Shaver & C. Hendrick (Eds.), *Sex and gender: Review of personality and social psychology* (Vol. 7, pp. 294–328). Beverly Hills, CA: Sage.

Arbelle, S., Benjamin, J., Golin, M., Kremer, I., Belmaker, R. H., & Ebstein, R. P. (2003). Relation of shyness in grade school children to the genotype for the long form of the serotonin transporter promoter region polymorphism. *American Journal of Psychiatry, 160*, 671–676.

Archer, J. (1970). Effects of population density on behavior in rodents. In J. H. Croobe (Ed.), *Social behaviors in birds and mammals*. New York, NY: Academic Press.

Archer, J. (1988). The sociobiology of bereavement: A reply to Littlefield and Rushton. *Journal of Personality and Social Psychology, 55*, 272–278.

Archer, J. (2004). Sex differences in aggression in real-world settings: A meta-analytic review. *Review of General Psychology, 8*(4), 291–322.

Archer, S. L. (1992). A feminist's approach to identity research. In G. R. Adams, T. P. Gullotta, & R. Montemayer (Eds.), *Adolescent identity formation* (pp. 25–49). Newbury Park, CA: Sage.

Ardrey, R. (1967). *African genesis*. New York, NY: Dell.

Aristotle. (1947). *Introduction to Aristotle, Nicomachean Ethics*. R. McBeon (Ed.). New York, NY: Random House.

Arkes, H. R., & Garske, J. P. (1977). *Psychological theories of motivation*. Belmont, CA: Brooks/Cole.

Arkoff, A. (1957). Resolution of approach-approach and avoidance-avoidance conflicts. *Journal of Abnormal and Social Psychology, 55*, 402–404.

Arkowitz, H. (1992). Integrative theories of therapy. In D. Freedheim (Ed.), *History of psychotherapy: A century of change*. Washington, DC: American Psychological Association.

Aronfreed, J. (1964). The origins of self-criticism. *Psychological Review, 71*, 193–218.

Ashmore, R. D. (1990). Sex, gender, and the individual. In L. A. Pervin (Ed.), *Handbook of personality* (pp. 486–526). New York, NY: Guilford.

Ashton, M. C., & Lee, K. (2010). On the cross-language replicability of personality factors. *Journal of Research in Personality, 44*, 436–441.

Ashton, M. C., Lee, K., Perugini, M., Szarota, P., De Vries, R. E., Di Blas, L., . . . & De Raad, B. (2004). A six-factor structure of personality-descriptive adjectives: Solutions from psycholexical studies in seven languages. *Journal of Personality and Social Psychology, 86*(2), 356–366.

Astin, A. N., Green, K. C., & Korn, W. S. (1987). *The American freshman: Twenty year trends*. Los Angeles, CA: University of California at Los Angeles, Higher Education Research Institute.

Atkinson, J. W. (1957). Motivational determinants of risk-taking behavior. *Psychological Review, 64*, 359–372.

Atkinson, J. W. (1964). *An introduction to motivation*. Princeton, NJ: Van Nostrand.

Atkinson, J. W., & Litwin, G. H. (1960). Achievement motive and test anxiety conceived as motive to approach success and motive to avoid failure. *Journal of Abnormal and Social Psychology, 60*, 52–63.

Atkinson, J. W., & Raynor, J. O. (Eds.). (1974). *Motivation and achievement*. Washington, DC: V. H. Winston.

Aunola, K., & Nurmi, J. E. (2005). The role of parenting styles in children's problem behavior. *Child development, 76*(6), 1144–1159.

Aunola, K., Stattin, H., & Nurmi, J. E. (2000). Parenting styles and adolescents' achievement strategies. *Journal of Adolescence, 23*(2), 205–222.

Ausubel, N. (Ed.). (1948). Applied psychology. In *A treasury of Jewish folklore*. New York, NY: Crown.

Averill, J. R. (1982). *Anger and aggression: An essay on emotion*. New York, NY: Springer-Verlag.

Ayllon, T., & Azrin, N. H. (1965). The measurement and reinforcement of behavior of psychotics. *Journal of Experimental Analysis of Behavior, 8*, 357–383.

Baker, L. A., Raine, A., Liu, J., & Jacobson, K. C. (2008). Differential genetic and environmental influences on reactive and proactive aggression in children. *Journal of Abnormal Child Psychology, 36*(8), 1265–1278.

Bakermans-Kranenburg, M. J., & van IJzendoorn, M. H. (2009). The first 10,000 Adult Attachment Interviews: Distributions of adult attachment representations in clinical and non-clinical groups. *Attachment & Human Development, 11*(3), 223–263.

Bakermans-Kranenburg, M. J., Van IJzendoorn, M. H., & Juffer, F. (2003). Less is more: Meta-analyses of sensitivity and attachment interventions in early childhood. *Psychological Bulletin, 129*, 195.

Bakermans-Kranenburg, M. J., Van IJzendoorn, M. H., & Juffer, F. (2005). Disorganized infant attachment and preventive interventions: A review and meta-analysis. *Infant Mental Health Journal, 26*, 191–216.

Balay, J., & Shevrin, H. (1988). The Subliminal Psychodynamic Activation method: A critical review. *American Psychologist, 43*, 161–174.

Baldwin, A. L. (1959). The effect of home environment on nursery school behavior. *Child Development, 20*, 49–62.

Baltes, P. B., & Schaie, K. W. (1973). *Life-span developmental psychology: Personality and socialization*. New York, NY: Academic Press.

Bandura, A. (1962). Social learning through imitation. In M. R. Jones (Ed.), *Nebraska Symposium on Motivation*. Lincoln, NE: University of Nebraska Press.

Bandura, A. (1965). Influence of models' reinforcement contingencies on the acquisition of imitative responses. *Journal of Personality and Social Psychology, 1*, 589–595.

Bandura, A. (1969). *Principles of behavior modification*. New York, NY: Molt.

Bandura, A. (1971). Psychotherapy based upon modeling principles. In A. E. Bergin & S. L. Garfield (Eds.), *Handbook of psychotherapy and behavior change*. New York, NY: Wiley.

Bandura, A. (1973). *Aggression: A social learning analysis*. Englewood Cliffs, NJ: Prentice-Hall.

Bandura, A. (1976). *Social learning theory*. Morristown, NJ: General Learning Press.

Bandura, A. (1977a). Self-efficacy: Toward a unifying theory of behavioral change. *Psychological Review, 84*, 191–215.

Bandura, A. (1977b). *Social learning theory*. Englewood Cliffs, NJ: Prentice-Hall.

Bandura, A. (1978). The self system in reciprocal determinism. *American Psychologist, 33*, 344–358.

Bandura, A. (1986). *Social foundations of thought and action: A social cognitive theory*. Englewood Cliffs, NJ: Prentice-Hall.

Bandura, A. (1989). Human agency in social cognitive theory. *American Psychologist, 44*, 1175–1184.

Bandura, A., Taylor, C. B. Williams, S. L., Mefford, I. N., & Barchas, J. D. (1985). Catecholamine secretion as a function of perceived coping self-efficacy. *Journal of Consulting and Clinical Psychology, 53*, 406–414.

Bandura, A., Adams, N. E., & Beyer, J. (1977). Cognitive processes mediating behavioral changes. *Journal of Personality and Social Psychology, 35*, 125–139.

Bandura, A., Grusec, J. E., & Menlove, F. L. (1966). Observational learning as a function of symbolization and incentive set. *Child Development, 37*, 499–506.

Bandura, A., Grusec, J. E., & Menlove, F. L. (1967). Vicarious extinction of avoidance behavior. *Journal of Personality and Social Psychology, 5*, 16–23.

Bandura, A., & Huston, A. (1961). Identification as a process of incidental learning. *Journal of Abnormal and Social Psychology, 63*, 311–318.

Bandura, A., & Jeffrey, R. W. (1973). Role of symbolic coding and rehearsal processes in observational learning. *Journal of Personality and Social Psychology, 26*, 122–130.

Bandura, A., & McDonald, F. J. (1963). Influence of social reinforcement and the behavior of models in shaping children's moral judgments. *Journal of Abnormal and Social Psychology, 67*, 274–281.

Bandura, A., & Mischel, W. (1965). Modification of self-imposed delay of reward through exposure to live and symbolic models. *Journal of Personality and Social Psychology, 2*, 698–705.

Bandura, A., O'Leary, A., Taylor, C. B., Gauthier, J., & Gossard, D. (1987). Perceived self-efficacy and pain control: Opioid and non-opioid mechanism. *Journal of Personality and Social Psychology, 53*, 563–571.

Bandura, A., Reese, L., & Adams, N. E. (1982). Microanalysis of action and fear arousal as a function of differential levels of perceived self-efficacy. *Journal of Personality and Social Psychology, 43*, 5–21.

Bandura, A., Ross, D., & Ross, S. A. (1961). Transmission of aggression through imitation of aggressive models. *Journal of Abnormal Social Psychology, 63*, 575–582.

Bandura, A., Ross, D., & Ross, S. A. (1963a). Imitation of film-mediated aggressive models. *Journal of Abnormal and Social Psychology, 66*, 3–11.

Bandura, A., Ross, D., & Ross, S. A. (1963b). Vicarious reinforcement and imitative learning. *Journal of Abnormal and Social Psychology, 67*, 601–607.

Bandura, A., & Walters, R. H. (1959). *Adolescent aggression*. New York, NY: Ronald.

Bandura, A., & Walters, R. H. (1963). *Social learning and personality development*. New York, NY: Holt.

Bandura, A., & Wood, R. (1989). Effect of perceived controllability and performance standards on self-regulation of complex decision making. *Journal of Personality and Social Psychology, 56*, 805–814.

Bannister, D., & Fransella, F. (1971). *Inquiring man*. Baltimore, MD: Penguin.

Barber, B. K. (1996). Parental psychological control: Revisiting a neglected construct. *Child Development, 67*(6), 3296–3319.

Barber, T. X., & Calverley, D. S. (1964). Experimental studies in "hypnotic" behavior: Suggested deafness evaluated by delayed auditory feedback. *British Journal of Psychology, 55*, 439–446.

Barclay, A. M. (1969). The effect of hostility on physiological fantasy responses. *Journal of Personality, 37*, 651–667.

Bargh, J. A., Chen, M., & Burrows, L. (1996). Automaticity of social behavior: Direct effects of trait construct and stereotype activation on action. *Journal of Personality and Social Psychology, 71*, 230–240.

Bargh, J. A., & Morsella, E. (2008). The unconscious mind. *Perspectives on Psychological Science, 3*(1), 73–79.

Barglow, P., Vaughn, B. E., & Molitor, N. (1987). Effects of maternal absence due to employment on the quality of infant-mother attachment in a low-risk sample. *Child Development, 58*, 945–954.

Barlow, D. H. (1988). *Anxiety and its disorders.* New York, NY: Guilford.

Barlow, D. H., Abel, G. G., & Blanchard, E. G. (1977). Gender identity change in a transsexual: An exorcism. *Archives of Sexual Behavior, 6*, 387–395.

Barker, R. G. (1960). Ecology and motivation. In M. R. Jones (Ed.), *Nebraska Symposium on Motivation* (Vol. 8). Lincoln, NE: University of Nebraska Press.

Barker, R. G. (1965). Explorations in ecological psychology. *American Psychologist, 20*, 1–13.

Barker, R. G. (1968). *Ecological psychology.* Stanford, CA: Stanford University Press.

Barker, R. G., Dembo, T., & Lewin, K. (1943). Frustration and regression. In R. G. Barker, J. S. Kounin, & H. F. Wright (Eds.), *Child behavior and development.* New York, NY: McGraw-Hill.

Barnett, M. A., Matthews, K. A., & Howard, J. A. (1979). Relationships between competitiveness and empathy in 6- and 7-year-olds. *Developmental Psychology, 15*, 221–222.

Barni, D., Alfieri, S., Marta, E., & Rosnati, R. (2013). Overall and unique similarities between parents' values and adolescent or emerging adult children's values. *Journal of Adolescence, 36*(6), 1135–1141.

Barni, D., Knafo, A., Ben-Arieh, A., & Haj-Yahia, M. M. (2014). Parent–child value similarity across and within cultures. *Journal of Cross-Cultural Psychology, 45*(6), 853–867.

Baron, J. N., & Reiss, P. C. (1985). Same time, next year: Aggregate analyses of the mass media on violent behavior. *American Sociological Review, 50*, 347–363.

Baron, R. A. (1974). The aggression-inhibiting influence of heightened sexual arousal. *Journal of Personality and Social Psychology, 30*, 318–322.

Baron, R. A. (1977). *Human aggression.* New York, NY: Plenum.

Baron, R. A. (1987). Effects of negative ions on interpersonal attraction: Evidence for intensification. *Journal of Personality and Social Psychology, 52*, 547–553.

Baron, R. A., Russell, G. W., & Arms, R. L. (1985). Negative ions and behavior: Impact on mood, memory, and aggression among Type A and Type B persons. *Journal of Personality and Social Psychology, 48*, 746–754.

Barry, H., Child, I., & Bacon, M. (1959). Relation of child training to subsistence economy. *American Anthropologist, 61*, 51–63.

Barzun, J. (1954). *God's country and mine.* Boston, MA: Atlantic Monthly.

Bateson, C., Jackson, D. D., Haley, J., & Weakland, J. H. (1956). Toward a theory of schizophrenia. *Behavioral Science, 1*, 251–264.

Batson, C. D., & Powell, A. A. (2003). Altruism and prosocial behavior. In T. Millon & M. J. Lerner (Eds.), *Handbook of Psychology* (Vol. 5, pp. 463–484). Hoboken, NJ: John Wiley & Sons, Inc.

Baumeister, R. F. (1986). *Identity: Cultural change and the struggle for self.* New York, NY: Oxford University Press.

Baumeister, R. F. (1987). How the self became a problem: A psychological review of historical research. *Journal of Personality and Social Psychology, 52*, 163–176.

Baumeister, R. F. (1990). Suicide as escape from self. *Psychological Review, 97*, 90–113.

Baumeister, R. F. (1993). Conceptions of self and identity: A modern retrospective on Allport's view. In K. H. Craik, R. Hogan, & R. N. Wolfe (Eds.), *Fifty years of personality psychology* (pp. 177–186). New York, NY: Plenum.

Baumeister, R. F., Bushman, B. J., & Campbell, W. K. (2000). Self-esteem, narcissism, and aggression: Does violence result from low self-esteem or from threatened egotism? *Current Directions in Psychological Science, 9*(1), 26–29.

Baumeister, R. F., Campbell, J. D., Krueger, J. I., & Vohs, K. D. (2003). Does high self-esteem cause better performance, interpersonal success, happiness, or healthier lifestyles? *Psychological science in the public interest, 4*(1), 1–44.

Baumeister, R. F., Dale, K., & Sommer, K. L. (1998). Freudian defense mechanisms and empirical findings in modern social psychology: Reaction formation, projection, displacement, undoing, isolation, sublimation, and denial. *Journal of Personality, 66*(6), 1081–1124.

Baumeister, R. F., Masicampo, E. J., & Vohs, K. D. (2011). Do conscious thoughts cause behavior? *Annual Review of Psychology, 62*, 331–361.

Baumeister, R. F., Smart, L., & Boden, J. M. (1996). Relation of threatened egotism to violence and aggression: The dark side of high self-esteem. *Psychological Review, 103*(1), 5–33.

Baumeister, R. F., & Tice, D. M. (1990). Point-counterpoints: Anxiety and social exclusion. *Journal of Social and Clinical Psychology, 9*, 165–195.

Baumrind, D. (1971). Current patterns of parental authority. *Developmental Psychology Monographs, 1*, 1–103.

Baumrind, D. (1972). Socialization and instrumental competence in young children. In W. W. Hartup (Ed.), *The young child: Reviews of research* (Vol. 2). Washington, DC: National Association for the Education of Young Children.

Baumrind, D. (1978). Parental disciplinary patterns and social competence in children. *Youth and Society, 9*, 239–276.

Baumrind, D. (1986). Sex differences in moral reasoning: Response to Walker's (1984). conclusion that there are none. *Child Development, 57*, 511–521.

Baumrind, D. (1989). The permanence of change and the impermanence of stability. *Human Development, 32*(3–4), 187–195.

Baumrind, D. (1991). The influence of parenting style on adolescent competence and substance use. *Journal of Early Adolescence, 11*(1), 56–95.

Baumrind, D. (2012). Differentiating between confrontive and coercive kinds of parental power-assertive disciplinary practices. *Human Development, 55,* 35–51.

Baumrind, D. (2013). Is a pejorative view of power assertion in the socialization process justified? *Journal of General Psychology, 17,* 420–427.

Baumrind, D., Larzelere, R. E., & Owens, E. B. (2010). Effects of preschool parents' power assertive patterns and practices on adolescent development. *Parenting: Science and Practice, 10*(3), 157–201.

Beach, F. (1955). The descent of instinct. *Psychological Review, 62,* 401–410.

Beck, A. T. (1967). *Depression. Clinical, experimental, and theoretical aspects.* New York, NY: Hoeber.

Beck, A. T. (1976). *Cognitive therapy and the emotional disorders.* New York, NY: International Universities Press.

Beck, A. T. (1984). Cognitive approaches to stress. In R. Woolfold & P. Lehrer (Eds.), *Principles and practice of stress management.* New York, NY: Guilford Press.

Beck, A. T., Rush, A. J., Shaw, B. F., & Emery, G. (1979). *Cognitive therapy of depression.* New York, NY: Guilford.

Becker, W. C. (1964). Consequences of different kinds of parental discipline. In M. L. Hoffman & L. W. Hoffman (Eds.), *Review of child development research* (Vol. 1). New York, NY: Russell Sage.

Beebe, B. (2004). Co-constructing mother-infant distress in face-to-face interactions: Contributions of microanalysis. *Zero to Three, 24,* 40–48.

Bell, P. A., & Byrne, D. (1978). Repression-sensitization. In H. London & J. E. Exner, Jr. (Eds.), *Dimensions of personality.* New York, NY: Wiley.

Bell, R. Q. (1965). Developmental psychology. *Annual Review of Psychology, 16,* 1–38.

Belsky, J. (1981). Early human experience: A family perspective. *Developmental Psychology, 17,* 3–23.

Belsky, J., Garduque, L., & Hrncir, E. (1984). Assuming performance, competence and executive capacity in infant play: Relations to home environment and security of attachment. *Developmental Psychology, 20,* 406–417.

Belsky, J., & Pluess, M. (2009). The nature (and nurture?) of plasticity in early human development. *Perspectives on Psychological Science, 4,* 345–351.

Belsky, J., & Rovine, M. (1937). Temperament and attachment security in the strange situation: An empirical rapprochement. *Child Development, 58,* 787–795.

Belsky, J., Sternberg, L. D., & Walker, A. (1982). The ecology of day-care. In M. Lamb (Ed.), *Childrearing in nontraditional families* (pp. 71–116). Hillsdale, NJ: Erlbaum.

Belson, W. A. (1978). *Television violence and the adolescent boy.* Teakfied Limited, England: Saxon House.

Bem, D. J., & Allen, A. (1974). On predicting some of the people some of the time: The search for cross-situational consistencies in behavior. *Psychological Review, 81,* 505–520.

Bem, D. J., & Funder, D. C. (1978). Predicting more of the people more of the time: Assessing the personality of situations. *Psychological Review, 85,* 485–501.

Bem, S. L. (1974). The measurement of psychological androgyny. *Journal of Consulting and Clinical Psychology, 42,* 165–172.

Bem, S. L. (1975). Sex-role adaptability: One consequence of psychological androgyny. *Journal of Personality and Social Psychology, 31,* 634–653.

Benn, R. K. (1986). Factors promoting secure attachment relationships between employed mothers and their sons. *Child Development, 57,* 1224–1231.

Bentham, J. (1779; 1948). *An introduction to the principles of morals and legislation.* Oxford: Blackwell.

Berglas, S., & Jones, E. E. (1978). Drug choice as a self-handicapping strategy in response to noncontingent success. *Journal of Personality and Social Psychology, 36,* 405–417.

Berkowitz, L. (1965a). The concept of aggressive drive: Some additional considerations. In L. Berkowitz (Ed.), *Advances in experimental social psychology* (Vol. 2). New York, NY: Academic Press.

Berkowitz, L. (1965b). Some aspects of observed aggression. *Journal of Personality and Social Psychology, 2,* 359–369.

Berkowitz, L. (1978). External determinants of impulsive aggression. In W. W. Hartup & J. de Wit (Eds.), *Origins of aggression.* The Hague, Netherlands: Mouton.

Berkowitz, L. (1983). Aversively stimulated aggression: Some parallels and differences in research with animals and humans. *American Psychologist, 38,* 1135–1144.

Berkowitz, L. (1989). Frustration aggression hypothesis: Examination and reformulation. *Psychological Bulletin, 106,* 59–72.

Berkowitz, L., & Geen, R. G. (1966). Film violence and the cue properties of available targets. *Journal of Personality and Social Psychology, 3,* 525–530.

Berkowitz, L., & Le Page, A. (1967). Weapons as aggression-eliciting stimuli. *Journal of Personality and Social Psychology, 7,* 202–207.

Berlyne, D. (1960). *Conflict, arousal, and curiosity.* New York, NY: McGraw-Hill.

Bernstein, B. (1964). Elaborated and restricted codes: Their social origins and some consequences. In J. Gumpery, & D. Hymes (Eds.), *The ethnography of communication* (Vol. 66, pp. 55–69) American Anthropologist Special Publication.

Bernstein, I. S., & Gordon, T. P. (1974). The function of aggression in primate societies. *American Scientist, 62,* 304–311.

Berry, D. S., & McArthur, L. Z. (1986). Perceiving character in faces: The impact of age-related craniofacial changes in social perception. *Psychological Bulletin, 100,* 3–18.

Berry, J., Kim, U., Power, S., Young, M., & Bujaki, J. (1989). Acculturation attitudes in plural societies. *Applied Psychology, 38,* 185–205.

Berry, J. W. (1967). Independence and conformity in subsistence-level societies. *Journal of Personality and Social Psychology, 7,* 415–418.

Berry, J. W. (1976). *Human ecology and cognitive style.* New York, NY: Russell Sage.

Berscheid, E. (2010). Love in the fourth dimension. *Annual Review of Psychology, 61,* 1–25.

Berscheid, E., & Walster, E. H. (1978). *Interpersonal attraction.* Reading, MA: Addison-Wesley.

Bettelheim, B. (1943). Individual and mass behavior in extreme situations. *Journal of Abnormal and Social Psychology, 38*(4), 417–452.

Bickman, L. (1971). The effect of another bystander's ability to help on bystander intervention in an emergency. *Journal of Experimental Social Psychology, 7*, 367–379.

Binet, A., & Henri, V. (1895). La psychologie individuelle. *Année psychologique, 2*, 411–463.

Binswanger, L. (1963). *Being-in-the-world: Selected papers of Ludwig Binswanger* (J. Needleman, Trans.). New York, NY: Basic Books.

Birren, J. E., Butler, R. N., Greenhouse, S. W., Sobolofe, C., & Yarrow, M. R. (1963). *Human aging: A biological and behavioral study*. Bethesda, MD: U.S. Public Health Service.

Blasband, D., & Peplau, L. A. (1985). Sexual exclusivity versus openness in gay male couples. *Archives of Sexual Behavior, 14*(5), 395–412.

Blasi, A. (1980). Bridging moral cognition and moral action: A critical review of the literature. *Psychological Bulletin, 88*, 593–637.

Bleidorn, W. (2012). Hitting the road to adulthood: Short-term personality development during a major life transition. *Personality and Social Psychology Bulletin, 38*(12), 1594–1608.

Bleidorn, W. (2015). What accounts for personality maturation in early adulthood? *Current Directions in Psychological Science, 24*(3), 245–252.

Block, J. (1961). *The Q-sort method in personality assessment and psychiatric research*. Springfield, IL: Charles C. Thomas.

Block, J. (1965). *The challenge of response sets: Unconfounding meaning, acquiescence, and social desirability in the MMPI*. New York, NY: Appleton-Century-Crofts.

Block, J. (1977). Advancing the psychology of personality: Paradigmatic shift or improving the quality of research. In D. Magnussen & N. S. Endler (Eds.), *Personality at the crossroads: Current issues in interactional psychology*. Hillsdale, NJ: Lawrence Erlbaum.

Block, J. (1993). Studying personality the long way. In D. C. Funder, R. D. Peake, C. Tomlinson-Keasey, & K. Widaman (Eds.), *Studying lives through time* (pp. 9–44). Washington, DC: American Psychological Association.

Block, J. (1995). A contrarian view of the five-factor approach to personality description. *Psychological Bulletin, 117*(2), 187–215.

Block, J. (2010). The five-factor framing of personality and beyond: Some ruminations. *Psychological Inquiry, 21*(1), 2–25.

Block, J., Block, J. H., & Harrington, D. M. (1974). Some misgivings about the matching familiar figures test as a measure of reflection-impulsivity. *Developmental Psychology, 10*, 611–632.

Block, J., Block, J. H., & Keyes, S. (1988). Longitudinal foretelling drug usage in adolescence: Early childhood personality and environmental precursors. *Child Development, 59*, 336–355.

Block, J. H. (1973). Conceptions of sex role: Some cross-cultural and longitudinal perspectives. *American Psychologist, 28*, 512–529.

Block, J. H. (1976). Issues, problems and pitfalls in assessing sex differences. *Merrill-Palmer Quarterly, 22*, 283–308.

Block, J. H. (September 1979). Personality development in males and females: The influence of differential socialization. Paper presented as part of the Master Lecture Series at the meeting of the American Psychological Association, New York.

Block, J. H., & Block, J. (1980). The role of ego-control and ego-resiliency in the organization of behavior. In W. A. Collins (Ed.), *Minnesota symposium on child development* (Vol. 13). Hillsdale, NJ: Lawrence Erlbaum.

Block, J. H., & Martin, B. (1955). Predicting the behavior of children under frustration. *Journal of Abnormal Social Psychology, 51*, 281–285.

Bluestone, C., & Tamis-LeMonda, C. S. (1999). Correlates of parenting styles in predominantly working- and middle-class African American mothers. *Journal of Marriage and the Family*, 881–893.

Blum, G. S. (1961). *A model of the mind*. New York, NY: Wiley.

Blyth, D. A., Simmons, R. G., Bucraft, R., Felt, D., Vancleave, E. F., & Bush, D. M. (1981). The effects of physical development on self-image and satisfaction with body-image for early adolescent males. In R. G. Simmons (Ed.), *Research in community and mental health* (Vol. 2, pp. 43–73). Greenwich, CT: JAI Press.

Bogenschutz, M. P., & Pommy, J. M. (2012). Therapeutic mechanisms of classic hallucinogens in the treatment of addictions: From indirect evidence to testable hypotheses. *Drug Testing and Analysis, 4*(7–8), 543–555.

Bohart, A. (1980). Toward a cognitive theory of catharsis. *Psychotherapy: Theory. Research and Practice, 17*, 192–201.

Bohart, A. (1993). Experiencing: The basis of psychotherapy. *Journal of Psychotherapy Integration, 3*, 51–67.

Bohart, A. C., & Watson, J. C. (2011). Person-centered psychotherapy and related experiential approaches. In S. B. Messer & A. S. Gurman (Eds.), *Essential psychotherapies: Theory and practice* (3rd ed., pp. 223–260). New York, NY: Guilford.

Book, A. S., Starzyk, K. B., & Quinsey, V. L. (2001). The relationship between testosterone and aggression: A meta-analysis. *Aggression and Violent Behavior, 6*(6), 579–599.

Booth-Kewley, S., & Friedman, H. S. (1987). Psychological predictors of heart disease: A quantitative review. *Psychological Bulletin, 101*, 343–362.

Borgida, E., & Nisbett, R. (1977). The differential impact of abstract vs. concrete information on decisions. *Journal of Applied Social Psychology, 7*, 258–271.

Bornstein, M. H. (1989). Sensitive periods in development: Structural characteristics and causal interpretations. *Psychological Bulletin, 105*, 179–197.

Bornstein, R. F., & Pittman, T. S. (Eds.), *Perception without awareness*. New York, NY: Guilford.

Boss, M. (1963). *Psychoanalysis and daseinanalysis*. (L. B. Lefebre, Trans.). New York, NY: Basic Books.

Bosson, J. K., Swann, W. B., & Pennebaker, J. W. (2000). Stalking the perfect measure of implicit self-esteem: The blind men and the elephant revisited? *Journal of Personality and Social Psychology, 79*(4), 631–643.

Botwin, M. D., & Buss, D. M. (1989). Structure of act-reported data: Is the five-factor model of personality recaptured?

Journal of Personality and Social Psychology, 56, 988–1001.

Botwin, M. D., Buss, D. M., & Shackelford, T. K. (1997). Personality and mate preferences: Five factors in mate selection and marital satisfaction. *Journal of Personality, 65*(1), 107–136.

Bouchard, T. J., Jr., Lykken, D. T., McGue, M., Segal, N. L., & Tellegen, A. (1990). Sources of human psychological differences: The Minnesota Study of Twins Reared Apart. *Science, 250,* 223–228.

Bourdage, J. S., Wiltshire, J., & Lee, K. (2015). Personality and workplace impression management: Correlates and implications. *Journal of Applied Psychology, 100*(2), 537–546.

Bowers, K. S. (1973). Situationalism in psychology: An analysis and critique. *Psychological Review, 80,* 307–336.

Bowlby, J. (1958). The nature of the child's tie to his mother. *International Journal of Psycho-Analysis, 39,* 350–373.

Bowlby, J. (1969). *Attachment and love: Attachment* (Vol. 1). New York, NY: Basic Books.

Bowman, M. L. (1989). Testing individual differences in ancient China. *American Psychologist, 44,* 576–578.

Brackbill, Y. (1962). *Research and clinical work with children.* Washington, DC: American Psychological Association.

Bradburn, N. M. (1963). Achievement and father dominance in Turkey. *Journal of Abnormal and Social Psychology, 67,* 464–468.

Brandstäder, J., & Greve, W. (1994).The aging self: Stabilizing and protective processes. *Developmental Review, 14,* 52–80.

Breger, L. (1974). *From instinct to identity.* Englewood Cliffs, NJ: Prentice-Hall.

Brehm, J. W. (1966). *A theory of psychological reactance.* New York, NY: Academic Press.

Brehm, J. W. (1972). *Responses to loss of freedom: A theory of psychological reactance.* Morristown, NJ: General Learning Press.

Brehm, S. S., & Brehm, J. W. (1981). *Psychological reactance: A theory of freedom and control.* New York, NY: Academic Press.

Breland, K., & Breland, M. (1961). The misbehavior of organisms. *American Psychologist, 16,* 681–684.

Brendgen, M., Dionne, G., Girard, A., Boivin, M., Vitaro, F., & Pérusse, D. (2005). Examining genetic and environmental effects on social aggression: A study of 6-year-old twins. *Child development, 76*(4), 930–946.

Brewin, C. R. (1985). Depression and causal attributions: What is their relation? *Psychological Bulletin, 98,* 297–309.

Briere, J., & Conte, J. (1993). Self-reported amnesia for abuse in adults molested as children. *Journal of Traumatic Stress, 6,* 21–31.

Briggs, S. P., & Cheek, J. M. (1988). On the nature of self-monitoring: Problems with assessment, problems with validity. *Journal of Personality and Social Psychology, 54,* 663–678.

Broadhurst, P. L. (1961). Analysis of maternal effects in the inheritance of behaviour. *Animal Behaviour, 9,* 129–141.

Brodie, F. (1981). *Richard Nixon: The shaping of his character.* New York, NY: Norton.

Brody, N. (1994). .5 + or –5 continuity and change in personal dispositions. In T. F. Heatherton & J. L. Weinberger (Eds.),

Can personality change? (pp. 59–82). Washington, DC: American Psychological Association.

Bronfenbrenner, U., & Ceci, S. J. (1993). Heredity, environment, and the question "how?"—A first approximation. In R. Plomin & G. E. McClearn (Eds.), *Nature, nurture and psychology* (pp. 313–324). Washington, DC: American Psychological Association.

Brotman, L. M., Gouley, K. K., Huang, K. Y., Rosenfelt, A., O'Neal, C., Klein, R. G., & Shrout, P. (2008). Preventive intervention for preschoolers at high risk for antisocial behavior: Long-term effects on child physical aggression and parenting practices. *Journal of Clinical Child & Adolescent Psychology, 37*(2), 386–396.

Brown, J. S. (1948). Gradients of approach and avoidance responses and their relation to level of motivation. *Journal of Comparative and Physiological Psychology, 41,* 450–465.

Brown, J. S. (1957). Principles of intrapersonal conflict. *Journal of Conflict Resolution, 1,* 135–154.

Brown, L. M., & Gilligan, C. (1992). *Meeting at the crossroads.* Cambridge, MA: Harvard University Press.

Brown, P., & Elliott, R. (1965). Control of aggression in a nursery school class. *Journal of Experimental Child Psychology, 2,* 103–107.

Browning, E. B. (1888). *A selection from the poetry of Elizabeth Barrett Browning.* London, UK: Smith, Elder & Co.

Brunner, J. S. (1956). A cognitive theory of personality. *Contemporary Psychology, 1,* 355–357.

Brunner, J. S., & Tagiuri, R. (1954). The perception of people. In G. Lindzey (Ed.), *Handbook of social psychology.* Reading, MA: Addison-Wesley.

Bryan, J. H., & Test, M. A. (1967). Models and helping: Naturalistic studies in aiding behavior. *Journal of Personality and Social Psychology, 6,* 400–407.

Bryan, J. H., & Walbek, N. (1970). Preaching and practicing generosity: Children's actions and reactions. *Child Development, 41,* 329–353.

Buhler, C. (1962). Genetic aspects of the self. *Annals of the New York Academy of Science, 96,* 730–764.

Burchinal, M., Lee, M., & Ramey, C. (1989). Type of day care and pre-school intellectual development in disadvantaged children. *Child Development, 60,* 128–137.

Burns, M. O., & Seligman, M. E. P. (1989). Explanatory style across the life span: Evidence for stability over 52 years. *Journal of Personality and Social Psychology, 56,* 471–477.

Burton, R. V. (1963). Generality of honesty reconsidered. *Psychological Review, 70,* 481–499.

Bushman, B. J., Baumeister, R. F., Thomaes, S., Ryu, E., Begeer, S., & West, S. G. (2009). Looking again, and harder, for a link between low self-esteem and aggression. *Journal of Personality, 77*(2), 427–446.

Buss, D. M. (1985). Human mate selection: Opposites are sometimes said to attract, but in fact we are likely to marry someone who is similar to us in almost every variable. *American Scientist, 73*(1), 47–51.

Buss, D. M. (1989). Sex differences in human mate preferences: Evolutionary hypotheses tested in 37 cultures. *Behavioral and Brain Sciences, 12*(1), 1–14.

Buss, D. M. (2003). *The evolution of desire: Strategies of human mating.* Basic books.

Buss, D. M. (Ed.). (2005). *The handbook of evolutionary psychology*. Hoboken, NJ: John Wiley & Sons.

Buss, D. M., & Barnes, M. (1986). Preferences in human mate selection. *Journal of Personality and Social Psychology, 50*, 559–570.

Buss, A. H., Plomin, R., & Willerman, L. (1973). The inheritance of temperaments. *Journal of Personality, 41*, 513–524.

Butcher, J. N. (Ed.) (1979). *New developments in the use of the MMPI*. Minneapolis, MN: University of Minnesota Press.

Butcher, J. N. (1999). *A beginner's guide to the MMPI-2*. Washington, DC: American Psychological Association.

Butcher, J. N., & Tellegen, A. (1978). Common methodological problems in MMPI research. *Journal of Consulting and Clinical Psychology, 46*, 620–628.

Butler, J. M., & Haigh, G. V. (1954). Changes in the relation between self-concepts and ideal concepts consequent upon client-centered counseling. In C. R. Rogers & R. F. Dymond (Eds.), *Psychotherapy and personality change*. Chicago, IL: University of Chicago Press.

Bylsma, L. M., Croon, M. A., Vingerhoets, A. J., & Rottenberg, J. (2011). When and for whom does crying improve mood? A daily diary study of 1004 crying episodes. *Journal of Research in Personality, 45*(4), 385–392.

Byrne, D. (1961). The repression-sensitization scale: Rationale, reliability, and validity. *Journal of Personality, 29*, 334–349.

Cairns, R. B. (1962). *Antecedents of social reinforcer effectiveness* (Unpublished manuscript). Indiana University, Bloomington.

Cairns, R. B. (1972). Attachment and dependency: A psychobiological and social learning synthesis. In J. Gewirtz (Ed.), *Attachment and dependency*. New York, NY: Winston.

Cairns, R. B. (1979). Social international methods: An introduction. In R. B. Cairns (Ed.), *The analysis of social interaction: Methods, issues and illustrations*. Hillsdale, NJ: Erlbaum.

Caldwell, W. V. (1968). *LSD psychotherapy: An exploration of psychedelic and psycholytic therapy*. New York, NY: Grove.

Cameron, P. (1972). Stereotypes about generational fun and happiness versus self-appraised fun and happiness. *The Gerontologist, 12*, 120–123.

Campbell, D. E., & Beets, J. L. (1978). Lunacy and the moon. *Psychological Bulletin, 85*, 1123–1129.

Campbell, J. (Ed.). (1971). *The portable Jung* (R. F. C. Hull, Trans.). New York, NY: Viking.

Campbell, J. D. (August 1993). *Clarity of the self-concept*. Invited address at the American Psychological Association Convention, Toronto, Canada.

Campbell, J. P. (1974). *Handbook for the Strong-Campbell Interest Inventory*. Stanford, CA: Stanford University Press.

Campbell, J. P. (1976). Psychometric theory. In M. D. Dunnette (Ed.), *Handbook of industrial and organizational psychology*. Chicago, IL: Rand McNally.

Cann, D. R., & Donderi, D. C. (1986). Jungian personality typology and the recall of everyday and archetypal dreams. *Journal of Personality and Social Psychology, 50*, 1021–1030.

Cantor, N. (1990). From thought to behavior: "Having" and "doing" in the study of personality and cognition. *American Psychologist, 45*, 735–750.

Cantor, N. (1994). Life task problem solving: Situational affordances and personal needs. *Personality and Social Psychology Bulletin, 20*, 235–243.

Cantor, N., & Kihlstrom, J. (1986). *Personality and social intelligence*. Englewood Cliffs, NJ: Prentice-Hall.

Cantor, N., & Zirkel, S. (1990). Personality, cognition, and purposive behavior. In L. A. Pervin (Ed.), *Handbook of personality* (pp. 135–164). New York, NY: Guilford.

Caprara, G. V., Passerini, S., Pastorelli, C., Renzi, P., & Zelli, A. (1986). Instigating and measuring interpersonal aggression and hostility: A methodological contribution. *Aggressive Behavior, 12*, 237–248.

Cardno, A. G., Marshall, E. J., Coid, B., Macdonald, A. M., Ribchester, T. R., Davies, N. J., . . . & Gottesman, I. I. (1999). Heritability estimates for psychotic disorders: The Maudsley twin psychosis series. *Archives of General Psychiatry, 56*(2), 162–168.

Carey, G., Goldsmith, H. H., Tellegen, A., & Gottesman, I. I. (1978). Genetics and personality inventories: The limits of replication with twin data. *Behavior Genetics, 8*, 299–313.

Carkhuff, R. R. (1969). *Helping and human relations. Vol. 1: Selection and training. Vol. 11: Practice and research*. New York, NY: Holt.

Carkhuff, R. R., & Berenson, B. G. (1967). *Beyond counseling and therapy*. New York, NY: Holt.

Carlsmith, L. (1964). Effect of early father-absence on scholastic aptitude. *Harvard Educational Review, 34*, 3–21.

Carlson, E. A. (1998). A prospective longitudinal study of attachment disorganization/disorientation. *Child Development, 69*, 1107–1128.

Carlson, L., & Carlson, A. (1984). Affect and psychological magnification: Derivations from Tomkins' script theory. *Journal of Personality, 52*, 36–45.

Carlson, M., Marcus-Newhall, A., & Miller, N. (1989). Evidence for a general construct of aggression. *Personality and Social Psychology Bulletin, 15*, 377–389.

Carter, J. E., & Heath, B. (1971). Somatotype methodology and kinesiology research. *Kinesiology Review, 2*, 10.

Carver, C. S. (1979). Reassertion and giving up: The interactive role of self-directed attention and outcome expectancy. *Journal of Personality and Social Psychology, 37*, 1859–1870 (b).

Carver, C. S. (1989). How should multifaceted personality constructs be tested? Issues illustrated by self-monitoring, attributional style, and hardiness. *Journal of Personality and Social Psychology, 56*, 577–585.

Carver, C. S., Blaney, P. H., & Scheier, M. F. (1979). Focus of attention, chronic expectancy and response to a feared stimulus. *Journal of Personality and Social Psychology, 37*, 1186–1195 (a).

Carver, C. S., & Scheier, M. F. (1981). *Attention and self-regulation: A control theory approach to human behavior*. New York, NY: Springer-Verlag.

Carver, C. S., & Scheier, M. F. (1982). Control theory: A useful conceptual framework for personality—social, clinical, and health psychology. *Psychological Bulletin, 92*, 111–135.

Carver, C. S., & Scheier, M. (1990). *Principles of self-regulation: Action and emotion*. New York, NY: Guilford Press.

Carver, C. S., & Scheier, M. F. (1998). *On the self-regulation of behavior*. Cambridge, MA: Cambridge University Press.

Carver, C. S., & Scheier, M. F. (2002). Control processes and self-organization as complementary principles underlying behavior. *Personality and Social Psychology Review, 6*(4), 304–315.

Carver, C. S., & White, T. L. (1994). Behavioral inhibition, behavioral activation, and affective responses to impending reward and punishment: The BIS/BAS Scales. *Journal of Personality and Social Psychology, 67*(2), 319–333.

Caspi, A. (1993). Why maladaptive behaviors persist: Sources of continuity and change across the life course. In D. C. Funder, R. D. Peake, C. Tomlinson-Keasey, & K. Widaman (Eds.), *Studying lives through time* (pp. 343–376). Washington, DC: American Psychological Association.

Caspi, A., & Bem, D. J. (1990). Personality continuity and change across the life course. In L. Pervin (Ed.), *Handbook of personality* (pp. 549–575). New York, NY: Guilford.

Caspi, A., Bem, D. J., & Elder, G. H. (1989). Continuities and consequences of interactional styles across the life course. *Journal of Personality, 57*(2), 375–406.

Caspi, A., Roberts, B. W., & Shiner, R. L. (2005). Personality development: Stability and change. *Annual Review of Psychology, 56*, 453–484.

Cass, V. C. (1979). Homosexuality identity formation: A theoretical model. *Journal of Homosexuality, 4*(3), 219–235.

Cass, V. C. (1984). Homosexual identity: A concept in need of definition. *Journal of Homosexuality, 9*(2–3), 105–126.

Cassidy, J., & Berlin, L. J. (1994). The insecure/ambivalent pattern of attachment: Theory and research. *Child Development, 65*(4), 971–991.

Cattell, R. B. (1949). *Manual for forms A and B: Sixteen Personality Factor Questionnaire*. Champaign, IL: Institute for Personality and Ability Testing.

Cattell, R. B. (1957). *Personality and motivation, structure and measurement*. Yonkers, NY: World Book.

Cattell, R. B. (1965). *The scientific analysis of personality*. Baltimore, MD: Penguin.

Cattell, R. B., Eber, H. W., & Tatsuoka, M. M. (1970). *Handbook for the Sixteen Personality Factor Questionnaire (16 PF)*. Champaign, IL: Institute for Personality and Ability Testing.

Cautela, J. R. (1977). The use of covert conditioning in modifying pain behavior. *Journal of Behavior Therapy and Experimental Psychiatry, 8*(1), 45–52.

Cervantes, R. C., & Castro, F. G. (1985). Stress, coping, and Mexican American mental health: A systematic review. *Hispanic Journal of Behavioral Sciences, 7*, 1–73.

Chabris, C. F., Lee, J. J., Cesarini, D., Benjamin, D. J., & Laibson, D. I. (2015). The fourth law of behavior genetics. *Current Directions in Psychological Science, 24*, 304–312.

Chang, L., Schwartz, D., Dodge, K. A., & McBride-Chang, C. (2003). Harsh parenting in relation to child emotion regulation and aggression. *Journal of Family Psychology, 17*(4), 598–606.

Chao, Y. Y., Scherer, Y. K., Wu, Y. W., Lucke, K. T., & Montgomery, C. A. (2013). The feasibility of an intervention combining self-efficacy theory and Wii Fit exergames in assisted living residents: A pilot study. *Geriatric Nursing, 34*, 377–382.

Chaplin, W. F., & Goldberg, L. R. (1985). A failure to replicate the Bern and Allen study of individual differences in cross-situational consistency. *Journal of Personality and Social Psychology, 47*, 1074–1090.

Chaplin, W. F., John, D. P., & Goldberg, L. R. (1988). Conceptions of traits and states: Dimensional attributes with ideals as prototypes. *Journal of Personality and Social Psychology, 54*, 541–557.

Charry, J. M., & Hawkinshire, F. B. W. (1981). Effects of atmospheric electricity on some substrates of disordered social behavior. *Journal of Personality and Social Psychology, 41*, 185–197.

Chase-Lansdale, P. L., & Owen, M. T. (1987). Maternal employment in a family context: Effects on infant-mother and infant-father attachments. *Child Development, 58*, 1505–1512.

Chatz, T. L. (1972). Recognizing and treating dangerous sex offenders. *Journal of Offender Therapy, 16*, 109–115.

Chazan, S. E. (1981). Development of object permanence as a correlate of dimensions of maternal care. *Developmental Psychology, 17*(1), 79–81.

Cheek, J. M. (1982). Aggregation, moderator variables, and the validity of personality tests: A peer-rating study. *Journal of Personality and Social Psychology, 43*, 1254–1269.

Chen, X., Dong, Q., & Zhou, H. (1997). Authoritative and authoritarian parenting practices and social and school performance in Chinese children. *International Journal of Behavioral Development, 21*(4), 855–873.

Chess, S., Thomas, A., & Birch, H. G. (1965). *Your child is a person*. New York, NY: Viking.

Chess, S., & Thomas, A. (1984). *Origins and evolution of behavior disorders*. New York, NY: Brunner/Mazel.

Child, I. L. (1968). Personality in culture. In E. F. Borgatta & W. W. Lambert (Eds.), *Handbook of personality theory and research*. Chicago, IL: Rand McNally.

Child, I. L., & Waterhouse, I. K. (1953). Frustration and the quality of performance: III. An experimental study. *Journal of Personality, 21*, 298–311.

Chipuer, H. M., Plomin, R., Pederson, N. L., McClearn, G. E., & Nesselroade, J. R. (1993). Genetic influence on family environment: The role of personality. *Developmental Psychology, 29*, 110–118.

Chiriboga, D. A. (1997). Crisis, challenge, and stability in the middle years. In M. Lachman & J. B. James (Eds.), *Multiple paths of midlife development* (pp. 293–322). Chicago, IL: University of Chicago Press.

Choe, D. E., Lane, J. D., Grabell, A. S., & Olson, S. L. (2013). Developmental precursors of young school-age children's hostile attribution bias. *Developmental Psychology, 49*(12), 2245–2256.

Christophersen, E. R. (1989). Injury control. *American Psychologist, 44*, 237–241.

Chwalisz, K., Diener, E., & Gallagher, D. (1988). Autonomic arousal feedback and emotional experience: Evidence from the spinal cord injured. *Journal of Personality and Social Psychology, 54*, 820–828.

Cialdini, R. B., Borden, R. J., Thorne, A., Walker, M. R., Freeman, S., & Sloan, L. R. (1976). Basking in reflected glory: Three (football) field studies. *Journal of Personality and Social Psychology, 34*(3), 366–375.

Cicirelli, V. G. (2010). Attachment relationships in old age. *Journal of Social and Personal Relationships, 27,* 191–199.

Clarke-Stewart, A. (1982). *Daycare.* Cambridge, MA: Harvard University Press.

Clemes, S. R. (1964). Repression and hypnotic amnesia. *Journal of Abnormal and Social Psychology, 69,* 62–69.

Clore, G. L., Ortony, A., & Foss, M. A. (1987). The psychological foundations of the affective lexicon. *Journal of Personality and Social Psychology, 53,* 751–766.

Coe, W. C. (1978). The credibility of posthypnotic amnesia: A contextualist's view. *International Journal of Classical and Experimental Hypnosis, 26,* 673–681.

Cofer, C. N., & Appley, M. H. (1964). *Motivation: Theory and research.* New York, NY: Wiley.

Cohen, D., & Nisbett, R. E. (1994). Self-protection and the culture of honor: Explaining southern violence. *Personality and Social Psychology Bulletin, 20*(5), 551–567.

Cohen, D., Nisbett, R. E., Bowdle, B. F., & Schwarz, N. (1996). Insult, aggression, and the southern culture of honor: An "experimental ethnography." *Journal of Personality and Social Psychology, 70*(5), 945–960.

Cohen, D. B. (1977). Neuroticism and dreaming sleep: A case for interactionism in personality of research. *British Journal of Social and Clinical Psychology, 16,* 153–163.

Cohen, J. (1988). *Statistical power analyses for the social sciences.* Hillsdale, NJ: Lawrence Erlbaum Associates.

Cohen, K. N., & Clark, J. A. (1984). Transitional object attachments in early childhood and personality characteristics in later life. *Personality and Social Psychology, 46,* 106–111.

Cohen, S., Doyle, W. J., Skoner, D. P., Rabin, B. S., & Gwaltney, J. M. (1997). Social ties and susceptibility to the common cold. *JAMA, 277,* 1940–1944.

Cohen, S., Frank, E., Doyle, W. J., Skoner, D. P., Rabin, B. S., & Gwaltney, J. M., Jr. (1998). Types of stressors that increase susceptibility to the common cold in healthy adults. *Health Psychology, 17,* 214.

Cohen, S., Line, S., Manuck, S. B., Rabin, B. S., Heise, E. R., & Kaplan, J. R. (1997). Chronic social stress, social status, and susceptibility to upper respiratory infections in nonhuman primates. *Psychosomatic Medicine, 59*(3), 213–221.

Cohen, S., & Wills, T. A. (1985). Stress, social support, and the buffering hypothesis. *Psychological Bulletin, 98,* 310–357.

Coifman, K. G., Bonanno, G. A., Ray, R. D., & Gross, J. J. (2007). Does repressive coping promote resilience? Affective-autonomic response discrepancy during bereavement. *Journal of Personality and Social, 92,* 745–758.

Colgan, S. M., Faragher, E. B., & Whorwell, P. J. (1988). Controlled trial of hypnotherapy in relapse prevention of duodenal ulceration. *Lancet, 11,* 1299–1300.

Collins, N. L., & Feeney, B. C. (2000). A safe haven: An attachment theory perspective on support seeking and caregiving in intimate relationships. *Journal of Personality and Social Psychology, 78*(6), 1053–1073.

Condry, J. (1977). Enemies of exploration: Self-initiated versus other-initiated learning. *Journal of Personality and Social Psychology, 35,* 459–477.

Conger, J. J. (1988). Hostages to Fortune: Youth, values and the public interest. *American Psychologist, 43,* 291–300.

Cook, J. M., Biyanova, T., Elhai, J., Schnurr, P. P., & Coyne, J. C. (2010). What do psychotherapists really do in practice? An Internet study of over 2,000 practitioners. *Psychotherapy: Theory, Research, Practice, Training, 47*(2), 260.

Cook, M., & Mineka, S. (1989). Observational conditioning of fear to fear-relevant versus fear-irrelevant stimuli in rhesus monkeys. *Journal of Abnormal Psychology, 98*(4), 448.

Cook, M., & Mineka, S. (1990). Selective associations in the observational conditioning of fear in rhesus monkeys. *Journal of Experimental Psychology: Animal Behavior Processes, 16*(4), 372.

Condon, T. J., & Allen, G. J. (1980). Role of psychoanalytic merging fantasies in systematic desensitization: A rigorous methodological examination. *Journal of Abnormal Psychology, 89,* 437–443.

Cooper, L. M. (1972). Hypnotic amnesia. In E. Fromm & R. E. Shor (Eds.), *Hypnosis: Research developments and perspectives.* Chicago, IL: Aldine-Atherton.

Cooper, R. M., & Zubek, J. P. (1958). Effects of enriched and restricted early environments on the learning ability of bright and dull rats. *Canadian Journal of Psychology, 12,* 159–164.

Cooper, W. H., & Withey, M. J. (2009). The strong situation hypothesis. *Personality and Social Psychology Review, 13*(1), 62–72.

Coopersmith, H. S. (1967). *The antecedents of self-esteem.* San Francisco, CA: Freeman.

Costa, P. T., & McCrae, R. R. (1977). Age differences in personality structures revisited: Studies in validity, stability and change. *International Journal of Aging and Human Development, 8,* 261–276.

Costa, P. T., & McCrae, R. R. (1992). *Revised NEO Personality Inventory (NEO-PI-R) and NEO Five-Factor Inventory (NEO-FFI) professional manual.* Odessa, FL: Psychological Assessment Resources, Inc.

Costa, P. T., & McCrae, R. R. (2008). The revised NEO personality inventory (NEO-PI-R). In G. J. Boyle, G. Mathews, & D. H. Saklofske, (Eds.). *The SAGE handbook of personality theory and assessment,* Vol. 2, (pp. 179–198). London, UK: Sage.

Costa, P. T., & Widiger, T. A. (1994). Introduction. In P. T. Costa & T. A. Widiger (Eds.), *Personality disorders and the five-factor model of personality* (pp. 1–12). Washington, DC: American Psychological Association.

Covert, M. V., Tangney, J. P., Maddux, J. E., & Heleno, N. M. (2003). Shame-proneness, guilt-proneness, and interpersonal problem solving: A social cognitive analysis. *Journal of Social and Clinical Psychology, 22*(1), 1–12.

Covington, M., & Omelich, C. (1979). Effort: The double-edged sword in school achievement. *Journal of Educational Psychology, 71,* 169–182.

Covington, M. V., & Beery, R. G. (1976). *Self-worth and school learning.* New York, NY: Holt.

Cowan, G., & Avants, S. K. (1988). Children's influence strategies: Structure, sex differences, and bilateral mother-child influences. *Child Development, 59,* 1303–1313.

Cowan, P. A. (1978). *Piaget: With feeling.* New York, NY: Holt, Rinehart, & Winston.

Cox, K., & McAdams, D. P. (2014). Meaning making during high and low point life story episodes predicts emotion regulation two years later: How the past informs the future. *Journal of Research in Personality, 50,* 66–70.

Craik, F. I., & Lockhart, R. S. (1972). Levels of processing: A framework for memory research. *Journal of Verbal Learning and Verbal Behavior, 11*(6), 671–684.

Cramer, P. (2000). Defense mechanisms in psychology today: Further processes for adaptation. *American Psychologist, 55*(6), 637–646.

Cramer, P., & Block, J. (1998). Preschool antecedents of defense mechanism use in young adults: A longitudinal study. *Journal of Personality and Social Psychology, 74*(1), 159–169.

Crandall, J. E. (1980). Adler's concept of social interest: Theory, measurement, and implications for adjustment. *Journal of Personality and Social Psychology, 39*, 481–495.

Crawford, C., Smith, M., & Krebs, D. (Eds.) (1987). *Sociobiology and psychology: Ideas, issues and applications.* Hillsdale, NJ: Erlbaum.

Crick, N. R., Ostrov, J. M., Burr, J. E., Cullerton-Sen, C., Jansen-Yeh, E., & Ralston, P. (2006). A longitudinal study of relational and physical aggression in preschool. *Journal of Applied Developmental Psychology, 27*(3), 254–268.

Critchfield, K. L., Levy, K. N., Clarkin, J. F., & Kernberg, O. F. (2008). The relational context of aggression in borderline personality disorder: Using adult attachment style to predict forms of hostility. *Journal of Clinical Psychology, 64*(1), 67–82.

Critelli, J. W., & Dupre, K. M. (1978). Self-disclosure and romantic attraction. *Journal of Social Psychology, 106*(l), 127–128.

Crits-Christoph, P., & Singer, J. L. (1983–84). An experimental investigation of the use of positive imagery in the treatment of phobias. *Imagination, Cognition, and Personality, 3*, 305–323.

Crocker, J., Luhtanen, R. K., Cooper, M. L., & Bouvrette, A. (2003). Contingencies of self-worth in college students: Theory and measurement. *Journal of Personality and Social Psychology, 85*(5), 894–908.

Crocker, J., & Major, B. (1989). Social stigma and self-esteem: The self-protective properties of stigma. *Psychological Review, 96*, 608–630.

Crocker, J., & Park, L. E. (2004). The costly pursuit of self-esteem. *Psychological Bulletin, 130*, 392–414.

Crocker, J., & Wolfe, C. T. (2001). Contingencies of self-worth. *Psychological Review, 108*, 593–623.

Crockett, L. J., Iturbide, M. I., Torres Stone, R. A., McGinley, M., Raffaelli, M., & Carlo, G. (2007). Acculturative stress, social support, and coping: Relations to psychological adjustment among Mexican American college students. *Cultural Diversity and Ethnic Minority Psychology, 13*, 347–355.

Cronbach, L. J. (1975). Beyond the two disciplines of scientific psychology. *American Psychologist, 30*, 116–127.

Csikszentmihalyi, M. (1990). *Flow.* New York, NY: Harper & Row.

Csikszentmihalyi, M., & LeFevre, J. (1989). Optimal experience in work and leisure. *Journal of Personality and Social Psychology, 56*, 815–822.

Cumming, E., & Henry, W. H. (1961). *Growing old.* New York, NY: Basic Books.

Cummins, D. (2005). Dominance, status, and social hierarchies. In D. M. Buss (Ed.), *The handbook of evolutionary psychology* (pp. 676–697). Hoboken, NJ: John Wiley & Sons.

Cunningham, M. R. (1988). What do you do when you're happy and blue? *Motivation and Emotion, 12*, 309–331.

Cutrona, C. E., Russell, D., & Jones, R. D. (1985). Cross-situational consistency in causal attributions: Does attributional style exist? *Journal of Personality and Social Psychology, 47*, 1043–1058.

Dabbs, J. M., & Morris, R. (1990). Testosterone, social class, and antisocial behavior in a sample of 4,462 men. *Psychological Science, 1*, 209–211.

Dahlstrom, W. G. (1969). Recurrent issues in the development of the MMPI. In J. N. Butcher (Ed.), *MMPI: Research developments and clinical applications.* New York, NY: McGraw-Hill.

Dahlstrom, W. G., & Dahlstrom, L. E. (1972). *An MMPI handbook: Clinical interpretation* (Vol. I, Rev. ed.). Minneapolis, MN: University of Minnesota Press.

Dahlstrom, W. G., & Dahlstrom, L. E. (1975). *An MMPI handbook: Research applications* (Vol. II, Rev. ed.). Minneapolis, MN: University of Minnesota Press.

Dahlstrom, W. G., & Welsh, G. S. (1960). *An MMPI handbook: A guide to use in clinical practice and research.* Minneapolis, MN: University of Minnesota Press.

Daly, M., & Wilson, M. I. (1996). Violence against stepchildren. *Current Directions in Psychological Science, 5*, 77–81.

Darwin, C. (1869). *On the origin of species by means of natural selection or the preservation of favoured races in the struggle for life.* New York, NY: Appleton.

Darwin, C. (1872; 1965). *The expression of the emotions in man and animals.* Chicago, IL: University of Chicago Press, 1965.

Darwin, C. (1873). *The descent of man, and selection in relation to sex.* New York, NY: Appleton.

Datan, N., Rodeheaver, D., & Hughes, F. (1987). Adult development and aging. *Annual Review of Psychology, 38*, 1, 53–80.

Davis, P. J., & Schwartz, G. (1987). Repression and the inaccessibility of affective memories. *Journal of Personality and Social Psychology, 52*, 155–162.

Davison, G. C. (1968). Elimination of a sadistic fantasy by a client-controlled counter-conditioning technique: A case study. *Journal of Abnormal Psychology, 73*, 84–89.

Davison, G. C. (2005). Issues and nonissues in the gay-affirmative treatment of patients who are gay, lesbian, or bisexual. *Clinical Psychology: Science and Practice, 12*(1), 25–28.

Davitz, J. (1952). The effects of previous training on post-frustration behavior. *Journal of Abnormal Social Psychology, 47*, 309–315.

De Angelis, T. (1993). Despite rise of violence by youth, solutions exist. *APA Monitor, 24*, 40.

Deary, I. J., & Brett, C. E. (2015). Predicting and retrodicting intelligence between childhood and old age in the 6-Day Sample of the Scottish Mental Survey 1947. *Intelligence, 50*, 1–9.

de Charms, R. (1968). *Personal causation.* New York, NY: Academic Press.

de Charms, R. (1972). Personal causation training in the schools. *Journal of Applied Social Psychology, 2*, 95–113.

de Charms, R. (1976). *Enhancing motivation: Change in the classroom*. New York, NY: Irvington.

de Charms, R., & Moeller, G. H. (1962). Values expressed in American children's readers: 1800–1950. *Journal of Abnormal and Social Psychology, 64*, 136–142.

Deci, E. L. (1975). *Intrinsic motivation*. New York, NY: Plenum.

Deci, E. L., & Ryan, R. M. (1985). The general causality orientations scale: Self-determination in personality. *Journal of Research in Personality, 19*(2), 109–134.

Deci, E. L., & Ryan, R. M. (2000). The "what" and "why" of goal pursuits: Human needs and the self-determination of behavior. *Psychological Inquiry, 11*(4), 227–268.

DeLongis, A., Folkman, S., & Lazarus, R. S. (1988). The impact of daily stress on health and mood: Psychological and social resources as mediators. *Journal of Personality and Social Psychology, 54*, 486–495.

Dement, W. C. (1960). The effect of dream deprivation. *Science, 131*, 1705–1707.

Dement, W. C. (1965). An essay on dreams: The role of physiology in understanding their nature. In F. Barron (Ed.), *New directions in psychology* (Vol. 2). New York, NY: Holt.

Dement, W. C., & Kleitman, N. (1957). The relation of eye movements during sleep to dream activity: An objective method for the study of dreaming. *Journal of Experimental Psychology, 53*, 339–346.

Dengerink, H. A., O'Leary, M. R., & Kasner, K. H. (1975). Individual differences in aggression responses to attack: Internal-external locus of control and field dependence-independence. *Journal of Research in Personality, 9*, 191–199.

De Pauw, S. S., & Mervielde, I. (2010). Temperament, personality and developmental psychopathology: A review based on the conceptual dimensions underlying childhood traits. *Child Psychiatry & Human Development, 41*, 313–329.

De Raad, B. (1992). The replicability of the big five personality dimensions in three word-classes of the Dutch language. *European Journal of Personality, 6*(1), 15–29.

De Raad, B. (2009). Structural models of personality. In P. J. Corr & Mathews (Eds.), *The Cambridge handbook of personality psychology*, (pp. 127–147). New York, NY: Cambridge Univesity Press.

De Raad, B., Barelds, D. P., Levert, E., Ostendorf, F., Mlačić, B., Blas, L. D., . . . & Church, A. T. (2010). Only three factors of personality description are fully replicable across languages: A comparison of 14 trait taxonomies. *Journal of Personality and Social Psychology, 98*(1), 160.

DeVore, I. (Ed.). (1965). *Primate behavior: Field studies of monkeys and apes*. New York, NY: Holt.

DiCaprio, N. S. (1974). *Personality theories: Guides to living*. Philadelphia, PA: Saunders.

DiCara, L. V. (1970). Learning in the autonomic nervous system. *Scientific American, 222*, 30–39.

Dicks-Mireaux, M. J. (1964). Extraversion-introversion in experimental psychology: Examples of experimental evidence and their theoretical implications. *Journal of Analytical Psychology, 9*, 117–128.

Digman, J. M., & Inouye, J. (1986). Further specification of the five robust factors of personality. *Journal of Personality and Social Psychology, 50*, 116–123.

Dijksterhuis, A., Preston, J., Wegner, D. M., & Aarts, H. (2008). Effects of subliminal priming of self and God on self-attribution of authorship for events. *Journal of Experimental Social Psychology, 44*(1), 2–9.

DiLalla, L. F. (2002). Behavior genetics of aggression in children: Review and future directions. *Developmental Review, 22*(4), 593–622.

Dixon, L. K., & Johnson, R. C. (1980). *The roots of individuality: A survey of human behavior genetics*. Monterey, CA: Brooks/Cole.

Dixon, N. F. (1971). *Subliminal perception: The nature of a controversy*. London, UK: McGraw-Hill.

Dodge, K. A. (1980). Social cognition and children's aggressive behavior. *Child Development, 51*, 162–170.

Dodge, K. A., & Coie, J. D. (1987). Social-information processing factors in reactive and proactive aggression in children's peer groups. *Journal of Personality and Social Psychology, 53*, 1146–1158.

Dodge, K. A., & Crick, N. R. (1990). Social information-processing bases of aggressive behavior in children. *Personality and Social Psychology Bulletin, 16*, 8–22.

Dodge, K. A., & Frame, C. L. (1982). Social cognitive biases and deficits in aggressive boys. *Child Development, 53*, 620–635.

Dodge, K. A., & Newman, J. P. (1981). Biased decision-making processes in aggressive boys. *Journal of Abnormal Psychology, 90*(4), 375–379.

Dodge, K. A., Price, J. M., Bachorowski, J. A., & Newman, J. P. (1990). Hostile attributional biases in severely aggressive adolescents. *Journal of Abnormal Psychology, 99*(4), 385–392.

Dollard, J., Doob, L. W., Miller, N. E., Mowrer, O. H., & Sears, R. R. (1939). *Frustration and aggression*. New Haven, CT: Yale University Press.

Dollard, J., & Miller, N. E. (1950). *Personality and psychotherapy*. New York, NY: McGraw-Hill.

Donnellan, M. B., Trzesniewski, K. H., Robins, R. W., Moffitt, T. E., & Caspi, A. (2005). Low self-esteem is related to aggression, antisocial behavior, and delinquency. *Psychological Science, 16*, 328–335.

Donnerstein, E. (1980). Aggressive erotica and violence toward women. *Journal of Personality and Social Psychology, 39*, 269–277.

Donnerstein, E., & Wilson, D. W. (1976). The effects of noise and perceived control upon ongoing and subsequent aggressive behavior. *Journal of Personality and Social Psychology, 34*, 774–781.

Donovan, G. H., Butry, D. T., Michael, Y. L., Prestemon, J. P., Liebhold, A. M., Gatziolis, D., & Mao, M. Y. (2013). The relationship between trees and human health: evidence from the spread of the emerald ash borer. *American journal of preventive medicine, 44*(2), 139–145.

Doob, A. N., & Wood, L. (1972). Catharsis and aggression: The effects of annoyance and retaliation on aggressive behavior. *Journal of Personality and Social Psychology, 22*, 156–162.

Dornbusch, S., Ritter, P., Liederman, P., Roberts, D., & Fraleight, M. (1987). The relation of parenting style to adolescent school performance. *Child Development, 58*, 1244–1257.

Drake, K., Belsky, J., & Fearon, R. M. (2014). From early attachment to engagement with learning in school: The role of self-regulation and persistence. *Developmental Psychology, 50*(5), 1350.

Draper, P., & Harpending, H. (1982). Father absence and reproductive strategy: An evolutionary perspective. *Journal of Anthropological Research*, 255–273.

Driscoll, R., Davis, K. E., & Lipetz, M. E. (1972). Parental interference and romantic love: The Romeo and Juliet effect. *Journal of Personality and Social Psychology, 24*, 1–10.

Dudek, S. Z., & Hall, W. B. (1991). Personality consistency: Eminent architects 25 years later. *Creativity Research Journal, 4*, 213–232.

Dulany, D. E., Jr. (1957). Avoidance learning of perceptual defense and vigilance. *Journal of Abnormal and Social Psychology, 55*, 333–338.

Dunlop, P. D., Lee, K., Ashton, M. C., Butcher, S. B., & Dykstra, A. (2015). Please accept my sincere and humble apologies: The HEXACO model of personality and the proclivity to apologize. *Personality and Individual Differences, 79*, 140–145.

Dunnette, M. D. (1976). Aptitudes, abilities, and skills. In M. D. Dunnette (Ed.), *Handbook of industrial and organizational psychology*. Chicago, IL: Rand McNally.

Dunnette, M. D., & Borman, W. C. (1979). Personnel selection and classification systems. *Annual Review of Psychology, 30*, 477–525.

Durante, K. M., Griskevicius, V., Simpson, J. A., Cantú, S. M., & Li, N. P. (2012). Ovulation leads women to perceive sexy cads as good dads. *Journal of Personality and Social Psychology, 103*, 292–305.

Dutton, D. G., & Aron, A. P. (1974). Some evidence for heightened sexual attraction under conditions of high anxiety. *Journal of Personality and Social Psychology, 30*, 510–517.

Duval, S., & Wicklund, R. A. (1972). *A theory of objective self-awareness*. New York, NY: Academic Press.

Duval, S., & Wicklund, R. A. (1973). Effects of objective self-awareness on attribution of causality. *Journal of Personality and Social Psychology, 9*, 17–31.

Dweck, C. S. (1975). The role of expectation and attribution in the alleviation of learned helplessness. *Journal of Personality and Social Psychology, 31*, 674–685.

Dweck, C. S., & Leggett, E. L. (1988). A social-cognitive approach to motivation and personality. *Psychological Review, 95*, 256–273.

Dweck, C. S. (1999). *Self-theories: Their role in motivation, personality and development*. Philadelphia, PA: Psychological Press.

Dweck, C. S. (2006). *Mindset: The new psychology of success*. New York, NY: Random House.

Eagle, M. N. (1984). *Recent developments in psychoanalysis: A critical evaluation*. New York, NY: McGraw-Hill.

Eagly, A. H., & Wood, W. (1999). The origins of sex differences in human behavior. *American Psychologist, 54*(6), 408–423.

Earley, P. C. (1989). Social loafing and collectivism: A comparison of the United States and the People's Republic of China. *Administrative Science Quarterly, 34*, 565–581.

Eaton, W. O., & Enns, L. R. (1986). Sex differences in human motor activity level. *Psychological Bulletin, 100*, 19–28.

Eaton, W. O., & Yu, A. P. (1989). Are sex differences in child motor activity level a function of sex differences in maturational status? *Child Development, 60*, 1005–1011.

Ebel, R. L. (1977). Comments on some problems of employment testing. *Personnel Psychology, 30*, 55–63.

Eckerman, C. O., & Rheingold, H. L. (1974). Infants' exploratory responses to toys and people. *Developmental Psychology, 10*, 255–259.

Edenberg, H. J., & Foroud, T. (2013). Genetics and alcoholism. *Nature Reviews Gastroenterology and Hepatology, 10*(8), 487–494.

Edmonds, G. W., Goldberg, L. R., Hampson, S. E., & Barckley, M. (2013). Personality stability from childhood to midlife: Relating teachers' assessments in elementary school to observer- and self-ratings 40 years later. *Journal of Research in Personality, 47*, 505–513.

Eckert, P. (2003). Language and adolescent peer groups. *Journal of Language and Social Psychology, 22*, 112–118.

Edenberg, H. J., & Foroud, T. (2013). Genetics and alcoholism. *Nature Reviews Gastroenterology and Hepatology, 10*(8), 487–494.

Edney, J. J. (1975). Territoriality and control: A field experiment. *Journal of Personality and Social Psychology, 31*, 1108–1115.

Edwards, A. L. (1954). *Manual for the Edwards Personal Preference Schedule*. New York, NY: Psychological Corporation.

Edwards, A. L. (1957). *The social desirability variable in personality research*. New York, NY: Dryden.

Edwards, A. L. (1959). *Edwards Personal Preference Schedule*. New York, NY: Psychological Corporation.

Edwards, A. L. (1962). The social desirability hypothesis: Theoretical implications for personality measurement. In S. Messick & J. Ross (Eds.), *Measurement in personality and cognition*. New York, NY: Wiley.

Edwards, A. L. (1964). Social desirability and performance on the MMPI. *Psychometrika, 29*, 295–308.

Egeland, J. A., Gerhard, D. S., Pauls, D. L., Sussex, J. N., Kidd, K. K., Allen, C. R., Hostetter, A. M., & Housman, D. E. (1987). Bipolar affective disorders linked to DNA markers on chromosome 11. *Nature, 325*, 783–787.

Eibl-Eibesfeldt, I. (1970). *Ethology: The biology of behavior*. New York, NY: Holt.

Eibl-Eibesfeldt, I. (1974). *Love and Hate*. New York, NY: Schocken.

Eibl-Eibesfeldt, I. (1977). Evolution of destructive aggression. *Aggressive Behavior, 3*, 127–144.

Eikeseth, S., Smith, T., Jahr, E., & Eldervik, S. (2007). Outcome for children with autism who began intensive behavioral treatment between ages 4 and 7. *Behavior Modification, 31*, 264–278.

Eisenberg, N., & Lennon, R. (1983). Sex differences in empathy and related capacities. *Psychological Bulletin, 94*, 100–131.

Eisenberg, N., Shell, R., Pasternak, J., Lennon, R., Belier, R., & Mathy, R. M. (1987). Prosocial development in middle childhood: A longitudinal study. *Developmental Psychology, 23*, 712–718.

Eisenberg, W., & Miller, P. A. (1987). The relation empathy to prosocial and related behaviors. *Psychological Bulletin, 101*, 91–119.

Eisenberg-Berg, N., & Geisheker, E. (1979). Content preachings and power of the model preacher: The effect on children's generosity. *Development Psychology, 15*, 168–175.

Eisenberger, N. I., Lieberman, M. D., & Williams, K. D. (2003). Does rejection hurt? An fMRI study of social exclusion. *Science, 302*, 290–292.

Ekman, P. (1993). Facial expression and emotion. *American Psychologist, 48*, 384–392.

Ekman, P. (2016). What scientists who study emotion agree about. *Perspectives on Psychological Science, 11*, 31–34.

Ekman, P., & Friesen, W. V. (1975). *Unmasking the face*. Englewood Cliffs, NJ: Prentice-Hall.

Ekman, P., Friesen, W. V., O'Sullivan, M., Chan, A., Tarlatzis, I. D., Heider, K., . . . & Tzavaras, A. (1987). Universals and cultural differences in the judgments of facial expressions emotion. *Journal of Personality and Social Psychology, 53*, 712–717.

Elder, G., Jr. (1986). Military times and turning points in men's lives. *Developmental Psychology, 2*, 233–245.

Elkind, D. (1970). *Children and adolescents: Interpretive essay on Jean Piaget*. New York, NY: Oxford University Press.

Elkind, D. (1979). *The child and society*. New York, NY: Oxford University Press.

Ellis, A. (1946). The validity of personality questionnaires. *Psychological Bulletin, 43*, 385–440.

Ellis, A. (1967). *Reason and emotion in psychotherapy*. New York, NY: Lyle Stuart.

Emmerich, W., Cocking, R. R., & Sigel, I. E. (1979). Relationships between cognitive and social functioning in preschool children. *Developmental Psychology, 15*, 495–504.

Emmons, R. A. (1989). The personal striving approach to personality. In L. A. Pervin (Ed.), *Goal concepts in personality and social psychology* (pp. 87–121). Hillsdale, NJ: Lawrence Erlbaum.

Emmons, R. A., & King, L. A. (1988). Conflict among personal strivings: Immediate and long-term implications for psychological and physical well-being. *Journal of Personality and Social Psychology, 5*, 1040–1048.

Endler, N. S. (1973). The person versus the situation—pseudo issue? A response to Alker. *Journal of Personality, 41*, 287–303.

Endler, N. S., & Hunt, J. (1968). S-R inventories of hostility and comparisons of the proportions of variance from persons, responses, and situations for hostility and anxiousness. *Journal of Personality and Social Psychology, 9*, 309–315.

Endler, N. S., & Magnussen, D. (1976). *Interactional psychology and personality*. Washington, DC: Hemisphere.

Entwisle, D. R. (1972). To dispel fantasies about fantasy-based measures of achievement motivation. *Psychological Bulletin, 77*, 377–391.

Epstein, L. (1976). Psychophysiological measurement in assessment. In M. Hersen & A. S. Bellack (Eds.), *Behavioral assessment*. New York, NY: Pergamon.

Epstein, S. (1973). The self-concept revisited or a theory of a theory. *American Psychologist, 28*, 405–416.

Epstein, S. (1977). Traits are alive and well. In D. Magnusson & N. S. Endler (Eds.), *Personality at the crossroads*. New York, NY: Wiley.

Epstein, S. (1979). The stability of behavior: I. On predicting most of the people much of the time. *Journal of Personality and Social Psychology, 37*, 1097–1126.

Epstein, S. (1980a). The self-concept: A review and the proposal of an integrated theory of personality. In E. Staub (Ed.), *Personality: Basic issues and current research*. Englewood Cliffs, NJ: Prentice-Hall.

Epstein, S. (1980b). The stability of behavior: II. Implications for psychological research. *American Psychologist, 35*, 790–866.

Erdelyi, M. H. (1974). A new look at the new look: Perceptual defense and vigilance. *Psychological Review, 81*, 1–25.

Erdelyi, M. H. (1992). Psychodynamics and the unconscious. *American Psychologist, 47*, 784–787.

Erdley, C. A., & Dweck, C. S. (1993). Children's implicit personality theories as predictors of their social judgments. *Child Development, 64*(3), 863–878.

Erhardt, A. A. (1987). A Transactional perspective on the development of gender differences. In J. M. Reinisch, L. A. Rosenbaum, & S. A. Sanders (Eds.), *Masculinity/femininity: Basic perspectives*. New York, NY: Oxford University Press.

Ericksen, C. W. (1958). Unconscious processes. In M. R. Jones (Ed.), *Nebraska symposium on motivation*. Lincoln, NE: University of Nebraska Press.

Ericksen, C. W. (1960). Discrimination and learning without awareness: A methodological survey and evaluation. *Psychological Review, 67*, 279–300.

Erikson, E. H. (1950). *Childhood and society*. New York, NY: Norton.

Erikson, E. H. (1958). *Young man Luther*. New York, NY: W. W. Norton.

Erikson, E. H. (1959). *Identity and the life cycle*. (Psychological Issues Monograph 1, Vol. 1, No. 1). New York, NY: International Universities Press.

Erikson, E. H. (1964). *Insight and responsibility*. New York, NY: Norton.

Erikson, E. H. (1966). The concept of identity in race relations: Notes and queries. *Daedalus, 95*, 145–171.

Erikson, E. H. (1968). *Identity: Youth and crisis*. New York, NY: Norton.

Erikson, E. H. (1969). *Gandhi's truth: On the origins of militant nonviolence*. New York, NY: W. W. Norton.

Erikson, E. H. (1976). *Toys and reasons*. New York, NY: Norton.

Eron, L. D., Walder, L. O., & Lefkowitz, M. M. (1971). *Learning of aggression in children*. Boston, MA: Little, Brown.

Escalona, S. K. (1968). *The roots of individuals: Normal patterns of development in infancy*. Chicago, IL: Aldine.

Evans, F. J., & Kihlstrom, J. F. (1973). Posthypnotic amnesia as disrupted retrieval. *Journal of Abnormal Psychology, 82*, 317–332.

Evans, R. B., & Koelseh, W. A. (1985). Psychoanalysis arrives in America. The 1909 Psychology Conference at Clark University. *American Psychologist, 40*, 942–948.

Exner, J. E. (1974). *The Rorschach: A comprehensive system*. New York, NY: Wiley.

Exner, J. E. (1976). Projective techniques. In I. B. Weiner (Ed.), *Clinical methods in psychology*. New York, NY: Wiley.

Exner, J. E. (1986). *The Rorschach: A comprehensive system. Volume 1: Basic foundations* (2nd ed.). New York, NY: Wiley.

Exner, J. E. (1991). *The Rorschach: A comprehensive system. Volume 2: Interpretation* (2nd ed.). New York, NY: Wiley.

Eysenck, H. J. (1947). *Dimensions of personality*. London, UK: Routledge.

Eysenck, H. J. (1952). *The structure of human personality*. London, UK: Methuen.

Eysenck, H. J. (1955). Cortical inhibition, figured after effect and theory of personality. *Journal of Abnormal and Social Psychology, 51*, 94–106.

Eysenck, H. J. (1967). *The biological basis of personality*. Springfield, IL: Charles C. Thomas.

Eysenck, H. J., & Eysenck, S. B. G. (1964). *The manual of the Eysenck personality inventory*. San Diego, CA: Educational and Industrial Testing Service.

Eysenck, H. J., & Rachman, S. (1965). *The causes and cures of neurosis: An introduction to modern behavior therapy based on learning theory and the principles of conditioning*. San Diego, CA: Knapp.

Fagot, B. I., & Leinbach, M. D. (1989). The young child's gender schema: Environmental input, internal organization. *Child Development, 60*(3), 663–672.

Fagot, B. I., Leinbach, M. D., & Hagan, R. (1986). Gender labeling and the adoption of sex-typed behaviors. *Developmental Psychology, 22*, 440–443.

Fairbairn, W. R. D. (1952). *Psycho-analytic studies of the personality*. New York, NY: Basic Books.

Fales, M. R., Frederick, D. A., Garcia, J. R., Gildersleeve, K. A., Haselton, M. G., & Fisher, H. E. (2016). Mating markets and bargaining hands: Mate preferences for attractiveness and resources in two national U.S. studies. *Personality and Individual Differences, 88*, 78–87.

Faraone, S. V., & Tsuang, M. T. (1985). Quantitative models of the genetic transmission of schizophrenia. *Psychological Bulletin, 98*, 41–66.

Farrell, E. W., & Dweck, C. (1985). The role of motivational processes in transfer of learning. As cited in Dweck, C. S. (1999). *Self-theories: Their role in motivation, personality and development*. Philadelphia, PA: Psychological Press.

Fearon, R. M. P., Van IJzendoorn, M. H., Fonagy, P., Bakermans-Kranenburg, M. J., Schuengel, C., & Bokhorst, C. L. (2006). In search of shared and nonshared environmental factors in security of attachment: A behavior-genetic study of the association between sensitivity and attachment security. *Developmental Psychology, 42*(6), 1026.

Feather, N. T. (1965). The relationship of expectation of success to need achievement and test anxiety. *Journal of Personality and Social Psychology, 1*, 118–126.

Feingold, A. (1988). Cognitive gender differences are disappearing. *American Psychologist, 43*, 95–103.

Feld, S. (1967). Longitudinal study of the origins of achievement strivings. *Journal of Personality and Social Psychology, 7*, 408–414.

Feningstein, A. (1987). On the nature of public and private self-consciousness. *Journal of Personality, 55*, 543–554.

Feng, J., Spence, I., & Pratt, J. (2007). Playing an action video game reduces gender differences in spatial cognition. *Psychological Science, 18*(10), 850–855.

Ferguson, T. I., & Rule, B. G. (1983). An attributional perspective on anger and aggression. In R. G. Geen & E. I. Donnerstein (Eds.), *Aggression: Theoretical and Empirical Reviews* (Vol. 1, pp. 41–74). New York, NY: Academic Press.

Feshbach, N. D. (1969). Sex differences in children's modes of aggressive responses toward outsiders. *Merrill-Palmer Quarterly, 15*, 249–258.

Feshbach, N. D. (1973). Cross-cultural studies of teaching styles in four-year-olds and their mothers. In A. D. Pick (Ed.), *Minnesota Symposia on Child Psychology: VII*. Minneapolis, MN: University of Minnesota Press.

Feshbach, N. D. (1975). The relationship of child rearing factors to children's aggression, empathy, and related positive and negative social behaviors. In J. de Wit & W. W. Hartup (Eds.), *Determinants and origins of aggressive behavior*. The Hague: Mouton.

Feshbach, N. D. (1978). Studies on empathic behavior in children. In B. A. Maher (Ed.), *Progress in experimental personality research*. New York, NY: Academic Press.

Feshbach, N. D. (1979). Empathy training: A field study in affective education. In S. Feshbach & A. Fraczek (Eds.), *Aggression and behavior change: Biological and social processes*. New York, NY: Praeger.

Feshbach, N. D., & Feshbach, S. (1969). The relationship between empathy and aggression in two age groups. *Developmental Psychology, 1*(2), 102–107.

Feshbach, N. D., & Feshbach, S. (2009). Empathy and education. In J. Decety & W. Ickes (Eds.). *The social neuroscience of empathy* (pp. 85–98). Cambridge MA: MIT Press.

Feshbach, N. D., & Roe, L. (1968). Empathy in six- and seven-year-olds. *Child Development, 39*, 133–145.

Feshbach, S. (1956). The catharsis hypothesis and some consequences of interaction with aggressive and neutral play objects. *Journal of Personality, 24*, 449–462.

Feshbach, S. (1964). The function of aggression and the regulation of aggressive drive. *Psychological Review, 71*, 257–272.

Feshbach, S. (1970). Aggression. In P. H. Mussen (Ed.), *Carmichael's manual of child psychology*. New York, NY: Wiley.

Feshbach, S. (1972). Effects of reality versus fantasy in filmed violence. In J. P. Murray, E. A. Rubinstein, & G. A. Comstock (Eds.), *Television and social behavior: Television and social learning* (Vol. II). Washington, DC: U.S. Government Printing Office.

Feshbach, S. (1974). The development and regulation of aggression: Some research gaps and a proposed cognitive approach. In W. W. Hartup & J. de Wit (Eds.), *Determinants and origins of aggressive behavior*. The Hague: Mouton.

Feshbach, S. (1978). The environment of personality. *American Psychologist, 33*, 447–455.

Feshbach, S. (1980). Child abuse and the dynamics of human aggression on violence. In G. Gerbner, E. Zigler, & C. Ross (Eds.), *Child abuse*. New York, NY: Oxford University Press.

Feshbach, S., Adelman, H., & Fuller, W. (1977). The prediction of reading and related academic problems. *Journal of Educational Psychology, 69*, 299–308.

Feshback, S., Fauvre, M., & Ballard-Campbell, M. (1983). *Learning to care*. Glenview, IL: Scott, Foresman.

Feshbach, S., & Feshbach, N. D. (1963). The influence of the stimulus object upon the complementary and supplementary projection of fear. *Journal of Abnormal and Social Psychology, 66,* 498–502.

Feshbach, S., & Singer, R. (1971). *Television and aggression.* San Francisco, CA: Jossey-Bass.

Feshbach, S., Stiles, W., & Bitter, E. (1967). The reinforcing effect of witnessing aggression. *Journal of Experimental Research in Personality, 2,* 133–139.

Festinger, L. (1957). *A theory of cognitive dissonance.* Stanford, CA: Stanford University Press.

Field, L. H., & Williams, M. (1970). The hormonal treatment of sexual offenders. *Medicine, Science, and the Law,* 27–34.

Fillenbaum, G. B. (1977). An examination of the vulnerability hypothesis. *International Journal of Aging and Human Development, 8,* 155–160.

Fineman, S. (1977). The achievement motive construct and its measurement: Where are we now? *British Journal of Psychology, 68*(1), 1–22.

Fisher, S. (1967). Projective methodologies. *Annual Review of Psychology, 18,* 165–190.

Fisher, S., & Cleveland, S. E. (1968). *Body image and personality* (Rev. ed.). New York, NY: Dover Publications.

Fisher, T. D. (2007). Sex of experimenter and social norm effects on reports of sexual behavior in young men and women. *Archives of Sexual Behavior, 36*(1), 89–100.

Fiske, S. T., & Taylor, S. E. (1984). *Social cognition.* Reading, MA: Addison-Wesley.

Flavell, J. H., Bothin, P. T., Fry, C. L., Wright, J. W., & Jarvis, P. E. (1968). *The development of role-taking and communication skills in children.* New York, NY: Wiley.

Fleeson, W. (2004). Moving personality beyond the person-situation debate: The challenge and the opportunity of within-person variability. *Current Directions in Psychological Science, 13*(2), 83–87.

Fleming, J., & Darley, J. M. (1990). The purposeful-action sequence and the "illusion of control": The effects of foreknowledge and target involvement on observers' judgments of others' control over random events. *Personality and Social Psychology Bulletin, 16,* 346–357.

Floderus-Myrhed, B., Pedersen, N., & Rasmuson, I. (1980). Assessment of heritability for personality, based on a short-form of the Eysenck Personality Inventory: A study of 12,898 twin pairs. *Behavior Genetics, 10*(2), 153–162.

Foersterling, F. (1985). Attributional retraining: A review. *Psychological Bulletin, 98,* 495–512.

Folkes, V. S. (1982). Communicating the causes of social rejection. *Journal of Experimental Social Psychology, 18,* 235–252.

Folkes, V. S. (1982). Forming relationships and the matching hypothesis. *Personality and Social Psychology Bulletin, 8,* 631–636.

Folkes, V. S. (1985). Mindlessness in social interaction, fact or fiction? *Journal of Personality and Social Psychology, 48,* 600–604.

Folkman, S., & Lazarus, R. S. (1988). Coping as a mediator of emotion. *Journal of Personality and Social Psychology, 54,* 466–475.

Folkman, S., & Lazarus, R. S., Dunkel-Schetter, C., DeLongis, A., & Gruen, R. (1986). The dynamics of a stressful encounter: Cognitive appraisal, coping, and encounter outcomes. *Journal of Personality and Social Psychology, 50,* 992–1003.

Fonagy, P., & Bateman, A. W. (2007). Mentalizing and borderline personality disorder. *Journal of Mental Health, 16*(1), 83–101.

Forgas, J. P., & Bower, G. H. (1987). Mood effects on person-perception judgments. *Journal of Personality and Social Psychology, 53,* 53–60.

Foulkes, D. (1990). Dreaming and consciousness. *European Journal of Cognitive Psychology, 2,* 39–55.

Fraley, R. C., & Roberts, B. W. (2005). Patterns of continuity: a dynamic model for conceptualizing the stability of individual differences in psychological constructs across the life course. *Psychological review, 112*(1), 60.

Fraley, R. C., Vicary, A. M., Brumbaugh, C. C., & Roisman, G. I. (2011). Patterns of stability in adult attachment: An empirical test of two models of continuity and change. *Journal of Personality and Social Psychology, 101,* 974–992.

Frank, J. D. (1935). Individual differences in certain aspects of the level of aspiration. *American Journal of Psychology, 47,* 119–128.

Frank, L. K. (1939). Projective methods for the study of personality. *Journal of Psychology, 8,* 343–389.

Frankl, V. E. (1963). *Man's search of meaning: An introduction to logotherapy* (I. Lasch, Trans.). New York, NY: Washington Square Press.

Fransella, F., & Adams, B. (1966). An illustration of the use of repertory grid technique in a clinical setting. *British Journal of Social and Clinical Psychology, 5,* 51–62.

Franz, C. E. (1994). Does thought content change as individuals age? A longitudinal study of midlife adults. In T. F. Heatherton & J. L. Weinberger (Eds.), *Can personality change* (pp. 227–250). Washington, DC: American Psychological Association.

Frazier, P. A. (1990). Victim attributions and post-rape trauma. *Journal of Personality and Social Psychology, 59*(2), 298–304.

Frazier, P. A. (1991). Self-blame as a mediator of postrape depressive symptoms. *Journal of Social and Clinical Psychology, 10,* 47–57.

Freedman, D. G. (1964). Smiling in blind infants and the issue of innate vs. acquired. *Journal of Child Psychology and Psychiatry, 5,* 171–184.

Freedman, J. L. (1975). *Crowding and behavior.* San Francisco, CA: Freeman.

Freedman, J. L. (1979). Reconciling apparent differences between the responses of humans and other animals to crowding. *Psychological Review, 86,* 80–85.

Freedman, J. L. (1984). Effect of television violence on aggressiveness, *Psychological Bulletin, 96,* 227–246.

Freedman, J. L., Levy, A. S., Buchanan, R. W., & Price, J. (1972). Crowding and human aggression. *Journal of Experimental Social Psychology, 8,* 528–548.

Freedman, J. L., Sears, D. O., & Carlsmith, J. M. (1978). *Social psychology* (2nd ed.). Englewood Cliffs, NJ: Prentice-Hall.

French, S. E., Seidman, E., Allen, L., & Aber, J. L. (2006). The development of ethnic identity during adolescence. *Developmental Psychology, 42*(1), 1–10.

Freud, A. (1946). *The ego and the mechanisms of defense*. New York, NY: International Universities Press.

Freud, A. (1958). Adolescence. *Psychoanalytic Study of the Child, 13*, 255–278.

Freud, A., & Dann, S. (1951). An experiment in group upbringing. *Psychoanalytic Study of the Child, 6*, 127–168.

Freud, S. (1911; 1959). Formulations regarding the two principles of mental functioning. In *Collected Papers* (Vol. IV). New York, NY: Basic Books.

Freud, S. (1915; 1934). *A general introduction to psychoanalysis*. New York, NY: Washington Square Press.

Freud, S. (1920; 1955). *Beyond the pleasure principle. The standard edition* (Vol. 18). London, UK: Hogarth.

Freud, S. (1925). *Collected papers*. London, UK: Hogarth.

Freud, S. (1935). *An autobiographical study* (James Strachey, Trans.). New York, NY: W. W. Norton and Co.

Freud, S. (1926; 1935). *The problem of anxiety*. New York, NY: W. W. Norton.

Freud, S. (1930; 1961). *Civilization and its discontents*. London, UK: Hogarth.

Freud, S. (1933; 1961). *New introductory lectures on psychoanalysis*. New York, NY: Norton.

Freund, A. M., & Ritter, J. O. (2009). Midlife crisis: A debate. *Gerontology, 55*(5), 582–591.

Freundl, P. C. (1977). *When is assertion aggressive?* (Unpublished doctoral dissertation). University of California, Los Angeles.

Friedman, H. S., & Booth-Kewley, S. (1988). Validity of the Type A construct: A reprise. *Psychological Bulletin, 104*, 381–384.

Frieze, I. H., & Chrisler, J. C. (2011). Editorial policy on the use of the terms "sex" and "gender." *Sex Roles, 64*(11–12), 789.

Frijda, N. H., & Swagerman, J. (1987). Can computers feel? Theory and design of an emotional system. *Cognition and Emotion, 1*, 35–258.

Frodi, A. (1977). Sexual arousal, situational restrictiveness, and aggressive behavior. *Journal of Research in Personality, 11*, 48–58.

Fromkin, H. L., Goldstein, I. H., & Brock, T. C. (1977). The role of "irrelevant" derogation in hostility catharsis: A field experiment. *Journal of Experimental Social Psychology, 13*, 239–252.

Fromm, E. (1941). *Escape from freedom*. New York, NY: Rinehart.

Fromm, E. (1955). *The sane society*. New York, NY: Rinehart.

Fromm, E. (1956). *The art of loving*. New York, NY: Harper & Row.

Fromm, E. (1964). *The heart of man*. New York, NY: Harper & Row.

Fromm, E. (1974). *Man for himself*. New York, NY: Rinehart.

Fuhrmann, B. S. (1986). *Adolescence. Adolescents*. Boston, MA: Little, Brown.

Funder, D. C. (1989). Accuracy in personality judgment and the dancing bear. In D. M. Buss & N. Cantor (Eds.), *Personality psychology: Recent trends and emerging directions* (pp. 210–223). New York, NY: Springer-Verlag.

Funder, D. C. (1991). Global traits: A neo-Allportian approach to personality. *Psychological Science, 2*, 31–39.

Funder, D. C., & Colvin, C. R. (1991). Explorations in behavioral consistency: Properties of persons, situations, and behaviors. *Journal of Personality and Social Psychology, 60*, 773–794.

Furstenberg, F. F., Jr., Brooks-Gunn, J., & Morgan, S. P. (1987). *Adolescent mothers in later life*. Cambridge, MA: Cambridge University Press.

Gabrenya, W. K., Wang, Y. E., & Latane, B. (1985). Social loafing on an optimizing task: Cross-cultural differences among Chinese and Americans. *Journal of Cross-Cultural Psychology, 16*, 223–242.

Galinsky, A. D., & Moskowitz, G. B. (2007). Further ironies of suppression: Stereotype and counter-stereotype accessibility. *Journal of Experimental Social Psychology, 43*, 833–841.

Gallagher, K. E., Lisco, C. G., Parrott, D. J., & Giancola, P. R. (2014). Effects of thought suppression on provoked men's alcohol-related physical aggression in the laboratory. *Psychology of Violence, 4*(1), 78–89.

Gallardo-Pujol, D., Andrés-Pueyo, A., & Maydeu-Olivares, A. (2013). MAOA genotype, social exclusion and aggression: An experimental test of a gene–environment interaction. *Genes, Brain and Behavior, 12*, 140–145.

Gallup, G. G., Jr. (1970). Chimpanzees: Self-recognition. *Science, 167*, 86–87.

Gallup, G. G., Jr. (1975). Towards an operational definition of self-awareness. In R. H. Tuttle (Ed.), *Socioecology and psychology of primates*. The Hague, Netherlands: Mouton.

Gallup, G. G., Jr. (1979). Self-awareness in primates. *American Scientist, 67*, 417–421.

Gallup, G. G., Jr., McClure, M. K., Hill, S. D., & Bundy, R. (1971). Capacity for self-recognition in differentially reared chimpanzees. *Psychological Record, 21*, 69–74.

Gamble, T. J., & Zigler, E. (1986). Effects of infant day care: Another look at the evidence. *American Journal of Orthopediatry, 56*, 26–41.

Gangestad, S., & Snyder, M. (1985). On the nature of self-monitoring: An examination of latent causal structure. In P. Shaker (Ed.), *Review of personality and social psychology* (Vol. 6, pp. 65–85). Beverly Hills, CA: Sage.

Gangestad, S. W., & Simpson, J. A. (1990). Toward an evolutionary history of female sociosexual variation. *Journal of Personality, 58*(1), 69–96.

Gangestad, S. W., & Snyder, M. (2000). Self-monitoring: Appraisal and reappraisal. *Psychological Bulletin, 126*, 530–555.

Gangestad, S. W., Thornhill, R., & Garver-Apgar, C. E. (2005). Adaptations to ovulation: Implications for sexual and social behavior. *Current Directions in Psychological Science, 14*(6), 312–316.

Gao, J., Wang, J., Zheng, P., Haardörfer, R., Kegler, M. C., Zhu, Y., & Fu, H. (2013). Effects of self-care, self-efficacy, social support on glycemic control in adults with type 2 diabetes. *BMC Family Practice, 14*, 1.

Garcia, J., & Koelling, R. A. (1966). Relation of cue to consequences in avoidance learning. *Psychonomic Science, 4*, 123–124.

Gardner, R. W., Holtzman, P. S., Klein, G. S., Linton, H. B., & Spence, D. P. (1959). *Cognitive control: A study of individual consistencies in cognitive behavior* (Psychological Issues Monograph 4). New York, NY: International Universities Press.

Garmezy, N. (1978). Current status of a sample of other high-risk research programs. In L. C. Wyne, R. C. Cromwell, & S. Mattlynke (Eds.), *The nature of schizophrenia:*

New approaches to research and treatment. New York, NY: Wiley.

Gay, P. (1988). *Freud. A life for our time.* New York, NY: W. W. Norton and Co.

Gaylord-Ross, R. J., Haring, T. G., Brun, C., & Pitts-Conway, V. (1984). The training and generalization of social interaction skills with autistic youths. *Journal of Applied Behavior Analysis, 17,* 229–247.

Gazzaniga, M. S. (1970). *The bisected brain.* New York, NY: Appleton-Century-Crofts.

Gazzaniga, M. S., & LeDoux, J. R. (1978). *The integrated mind.* New York, NY: Plenum.

Geisler, C. (1986). The use of subliminal psychodynamic activation in the study of regression. *Journal of Personality and Social Psychology, 5,* 844–851.

George, A. L., & George, J. L. (1964). *Woodrow Wilson and Colonel House: A personality, study.* New York, NY: Dover.

Gerardo, C. J., & Bohan, J. B. (1909–1921; 1971). Development of a sense of self-identity in children. *Child Development, 42*(6), 1909–1921.

Gerbner, G., Ross, C. J., & Zigler, E. (1980). *Child abuse: An agenda for action.* New York, NY: Oxford University Press.

Gershoff, E. T. (2002). Corporal punishment by parents and associated child behaviors and experiences: A meta-analytic and theoretical review. *Psychological Bulletin, 128*(4), 539–579.

Gershoff, E. T. (2013). Spanking and child development: We know enough now to stop hitting our children. *Child Development Perspectives, 7,* 133–137.

Gerwirtz, J. L. (1961). A learning analysis of the effects of normal stimulation, privation, and deprivation on the acquisition of social motivation and attachment. In B. M. Foss (Ed.), *Determinants of infant behavior* (Vol. 1). New York, NY: Wiley.

Gewirtz, J. L. (1972). *Attachment and dependency.* Washington, DC: V. H. Winston and Sons.

Gewirtz, J. L., & Boyd, E. F. (1977). Experiments on mother-infant interaction underlying mutual attachment acquisition: The infant conditions the mother. In *Attachment behavior* (pp. 109–143). New York, NY: Springer US.

Giancola, P. R. (2004). Executive functioning and alcohol-related aggression. *Journal of Abnormal Psychology, 113*(4), 541–555.

Gibbon, F. X. (1986). Social comparison and depression: Company's effect on misery. *Journal of Personality and Social Psychology, 51,* 140–148.

Gil, D. G. (1970). *Violence against children: Physical child abuse in the United States.* Cambridge, MA: Harvard University Press.

Gilbert, D. (2015). *The American class structure in an age of growing inequality.* Newbury Park, CA: Sage.

Gilbert, D. T. (1989). Thinking lightly about others: Automatic components of the social inference process. In J. S. Uleman & J. A. Bargh (Eds.), *Unintended thought* (pp. 189–211). New York, NY: Guilford.

Gilbert, D. T., Pelham, B. W., & Krull, D. S. (1988). On cognitive busyness: When person perceivers meet persons perceived. *Journal of Personality and Social Psychology, 54,* 733–740.

Gildersleeve, K., Haselton, M. G., & Fales, M. R. (2014). Do women's mate preferences change across the ovulatory cycle? A meta-analytic review. *Psychological Bulletin, 140,* 1205–1259.

Gilligan, C. (1982). *In a different voice: Psychological theory and women's development.* Cambridge, MA: Harvard University Press.

Gilligan, C., Brown, L., & Rogers, A. (1990). Psyche embedded: A place for body, relationships, and culture in personality theory. In A. I. Rabin, R. A. Zucker, R. A. Emmons, & S. Frank (Eds.), *Studying persons and lives* (pp. 86–147). New York, NY: Springer.

Ginsberg, H. J., & Miller, S. M. (1982). Sex differences in children's risk-taking behavior. *Child Development, 53,* 426–428.

Glass, D. C., & Singer, J. E. (1972). *Urban stress.* New York, NY: Academic Press.

Gleason, J. B. (1973). Code switching in children's language. In T. E. Moore (Ed.), *Cognitive development and the acquisition of language.* New York, NY: Academic Press.

Goffman, E. (1961). *Asylums.* Garden City, NY: Doubleday.

Goldberg, S. (2000). *Attachment and development.* London, UK: Arnold.

Goldfarb, W. (1945). Psychological privation in infancy and subsequent adjustment. *American Journal of Orthopsychiatry, 15,* 247–255.

Goldfried, M. R. (1976). Behavioral assessment. In I. B. Weiner (Ed.), *Clinical methods in psychology.* New York, NY: Interscience-Wiley.

Goldsmith, H. H., Buss, K. A., & Lemery, K. S. (1997). Toddler and childhood temperament: Expanded content, stronger genetic evidence, new evidence for the importance of environment. *Developmental Psychology, 33,* 891–905.

Goldstein, A. P. (1982). Problem-solving training. In A. P. Goldstein, E. G. Cart, W. S. Davidson II, & P. Weber (Eds.), *In response to aggression: Methods of control and personal alternatives.* Elmford, NY: Pergamon Press.

Goldstein, A. P., & Michaels, G. Y. (1985). *Empathy: Developmental training and consequences.* Hillsdale, NJ: Erlbaum.

Goodall, J. (1986). *The chimpanzees of Gambe: Patterns of behavior.* Cambridge, MA: Harvard University Press.

Goodwin, D. W., Schulsinger, F., Hermansen, L., Guze, S. B., & Winokur, G. (1973). Alcohol problems in adoptees raised apart from alcoholic biological parents. *Archives of General Psychiatry, 28,* 238–243.

Gottesman, I. I. (1993). Origins of schizophrenia: Past as prologue. In R. Plomin & G. E. McClearn (Eds.), *Nature, nurture and psychology* (pp. 231–244). Washington, DC: American Psychological Association.

Gottesman, I. I., & Shields, J. (1966). Contributions of twin studies to perspectives on schizophrenia. In B. Maher (Ed.), *Progress in experimental personality research* (Vol. 3). New York, NY: Academic Press.

Gottesman, I. I., & Shields, J. (1972). *Schizophrenia and genetics: A twin study vantage point.* New York, NY: Academic Press.

Gottman, J. M. (1979). *Marital interaction: Experimental investigations.* New York, NY: Academic Press.

Gough, H. G. (1960). The Adjective Checklist as a personality assessment research technique. *Psychological Reports, 6,* 107–122.

Gough, H. G. (1965). Conceptual analysis of psychological test scores and other diagnostic variables. *Journal of Abnormal Psychology, 70*, 294–302.

Gould, K. L. (1972). The phases of adult life: A study in developmental psychology. *American Journal of Psychiatry, 129*, 521–531.

Gould, K. L. (1978). *Transformation.* New York, NY: Simon and Schuster.

Gould, R. (1975). Adult life stages: Growth toward self-tolerance. *Psychology Today, 8*, 74–78.

Graham, J. R. (1977). *The MMPI: A practical guide.* New York, NY: Oxford University Press.

Graham, S. (1984). Communicated sympathy and anger to black and white children: The cognitive (attributional) consequences of affective cues. *Journal of Personality and Social Psychology, 47*, 4054.

Granick, S., & Patterson, R. D. (1972). *Human aging. II: An eleven-year follow-up biomedical and behavioral study.* Bethesda, MD: U.S. Public Health Service.

Gray, H., & Wheelwright, J. (1964). Jung's psychological types, their frequency and occurrence. *Journal of General Psychology, 34*, 3–17.

Gray, J. A. (1981). A critique of Eysenck's theory of personality. In *A Model for Personality* (pp. 246–276). Berlin–Heidelberg, Germany: Springer.

Gray, J. R., & Burgess, G. C. (2004). Personality differences in cognitive control? BAS, processing efficiency, and the prefrontal cortex. *Journal of Research in Personality, 38*(1), 35–36.

Gray, L., Miller, L. W., Philipp, B. L., & Blass, E. M. (2002). Breastfeeding is analgesic in healthy newborns. *Pediatrics, 109*, 590–593.

Gray, L., Watt, L., & Blass, E. M. (2000). Skin-to-skin contact is analgesic in healthy newborns. *Pediatrics, 105*, e14.

Greenberg, L. S., & Safran, J. D. (1987). *Emotion in psychotherapy.* New York, NY: Guilford

Greenberg, L. S., Rice, L. N., & Elliott, R. (1993). *Facilitating emotional change: The moment-by-moment process.* New York, NY: Guilford.

Greenspoon, J. (1962). Verbal conditioning and clinical psychology. In A. J. Bachrach (Ed.), *Experimental foundations of clinical psychology.* New York, NY: Basic Books.

Greenwald, A. G. (1992). New look 3: Unconscious cognition reclaimed. *American Psychologist, 47*, 766–779.

Griffin, D. W., & Bartholomew, K. (1994). Models of the self and other: Fundamental dimensions underlying measures of adult attachment. *Journal of Personality and Social Psychology, 67*(3), 430.

Grosskurth, P. (1986). *Melanie Klein: Her world and her work.* New York, NY: Alfred A. Knopf.

Grotevant, H. D., & Adams, G. R. (1984). Development of an object measure to assess ego identity in adolescence: Validation and replication. *Journal of Youth and Adolescence, 13*, 419–438.

Guardo, C. J., & Bohan, J. B. (1909–1921). Development of a sense of self-identity in children. *Child Development, 1971, 42.*

Guilford, J. P. (1940). *An inventory of factors STDCR.* Beverly Hills, CA: Sheridan Supply.

Guilford, J. P., & Martin, H. G. (1943). *The Guilford-Martin inventory of factors GAMIN: Manual of directions and norms.* Beverly Hills, CA: Sheridan Supply.

Guilford, J. P., & Zimmerman, W. S. (1956). Fourteen dimensions of temperament. *Psychological Monographs, 70* (No. 10).

Gur, R. C., & Sackheim, H. A. (1979). Self-deception: A concept in search of a phenomenon. *Journal of Personality and Social Psychology, 37*, 147–169.

Guttman, D. (1977). The cross-cultural perspective: Notes toward a comparative psychology of aging. In J. E. Birren & K. W. Schaie (Eds.), *Handbook of the psychology of aging.* Princeton, NJ: Van Nostrand.

Hahlweg, K., & Markman, H. J. (1988). Effectiveness of behavioral marital therapy. Empirical status of behavioral techniques in preventing and alleviating marital distress. *Journal of Consulting and Clinical Psychology, 56*, 440–447.

Haley, G. A. (1974). Eye movement responses of repressors and sensitizers to a stressful film. *Journal of Research in Personality, 8*, 88–94.

Halfall, S. E., & Lieberman, J. R. (1987). Personality and social resources in immediate and continued stress resistance among women. *Journal of Personality and Psychology, 52*, 18–26.

Hall, C. S., & Lindzey, G. (1970). *Theories of personality* (2nd ed.). New York, NY: Wiley.

Hall, W. B., & MacKinnon, D. W. (1969). Personality inventories as predictors of creativity among architects. *Journal of Applied Psychology, 53*, 322–326.

Hamachek, D. E. (1976). Development of dynamics of the self. In James F. Adams (Ed.), *Understanding adolescence: Current developments in adolescent psychology.* Boston, MA: Allyn and Bacon.

Hamer, D., & Sirota, L. (2000). Beware the chopsticks gene. *Molecular Psychiatry, 5*, 11–13.

Hamilton, J. C., Greenberg, J., Pyszczynski, T., & Cather, C. (1993). A self-regulatory perspective on psychopathology and psychotherapy. *Journal of Psychotherapy Integration, 3*, 205–249.

Hammock, T., & Brehm, J. W. (1966). The attractiveness of choice alternatives when freedom to choose is eliminated by a social agent. *Journal of Personality, 34*, 546–554.

Hammond, D. C. (Ed.). (1990). *Handbook of hypnotic suggestions and metaphors.* New York, NY: Norton.

Hampson, J. L. (1965). Determinants of psychosexual orientation. In F. A. Beach (Ed.), *Sex and behavior.* New York, NY: Wiley.

Haran, H., & Kaplan, R. M. (1977). *Psychology: Personal and social adjustment.* New York, NY: Harper & Row.

Hare, B., Melis, A. P., Woods, V., Hastings, S., & Wrangham, R. (2007). Tolerance allows bonobos to outperform chimpanzees on a cooperative task. *Current Biology, 17*, 619–623.

Harlow, H. F. (1953). Motivation as a factor in the acquisition of new responses. In M. R. Jones (Ed.), *Nebraska symposium on motivation.* Lincoln, NE: University of Nebraska Press.

Harlow, H. F. (1958). The nature of love. *American Psychologist, 13*, 673–685.

Harlow, H. F. (1971). *Learning to love.* San Francisco, CA: Albion.

Harlow, H. F., & Suomi, S. J. (1971). Social recovery by isolation-reared monkeys. *Proceedings of the National Academy of Sciences, 68,* 1534–1558.

Harman, H. H. (1967). *Modern factor analysis* (2nd ed.). Chicago, IL: University of Chicago Press.

Harris, M. A., Brett, C. E., Johnson, W., & Deary, I. J. (2016). Personality stability from age 14 to age 77 years. *Psychology and Aging, 31*(8), 862–874.

Harris, M. B. (1974). Mediators between frustration and aggression in a field experiment. *Journal of Experimental Social Psychology, 10,* 561–571.

Harris, R. L., Ellicott, A. M., & Holmes, D. S. (1986). The timing of psychosocial transitions and changes in women's lives: An examination of women aged 45 to 60. *Journal of Personality and Social Psychology, 51,* 409–416.

Hart, S. A., Petrill, S. A., Deckard, K. D., & Thompson, L. A. (2007). SES and CHAOS as environmental mediators of cognitive ability: A longitudinal genetic analysis. *Intelligence, 35,* 233–242.

Harter, S. (1982). The perceived competence scale for children. *Child Development, 53,* 87–97.

Harter, S. (1983a). Developmental perspectives on the self-system. In P. H. Mussen (Ed.), *Handbook of child psychology*; E. M. Hetherington (Ed.), *Volume IV: Socialization, personality, and social development.* New York, NY: Wiley.

Harter, S. (1983b). Developmental perspectives on the self system. In P. H. Mussen (Ed.), *Revised Carmichael manual of child development* (Vol. IV). New York, NY: Harper.

Harter, S. (1990). Processes underlying adolescent self-concept formation. In R. Montemayor, G. R. Adams, & T. P. Gullotta (Eds.), *From childhood to adolescence* (pp. 205–239). Newbury Park, CA: Sage.

Hartmann, D. P. (1977). Considerations in the choice of interobserver reliability estimates. *Journal of Applied Behavioral Analysis, 10,* 103–116.

Hartmann, E. (1965). The D-State: A review and discussion of studies on the physiological state concomitant with dreaming. *New England Journal of Medicine, 273,* 30–35.

Hartmann, H. (1958). *Ego psychology and the problem of adaptation.* New York, NY: International Universities Press.

Hartmann, H. (1964). *Essays on ego psychology: Selected problems in psychoanalytic theory.* New York, NY: International Universities Press.

Hartmann, H., Kris, E., & Loewenstein, R. M. (1946). Comments on the formation of psychic structure. *Psychoanalytic study of the child,* 11–18.

Hartnagel, T. F., Teevan, J. J., & McIntyre, J. J. (1979). Television violence and violent behavior. *Social Forces, 54,* 341–351.

Hartshorne, H., & May, M. A. (1928). *Studies in the nature of character. Vol. 1. Studies in deceit.* New York, NY: Macmillan.

Hartshorne, H., May, M. A., & Mailer, J. B. (1929). *Studies in service and self control.* New York, NY: Macmillan.

Hartshorne, H., May, M. A., & Shuttleworth, F. H. (1930). *Studies in the nature of character. Vol. 3. Studies in the organization of character.* New York, NY: Macmillan.

Harvey, J. H., Orbuch, T. L., Chwalisz, K. D., & Garwood, G. (1991). Coping with sexual assault: The roles of account-making and confiding. *Journal of Traumatic Stress, 4,* 515–531.

Harvey, J. H., Orbuch, T. L., & Weber, A. L. (August 1993). *Restoring identity and control by account-making after major trauma.* Paper presented as part of a symposium on "Narrative Self-Interpretation," American Psychological Association Convention, Toronto, Canada.

Hatfield, E. (1983). What do women and men want from love and sex? In E. R. Allgeier & N. B. McCormick (Eds.), *Changing boundaries: Gender roles and sexual behavior.* Palo Alto, CA: Mayfield.

Hatfield, E. (1988). Passionate and compassionate love. In R. J. Sternberg & M. L. Barma (Eds.), *The psychology of love.* New Haven: Yale University Press.

Hatfield, E. C., Pillemer, J. T., O'Brien, M. U., & Le, Y. C. L. (2008). The endurance of love: Passionate and companionate love in newlywed and long-term marriages. *Interpersona, 2*(1), 35–64.

Hatfield, E., & Sprecher, S. (1986). Measuring passionate love in intimate love. *Journal of Adolescence, 9,* 383–410.

Hatfield, E., & Walster, G. W. (1981). *A new look at love.* Reading, MA: Addison-Wesley.

Hauser, S. T., & Kasendorf, E. (1983). *Black and white identity formation.* Malabar, Florida: Robert E. Krieger Publishing Co.

Havighurst, R. J., Neugarten, B. L., & Tobin, S. S. (1968). Disengagement and patterns of aging. In B. L. Neugarten (Ed.), *Middle age and aging.* Chicago, IL: University of Chicago Press.

Hawkins, R. P., Peterson, R. F., Schweid, E., & Bijou, S. W. (1966). Behavior therapy in the home: Amelioration of parent-child relations with the parent in a therapeutic role. *Journal of Experimental Child Psychology, 4,* 99–107.

Hay, D. F. (1979). Cooperative interactions and sharing between very young children and their parents. *Developmental Psychology, 15,* 647–653.

Hayes, A. F. (1995). Age preferences for same- and opposite-sex partners. *Journal of social psychology, 135,* 125–133.

Haynes, S. N., Richard, D. C. S., & Kubany, E. S. (1995). Content validity in psychological assessment: A functional approach to concepts and methods. *Psychological Assessment, 7,* 238–247.

Hazan, C., & Shaver, P. (1987). Romantic love conceptualized as an attachment process. *Journal of Personality and Social Psychology, 52,* 511–524.

Healey, M. D., & Ellis, B. J. (2007). Birth order, conscientiousness, and openness to experience: Tests of the family-niche model of personality using a within-family methodology. *Evolution and Human Behavior, 28,* 55–59.

Heatherton, T. F., & Nichols, P. A. (1994). Conceptual issues in assessing whether personality can change. In T. F. Heatherton & J. L. Weinberger (Eds.), *Can personality change?* (pp. 3–18). Washington, DC: American Psychological Association.

Heckhausen, H., & Roelofsen, I. (1962). Anfange und Entwicklung der Leistungsmotivation: (I) Im Wetteifer des Kleinkindes. *Psychologisches Forschungen, 26,* 313–397.

Heckhausen, J., Dixon, R. A., & Baltes, P. B. (1989). Gains and losses in development throughout adulthood as perceived by different adult age groups. *Developmental Psychology*, *25*, 109–121.

Heider, F. (1944). Social perception and phenomenal causation. *Psychological Review*, *51*, 358–374.

Heider, F. (1958). *The psychology of interpersonal relations*. New York, NY: Wiley.

Heimberg, R. G. (1989). *Cognitive and behavioral treatments for social phobia: A critical analysis*, *9*, 187–188.

Heller, K., Davis, J. D., & Myers, R. A. (1966). The effects of interviewer style in a standardized interview. *Journal of Consulting Psychology*, *30*, 501–508.

Helmreich, R., & Stapp, J. (1974). Short forms of the Texas social behavior inventory (TSBI), an objective measure of self-esteem. *Bulletin of the Psychonomic Society*, *4*, 473–475.

Helmreich, R. L., & Spence, J. T. (1978). The work and family orientation questionnaire: An objective instrument to assess components of achievement motivation and attitudes toward family and career. *JSAS Catalog of Selected Documents in Psychology*, *8*, 35.

Helson, R. (1982). Critics and their texts: An approach to Jung's theory of cognition and personality. *Journal of Personality and Social Psychology*, *43*, 409–418.

Helson, R. (1993). Comparing longitudinal studies of adult development: Toward a paradigm of tension between stability and change. In D. C. Funder, R. D. Parke, C. Tomlinson-Keasey, & K. Widaman (Eds.), *Studying lives through time* (pp. 93–120). Washington, DC: American Psychological Association.

Helson, R., Mitchell, V., & Moane, G. (1984). Personality and patterns of adherence and nonadherence to the social clock. *Journal of Personality and Social Psychology*, *46*, 1079–1096.

Helson, R., & Stewart, A. (1994). Personality change in adulthood. In T. F. Heatherton & J. Weinberger (Eds.), *Can personality change?* (pp. 201–226). Washington, DC: American Psychological Association.

Henderson, N. D. (1982). Human behavior genetics. *Annual Review of Psychology*, *33*, 403–440.

Hendrick, C. (Ed.) (1989). *Close relationships: Review of personality and social psychology*, *10*. Newbury Park, CA: Sage.

Hendrick, C., & Hendrick, S. S. (1990). A relationship-specific version of the Love Attitudes Scale. *Journal of Social Behavior and Personality*, *5*(4), 239–248.

Henrich, J., & Gil-White, F. J. (2001). The evolution of prestige: Freely conferred deference as a mechanism for enhancing the benefits of cultural transmission. *Evolution and human behavior*, *22*, 165–196.

Hepworth, J. T., & West, S. G. (1988). Lynchings and the economy: A time-series reanalysis of Hovland and Sears (1940). *Journal of Personality and Social Psychology*, *55*, 239–247.

Herbert, J. (1970). Hormones and reproductive behaviors in Rhesus and Talapoin monkeys. *Journal of Reproduction and Fertility* (supplement), *11*, 119–140.

Hermans, H. J. M. (1987). The dream in the process of valuation: A method of interpretation. *Journal of Personality and Social Psychology*, *53*, 163–175.

Hess, E. H. (1965). Attitude and pupil size. *Scientific American*, *212*, 46–54.

Hicks, D. J. (1968). Effects of co-observer's sanctions and adult presence on imitative aggression. *Child Development*, *39*, 303–309.

Hicks, L. H., & Birren, J. E. (1970). Aging, brain damage, and psychomotor slowing. *Psychological Bulletin*, *74*, 377–396.

Higgins, E. T. (1987). Self-discrepancy: A theory relating self and affect. *Psychological Review*, *94*, 319–340.

Higgins, E. T. (1989). Knowledge accessibility and activation: Subjectivity and suffering from unconscious sources. In J. S. Uleman & J. A. Bargh (Eds.), *Unintended thought* (pp. 75–123). New York, NY: Guilford.

Higgins, E. T., Strauman, T., & Klein, R. (1986). Standards and the process of self-evaluation. In R. M. Sorrentino, & E. T. Higgins (Eds.), *Handbook of motivation and cognition* (pp. 23–63). New York, NY: Guilford Press.

Hilgard, E. R. (1949). Human motives and the concept of the self. *American Psychologist*, *4*, 374–382.

Hilgard, E. R. (1973). A neodissociation interpretation of pain reduction in hypnosis. *Psychological Review*, *80*, 396–411.

Hilgard, E. R., Atkinson, R. C., & Atkinson, R. L. (1975). *Introduction to psychology* (6th ed.). New York, NY: Harcourt, Brace, Jovanovich.

Hilgard, J. R. (1970). *Personality and hypnosis*. Chicago, IL: University of Chicago Press.

Hinde, R. A. (1960). Energy models of motivation. *Symposium of the Society of Experimental Biology*, *14*, 199–213.

Hineline, P. N. (1980). The language of behavior analysis: Its community, its functions, and its limitations. *Behaviorism*, *8*, 67–86.

Hirai, T. (1974). *Psychophysiology of Zen*. Tokyo, Japan: Igaku Shoin.

Hiroto, D. S., & Seligman, M. E. P. (1975). Generality of learned helplessness in man. *Journal of Personality of Social Psychology*, *31*, 311–327.

Hoare, C. H. (1990). Psychosocial identity development and cultural others. *Journal of Counseling and Development*, *70*, 45–53.

Hobfoll, S. E., & Lieberman, J. R. (1987). Personality and social resources in immediate and continued stress resistance among women. *Journal of Personality and Social Psychology*, *52*, 18–26.

Hochchild, A. (1983). *The managed heart: The commercialization of human feeling*. Berkeley, CA: University of California Press.

Hoeve, M., Dubas, J. S., Eichelsheim, V. I., Van Der Laan, P. H., Smeenk, W., & Gerris, J. R. (2009). The relationship between parenting and delinquency: A meta-analysis. *Journal of Abnormal Child Psychology*, *37*(6), 749–775.

Hoffman, M. L. (1970). Conscience, personality, and socialization techniques. *Human Development*, *13*, 90–126.

Hoffman, M. L. (1975). Altruistic behavior and the parent-child relationship. *Journal of Personality and Social Psychology*, *31*, 937–943.

Hoffman, M. L. (1975). Developmental synthesis of affect and cognition and its implications for altruistic motivation. *Developmental psychology*, *11*(5), 607.

Hoffman, M. L. (2000). *Empathy and moral development: Implications for caring and justice*. Cambridge, MA: Cambridge University Press.

Hofmann, S. G., Asnaani, A., Vonk, I. J., Sawyer, A. T., & Fang, A. (2012). The efficacy of cognitive behavioral therapy: A review of meta-analyses. *Cognitive Therapy and Research, 36*, 427–440.

Hofstader, D. (1979). *Godel, Escher, & Bach*. New York, NY: Vintage.

Hofstee, W. K., Kiers, H. A., De Raad, B., Goldberg, L. R., & Ostendorf, F. (1997). A comparison of Big-Five structures of personality traits in Dutch, English, and German. *European Journal of Personality, 11*(1), 15–31.

Hogan, R. (1976). *Personality theory*. Englewood Cliffs, NJ: Prentice-Hall.

Hogan, R., DeSoto, C. B., & Solano, C. (1977). Traits, tests, and personality research. *American Psychologist, 32,* 255–264.

Hogan, R., & Hogan, J. (1992). *Hogan Personality Inventory manual*. Tulsa, OK: Hogan Assessment Systems.

Hokanson, J. E., & Burgess, M. (1962). The effects of three types of aggression on vascular processes. *Journal of Abnormal and Social Psychology, 64*, 446–449.

Hollingworth, H. L. (1920). *Psychology of the functional neurotic*. New York, NY: Appleton-Century.

Holmes, T. H., & Rahe, R. H. (1967). The social readjustment rating scale. *Journal of Psychosomatic Research, 11,* 213–218.

Holt, E. B. (1931). *Animal drive and the learning process, an essay toward radical empiricism* (Vol. 1). New York, NY: Holt.

Holzman, D. C. (2010). What's in a color? The unique human health effects of blue light. *Environmental Health Perspectives, 118*(1), A22.

Hong, K. (1978). The transitional phenomena: A theoretical integration. *Psychoanalytic Study of the Child, 33*, 47–79.

Horney, K. (1937). *Neurotic personality of our times*. New York, NY: Norton.

Horney, K. (1945). *Our inner conflicts*. New York, NY: Norton.

Horowitz, M. J. (1988). *Introduction to psychodynamics*. New York, NY: Basic Books.

Horrocks, J. E. (1969). *The psychology of adolescence*. Boston, MA: Houghton Muffin.

Horrocks, J. E. (1976). Development and dynamics of the self. In J. F. Adams (Ed.), *Understanding adolescence*. Boston, MA: Allyn and Bacon.

Hottes, T. S., Bogaert, L., Rhodes, A. E., Brennan, D. J., & Gesink, D. (2016). Lifetime prevalence of suicide attempts among sexual minority adults by study sampling strategies: A systematic review and meta-analysis. *American Journal of Public Health, 106*(5), e1–e12.

Hough, R. L., McGarvey, W., Graham, J., & Timbers, D. (1985). Cultural variations in the modeling of life change–illness relationships. Unpublished 1982 manuscript cited in Cervantes, R. C., & Castro, F. G. (1985) Stress, coping, and Mexican American Mental Health: A systematic review. *Hispanic Journal of Behavioral Sciences, 7*, 1–73.

House, J. S., Landis, K. R., & Umberson, D. (1988). Social relationships and health. *Science, 241*(4865), 540–545.

Houston, B. K. (1988). Cardiovascular and neuroendocrine reactivity, global Type A and components of Type A behavior. In B. K. Houston & C. R. Snyder (Eds.), *Type A behavior pattern: Research, theory, and intervention* (pp. 212–253). New York, NY: Wiley.

Howard, A., & Bray, D. (1988). *Managerial lives in transition: Advancing age and changing times*. New York, NY: Guilford.

Howard, G. S. (1991). Culture tales: A narrative approach to thinking, cross-cultural psychology, and psychotherapy. *American Psychologist, 46*, 187–197.

Howe, D. (2011). *Attachment across the lifecourse: A brief introduction*. New York, NY: Palgrave Macmillan.

Howes, D. H., & Solomon, R. L. (1951). Visual duration threshold as a function of word-probability. *Journal of Experimental Psychology, 41*, 401–410.

Huesmann, L. R., & Eron, L. D. (1986). *Television and the aggressive child: A cross-national comparison*. Hillsdale, NJ: Erlbaum.

Huesmann, L. R., Eron, L. D., Lefkowitz, M. M., & Walder, L. O. (1984). The stability of aggression over time and generations. *Developmental Psychology, 20*, 1120–1134.

Huesmann, L. R., Lagerspetz, K., & Eron, L. D. (1983). Intervening variables in the television violence-aggression relation: Evidence from the two countries. *Developmental Psychology, 19*, 71–77.

Hull, C. L. (1943). *Principles of behavior*. New York, NY: Appleton-Century-Crofts.

Hull, C. L. (1951). *Essentials of behavior*. New Haven, CT: Yale University Press.

Hull, C. L. (1952). *A behavior system: An introduction to behavior theory concerning the individual organism*. New Haven, CT: Yale University Press.

Hull, J. G., & VanTreuren, R. R. (1986). Experimental social psychology, and the causes and effects of alcohol consumption. In H. D. Cappell (Ed.), *Research advances in alcohol and drug problems*. New York, NY: Plenum Press.

Hull, J. G., VanTreuren, R. R., & Vernelli, S. (1987). Hardiness and health: A critique and alternative approach. *Journal of Personality and Social Psychology, 53*, 518–530.

Hunter, E. J. (1976). The prisoner of war: Coping with the stress of isolation. In R. H. Moos (Ed.), *Human adaptation: Coping with life crises*. Lexington, MA: Heath.

Huntingford, F. A. (1987). Animals fight, but do not make war. In J. Groebel & R. A. Hinde (Eds.), *Aggression and war*. Cambridge, MA: Cambridge University Press.

Huppertz, C., Bartels, M., de Zeeuw, E. L., van Beijsterveldt, C. E., Hudziak, J. J., Willemsen, G., . . . & de Geus, E. J. (2016). Individual differences in exercise behavior: Stability and change in genetic and environmental determinants from age 7 to 18. *Behavior Genetics, 46*(5), 665–679.

Huston, A. C. (1983). Sex-typing. In P. H. Mussen (Ed.), *Handbook of child psychology;* E. M. Hetherington (Ed.), *Volume IV: Socialization, personality, and social development*. New York, NY: John Wiley & Sons.

Hutchings, B., & Mednick, S. A. (1977). Criminality in adoptees and their adoptive and biological parents: A pilot study. In S. Mednick & K. O. Christiansen (Eds.), *Biosocial bases of criminal behavior*. New York, NY: Gardner.

Huxley, A. (1954). *The doors of perception*. New York, NY: Harper & Row.

Hyde, J. S. (1984). How large are sex differences in aggression? A developmental meta-analysis. *Developmental Psychology, 20*, 722–736.

Hyde, J. S. (2014). Gender similarities and differences. *Annual Review of Psychology, 65,* 373–398.

Hyde, J. S., Lindberg, S. M., Linn, M. C., Ellis, A. B., & Williams, C. C. (2008). Gender similarities characterize math performance. *Science, 321*(5888), 494–495.

Hyde, J. S., & Linn, M. C. (1988). Gender differences in verbal ability: A meta-analysis. *Psychological Bulletin, 104,* 53–69.

Hyde, J. S., Fennema, E., & Lamon, S. J. (1990). Gender differences in mathematics performance: A meta-analysis. *Psychological Bulletin, 107,* 139–155.

Inkeles, A. (1968). Society, social structure, and child socialization. In J. A. Clausen (Ed.), *Socialization and society.* Boston, MA: Little, Brown.

Inkeles, A., & Rossi, P. H. (1966). National comparisons of occupational prestige. *American Journal of Sociology, 61,* 329–339.

Isabella, R. A., Belsky, J., & von Eye, A. (1989). Origin of infant-mother attachment: An examination of interactional synchrony during the infant's first year. *Developmental Psychology, 25,* 12–21.

Isen, A. M., Nygren, T. E., & Ashby, F. G. (1988). Influence of positive affect on the subjective utility of gains and losses: It is just not worth the risk. *Journal of Personality and Social Psychology, 55,* 710–717.

Ittelson, W. H., Proshansky, H. M., Rivlin, L. G., & Winkel, G. H. (1974). *An introduction to environmental psychology.* New York, NY: Holt.

Izard, C. E. (1977). *Human emotions.* New York, NY: Plenum.

Izard, C. E. (1992). Basic emotions, relations among emotions, and emotion-cognition relations. *Psychological Review, 99,* 561–565.

Jacklin, C. N. (1989). Female and male: Issues of gender. *American Psychologist, 44,* 127–133.

Jackson, D. H., & Messick, S. (1962). Response styles and the assessment of psychopathology. In S. Messick & J. Ross (Eds.), *Measurement of personality and cognition.* New York, NY: Wiley.

Jackson, J. J., Hill, P. L., Payne, B. R., Roberts, B. W., & Stine-Morrow, E. A. (2012). Can an old dog learn (and want to experience) new tricks? Cognitive training increases openness to experience in older adults. *Psychology and Aging, 27,* 286.

Jacobsen, T., Edelstein, W., & Hoffman, V. (1994). A longitudinal study of the relation between representations of attachment in childhood and cognitive functioning in childhood and adolescence. *Developmental Psychology, 30,* 112–124.

Jaffe, Y. (1975). *Sex and aggression: An intimate relationship.* (Unpublished doctoral dissertation). University of California, Los Angeles.

Jaffe, Y., Malamuth, N., Feingold, J., & Feshbach, S. (1974). Sexual arousal and behavioral aggression. *Journal of Personality and Social Psychology, 30,* 759–764.

Jaffee, S., & Hyde, J. S. (2000). Gender differences in moral orientation. *Psychological Bulletin, 126*(5), 703–726.

James, W. (1890; 1952). *The principles of psychology.* Chicago, IL: The Encyclopedia Britannica.

James, W. T. (1951). Social organization among dogs of different temperaments: Terriers and beagles reared together. *Journal of Comparative Physiological Psychology, 44,* 71–77.

Jang, K. L., McCrae, R. R., Angleitner, A., Riemann, R., & Livesley, W. J. (1998). Heritability of facet-level traits in a cross-cultural twin sample: Support for a hierarchical model of personality. *Journal of Personality and Social Psychology, 74*(6), 1556–1565.

Janoff-Bulman, R. (1989). Assumptive worlds and the stress of traumatic events: Applications of the schema construct. *Social Cognition, 7,* 113–138.

Janoff-Bulman, R. (1992). *Shattered assumptions.* New York, NY: Free Press.

Jenkins, A. H. (1982). *The psychology of the Afro-American.* New York, NY: Pergamon.

Jensen, G. D., & Tolman, C. W. (1962). Activity level of the mother monkey, *Macaca nemestrina,* as affected by various conditions of sensory access to the infant following separation. *Animal Behaviour, 10,* 228–230.

Jensen, G. D., & Tolman, C. W. (1962). Mother-infant relationship in the monkey, *Macaca nemestrina*: The effect of brief separation and mother-infant specificity. *Journal of Comparative and Physiological Psychology, 55,* 131–136.

Jerremalm, A., Jannson, L., & Ost, L. G. (1986). Cognitive and physiological reactivity and the effects of different behavioral methods in the treatment of social phobia. *Behavior Research and Therapy, 24,* 171–180.

Jessor, R., Graves, T. D., Hanson, R. C., & Jessor, S. L. (1968). *Society, personality, and deviant behavior.* New York, NY: Holt.

John, O. P. (1990). The "big five" factor taxonomy: Dimensions of personality in the natural language and in questionnaires. In L. A. Pervin (Ed.), *Handbook of personality* (pp. 66–100). New York, NY: Guilford.

Johnson, D. W., & Norem-Hebeisen, A. (1977). Attitudes toward interdependence among persons and psychological health. *Psychological Reports, 40,* 843–850.

Johnson, R. C., McClearn, G. E., Yuen, S., Nagoshi, C. T., Ahem, F. M., & Cole, R. E. (1985). Galton's data a century later. *American Psychologist, 40,* 875–892.

Johnson, R. N. (1972). *Aggression in man and animals.* Philadelphia, PA: Saunders.

Johnson, W., & Krueger, R. F. (2004). Genetic and environmental structure of adjectives describing the domains of the big five model of personality: A nationwide US twin study. *Journal of Research in Personality, 38*(5), 448–472.

Jones, E. (1953–1957). *The life and work of Sigmund Freud* (Vols. I–III). New York, NY: Basic Books.

Jones, E. E. (1979). The rocky road from acts to dispositions. *American Psychologist, 34,* 107–117.

Jones, E. E., & Davis, K. E. (1965). From acts to dispositions: The attribution process in person perception. In L. Berkowitz (Ed.), *Advances in experimental social psychology* (Vol. 2). New York, NY: Academic Press.

Jones, E. E., & Nisbett, R. E. (1971). *The actor and observer: Divergent perceptions of the causes of behavior.* Morristown, NJ: General Learning Press.

Jones, J. D., Cassidy, J., & Shaver, P. R. (2015). Adult attachment style and parenting. In J. A. Simpson & W. S. Rholes (Eds.), *Attachment theory and research: New directions and emerging themes* (pp. 234–260). New York, NY: Guilford Press.

Jones, R. M. (1992). Ego identity and adolescent problem behavior. In G. R. Adams, T. P. Gullotta, & R. Montemayer (Eds.), *Adolescent identity formation* (pp. 216–233). Newbury Park, CA: Sage.

Jordan, J. V., Kaplan, A. G., Miller, J. B., Sliver, I. P., & Surrey, J. L. (1991). *Women's growth in connection*. New York, NY: Guilford.

Jorgensen, K., Andersen, T. J., & Dam, H. (2000). The diagnostic efficiency of the Rorschach Depression Index and the Schizophrenia Index: A review. *Assessment, 7*, 259–280.

Josselson, R. L. (1988). *Finding herself: Pathways of identity development in women*. New York, NY: Jossey-Bass.

Joussemet, M., Vitaro, F., Barker, E. D., Côté, S., Nagin, D. S., Zoccolillo, M., & Tremblay, R. E. (2008). Controlling parenting and physical aggression during elementary school. *Child Development, 79*(2), 411–425.

Judge, T. A., Woolf, E. F., & Hurst, C. (2009). Is emotional labor more difficult for some than for others? A multilevel, experience-sampling study. *Personnel Psychology, 62*, 57–88.

Jung, C. (1904; 1973). Studies in word association. In *Experimental researches, collected works* (Vol. 2). Princeton, NJ: Princeton University Press.

Jung, C. (1916). *Analytical psychology*. New York, NY: Moffat, Yard.

Jung, C. (1936; 1959). *The concept of the collective unconscious*. In *Collected work* (Vol. 9, Part I). Princeton, NJ: Princeton University Press.

Jung, C. (1959). *The basic writings of C. G. Jung* (V. de Laszlo, Ed.). New York, NY: Random House.

Kachadourian, L. K., Homish, G. G., Quigley, B. M., & Leonard, K. E. (2012). Alcohol expectancies, alcohol use, and hostility as longitudinal predictors of alcohol-related aggression. *Psychology of Addictive Behaviors, 26*(3), 414–422.

Kadushin, A. (1970). *Adopting older children*. New York, NY: Columbia University Press.

Kagan, J. (1966). Developmental studies in reflection and analysis. In A. H. Kidd & J. L. Rivoire (Eds.), *Perceptual development in children*. New York, NY: International Universities Press.

Kagan, J. (1989). Temperamental contributions to social behavior. *American Psychologist, 44*, 668–674.

Kagan, J., Arcus, D., & Snidman, N. (1993). The idea of temperament: Where do we go from here? In R. Plomin & G. E. McClearn (Eds.), *Nature, nurture and psychology* (pp. 197–212). Washington, DC: American Psychological Association.

Kagan, J., Klein, R. E., Finley, G. E., Rogoff, B., Nolan, E., & Kogan, N. (1970). Individual variation in cognitive processes. In P. H. Mussen (Ed.), *Carmichael's manual of child psychology* (Vol. 1). New York, NY: Wiley.

Kagan, J., & Moss, H. A. (1959). Stability and validity of achievement fantasy. *Journal of Abnormal and Social Psychology, 58*, 357–364.

Kagan, J., & Moss, H. A. (1962). *Birth to maturity*. New York, NY: Wiley.

Kagan, J., & Snidman, N. (1991). Infant predictors of inhibited and uninhibited profiles. *Psychological Science, 2*, 40–44.

Kagan, S., & Madsen, M. C. (1971). Cooperation and competition of Mexican, Mexican-American, and Anglo children of two ages. *Developmental Psychology, 5*, 32–39.

Kagitcibasi, E., & Berry, J. W. (1989). Cross-cultural psychology: Current research and trends. *Annual Review of Psychology, 46*, 493–531.

Kahneman, D. (2011). *Thinking fast and slow*. New York, NY: Farrar, Straus, and Giroux.

Kahneman, D., & Tversky, A. (1979). Prospect theory: An analysis of decision under risk. *Econometrica: Journal of the Econometric Society*, 263–291.

Kallman, W. M., & Feuerstein, M. (1977). Psychophysiological procedures. In A. R. Ciminero, K. S. Calhoun, & H. E. Adams (Eds.), *Handbook of behavioral assessment*. New York, NY: Interscience-Wiley.

Kamiya, J. (1969). Operant control of the EEG and some of its reported effects on consciousness. In C. T. Tart (Ed.), *Altered states of consciousness*. New York, NY: Wiley.

Kanfer, F. H. (1970). Self-regulation: Research, issues and speculations. In C. Neuringer & J. L. Michael (Eds.), *Behavior modification in clinical psychology*. New York, NY: Appleton-Century-Crofts.

Kanfer, F. H., & Marston, A. R. (1963). Determinants of self-reinforcement in human learning. *Journal of Experimental Psychology, 66*, 245–254.

Kanfer, F. H., & Saslow, G. (1969). Behavioral diagnosis. In C. M. Franks (Ed.), *Behavior therapy: Appraisal and status*. New York, NY: McGraw-Hill.

Kaplan, R. M., & Saccuzzo, D. S. (1981). *Psychological testing: Principles and applications*. Belmont, CA: Brooks/Cole.

Kardiner, A. (1945). *The psychological frontier of society*. New York, NY: Columbia University Press.

Kasser, T., & Ryan, R. M. (1996). Further examining the American dream: Differential correlates of intrinsic and extrinsic goals. *Personality and Social Psychology Bulletin, 22*(3), 280–287.

Kastenbaum, R., Derbin, V., Sabatini, P., & Ant, S. (1972). "The age of me": Towards personal and interpersonal definitions of functional aging. *International Journal of Aging and Human Development, 3*, 197–211.

Kawabata, Y., Alink, L. R., Tseng, W. L., Van Ijzendoorn, M. H., & Crick, N. R. (2011). Maternal and paternal parenting styles associated with relational aggression in children and adolescents: A conceptual analysis and meta-analytic review. *Developmental Review, 31*(4), 240–278.

Kaufman, H., & Feshbach, S. (1963). Displaced aggression and its modification through exposure to antiaggressive communications. *Journal of Abnormal and Social Psychology, 67*, 79–83.

Kazdin, A. E. (1977). Artifact, bias, & complexity of assessment: The ABCs of reliability. *Journal of Applied Behavior Analysis, 10*, 141–150.

Kazdin, A. E., Bass, D., Siegal, T., & Thomas, C. (1989). Cognitive-behavioral therapy and relationship therapy in the treatment of children referred for antisocial behavior. *Journal of Consulting and Clinical Psychology, 57*, 522–535.

Keiner, J. (1857). Klexographien, Part VI. In R. Pissin (Ed.), *Keiners Werke*. Berlin, Germany: Bong & Co.

Kelley, C. K., & King, G. D. (1979). Behavioral correlates of the 2-7-8 MMPI profile type in students at a university mental health center. *Journal of Consulting and Clinical Psychology, 47*, 679–685.

Kelley, H. H. (1967). Attribution theory in social psychology. In D. Levine (Ed.), *Nebraska symposium on motivation*. Lincoln, NE: University of Nebraska Press.

Kelley, H. H. (1983). Love and commitment. In H. H. Kelley, E. Berscheid, A. Christensen, J. H. Harvey, T. L. Huston, G. Luimger, E. McClintock, L. A. Peplau, & D. R. Peterson (Eds.), *Close relationships*. New York, NY: W. H. Freeman & Co.

Kelly, G. A. (1955). *The psychology of personal constructs*. New York, NY: Norton.

Kelly, G. A. (1958). Man's construction of his alternatives. In G. Lindzey (Ed.), *Assessment of human motives*. New York, NY: Grove.

Kelly, G. A. (1966; 1970). A summary statement of cognitive-oriented comprehensive theory of behavior. In J. C. Mancuso (Ed.), *Readings for a cognitive theory of personality*. New York, NY: Holt.

Kempe, R. S., & Kempe, C. H. (1978). *Child abuse*. Cambridge, MA: Harvard University Press.

Keniston, K. (1967). The sources of student dissent. *Journal of Social Issues, 22*, 108–137.

Kenrick, D. T., & Keefe, R. C. (1992). Age preferences in mates reflect sex differences in human reproductive strategies. *Behavioral and Brain Sciences, 15*(1), 75–79.

Kernberg, O. F. (1975). *Borderline conditions and pathological narcissism*. New York, NY: Jason Aronson.

Kernis, M. H., Cornell, D. P., Sun, C., Berry, A., & Harlow, T. (1993). There's more to self-esteem than whether it is high or low: The importance of stability of self-esteem. *Journal of Personality and Social Psychology, 65*, 1190–1204.

Kernis, M. H., Grannemann, B. D., & Mathis, L. C. (1991). Stability of self-esteem as a moderator of the relation between level of self-esteem and depression. *Journal of Personality and Social Psychology, 61*, 80–84.

Khoshaba, D. M., & Maddi, S. R. (1999). Early experiences in hardiness development. *Consulting Psychology Journal: Practice and Research, 51*(2), 106–116.

Kihlstrom, J. F. (1987). The cognitive unconscious. *Science, 237*, 1445–1452.

Kihlstrom, J. F. (1990). The psychological unconscious. In L. A. Pervin (Ed.), *Handbook of personality* (pp. 445–464). New York, NY: Guilford.

Kihlstrom, J. F. (2002). The unconscious. In V. Ramachandran (Ed.), *Encyclopedia of the human brain*, (Vol. 4, pp. 635–646). San Diego, CA: Academic Press.

Kihlstrom, J. F. (2007). Consciousness in hypnosis. In P. D. Zelanzo, M. Moscovitch, & E. Thompson (Eds.), *Cambridge handbook of consciousness* (pp. 445–479). Cambridge, MA: Cambridge University Press.

Kihlstrom, J. F. (2013). Unconscious processes. In D. Reisberg (Ed.), *The Oxford handbook of cognitive psychology* (pp. 176–180). New York, NY: Oxford University Press.

Kim, H. S., Sherman, D. K., & Taylor, S. E. (2008). Culture and social support. *American Psychologist, 63*(6), 518–526.

Kimble, G. A., Garmezy, N., & Zigler, E. (1974). *Principles of general psychology* (4th ed.) New York, NY: Ronald.

King, L. F., Armitage, S. G., & Tilton, J. (1960). A therapeutic approach to schizophrenia of extreme pathology. *Journal of Abnormal and Social Psychology, 61*, 276–286.

Kinsey, A. C., Pomeroy, W. B., & Martin, C. E. (1948). *Sexual behavior in the human male*. Philadelphia, PA: Saunders.

Kinsey, A. C., Pomeroy, W. B., Martin, C. E., & Gebhard, P. H. (1953). *Sexual behavior in the human female*. Philadelphia, PA: Saunders.

Kirsch, I. (1985). Self-efficacy and expectancy: Old wine with new labels. *Journal of Personality and Social Psychology, 49*, 824–830.

Klein, G. S. (1967). Peremptory ideation: Structure and force in motivated ideas. In R. Jessor & S. Feshbach (Eds.), *Cognition, personality and clinical psychology*. San Francisco, CA: Jossey-Bass.

Klein, G. S. (1969). Freud's two theories of sexuality. In L. Breger (Ed.), *Clinical-cognitive psychology*. Englewood Cliffs, NJ: Prentice-Hall.

Klein, G. S. (1970). *Perception, motives and personality*. New York, NY: Knopf.

Klein, K. B., & Spiegel, D. (1989). Modulation of gastric acid secretion by hypnosis. *Gastroenterology, 96*, 1383–1387.

Klein, M. (1937). *The psycho-analysis of children* (2nd ed.). London, UK: Hogarth.

Klein, M. (1948). *Contributions to psychoanalysis, 1921–45*. London, UK: Hogarth.

Klein, R. (1970). *Some factors influencing empathy in six and seven year old children varying in ethnic background* (Unpublished doctoral dissertation). University of California, Los Angeles.

Kleinmuntz, A., & Szucko, J. J. (1984a). A field study of the fallibility of polygraphic lie detection. *Nature, 308*, 449–450.

Kleinmuntz, A., & Szucko, J. J. (1984b). Lie detection in ancient and modern times. *American Psychologist, 39*, 766–776.

Klimstra, T. A., Hale, W. W. III, Raaijmakers, Q. A. W., Branje, S. J. T., & Meeus, W. H. J. (2009). Maturation of personality in adolescence. *Journal of Personality and Social Psychology: Personality Processes and Individual Differences, 96*, 898–912.

Kline, N. (1962). Drugs are the greatest practical advance in the history of psychiatry. *New Medical Material, 4*, 49.

Kline, P. (1972). *Fact and fancy in Freudian theory*. London, UK: Methuen.

Klineberg, O. (1935). *Race differences*. New York, NY: Harper & Brothers.

Klinger, E. (1966). Fantasy need achievement as a motivational construct. *Psychological Bulletin, 66*, 291–303.

Klinger, E. (1987). Current concerns and disengagement from incentives. In F. Halisch & J. Kuhl (Eds.), *Motivation, intention, and volition* (pp. 337–347). New York, NY: Springer-Verlag.

Klopfer, B. (Ed.), (1954; 1970). *Developments in the Rorschach technique*. Yonkers, NY: World Book.

Klopfer, W. G., & Taulbee, E. S. (1976). Projective tests. *Annual Review of Psychology, 26*, 543–568.

Knight, G. P., & Kagan, S. (1977). Development of pro-social and competitive behaviors in Anglo-American and Mexican-American children. *Child Development, 48,* 1385–1394.

Knott, P. D., Lasater, L., & Shuman, R. (1974). Aggression: Guilt and conditionability for aggressiveness. *Journal of Personality, 42,* 332–344.

Kobasa, S. C. (1979). Stressful life events, personality, and health: An inquiry into hardiness. *Journal of Personality and Social Psychology, 37,* 1–11.

Kobasa, S. C. (1982). The hardy personality: Toward a social psychology of stress and health. In G. Sanders & J. Suls (Eds.), *Social psychology of health and illness* (pp. 3–32). Hillsdale, NI: Erlbaum.

Kobasa, S. C., & Maddi, S. R. (1977). Existential personality theory. In R. J. Corsini (Ed.), *Current personality theory* (pp. 243–276). Itasca, IL: F. E. Peacock.

Kobasa, S. C., Maddi, S. R., Puccetti, M., & Zola, J. (1986). Relative effectiveness of hardiness, exercise and social support as resources against illness. *Journal of Psychosomatic Research, 29,* 525–533.

Kohlberg, L. (1958). *The development of modes of moral thinking and choice in the years ten to sixteen* (Unpublished doctoral dissertation). University of Chicago, Chicago, IL.

Kohlberg, L. (1966). A cognitive-developmental analysis of children's sex-role concepts and attitudes. In E. Maccoby (Ed.), *The development of sex differences.* Stanford, CA: Stanford University Press.

Kohlberg, L. (1969a). Stage and sequence: The cognitive-developmental approach to socialization. In D. Goslin (Ed.), *Handbook of socialization theory and research.* Chicago, IL: Rand McNally.

Kohlberg, L. (1969b). *Stages in the development of moral thought and action.* New York, NY: Holt.

Kohlberg, L. (1976). Moral stages and moralization: The cognitive-developmental approach. In T. Lickona (Ed.), *Moral development and behavior: Theory, research and social issues.* New York, NY: Holt.

Kohut, H. (1971). *The analysis of the self: A systematic approach to the psychoanalytic treatment of narcissistic personality disorders* (Monograph Series of the Psychoanalytic Study of the Child, No. 41). New York, NY: International Universities Press.

Kohut, H. (1977). *The restoration of the self.* New York, NY: International Universities Press.

Kohut, H. (1984a). *How does analysis cure?* Chicago, IL: University of Chicago Press.

Kohut, H. (1984b). *How does analysis work?* Arnold Goldberg (Ed.), Paul Stepansky (Collaborator). Chicago, IL: University of Chicago Press.

Konecni, V. J. (1975). Annoyance, type and duration of postannoyance activity, and aggression: The "cathartic effect." *Journal of Experimental Psychology: General, 104*(1), 76–102.

Kopp, C. B. (1987). The growth of self-regulation. Caregivers and children. In N. Eisenberg (Ed.), *New directions in developmental psychology.* New York, NY: Wiley.

Kornadt, H. J. (1983). A cross-cultural analysis of the development of aggression. In J. B. Derigowski, S. Dzinvawiec, & R. C. Annis (Eds.), *Expiscations in Cross-Cultural Psychology* (pp. 285–297). Selected papers from the Sixth International Conference of the International Association for Cross-Cultural Psychology. Lisse, Netherlands: Swets and Zeitlinger B. V.

Kornienko, O., Santos, C. E., Martin, C. L., & Granger, K. L. (2016). Peer influence on gender identity development in adolescence. *Developmental Psychology, 52*(10), 1578–1592.

Krasner, L., & Ullman, L. P. (1973). *Behavior influence and personality.* New York, NY: Holt.

Kretschmer, E. (1925). *Physique and character.* New York, NY: Harcourt, Brace.

Kreuz, L. E., & Rose, R. M. (1972). Assessment of aggressive behaviors and plasma testosterone in a young criminal population. *Psychosomatic Medicine, 34,* 321–332.

Krizan, Z., & Suls, J. (2008). Are implicit and explicit measures of self-esteem related? A meta-analysis for the Name-Letter Test. *Personality and Individual Differences, 44*(2), 521–531.

Kroger, J. (1992). Intrapsychic dimensions of identity during late adolescence. In G. R. Adams, T. P. Gullotta, & R. Montemayer (Eds.), *Adolescent identity formation* (p. 122–144). Newbury Park, CA: Sage.

Kroger, J., Martinussen, M., & Marcia, J. E. (2010). Identity status change during adolescence and young adulthood: A meta-analysis. *Journal of Adolescence, 33*(5), 683–698.

Krueger, R. F., Moffitt, T. E., Caspi, A., Bleske, A., & Silva, P. A. (1998). Assortative mating for antisocial behavior: Developmental and methodological implications. *Behavior Genetics, 28,* 173–186.

Kruijt, J. (1964). *Ontogeny of social behavior in Burmese red jungle fowl* (Gallus gallus spodiceus) (Behavior Supp. 12). Leiden, Netherlands: Brill.

Kuder, G. F., & Richardson, M. W. (1937). The theory of the estimation of reliability, *Psychometrika, 2,* 151–160.

Kuiper, N. A., MacDonald, M. R., & Deny, P. A. (1983). Parameters of a depressive self-schema. In J. Suls & A. G. Greenwald (Eds.), *Psychological perspectives on the self.* Hillsdale, NJ: Erlbaum.

Kukla, A. (1972). Attributional determinants of achievement-related behavior. *Journal of Personality and Social Psychology, 21,* 166–174.

Kukla, A. (1980). The modem language of consciousness. In L. Michaels & C. Ricks (Eds.), *The state of the language.* Berkeley, CA: University of California Press.

Kuo, F. E., & Sullivan, W. C. (2001). Environment and crime in the inner city: Does vegetation reduce crime?. *Environment and behavior, 33*(3), 343–367.

Kurtines, W., & Greif, E. B. (1974). The development of moral thought: Review and evaluation of Kohlberg's approach. *Psychological Bulletin, 81,* 453–470.

Laan, A. J., Van Assen, M. A., & Vingerhoets, A. J. (2012). Individual differences in adult crying: The role of attachment styles. *Social Behavior and Personality: An International Journal, 40*(3), 453–471.

Lack, D. L. (1943). *The life of the robin.* Cambridge, MA: Cambridge University Press.

Lachman, M. E., Lewkowicz, C., Marcus, A., & Peng, Y. (1994). Images of midlife development among young, middle-aged, and older adults. *Journal of Adult Development, 1*(4), 201–211.

La Freniere, P., Strayer, F. F., & Gauthier, R. (1984). The emergence of same sex affiliative preferences among preschool peers: A developmental ethological perspective. *Child Development, 55*, 1958–1965.

La Fromboise, T., Coleman, H. L. K., & Gerton, J. (1993). Psychological impact of biculturalism: Evidence and theory. *Psychological Bulletin, 114*, 395–412.

Lagerspetz, K. (1969). Aggression and aggressiveness in laboratory mice. In S. Garattini & E. B. Sigg (Eds.), *Aggressive behavior*. Amsterdam, Netherlands: Excerpta Medica.

Lagerspetz, K. (1979). Modification of aggressiveness in mice. In S. Feshbach & A. Fraczek (Eds.), *Aggression and behavior change: Biological and social processes*. New York, NY: Praeger.

Lagerspetz, K. M., Bjorkgvist, K., & Peltoren, T. (1988). Is indirect aggression typical of females? Gender differences in aggressiveness in 11 to 12 year old children. *Aggressive Behavior, 14*, 403–414.

Laing, R. D. (1965). *The divided self. An existential study in sanity and madness*. Baltimore, MD: Penguin.

Lamb, D. (1978). Anxiety. In H. London & J. E. Exner (Eds.), *Dimensions of personality*. New York, NY: John Wiley.

Lamb, M. E. (1977). Father-infant and mother-infant interaction in the first year of life. *Child Development, 48*, 167–181.

Lamb, M. E. (Ed.) (1978). *Social and personality development*. New York, NY: Holt, Rinehart, & Winston.

Lamb, M. E. (1982). Maternal employment and child development: A review. In M. E. Lamb (Ed.), *Nontraditional families: Parenting and child development* (pp. 43–69). Hillsdale, NJ: Erlbaum.

Lambe, S., Hamilton-Giachritsis, C., Garner, E., & Walker, J. (2016). The role of narcissism in aggression and violence: A systematic review. *Trauma, Violence, & Abuse*. doi: 10.1177/1524838016650190

Lambert, A. J., Good, K. S., & Kirk, I. J. (2010). Testing the repression hypothesis: Effects of emotional valence on memory suppression in the think–no think task. *Consciousness and Cognition, 19*(1), 281–293.

Landrine, H. (1992). Clinical implications of cultural differences: The referential versus indexical self. *Clinical Psychology Review, 12*, 401–415.

Lang, P. J. (1971). The application of psychophysiological methods to the study of psychotherapy and behavior modification. In A. E. Bergin & S. L. Garfield (Eds.), *Handbook of psychotherapy and behavior change*. New York, NY: Wiley.

Langer, E. J. (1975). The illusion of control. *Journal of Personality and Social Psychology, 32*, 311–328.

Langer, E. J. (1989a). *Mindfulness*. Reading, MA: Addison-Wesley.

Langer, E. J. (1989b). Minding matters: The consequences of mindlessness-mindfulness. In L. Berkowitz (Ed.), *Advances in Experimental Social Psychology* (Vol. 22, pp. 137–173). San Diego: Academic Press.

Langer, E. J., Blank, A., & Chanowitz, B. (1978). The mindlessness of ostensibly thoughtful action: The role of "placebic" information in interpersonal interaction. *Journal of Personality and Social Psychology, 36*, 635–642.

Langer, E. J., & Rodin, J. (1976). The effects of choice and enhanced personal responsibility for the aged: A field experiment in an institutional setting. *Journal of Personality and Social Psychology, 34*, 191–98.

Langergraber, K., Schubert, G., Rowney, C., Wrangham, R., Zommers, Z., & Vigilant, L. (2011). Genetic differentiation and the evolution of cooperation in chimpanzees and humans. *Proceedings of the Royal Society B: Biological Sciences, 278*(1717), 2546–2552.

Langlois, J. H., & Downs, A. C. (1980). Mothers, fathers, and peers as socialization agents of sex-typed play behaviors in young children. *Child Development*, 1237–1247.

Larrick, R. P., Timmerman, T. A., Carton, A. M., & Abrevaya, J. (2011). Temper, temperature, and temptation: Heat-related retaliation in baseball. *Psychological Science, 22*(4), 423–428.

Larsen, R. J., & Ketelaar, T. (1991). Personality and susceptibility to positive and negative emotional states. *Journal of Personality and Social Psychology, 61*(1), 132–140.

Larson, R. J., & Diener, E. (1985). A multitrait-multimethod examination of affect structure: Hedonic level and emotional intensity. *Personality and Individual Differences, 6*, 631–636.

Larson, R. J., & Diener, E. (1987). Affect intensity as an individual difference characteristic: A review. *Journal of Research in Personality, 21*, 1–39.

Larson, R. J., Diener, E., & Cropanzano, R. S. (1987). Cognitive operations associated with individual differences in affect intensity. *Journal of Personality and Social Psychology, 53*, 767–774.

Lashley, K. S. (1930). The mechanism of vision: I. A method for rapid analysis of pattern-vision in the rat. *Pedagogical Seminary and Journal of Genetic Psychology, 37*, 453–460.

Last, U. (1975). *Motives, styles, contents and products of identification in the authority figure* (Unpublished doctoral dissertation). Hebrew University, Jerusalem, Israel.

Lawson, R. (1965). *Frustration: The development of a scientific concept*. New York, NY: Macmillan.

Lazarus, A. A. (1971). *Behavior therapy and beyond*. New York, NY: McGraw-Hill.

Lazarus, R. S. (1966). *Psychological stress and the coping process*. New York, NY: McGraw-Hill.

Lazarus, R. S. (1982). Thoughts on the relation between emotion and cognition. *American Psychologist, 37*, 1019–1024.

Lazarus, R. S. (1985). Puzzles in the study of daily hassles. *Journal of Behavioral Medicine, 7*, 375–389.

Lazarus, R. S. (1991). *Emotion & adaptation*. New York, NY: Oxford University Press.

Lazarus, R. S., & Alfert, E. (1964). The short circuiting of threat by experimentally altering cognitive appraisal. *Journal of Abnormal and Social Psychology, 69*, 195–205.

Lazarus, R. S., & Averill, J. R. (1972). Emotion and cognition: With special reference to anxiety. In C. D. Spielberger (Ed.), *Anxiety: Current trends in theory and research*. New York, NY: Academic Press.

Lazarus, R. S., & Smith, C. A. (1988). Knowledge and appraisal in the cognition–emotion relationship. *Cognition and Emotion, 2*, 281–300.

Leary, M. R., & Baumeister, R. F. (2000). The nature and function of self-esteem: Sociometer theory. *Advances in Experimental Social Psychology, 32*, 1–62.

Leary, M. R., Tambor, E. S., Terdal, S. K., & Downs, D. L. (1995). Self-esteem as an interpersonal monitor: The sociometer hypothesis. *Journal of Personality and Social Psychology, 68,* 518–530.

LeBoeuf, B. J., & Peterson, R. S. (1969). Social status and mating activity in elephant seals. *Science, 163,* 91–93.

Lecky, P. (1945). *Self-consistency: A theory of personality.* New York, NY: Island Press Co-operative.

Lee, K., & Ashton, M. C. (2004). Psychometric properties of the HEXACO Personality Inventory. *Multivariate Behavioral Research, 39,* 329–358.

Lefcourt, H. M. (1973). The function of illusions of control and freedom. *American Psychologist, 28,* 417–425.

Lefcourt, H. M. (1976). *Locus of control.* Hillsdale, NJ: Lawrence Erlbaum.

Lefcourt, H. M., Von Baeyer, C. L., Ware, E. E., & Cox, C. J. (1979). The multidimensional-multiattributional causality scale: The development of a goal specific locus of control scale. *Canadian Journal of Behavioral Science, 11,* 286–304.

Lefkowitz, M. M., Eron, L. D., Walder, L. O., & Huesmann, L. R. (1977). *Growing up to be violent.* New York, NY: Pergamon.

Lehman, C. H., & Witty, P. A. (1934). Faculty psychology and personality traits. *American Journal of Psychology, 44,* 486–500.

Lehman, D. R., Wortman, C. B., & Williams, A. F. (1987). Long-term effects of losing a spouse or child in a motor vehicle crash. *Journal of Personality and Social Psychology, 52,* 218–231.

Lehrman, D. S. (1953). A critique of Konrad Lorenz's theory of instinctive behavior. *Quarterly Review of Biology, 28,* 337–363.

Lehrman, D. S. (1970). Semantic and conceptual issues in the nature-nurture problem. In L. R. Aronson, E. Tobach, D. S. Lehrman, & J. S. Rosenblatt (Eds.), *Development and evolution of behavior.* San Francisco, CA: Freeman.

Lehrman, H. C. (1953). *Age and achievement.* Princeton, NJ: Princeton University Press.

Lennenberg, E. H. (1967). *Biological foundations of language.* New York, NY: Wiley.

Leonard, K. E. (1989). The impact of explicit aggressive and implicit nonaggressive cues on aggression in intoxicated and sober males. *Personality and Social Psychology Bulletin, 15,* 390–400.

Lepper, M. R., Greene, D., & Nisbett, R. E. (1973). Undermining children's intrinsic interest with extrinsic reward: A test of the overjustification hypothesis. *Journal of Personality and Social Psychology, 28,* 129–137.

Lerner, J. S., Li, Y., Valdesolo, P., & Kassam, K. S. (2015). Emotion and decision making. *Annual Review of Psychology, 66,* 799–823.

Lesch, K. P., Bengel, D., Heils, A., & Sabol, S. Z. (1996). Association of anxiety-related traits with a polymorphism in the serotonin transporter gene regulatory region. *Science, 274,* 1527–1531.

Levant, R. F., & Schlien, J. M. (1984). *Client-centered therapy and the person-centered approach.* New York, NY: Praeger.

Leventhal, H. (1984). A perceptual-motor theory of emotion. In L. Berkowitz (Ed.), *Advances in experimental social psychology.* New York, NY: Academic Press.

Levinson, D. J. (1978). *The seasons of a man's life.* New York, NY: Ballantine.

Levinson, D. J. (1986). A conception of adult development. *American Psychologist, 41,* 3–13.

Levis, D. J. (1976). Learned helplessness: A reply and an alternative S-R interpretation. *Journal of Experimental Psychology: General, 105,* 47–65.

Levy, K. N. (2005). The implications of attachment theory and research for understanding borderline personality disorder. *Development and Psychopathology, 17*(4), 959–986.

Levy, S. M. (1981). The aging woman: Developmental issues and mental health needs. *Professional Psychology, 12,* 92–101.

Lewicki, P. (1986). *Nonconscious social information processing.* New York, NY: Academic Press.

Lewicki, P., Hill, T., & Czyzewska, M. (1992). Non-conscious acquisition of information. *American Psychologist, 47,* 788–791.

Lewin, K. (1935). *A dynamic theory of personality.* New York, NY: McGraw-Hill.

Lewin, K., Dembo, T., Festlinger, L., & Sears, P. S. (1944). Level of aspiration. In J. McV. Hunt (Ed.), *Personality and the behavioral disorders* (Vol. 1). New York, NY: Ronald.

Lewinsohn, P. M., Mischel, W., Chaplin, W., & Barton, R. (1980). Social competence and depression: The role of illusory self-perception. *Journal of Abnormal Psychology, 89,* 203–212.

Lewis, M. (1987). Early sex role behavior and school adjustment. In J. M. Reinisch, L. A. Rosenbaum, & S. A. Sanders (Eds.), *Masculinity/femininity: Basic perspectives.* New York, NY: Oxford University Press.

Lewis, M., & Brooks-Gunn, J. (1979). *Social cognition and the acquisition of self.* New York, NY: Plenum.

Lewis, M., & Feisking, C. (1989). Infant, mother, and mother-infant interaction behavior and subsequent attachment. *Child Development, 60,* 831–837.

Lewis, M., Sullivan, M. W., Stanger, C., & Weiss, M. (1989). Self-development and self-conscious emotions. *Child Development, 60,* 146–156.

Lewis, M. J. (1990). Self-knowledge and social development in early life. In L. A. Pervin (Ed.), *Handbook of personality* (pp. 277–300). New York, NY: Guilford.

Lewis, O. (1961). *Children of Sanchez.* New York, NY: Random House.

Lewis, W. A., & Bucher, A. M. (1992). Anger, catharsis, the reformulated frustration-aggression hypothesis, and health consequences. *Psychotherapy, 29,* 385–392.

Ley, R. G. (1979). Cerebral asymmetries, emotional experience, and imagery: Implications for psychotherapy. In A. A. Sheilah & J. T. Shaffer (Eds.), *The potential of fantasy and imagination.* New York, NY: Brandon House.

Leyens, J. P., Camino, L., Parke, R. D., & Berkowitz, L. (1975). Effects of movie violence on aggression in a field setting as a function of group dominance and cohesion. *Journal of Personality and Social Psychology, 32,* 346–360.

Liebert, R. M., & Allen, K. M. (1967). *The effects of rule structure and reward magnitude on the acquisition and adoption of self-reward criteria* (Unpublished manuscript). Vanderbilt University, Nashville, TN.

Liebert, R. M., & Spiegler, M. D. (1974). *Personality: Strategies for the study of man* (Rev. ed.) Homewood, IL: Dorsey Press.

Lilienfeld, S. O., Wood, J. M., & Garb, H. N. (2000) The scientific status of projective techniques. *Psychological Science in the Public Interest, 1*, 27–66.

Lindzey, G. (1952). The Thematic Apperception Test: Interpretive assumptions and related empirical evidence. *Psychological Bulletin, 49*, 1–25.

Lindzey, G. (1967a). Behavior and morphological variation. In J. N. Spuhler (Ed.), *Genetic diversity and human behavior*. Chicago, IL: Aldine.

Lindzey, G. (1967b). Some remarks concerning incest, the incest taboo, and psychoanalytic theory. *American Psychologist, 22*, 1051–1059.

Linville, P. W. (1982). Affective consequences of complexity regarding self and others. In M. S. Clark & S. T. Fiske (Eds.), *Affect and cognition: The 17th Annual Carnegie Symposium on Cognition*. Hillsdale, NJ: Erlbaum.

Linville, P. W. (1985). Self-complexity and affective extremity: Don't put all your eggs in one cognitive basket. *Social Cognition, 3*, 94–120.

Linville, P. W. (1987). Self-complexity as a cognitive buffer against stress-related illness and depression. *Journal of Personality and Social Psychology, 52*(4), 663–676.

Linz, D., Donnerstein, E., Bross, M., & Chapin, M. (1986). Mitigating the influence of violence on television and sexual violence in the media. In R. J. Blanchard & D. C. Blanchard (Eds.), *Advances in the study of aggression* (Vol. 2). Orlando, FL: Academic Press.

Lissner, K. (1933). Die Entspannung von Bedurfnissen durch Ersatzhandlungen. *Psychologische Forschung, 18*, 218–250.

Little, A. C., Burt, D. M., & Perrett, D. I. (2006). Assortative mating for perceived facial personality traits. *Personality and Individual Differences, 40*(5), 973–984.

Little, B. R. (1989). Personal projects analysis: Trivial pursuits, magnificent obsessions, and the search for coherence. In D. M. Buss & N. Cantor (Eds.), *Personality psychology: Recent trends and emerging directions* (pp. 15–31) New York, NY: Springer-Verlag.

Littlefield, C. H., & Rushton, J. P. (1986). When a child dies: The sociobiology of bereavement. *Journal of Personality and Social Psychology, 51*, 797–802.

Livson, N., & Peskin, H. (1980). Perspectives on adolescence from longitudinal research. In J. Adelson (Ed.), *Handbook of adolescent psychology* (pp. 47–98). New York, NY: Wiley.

Loeb, A., Beck, A. T., Diggory, J. C., & Tuthill, R. (1967). Expectancy, level of aspiration, performance, and self-evaluation in depression. *Proceedings of the 75th Annual Convention of the American Psychological Association, 2*, 193–194.

Loehlin, J. C. (1989). Partitioning environmental and genetic contributions to behavioral development. *American Psychologist, 44*, 1285–1292.

Loehlin, J. C., & Nicholls, R. C. (1976). *Heredity, environment, and personality*. Austin, TX: University of Texas Press.

Loevinger, J. (1976). *Ego development*. San Francisco, CA: Jossey-Bass.

Loftus, E. F. (Ed.). (1992). Science watch. *American Psychologist, 47*, 761–809.

Loftus, E. F. (1993). The reality of repressed memories. *American Psychologist, 48*, 518–537.

Lohr, V. I. (2011). Greening the human environment: The untold benefits. In *XXVIII International Horticultural Congress on Science and Horticulture for People (IHC2010): Colloquia and Overview 916* (pp. 159–170).

Lomangino, L. (1969). *The depiction of subliminally and supraliminally presented aggressive stimuli and its effect on the cognitive functioning of schizophrenics* (Unpublished doctoral dissertation). Fordham University, New York, NY.

London, P. (1970). The rescuers: Motivational hypotheses about Christians who saved Jews from the Nazis. In J. R. McCaulay & L. Berkowitz (Eds.), *Altruism and helping behavior*. New York, NY: Academic Press.

Loo, C. M. (1972). The effects of spatial density on the social behavior of children. *Journal of Applied Social Psychology, 2*, 372–381.

Lorenz, K. (1935). Der Kumpan in der Umwelt des Vogels. *Journal für Ornithologie, 83*, 137–213, 289–413.

Lorenz, K. (1950). The comparative method in studying innate behaviour patterns. *Symposium of the Society of Experimental Biology, 4*, 221–268.

Lorenz, K. (1966). *On aggression*. New York, NY: Bantam.

Lovaas, O. I. (1968). Some studies on the treatment of childhood schizophrenia. In J. M. Shlien (Ed.), *Research in psychotherapy*. Washington, DC: American Psychological Association.

Lovaas, O. I. (1987). Behavioral treatment and normal education and intellectual functioning in young autistic children. *Journal of Consulting and Clinical Psychology, 55*, 3–9.

Lovaas, O. I., Freitag, G., Gold, V. I., & Kassorla, I. C. (1965). Experimental studies in childhood schizophrenia: 1. Analysis of self-destructive behavior. *Journal of Experimental Child Psychology, 2*, 67–84.

Lowenthal, M. F., Thurnher, M., & Chiriboga, D. (1975). *Four stages of life-span*. San Francisco, CA: Jossey-Bass.

Lubin, B., Wallis, R. R., & Paine, C. (1971). Patterns of psychological test usage in the United States, 1935–1969. *Professional Psychology, 2*, 70–74.

Luborsky, L. (1967). Momentary forgetting during psychotherapy and psychoanalysis: A theory and research method. In R. R. Holt (Ed.), *Motives and thought: Psychoanalytic essays in honor of David Rappaport* (Psychological Issues Monograph 18/19). New York, NY: International Universities Press.

Luborsky, L., & Crits-Christoph, P. (1990). *Understanding transference: The CCRT method*. New York, NY: Basic Books.

Luck, P. W., & Heiss, J. (1972). Social determinants of self-esteem in adult males. *Sociology and Social Research, 57*, 69–84.

Luyckx, K., Goossens, L., & Soenens, B. (2006). A developmental contextual perspective on identity construction in emerging adulthood: Change dynamics in commitment formation and commitment evaluation. *Developmental Psychology, 42*, 366–380.

Luyckx, K., Schwartz, S. J., Berzonsky, M. D., Soenens, B., Vansteenkiste, M., Smits, I., & Goossens, L. (2008). Capturing ruminative exploration: Extending the four-dimensional model of identity formation in late adolescence. *Journal of Research in Personality, 42,* 58–82.

Luyckx, K., Teppers, E., Klimstra, T., & Rassert, J. (2014). Identity processes and personality traits and types in adolescence: Directionality of effects and developmental trajectories. *Developmental Psychology, 50,* 2144–2153.

Lykken, D. T., McGue, M., Tellegen, A., & Bouchard, T. J., Jr. (1992). Emergenesis: Genetic traits that may not run in families. *American Psychologist, 47,* 1565–1577.

Maccoby, E. E. (1988). Gender as a social category. *Developmental Psychology, 24,* 755–765.

Maccoby, E. E., & Feldman, S. S. (1972). Mother attachment and stranger reactions in the third year of life. *Monographs of the Society for Research in Child Development, 37*(1), 1–86.

Maccoby, E. E., & Jacklin, C. N. (1974). *The psychology of sex differences.* Stanford, CA: Stanford University Press.

Maccoby, E. E., & Jacklin, C. N. (1980). Sex differences in aggression: A rejoinder and reprise. *Child Development, 51,* 964–980.

MacDonald, G., & Leary, M. R. (2005). Why does social exclusion hurt? The relationship between social and physical pain. *Psychological Bulletin, 131,* 202–223.

MacFarlane, J. W., Allen, L., & Honzik, M. P. (1954). A development study of the behavior problems of normal children between 20 months and 14 years. *University of California Publications in Child Development, 2.*

MacKay, D. G. (1987). *The organization of perception and action: A theory for language and other cognitive skills.* Berlin, Germany: Springer-Verlag.

MacKinnon, D. W. (1962). The nature and nurture of creative talent. *American Psychologist, 17,* 484–495.

Maddi, S. R. (1976). *Personality theories: A comparative analysis* (3rd ed.). Homewood, IL: Dorsey.

Maddi, S. R. (1988). On the problem of accepting facticity and pursuing possibility. In S. B. Messer, L. A. Sass, & R. L. Woolfolk (Eds.), *Hermeneutics and psychological theory: Interpretative perspectives on personality, psychotherapy and psychopathology.* New Brunswick, NJ: Rutgers University Press.

Maddi, S. R. (2002). The story of hardiness. *Consulting Psychology Journal: Practice and Research, 54*(3), 173–185.

Maddi, S. R., Bartone, P. T., & Puccetti, M. C. (1987). Stressful events are indeed a factor in physical illness: Reply to Schroeder and Costa (1984). *Journal of Personality and Social Psychology, 52,* 833–843.

Maddi, S. R., Harvey, R. H., Khoshaba, D. M., Fazel, M., & Resurreccion, N. (2009). Hardiness training facilitates performance in college. *Journal of Positive Psychology, 4*(6), 566–577.

Maddi, S. R., Kahn, S., & Maddi, K. L. (1998). The effectiveness of hardiness training. *Consulting Psychology Journal: Practice and Research, 50*(2), 78.

Maddox, G. L. (1970). Fact and artifact: Evidence bearing on disengagement theory. In E. Palmore (Ed.), *Normal aging.* Durham, NC: Duke University Press.

Maddux, J. E., Norton, L. W., & Stoltenberg, C. D. (1986). Self-efficacy expectancy, outcome expectancy, and outcome value: Relative effects on behavioral intentions. *Journal of Personality on Social Psychology, 51,* 783–789.

Madsen, M. C., & Shapira, A. (1970). Cooperative and competitive behavior of urban Afro-American, Anglo-American, Mexican-American, and Mexican village children. *Developmental Psychology, 3,* 16–20.

Maduro, R. J., & Wheelwright, J. B. (1977). Analytical psychology. In R. J. Corsini (Ed.), *Current personality theories.* Itasca, IL: F. E. Peacock.

Magnussen, D. (1990). Personality development from an interactional perspective. In L. A. Pervin (Ed.), *Handbook of personality* (pp. 193–224). New York, NY: Guilford.

Magnussen, D., & Endler, N. S. (1977). Interactional psychology: Present status and future prospects. In D. Magnussen & N. S. Endler (Eds.), *Personality at the crossroads: Current issues in interactional psychology* (pp. 99–111). Hillsdale, NJ: Lawrence Erlbaum.

Mahler, M. S. (1968). *On human symbiosis and the vicissitudes of individuation.* New York, NY: International Universities Press.

Mahler, V. (1933). Ersatzhandlungen verschiedenen Realitatsgrade. *Psychologische Forschung, 18,* 26–89.

Mahone, C. H. (1960). Fear of failure and unrealistic vocational aspiration. *Journal of Abnormal and Social Psychology, 60,* 253–261.

Mahoney, M. (1974). *Cognition and behavior modification.* Cambridge, MA: Ballinger.

Mahoney, M. (1991). *Human change processes.* New York, NY: Basic Books.

Mahoney, M. (1985). Psychotherapy and human change processes. In M. J. Mahoney & A. Freeman (Eds.), *Cognition and psychotherapy* (pp. 3–48). New York, NY: Plenum.

Mahrer, A. R. (1956). The role of expectancy in delayed reinforcement. *Journal of Experimental Psychology, 52,* 101–105.

Maier, N. R. F. (1949). *Frustration: The study of behavior without a goal.* New York, NY: McGraw-Hill.

Main, M. (1990). Cross-cultural studies of attachment organization: Recent studies, changing methodologies, and the concept of conditional strategies. *Human Development, 33*(1), 48–61.

Main, M., & Cassidy, J. (1988). Categories of responses to reunion with the parent at age 6: Predictable from infant attachment classification and stable over a one month period. *Developmental Psychology, 24,* 415–426.

Main, M., Goldwyn, R., & Hesse, E. (2003). The Adult Attachment Interview classification and scoring system (version 7.2).

Main, M., Kaplan, K., & Cassidy, J. (1985). Security in infancy, childhood and adulthood: A move to the level of representation. In I. Bretherton & E. Waters (Eds.), *Growing points of attachment theory and research. Monographs of The Society for Research in Child Development, 50,* Serial No. 209 (1–2), 66–104.

Main, M., & Solomon, J. (1986). Discovery of an insecure-disorganized/disoriented attachment pattern. In T. Brazelton, T. Berry, & M. W. Yogman (Eds.), *Affective development in infancy* (pp. 95–124). Westport, CT: Ablex Publishing.

Main, M., & Solomon, J. (1990). Procedures for identifying infants as disorganized/disoriented during the Ainsworth Strange Situation. In M. T. Greenberg, D. Cicchetti, & E. M. Cummings (Eds.), *Attachment in preschool years:*

Theory, research, and intervention (pp. 121–160). Chicago, IL: University of Chicago.

Mair, M. (1988). *Between psychology and psychotherapy.* New York, NY: Routledge.

Major, B., Kaiser, C. R., O'Brien, L. T., & McCoy, S. K. (2007). Perceived discrimination as worldview threat or worldview confirmation: Implications for self-esteem. *Journal of Personality and Social Psychology, 92*(6), 1068–1086.

Malamuth, N. M. (1983). Factors associated with rape as predictors of laboratory aggression against women. *Journal of Personality and Social Psychology, 45,* 433–442.

Malamuth, N. M., Feshbach, S., & Jaffe, Y. (1977). Sexual arousal and aggression: Recent experiments and theoretical issues. In A. Peplau & C. Hammen (Eds.), *Journal of Social Issues, 33,* 110–133.

Malamuth, N. M., Feshbach, S., & Jaffe, Y., Haber, S. F., & Feshbach, S. (1980). Testing hypotheses regarding rape: Exposure to sexual violence, sex differences, and the "normality" of rapists. *Journal of Research in Personality, 14,* 121–137.

Malcolm-Smith, S., & Solms, M. (2004). Incidence of Threat in Dreams: A Response to Revonsuo's Threat Simulation Theory. *Dreaming, 14*(4), 220.

Malouff, J. M., Thorsteinsson, E. B., Schutte, N. S., Bhullar, N., & Rooke, S. E. (2010). The five-factor model of personality and relationship satisfaction of intimate partners: A meta-analysis. *Journal of Research in Personality, 44,* 124–127.

Maltzman, I. (1966). Awareness: Cognitive psychology vs. behaviorism. *Journal of Experimental Research in Personality, 1,* 161–165.

Manning, M. M., & Wright, T. L. (1983). Self-efficacy expectancies, and the persistence of pain control in childbirth. *Journal of Personality and Social Psychology, 45,* 421–431.

Manning, S. A., & Taylor, D. A. (1975). Effects of viewed violence and aggression: Stimulation and catharsis. *Journal of Personality and Social Psychology, 31,* 180–188.

Marcia. J. E. (1980). Identity in adolescence. In J. Adelson (Ed.), *Handbook of adolescent psychology.* New York, NY: Wiley.

Marcus, R. F., Telleen, S., & Poke, E. J. (1979). Relation between cooperation and empathy in young children. *Developmental Psychology, 15,* 346–347.

Marijuana and Health: Seventh Annual Report to the United States Congress from the Secretary of Health, Education, and Welfare. (1977). Washington, DC: U.S. Government Printing Office.

Marin, G. V., Marin, G., Otero-Sabogal, R., Sabogal, F., & Perez-Stable, E. (1987). *Cultural differences in attitudes toward smoking: Developing messages using the theory of reasoned action* (Tech. Rep.). (Available from Box 0320, 400 Parnassus Ave., San Francisco, CA 94117).

Markstrom-Adams, C. (1992). A consideration of intervening factors in adolescent identity formation. In G. R. Adams, T. P. Gullotta, & R. Montemayer (Eds.), *Adolescent identity formation* (pp. 173–192). Newbury Park, CA: Sage.

Markstrom-Adams, C., & Berman, R. (August 1993). *Identity formation among Canadian Jewish adolescents in minority and majority community contexts.* Paper presented as part of a symposium on "Cultural Contexts of Identity Formation: Some International Perspectives," American Psychological Association Convention, Toronto, Canada.

Markstrom-Adams, C., Berman, R. C., & Brusch, G. (1993). *Identity formation among Jewish adolescents in dissonant and consonant community contexts.* Paper submitted for publication.

Markus, H. (1977). Self-schemata and processing information about the self. *Journal of Personality and Social Psychology, 35,* 63–78.

Markus, H., Crane, M., Bernstein, S., & Siladi, M. (1982). Self-schemas and gender. *Journal of Personality and Social Psychology, 42,* 38–50.

Markus, H., & Kitayama, S. (1991). Culture and the self: Implications for cognition, emotion, and motivation. *Psychological Review, 98,* 224–253.

Markus, H., & Kunda, Z. (1986). Stability and malleability of the self-concept. *Journal of Personality and Social Psychology, 51,* 858–866.

Markus, H., & Nurius, P. (1988). Possible selves. *American Psychologist, 41,* 954–969.

Markus, H., & Wurf, E. (1987). The dynamic self-concept: A social psychological perspective. *Annual Review of Psychology, 38,* 299–337.

Markus, H. R., & Schwartz, B. (2010). Does choice mean freedom and well-being? *Journal of Consumer Research, 37*(2), 344–355.

Marsden, G. (1971). Content analysis studies of psychotherapy: 1954 through 1968. In A. F. Bergin & S. L. Garfield (Eds.), *Handbook of psychotherapy and behavior change.* New York, NY: Wiley.

Marsh, K. L., & Weary, G. (1989). Depression and attributional complexity. *Personality and Social Psychology Bulletin, 15,* 325–336.

Marshall, G. D., & Zimbardo, P. G. (1979). Affective consequences of inadequately explained physiological arousal. *Journal of Personality and Social Psychology, 37,* 970–988.

Martin, C. L., & Halverson, C. F., Jr. (1981). A schematic processing model of sex-typing and stereotyping in young children. *Child Development, 52,* 1119–1134.

Martin, C. L., & Halverson, C. F., Jr. (1987). The roles of cognition in sex-roles and sex-typing. In D. B. Carter (Ed.), *Current conceptions of sex roles and sex-typing: Theory and research.* New York, NY: Praeger.

Martin, C. L., & Ruble, D. N. (2010). Patterns of gender development. *Annual Review of Psychology, 61,* 353–381.

Martin, L. L., & Tesser, A. (1989). Toward a motivational and structural theory of ruminative thought. In J. S. Uleman & J. A. Bargh (Eds.), *Unintended thought* (pp. 306–326). New York, NY: Guilford.

Martindale, A. E., & Martindale, C. (1988). Metaphorical equivalence of elements and temperaments: Empirical studies of Bachelard's theory of imagination. *Journal of Personality and Social Psychology, 55,* 836–848.

Martindale, D. A. (1971). Territorial dominance behavior in dyadic verbal interactions. *Proceedings of the 79th Annual Convention of the American Psychological Association, 6,* 305–306.

Maslach, C. (1979). Negative emotional biasing of unexplained arousal. *Journal of Personality and Social Psychology, 37,* 953–969.

Maslow, A. H. (1941). Deprivation, threat and frustration. *Psychological Review, 48,* 364–366.

Maslow, A. H. (1943). A theory of human motivation. *Psychological Review, 50,* 370–396.

Maslow, A. H. (1971). *The farther reaches of human nature.* New York, NY: Viking.

Masson, J. M. (1985). *The assault on truth: Freud's suppression of the seduction theory.* New York, NY: Penguin.

Masten, A. S., Best, K. M., & Garmezy, N. (1990). Resilience and development: Contributions from the study of children who overcome adversity. *Development and Psychopathology, 2,* 425–444.

Masters, W., & Johnson, V. (1966). *Human sexual response.* Boston, MA: Little, Brown.

Matarazzo, J. D., & Wiens, A. N. (1972). *The interview: Research on its anatomy and structure.* Chicago, IL: Aldino-Atherton.

Matarazzo, J. D., Wiens, A. N., Matarazzo, R. G., & Saslow, G. (1968). Speech and silence behavior in clinical psychotherapy and its laboratory correlates. In J. Shlien, H. Hunt, J. D. Matarazzo, & C. Savage (Eds.), *Research in psychotherapy* (Vol. 3). Washington, DC: American Psychological Association.

Matas, L., Arend, R. A., & Sroufe, L. A. (1978). Continuity of adaptation in the second year: The relationship between quality of attachment and later competence. *Child Development, 49,* 483–494.

Matheny, A., Jr., Wilson, R. S., & Thaben, A. S. (1987). Home and mother: Relations with infant temperament. *Developmental Psychology, 23,* 323–331.

Matsumoto, D., Yoo, S. H., Nakagawa, S., & Members of Multinational Study of Cultural Display Rules. (2008). Culture, emotion regulation, and adjustment. *Journal of Personality and Social Psychology, 94*(6), 925–937.

Matthews, K. A. (1988). Coronary heart disease and Type A behaviors: Update and alternative to the Booth-Kewley and Friedman (1987) quantitative review. *Psychological Bulletin, 104,* 373–380.

Matthews, K. A., Batson, C. D., Horn, J., & Rosenman, R. H. (1981). Principles in his nature which interest him in the fortune of others . . . The heritability of empathic concern for others. *Journal of Personality, 49,* 237–247.

Matthews, K. A., Gump, B. B., Harris, K. F., Haney T. L., & Barefoot, J. C. (2004). Hostile behaviors predict cardiovascular mortality among men enrolled in the multiple risk factor intervention trial. *Circulation, 109,* 66–70.

Mazis, M. B. (1975). Antipollution measures and psychological reactance theory: A field experiment. *Journal of Personality and Social Psychology, 31,* 546–660.

McAdams, D. P. (1988). *Power, intimacy, and the life story.* New York, NY: Guilford.

McAdams, D. P. (1989). The development of a narrative identity. In D. M. Buss & N. Cantor (Eds.), *Personality psychology: Recent trends and emerging directions* (pp. 160–176). New York, NY: Springer-Verlag.

McAdams, D. P. (1990). Unity and purpose in human lives: The emergence of identity as a life story. In A. I. Rabin, R. A.

Zucker, R. A. Emmons, & S. Frank (Eds.), *Studying persons and lives* (pp. 148–200). New York, NY: Springer.

McAdams, D. P. (August, 1993). *Generative lives: Suffering, redemption, and personal destiny.* Paper presented at the American Psychological Association Convention, Toronto, Canada.

McAdams, D. P. (1994). Can personality change? Levels of stability and growth in personality across the life span. In T. F. Heatherton & J. L. Weinberger (Eds.), *Can personality change?* (pp. 299–314). Washington, DC: American Psychological Association.

McAdams, D. P. (2001). The psychology of life stories. *Review of General Psychology, 5,* 100–122.

McAdams, D. P. (2013). *The redemptive self: Stories Americans live by* (Rev. and expanded ed.). New York, NY: Oxford University Press.

McAdams, D. P., de St. Aubin, E., & Logan, R. L. (1993). Generativity among young, midlife, and older adults, *Psychology and Aging, 8,* 221–230.

McAdams, D. P., & McLean, K. C. (2013). Narrative identity. *Current Directions in Psychological Science, 22,* 233–238.

McClearn, G. E. (1962). The inheritance of behavior. In L. Postman (Ed.), *Psychology in the making.* New York, NY: Knopf.

McClelland, D. C. (1958). Methods of measuring human motivation. In J. W. Atkinson (Ed.), *Motives in fantasy, action, and society.* Princeton, NJ: Van Nostrand.

McClelland, D. C. (1961). *The achieving society.* Princeton, NJ: Van Nostrand.

McClelland, D. C., & Atkinson, J. W. (1948). The projective expression of needs: I. The effect of different intensities of the hunger drive on perception. *Journal of Psychology, 25,* 205–222.

McClelland, D. C., Davis, W. N., Kahn, R., & Wanner, E. (1972). *The drinking man.* New York, NY: Free Press.

McClelland, D. C., & Pilon, D. A. (1983). Sources of adult motives in patterns of parent behavior in early childhood. *Journal of Personality and Social Psychology, 44,* 564–574.

McCrae, R. R., & Costa, P. T., Jr. (1984). *Emerging lives, enduring disposition: Personality in adulthood.* Boston, MA: Little, Brown.

McCrae, R. R., & Costa, P. T., Jr. (1987). Validation of the five-factor model of personality across instruments and raters. *Journal of Personality and Social Psychology, 1,* 81–90.

McCrae, R. R., & Costa, P. T., Jr. (1990). *Personality in adulthood.* New York, NY: Guilford.

McCrae, R. R., & Costa, P. T., Jr. (1997). Personality trait structure as a human universal. *American Psychologist, 52,* 509–516.

McCrae, R. R., & Costa, P. T. (2003). *Personality in adulthood: A five-factor theory perspective.* New York, NY: Guilford.

McCrae, R. R., & Costa, P. T. (2008). Empirical and theoretical status of the five-factor model of personality traits. In G. J. Boyle, G. Mathews, & D. H. Saklofske (Eds.), *The SAGE handbook of personality theory and assessment* (Vol. 1, pp. 273–294). Los Angeles, CA: Sage.

McCrae, R. R., Costa, P. T., Jr., & Martin, T. A. (2005). The NEO–PI–3: A more readable revised NEO personality inventory, *Journal of Personality Assessment, 84,* 261–270.

McCrae, R. R., & John, O. P. (1992). An introduction to the five factor model and its applications. *Journal of Personality, 60,* 175–215.

McGinnies, E. (1949). Emotionality and perceptual defense. *Psychological Review, 56,* 244–251.

McGlothlin, W. H., & Arnold, D. D. (1971). LSD revisited. *Archives of General Psychiatry, 24,* 35–49.

McGlothlin, W. H., Cohen, S., & McGlothlin, M. S. (1967). Long lasting effects of LSD on normals. *Archives of General Psychiatry, 17,* 521–532.

McGrath, M. J., & Cohen, D. B. (1978). REM sleep facilitation of adaptive waking behaviors: A review of the literature. *Psychological Bulletin, 85,* 24–57.

McGue, M. (1999). The behavioral genetics of alcoholism. *Current Directions in Psychological Science, 8*(4), 109–115.

McGue, M., & Lykken, D. T. (1992). Genetic influence on risk of divorce. *Psychological Science, 3,* 368–373.

McGuire, J., Martin, C. L., Fabes, R. A., & Hanish, L. D. (2007). The role of "gender enforcers" in young children's peer interactions. Poster presented at Biennial Meeting of the Society for Research in Child Development, Boston, MA.

McGuire, W. J., & Padawer-Singer, A. (1976). Trait salience in the spontaneous self-concept. *Journal of Personality and Social Psychology, 33,* 743–754.

McKinley, D. G. (1964). *Social class and family life.* New York, NY: Free Press.

Mednick, S., & Christiansen, K. O. (1977). *Biosocial bases of criminal behavior.* New York, NY: Gardner.

Mednick, S. A., Brennan, P., & Kandel, E. (1988). Predisposition to violence. *Aggressive Behavior, 14,* 25–33.

Mednick, S. A., Moffitt, T. E., & Stack, S. (1987). *The causes of crime: New biological approaches.* New York, NY: Cambridge University Press.

Meehl, P. E. (1954). *Clinical versus statistical prediction.* Minneapolis, MN: University of Minnesota Press.

Meehl, P. E. (1962). Schizotaxia, schizotypy, schizophrenia. *American Psychologist, 17,* 827–838.

Meeus, W. (1996). Studies on identity development in adolescence: An overview of research and some new data. *Journal of Youth and Adolescence, 25*(5), 569–598.

Megargee, E. I. (1966). Undercontrolled and overcontrolled personality types in extreme antisocial aggression. *Psychological Monographs, 80* (Whole No. 611).

Megargee, E. I., & Mendelsohn, G. A. (1962). A cross validation of twelve MMPI indices of hostility and control. *Journal of Abnormal and Social Psychology, 65,* 431–438.

Meiselman, K. (1979). *Incest: A psychological study of causes and effects with treatment recommendations.* San Francisco, CA: Jossey-Bass.

Meltzoff, A. N., & Decety, J. (2003). What imitation tells us about social cognition: A rapprochement between developmental psychology and cognitive neuroscience. *Philosophical Transactions of the Royal Society, London: Biological Sciences, 358,* 491–500.

Mendelsohn, G. A. (1993). It's time to put theories of personality in their place, or, Allport and Stagner got it right, why can't we? In K. H. Craik, R. Hogan, & R. N. Wolfe (Eds.), *Fifty years of personality psychology* (pp. 103–118). New York, NY: Plenum.

Menzies, E. S. (1974). *Preference in television content among violent prisoners* (FCI Research Reports). Tallahassee, FL: Federal Correctional Institution.

Merton, R. K. (1957). *Social theory and social structure.* Glencoe, IL: Free Press.

Mervielde, I., De Clercq, B., De Fruyt, F., & Van Leeuwen, K. (2005). Temperament, personality, and developmental psychopathology as childhood antecedents of personality disorders. *Journal of Personality Disorders, 19,* 171–201.

Messick, S. (1975). The standard problem: Meaning and values in measurement and evaluation. *American Psychologist, 30,* 955–966.

Messick, S., & Jackson, D. N. (1961). Acquiescence and the factorial interpretation of the MMPI. *Psychological Bulletin, 58,* 299–304.

Meyer, H. H., Walker, W. B., & Litwin, G. H. (1961). Motive patterns and risk preferences associated with entrepreneurship. *Journal of Abnormal and Social Psychology, 63,* 570–574.

Midlarsky, E., & Bryan, J. H. (1972). Affect expressions and children's imitative altruism. *Journal of Experimental Research in Personality, 6,* 195–203.

Mikulincer, M., & Shaver, P. R. (2001). Attachment theory and intergroup bias: Evidence that priming the secure base schema attenuates negative reactions to out-groups. *Journal of Personality and Social Psychology, 81,* 97–115.

Mikulincer, M., Shaver, P. R., Gillath, O., & Nitzberg, R. A. (2005). Attachment, caregiving, and altruism. *Journal of Personality and Social Psychology, 89,* 817–839.

Mikulincer, M., Shaver, P. R., & Pereg, D. (2003). Attachment theory and affect regulation: The dynamics, development, and cognitive consequences of attachment-related strategies. *Motivation and Emotion, 27,* 77–102.

Miles, D. R., & Carey, G. (1997). Genetic and environmental architecture on human aggression. *Journal of Personality and Social Psychology, 72*(1), 207.

Milevsky, A., Schlechter, M., Netter, S., & Keehn, D. (2007). Maternal and paternal parenting styles in adolescents: Associations with self-esteem, depression and life-satisfaction. *Journal of Child and Family Studies, 16*(1), 39–47.

Milgram, S. (1963). Behavioral study of obedience. *Journal of Abnormal and Social Psychology, 67,* 371–378.

Milgram, S. (1974). *Obedience to authority.* New York, NY: Harper & Row.

Milgram, S., & Shotland, R. L. (1973). *Television and antisocial behavior: Field experiments.* New York, NY: Academic Press.

Miller, D. R., & Swanson, G. E. (1960). *Inner conflict and defense.* New York, NY: Holt.

Miller, I. W., III, & Norman, W. H. (1979). Learned helplessness: A review and attribution-theory model. *Psychological Bulletin, 86,* 93–118.

Miller, M. M. (1959). Treatment of chronic alcoholism by hypnotic aversion. *Journal of the American Medical Association, 171,* 1492–1495.

Miller, N. E. (1941). The frustration-aggression hypothesis. *Psychological Review, 48*, 337–342.

Miller, N. E. (1944). Experimental studies in conflict. In J. McV. Hunt (Ed.), *Personality and the behavioral disorders* (Vol. 1). New York, NY: Ronald.

Miller, N. E. (1959). Liberalization of basic S-R concepts: Extensions to conflict, motivation, and social learning. In S. Koch (Ed.), *Psychology: A study of a science* (Vol. 2). New York, NY: McGraw-Hill.

Miller, N. E., & Banuazizi, A. (1968). Instrumental learning by curarized rats of a specific visceral response, intestinal or cardiac. *Journal of Comparative and Physiological Psychology, 65*, 1–17.

Miller, N. E., & Bugelski, R. (1948). Minor studies in aggression. II. The influence of frustration imposed by the in-group attitudes expressed toward out-groups. *Journal of Psychology, 25*, 437–442.

Miller, N. E., & Dollard, J. (1941). *Social learning and imitation*. New Haven, CT: Yale University Press.

Miller, P. A., & Eisenberg, N. (1988). The relation of empathy to aggressive and externalizing/antisocial behavior. *Psychological Bulletin, 103*, 324–344.

Miller, W. R., & C'deBaca, J. (1994). Quantum change: Toward a psychology of transformation. In T. F. Heatherton & J. L. Weinberger (Eds.), *Can personality change?* (pp. 253–280). Washington, DC: American Psychological Association.

Millett, R. A. (1960). Measures of learning and conditioning. In H. J. Eysenck (Ed.), *Experiments in personality* (Vol. II). London, UK: Routledge.

Mischel, W. (1961). Delay of gratification, need for achievement, and acquiescence in another culture. *Journal of Abnormal and Social Psychology, 62*, 543–552.

Mischel, W. (1966). A social learning theory view of sex differences in behavior. In E. E. Maccoby (Ed.), *The development of sex differences*. Stanford, CA: Stanford University Press.

Mischel, W. (1968). *Personality and assessment*. New York, NY: Wiley.

Mischel, W. (1971). *Introduction to personality*. New York, NY: Holt.

Mischel, W. (1973). Toward a cognitive social learning reconceptualization of personality. *Psychological Review, 80*, 252–283.

Mischel, W. (1974a). Cognitive appraisals and transformations in self-control. In B. Weiner (Ed.), *Cognitive views of human motivation*. New York, NY: Academic Press.

Mischel, W. (1974b). Process in delay of gratification. In L. Berkowitz (Ed.), *Advances in experimental social psychology* (Vol. 7). New York, NY: Academic Press.

Mischel, W. (1977). On the future of personality measurement. *American Psychologist, 32*, 246–254.

Mischel, W. (1979). On the interface of cognition and personality: Beyond the person-situation debate. *American Psychologist, 34*, 740–754.

Mischel, W. (1984). Convergences and challenges in the search for consistency. *American Psychologist, 39*, 351–364.

Mischel, W. (2009). From personality and assessment (1968) to personality science, 2009. *Journal of Research in Personality, 43*(2), 282–290.

Mischel, W., & Ebbesen, E. B. (1970). Attention in delay of gratification. *Journal of Personality and Social Psychology, 16*, 329–337.

Mischel, W., Ebbesen, E. B., & Zeiss, A. R. (1972). Cognitive and attentional mechanisms in delay of gratification. *Journal of Personality and Social Psychology, 21*, 204–218.

Mischel, W., & Mischel, H. N. (1976). A cognitive social learning approach to morality and self-regulation. In T. Lickona (Ed.), *Moral development and behavior: Theory, research and social issues*. New York, NY: Holt.

Mischel, W., & Mischel, H. N. (1977). Self-control and the self. In T. Mischel (Ed.), *The Self: Psychological and philosophical issues*. Totowa, NJ: Rowan and Littlefield.

Mischel, W., & Peake, P. K. (1982). Beyond déjà vu in the search for cross-situational consistency. *Psychological Review, 89*, 730–755.

Mischel, W., Peake, P. K., & Zeiss, A. (1972). Cognitive and attentional mechanisms in delay of gratification. *Journal of Personality and Social Psychology, 21*, 204–218.

Mischel, W., Shoda, Y., & Peake, P. K. (1988). The nature of adolescent competencies predicted by preschool delay of gratification. *Journal of Personality and Social Psychology, 54*, 687–696.

Mitchell, C., & Stuart, R. B. (1984). Effects of self-efficacy on dropout from obesity treatment. *Journal of Consulting and Clinical Psychology, 52*, 1100–1101.

Mitchell, J. E., Baker, L. A., & Jacklin, C. N. (1989). Masculinity and femininity in twin children: Genetic and environmental factors. *Child Development, 60*, 1475–1485.

Miu, A. C., Vulturar, R., Chiş, A., Ungureanu, L., & Gross, J. J. (2013). Reappraisal as a mediator in the link between 5-HTTLPR and social anxiety symptoms. *Emotion, 13*(6), 1012–1022.

Moffitt, T. E. (2005). The new look of behavioral genetics in developmental psychopathology: Gene-environment interplay in antisocial behaviors. *Psychological Bulletin, 131*(4), 533–554.

Money, J. (Ed.). (1965). *Sex research, new developments*. New York, NY: Holt.

Monte, C. F. (1977). *Beneath the mask*. New York, NY: Praeger.

Monteith, M., Berkowitz, L., Kruglanski, A., & Blair, C. (1990). *The influence of physical discomfort on experienced anger and anger related ideas, judgments, & memories*. Manuscript in preparation.

Montemayor, R., & Eisen, M. (1977). The development of self-conceptions from childhood to adolescence. *Developmental Psychology, 13*, 314–319.

Moos, R. H. (1973). Conceptualizations of human environment. *American Psychologist, 28*, 652–665.

Morash, M. A. (1980). Working class membership and the adolescent identity crisis. *Adolescence, 15*, 313–320.

Mor, N., & Winquist, J. (2002). Self-focused attention and negative affect: A meta-analysis. *Psychological Bulletin, 128*, 638–662.

Morokoff, P. J. (1985). Effects of sex guilt, repression, sexual "arousability," and sexual experience on female sexual arousal during erotica and fantasy. *Journal of Personality and Social Psychology, 49*, 177–187.

Morris, J. L. (1966). Propensity for risk taking as a determinant of vocational choice: An extension of the theory of achievement motivation. *Journal of Personality and Social Psychology, 3,* 328–335.

Moss, H. A., & Kagan, J. (1961). Stability of achievement and recognition seeking behaviors from early childhood through adulthood. *Journal of Abnormal and Social Psychology, 62,* 504–513.

Mõttus, R., Luciano, M., Starr, J. M., Pollard, M. C., & Deary, I. J. (2013). Personality traits and inflammation in men and women in their early 70s: The Lothian Birth Cohort 1936 study of healthy aging. *Psychosomatic Medicine, 75,* 11–19.

Mowrer, O. H. (1960). *Learning theory and behavior.* New York, NY: Wiley.

Mowrer, O. H., & Viek, P. (1948). An experimental analogue of fear from a sense of helplessness. *Journal of Abnormal and Social Psychology, 43,* 193–200.

Moyer, K. E. (1971). The physiology of aggression and the implications for aggression control. In J. L. Singer (Ed.), *The control of aggression and violence.* New York, NY: Academic Press.

Mukherjee, B. N., & Sinha, R. (1970). Achievement values and self-ideal discrepancies in college students, *Personality: An International Journal, 1,* 275–301.

Muller, M. N., & Mitani, J. C. (2005). Conflict and cooperation in wild chimpanzees. *Advances in the Study of Behavior, 35,* 275–331.

Munroe, R. H., Shimmin, H. S., & Munroe, R. L. (1984). Gender understanding and sex-role preferences in four cultures. *Developmental Psychology, 20,* 673–682.

Murray, H. A. (1933). The effect of fear upon estimates of the maliciousness of other personalities. *Journal of Social Psychology, 4,* 310–329.

Murray, H. A. (1938). *Explorations in personality: A clinical and experimental study of fifty men of college age.* New York, NY: Oxford University Press.

Murray, H. A. (1943). *Thematic apperception test.* Cambridge, MA: Harvard University Press.

Murstein, B. I. (1963). *Theory and research in projective techniques.* New York, NY: Wiley.

Mussen, P. H. (1977). The development of personality and social behavior. In P. Mussen & M. R. Rosenzweig (Eds.), *Psychology: An introduction.* Lexington, MA: D. C. Heath.

Mussen, P. H., & Eisenberg-Berg, N. (1977). *The roots of caring, sharing, and helping: The development of prosocial behavior in children.* San Francisco, CA: Freeman.

Myers, I. (1962). *The Myers-Briggs Type Indicator.* Princeton, NJ: Educational Testing Service.

Myers, L. J., Speight, S. L., Highlen, P. S., Cox, C. I., Reynolds, A. L., Adams, E. M., & Hanley, C. P. (1990). Identity development and worldview: Toward an optimal conceptualization. *Journal of Counseling and Development, 70,* 64–71.

Myrtek, M. (2001). Meta-analyses of prospective studies on coronary heart disease, type A personality, and hostility. *International Journal of Cardiology, 79*(2), 245–251.

Nadon, R., Laurence, J. R., & Perry, C. (1987). Multiple predictors of hypnotic susceptibility. *Journal of Personality and Social Psychology, 53,* 948–960.

Nasby, W., Hayden, B., & DePaulo, B. M. (1980). Attributional bias among aggressive boys to interpret unambiguous social stimuli as displays of hostility. *Journal of Abnormal Psychology, 89*(3), 459–468.

Nation, J. R., Cooney, J. B., & Gartrell, K. E. (1979). Durability and generalizability of persistence training. *Journal of Abnormal Psychology, 88*(2), 121–136.

Neisser, U. (1988). Five kinds of self-knowledge. *Philosophical Psychology, 1,* 35–59.

Nelson, J. D., Gelfand, D. M., & Hartmann, D. P. (1969). Children's aggression following competition and exposure to an aggressive model. *Child Development, 40,* 1085–1097.

Neugarten, B. L. (1977). Personality and aging. In J. E. Birren & K. W. Schaie (Eds.), *Handbook of the psychology of aging.* New York, NY: Van Nostrand Reinhold.

Newcomb, T. (1943). *Personality and social change.* New York, NY: Dryden.

Newson, J., & Newson, E. (1968). *Four years old in an urban community.* Chicago, IL: Aldine.

Newson, J., & Newson, E. (1976). Cultural aspects of child rearing in the English-speaking world. In A. Skolnick (Ed.), *Rethinking childhood.* Boston, MA: Little, Brown.

Nguyen, A. M. D., & Benet-Martínez, V. (2013). Biculturalism and adjustment: A meta-analysis. *Journal of Cross-Cultural Psychology, 44*(1), 122–159.

Nicholls, J. G. (1984). Conceptions of ability and achievement motivation. In R. E. Ames & C. Ames (Eds.), *Motivation in education* (Vol. 1, pp. 39–73). San Francisco, CA: Academic Press.

Nichols, M. P., & Efran, J. S. (1985). Catharsis in psychotherapy: A new perspective. *Psychotherapy, 22,* 46–58.

Nickel, T. W. (1974). The attribution of intention as a critical factor in the relation between frustration and aggression. *Journal of Personality, 42,* 482–492.

Niedenthal, P. M., Brauer, M., Robin, L., & Innes-Ker, A. H. (2002). Adult attachment and the perception of facial expression of emotion. *Journal of Personality and Social Psychology, 82,* 419–433.

Niedenthal, P. M., Cantor, N., & Kihlstrom, J. F. (1985). Prototype matching: A strategy for social decision making. *Journal of Personality and Social Psychology, 48*(3), 575–584.

Niedenthal, P. M., Halberstadt J. B., & Setterlund, M. B. (1997). Being happy and seeing "happy": Emotional state mediates visual word recognition. *Cognition & Emotion 11,* 403–432.

Niedenthal, P. M., & Ric, F. (2017). *The psychology of emotions.* New York, NY: Routledge.

Niedenthal, P. M., & Setterlund, M. B. (1994). Emotion congruence in perception. *Personality and Social Psychology Bulletin, 20*(4), 401–411.

Niedenthal, P. M., Setterlund, M. B., & Jones, D. (1994). The emotional organization of perceptual memory. In P. M. Niedenthal & S. Kitayama (Eds.), *The heart's eye: Emotional influences in perception and attention* (pp. 180–201). New York, NY: Academic Press.

Niedenthal, P. M., Setterlund, M. B., & Wherry, M. B. (1992). Possible self-complexity and affective reactions to goal-relevant evaluation. *Journal of Personality and Social Psychology, 63*(1), 5–16.

Niedenthal, P. M., Tangney, J. P., & Gavanski, I. (1994). "If only I weren't" versus "If only I hadn't": Distinguishing shame and guilt in counterfactual thinking. *Journal of Personality and Social Psychology, 67*(4), 585–595.

Niiya, Y., Ellsworth, P. C., & Yamaguchi, S. (2006). Amae in Japan and the United States: An exploration of a "culturally unique" emotion. *Emotion, 6,* 279.

Nisan, M., & Kohlberg, L. (1982). Universality and variation in moral judgment: A longitudinal and cross-sectional study in Turkey. *Child Development, 53,* 865–876.

Nisbett, R. E. (1993). Violence and US regional culture. *American Psychologist, 48*(4), 441–449.

Nisbett, R. E., & Borgida, E. (1975). Attribution and the psychology of prediction. *Journal of Personality and Social Psychology, 32,* 932–943.

Nisbett, R. E., & Schachter, S. (1966). Cognitive manipulation of pain. *Journal of Experimental Social Psychology, 2,* 227–236.

Nobles, W. (1989). Psychological nigrescence: An Afrocentric view. *Counseling Psychologist, 17,* 253–257.

Norem, J. K. (1989). Cognitive strategies as personality: Effectiveness, specificity, flexibility, and change. In D. M. Buss & N. Cantor (Eds.), *Personality psychology: Recent trends and emerging directions* (pp. 45–60). New York, NY: Springer-Verlag.

Norem-Hebeisen, A. A., & Johnson, D. W. (1981). The relationship between cooperative, competitive, and individualistic attitudes and differentiated aspects of self-esteem. *Journal of Personality, 49,* 415–426.

Norman, W. T. (1963). Toward an adequate taxonomy of personality attributes: Replicated factor structure in peer nomination personality ratings. *Journal of Abnormal and Social Psychology, 66,* 574–583.

Norman, W. T. (1967). On estimating psychological relationships: Social desirability and self-report. *Psychological Bulletin, 67,* 273–293.

Novaco, R. W. (1975). *Anger control: The development and evaluation of an experimental treatment.* Lexington, MA: Lexington Books.

Novaco, R. W. (1985). Anger and its therapeutic regulations. In M. A. Chesney & R. Rosenman (Eds.), *Anger and hostility in cardiovascular and behavioral disorders.* New York, NY: Hemisphere.

Nunnally, J. C. (1978). *Psychometric theory* (2nd ed.). New York, NY: McGraw-Hill.

Nuttin, J. M., Jr. (1985). Narcissism beyond Gestalt and awareness: The name-letter effect. *European Journal of Social Psychology, 15,* 353–361.

Ochse, R., & Plug, C. (1986). Cross-cultural investigation of the validity of Erikson's theory of personality development. *Journal of Personality and Social Psychology, 50,* 1240–1252.

Offer, D. (1969). *The psychological world of the teenager.* New York, NY: Basic Books.

Offer, D., & Offer, J. B. (1975). *From teenage to young manhood.* New York, NY: Basic Books.

Oliner, S. P., & Oliner, P. M. (1988). *The altruistic personality: Rescuers of Jews in Nazi Europe.* New York, NY: Free Press.

Olowse, A. A. (1984). A cross-cultural study of adolescent self-concept. *Journal of Adolescence, 6,* 263–274.

Olweus, D. (1973). Personality and aggression. In J. K. Cole & D. D. Jensen (Eds.), *Nebraska Symposium on Motivation* (Vol. 21). Lincoln, NE: University of Nebraska Press.

Olweus, D. (1974). Personality factors and aggression: With special reference to violence within the peer group. In J. de Wit & W. W. Hartup (Eds.), *Determinants and origins of aggressive behavior.* The Hague, Netherlands: Mouton.

Olweus, D. (1976). *Aggression in the schools: Bullies and whipping boys.* Washington, DC: Hemisphere.

Olweus, D. (1977a). A critical analysis of the "modern" interactionist position. In D. Magnussen & N. S. Endler (Eds.), *Personality at the crossroads: Current issues in interactional psychology.* Hillsdale, NJ: Lawrence Erlbaum.

Olweus, D. (1977b). Aggression and peer acceptance in preadolescent boys. Two short-term longitudinal studies of ratings. *Child Development, 48,* 1301–1313.

Olweus, D. (1979). Stability of aggressive reaction patterns in males: A review. *Psychological Bulletin, 86,* 852–875.

Olweus, D. (1980). Familial and temperamental determinants of aggressive behavior in adolescent boys: A causal analysis. *Developmental Psychology, 16,* 644–666.

Olweus, D. (1986). Aggression and hormones: Behavioral relationship with testosterone and adrenaline. In D. Olweus, J. Block, & M. Radke-Yarrow (Eds.), *Development of antisocial and prosocial behavior: Research, theories, and issues.* Orlando, FL: Academic Press.

Olweus, D., Mattisson, A., Schalling, D., & Lam, H. (1980). Testosterone, aggression, physical, and personality dimensions in normal adolescent males. *Psychosomatic Medicine, 42,* 253–269.

Ones, D. S., Viswesvaran, C., & Reiss, A. D. (1996). Role of social desirability in personality testing for personnel selection: The red herring. *Journal of Applied Psychology, 81*(6), 660–679.

Opler, M. K. (Ed.). (1959). *Culture and mental health.* New York, NY: Macmillan.

Opler, M. K. (Ed.). (1967). *Culture and social psychiatry.* New York, NY: Atherton.

Orlinsky, D., & Howard, B. (1967). The good hour. *Archives of General Psychiatry, 16,* 621–632.

Orne, M. T. (1959). The nature of hypnosis: Artifact and essence. *Journal of Abnormal and Social Psychology, 58,* 277–299.

Orne, M. T. (1962). On the social psychology of the psychological experiment. *American Psychologist, 17,* 776–783.

Orne, M. T. (1975). Hypnosis. In G. Lindzey, C. Hall, & R. F. Thompson (Eds.), *Psychology.* New York, NY: Worth.

Ornstein, R. E. (1972). *The psychology of consciousness.* San Francisco, CA: Freeman.

Ortony, A., & Turner, T. J. (1990). What's basic about basic emotions? *Psychological Review, 97,* 315–331.

Orvis, B. R., Cunningham, J. D., & Kelley, H. H. (1975). A closer examination of causal inference: The role of consensus, distinctiveness, and consistency information. *Journal of Personality and Social Psychology, 32,* 605–616.

Ostwald, P., & Bittner, E. (1968). Life adjustment after severe persecution. *American Journal of Psychiatry, 124,* 87–94.

Otsuka, K., Taguri, M., Dennis, C. L., Wakutani, K., Awano, M., Yamaguchi, T., & Jimba, M. (2014). Effectiveness of a breastfeeding self-efficacy intervention: Do hospital practices make a difference? *Maternal and Child Health Journal, 18,* 296–306.

Oyserman, D., Coon, H. M., & Kemmelmeier, M. (2002). Rethinking individualism and collectivism: Evaluation of theoretical assumptions and meta-analyses. *Psychological Bulletin, 128*(1), 3–72.

Ozer, D. J., & Gjerde, P. F. (1989). Patterns of personality consistency and change from childhood through adolescence. *Journal of Personality, 57,* 483–507.

Paivio, A. (1971). *Imagery and verbal processes.* New York, NY: Holt.

Parke, R. D. (1970). The role of punishment in the socialization process. In R. A. Hoppe, G. A. Milton, & E. C. Simmel (Eds.), *Early experiences and the processes of socialization.* New York, NY: Academic Press.

Parke, R. D., & Colmer, C. W. (1975). Child abuse: An interdisciplinary analysis. In E. M. Hetherington (Ed.), *Review of child development research* (Vol. 5, pp. 509–590). Chicago, IL: University of Chicago Press.

Parke, R. D., & Slaby, R. G. (1983). The development of aggression. In P. H. Mussen (Gen. Ed.) & E. M. Hetherington (Vol. Ed.), *Handbook of child psychology: Vol. 4, Socialization, personality, and social development* (4th ed., pp. 547–641). New York, NY: Wiley.

Parke, R. D., & Suomi, S. J. (1980). Adult male-infant relationships: Human and nonprimate evidence. In K. Immelmann, G. Barlow, M. Main, & L. Petrinovitch (Eds.), *Behavioral development: The Bielefeld interdisciplinary project.* New York, NY: Cambridge University Press.

Parke, R. D., & Walters, R. H. (1967). Some factors influencing the efficacy of punishment training for inducing response inhibitions. *Monographs of the Society for Research in Child Development, 32* (1, Serial No. 109).

Parker, G., Tupling, H., & Brown, L. B. (1979). A parental bonding instrument. *British Journal of Medical Psychology, 52,* 1–10.

Passini, F. T., & Norman, W. T. (1966). A universal conception of personality structure? *Journal of Personality and Social Psychology, 4,* 44–49.

Passman, R., & Weisberg, P. (1975). Mothers and blankets as agents for promoting play and exploration by young children in a novel environment. *Developmental Psychology, 11,* 170–177.

Patterson, C. J. (1982). Self-control and self-regulation in childhood. In T. Field & A. Huston-Stein (Eds.), *Review of human development.* New York, NY: Wiley.

Patterson, C. J., & Mischel, W. (1976). Effects of temptation-inhibiting and task-facilitating plans on self-control. *Journal of Personality and Social Psychology, 33,* 209–217.

Patterson, G. R. (1979). Treatment for children with conduct problems: A review of outcome studies. In S. Feshbach & A. Fraczek (Eds.), *Aggression and behavior change: Biological and social processes,* (pp. 83–138). New York, NY: Praeger.

Patterson, G. R. (1982). *Coercive family process.* Eugene, OR: Castalia Press.

Patterson, G. R., & Bank, L. (1989). Some amplifying mechanisms for pathological processes in families. In M. Gunner (Ed.), *Minnesota symposium on child psychology.* Hillsdale, NJ: Lawrence Erlbaum Associates.

Patterson, G. R., Chamberlain, P., & Reid, J. B. (1982). A comparative evaluation of a parent training program. *Behavior Therapy, 13,* 638–650.

Patterson, G. R., Cobb, J. A., & Ray, R. S. (1973). Asocial engineering technology for retraining the families of aggressive boys. In H. E. Adams & I. P. Unibel (Eds.), *Issues and trends in behavior therapy.* Springfield, IL: Charles C. Thomas.

Patterson, G. R., Littman, R. A., & Bricker, W. (1967). Assertive behavior in children: A step toward a theory of aggression. *Monographs of the Society for Research in Child Development, 32*(5, Serial No. 113).

Patterson, S. J., Sochting, I., & Marcia, J. E. (1992). The inner space and beyond: Women and identity. In G. R. Adams, I. P. Gullotta, & R. Montemayer (Eds.), *Adolescent identity formation* (pp. 9–24). Newbury Park, CA: Sage.

Paul, G. L. (1966). *Insight vs. desensitization in psychotherapy.* Stanford, CA: Stanford University Press.

Paunonen, S. V., & Jackson, D. N. (1985). Idiographic measurement strategies for personality and prediction: Some unredeemed promissory notes. *Psychological Review, 92,* 486–511.

Pedersen, P. (1987). Ten frequent assumptions of cultural bias in counseling. *Journal of multicultural counseling and development, 15*(1), 16–24.

Peeke, H. R. S., Wyers, E. J., & Herz, M. J. (1969). Waning of the aggressive response to male models in the three spined stickleback (Gasterosteus aculeatus L.). *Animal Behavior, 17,* 224–228.

Pelto, P. (1968). The difference between tight and loose societies. *Transaction,* 37–40.

Penk, W. E., Carpenter, J. C., & Rylee, K. E. (1979). MMPI correlates of social and physical anhedonia. *Journal of Consulting and Clinical Psychology, 47,* 1046–1052.

Pennebaker, J. W. (1989). Stream of consciousness and stress: Levels of thinking. In J. S. Uleman & J. A. Bargh (Eds.), *Unintended thought* (pp. 327–350). New York, NY: Guilford.

Pennebaker, J. W. (1990). *Opening up.* New York, NY: William Morrow.

Pennebaker, J. W., & Smyth, J. M. (2016). *Opening up by writing it down.* New York, NY: Guilford.

Peplau, L. A. (July 3–8, 1988). *Research on lesbian and gay relationships. A decade review.* Paper presented at the 4th International Congress on Personal Relationships held at the University of British Columbia, Vancouver, Canada.

Peplau, L. A., Rubin, A., & Hill, C. T. (1977). Sexual intimacy in dating relationships. *Journal of Social Issues, 33,* 86–109.

Penman, D., & Duck, S. (1987). *Intimate relationships: Development, dynamics, deterioration.* Newbury Park, CA: Sage.

Pervin, L. A. (Ed.). (1989). *Goal concepts in personality and social psychology.* Hillsdale, NJ: Lawrence Erlbaum.

Petersen, A. C. (1988). Adolescent development. *Annual Review of Psychology, 39,* 583–607.

Peterson, C., & Barrett, L. C. (1987). Explanatory style and academic performance among university freshmen. *Journal of Personality and Social Psychology, 53,* 603–607.

Peterson, C., Seligman, M. E. P., & Vaillant, G. (1988). Pessimistic explanatory style is a risk factor for physical illness: A thirty-five year longitudinal study. *Journal of Personality and Social Psychology, 55,* 23–27.

Peterson, C., Semmel, A., von Baeyer, C., Abramson, L. Y., Metalsky, G. I., & Seligman, M. E. P. (1982). The Attributional Style Questionnaire. *Cognitive Therapy and Research, 6*, 287–299.

Peterson, D. R. (1983). Conflict. In H. H. Kelley, E. Berscheid, A. Christenson, J. H. Harvey, T. L. Huston, G. Levinger, E. McClintock, L. A. Peplau, & D. R. Peterson (Eds.), *Close relationships*. New York, NY: W. H. Freeman.

Pfeifer, J. H., Dapretto, M., & Lieberman, M. D. (2009). The neural foundations of evaluative self-knowledge in middle childhood, early adolescence and adulthood. In P. D. Zelazo, M. Chandler, & E. Crone (Eds.), *Developmental social cognitive neuroscience* (pp. 141–163). New York, NY: Routledge.

Phares, E. J. (1976). *Locus of control in personality*. Morristown, NJ: General Learning Press.

Phillips, D., McCartney, K., & Scan, S. (1987). Child-care quality and children's social development. *Developmental Psychology, 23*, 537–543.

Phillips, D. J. (1983). The impact of mass media violence on U.S. homicides. *American Sociological Review, 48*, 560–568.

Phillips, D. J., & Hensley, J. E. (1984). When violence is rewarded or punished: The impact of mass media stories on homicide. *Journal of Communication, 34*(3), 101–116.

Phinney, J. S. (1990). Ethnic identity in adolescents and adults: A review of research. *Psychological Bulletin, 108*, 499–514.

Phinney, J. S. (1991). Ethnic identity and self-esteem: A review and integration. *Hispanic Journal of Behavioral Sciences, 13*, 193–208.

Phinney, J. S., & Chavira, V. (1992). Ethnic identity and self-esteem: An exploratory longitudinal study. *Journal of Adolescence, 15*, 271–281.

Phinney, J. S., & Rosenthal, D. A. (1992). Ethnic identity in adolescence: Process, context, and outcome. In G. R. Adams, T. P. Gullotta, & R. Montemayer (Eds.), *Adolescent identity formation* (pp. 145–172). Newbury Park, CA: Sage.

Pianka, E. R. (1970). On r- and K-selection. *American Naturalist, 104*, 592–597.

Piccione, C., Hilgard, E. R., & Zimbardo, P. G. (1989). On the degree of stability of measured hypnotizability over a 25-year period. *Journal of Personality and Social Psychology, 56*, 289–295.

Pihl, R. O., Assaad, J. M., & Hoaken, P. N. (2003). The alcohol-aggression relationship and differential sensitivity to alcohol. *Aggressive Behavior, 29*(4), 302–315.

Piliavin, I. M., Rodin, J., & Piliavin, J. A. (1969). Good Samaritanism: An underground phenomenon? *Journal of Personality and Social Psychology, 13*, 289–299.

Pilleri, G., & Knuckey, J. (1969). Behaviour patterns of some delphinidae observed in the western Mediterranean. *Zeitschrift für Tierpsychologie, 26*(1), 48–72.

Pitkänen-Pulkkinen, L. (1979). Self-control as a prerequisite for constructive behavior. In S. Feshbach & A. Fraczek (Eds.), *Aggression and behavior change: Biological and social processes*. New York, NY: Praeger.

Pitkänen-Pulkkinen, L. (1982). Self-control and continuity from childhood to adolescence. In P. B. Baltes and O. G. Brim (Eds.), *Life-span development and behavior* (Vol. 4). New York, NY: Academic Press.

Plato. (1972). *The symposium* (W. Hamilton, Trans.). London, UK: Penguin Books Ltd.

Plomin, R. (1986). *Development, genetics, and psychology*. Hillsdale, NJ: Erlbaum.

Plomin, R. (1989). Environment and genes. *American Psychologist, 44*, 105–111.

Plomin, R., Chipuer, H. M., & Loehlin, J. C. (1990). Behavioral genetics and personality. In L. A. Pervin (Ed.), *Handbook of personality* (pp. 225–243). New York, NY: Guilford.

Plomin, R., Corely, R., DeFries, J. C., & Fulker, D. W. (1990). Individual differences in television viewing in early childhood: Nature as well as nurture. *Psychological Science, 1*, 371–377.

Plutchik, R. (1980) *Emotions: A psychoevolutionary synthesis*. New York, NY: Harper and Row.

Plutchik, R. (1994). *The psychology and biology of emotion*. New York, NY: Harper Collins.

Polansky, N., Freeman, W., Horowitz, M., Irwin, L., Papanis, N., Rappaport, D., & Whaley, F. (1949). Problems of interpersonal relations in research on groups. *Human Relations, 2*, 281–291.

Polderman, T. J., Benyamin, B., De Leeuw, C. A., Sullivan, P. F., Van Bochoven, A., Visscher, P. M., & Posthuma, D. (2015). Meta-analysis of the heritability of human traits based on fifty years of twin studies. *Nature Genetics, 47*, 702–709.

Posner, M. I., & Rothbart, M. K. (1989). Intentional chapters on unintended thoughts. In J. S. Uleman & J. A. Bargh (Eds.), *Unintended thought* (pp. 450–470). New York, NY: Guilford.

Powers, W. T. (1973). *Behavior: The control of perception*. Chicago, IL: Aldine.

Pratt, M. W., Kerig, P., Cowan, P. A., & Cowan, C. P. (1988). Mothers and fathers teaching three year olds: Authoritative parenting and adult scaffolding of young children's learning. *Developmental Psychology, 24*, 832–839.

Price, R. H., & Bouffard, D. L. (1974). Behavioral appropriateness and situational constraint as dimensions of social behavior. *Journal of Personality and Social Psychology, 30*(4), 579–586.

Proshansky, H., & Newton, P. (1973). Colour: The nature and meaning of Negro self-identity. In P. Watson (Ed.), *Psychology and race* (pp. 176–212). Chicago, IL: Aldine.

Provence, S., & Lipton, R. C. (1962). *Infants in institutions*. New York, NY: International Universities Press.

Querido, J. G., Warner, T. D., & Eyberg, S. M. (2002). Parenting styles and child behavior in African American families of preschool children. *Journal of Clinical Child and Adolescent Psychology, 31*(2), 272–277.

Quinn, P. C., & Liben, L. S. (2008). A sex difference in mental rotation in young infants. *Psychological Science, 19*(11), 1067–1070.

Quintana, S. M. (2007). Racial and ethnic identity: Developmental perspectives and research. *Journal of Counseling Psychology, 54*(3), 259–270.

Rabkin, J. G., & Streuning, E. L. (1976). Life events, stress, and illness. *Science, 194*, 1013–1020.

Rabkin, L. Y., & Rabkin, K. (1974). Children of the kibbutz. *Readings in Psychology Today* (3rd ed.). Del Mar, CA: CRM.

Radke-Yarrow, M., Zahn-Waxler, C., & Chapman, M. (1983). Children's prosocial dispositions and behavior.

In P. H. Mussen (Ed.), *Handbook of child psychology*; E. M. Hetherington (Ed.), *Volume IV: Socialization, personality, and social development*. New York, NY: Wiley.

Rahe, R. H. (1974). The pathway between subjects' recent life change and their near-future illness reports: Representative results and methodological issues. In B. S. Dohrenwend & B. P. Dohrenwend (Eds.), *Stressful life events: Their nature and effects*. New York, NY: Wiley.

Raifman, J., Moscoe, E., Austin, S. B., & McConnell, M. (2017). Difference-in-differences analysis of the association between state same-sex marriage policies and adolescent suicide attempts. *JAMA Pediatrics, 171*, 350–356.

Rainwater, L. (1966). Crucible of identity. The Negro lower-class family. *Daedalus, 95*, 172–216.

Ramirez, M. (1983). *Psychology of the Americas: Mestizo perspectives on personality and mental health*. New York, NY: Pergamon.

Ramirez, M. (1991). *Psychotherapy and counseling with minorities*. New York, NY: Pergamon.

Rapaport, D. (1942). *Emotions and memory*. Baltimore, MD: Williams & Wilkins.

Rapaport, D. (1959). The structure of psychoanalytic theory. In S. Koch (Ed.), *Psychology: A study of a science* (Vol. 3). New York, NY: McGraw-Hill.

Rapaport, D. (1960). *The structure of psychoanalytic theory: A systematizing attempt* (Psychological Issues Monograph 6). New York, NY: International Universities Press.

Rathbun, C., McLaughlin, H., Bennett, O., & Garland, J. A. (1965). Later adjustment of children following radical separation from family and culture. *American Journal of Orthopsychiatry, 35*, 604–609.

Raush, H. L., Barry, W. A., Hertel, R. K., & Swain, M. A. (1974). *Communication, conflict and marriage*. San Francisco, CA: Jossey-Bass.

Rauthmann, J. F., Gallardo-Pujol, D., Guillaume, E. M., Todd, E., Nave, C. S., Sherman, R. A., . . . & Funder, D. C. (2014). The Situational Eight DIAMONDS: A taxonomy of major dimensions of situation characteristics. *Journal of Personality and Social Psychology, 107*(4), 677–718.

Ravitz, P., Maunder, R., Hunter, J., Sthankiya, B., & Lancee, W. (2010). Adult attachment measures: A 25-year review. *Journal of Psychosomatic Research, 69*(4), 419–432.

Raynor, J. O. (1970). Relationships between achievement-related motives, future orientation, and academic performance. *Journal of Personality and Social Psychology, 15*, 28–33.

Read, D., Adams, G. R., & Dobson, W. R. (1984). Ego-identity, status, personality and social influence style. *Journal of Personality and Social Psychology, 46*, 169–177.

Reddy, V. (2003). On being the object of attention: Implications for self-other consciousness. *Trends in Cognitive Sciences, 7*, 397–402.

Reid, J. B. (1986). Social-interactional patterns in families of abused and nonabused children. In C. Zahn-Waxler, E. M. Cummings, & R. Iannotti (Eds.), *Altruism and aggression*. New York, NY: Cambridge University Press.

Reid, J. D., & Willis, S. L. (1999). Middle age: New thoughts, new directions. In S.L. Willis and J.B. Reid (Eds.), *Life in the middle: Psychological and social development in middle age*, 276–280. Academic Press, San Diego, CA.

Reisenzein, R. (1983). The Schachter theory of emotion: Two decades later. *Psychological Bulletin, 94*, 239–264.

Reiss, D. (1993). Genes and the environment: Siblings and synthesis. In R. Plomin & G. E. McClearn (Eds.), *Nature, nurture and psychology* (pp. 417–432). Washington, DC: American Psychological Association.

Remafedi, G., French, S., Story, M., Resnick, M. D., & Blum, R. (1998). The relationship between suicide risk and sexual orientation: Results of a population-based study. *American Journal of Public Health, 88*, 57–60.

Remmers, H. H., & Radler, D. H. (1957). *The American teenager*. Indianapolis, IN: Bobbs-Merrill.

Revonsuo, A. (2000). The reinterpretation of dreams: An evolutionary hypothesis of the function of dreaming. *Behavioral and Brain Sciences, 23*(6), 877–901.

Reyker, J. (1967). Hypnosis in research on psychopathology. In J. E. Gordon (Ed.), *Handbook of clinical and experimental hypnosis*. New York, NY: Macmillan.

Reykowski, J. (1979). Intrinsic motivation and intrinsic inhibition of aggressive behavior. In S. Feshbach & A. Fraczek (Eds.), *Aggression and behavior change: Biological and social processes*. New York, NY: Praeger.

Rhee, S. H., & Waldman, I. D. (2002). Genetic and environmental influences on antisocial behavior: A meta-analysis of twin and adoption studies. *Psychological Bulletin, 128*(3), 490–529.

Rheingold, H. L. (1956). The modification of social responsiveness in institutional babies. *Monographs of the Society for Research in Child Development, 21*(2, Whole No. 63).

Rholes, W., & Simpson, J. A. (2004). *Adult attachment: Theory, research, and clinical implications*. New York, NY: Guilford.

Ribble, M. (1943). *The rights of infants*. New York, NY: Columbia University Press.

Richter, C. P. (1958). The phenomenon of unexplained sudden death in animals and man. In W. H. Gant (Ed.), *Physiological basis of psychiatry*. Springfield, IL: Charles C. Thomas.

Rick, S., & Loewenstein, G. (2008). The role of emotion in economic behavior. In M. Lewis, J. M. Haviland-Jones, & L. F. Barrett (Eds.), *Handbook of emotions* (3rd ed.). New York, NY: Guilford.

Ricoeur, P. (1983). Narrative and hermeneutics. In J. Fisher (Ed.), *Perspective on the work of Monroe C. Beardsley* (pp. 149–162). Philadelphia, PA: Temple University Press.

Riegel, K. (1975). Adult life-crises: A diabetic interpretation of development. In M. Dutan & L. H. Ginsberg (Eds.), *Life span developmental psychology: Normative life crises*. New York, NY: Academic Press.

Riemann, R., Angleitner, A., & Strelau, J. (1997). Genetic and environmental influences on personality: A study of twins reared together using the self-and peer report NEO-FFI scales. *Journal of Personality, 65*(3), 449–475.

Rietveld, C. A., Conley, D., Eriksson, E., Esko, T., Medland, S. E., Vinkhuyzen, A. A. E., . . . Social Science Genetic Association Consortium. (2014). Replicability and robustness of GWAS for behavioral traits. *Psychological Science, 25*, 1975–1986.

Rietveld, C. A., Conley, D., Eriksson, N., Esko, T., Medland, S. E., Vinkhuyzen, A. A., . . . & Domingue, B. W. (2014). Replicability and robustness of genome-wide-association studies for behavioral traits. *Psychological science, 25*(11), 1975–1986.

Riggins-Caspers, K. M., Cadoret, R. J., Knutson, J. F., & Langbehn, D. (2003). Biology-environment interaction and evocative biology-environment correlation: Contributions of harsh discipline and parental psychopathology to problem adolescent behaviors. *Behavior Genetics, 33*(3), 205–220.

Ritu, K., & Sukhdeep, G. (1986). Relations between acceptance-rejection and self-esteem. *Indian Psychology Review, 30*, 15–21.

Robbins, C. J. (1988). Attributions and depression: Why is the literature so inconsistent? *Journal of Personality and Social Psychology, 54*, 880–889.

Robbins, K., & McAdam, D. (1974). Interhemispheric alpha symmetry and imagery mode. *Brain and Language, 1*, 189–193.

Roberti, J. W. (2004). A review of behavioral and biological correlates of sensation seeking. *Journal of research in personality, 38*(3), 256–279.

Roberts, B. W., & Caspi, A. (2005). The cumulative continuity model of personality development: Striking a balance between continuity and change in personality traits across the life course. In U. M. Staudinger, & U. Lindenberger (Eds.), *Understanding human development* (pp. 183–214). New York, NY: Springer US.

Roberts, B. W., & DelVecchio, W. F. (2000). The rank-order consistency of personality traits from childhood to old age: A quantitative review of longitudinal studies. *Psychological Bulletin, 126*(1), 3–25.

Roberts, B. W., Walton, K. E., & Viechtbauer, W. (2006). Patterns of mean-level change in personality traits across the life course: A meta-analysis of longitudinal studies. *Psychological Bulletin, 132*(1), 1–25.

Roberts, B. W., Wood, D., & Caspi, A. (2008). The development of personality traits in adulthood. In O. P. John, R. W. Robins, & L. A. Pervin (Eds.), *Handbook of personality: Theory and research* (3rd ed., pp. 375–398). New York, NY: Guilford.

Rochat, P. (2001). *The infant's world.* Cambridge, MA: Harvard University Press.

Rodgers, D. A. (1966). Factors underlying differences in alcohol preference among inbred strains of mice. *Psychosomatic Medicine, 28*, 498–513.

Rodgers, D. A., & McClearn, G. E. (1962). Alcohol preference of mice. In E. L. Bliss (Ed.), *Roots of behavior.* New York, NY: Harper & Row.

Rodin, J., Elias, M., Silberstein, L. R., & Wagner, A. (1988). Combined behavioral and pharmacological treatment for obesity: Predictors of successful weight maintenance. *Journal of Consulting and Clinical Psychology, 56*, 399–404.

Rodin, J., & Langer, E. J. (1977). Long-term effects of a control-relevant intervention with the institutionalized aged. *Journal of Personality and Social Psychology, 35*, 897–902.

Rodin, J., & Langer, E. J. (1980). Aging labels: The decline of control and the fall of self-esteem. *Journal of Social Issues, 36*, 12–29.

Rogers, C. R. (1959). A theory of therapy, personality, and interpersonal relationships, as developed in the client-centered framework. In S. Koch (Ed.), *Psychology: A study of a science* (Vol. 3). New York, NY: McGraw-Hill.

Rogers, C. R. (1961). *On becoming a person.* Boston, MA: Houghton Muffin.

Rogers, C. R. (1963). Actualizing tendency in relation to "motives" and to consciousness. In M. R. Jones (Ed.), *Nebraska symposium on motivation.* Lincoln, NE: University of Nebraska Press.

Rogers, C. R. (1980). *A way of being.* Boston, MA: Houghton Muffin.

Rogers, C. R. (1983). *Freedom to learn for the '80's.* Columbus, OH: Charles E. Merrill.

Rogers, C. R., & Dymond, R. F. (Eds.). (1954). *Psychotherapy and personality change.* Chicago, IL: University of Chicago Press.

Rogers, C. R., Gendlin, E. T., Kiesler, D. J., & Truax, C. B. (1967). *The therapeutic relationship and its impact.* Madison, WI: University of Wisconsin Press.

Rogers, T. B., Kuiper, N. A., & Kirker, W. S. (1977). Self-reference and the encoding of personal information. *Journal of Personality and Social Psychology, 35*(9), 677–688.

Rohner, R. P. (1986). *The warmth dimension.* Beverly Hills, CA: Sage.

Roisman, G. I., & Fraley, R. C. (2008). A behavior-genetic study of parenting quality, infant attachment security, and their covariation in a nationally representative sample. *Developmental Psychology, 44*, 831.

Roisman, G. I., Holland, A., Fortuna, K., Fraley, R. C., Clausell, E., & Clarke, A. (2007). The adult attachment interview and self-reports of attachment style: An empirical rapprochement. *Journal of Personality and Social Psychology, 92*(4), 678–697.

Roizen, J. (2002). Epidemiological issues in alcohol-related violence. In M. Galanter (Ed.), *Recent developments in alcoholism* (Vol. 13, pp. 7–40). New York, NY: Kluwer Academic Publishers.

Rorer, L. G., & Goldberg, L. R. (1965). Acquiescence in the MMPI? *Educational and Psychological Measurement, 25*, 801–817.

Rorschach, H. (1921). *Psychodiagnostik* (Hans Huber, Trans., Verlag, 1942). Bern, Switzerland: Bircher.

Rose, R. J., Koskenvuo, M., Kaprio, J., Sarna, S., & Langinvainio, H. (1988). Shared genes, shared experiences, and similarity of personality: Data from 14,288 adult Finnish co-twins. *Journal of Personality and Social Psychology, 54*, 161–171.

Rosenbaum, R. (1992). Psychotherapy and integration in India. *Journal of Psychotherapy Integration, 2*, 65–70.

Rosenberg, M. (1965). *Society and the adolescent self-image.* Princeton, NJ: Princeton University Press.

Rosenberg, M. (1979). *Conceiving the self.* New York, NY: Basic Books.

Rosenberg, M. (1985). Self-concept and psychological wellbeing in adolescence. In R. L. Leahy (Ed.), *The development of the self* (pp. 205–246). New York, NY: Academic Press.

Rosenberg, M., & Pearlin, L. I. (1978). Social class and self-esteem among children and adults. *American Journal of Sociology, 84*, 53–77.

Rosenthal, D. (1970). *Genetic theory and abnormal behavior.* New York, NY: McGraw-Hill.

Rosenthal, R., & Jacobson, L. (1968). *Pygmalion in the classroom: Teacher expectation and pupils' intellectual development*. New York, NY: Holt.

Ross, H. S., & Goldman, B. D. (1977). Establishing new social relations in infancy. In T. Alloway, P. Pliner, & L. Krames (Eds.), *Attachment behavior: Advances in the study of communication and affect* (Vol. 3). New York, NY: Plenum.

Ross, L. (1977). The intuitive psychologist and his shortcomings. Distortions in the attribution process. In L. Berkowitz (Ed.), *Advances in experimental social psychology* (Vol. 10). New York, NY: Academic Press.

Rotter, J. B. (1954). *Social learning and clinical psychology*. Englewood Cliffs, NJ: Prentice-Hall.

Rotter, J. B. (1966). Generalized expectancies for internal versus external control of reinforcements. *Psychological Monographs, 80*(1, Whole No. 609).

Rotter, J. B. (1972). *Applications of a social learning theory of personality*. New York, NY: Holt.

Rotter, J. B. (1975). Some problems and misconceptions related to the construct of internal versus external control of reinforcement. *Journal of Consulting and Clinical Psychology, 43*, 55–67.

Rotter, J. B. (1980). Interpersonal trust, trustworthiness, and gullibility. *American Psychologist, 35*, 1–7.

Rotter, J. B., Chance, J. E., & Phares, E. J. (1972). An introduction to social learning theory. In J. B. Rotter, J. E. Chance, & E. J. Phares (Eds.), *Applications of a social learning theory of personality*. New York, NY: Holt.

Rotton, J., & Cohn, E. G. (2001). Temperature, routine activities, and domestic violence: A reanalysis. *Violence and Victims, 16*(2), 203–215.

Rotton, J., & Frey, J. (1985). Air pollution, weather, and violent crimes: Concomitant time-series analysis of archival data. *Journal of Personality and Social Psychology, 49*, 1207–1220.

Rowe, D. C. (1993). Genetic perspectives on personality. In R. Plomin & G. E. McClearn (Eds.), *Nature, nurture, and psychology* (pp. 179–196). Washington, DC: American Psychological Association.

Rowe, D. C. (1994). *The limits of family influence*. New York, NY: Guilford.

Rozin, P., & Fallon, A. E. (1987). A perspective on disgust. *Psychological Review, 94*, 23–41.

Rubin, R. T. (1987). The neuroendocrinology and neurochemistry of antisocial behavior. In S. A. Mednick, T. E. Moffitt, & S. A. Stack (Eds.), *The causes of crime* (pp. 239–262). Cambridge, MA: Cambridge University Press.

Rubin, Z. (1970). Measurement of romantic love. *Journal of Personality and Social Psychology, 16*, 265–273.

Rubin, Z. (1973). *Liking and loving: An invitation to social psychology*. New York, NY: Holt.

Ruble, D. N., & Brooks-Gunn, J. (1982). The experience of menarche. *Child Development*, 1557–1566.

Ruble, D. N., Parsons, J. E., & Ross, J. (1976). Self-evaluative responses of children in an achievement setting. *Child Development, 47*, 990–997.

Rule, B. G., & Neasdale, A. R. (1976). Emotional arousal and aggressive behavior. *Psychological Bulletin, 83*, 851–863.

Rule, B. G., Taylor, B., & Dobbs, A. R. (1987). Priming effects of heat on aggressive thoughts. *Social Cognition, 5*, 131–144.

Runyan, W. M. (1982). *Life histories and psychobiography*. New York, NY: Oxford University Press.

Runyan, W. M. (1988). Progress in psychobiography. *Journal of Personality, 56*, 295–321.

Rushton, J. P. (1976). Socialization and the altruistic behavior of children. *Psychological Bulletin, 83*, 898–913.

Rushton, J. P., Brainerd, D. J., & Pressley, M. (1983). Behavioral development and construct validity: The principle of aggregation. *Psychological Bulletin, 94*, 18–38.

Rushton, J. P., Fulker, D. W., Neale, M. C., Nias, D. K. B., & Eysenck, H. J. (1986). Altruism and aggression: The heritability of individual differences. *Journal of Personality and Social Psychology, 50*, 1192–1198.

Russell, J. A. (1980). A circumplex model of affect. *Journal of Personality and Social Psychology, 39*, 1161–1178.

Russell, J. A. (1983). Pancultural aspects of the human conceptual organization of emotions. *Journal of Personality and Social Psychology, 45*, 1281–1288.

Rutter, M. (1979). Maternal deprivation, 1972–1978: New findings, new concepts, new approaches. *Child Development, 50*, 283–305.

Rutter, M. (1980). *Changing youth in a changing society. Patterns of adolescent development and disorder*. Cambridge, MA: Harvard University Press.

Rutter, M., & Garmezy, N. (1983). Developmental psychopathology. In P. H. Mussen (Ed.), *Handbook of child psychology*; E. M. Hetherington (Ed.), *Volume IV: Socialization, personality, and social development*. New York, NY: Wiley.

Ryan, R. M., & Deci, E. L. (2000). Self-determination theory and the facilitation of intrinsic motivation, social development, and well-being. *American Psychologist, 55*(1), 68–78.

Ryan, R. M., Huta, V., & Deci, E. L. (2006). Living well: A self determination theory perspective on eudaimonia. *Journal of Happiness Studies, 9*, 139–170.

Ryan, R. M., & Lynch, J. H. (1989). Emotional autonomy versus detachment: Revisiting the vicissitudes of adolescence and young adulthood. *Child Development, 60*, 340–356.

Ryan, R. M., Rigby, C. S., & Przybylski, A. (2006). The motivational pull of video games: A self-determination theory approach. *Motivation and Emotion, 30*(4), 344–360.

Ryff, D. C. (1982). Self-perceived personality change in adulthood and aging. *Journal of Personality and Social Psychology, 42*, 108–115.

Saccuzzo, D. P. (1975). Canonical correlation as a method of assessing the correlates of good and bad therapy hours. *Psychotherapy: Theory, research, and practice*. Menasha, WI: American Psychological Association.

Sagi, A., & Hoffman, M. L. (1976). Empathic distress in newborns. *Developmental Psychology, 12*, 175–176.

Sameroff, A. J. (1975). Early influences in development: Factor fancy? *Merrill-Palmer Quarterly, 21*(4), 267–294.

Sameroff, A. J. (March 1979). *Theoretical and empirical issues in the operationalization of transactional research*. Paper presented at the biennial meeting of the Society for Research in Child Development, San Francisco, CA.

Sameroff, A. J., & Chandler, M. J. (1975). Reproductive right and the continuum of caretaking casualty. In F. D. Horowitz (Ed.), *Review of child development research* (Vol. 4). Chicago, IL: University of Chicago Press.

Sampson, R. J., & Laub, J. H. (1990). Crime and deviance over the life course: The salience of adult social bonds. *American Sociological Review, 55*, 609–627.

Samson, D. R., Crittenden, A. N., Mabulla, I. A., Mabulla, A. Z., & Nunn, C. L. (2017). Hadza sleep biology: Evidence for flexible sleep-wake patterns in hunter-gatherers. *American Journal of Physical Anthropology, 162*(3), 573–582.

Sarason, B. R., Shearing, E. N., Pierce, G. R., & Sarason, I. G. (1987). Interrelations of social support measures: Theoretical and practical implications. *Journal of Personality and Social Psychology, 52*, 813–832.

Sarason, I. G. (1978). The test anxiety scale: Concept and research. In C. D. Spielberger & I. G. Sarason (Eds.), *Stress and anxiety* (Vol. 5). Washington, DC: Hemisphere.

Sarason, I. G., Smith, R. E., & Diener, E. (1975). Personality research: Components of variance attributable to the person and the situation. *Journal of Personality and Social Psychology, 3*, 199–204.

Sarason, S. B., Davidson, K. S., Lightchal, F., Waite, R. R., & Ruebush, B. K. (1960). *Anxiety in elementary school children.* New York, NY: Wiley.

Sarbin, T. R. (1942). A contribution to the study of actuarial and individual method of predictions. *American Journal of Sociology, 48*, 593–602.

Sassin, J. F., Parker, D. C., Mace, J. W., Gotlin, R. W., Johnson, L. C., & Rossman, L. G. (1969). Human growth hormone release: Relation to slow-wave sleep and sleep-waking cycles. *Science, 165*(3892), 513–515.

Saudino, K. J. (2005). Behavioral genetics and child temperament. *Journal of Developmental and Behavioral Pediatrics, 26*, 214–223.

Scarr, S., & Carter-Saltzman, L. (1979). Twin method: Defense of a critical assumption. *Behavior Genetics, 9*, 527–542.

Scarr, S., & Carter-Saltzman, L. (1985). Behavior genetics and intelligence. In R. J. Sternberg (Ed.), *Handbook of human intelligence*. New York, NY: Cambridge University Press.

Schaal, B., Tremblay, R. E., Soussignan, R., & Susman, E. J. (1996). Male testosterone linked to high social dominance but low physical aggression in early adolescence. *Journal of the American Academy of Child & Adolescent Psychiatry, 35*(10), 1322–1330.

Schachter, S. (1959). *The psychology of affiliation*. Stanford, CA: Stanford University Press.

Schachter, S. (1964). The interaction of cognitive and physiological determinants of emotional state. In L. Berkowitz (Ed.), *Advances in experimental social psychology* (Vol. 1). New York, NY: Academic Press.

Schachter, S., & Singer, J. E. (1962). Cognitive, social, and physiological determinants of emotional state. *Psychological Review, 69*, 379–399.

Schafer, R. (1960). The loving and beloved super ego in Freud's structural theory. In O. Fenichel et al. (Eds.), *Psychoanalytic study of the child* (Vol. 15). New York, NY: International Universities Press.

Schafer, R. (1976). *A new language for psychoanalysis*. New Haven, CT: Yale University Press.

Schafer, R. (1992). *Retelling a life*. New York, NY: Basic Books.

Schanberg, S. M., & Kuhn, C. M. (1980). Maternal deprivation: An animal model of psychosocial dwarfism. In E. Vadin, T. L. Sourkes, & M. E. Youdin (Eds.), *Enzymes and neurotransmitters*. New York, NY: Wiley.

Schanberg, S. M., & Kuhn, C. M. (1980). Maternal deprivation: An animal model of psychosocial dwarfism. *Enzymes and neurotransmitters in mental disease*, 373–393.

Schinka, J. A., Busch, R. M., & Robichaux-Keene, N. (2004). A meta-analysis of the association between the serotonin transporter gene polymorphism (5-HTTLPR) and trait anxiety. *Molecular Psychiatry, 9*, 197–202.

Schlosberg, H. (1954). Three dimensions of emotion. *Psychological Review, 61*, 81–88.

Schlotz, W., Schulz, P., Hellhammer, J., Stone, A. A., & Hellhammer, D. H. (2006). Trait anxiety moderates the impact of performance pressure on salivary cortisol in everyday life. *Psychoneuroendocrinology, 31*, 459–472.

Schludermann, S. M., & Schludermann, E. H. (1983). Sociocultural change and adolescents' perceptions of parent behavior. *Developmental Psychology, 19*(5), 674–685.

Schmidt, G., & Weiner, B. (1988). An attribution-affect-action theory of behavior: Replications of judgments of help giving. *Personality and Social Psychology Bulletin, 14*, 610–621.

Schneider, D. J. (1973). Implicit theory: A review. *Psychological Bulletin, 79*, 294–309.

Schuckit, M. A. (1987). Biological vulnerability to alcoholism. *Journal of Consulting and Clinical Psychology, 55*, 301–309.

Schuerger, J. M., Zarrella, K. L., & Hotz, A. S. (1989). Factors that influence the temporal stability of personality by questionnaire. *Journal of Personality and Social Psychology, 56*, 777–783.

Schultz, D. (1976). *Theories of personality*. Belmont, CA: Brooks/Cole.

Schwartz, B. (2004). *The paradox of choice: Why more is less*. New York, NY: Ecco.

Schwartz, S. J., Syed, M., Yip, T., Knight, G. P., Umaña-Taylor, A. J., Rivas-Drake, D., & Lee, R. M. (2014). Methodological issues in ethnic and racial identity research with ethnic minority populations: Theoretical precision, measurement issues, and research designs. *Child Development, 85*(1), 58–76.

Schweder, R. A., & Bourne, D. J. (1984). Does the concept of the person vary cross-culturally? In R. A. Schweder & R. A. LeVine (Eds.), *Culture theory: Essays in mind, self, and emotion*. Cambridge, England: Cambridge University Press, 158–199.

Scott, J. P. (1958). *Aggression*. Chicago, IL: University of Chicago Press.

Sears, R. R., Ran, L., & Alpert, R. (1965). *Identification and child rearing*. Stanford, CA: Stanford University Press.

Seeman, M. (1963). Alienation and social learning in a reformatory. *American Journal of Sociology, 69*, 270–284.

Seeman, M., & Evans, J. W. (1962). Alienation and learning in a hospital setting. *American Sociological Review, 27*, 772–783.

Seeman, M., & Evans, J. W. (1962). Alienation and learning in a hospital setting. *American Sociological Review, 27*(6), 772–782.

Segal, H. (1973). *Introduction to the work of Melanie Klein*. New York, NY: Basic Books.

Seligman, M. E. P., & Beagley, G. (1975). Learned helplessness in the rat. *Journal of Comparative and Physiological Psychology, 88*, 534–541.

Seligman, M. E. P. (1975). *Helplessness: On depression, development, and death.* San Francisco, CA: Freeman.

Seligman, M. E. P. (1990). *Learned optimism.* New York, NY: Knopf.

Seligman, M. E. P. (2011). *Flourish: A visionary new understanding of happiness and well-being.* New York, NY: Free Press, A division of Simon and Schuster.

Seligman, M. E. P., & Maier, S. F. (1967). Failure to escape traumatic shock. *Journal of Experimental Psychology, 74,* 1–9.

Sellers, R. M., Copeland-Linder, N., Martin, P. P., & Lewis, R. H. (2006). Racial identity matters: The relationship between racial discrimination and psychological functioning in African American adolescents. *Journal of Research on Adolescence, 16*(2), 187–216.

Service, E. R. (1966). *The hunters.* Englewood Cliffs, NJ: Prentice-Hall.

Setterlund, M. B., & Niedenthal, P. M. (1993). "Who am I? Why am I here?" Self-esteem, self-clarity, and prototype matching. *Journal of Personality and Social Psychology, 65*(4), 769.

Shafer, A. B. (2001). The big five and sexuality trait terms as predictors of relationships and sex. *Journal of Research in Personality, 35,* 313–338.

Shakow, D., & Rapaport, D. (1964). The influence of Freud on American psychology. *Psychological Issues, 4,* 1–243.

Shapira, A., & Madsen, M. C. (1974). Between and within group cooperation and competitive behavior among kibbutz and non-kibbutz children. *Developmental Psychology, 10,* 140–145.

Shapiro, D., & Giber, D. (1978). Meditation and psychotherapeutic effects. *Archives of General Psychiatry, 35,* 294–302.

Shapiro, D., & Surwit, R. S. (1976). Learned control of physiological functions and disease. In H. Leitenberg (Ed.), *Handbook of behavior modification and behavior therapy.* Englewood Cliffs, NJ: Prentice-Hall.

Shapiro, D. J., & Alexander, I. E. (1969). Extroversion-introversion: Affiliation and anxiety. *Journal of Personality, 37,* 387–406.

Shaver, P., & Hazan, C. (1988). A biased overview of the study of love. *Journal of Social and Personal Relationships, 5,* 473–501.

Shaver, P., Hazan, C., & Bradshaw, D. (1988). Love as attachment. In R. J. Sternberg & M. L. Barma (Eds.), *The psychology of love.* New Haven, CT: Yale University Press.

Shaver, P., Schwartz, J., Kirson, D., & O'Connor, C. (1987). Emotion knowledge: Further exploration of a prototype approach. *Journal of Personality and Social Psychology, 52,* 1061–1086.

Shedler, J., Mayman, M., & Manis, M. (1993). The illusion of mental health. *American Psychologist, 48,* 1117–1131.

Sheehan, G. (1978). *Running and being.* New York, NY: Warner.

Sheehy, G. (1976). *Passages.* New York, NY: Dutton.

Sheldon, W. H. (1954). *Atlas of men.* New York, NY: Harper & Brothers.

Sheldon, W. H., & Stevens, S. S. (1942). *The varieties of temperament: A psychology of constitutional differences.* New York, NY: Harper.

Sheldon, W. H., & Tucker, W. B. (1940). *The varieties of human physique: An introduction to constitutional psychology.* New York, NY: Harper.

Sherif, M., Harvey, O. J., White, B. J., Hood, W. R., & Sherif, C. (1961). *Intergroup conflict and cooperation: The rober's cave experiment.* Norman, OK: University of Oklahoma Book Exchange.

Shevrin, H. (1974). Brain wave correlates of subliminal stimulation, unconscious attention, primary and secondary process thinking and repressiveness. In M. Mayman (Ed.). *Psychoanalytic research: Three approaches to the experimental study of subliminal processes* [Psychological Issues Monograph 30]. New York, NY: International Universities Press.

Shevrin, H., & Dickman, S. (1980). The psychological unconscious: A necessary assumption for all psychological theory. *American Psychologist, 35,* 421–434.

Shields, J. (1976). Heredity and environment. In H. J. Eysenck & G. D. Wilson (Eds.), *A textbook of human psychology.* Baltimore, MD: University Park Press.

Showers, C. (1992). Evaluatively integrative thinking about characteristics of the self. *Personality and Social Psychology Bulletin, 18,* 719–729.

Shulman, S., Elicker, J., & Sroufe, L. A. (1994). Stages of friendship growth in preadolescence as related to attachment history. *Journal of social and personal relationships, 11*(3), 341–361.

Shure, M., & Spivack, G. (1972). Means-ends thinking, adjustment and social class among elementary school-aged children. *Journal of Consulting and Clinical Psychology, 38,* 348–353.

Siegman, A. W., Townsend, S. T., Civelek, A. C., & Blumenthal, R. S. (2000). Antagonistic behavior, dominance, hostility, and coronary heart disease. *Psychosomatic Medicine, 62,* 248–257.

Signorella, M. L., Jamison, W., & Krupa, M. H. (1989). Predicting spatial performance from gender stereotyping in activity preferences and in self-concept. *Developmental Psychology, 25,* 89–95.

Silverman, L. H. (1976). Psychoanalytic theory: "The reports of my death are greatly exaggerated." *American Psychologist, 31,* 621–637.

Silverman, L. H. (1983). The subliminal psychodynamic activation method: Overview and comprehensive listing of studies. In. J. Masling (Ed.), *Empirical studies of psychoanalytic theories* (Vol. 1, pp. 69–100). Hillsboro, NJ: Erlbaum.

Silverman, L. H. (1985). Research on psychoanalytic psychodynamic propositions. *Clinical Psychology Review, 5,* 247–257.

Silverman, L. H., Bronstein, A., & Mendelsohn, E. (1976). The further use of the subliminal psychodynamic activation method for the experimental study of the clinical theory of psychoanalysis: On the specificity of relationships between manifest psychopathology and unconscious conflict. *Psychotherapy: Theory, Research and Practice, 13,* 2–16.

Silvia, P. J., & Phillips, A. G. (2004). Self-awareness, self-evaluation, and creativity. *Personality and Social Psychology Bulletin, 30*(8), 1009–1017.

Simmons, R. G., & Blyth, D. A. (1987). *Moving into adolescence: The impact of pubertal change and school contact.* New York, NY: Aldine.

Simonds, P. F. (1977). Peers, parents and primates: The developing network of attachments. In T. Alloway, P. Pliner, &

L. Krames (Eds.), *Attachment behavior: Advances in the study of communication and affect*. New York, NY: Plenum.

Simonton, D. K. (1988a) Age and outstanding achievement: What do we know after a century of research? *Psychological Bulletin, 104*, 251–267.

Simonton, D. K. (1988b) *Scientific genius: A psychology of science*. Cambridge, England: Cambridge University Press.

Simpson, J. A., Campbell, B., & Berscheid, E. (1986). The association between romantic love and marriage: Kephart (1967) twice revisited. *Personality and Social Psychology Bulletin, 12*(3), 363–372.

Singer, J. A. (2004). Narrative identity and meaning making across the adult lifespan: An introduction. *Journal of Personality, 72*(3), 437–460.

Singer, J. L. (1966). *Daydreaming*. New York, NY: Random House.

Singer, J. L. (1973). *The child's world of make believe*. New York, NY: Academic Press.

Singer, J. L. (1974). *Imagery and daydream methods in psychotherapy and behavior modification*. New York, NY: Academic Press.

Singer, J. L., & Bonanno, G. A. (1990). Personality and private experience: Individual variations in consciousness and in attention to subjective phenomena. In L. A. Pervin (Ed.), *Handbook of personality* (pp. 419–444). New York, NY: Guilford.

Singer, J. L., & Kolligian, J., Jr. (1987). Personality: Developments in the study of private experience. In M. R. Rosenzweig & L. M. Porter (Eds.), *Annual Review of Psychology, 38*, 533–574.

Singer, J. L., & Singer, D. G. (1986). Family experience and television viewing as predictive of children's imagination, restlessness, and aggression. *Journal of Social Issues, 42*, 107–124.

Skinner, B. F. (1938). *The behavior of organisms*. New York, NY: Appleton-Century-Crofts.

Skinner, B. F. (1948). *Walden two*. New York, NY: Macmillan.

Skinner, B. F. (1953). *Science and human behavior*. New York, NY: Macmillan.

Skinner, B. F. (1963). Operant behavior. *American Psychologist, 18*, 503–515.

Skinner, B. F. (1971). *Beyond freedom and dignity*. New York, NY: Knopf.

Slade, A. (1987). Quality of attachment and early symbolic play. *Developmental Psychology, 23*, 78–85.

Slavin, L. A., Rainer, K. L., McCreary, M. L., & Gowda, K. K. (1990). Toward a multicultural model of the stress process. *Journal of Counseling and Development, 70*, 156–163.

Šmigelskas, K., Žemaitienė, N., Julkunen, J., & Kauhanen, J. (2015). Type A behavior pattern is not a predictor of premature mortality. *International Journal of Behavioral Medicine, 22*, 161–169.

Smith, B. L. (2012). The case against spanking. *Monitor on Psychology, 43*, 60.

Smith, C. A., & Ellsworth, C. (1985). Patterns of cognitive appraisal in emotion. *Journal of Personality and Social Psychology, 48*, 813–838.

Smith, C. A., & Ellsworth, C. (1987). Patterns of appraisal and emotion related to taking an exam. *Journal of Personality and Social Psychology, 52*, 475–488.

Smith, C. A., & Lazarus, R. S. (1990) Emotion and adaptation. In L. A. Pervin (Ed.), *Handbook of personality: Theory and research* (pp. 609–637). New York, NY: Guilford.

Smith, D. L. (1988). Psychotherapy and narration: The contribution of Paul Ricoeur. *The Humanistic Psychologist, 16*, 323–331.

Smith, P. B., & Bond, M. H. (1993). *Social psychology across cultures*. Boston, MA: Allyn & Bacon.

Smith, P. B., & Pederson, D. R. (1988). Maternal sensitivity and patterns of infant-mother attachment. *Child Development, 59*, 1097–1101.

Smith, P. K., & Daglish, L. (1977). Sex differences in parent and infant behavior in the home. *Child Development, 48*, 1250–1254.

Smith, R., Smythe, L., & Lien, D. (1972). Inhibition of helping behavior by a similar or dissimilar nonreactive fellow bystander. *Journal of Personality and Social Psychology, 23*, 414–419.

Smith, R. T. (1963). A comparison of socioenvironmental factors in monozygotic and dizygotic twins: Testing an assumption. In S. G. Vandenberg (Ed.), *Methods and goals in human behavior genetics*. New York, NY: Academic Press.

Smith, R. T. (1965). A comparison of socioenvironmental factors in monozygotic and dizygotic twins, testing an assumption. *Methods and goals in human behavior genetics*, 45–61.

Smollar, J., & Youniss, J. (1985). Adolescent self-concept development. In R. L. Leahy (Ed.), *The development of the self* (pp. 247–266). New York, NY: Academic Press.

Snow, C. (1987). Relevance of the notion of a critical period to language acquisition. In M. H. Bernstein (Ed.), *Sensitive periods in development: Interdisciplinary perspectives* (pp. 183–209). Hillsdale, NJ: Erlbaum.

Snyder, M. (1974). Self-monitoring of expressive behavior. *Journal of Personality and Social Psychology, 30*, 526–537.

Snyder, M. (1987). *Public appearances/private realities: The psychology of self-monitoring*. New York, NY: W. H. Freeman.

Snyder, M., & Gangestad, S. (1986). The nature of self-monitoring. *Journal of Personality and Social Psychology, 51*, 125–139.

Snyder, M., Gangestad, S., & Simpson, J. A. (1983). Choosing friends as activity partners: The role of self-monitoring. *Journal of Personality and Social Psychology, 45*(5), 1061–1072.

Snyder, M., & Simpson, J. A. (1987). Orientation toward romantic relationships. In D. Perlman & S. Duck (Eds.), *Intimate relationships: Development, dynamics, deterioration*. Newbury Park, CA: Sage.

Soldz, S., & Vaillant, G. E. (1999). The big five personality traits and the life course: A 45-year longitudinal study. *Journal of Research in Personality, 33*(2), 208–232.

Sommer, R., & Ross, H. (1958). Social interaction on a geriatric ward. *International Journal of Social Psychiatry, 4*, 128–133.

Sommershield, H., & Reyker, J. (1973). Posthypnotic conflict, repression and psychopathology. *Journal of Abnormal Psychology, 82*, 278–290.

Sorenson, R. C. (1973). *Adolescent sexuality in contemporary America: Personal values and sexual behavior ages 13–19*. New York, NY: Abrams.

Spanos, N. P. (1986). Hypnosis and the modification of hypnotic susceptibility: A social psychological perspective. In P. L. N. Naish (Ed.), *What is hypnosis? Current theories and research* (pp. 85–120). Philadelphia, PA: Open University Press.

Spanos, N. P., Lush, N. I., & Gwynn, M. I. (1989). Cognitive skill-training enhancement of hypnotizability: Generalization effects and trance logic responding. *Journal of Personality and Social Psychology, 56,* 795–804.

Specht, J., Egloff, B., & Schmukle, S. C. (2011). Stability and change of personality across the life course: The impact of age and major life events on mean-level and rank-order stability of the big five. *Journal of Personality and Social Psychology, 101*(4), 862–882.

Spence, D. P. (1982). *Narrative truth and historical truth.* New York, NY: Norton.

Spence, J. T., & Helmrich, R. L. (1978). *Masculinity and femininity: Their psychological dimensions, correlates, and antecedents.* Austin, TX: University of Texas Press.

Spera, C. (2005). A review of the relationship among parenting practices, parenting styles, and adolescent school achievement. *Educational psychology review, 17*(2), 125–146.

Sperry, R. W. (1964). The great cerebral commissure. *Scientific American, 210,* 42–52.

Sperry, R. W. (1968). Hemisphere deconnection and unity in conscious awareness. *American Psychologist, 23,* 723–733.

Spielberger, C. D. (1962). The role of awareness in verbal conditioning. In C. W. Eriksen (Ed.), *Behavior and awareness.* Durham, NC: Duke University Press.

Spielberger, C. D. (1971a). Anxiety as an emotional state. In C. D. Spielberger (Ed.), *Anxiety: Current trends in theory and research* (Vol. 1). New York, NY: Academic Press.

Spielberger, C. D. (Ed.) (1971b). *Anxiety: Current trends in theory and research* (Vol. II). New York, NY: Academic Press.

Spielberger, C. D., Gorsuch, R. L., & Lushene, R. E. (1970). *Manual for the state-trait anxiety inventory.* Palo Alto, CA: Consulting Psychologists Press.

Spielberger, C. D., Gorsuch, R. L., Lushene, R., Vagg, P. R., & Jacobs, G. A. (1983). State-Trait Anxiety Inventory (STAI). Menlo Park, CA: Mind Garden.

Spinetta, J. J., & Rigler, D. (1972). The child-abusing parent: A psychological review. *Psychological Bulletin, 77,* 296–304.

Spitz, R. A. (1945). Hospitalism. An inquiry into the genesis of psychiatric conditions in early childhood. In O. Fenichel et al. (Eds.), *The psychoanalytic study of the child* (Vol. 1). New York, NY: International Universities Press.

Spivack, G., & Levine, M. (1963). *Self-regulation in acting-out and normal adolescents* (Report M-4351). Washington, DC: National Institutes of Health.

Spivack, G., & Shure, M. B. (1974). *Social adjustment of young children: A cognitive approach to solving real-life problems.* San Francisco, CA: Jossey-Bass.

Sroufe, L. A. (2005). Attachment and development: A prospective, longitudinal study from birth to adulthood. *Attachment & Human Development, 7*(4), 349–367.

Sroufe, L. A., Carlson, E., & Shulman, S. (1993). Individuals in relationships: Development from infancy through adolescence. In D. C. Funder, R. D. Parke, C. Tomlinson-Keasey, & K. Widaman (Eds.), *Studying lives through time* (pp. 315–342). Washington, DC: American Psychological Association.

Sroufe, L. A., Egeland, B., Carlson, E., & Collins, W. A. (2005). *The development of the person: The Minnesota study of risk and adaptation from birth to adulthood.* New York, NY: Guilford.

Sroufe, L. A., Fox, N., & Pancake, V. (1983). Attachment and dependency in developmental perspective. *Child Development, 54,* 1615–1627.

Sroufe, L. A., & Waters, E. (1977a). Attachment as an organizational construct. *Child Development, 48,* 1184–1199.

Sroufe, L. A., & Waters, E. (1977b). Heart rate as a convergent measure in clinical and developmental research. *American Behavioral Scientist, 20*(3), 295–318.

Stangor, C., & Ruble, D. N. (1989). Differential influences of gender schemata and gender constancy on children's information processing and behavior. *Social Cognition, 7,* 353–372.

Staub, E. (1972). Instigation to goodness: The role of social norms and interpersonal influence. *Journal of Social Issues, 28,* 131–150.

Staub, E. (1974). Helping a distressed person: Social, personality, and stimulus determinants. In L. Berkowitz (Ed.), *Advances in experimental social psychology* (Vol. 7). New York, NY: Academic Press.

Steck, L., Levitan, D., MacLane, D., & Kelley, H. H. (1982). Care, need and conceptions of love. *Journal of Personality and Social Psychology, 43,* 481–491.

Steele, C. M., & Josephs, R. A. (1988). Drinking your troubles away. II: An attention-allocation model of alcohol's effect on psychological stress. *Journal of Abnormal Psychology, 97*(2), 196–205.

Stein, A., & Friedrich, L. K. (1971). Television content and young children's behavior. In J. P. Murray, E. A. Rubinstein, & G. A. Comstock (Eds.), *Television and social behavior: Television and social learning* (Vol. 2). Washington, DC: U.S. Government Printing Office.

Steinberg, L., Elman, J. D., & Mounts, Nina S. (1989). Authoritative parenting, psychosocial maturity, and academic success among adolescents. *Child Development, 60,* 1424–1436.

Steinberg, L., Lamborn, S. D., Dornbusch, S. M., & Darling, N. (1992). Impact of parenting practices on adolescent achievement: Authoritative parenting, school involvement, and encouragement to succeed. *Child Development, 63*(5), 1266–1281.

Steinberg, L., & Silverberg, L. (1986). The vicissitudes of autonomy in adolescence. *Child Development, 57,* 841–851.

Stephenson, W. (1953). *The study of behavior.* Chicago, IL: University of Chicago Press.

Stern, D. N. (1985). *The interpersonal world of the infant.* New York, NY: Basic Books.

Sternberg, R. J. (1979). *Human intelligence: Perspectives on its theory and measurement.* Norwood, NJ: Ablex Publishing.

Sternberg, R. J. (1986). A triangular theory of love. *Psychological Review, 93,* 119–135.

Sternberg, R. J. (1997). Construct validation of a triangular love scale. *European Journal of Social Psychology, 27*(3), 313–335.

Sternberg, R. J., & Grajek, S. (1984). The nature of love. *Journal of Personality and Social Psychology, 47,* 312–329.

Sternberg, R. J., & Kolligian, J. (Eds.). (1990). *Competence considered.* New Haven, CT: Yale University Press.

Stevenson, H. C., Jr. (August 1993). *New theoretical considerations in assessing racial socialization attitudes in African American youth: Getting an Eye's view of the "WE."* Paper presented as part of an invited symposium on "Cultural Contexts of Identity Formation—Some International Perspectives," American Psychological Association Convention, Toronto, Canada.

Stewart, A. J., & Gold-Steinberg, S. (1990). Midlife women's political consciousness: Case studies of psychosocial development and political commitment. *Psychology of Women Quarterly, 14,* 4.

Stewart, A. J., & Healy, J. M., Jr. (1989). Linking individual development and social changes. *American Psychologist, 44,* 30–42.

Stewart, K. (1969). Dream theory in Malaya. In C. T. Tart (Ed.), *Altered states of consciousness.* New York, NY: Wiley.

Stipek, D., Weiner, B., & Li, K. (1989). Testing some attribution-emotion relations in the People's Republic of China. *Journal of Personality and Social Psychology, 56,* 109–116.

Stokols, D. (1978). Environmental psychology. In L. W. Porter & M. R. Rosenzweig (Eds.), *Annual review of psychology* (Vol. 29). Palo Alto, CA: Annual Reviews.

Stoller, R. J. (1979). *Sexual excitement: Dynamics of erotic life.* New York, NY: Pantheon Books.

Storbeck, J., & Clore, G. L. (2007). On the interdependence of cognition and emotion. *Cognition and Emotion, 21*(6), 1212–1237.

Storms, M. D. (1973). Videotape and the attribution process: Reversion actors' and observers' points of view. *Journal of Personality and Social Psychology, 27,* 165–175.

Stotland, E., & Dunn, R. E. (1962). Identification, authoritarian defensiveness, self-esteem, and birth order. *Psychological Monographs, 76* (No. 528).

Strack, F. (2016). Reflection on the Smiling Registered Replication Report. *Perspectives on Psychological Science,* doi: 10.1177/1745691616674460.

Strack, F., Martin, L. L., & Stepper, S. (1988). Inhibiting and facilitating conditions of the human smile: A nonobtrusive test of the facial feedback hypothesis. *Journal of Personality and Social Psychology, 54,* 768.

Stratton, G. M. (1923). *Anger: Its religious and moral significance.* New York, NY: Macmillan.

Straus, M. A. (1968). Communication, creativity and problem solving ability of middle and working class families in three societies. *American Journal of Sociology, 73,* 417–431.

Strong, D. R., Greene, R. L., & Schinka, J. A. (2000). A taxometric analysis of MMPI-2 infrequency scales F and F(p)] in clinical settings. *Psychological Assessment, 12,* 166–173.

Strong, E. K. (1943). *Vocational interests of men and women.* Stanford, CA: Stanford University Press.

Struhsaker, T., & Leland, L. (1987). Columbines: Infanticide by adult males. In B. B. Smith, D. L. Cheney, R. M. Seyfarth, R. W. Wranghaus, & T. T. Struhsaker, *Primate societies.* Chicago, IL: University of Chicago Press.

Stücke, T. S., & Sporer, S. L. (2002). When a grandiose self-image is threatened: Narcissism and self-concept clarity as predictors of negative emotions and aggression following ego-threat. *Journal of Personality, 70*(4), 509–532.

Stupica, B. (2016). Rounding the bases with a secure base. *Attachment & Human Development, 18,* 373–390.

Stupica, B., Sherman, L. J., & Cassidy, J. (2011). Newborn irritability moderates the association between infant attachment security and toddler exploration and sociability. *Child Development, 82,* 1381–1389.

Sullivan, H. S. (1953). *The interpersonal theory of psychiatry.* New York, NY: Norton.

Suomi, S. J. (1977). Development of attachment and other social behaviors in Rhesus monkeys. In T. Alloway, P. Pliner, & L. Krames (Eds.), *Attachment behavior: Advances in the study of communication and affect.* New York, NY: Plenum.

Suomi, S. J., Harlow, H. F., & Kimball, S. D. (1971). Behavioral effects of prolonged partial social isolation in the rhesus monkey. *Psychological Reports, 29,* 1171–1177.

Susman, E. J., Inoff-Germain, G., Nottelmann, E. D., Loriaux, D. L., Cutler, G. B., Jr., & Chrauses, G. P. (1987). Hormones, emotional dispositions and aggressive attributes in young adolescents. *Child Development, 58,* 1114–1134.

Swann, W. B., Jr. (2011). Self-verification theory. In P. A. M. Van Lange, A. W. Kruglanski, & E. T. Higgins (Eds.), *Handbook of theories of social psychology* (Vol. 2, pp. 23–42). London, UK: Sage.

Swann, W. B., Griffin, J. J., Predmore, A. C., & Gaines, B. (1987). Cognitive-affective crossfire: When self-consistency meets self-enhancement. *Journal of Personality and Social Psychology, 52,* 881–889.

Swann, W. B., & Hill, C. A. (1982). When our identities are mistaken: Reaffirming self-conceptions through social interaction. *Journal of Personality and Social Psychology, 43,* 59–66.

Swann, W. B., & Read, S. J. (1981). Self-verification processes: How we sustain our self-conception. *Journal of Experimental Social Psychology, 17,* 351–372.

Symons, C. S., & Johnson, B. T. (1997). The self-reference effect in memory: A meta-analysis. *Psychological Bulletin, 121*(3), 371–394.

Taffel, C. (1955). Anxiety and conditioning in verbal learning. *Journal of Abnormal and Social Psychology, 51,* 496–501.

Tagiuri, R. (1969). Person perception. In G. Lindzey & E. Aronson (Eds.), *Handbook of social psychology* (Vol. 3). Reading, MA: Addison-Wesley.

Tamis-LeMonda, C. S., Briggs, R. D., McClowry, S. G., & Snow, D. L. (2009). Maternal control and sensitivity, child gender, and maternal education in relation to children's behavioral outcomes in African American families. *Journal of Applied Developmental Psychology, 30*(3), 321–331.

Tait, R., & Silver, R. C. (1989). Coming to terms with major negative life events. In J. S. Uleman & J. A. Bargh (Eds.), *Unintended thought* (pp. 351–382). New York, NY: Guilford.

Tangney, J. P. (1991). Moral affect: the good, the bad, and the ugly. *Journal of personality and social psychology, 61*(4), 598.

Taylor, M. D., Whiteman, M. C., Fowkes, G. R., Lee, A. J., Allerhand, M., & Deary, I. J. (2009). Five Factor Model personality traits and all-cause mortality in the Edinburgh Artery Study cohort. *Psychosomatic Medicine, 71,* 631–641.

Taylor, J. A. (1953). A personality scale of manifest anxiety. *Journal of Abnormal and Social Psychology*, *48*, 285–290.

Taylor, R. B., & Lanni, J. C. (1981). Territorial dominance: The influence of the resident advantage in triadic decision making. *Journal of Personality and Social Psychology*, *41*, 900–915.

Taylor, S., & Gammon, C. (1975). Effects of type and dose of alcohol on human physical aggression. *Journal of Personality and Social Psychology*, *32*, 169–175.

Taylor, S. E. (2011). Social support: A review. In H. S. Friendman (Ed.), *Oxford handbook of health psychology* (pp. 189–214). New York, NY: Oxford University Press

Taylor, S. E., & Brown, J. D. (1988). Illusion and well-being: A social psychological perspective on mental health. *Psychological Bulletin*, *103*, 193–210.

Tedeschi, J. T. (1983). Social influence theory and aggression. In R. G. Geen & E. I. Donnerstein (Eds.), *Aggression: Theoretical and empirical reviews* (Vol. 1, pp. 135–162). New York, NY: Academic Press.

Teleki, G. (1973). *The predatory behavior of wild chimpanzees*. Lewisburg, PA: Bucknell University Press.

Tellegen, A., & Atkinson, G. (1974). Openness to absorbing and self-altering experiences ("absorption"), a trait related to hypnotic susceptibility. *Journal of Abnormal Psychology*, *83*, 268–277.

Tellegen, A., Lykken, T., Bouchard, T. J., Jr., Wilcox, K. J., Segal, N. L., Rich, S. (1988). Personality similarity in twins reared apart and together. *Journal of Personality and Social Psychology*, *54*, 1031–1039.

Tempone, V. J. (1964). Extension of the repression-sensitization hypothesis to success and failure experience. *Psychological Reports*, *15*, 39–45.

Tenopyr, M. L. (1977). Content-construct confusion. *Personnel Psychology*, *30*, 47–54.

Temrin, H., Buchmayer, S., & Enquist, M. (2000). Step–parents and infanticide: New data contradict evolutionary predictions. *Proceedings of the Royal Society of London B: Biological Sciences*, *267*, 943–945.

Tesser, A. (1993). The importance of heritability in psychological research: The case of attitudes. *Psychological Review*, *100*, 129–142.

Tesser, A., Crepaz, N. Collins, J. C., Cornell, D., & Beach, S. R. H. (2000). Confluence of self-esteem regulation mechanisms: On integrating the self-zoo. *Personality and Social Psychology Bulletin*, *26*, 1476–1489.

Thoits, P. A. (1995). Stress, coping, and social support processes: Where are we? What next?. *Journal of health and social behavior*, 53–79.

Thomas, A., & Chess, S. (1976). Behavioral individuality in childhood. In L. Aronson, E. Tabach, D. Lehrmon, & J. Rosenblatt (Eds.), *Development and evolution of behavior*. San Francisco, CA: Freeman.

Thomas, A., Chess, S., Birch, H. G., Hertzig, M. L., & Korn, S. J. (1963). *Behavioral individuality in early childhood*. New York, NY: New York University Press.

Thomas, A., Chess, S., Birch, H. G., Hertzig, M. L., & Korn, S. J. (1968). *Temperament and behavior disorders in children*. New York, NY: New York University Press.

Thompson, R. A. (1993). Socioemotional development: Enduring issues and new challenges. *Developmental Review*, *13*, 372–402.

Thompson, R. A., Connell, J. P., & Bridger, L. J. (1988). Temperament, emotion, and social interactive behavior in the strange situation: A component process analysis of attachment system functioning. *Child Development*, *59*, 1102–1110.

Thompson, W. R. (1954). The inheritance and development of intelligence. *Association for Research in Nervous and Mental Diseases: Research Pub.*, *33*, 209–231.

Thorndike, E. L. (1906). *Principles of teaching*. New York, NY: Seiler.

Thorne, A. (1987). The press of personality: A study of conversations between introverts and extroverts. *Journal of Personality and Social Psychology*, *53*, 718–726.

Tieger, T. (1980). On the biological basis of sex differences in aggression. *Child Development*, *51*, 943–963.

Timmerman, T. A. (2007). "It was a thought pitch": Personal, situational, and target influences on hit-by-pitch events across time. *Journal of Applied Psychology*, *92*(3), 876–884.

Tinbergen, N. (1951). *The study of instinct*. London, UK: Oxford University Press.

Tinbergen, N. (1953). Fighting and threat in animals. *New Biology*, *14*, 9–24.

Tinbergen, N. (1968). On war and peace in animals and man. *Science*, *160*, 1411–1418.

Tizard, B. (1977). *Adoption: A second change*. London, UK: Open Books.

Tizard, B., & Hodges, J. (1978). The effect of early institutional rearing on the development of eight-year-old children. *Journal of Child Psychology and Psychiatry*, *19*, 99–118.

Tizard, B., & Rees, J. (1975). The effect of early institutional rearing on the behavior problems and affectional relationships of four-year-old children. *Journal of Child Psychology and Psychiatry*, *16*, 61–74.

Todd, J. T., & Bohart, A. C. (1994). *Foundations of clinical and counseling psychology* (2nd ed.). New York, NY: Harpercollins.

Toch, H. (1969). *Violent men*. Chicago, IL: Aldine.

Tolman, A. E., Diekmann, K. A., & McCartney, K. (1989). Social connectedness and mothering: Effects of maternal employment and maternal absence. *Journal of Personality and Social Psychology*, *56*, 942–949.

Tomkins, S. S. (1947). *The Thematic Apperception Test: The theory and technique of interpretation*. New York, NY: Grune & Stratton.

Tomkins, S. S. (1970). Affect as the primary motivational system. In M. B. Arnold (Ed.), *Feelings and emotions*. New York, NY: Academic Press.

Tomkins, S. S. (1980) Affect as amplification: Some modification in theory. In R. Plutchik & H. Kellerman (Eds.), *Emotion: Theory, research and experience: Vol. 1, Theories of emotion*. New York, NY: Academic Press.

Tongas, P. N. (1979). The Kaiser-Permanente smoking control program: Its purpose and implications for an HMO. *Professional Psychology*, *10*, 409–418.

Towers, H., Spotts, E. L., & Neiderhiser, J. M. (2003). Genetic and environmental influences on parenting and marital relationships: Current findings and future directions. *Marriage & Family Review*, *33*(1), 11–29.

Trevarthen, C. (1983). Emotions in infancy: Regulators of contacts and relationships with persons. In K. Scherer & P. Ekman, (Eds.), *Approaches to emotion*. Hillsdale, NJ: Erlbaum.

Triandis, H. C. (1989). The self and social behavior in different cultural contexts. *Psychological Review, 96*, 506–520.

Triandis, H. C. (2002). Individualism-collectivism and personality. *Journal of personality, 69*(6), 907–924.

Troiden, R. R. (1988). Homosexual identity development. *Journal of Adolescent Health Care, 9*, 105–113.

Troll, L. E., Neugarten, B. L., & Kraines, R. J. (1969). Similarities in values and other personality characteristics in college students and their parents. *Merrill-Palmer Quarterly, 15*, 323–326.

Trope, Y. (1975). Seeking information about one's own ability as a determinant of choice among tasks. *Journal of Personality and Social Psychology, 32*, 1004–1013.

Truax, C. B., & Carkhuff, R. R. (1967). *Toward effective counseling and psychotherapy: Training and practice*. Chicago, IL: Aldine.

Truax, C. B., & Mitchell, K. M. (1971). Research on certain therapist interpersonal skills in relation to process and outcome. In A. E. Bergin & S. L. Garfield (Eds.), *Handbook of psychotherapy and behavior change*. New York, NY: Wiley.

Truax, C. B., Wargo, D. G., Frank, J. D., Imber, S. D., Battle, C. C., Hoehn-Saric, R., Nash, E. H., & Stone, A. R. (1966). Therapist empathy, genuineness and warmth and patient therapeutic outcome. *Journal of Consulting Psychology, 30*, 395–401.

Trzesniewski, K. H., Donnellan, M. B., Moffitt, T. E., Robins, R. W., Poulton, R., & Caspi, A. (2006). Low self-esteem during adolescence predicts poor health, criminal behavior, and limited economic prospects during adulthood. *Developmental Psychology, 42*, 381.

Tucker-Drob, E. M., & Bates, T. C. (2016). Large cross-national differences in gene × socioeconomic status interaction on intelligence. *Psychological Science, 27*(2), 138–149.

Turiel, E. (1966). An experimental test of the sequentiality of developmental states in the child's moral judgments. *Journal of Personality and Social Psychology, 3*, 611–618.

Turkheimer, E., Haley, A. P., Waldron, M., & Gottesman, I. (2003). Socioeconomic status modifies heritability of IQ in young children. *Psychological Science, 14*, 623–628.

Turkheimer, E., Pettersson, E., & Horn, E. E. (2014). A phenotypic null hypothesis for the genetics of personality. *Annual Review of Psychology, 65*, 515–540.

Turner, E. A., Chandler, M., & Heffer, R. W. (2009). The influence of parenting styles, achievement motivation, and self-efficacy on academic performance in college students. *Journal of College Student Development, 50*(3), 337–346.

Turner, J. A., & Clancy, L. (1988). Comparison of operant behavioral and cognitive-behavioral group treatment for chronic low back pain. *Journal of Consulting and Clinical Psychology, 56*, 261–266.

Tversky, A., & Kahneman, D. (1971). Belief in the law of small numbers. *Psychological Bulletin, 76*, 105–110.

Tversky, A., & Kahneman, D. (1980). Causal schemas in judgments under uncertainty. In M. Fishbein (Ed.), *Progress in social psychology*. Hillsdale, NJ: Lawrence Erlbaum.

Tversky, A., & Kahneman, D., (1981). The framing of decisions and the psychology of choice. *Science, 211*, 453–458.

Twenge, J. M., & Campbell, W. K. (2002). Self-esteem and socioeconomic status: A meta-analytic review. *Personality and Social Psychology Review, 6*(1), 59–71.

Tyler, L. E. (1969). *The work of the counselor* (3rd ed.). New York, NY: Appleton-Century-Crofts.

Tyler, L. E. (1971). *Tests and measurements* (2nd ed.). Englewood Cliffs, NJ: Prentice-Hall.

Uleman, J. S., & Bargh, J. A. (Eds.). (1989). *Unintended thought*. New York, NY: Guilford.

Ulrich, R. (1984). View through a window may influence recovery. *Science, 224*(4647), 224–225.

Umaña-Taylor, A. J., Quintana, S. M., Lee, R. M., Cross, W. E., Rivas-Drake, D., Schwartz, S. J., . . . & Seaton, E. (2014). Ethnic and racial identity during adolescence and into young adulthood: An integrated conceptualization. *Child Development, 85*(1), 21–39.

U.S. Bureau of the Census. (1986). *Fertility of American women* (Current Population Reports, Series P-20, No. 406). Washington, DC: U.S. Government Printing Office.

U.S. Bureau of the Census. (1993). *Statistical abstract of the United States*. Washington, DC: U.S. Government Printing Office.

Vaillancourt, T., deCatanzaro, D., Duku, E., & Muir, C. (2009). Androgen dynamics in the context of children's peer relations: An examination of the links between testosterone and peer victimization. *Aggressive Behavior, 35*, 103–113.

Vaillant, G. E. (1993). *The wisdom of the ego*. Cambridge, MA: Harvard University Press.

Valins, S. (1966). Cognitive effects of false heart-rate feedback. *Journal of Personality and Social Psychology, 4*, 400–408.

Valzelli, L. (1976). Drugs and aggressiveness. In K. Moyer (Ed.), *Physiology of aggression and implications for control*. New York, NY: Raven.

Vandell, P. L., Henderson, V. K., & Wilson, K. S. (1988) A longitudinal study of children with daycare experiences of varying quality. *Child Development, 59*, 1286–1292.

Van Hook, E., & Higgins, E. T. (1988). Self-related problems beyond the self-concept: Motivational consequences of discrepant self-guides. *Journal of Personality and Social Psychology, 55*, 625–633.

Van Ijzendoorn, M. H., & Kroonenberg, P. M. (1988). Trans-cultural patterns of attachment: A meta-analysis of the strange situation. *Child Development, 59*, 147–156.

Van Ijzendoorn, M. H., Schuengel, C., & Bakermans–Kranenburg, M. J. (1999). Disorganized attachment in early childhood: Meta-analysis of precursors, concomitants, and sequelae. *Development and Psychopathology, 11*, 225–250.

Van Lawick-Goodall, J. (1968a). Tool-using bird: The Egyptian vulture. *National Geographic, 133*, 631–641.

Van Lawick-Goodall, J. (1968b). The behavior of free-living chimpanzees in the Gombe Stream Reserve. *Animal Behavior Monographs, 1*, 161–311.

Valli, K., & Revonsuo, A. (2009). The threat simulation theory in light of recent empirical evidence: A review. *The American Journal of Psychology, 122*, 17–38.

Valli, K., Revonsuo, A., Pälkäs, O., Ismail, K. H., Ali, K. J., & Punamäki, R. L. (2005). The threat simulation theory of the evolutionary function of dreaming: Evidence from dreams of traumatized children. *Consciousness and cognition, 14*(1), 188–218.

Vandell, P. L., Henderson, V. K., & Wilson, K. S. (1988). A longitudinal study of children with daycare experiences of varying quality. *Child Development, 59,* 1286–1292.

Vaughn, B. E., Lefever, G., Sefier, R., & Barglow, P. (1989). Attachment behavior, attachment security and temperament during infancy. *Child Development, 60,* 728–737.

Veroff, J. (1969). Social comparison and the development of achievement motivation. In C. P. Smith (Ed.), *Achievement-related motives in children.* New York, NY: Russell Sage.

Veroff, J., Atkinson, J. W., Feld, S. C., & Gurin, G. (1960). The use of thematic apperception to assess motivation in a nationwide interview study. *Psychological Monographs, 74* (No. 12).

Verschueren, M., Rassart, J., Claes, L., Moons, P., & Luyckx, K. (2017). Identity statuses throughout adolescence and emerging adulthood: A large-scale study into gender, age, and contextual differences. *Psychologica Belgica, 57*(1), 32–42.

Vertes, R. P. (2004). Memory consolidation in sleep: Dream or reality. *Neuron, 44*(1), 135–148.

Vignoles, V. L., Owe, E., Becker, M., Smith, P. B., Easterbrook, M. J., Brown, R., . . . & Bond, M. H. (2016). Beyond the 'east–west' dichotomy: Global variation in cultural models of selfhood. *Journal of Experimental Psychology: General, 145*(8), 966–1000.

Volosinov, V. N. (1976). *Freudianism: A Marxist critique.* New York, NY: Academic Press.

Wade, T. D., & Kendler, K. S. (2000). The genetic epidemiology of parental discipline. *Psychological Medicine, 30*(6), 1303–1313.

Wagenmakers, E. J., Beek, T., Dijkhoff, L., Gronau, Q. F., Acosta, A., Adams, R. B., Jr., . . . & Bulnes, L. C. (2016). Registered replication report: Strack, Martin, & Stepper (1988). *Perspectives on Psychological Science, 11*(6), 917–928.

Walker, L. J. (1984). Sex differences in the development of word reasoning: A critical review. *Child Development, 55,* 677–691.

Walker, L. J. (1989). A longitudinal study of moral reasoning. *Child Development, 60,* 157–166.

Walker, M. P., & Stickgold, R. (2004). Sleep-dependent learning and memory consolidation. *Neuron, 44*(1), 121–133.

Waller, N. G. (1999). Evaluating the structure of personality. In C. R. Cloninger (Ed.), *Personality and psychopathology* (pp. 155–197). Arlington, VA: American Psychiatric Association.

Walster, E., Hatfield, E., Aronson, V., Abrahams, D., & Rottman, L. (1966). Importance of physical attractiveness in dating behavior. *Journal of Personality and Social Psychology, 4,* 508–516.

Walters, R. H., & Brown, M. (1963). Studies of reinforcement of aggression: III. Transfer of responses to an interpersonal situation. *Child Development, 34,* 536–571.

Wapner, S. (1976). Commentary: Process and context in the conception of cognitive style. In S. Messick (Ed.), *Individuality in learning: Implications of cognitive styles and creativity for human development* (pp. 73–78). San Francisco, CA: Jossey-Bass.

Wapner, S., & Hiatt, F. L. (August 1993). *The holistic, developmental, systems-oriented approach.* Paper presented as part of a symposium on "Psychology's 'World Views': General Approaches to Understanding Human Behavior," American Psychological Association Convention, Toronto, Canada.

Washburn, S. L. (1978). Human behavior and the behavior of other animals. *American Psychologist, 33,* 405–418.

Waterman, A. S. (1982). Identity development from adolescence to adulthood: An extension of theory and a review of research. *Developmental Psychology, 18,* 341–358.

Waterman, A. S. (1992). Identity as an aspect of optimal psychological functioning. In G. R. Adams, T. P. Gullotta, & R. Montemayer (Eds.), *Adolescent identity formation* (pp. 50–72). Newbury Park, CA: Sage.

Waterman, A. S. (1981). Individualism and interdependence. *American Psychologist, 36,* 762–773.

Waters, E. (1978). The reliability and stability of individual differences in infant-mother attachment. *Child Development, 49,* 483–494.

Waters, E., & Crandall, V. J. (1964). Social class and obscured maternal behaviors from 1940 to 1960. *Child Development, 35,* 1021–1032.

Watkins, R. P., Peterson, R. F., Schweid, E., & Bijou, S. W. (1966). Behavior therapy in the home: Amelioration of problem parent-child relations with the parent in a therapeutic role. *Journal of Experimental Child Psychology, 4,* 99–107.

Watson, D., Klohnen, E. C., Casillas, A., Nus Simms, E., Haig, J., & Berry, D. S. (2004). Match makers and deal breakers: Analyses of assortative mating in newlywed couples. *Journal of Personality, 72*(5), 1029–1068.

Watson, G. A. (1957). Some personality differences in children related to strict or permissive parental discipline. *Journal of Psychology, 44,* 227–249.

Watson, J. B. (1930). *Behaviorism* (Rev. ed.). New York, NY: Norton.

Weary, G. B. (1978). Self-serving biases in the attribution process: A re-examination of the fact or fiction question. *Journal of Personality and Social Psychology, 36,* 56–71.

Weatherhead, P. J., & Robertson, R. J. (1979). Offspring quality and the polygyny threshold: "The sexy son hypothesis." *American Naturalist, 113,* 201–208.

Webb, J. T. (1970). *The relation of MMPI two-point codes to age, sex, and education level in a representative nationwide sample of psychiatric outpatients.* Paper presented at Southeastern Psychological Association meetings, Louisville, KY.

Webb, W. B. (1975). *Sleep, the gentle tyrant.* Englewood Cliffs, NJ: Prentice-Hall.

Webb, W. B., & Bonnet, M. H. (1979). Sleep and dreams. In M. E. Meyer (Ed.), *Foundations of contemporary psychology.* New York, NY: Oxford University Press.

Webb, W. B., & Cartwright, R. D. (1978). Sleep and dreams. *Annual Review of Psychology, 29,* 223–252.

Weber, M. (1904; 1958). *The Protestant ethic and the spirit of capitalism.* New York, NY: Scribner's.

Wegner, D. M. (1994). Ironic processes of mental control. *Psychological Review, 101,* 34–52.

Wegner, D. M. (2002). *The illusion of conscious will.* Cambridge MA: MIT Press.

Wegner, D. M. (2004). Précis of the illusion of conscious will. *Behavioral and Brain Sciences, 27*(5), 649–659.

Wegner, D. M., & Erber, R. (1992). The hyperaccessibility of suppressed thought. *Journal of Personality and Social Psychology, 63,* 903–912.

Wegner, D. M., & Vallacher, R. R. (1977). *Implicit psychology.* New York, NY: Oxford University Press.

Weinberger, D. A., Schwartz, G., & Davidson, R. (1979). Low-anxious, high-anxious and repressive coping styles: Psychometric patterns and behavioral and physiological responses to stress. *Journal of Abnormal Psychology, 88,* 369–380.

Weinberger, J. L. (1994). Can personality change? In T. F. Heatherton & J. L. Weinberger (Eds.), *Can personality change?* (pp. 33–350). Washington, DC: American Psychological Association.

Weiner, B. (1966). Effects of motivation on the availability and retrieval of memory traces. *Psychological Bulletin, 65,* 24–37.

Weiner, B. (1978). Achievement strivings. In H. London & J. Exner (Eds.), *Dimensions of personality.* New York, NY: Wiley.

Weiner, B. (1979). A theory of motivation for some classroom experiences. *Journal of Educational Psychology, 71,* 3–25.

Weiner, B. (1980). A cognitive (attribution) -emotion-action model of motivated behavior: An analysis of judgments of help-giving. *Journal of Personality and Social Psychology, 39,* 186–200.

Weiner, B. (1985). An attributional theory of achievement motivations and emotion. *Psychological Review, 92,* 548–573.

Weiner, B. (1986). *An attributional theory of motivation and emotion.* New York, NY: Springer-Verlag.

Weiner, B. (1993). On sin versus sickness: A theory of perceived responsibility and social motivation. *American Psychologist, 48,* 957–965.

Weiner, B., & Kukla, A. (1970). An attributional analysis of achievement motivation. *Journal of Personality and Social Psychology, 15,* 1–20.

Weiner, B., Perry, R. P., & Magnusson, J. (1988). An attributional analysis of reactions to stigmas. *Journal of Personality and Social Psychology, 55,* 738–748.

Weiner, B., Russell, D., & Lerman, D. (1978). Affective consequences of causal ascriptions. In J. H. Harvey, W. J. Ickes, & R. F. Kidd (Eds.), *New directions in attribution research* (Vol. 2). Hillsdale, NJ: Lawrence Erlbaum.

Weiner, B., Russell, D., & Lerman, D. (1979). The cognition-emotion process in achievement-related contexts. *Journal of Personality and Social Psychology, 37,* 1211–1220.

Weinraub, M., Brooks, J., & Lewis, M. (1977). The social network: A reconsideration of the concept of attachment. *Human Development, 20,* 31–47.

Weisman, A. D. (1973). Coping with untimely death. *Psychiatry, 36,* 366–378.

Weisz, J. R., Suwanlert, S., Chaiyasit, W. C., & Walter, B. R. (1987). Over- and uncontrolled referral problems among children and adolescents from Thailand and the United States: The Wat and Wai of cultural differences. *Journal of Consulting and Clinical Psychology, 55,* 719–726.

Weitzenhoffer, A. M., & Hilgard, E. R. (1962). *Stanford hypnotic susceptibility scale.* Stanford, CA: Stanford University Press.

Wells, B. W. P. (1972). The psycho-social influence of building environment: Sociometric findings in large and small office spaces. In R. Gutman (Ed.), *People and buildings.* New York, NY: Basic Books.

Wells, W. D. (1971). *Television and aggression: Replication of an experimental field study.* Unpublished manuscript, University of Chicago, Chicago, IL.

Wenke, D., Fleming, S. M., & Haggard, P. (2010). Subliminal priming of actions influences sense of control over effects of action. *Cognition, 115*(1), 26–38.

Werner, C. M., Brown, B. B., & Damron, G. (1981). Territorial marking in a game arcade. *Journal of Personality and Social Psychology, 41,* 1094–1104.

Werner, E. E. (2013). What can we learn about resilience from large-scale longitudinal studies? In S. Goldstein & R. B. Brooks (Eds.) *Handbook of Resilience in Children* (pp. 87–102). New York, NY: Springer US.

Werner, E. E., & Smith, R. S. (1982). *Vulnerable but invincible: A study of resilient children.* New York, NY: McGraw-Hill.

Westen, D., Ludolph, P., Lerner, H., Ruffins, S., & Wiss, F. C. (1990). Object relations in borderline adolescents. *Journal of the American Academy of Child and Adolescent Psychiatry, 29,* 338–348.

Wethington, E. (2000). Expecting stress: Americans and the "midlife crisis." *Motivation and Emotion, 24*(2), 85–103.

Whalen, C., & Schriebman, L. (2004). Joint attention training for children with autism using behavior modification procedures. *Journal of Child Psychology and Psychiatry, 44,* 456–468.

White, G. L. (1981). Some correlates of romantic jealousy. *Journal of Personality, 149,* 129–146.

White, G. L., & La Barba, R. C. (1976). The effects of tactile and kinesthetic stimulation on neonatal development in the premature infant. *Journal of Developmental Psychobiology, 9,* 569–577.

White, R. M. (1975). *Sleep length and variability: Measurement and interrelationships* (Unpublished doctoral dissertation). University of Florida, Gainesville, FL.

White, R. W. (Ed.) (1966). *The study of lives.* New York, NY: Atherton.

Whiteman, M. (1967). Children's conceptions of psychological causality. *Child Development, 38,* 143–155.

Whiting, B. B. (1966). *Six cultures: Studies of child rearing.* New York, NY: Wiley.

Whiting, B. B. (Ed.). (1966). *Six cultures series* (Vol. I–VII). New York, NY: Wiley.

Whiting, B. B., & Whiting, J. W. M. (1975). *Children of six cultures.* Cambridge, MA: Harvard University Press.

Whiting, J. W. M. (1954). The cross-cultural method. In G. Lindzey (Ed.), *Handbook of social psychology.* Reading, MA: Addison-Wesley.

Whiting, J. W. M. (1968). Methods and problems in cross-cultural research. In G. Lindzey & E. Aronson (Eds.), *Handbook of social psychology* (Vol. 2). Reading, MA: Addison-Wesley.

Whiting, J. W. M., & Child, I. L. (1953). *Child training and personality*. New Haven, CT: Yale University Press.

Whiting, J. W. M., Kluckhohn, R., & Anthony, A. (1958). The function of male initiation ceremonies at puberty. In E. E. Maccoby, T. M. Newcomb, & E. L. Hartley (Eds.), *Readings in social psychology* (3rd ed.). New York, NY: Holt.

Wicker, A. W. (1968). Undermanning, performances, and students' subjective experiences in behavioral settings of large and small high schools. *Journal of Personality and Social Psychology, 10*, 255–261.

Wicker, A. W., & Kirmeyer, S. (1977). From church to laboratory to national park: A program of research on excess and insufficient populations in behavior settings. In D. Stokols (Ed.), *Perspectives on environment and behavior*. New York, NY: Plenum.

Widiger, T. A., & Frances, A. J. (1994). Toward a dimensional model for the personality disorders. In P. T. Costa & T. A. Widiger (Eds.), *Personality disorders and the five-factor model of personality* (pp. 19–40). Washington, DC: American Psychological Association.

Widom, C. S. (1989). Does violence beget violence? A critical examination of the literature. *Psychological Bulletin, 106*, 3–28.

Wiens, A. H. (1976). The assessment interview. In I. B. Weiner (Ed.), *Clinical methods in psychology*. New York, NY: Wiley.

Wiggins, J. S. (1959). Interrelationships among MMPI measures of dissimulation under standard and social desirability instructions. *Journal of Consulting Psychology, 23*, 419–427.

Wiggins, J. S. (1962). Strategic, method, & stylistic variance in the MMPI. *Psychological Bulletin, 59*, 224–242.

Wiggins, J. S. (1973). *Personality and prediction: Principles of personality assessment*. Reading, MA: Addison-Wesley.

Wiggins, J. S., Renner, K. E., Clore, G. L., & Rose, R. J. (1971). *The psychology of personality*. Reading, MA: Addison-Wesley.

Williams, L. M. (1992). Adult memories of childhood abuse: Preliminary findings from a longitudinal study. *The Advisor: American Professional Society on the Abuse of Children, 5*(3), 19–21.

Williamsen, J. A., Johnson, H. J., & Eriksen, C. W. (1965). Some characteristics of posthypnotic amnesia. *Journal of Abnormal Psychology, 70*, 123–131.

Wilson, E. O. (1975). *Sociobiology: The new synthesis*. Cambridge, MA: Harvard University Press.

Wilson, E. O. (1977). Biology and the social sciences. *Daedalus, 11*, 127–140.

Wilson, E. O. (2000). *Sociobiology: The New Synthesis, 25th Anniversary Edition*. Cambridge, MA: Harvard University Press.

Wilson, G. (1978). Introversion/extraversion. In H. London & J. E. Exner, Jr. (Eds.), *Dimensions of personality*. New York, NY: Wiley.

Wilson, J. Q., & Herrnstein, R. J. (1985). *Crime and human nature*. New York, NY: Simon & Schuster.

Wilson, T. D., & Linville, P. W. (1982). Improving the academic performance of college freshmen: Attribution theory revisited. *Journal of Personality and Social Psychology, 42*, 367–376.

Wilson, T. D., & Linville, P. W. (1985). Improving the performance of college freshmen with attributional techniques. *Journal of Personality and Social Psychology, 49*, 287–293.

Wine, J. D. (1971). Test anxiety and direction of attention. *Psychological Bulletin, 76*, 92–104.

Winget, C., Kramer, M., & Whitman, R. (1972). Dreams and demography. *Canadian Psychiatric Association Journal, 17*, 203–208.

Winnicott, D. W. (1953). Transitional objects and transitional phenomena. *International Journal of Psychoanalysis, 34*, 89–97.

Winston, H. D., & Lindzey, G. (1964). Albinism and water escape performance in the mouse. *Science, 144*, 189–191.

Winter, D. L., & Carlson, L. A. (1988). Using motive scores in the psychobiographical study of an individual. The case of Richard Nixon. *Journal of Personality, 56*, 75–104.

Winterbottom, M. R. (1953). *The relation of childhood training in independence to achievement motivation* (Unpublished doctoral dissertation). University of Michigan, Ann Arbor, MI.

Witkin, H. A., Dyk, R. B., Faterson, H. F., Goodenough, D. R., & Karp, S. A. (1962). *Psychological differentiation*. New York, NY: Wiley.

Witkin, H. A., Mednick, S. A., Schulsinger, F., Bakkestrom, E., Christianses, K. O., Goodenough, D. R., . . . & Stocking, M. (1976). Criminality in XYY and XXY men. *Science, 196*, 547–555.

Witkin, H. A., & Goodenough, D. (1981). *Cognitive styles: Essences and origins*. New York, NY: International Universities Press.

Wolf, T. M. (1973). Effects of live modeled sex-inappropriate play behavior in a naturalistic setting. *Developmental Psychology, 9*, 120–124.

Wollmer, M. A., de Boer, C., Kalak, N., Beck, J., Götz, T., Schmidt, T., . . . & Sönmez, D. (2012). Facing depression with botulinum toxin: A randomized controlled trial. *Journal of Psychiatric Research, 46*(5), 574–581.

Wolk, S., & DuCette, J. (1974). Intentional performance and incidental learning as a function of personality and task dimensions. *Journal of Personality and Social Psychology, 29*, 90–101.

Wolpe, J. (1958). *Psychotherapy by reciprocal inhibition*. Stanford, CA: Stanford University Press.

Wolpe, J. (1969). *The practice of behavior therapy*. New York, NY: Pergamon.

Wood, A., Lupyan, G., Sherrin, S., & Niedenthal, P. (2016). Altering sensorimotor feedback disrupts visual discrimination of facial expressions. *Psychonomic Bulletin & Review, 23*(4), 1150–1156.

Wood, J. M., Nezworski, M. T., & Stejskal, W. J. (1996). The comprehensive system for the Rorschach: A critical examination. *Psychological Science, 7*, 3–11.

Woodworth, R. S. (1920). *Personal data sheet*. Chicago, IL: Stoelting.

Worchel, S. (1974). The effect of three types of arbitrary thwarting on the instigation to aggression. *Journal of Personality, 42*, 300–318.

Wortman, C. B., & Brehm, J. W. (1975). Responses to uncontrollable outcomes: An integration of reactance theory and the learned helplessness model. In L. Berkowitz (Ed.),

Advances in experimental social psychology (Vol. 8). New York, NY: Academic Press.

Wortman, C. B., & Silver, R. C. (1989). The myths of coping with loss. *Journal of Consulting and Clinical Psychology, 57,* 349–357.

Wrightsman, L. (1977). *Social psychology* (2nd ed.). Belmont, CA: Brooks/Cole.

Wu, C. C., Samanez-Larkin, G. R., Katovich, K., & Knutson, B. (2014). Affective traits link to reliable neural markers of incentive anticipation. *Neuroimage, 84,* 279–289.

Wylie, R. G. (1974). *The self-concept: A review of methodological considerations and measuring instruments* (Rev. ed., Vol. 1). Lincoln, NE: University of Nebraska Press.

Wylie, R. G. (1979). *The self-concept: Theory and research on selected topics* (Vol. 2). Lincoln, NE: University of Nebraska Press.

Xu, Y., Farver, J. M., Zhang, Z., Zeng, Q., Yu, L., & Cai, B. (2005). Mainland Chinese parenting styles and parent-child interaction. *International Journal of Behavioral Development, 29,* 524–531.

Yando, R. M., & Kagan, J. (1970). The effect of task complexity on reflection-impulsivity. *Cognitive Psychology, 1*(2), 192–200.

Yates, A. B. (1962). *Frustration and conflict.* London, UK: Methuen.

Yee, B. W. K. (1987). Adaptation in old age: Japanese and Vietnamese elderly women. *Asian American Psychological Association Journal, 12,* 38–50.

Young, P. T. (1943). *Emotion in man and animal.* New York, NY: Wiley.

Zadra, A., Desjardins, S., & Marcotte, E. (2005). Evolutionary function of dreams: A test of the threat simulation theory in recurrent dreams. *Consciousness and Cognition, 15*(2), 450–463.

Zahn-Waxler, C., & Radke-Yarrow, M. (1982). The development of altrusion: Alternative research strategies. In N. Eisenberg-Berg (Ed.), *The development of prosocial behavior.* New York, NY: Academic Press.

Zajonc, R. B. (1980). Feeling and thinking: Preferences need no inferences. *American Psychologist, 39,* 151–175.

Zaleski, Z. (1984). Sensation seeking and risk taking behavior. *Personality and individual differences, 5,* 607–608.

Zeichner, A., & Reidy, D. E. (2009). Are homophobic men attracted to or repulsed by homosexual men? Effects of gay male erotica on anger, fear, happiness, and disgust. *Psychology of Men & Masculinity, 10,* 231.

Zelenski, J. M., & Larsen, R. J. (2000). The distribution of basic emotions in everyday life: A state and trait perspective from experience sampling data. *Journal of Research in Personality, 34*(2), 178–197.

Zigler, E., & Yospe, L. (1960). Perceptual defense and the problem of response suppression. *Journal of Personality, 28,* 220–239.

Zillman, D. (1971). Excitation transfer in communication-mediated aggressive behavior. *Journal of Experimental Social Psychology, 7,* 419–434.

Zillman, D. (1978). Attribution and misattribution of excitatory reactions. In J. H. Harvey, W. J. Ickes, & R. F. Kidd (Eds.), *New directions in attribution research* (Vol. 2). Hillsdale, NJ: Lawrence Erlbaum.

Zillman, D. (1984). *Connections between sex and aggression.* Hillsdale, NJ: Lawrence Erlbaum.

Zillman, D., Bryant, J., Comiskey, P., & Medoff, N. (1981). Excitation and hedonic valence in the effect of erotica on motivated intermale aggression. *European Journal of Social Psychology, 11,* 233–252.

Zillman, P., & Cantor, J. R. (1976). Effect of timing of information about mitigating circumstances on emotional responses to provocation and retaliatory behavior. *Journal of Experimental Social Psychology, 12,* 38–55.

Zillman, D., Katcher, A. H., & Milarsky, B. (1972). Excitation transfer from physical exercise to subsequent aggressive behavior. *Journal of Experimental Social Psychology, 8,* 247–259.

Zinberg, N. E. (Ed.). (1977). *Alternate states of consciousness.* New York, NY: Free Press.

Zubin, J., Eron, L. D., & Schumer, F. (1965). *An experimental approach to projective techniques.* New York, NY: Wiley.

Zuckerman, M., Koestner, R., DeBoy, T., Garcia, T., Maresca, B. C., & Sartoris, J. M. (1988). To predict some of the people some of the time: A reexamination of the moderator variable approach in personality theory. *Journal of Personality and Social Psychology, 54,* 1006–1019.

Name Index

Aaronson, B., 313
Aarts, H., 302
Aber, J. L., 198
Abramson, L. Y., 105, 324, 325
Abrevaya, J., 363
Acklin, M. W., 150
Adams, E. M., 197, 198
Adams, G. R., 195, 196
Adams, H. E., 57
Adams, N. E., 102
Adler, A., 39, 41, 46, 61, 62, 67–68, 190, 217
Adorno, I. W., 71
Ainsworth, M., 130, 222–223, 226
Alden, L. E., 104
Aldis, O., 205
Aleixo, M. A., 280
Alexander, I. E., 63
Alexander, M. G., 154
Alfert, E., 171
Alfieri, S., 248
Alink, L. R., 230
Allen, A., 167–168
Allen, K. M., 101
Allen, L., 198
Alloy, L. B., 324
Allport, G., 17, 63, 109, 116, 159
Allred, K. D., 294
Almeida, D. M., 290
Alpert, R., 231
Altman, I., 33, 37
Alves, M. C., 280
Andersen, T. J., 150
Anderson, C. A., 35–36, 356, 359, 363
Anderson, K. B., 363
Anderson, M. C., 56
Andrés-Pueyo, A., 11
Ang, R. P., 238
Ansbacher, H. L., 67
Ansbacher, R. R., 67
Ant, S., 250
Antill, J. K., 205
Arbelle, S., 18
Archer, J., 9, 203, 205
Archer, S. L., 197
Arcus, D., 17
Ardrey, R., 358
Aristotle, 128, 346
Arkes, H. R., 113
Arkoff, A., 266
Arkowitz, H., 387
Arnold, D. D., 313
Aronfreed, J., 233
Ashby, F. G., 287
Ashmore, R. D., 201, 202, 203, 208, 209
Ashton, M. C., 66, 147, 163
Asnaani, A., 105
Assaad, J. M., 360
Atkinson, J., 334–335
Atkinson, J. W., 152, 335
Aunola, K., 229, 230
Austin, S. B., 200

Averill, J. R., 171, 278, 368
Ayllon, T., 96
Azrin, N. H., 96

Bachorowski, J. A., 373
Bacon, M., 33, 34
Baker, L. A., 206, 361
Bakermans-Kranenburg, M. J., 224
Baldwin, A. L., 228
Ballard-Campbell, M., 238
Baltes, P. B., 251
Bandura, A., 41, 86, 89, 99–104, 153, 186, 190, 233, 270, 327, 365, 368–369
Bank, L., 369
Bannister, D., 118, 121
Barber, B. K., 229
Barber, T. X., 311
Barckley, M., 243
Bargh, J. A., 254, 304
Barker, R., 36
Barker, R. G., 273
Barlow, D. H., 186
Barnes, M., 353
Barnett, M. A., 238
Barni, D., 248
Barrett, L. C., 337
Barry, H., 33, 34
Bartholomew, K., 226
Barton, R., 188
Bartone, P. T., 289
Barzun, J., 130
Bateman, A. W., 227
Bates, T. C., 20
Batson, C. D., 234
Baumeister, R. F., 10, 32, 58, 176, 184, 186, 187, 193, 298, 373
Baumrind, D., 228–231, 233
Beagley, G., 323
Beck, A. T., 68, 102, 104, 105
Becker, W. C., 228
Beebe, B., 223
Beets, J. L., 36
Bell, P. A., 139
Bell, S. M., 222
Belsky, J., 216, 218, 224–225
Bem, D. J., 167–168, 242, 245
Bem, S. L., 208
Ben-Arieh, A., 248
Benet-Martínez, V., 199
Benjamin, D. J., 22
Bentham, J., 47
Berkowitz, L., 365, 368, 370
Berlin, L. J., 224
Berlyne, D., 264
Berman, R. C., 195
Bernheim, H., 44
Bernstein, I. S., 359
Bernstein, S., 180
Berry, A. 184
Berry, J., 199
Berry, J. W., 7, 33, 34, 230

Berscheid, E., 130, 347, 349, 350
Best, K. M., 110
Bhullar, N., 353
Binet, A., 130
Binswanger, L., 115, 116
Birch, H. G., 216, 245
Birren, J. E., 254, 255–256
Bitter, E., 373
Bittner, E., 249
Björkqvist, K., 205
Blair, C., 368
Blaney, P. H., 187
Blank, A., 299, 300
Blasband, D., 354
Blass, E. M., 222
Blehar, M. C., 130
Bleidoorn, W., 248
Blelsky, J., 225
Bleske, A., 353
Block, J., 152, 235, 242, 244, 245
Block, J. H., 162, 163, 205, 235
Bluestone, C., 230
Blum, G. S., 310
Blum, R., 200
Blumenthal, R. S., 291
Blysma, L. M., 293
Blyth, D. A., 247
Boden, J. M., 184, 373
Bogaert, L., 200
Bogenschutz, M. P., 313
Bohart, A., 108, 109, 293, 374
Boivin, M., 361
Bokhorst, C. L., 227
Bonanno, G. A., 59, 315
Bond, M. H., 29
Bonnet, M. H., 305
Book, A. S., 247
Bornstein, M. H., 218
Boss, M., 115
Bosson, J. K., 181
Botwin, M. D., 353
Bouffard, D. L., 26
Bourdage, J. S., 163
Bouvrette, A., 183
Bowdle, B. F., 35
Bower, G. H., 287
Bowlby, J., 70, 77, 219, 221, 222
Bowman, M. L., 128
Boyd, E. F., 218, 222
Bradshaw, D., 352, 353
Brainerd, D. J., 169
Brandstädter, J., 252, 257
Brauer, M., 227
Bray, D., 253
Brehm, J. W., 326, 327
Brehm, S. S., 327
Breland, K., 97
Breland, M., 97
Brendgen, M., 361
Brennan, D. J., 200
Brennan, P., 21

Brett, C. E., 255
Breuer, J., 45, 63
Brewin, C. R., 325
Bricker, W., 369
Briere, J., 56
Briggs, R. D., 230
Briggs, S. P., 185
Broadhurst, P. L., 13
Brock, T. C., 374
Brody, N., 244
Bronfrenbenner, U., 22–23
Brooks-Gunn, J., 28, 179, 247
Brotman, L. M., 372
Brown, J. D., 176, 188, 189, 327
Brown, J. S., 265, 267
Brown, L., 30
Brown, L. M., 30, 208
Brown, M., 369
Brown, P., 369
Browning, E. Barrett, 346
Bruner, J. S., 118, 122
Brusch, G., 195
Bryan, J. H., 101, 237
Bryant, J., 368
Buber, M., 115
Buchanan, R. W., 363
Bucher, A. M., 374
Buchmayer, S., 9
Bugelski, R., 58
Bühler, C., 249, 251, 252, 253, 257
Burgess, G. C., 161
Burgess, M., 374
Burrows, L., 254
Burt, D. M., 353
Busch, R. M., 18
Bushman, B. J., 356, 359, 360, 373, 374
Buss, A. H., 17
Buss, D. M., 8, 353
Buss, K. A., 17
Butcher, J. N., 144
Butry, D. T., 363
Byrne, D., 58, 138, 139, 144

Cadoret, R. J., 361
Caldwell, W. V., 313
Calverley, D. S., 311
Cameron, P., 250
Campbell, B., 349
Campbell, D. E., 36
Campbell, J., 63, 64
Campbell, J. D., 176, 183, 184
Campbell, W. K., 28, 373
Camus, A., 115
Cantor, H., 274
Cantor, J. R., 375
Cantor, N., 185
Cantú, S. M., 9
Caprara, G. V., 373
Cardno, A. G., 20
Carey, G., 361
Carlson, E., 224, 245
Carlson, M., 374
Carpenter, J. C., 144
Carter-Saltzman, L., 15, 27
Carton, A. M., 363
Cartwright, R. D., 308
Carver, C. S., 161, 186, 187, 252, 299, 325
Caspi, A., 242, 244, 245, 248, 353, 374
Cass, V. C., 199
Cassidy, J., 130, 218, 224, 226
Castro, F. G., 293
Cattell, R. B., 146–147, 159, 160, 162–163
Cautela, J. R., 105
Ceci, S. J., 22–23
Cervantes, R. C., 293
Cesarini, D., 22

Chabris, C. F., 22
Chamberlain, P., 96
Chandler, M., 230
Chandler, M. J., 216
Chang, L., 372
Chanowitz, B., 299, 300
Chao, Y. Y., 102
Chaplin, W., 188
Chaplin, W. F., 168
Chapman, M., 238
Charcot, J. M., 44
Chavira, V., 198–199
Chazan, S. E., 79
Cheek, J. M., 167, 169, 185
Chen, M., 254
Chen, X., 230
Chess, S., 216, 245, 360
Child, I., 33, 34
Chipuer, H. M., 22
Chirigoba, D. A., 251
Choe, D. E., 373
Chrisler, J. C., 201
Chwalisz, K., 281
Cialdin, R. B., 188
Cicirelli, V. G., 227
Civelek, A. C., 291
Claes, L., 197
Clarkin, J. F., 227
Clore, G. L., 279
Cobb, J. A., 96
Cocking, R. R., 235
Coe, W. C., 311
Cohen, D., 35, 363
Cohen, D. B., 308
Cohen, J., 203
Cohen, S., 292, 313
Cohn, E. G., 363
Coifman, K. G., 59
Coleman, H. L. K., 199
Colgan, S. M., 311
Collins, N. L., 353
Collins, W. A., 224
Collmer, C. W., 372
Colvin, C. R., 170
Comiskey, P., 368
Condry, J., 328
Conley, D., 22
Conte, J., 56
Cook, M., 5
Coon, H. M., 198
Cooney, J. B., 94
Cooper, M. L., 183
Cooper, R. M., 13
Cooper, W. H., 26
Coopersmith, H. S., 183
Copernicus, 46
Copland-Linder, N., 199
Corley, R., 20
Cornell, D. P. 184
Costa, P. T., 66, 147, 161, 162, 242, 253
Covert, M. V., 284
Cowan, P. A., 232
Cox, C. I., 197, 198
Cox, K., 210
Craik, F. I., 177
Cramer, P., 59, 152
Crane, M., 180
Crick, N., 372
Crick, N. R., 230, 373
Critchfield, K. L., 227
Critelli, J. W., 347
Crits-Christoph, P., 104
Crittenden, A. N., 305
Crocker, J., 28, 183, 184, 188
Crockett, L. J., 293
Croon, M. A., 293

Cropanzano, R. S., 286
Csikszentmihalyi, M., 329
Cumming, E., 256
Cunningham, J. D., 164
Cunningham, M. R., 287
Cutrona, C. E., 325
Czyzewska, M., 303

Dabbs, J. M., 360
Daglish, L., 205
Dahlstrom, W. G., 144
Dale, K., 58
Daly, M., 9
Dapretto, M., 237
Darley, J. M., 327
Darling, N., 230
Darwin, C., 3, 7, 44, 46, 87, 108, 129, 262, 358
Darwin, E., 129
Datan, N., 254
Davidson, R., 58
da Vinci, L., 271
Davis, J. D., 153
Davis, K. E., 164
Davis, P. J., 58
Davison, G. C., 105, 200
Davitz, J., 368
Deary, I. J., 255
deCatanzaro, D., 247
Decety, J., 237
Deci, E. L., 328, 329, 330
Deci, R., 330
Deckard, K. D., 27
De Clercq, B., 216
De Fries, J. C., 20
De Fruyt, F., 216
DeLongis, A., 290, 291
Del Veccio, W. F., 242
Dembo, T., 273, 335
Dement, W. C., 306, 307
Demosthenes, 67, 68
DeNeve, K. M., 363
DePaulo, B. M., 373
De Pauw, S. S., 216
De Raad, B., 162
Derbin, V., 250
Desjardins, S., 309
DeSoto, C. B., 169
de St. Aubin, E., 253
Devore, I., 205
Dicks-Mireaux, M. J., 66
Diener, E., 286, 291
Diggory, J. C., 102
Dijksterhuis, A., 302
DiLalla, L. F., 361
Dionne, G., 361
Dixon, R. A., 251
Dobbs, A. R., 368
Dodge, K. A., 367, 372, 373
Dollard, J., 86, 88–91, 92, 98, 190, 221, 263, 365
Domingue, B. W., 22
Dong, Q., 230
Donnellan, M. B., 184, 374
Donnerstein, E., 363
Donovan, G. H., 363
Doob, A. N., 374
Dornbusch, S., 228, 229
Dornbusch, S. M., 230
Dorr, N., 363
Downs, A. C., 206
Downs, D. L., 10
Drake, K., 225
Draper, P., 8
DuCette, J., 322
Duck, S., 351
Dudek, S. Z., 253
Duku, E., 247

Dunkel-Shetter, C., 291
Dunlop, P. D., 163
Dupre, K. M., 347
Durante, K. M., 9
Duval, S., 186
Dweck, C. S., 105, 330, 338, 339
Dymond, R. F., 111

Eagle, M. N., 80
Eagley, A. H., 353
Earley, P. C., 29
Ebbesen, E. B., 269
Eber, H., 147
Eckert, P., 248
Edelstein, W., 225
Edenberg, H. J., 21
Edmonds, G. W., 243
Edwards, A. L., 143, 147
Efran, J. S., 374
Egeland, B., 224
Egloff, B., 245
Eibl-Eibesfeldt, I., 9, 355, 358
Eikeseth, S., 96
Einstein, A., 44
Eisenberg, W., 238
Eisenberger, N. I., 10
Ekman, P., 9, 10, 285
Elder, G., 253
Elder, G. H., 242
Eldervik, S., 96
Elicker, J., 224
Elkind, D., 246
Elliot, R., 369, 374
Ellis, A., 68
Ellis, A. B., 203
Ellis, B. J., 69
Ellsworth, C., 284
Ellsworth, P. C., 10
Elmen, J. D., 228
Emmerich, W., 235
Emmons, R. A., 274
Endler, N. S., 166, 167
Enquist, M., 9
Epstein, L., 169
Epstein, S., 183
Erb, W., 44
Erber, R., 301
Erdelyi, M. H., 303
Erdley, C. A., 339
Eriksen, C. W., 311
Erikson, E., 39, 41, 62, 73–75, 72, 193, 198, 210,
    249, 250, 257, 274
Eriksson, N., 22
Eron, L. D., 150, 373
Escalona, S. K., 77
Esko, T., 22
Evans, J. W., 322
Evans, R. B., 66, 311
Exner, J. E., 150, 152
Eyberg, S. M., 230
Eysenck, H. J., 18, 66, 159–160, 162, 163
Eysenck, S. B. J., 18

Fabes, R. A., 206
Fagot, B. I., 205, 207
Fairbairn, W. R. D., 72
Fales, M. R., 8, 9
Fallon, A. E., 285
Fang, A., 105
Faragher, E. B., 311
Faraone, S. V., 20
Farrell, E. W., 339
Fauvre, M., 238
Fazel, M., 294
Fearon, R. M. P., 227
Feather, N. T., 332

Feeny, B. C., 353
Feisking, C., 223
Feld, S., 332
Feng, J., 203
Fenigstein, A., 187
Ferguson, T. I., 368
Feshbach, N., 237, 238, 358, 375
Feshbach, N. D., 57, 205, 237, 238
Feshbach, S., 57, 238, 315, 365, 366, 371, 373, 374
Festinger, L., 189, 335
Feuerstein, M., 154
Fillenbaum, G. B., 255
Fineman, S., 152
Fischer, T. D., 154, 203
Fisher, S., 150
Fiske, S. T., 327
Flanagan, M., 363
Fleeson, W., 26
Fleming, J., 327
Fleming, S. M., 302
Fliess, W., 50, 63
Foersterling, F., 339
Folkes, V. S., 283, 349
Folkman, S., 290, 291, 292
Fonagy, P., 227
Forgas, J. P., 287
Foroud, T., 21
Foulkes, D., 306
Fraley, R. C., 245
Frame, C. L., 367
Frank, J. D., 335
Frankl, V., 116
Fransella, F., 118, 121
Franz, C. E., 253
Freedman, D. G., 9
Freedman, J. L., 363
French, S., 200
French, S. E., 198
Frenkl-Brunswick, E., 55
Freud, Amalia, 44
Freud, Anna, 72, 75–76, 78
Freud, S., 39, 41, 43, 44–59, 61–62, 66, 67, 68, 70,
    72, 75, 78, 81, 109, 114, 117, 119, 175, 190,
    261, 262, 263, 268, 269, 271, 298, 330, 346,
    353, 364, 386
Freund, A. M., 250, 252
Friesen, W. V., 9, 285
Frieze, I. H., 201
Frijda, N. H., 285
Fromkin, H. L., 374
Fromm, E., 39, 41, 62, 70–72, 67, 109, 354
Fuhrmann, B. S., 196
Fulker, D. W., 20
Funder, D. C., 168, 170
Furstenberg, F. F., 28

Gabrenya, W. K., 29
Galen, 128–129, 158
Galinsky, A. D., 55
Gall, J., 262
Gallagher, D., 281
Gallardo-Pujol, D., 11
Gallegher, K. E., 360
Gallup, G. G., 178–179
Galton, F., 129–130
Gammon, C., 359
Gandhi, 73
Gangestad, S., 8, 9, 185
Gao, J., 102
Garb, H. N., 150
Gardner, R. W., 76
Garduque, L., 224–225
Garmazy, N., 110
Garner, E., 374
Garske, J. P., 113
Gartrell, K. E., 94

Garver-Apgar, C. E., 9
Gatziolis, D., 363
Gauthier, R., 205
Gavanski, I., 284
Gay, P., 45, 50, 51, 54, 63
Gaylord-Ross, R. J., 96
Gazzaniga, M. S., 314
Geen, R. G., 370
Gelfand, D. M., 369
Gershoff, E. T., 95
Gerton, J., 199
Gesink, D., 200
Gewirtz, J. L., 218, 222
Giancola, P. R., 360
Gibbon, F. X., 188
Gilbert, D., 28
Gilbert, D. T., 165, 299
Gildersleeve, K., 9
Gilgan, C., 30, 208, 233, 238
Girard, A., 361
Gjerde, P. F., 243
Glass, D. C., 320
Gleason, J. B., 123
Goh, D. H., 238
Goldberg, L. R., 168, 171, 243
Goldberg, S., 162, 223
Goldsmith, H. H., 17
Goldstein, A. P., 375
Goldstein, I. H., 374
Goldwyn, R., 226
Good, K. S., 56
Goodall, J., 358
Goodenough, D., 31
Goodwin, D. W., 21
Goossens, L., 197
Gordon, T. P., 359
Gorsuch, R. L., 170, 171
Gottesman, I. I., 20, 21
Gottman, J. M., 355
Gough, H. G., 169
Gould, K. L., 249
Gouley, K. K., 372
Gowda, K. K., 293
Grabell, A. S., 373
Graham, J., 293
Graham, S., 337
Grajek, S., 348
Granger, K. L., 206
Grannemann, B. D., 184
Gray, J. A., 160–161
Gray, J. R., 161
Gray, L., 222
Green, C., 56
Greenberg, L. S., 374
Greene, D., 328
Greenspoon, J., 153
Greenwald, A. G., 303
Greif, E. B., 233
Greve, W., 252, 257
Griffin, D. W., 226
Griskevicius, V., 9
Gross, J., 59
Grosskurth, P., 78
Gruen, R., 291
Grusec, J. E., 101, 369
Guilford, J. P., 146–147
Gullota, T. P., 196

Hagan, R., 205
Haggard, P., 302
Haj-Yahia, M. M., 248
Haley, G. A., 139
Hall, W. B., 169, 253
Halverson, C. F., 208
Ham, H., 150

Hamachek, D. E., 247
Hamer, D., 22
Hamilton, J. C., 186
Hamilton-Giachritsis, C., 374
Hammock, T., 326
Hammond, D. C., 311
Hampson, S. E., 243
Hanish, L. D., 206
Hanley, C. P., 197, 198
Hare, B., 234
Harlow, H., 70, 77, 221
Harlow, T., 184
Harpending, H., 8
Harris, M. A., 255
Harris, M. B., 366
Hart, S. A., 27
Harter, S., 179, 180, 181, 183
Hartmann, D. P., 369
Hartmann, H., 72, 76
Hartshorne, H., 169
Harvey, J. H., 209–210
Harvey, R. H., 294
Hasselton, M. G., 9
Hastings, S., 234
Hatfield, E., 349, 350, 351, 355
Hauser, S. T., 195
Havighurst, R. J., 257
Hay, D. F., 235
Hayden, B., 373
Haynes, A. F., 136
Hays, A. F., 354
Hazan, C., 226, 351, 352, 353
Healy, M. D., 69
Heatherton, T. F., 253
Heckhausen, H., 334
Heckhausen, J., 251
Heffer, R. W., 230
Heidegger, M., 115
Heider, F., 164, 189
Heleno, N. M., 284
Heller, K., 153
Hellhammer, D. H., 155
Hellhammer, J., 155
Helmreich, R., 148
Helson, R., 242, 243, 253
Henderson, N. D., 18
Hendrick, C., 347, 351
Hendrick, S. S., 347
Henry, W. H., 256
Hepworth, J. T., 366
Herbert, J., 360
Hermans, H. J. M., 308
Herrnstein, R. J., 21
Hesse, E., 226
Hicks, D. J., 369
Hicks, L. H., 254
Higgins, E. T., 112, 182, 282, 283, 301, 302
Highlen, P. S., 197, 198
Hilgard, E. R., 309, 382
Hilgard, J. R., 310, 311
Hill, C. A., 189
Hill, C. T., 354
Hill, T., 303
Hineline, P. N., 86, 92
Hiroto, D. S., 323
Hoaken, P. N., 360
Hoare, C. H., 175
Hochschild, A., 279
Hoeve, M., 230
Hoffman, M. L., 237
Hofmann, S. G., 105
Hofmann, V., 225
Hofstader, D., 299
Hofstree, W. K., 161
Hogan, J., 163
Hogan, R., 163, 169

Hokanson, J. E., 374
Hollingworth, H. L., 130
Holmes, T. H., 289
Holzman, D. C., 305
Homish, G. G., 373
Hong, K., 80
Horn, E. E., 17
Horney, K., 39, 41, 62, 67, 68–70
Horowitz, M. J., 62
Hottes, T. S., 200
Hotz, A. S., 144
Hough, R. L., 293
House, J. S., 292
Howard, A., 253
Howard, B., 153
Howard, G. S., 209
Howard, J. A., 238
Howe, D., 223
Hrncir, E., 224–225
Huang, K. Y., 372
Huesmann L. R., 372
Hughes, F., 254
Hull, C., 86–87, 90, 92
Hull, J. G., 294, 360
Hunter, E. J., 249
Hunter, J., 226
Huntingford, F. A., 358
Huppertz, C., 20
Hurst, C., 279
Huta, V., 330
Huxley, A., 313
Hyde, J. S., 203, 204, 233

Innes-Ker, A. H., 227
Isabella, R. A., 218
Isen, A. M., 287
Ittelson, W. H., 37
Izard, C. E., 285

Jacklin, C. N., 203, 205, 206, 231
Jackson, D. H., 143
Jackson, D. N., 168
Jackson, J. J., 255
Jacobsen, T., 225
Jacobson, K. C., 361
Jaffe, S., 233
Jahr, E., 96
James, W., 175, 188, 279
Jannson, L., 104
Jensen, G. D., 220
Jerremalm, A., 104
John, D. P., 171
John, O. P., 161, 162
Johnson, B. T., 177
Johnson, D. W., 32
Johnson, H. J., 311
Johnson, R. C., 130
Johnson, W., 255
Jones, D., 287
Jones, E. E., 157, 164
Jones, J. D., 130
Jones, R. D., 325
Jones, R. M., 196
Jordan, J. V., 1991, 30
Jorgensen, K., 150
Josephs, R. A., 360
Josselson, R. L., 196
Joussemet, M., 372
Judge, T. A., 279
Juffer, F., 224
Julkunen, J., 291
Jung, C., 39, 41, 46, 54, 61, 62–67, 109, 159

Kachadourian, L. K., 373
Kagan, J., 17, 332
Kagan, S., 236

Kagitcibasi, E., 230
Kahn, S., 294
Kahneman, D., 266, 299
Kaiser, C. R., 184
Kallman, W. M., 154
Kandel, E., 21
Kanfer, F. H., 101–102, 186
Kaplan, K., 226
Kaplan, R. M., 139
Kardiner, A., 72
Kasendorf, E., 195
Kassam, K. S., 278
Kasser, T., 330
Kastenbaum, R., 250
Katcher, A. H., 363
Katovich, K., 155
Kauhanen, J., 291
Kawabata, Y., 230
Keefe, R. C., 353
Keehn, D., 230
Keiner, J., 148
Kelley, H. H., 157, 164, 347
Kelly, G., 39, 41, 107–108, 117–123, 190, 386
Kemmelmeier, M., 198
Kendler, K. D., 361
Kenrick, D. T., 353
Kernberg, O. F., 227
Kernis, M. H., 184
Kessler, R. C., 290
Kettelaar, T., 161
Khoshbasa, D. M., 294
Kierkegaard, S., 115
Kihlstrom, J. F., 185, 300, 302–303, 309
Kihlstrom, W. A., 311
Kim, H. S., 294
King, L. A., 274
Kirk, I. J., 56
Kirker, W. S., 177
Kirmeyer, S., 36
Kitayama, S., 30, 31, 176
Klein, G., 76
Klein, G. S., 48, 81, 311
Klein, M., 72, 78
Klein, R., 282, 283
Klein, R. G., 372
Kleitman, N., 306
Klimstra, T., 197
Klimstra, T. A., 248
Kline, P., 72
Klinger, E., 273
Klopfer, B., 150
Knafo, A., 248
Knight, G. P., 236
Knuckey, J., 235
Knutson, B., 155
Knutson, J. F., 361
Kobasa, S. C., 116, 287, 294
Koelseh, W. A., 66
Kohlberg, L., 207, 208, 232–234, 238, 246
Kohut, H., 62, 72, 80, 81, 319
Kolligian, J., 116, 339
Konecni, V. J., 374
Kornienko, O., 206
Kraines, R. J., 249
Kramer, M., 308
Kretschmer, 158
Kreuz, L. E., 360
Krizan, Z., 181
Kroger, J., 196
Kruger, J. I., 184
Kruger, R. F., 353
Kruglanski, A., 368
Krull, D. S., 165
Kubany, E. S., 136
Kuhn, C. M., 222
Kuiper, N. A., 177

Kukla, A., 332, 341
Kunda, Z., 181
Kuo, F. E., 363
Kurtines, W., 233

Laan, A. J., 293
LaBarba, R. C., 222
Lachman, M. E., 252
Lack, D. L., 357
La Freniere, P., 205
LaFromboise, T., 199
Lagerspetz, K., 205
Laibson, D. I., 22
Lamb, M. E., 171
Lambe, S., 374
Lambert, A. J., 56
Lamborn, S. D., 230
Lancee, W., 226
Landis, K. R., 292
Landrine, H., 30, 31, 185
Lane, J. D., 373
Langbehn, D., 361
Lange, C., 279
Langer, E. J., 256, 299, 300, 327
Langergraber, K., 235
Langlois, J. H., 206
Larrick, R. P., 363
Larsen, R. J., 161, 286
Laub, J. H., 243
Lazarus, R. S., 171, 282, 284, 290, 291, 292
Le, Y. C. L., 350
Leary, M. R., 10, 184
LeBoeuf, B. J., 357
Lecky, P., 189
LeDoux, J. R., 314
Lee, J. J., 22
Lee, K., 66, 147, 163
Lefcourt, H. M., 322, 323
LeFevre, J., 329
Lefkowitz, M. M., 373
Leggett, E. L., 105, 330, 339
Lehman, D. R., 289
Lehrman, D. S., 334
Leinbach, M. D., 205, 207
Leland, L., 358
Lemery, K. S., 17
Lennenberg, E. H., 217
Leonard, K. E., 373
LePage, A., 370
Lepper, M. R., 328
Lerner, J. S., 278
Lesch, K. P., 6, 18
Levinson, D., 251–252
Levinson, D. J., 249
Levis, D. J., 323
Levitan, D., 347
Levy, A. S., 363
Levy, K. N., 227
Levy, S. M., 257
Lewicki, P., 301, 303
Lewin, K., 26, 263, 265, 272, 273, 330, 335, 386
Lewinsohn, P. M., 188
Lewis, M., 178, 179, 193, 202, 223
Lewis, R. H., 199
Lewis, W. A., 374
Lewkowicz, C., 252
Li, K., 31
Li, N. P., 9
Li, Y., 278
Liben, L. S., 203
Lieberman, M. D., 10
Liebert, R. M., 101
Liebhold, A. M., 363
Lilienfeld, S. O., 150
Lindberg, S. M., 203
Linn, M. C., 203

Linneville, P. W., 338
Linville, P. W., 182
Lisco, C. G., 360
Lissner, K., 272
Little, A. C., 353
Little, B. R., 274
Littman, R. A., 369
Litwin, G. H., 332, 335
Liu, J., 361
Livson, N., 245
Locke, J., 297
Lockhart, R. S., 177
Loeb, A., 102
Loehlin, J. C., 18, 22
Loevinger, J., 269
Loftus, E., 56
Logan, R. L., 253
Lohr, B. A., 57
Lohr, V. I., 363
London, P., 237
Loo, C. M., 363
Lorenz, K., 357, 358
Lovaas, O. I., 96
Lowenstein, G., 278
Lubin, B., 144
Lucke, K. T., 102
Luhtanen, R. K., 183
Lupyan, G., 280
Lushene, R., 170, 171
Luther, M., 73
Luyckx, K., 197
Lykken, D. T., 20, 22
Lynch, J. H., 248

Mabulla, A. Z., 305
Mabulla, I. A., 305
Maccoby, E. E., 203, 205, 231
MacDonald, G., 10
MacKinnon, D. W., 169
Maddi, K. L., 294
Maddi, S. R., 116, 289, 294
Maddux, J. E., 103, 284
Madsen, M. C., 236
Magnusson, D., 166, 167
Magnusson, J., 342
Mahler, M., 77, 79
Mahler, M. S., 272
Mahone, C. H., 332
Mahoney, M., 104, 327
Mahrer, A. R., 270, 271
Maier, N. R. F., 273
Maier, S. F., 323
Main, M., 222, 224, 226
Mair, M., 209
Major, B., 28, 184
Malcolm-Smith, S., 309
Malouff, J. M., 353
Manning, M. M., 103
Manning, S. A., 374
Mao, M. Y., 363
Marcia, J., 193, 194–197, 198, 199, 200
Marcotte, E., 309
Marcus, A., 252
Marcus, R. F., 238
Marcus-Newhall, A., 373
Markstrom-Adams, C., 195, 196
Markus, H., 30, 31, 176, 180, 181, 182, 264
Marsden, G., 153
Marsh, K. L., 183
Marshall, G. D., 281
Marston, A. R., 101–102
Marta, E., 248
Martin, C. L., 206, 208
Martin, L. L., 279, 299, 300
Martin, P. P., 199
Martin, T. A., 66

Martindale, A. E., 158
Martindale, C., 158
Martinussen, M., 196
Masicampo, E., J., 298
Maslach, C., 281
Maslow, A., 39, 41, 107, 109, 110, 112–115, 190, 366
Masson, J. M., 51
Masten, A. S., 110
Matarazzo, J. D., 153
Matarazzo, R. G., 153
Mathis, L. C., 184
Matsumoto, D., 32
Matthews, K. A., 238, 291
Maunder, R., 226
May, M. A., 169
Maydeu-Olivares, A., 11
Mazis, M. B., 327
McAdams, D., 193, 194–197, 209, 210–212, 253
McArthur, L. Z., 7
McBride-Chang, C., 372
McClearn, G. E., 13
McClelland, D. C., 152, 332–333
McClowry, S. G., 230
McCoy, S. K., 184
McCrae, R. R., 66, 161, 162, 242, 253
McCreary, M. L., 293
McDonald, F. J., 233
McGarvey, W., 293
McGlothlin, M. S., 313
McGlothlin, W. H., 313
McGrath, M. J., 308
McGue, M., 20, 21, 22
McGuire, J., 206
McLane, D., 347
McLean, K. C., 212
McRae, R. R., 147
Medland, S. E., 22
Mednick, S. A., 21
Medoff, N., 368
Meeus, W., 197
Melis, A. P., 234
Meltzoff, A. N., 237
Mendelsohn, G. A., 386
Menlove, F. L., 101, 369
Mervielde, I., 216
Messick, S., 143
Metalsky, G. I., 324
Meyer, H. H., 332
Michael, Y. L., 363
Michelangelo, 271
Midlarsky, E., 237
Mikulincer, M., 227
Milarsky, B., 363
Miles, D. R., 361
Milevsky, A., 230
Milgram, S., 371
Miller, D. R., 28
Miller, I. W., 324
Miller, L. W., 222
Miller, M. M., 105
Miller, N., 41, 86, 88–91, 92, 98, 190, 221, 263, 265,
    266–267, 268, 334, 365, 366, 373
Miller, N. E., 58
Miller, P. A., 238
Mineka, S., 5
Mischel, H. N., 234
Mischel, W., 26, 41, 99, 103, 122, 157, 159, 163–164,
    166, 188, 234, 269, 270
Mitani, J. C., 234
Mitchell, C., 102
Mitchell, J. E., 206
Mitchell, K. M., 153
Miu, A. C., 18
Moffitt, T. E., 21, 353, 361, 374
Monte, C. F., 53
Monteith, M., 368

Montemayor, R., 195
Montgomery, C. A., 102
Moons, P., 197
Mor, N., 186
Morash, M. A., 197
Morgan, C., 150
Morgan, S. P., 28
Morokoff, P. J., 57, 58
Morris, J. L., 332
Morris, R., 360
Morsella, E., 304
Moscoe, E., 200
Moskowitz, G. B., 55
Moss, H. A., 332
Mõttus, R., 256
Mounts, N. S., 228
Mowrer, O. H., 282, 322
Moyer, K. E., 360
Muir, C., 247
Mukherjee, B. N., 332
Muller, M. N., 234
Munroe, R. H., 207
Munroe, R. L., 207
Murray, H., 57, 147, 150, 261, 262, 330–331
Murstein, B. I., 152
Myers, L. J., 197, 198
Myers, R. A., 153
Myrtek, M., 291

Nasby, W., 373
Nation, J. R., 94
Neasdale, A. R., 281
Neiderhiser, J. M., 361
Nelson, J. D., 369
Netter, S., 230
Neugarten, B. L., 249, 257
Newcomb, T., 249
Newman, J. P., 373
Nezworski, M. T., 150
Nguyen, A. M. D., 199
Nichols, M. P., 374
Nichols, P. A., 253
Nichols, R. C., 18
Nickel, T. W., 367
Niedenthal, P., 280
Niedenthal, P. M., 183, 185, 227, 278, 284, 287
Niiya, Y., 10
Nisbett, R. E., 34–35, 157, 164, 281, 328, 363
Nitzberg, R. A., 227
Norem, J. K., 325
Norem-Hebeisen, A., 32
Norem-Hebeisen, A. A., 32
Norman, W. H., 324
Norman, W. T., 165
Norton, L. W., 103
Nunn, C. L., 305
Nurius, P., 182
Nurmi, J. E., 229, 230
Nuttin, J. M., 180
Nygren, T. E., 287

O'Brien, L. T., 184
O'Brien, M. U., 350
Ochse, R., 75
Odbert, H. S., 146
Offer, D., 248
Offer, J. B., 248
Oliner, P. M., 237, 238
Oliner, S. P., 237, 238
Oliveira, J. M., 280
Olson, S. L., 373
Olweus, D., 170, 247, 360, 371, 372, 373
O'Neal, C., 372
Ones, D. S., 143
Orbuch, T. L., 209–210
Orlinsky, D., 153

Orne, M. T., 311
Ornstein, R. E., 297
Ortony, A., 286
Orvis, B. R., 164
Osmond, H., 313
Ost, L. G., 104
Ostwald, P., 249
Otsuka, K., 102
Oyserman, D., 198
Ozer, D. J., 243

Paine, C., 144
Paivio, A., 315
Park, L. E., 188
Parke, R. D., 101, 205, 371, 372
Parrott, D. J., 360
Passini, F. T., 165
Passman, R., 80
Patterson, G. R., 96, 369
Patterson, S. J., 196
Paunonen, S. V., 168
Pavlov, I., 265
Peake, P. K., 270
Pearlin, L. I., 28
Pederson, D. R., 223
Pederson, P., 31
Pelham, B. W., 165
Pelto, P., 34
Peltorer, T., 205
Peng, Y., 252
Penk, W. E., 144
Penman, D., 351
Pennebaker, J. W., 181, 291, 293
Peplau, L. A., 354
Pereg, D., 227
Perret, D. I., 353
Perry, R. P., 342
Pérusse, D., 361
Pervin, L. A., 273
Peskin, H., 245
Petersen, A. C., 246, 247, 355
Peterson, C., 325, 337
Peterson, R. S., 357
Petrill, S. A., 27
Pettersson, E., 17
Pfeifer, J. H., 237
Phares, E. J., 322
Philipp, B. L., 222
Phillips, A. G., 187
Phinney, J. S., 198–199
Piccione, C., 309
Pihl, R. O., 360
Pileri, G., 235
Piliavin, I. M., 342
Piliavin, J. A., 342
Pillemer, J. T., 350
Pitkänen-Pulkkinnen, L., 375
Plato, 346
Pleuss, M., 216
Plomin, R., 17, 20, 22, 361
Plug, C., 75
Plutchik, R., 278, 285, 286
Poke, E. J., 238
Polderman, T. J., 2015
Pommy, J. M., 313
Powell, A. A., 234
Powers, W. T., 299
Pressley, M., 169
Prestemon, J. P., 363
Preston, J., 302
Price, J., 363
Price, J. M., 373
Price, R. H., 26
Prince, M., 261
Proshansky, H. M., 37
Przybylski, A., 329

Puccetti, M. C., 289

Querido, J. G., 230
Quigley, B. M., 373
Quinn, P. C., 203
Quinsey, V. L., 247
Quintana, S. M., 198

Rabkin, J. G., 289
Radke-Yarrow, M., 235, 237, 238
Radler, D. H., 248
Rahe, R. H., 288, 289
Raifman, J., 200
Raine, A., 361
Ramirez, M., 30, 31
Ranier, K. L., 293
Rapaport, D., 46, 55, 72, 76, 79
Rassart, J., 197
Rau, L., 231
Raush, H. L., 355
Rauthman, J. F., 26
Ravitz, P., 226
Ray, R. D., 59
Ray, R. S., 96
Raynor, J. O., 332
Read, S. J., 189
Reddy, V., 237
Reese, L., 102
Reid, J. B., 96, 372
Reid, J. D., 251
Reidy, D. E., 57
Reisenzein, R., 281
Reiss, A. D., 143
Reiss, D., 22
Remafadi, G., 200
Remmers, H. H., 248
Resnick, M. D., 200
Resureccion, N., 294
Revonsuo, A., 309
Reykowski, J., 359
Reynolds, A. L., 197, 198
Rhee, S. H., 361
Rhodes, A. E., 200
Rholes, W., 227
Ribble, M., 77
Ric, F., 278
Rice, L. N., 374
Richard, D. C. S., 136
Richter, C. P., 323
Rick, S., 278
Ricoeur, P., 209
Rietveld, C. A., 22
Rigby, C. S., 329
Riggins-Caspers, K. M., 361
Ritter, J. O., 250, 252
Rivlin, L. G., 37
Robbins, C. J., 325
Roberti, J. W., 26
Roberts, B. W., 242, 245, 248
Robertson, R. J., 8
Robichaux-Keene, N., 18
Robin, L., 227
Robins, R. W., 374
Rochat, P., 237
Rodeheaver, D., 254
Rodgers, D. A., 13
Rodin, J., 256, 342
Roelofsen, I., 334
Rogers, A., 30
Rogers, C., 39, 41, 80, 107, 109–112, 114, 175, 190, 244, 319, 386
Rogers, T. B., 177
Rohner, R. P., 230
Roisman, G. I., 226, 227
Roizen, J., 359
Rooke, S. E., 353

Roosevelt, T., 68
Rorschach, H., 149–150
Rose, R. J., 18
Rose, R. M., 360
Rosenbaum, R., 349
Rosenberg, M., 28, 148, 181
Rosenfelt, A., 372
Rosenthal, D. A., 198
Rosnati, R., 248
Ross, D., 100, 368
Ross, L., 165
Ross, S, A., 100, 368
Rottenburg, J., 293
Rotter, J., 41, 98–99, 102, 190
Rotter, J. B., 320, 321–322
Rotton, J., 363
Rousseau, J., 72
Rowe, D. C., 21
Rozin, P., 285
Rubin, A., 354
Rubin, Z., 138, 347
Ruble, D. N., 206, 208, 247
Rule, B. G., 281 368
Rushto, J. P., 18
Rushton, J. P., 169, 237
Russell, D., 325
Ryan, R. M., 248, 329, 330
Ryff, D. C., 251
Rylee, K. E., 144

Sabatini, P., 250
Saccuzzo, D. P., 153
Saccuzzo, D. S., 139
Safran, J. D., 374
Sagi, A., 237
Samanez-Larkin, G. R., 155
Sameroff, A. J., 216
Sampson, R. J., 243
Samson, D. R., 305
Santos, C. E., 206
Sarason, I. G., 186
Sartre, J. P., 115
Saslow, G., 153
Sassin, J. F., 305
Sawyer, A. T., 105
Scarr, S., 15, 27
Schaal, B., 360
Schachter, S., 69, 280, 281
Schafer, R., 72, 81–82
Scheier, M., 252, 299
Scheier, M. F., 186
Scherer, Y. K., 102
Schinka, J. A., 18
Schlechter, M., 230
Schlotz, W., 155
Schmidt, G., 342
Schneider, D. J., 122
Schriebman, L., 96
Schuckit, M. A., 21
Schuengel, C., 224
Schuengel, C., 227
Schuerger, J. M., 144
Schukle, S. C., 245
Schultz, D., 113
Schulz, P., 155
Schumer, F., 150
Schutte, N. S., 353
Schwartz, B., 264
Schwartz, D., 372
Schwartz, G., 58
Schwartz, S. J., 198
Schwarz, N., 35
Scott, J. P., 359
Sears, P. S., 335
Sears, R. R., 231
Seeman, M., 322

Seidman, E., 198
Seligman, M. E. P., 32, 105, 323, 324, 325
Sellers, R. M., 199
Setterlund, M. B., 183, 287
Shackelford, T. K., 353
Shafer, A. B., 163
Shakespeare, W., 250
Shakow, D., 46
Shanberg, S. M., 222
Shapira, A., 236
Shaver, P., 130, 226, 227, 351, 352, 353
Shedler, J., 59
Sheehy, G., 252
Sheldon, W., 158, 159
Sheldon, W. H., 158
Sherman, D. K., 294
Sherman, L. J., 218
Sherrin, S., 280
Shields, J., 18
Shimmin, H. S., 207
Shiner, R. L., 245
Shoda, Y., 270
Showers, C., 183
Shrout, P., 372
Shulman, S., 224, 245
Shure, M. B., 375
Shuttleworth, F. H., 169
Siegman, A. W., 291
Sigel, I. E., 235
Siladi, M., 180
Silva, P. A., 353
Silver, R. C., 290, 300
Silverberg, L., 248
Silvia, P. J., 187
Simmons, R. G., 247
Simonds, P. F., 220
Simonton, D. K., 334
Simpson, J. A., 8, 9, 227, 349, 351
Singer, J. A., 209
Singer, J. E., 280, 281, 320
Singer, J. L., 104, 116, 308, 315
Sinha, R., 332
Sirota, L., 22
Skinner, B. F., 41, 86, 87, 89, 91–98, 99, 100, 101,
    117, 190, 222, 319–320
Slaby, R. G., 371
Slade, A., 225
Slavin, L. A., 293
Smart, L., 184, 373
Šmigelskas, K., 291
Smith, B. L., 95
Smith, C. A., 282, 284, 292
Smith, D. L., 209
Smith, P. B., 29, 223
Smith, P. K., 205
Smith, R. S., 110
Smith, R. T., 15
Smith, T., 96
Smith, T. W., 294
Smollar, J., 181
Smyth, J. M., 293
Snidman, N., 17
Snow, C., 218
Snow, D. L., 230
Snyder, M., 26, 185, 188, 351
Sobreira, G. 280
Sochting, I., 196
Soenens, B., 197
Solano, C., 169
Soldz, S., 254
Solms, M., 309
Solomon, J., 222
Sommer, K. L., 58
Soussignan, R., 360
Spanos, N. P., 311
Specht, J., 245

Speight, S. L., 197, 198
Spence, D., 82
Spera, C., 229
Sperry, R. W., 314
Spiegel, D., 311
Spielberger, C. D., 170, 171, 303
Spielberger, C. S., 148
Spitz, R., 70, 77
Spivack, G., 375
Sporer, S. L., 373–374
Spotts, E. L., 361
Sprecher, S., 350
Sroufe, L. A., 222, 224, 225, 227, 245
Stack, S., 21
Stangor, C., 208
Stanley-Hall, G., 66
Stapp, J., 148
Starzyk, K. B., 247
Stattin, H., 230
Staub, E., 238
Stayton, D. J., 222
Steck, L., 347, 350
Steele, C. M., 360
Steinberg, L., 228, 230, 248
Stejskal, W. J., 150
Stephenson, W., 111
Stepper, S., 279
Sternberg, R. J., 339, 347, 348
Stevens, S. S., 158
Stevenson, H. C., 30
Stewart, A., 243, 253
Sthankiya, B., 226
Stickgold, R., 308
Stiles, W., 373
Stipek, D., 31
Stoller, R. J., 345
Stoltenberg, C. D., 103
Stone, A. A., 155
Storbeck, J., 279
Storms, M. D., 165
Story, M., 200
Strack, F., 279, 280
Strauman, T., 282, 283
Strayer, F. F., 205
Streuning, E. L., 289
Struhsaker, T., 358
Stuart, R. B., 102
Stücke, T. S., 373–374
Stupica, B., 218, 223
Sullivan, H. S., 67
Sullivan, W. C., 363
Suls, J., 181
Sun, C. 184
Suomi, S. J., 205, 220
Susman, E. J., 247, 360
Swagerman, J., 285
Swann, W. B., 181, 189
Swanson, G. E., 28
Symons, C. S., 177

Taffel, C., 303
Tagiuri, R., 57, 122
Tagney, J. P., 284
Tait, R., 300
Tambor, E. S., 10
Tamis-LeMonda, C. S., 230
Tangney, J. P., 284
Tatsuoka, M. M., 147
Taylor, B., 368
Taylor, D. A., 374
Taylor, J. A., 144
Taylor, M. D., 256
Taylor, S., 359
Taylor, S. E., 176, 188, 189, 292, 294, 327
Teasdale, J. D., 105, 324
Tedeschi, J. T., 356

Teleki, G., 234
Telleen, S., 238
Temrin, H., 9
Teppers, E., 197
Terdal, S. K., 10
Tesser, A., 20, 299, 300
Test, M. A., 101
Theophrastus, 128, 129
Thoits, P. A., 292
Thomas, A., 216, 245, 360
Thompson, L. A., 27
Thompson, R. A., 286
Thompson, W. R., 13
Thorne, A., 66
Thornhill, R., 9
Thorsteinsson, E. B., 353
Tice, D. M., 10
Tieger, T., 205
Tillich, P., 115
Timbers, D., 293
Timmerman, T. A., 363
Tinbergen, N., 357
Tobin, S. S., 257
Tolman, C. W., 220
Tomkins, S. S., 278
Tongas, P. N., 105
Towers, H., 361
Townsend, S. T., 291
Tremblay, R. E., 360
Treuren, R. R., 294
Triandis, H. C., 30, 31, 32
Troiden, R. R., 200
Troll, L. E., 249
Trope, Y., 335
Truax, C. B., 153
Trucker-Drob, E. M., 20
Trzesniewski, K. H., 184, 374
Tseng, W. L., 230
Turkheimer, E., 17, 19, 22
Turner, E. A., 230
Turner, T. J., 286
Tuthill, R., 102
Tversky, A., 266
Twenge, J. M., 28
Tyler, L. E., 153

U.S. Youth Soccer, 340
Umaña-Taylor, A. J., 198
Umberson, D., 292

Vaillancourt, T., 247
Vaillant, G., 253, 254, 325
Valdesolo, P., 278
Valins, S., 281
Vallacher, R. R., 122, 123
Valli, K., 309
van Assen, M. A., 293
Van Hook, E., 182
van IJzendoorn, M. H., 224, 226, 227, 230
Van Lawick-Goodall, J., 357
Van Leeuwen, K., 216
VanTreuren, R. R., 360
Vernelli, S., 294
Verschueren, M., 197
Vertes, R. P., 308
Viechtbauer, W., 242
Viek, P., 322

Vignoles, V. L., 176
Vingerhoets, A. J., 293
Vinkhuyzen, A. A., 22
Viswesvaran, C., 143
Vitaro, F., 361
Vohs, K. D., 184, 298
Volosinov, V. N., 48
von Eye, A., 218
von Helmholtz, H., 47
Vonk, I. J., 105

Wade, T. D., 361
Wagenmakers, E. J., 280
Waldman, I. D., 361
Walker, J., 374
Walker, L. J., 233
Walker, M. P., 308
Walker, W. B., 332
Wall, S., 130
Wallis, R. R., 144
Walster, E., 349
Walster, E. H., 349, 350
Walster, G. W., 349, 355
Walters, R. H., 99, 369
Walton, K. E., 242
Warner, T. D., 230
Waterman, A. S., 32, 196
Waters, E., 130, 222
Watson, D., 353
Watson, G. A., 228
Watson, J. B., 262
Watson, J. C., 109
Watt, L., 222
Weary, G., 183, 188
Weatherhead, P. J., 8
Webb, W. B., 305, 308
Weber, A. L., 209–210
Weber, M., 332
Wegner, D. M., 55, 122, 123, 298, 299, 300, 301, 302
Weinberger, D. A., 58
Weinberger, J. L., 243
Weiner, B., 31, 55, 283, 336, 341, 342, 368, 387
Weisberg, P., 80
Weisman, A. D., 249
Weisz, J. R., 29
Weitzenhoffer, A. M., 309
Welsh, G. S., 144
Wenke, D., 302
Werner, E. E., 110
West, S. G., 366
Westen, D., 79
Wethington, E., 251, 252, 290
Whalen, C., 96
Wherry, M. B., 183
White, G. L., 222, 355
White, R. M., 304
White, T. L., 161
Whiting, B. B., 205, 236
Whiting, J. W. M., 236
Whitman, R., 308
Whorwell, P. G., 311
Wicker, A. W., 36
Wicklund, R. A., 186
Widom, C. S., 372
Wiens, A. H., 153
Wiens, A. N., 153
Willerman, L., 17

Williams, A. F., 289
Williams, C. C., 203
Williams, K. D., 10
Williams, L. M., 56
Williamsen, J. A., 311
Willis, S. L., 251
Wills, T. A., 292
Wilson, D. W., 363
Wilson, E. O., 7, 234, 235
Wilson, G., 18, 66
Wilson, J. Q., 21
Wilson, M. I., 9
Wilson, T. D., 338
Wine, J. D., 186
Winget, C., 308
Winkel, G. H., 37
Winnicott, D., 80
Winquist, J., 186
Withey, M. J., 26
Witkin, H. A., 31
Wolf, E. F., 279
Wolfe, C. T., 183, 188
Wolk, S., 322
Wollmer, M. A., 280
Wood, A., 280
Wood, D., 248
Wood, J. M., 150
Wood, L., 374
Wood, R., 103
Wood, W., 353
Woods, V., 234
Woodworth, R. S., 143
Worchel, S., 367
Wortman, C. B., 289, 290
Wrangham, R., 234
Wright, L. W., 57
Wright, T. L., 103
Wu, C. C., 155
Wu, Y. W., 102
Wurf, E., 180, 181

Xua, Y., 230

Yamaguchi, S., 10
Youness, J., 181

Zadra, A., 309
Zahn-Waxler, C., 235, 237, 238
Zalesky, Z., 26
Zarrella, K. L., 144
Zeichner, A., 57
Zeiss, A., 269
Zelenski, J. M., 286
Žemaitienė, N., 291
Zhou, H., 230
Zillman, D., 281, 363, 368
Zillman, P., 375
Zimbardo, P. G., 281, 309
Zimmerman, W. S., 146
Zirkel, S., 274
Zubek, J. P., 13
Zubin, J., 150
Zuckerman, M., 168

Subject Index

AAI (Adult Attachment Interview), 226–227
Absolute stability, 242–243
Account, 210
ACE model, heritability, 16–17
Achievement motivation, 330–339
    Atkinson's theory of, 334–335
    and attributions of responsibility, 340–342
    and competence, 339–340
    and economic development, 332–333
Achievement needs
    defined, 330–331
    development of, 334
    measurement of, 331
    as personality structure, 331–332
Achievement performance, 337
Achievement strivings
    attribution theory and, 336–339
    explanatory style and, 337
Acquiescence, 143
Acquired drives, 88, 89–90
Actor-observer differences, 165
Actualized person, 114
Adolescence, 245–249
    and autonomy and conformity, 247–248
    biological changes in, 246–247
    continuity between adolescents and parents in, 248–249
    and emerging adulthood, 245–249
    individual variations in, 247
    trait level changes, 248
Adult Attachment Interview (AAI), 226–227
Adult development, 249–254
    childhood attachment and, 226–227
    continuity and change in, 252–254
    midlife crisis in, 251–252
    stages of, 250–251
Affect, 277
Agape, 346
Age, and outstanding achievements, 334. *See also* Old age
Agent, self as, 178
Aggregation techniques, 168–169
Aggression, 281, 356–361
    and aggressive cues, 370
    alcohol, drugs, and, 359–360
    altruism and, 18–19
    biological aspects of, 357–359
    catharsis and regulation of, 374–375
    child abuse and, 372
    child-rearing practices and, 371–372
    climate and, 35–36
    cultural influences on, 361–362
    defined, 356–357
    ethological research on, 357–358
    and frustration, 273, 365–368
    genetics and, 360–361
    and hostile attribution bias, 373
    inhibitors, 358
    instinct of, 48, 384
    instrumental, 357
    intrinsic, 359
    learning theory models of, 365–371
    modeling of, 100–101, 368–369

    and narcissism, 373–374
    and noise, 362–363
    as personality trait, 372–374
    and physical environment, 362–363
    physiological influences on, 359–360
    psychoanalytic theory of, 39, 364–365
    and reinforcement, 369–370
    releasers, 357, 364
    sex hormones and, 360
    social influence and, 370–371
    temperature and, 35–36
Aggressive drive, 356–357, 358–359
Agreeableness, 161–163
Alcohol
    and aggression, 359–360
    as drug, 312
    preference, 13, 21
Alcoholism
    biological basis, 13, 21
    and culture, 32
Alienation, 71
Alleocentric, 32
Altered states of consciousness, 297, 304–313, 315
    dreams, 306–309
    drugs, 312–313
    fantasy, 315
    hypnosis, 309–311
    sleep, 304–305
Altruism, 234–235, 237
    and aggression, 18–19
    altruistic personality, 238
Ambivalent behavior, 266–267
Ambivalent/resistant, 224
Amnesia, 303, 309, 311
Anal stage, 49–50
Analysis of variance, 167
Analytic psychology, 62–66
Androgyny, 208
Anger, 284, 285
    and achievement performance, 337
    and aggression, 358–359, 375
Anhedonia, 145
Anima, 64
Animus, 64
Anxiety, 69–70, 115–116, 121–122
    and aggression, 373
    existential, 115
    hierarchy, 104
    and psychoanalytic theory, 53–54
    state, 170–171
    trait, 170–171
Anxious/resistant attachment, 222
Appraisal
    approach to emotions, 284–285
    and problem-focused coping, 292
Approach-approach conflict, 265–266, 268
Approach-avoidance conflict, 266, 266–267
ARAS (ascending reticular activating), 160
Arbitrariness, 367
Archetypes, 64–65
Army Alpha, 130

Arousal theories of emotions, 280–281. *See also* Sexual arousal
Ascending reticular activating system (ARAS/RAS), 160
Associationist (stimulus-response) learning theory, 86–91
    habits and drives, 87–88
    personality development, 88–91
Association of Humanistic Psychology, 108
Attachment, 72, 77–78, 80, 218–227
    adult outcomes, 227
    in adults, measurement of, 226–227
    ambivalent/resistant, 224, 225
    anxious/resistant, 222
    avoidant, 222, 223–224, 225
    and caregiving, 223–224
    characteristics of, 219–222
    childhood outcomes, 224–225
    cultural variations in, 225–226
    disorganized/disoriented, 222, 224
    feeding and, 221
    insecure, 227
    secure, 222, 223, 224, 226–227
    and Strange Situation, 222
    styles, intimacy and, 351–353
    universality of, 220–222
Attachment style, 222
Attribution
    causal, 105
    and depression, 324
Attributional style, 325
Attributional theory, 164–166, 283–284, 336–339
Attributional training, 338
Attributions of responsibility, 340–342
    evaluation, 341–342
    helping behavior, 342
Authenticity, 115
Authoritarianism, 71
Authoritative parenting, 229–231
Autism, 95
Automatic, 299
Automaticity, 300–301
Autonomous motivation, 329
Autonomous style, 226
Autonomy, 247–248
    primary, 76
    secondary, 76
Aversive imagery, 105
Avoidance-avoidance conflict, 265–266
Avoidance learning, 93
Avoidant attachment, 222, 223–224
Awareness, learning without, 303

B values, 114
Balancing selection, 12
BAS (behavioral activation system), 160–161
Behavior
    decreasing, 94–95
    genetic aspects of, 13–23
    increasing, 93–94
Behavioral activation system (BAS), 160–161
Behavioral assessment, 152–155
Behavioral dynamics, 39, 40
Behavioral inhibition system (BIS), 160–161
Behavioral observations. *See* Behavioral assessment
Behavioral techniques. *See* Behavioral assessment
Behaviorism, 108, 111, 262–263
    radical, 86, 92
Behavior modification, 96
    cognitive, 103–105
Behavior settings, 36–37
Belonging, need for, 10, 12
Big Five model of personality, 147, 157, 161–163
Birth order, and personality development, 69
Birth trauma, 54
BIS (behavioral inhibition system), 160–161
Bodily functions, hypnosis and control of, 310–311
Body type, 158–159

Bonding, 219
Borderline Personality Disorder, 227
Bound energy, 47
Broad band personality traits, 162

California Psychological Inventory (CPI), 18
Castration anxiety, 50
Catharsis, 374
Cathexis, 47
Causal attributions, 105, 283–284, 335
    consequences of, 336–337
Cerebral arteriosclerosis, 254
Challenge, 116
Child abuse, 372
Child-rearing, 27
    and culture, 29
    and discipline patterns, 29
    patterns, 228–231
    practices, aggression and, 371–372
Choice, 115
Chronically accessible schemas, 302
Classical conditioning, 91
Client-centered therapy, 111–112
Climate
    and aggression, 35–36
    and personality, 33–35
Cognitive appraisal, 171
Cognitive approaches/theories
    emotions, 282–285
    moral development, 232–233
    personality, 40, 41
Cognitive behavior modification, 104–105
    imagery, 104, 105
    other cognitive changes, 105
Cognitive prototype, 103
Cognitive styles, 76–77
Coherence, 242–243
Collective unconscious, 64–65
Collectivistic cultures, 31
College Board, 136
Commitment, 116
Companionate love, 350–351
Competence, 339–340
    integrating perceived control with achievement motivation and, 340
    mindset, 339–340
Complexes, 65
Conceptual orientation, 28
Concordance, 20–21
Concrete reciprocal hedonism, 232
Concurrent validity, 137
Conditional positive regard, 110
Conditions of worth, 110
Conflict, 264–268
    approach-approach, 265–266, 268
    approach-avoidance, 265–266
    avoidance-avoidance, 265–266
    discriminative, 265
    and displacement, 268
    Lewin's classification system, 265–266
    Miller's model, 266–268
    spatial, 265
    stable, 265
    temporal, 265
    unstable, 265
Conformity, 71, 247–248, 370–371
Conscientiousness, 161–163
Consciousness, 297–298. *See also* Altered states of consciousness; Awareness
    fantasy and, 315–316
    relationship of, to nonconscious information processing, 298–304
    relationship of self to, 302–303
    split-brain experiments and, 313–315
Consequence, of actions, 266–268
Constitutional source traits, 159
Constructed environments, 36
Constructive alternativism, 118–119

Construct validity, 138–139
Continuous distribution, 159
Content validity, 136
Continuity, 193, 241–245
   and change, 241–245, 252–254
   vs. stages, 217–218
Control, 116
   efforts to preserve sense of personal, 326–329
   external, 99, 320–321
   illusion of, 327
   internal, 99, 320–321
   lawfulness and, 92–93
   locus of, 99, 320–322
   perceived, 320–330
Controllability, 336
Controlled motivation, 329
Control theories, 299
Conventional stage, 232
Convergent validity, 139
Cooperation, 235–236
   cross-cultural, 236
Coping, 69, 72, 75–76
   appraisal and problem-focused, 292
   with stress, 291
Cordelia complex, 55
Correlation coefficient, 14
Creative self, 68
Criminality
   heritability of, 21
   and the moon, 36
   and temperature, 35–36
Criterion validity, 136–138
Critical periods, 217–218
Cross-lagged design, 244
Cross-sectional research design, 244
Crowding, 362–363
Crying, 293
Cues, 88–89
   aggressive, 357, 370
   situation and discriminative, 103
Culture
   and aggression, 29, 361–362
   and alcoholism, 21
   and attachment, 225–226
   and cooperation, 236
   greater recognition of influence, 73
   individualistic vs. collectivistic, 31
   influence on personality, 28–33
   and self, 176
   and stress, 293–294
Current concerns, 208–209
Cybernetic system, 299

D values, 114
Death instinct, 47, 48, 363
Death wish, 47, 59
Decision/Commitment component, 347
Defense mechanisms, 40, 54–59
   individual differences in, 58–59
   other types of, 57–58
   perceptual defense, 57
   repression and unconscious, 54–56
   against stress, 59
Defensive pessimism, 325–326
Delay of gratification. *See* Impulse control and delay of gratification
Delta waves, 306
Demand characteristics, 118
Demography, old age, 257
Denial, 57, 59
Density, 37
Deoxyribonucleic acid (DNA), 4–5
Depression, 29, 32, 35
   attachment style and, 227
   and learned helplessness, 324
Destructiveness, 71

Determinism, 3, 48–49, 319
Developmental influences, 371–372
Differential effect, 166
Directional selection, 12
Discipline patterns, parental, 228–231
Discordance, 20
Discriminant validity, 139
Discriminative conflict, 265
Discriminative cues, 103
Discriminative stimuli, 94
Disengagement, 256–257
Disgust, 285
Dismissing style, 226, 227
Disorganized/disoriented attachment, 222, 224
Displacement, 57–58, 271–272
   conflict and, 268
Dissociation, 261
Dizygotic (DZ) twins, studies of, 13–19
DNA (deoxyribonucleic acid), 4–5, 22
Dreams, 46, 48–49, 306–309
   deprivation of, 306, 307
   function of, 307–308
   latent content of, 48–49
   manifest content of, 49
   study of, 306
Drive-instigated hostility, 356
Drive reduction, 87, 90–91, 97
Drives, 87–88
   acquired or secondary, 88, 89–90
   habits and, 87–88
   primary, 88
Drive therapy, disenchantment with, 72
Drugs, 312–313
   and aggression, 359–360

Ecological perspective on personality, 31–32
Economic development, achievement motivation
     and, 332–333
Ectomorphic physiques, 158
Educational Testing Service, 136–137
Edwards Personal Preference Schedule (EPPS), 147–148
EEG (electroencephalography), 155
Ego, 51, 52–53, 54, 73–75
   control, 242, 269
   functions, conflict-free, 76
   psychology, psychoanalytic, 72, 75–77, 79
Ego integrity, 257
Ego-resiliency, 242
Electra complex, 50
Electroencephalography (EEG), 155
Emerging adulthood, 245–249
Emotion(s), 277–279, 349
   appraisal approach to, 284–285
   areas of study of, 279
   arousal theories of, 280–281
   attributional approach to, 283–284
   basic, 285–286
   body as source of, 279–280
   cognitive theories of, 282–285
   definition of, 278–279
   facial expressions and, 9–10, 279–280
   individual differences in emotional reactivity, 286
   and personal construct theory, 121–122
   recent developments in theories of, 285–286
   structure of, 285–286
   two-factor model, 280–281
Emotional style, 286
Empathy, 111, 237–238, 375
Empirical approaches, objective personality tests, 144–145
Endomorphic body builds, 158
Energy
   disenchantment with psychic, 73
   Freud's concept of psychological energy, 47–48
Entity theorists, 339
Entropy, 47

Environment(s)
in ACE model, 16–17
constructed, 36
effect, nonshared, 21–22
natural, 33–36
nonshared environment effect, 16–17, 21–22
physical, and aggression, 362–363
summary of effects of, 37
Environment mold traits, 159
Eros, 48, 346
Error variability, 132
Error variance, 132
Escape learning, 93
Ethnic identity, 197–199
Ethological research, on aggression, 357–359
Evaluation, 341–342
Evolution, Darwinian theory, 3, 7, 44, 46, 87, 108, 129, 262, 358
Evolutionary psychology, 7–9
Exclusion, belonging and, 10, 12
Existential humanism, 115–116
Expectancy, 98, 99, 367
and delay of gratification, 270–271
Expectancy-value theory, 98–99
Expectations, outcome, 102
Expected-reward condition, 328
Experience corollary, 119–120
Explanatory style, and achievement strivings, 337
External control, 99, 320–321
Extinction, 94
Extinction burst, 94
Extraversion, 18, 160–163
Extrinsic motivation, 327–329
Extroversion, 65–66, 159, 160

Face validity, tests based on, 143–144
Facets, 162
Facial expressions, 6, 11
and emotions, 9–10, 279–280
Facial feedback model, 279–280
Factor analysis, 146–147
Cattell and, 146–147, 159
Guilford's work, 146
16 P-F, 144, 147
Family
greater recognition of influence of, 73
socialization and, 228–231
Fantasy, 269, 271–272, 374
and consciousness, 315–316
Fear, 10, 89
Feeding, and attachment, 221
Feeling, thinking vs., 66
Femininity, 206
Fixation, 51
and frustration, 273
Five Factor Model (FFM), 147, 161
Flow, of experience, 328
fMRI (functional magnetic resonance imaging, 10, 155
Focus of convenience, 119
Foreclosure, 195
Free association, 40, 45, 48, 51
Freedom, 71, 115, 319–320
Freedom of movement, 99
Free energy, 47–48
Free will, 320
Freudian slips, 49
Frustration, 269–270, 273
and aggression, 263, 273, 365–368
and enhanced goal striving, 273
and fixation, 273
and regression, 273
Frustration-aggression
hypothesis, 263, 365–368
Functional magnetic resonance imaging (fMRI), 10, 155
Fundamental attributional error, 165

Gender, 201
and moral development, 233
Gender identity, 201–209
gender differences, 201–207
gender typing, 201–209
identity status theory, 197
Gender schema theory, 208
Generalization, mediated, 89–90
General source traits, 159
Generosity and caring, 237
Genes, 4–5, 13–23
Genetics
and aggression, 360–361
heritability and, 12–23. See also Heritability
human genome, 4–5
molecular, 22
nonshared environment effect and, 16–17, 21–22
role of, 4–5, 22–23
social exclusion and, 12
Genital stage, 49–50
Genome, 4–5
Genome Wide Association Studies (GWAS), 22
Genotype vs. phenotype, 16
Gerontology, 255
Gestalt psychology, 40, 263
Goals, 98, 99, 273–274
Goal striving, frustration and enhanced, 273
Gonadotropic hormones, 246
Google, 251
Grade-point average (GPA), 136–137
Guilford-Zimmerman Temperament Survey, 146
Guilt, 52, 53, 54, 57, 58–59, 115, 121, 284, 285
GWAS (Genome Wide Association Studies), 22

Habits, and drives, 87–88
Habitual responses, 160
Hardiness, 116, 293
individual differences in stress reactions and, 294
Hassles, 290
Hate, 354–356. See also Aggression
Hedonism, 46–47, 52
concrete reciprocal, 232
Helping behavior, 342
Hemispheres of brain, 313–315
Heritability
ACE model, 16–17
criticisms of, 22–23
estimates, sample and, 19–20
experimental study of, 12–13
mental illness and social problems, 20–21
molecular genetics, 22
nonshared environment effect, 21–22
study of, through human research, 13–20
HEXACO-PI, 147
Holistic approach, 108
Homeostasis, 46–47
Homicide, 361–362
Hormonal changes, and behavior, 246–247
Hostile attribution bias, 373
Human genome, 4–5
Human research, heritability, 13–20
Humanism, 108–109
existential, 115–116
organismic, 112–114
Humanistic theory, 108–109
Humans
similarity of all, 4–12
uniqueness of, 12–23
Humor, 48–49
Hypnosis, 44–45, 309–311
defined, 309–311
reducing anxiety through, 54
and unconscious motives, 54

Id, 51, 52, 53, 54, 75–76, 77, 81
Ideal self, 111–112, 182
Ideocentric, 32
Identity, 193
    achievement, 194, 195–196
    diffusion, 194, 195–196
    ethnic, 197–199
    foreclosure, 194, 195–196
    formation, stages of, 194–197
    gender, 201–209
    moratorium, 194, 195–196
    narrative and, 209–212
    statuses, 194, 195–196, 197
Idiographic data, 98
Illusion of control, 327
Imageos, 212
Imagery, 104, 105, 315
    aversive, 105
Imaginary images, 269–270
Imitation, 99, 368–369
Implicit psychology, 107–108, 122–123
Impulse control and delay of gratification, 268–270
    expectancy, 270–271
    imaginary images, 269–270
    learning theory approaches, 270
Incest taboo, 46, 50
Incremental theorists, 339
Individual corollary, 119
Individual differences, 129–130, 132, 133, 134, 385
    in defensive preferences, 58–59
    in emotional reactivity, 286
    in learned helplessness, 325
    in stress reactions and hardiness, 294
Individualism, and mental health, 32–33
Individualistic cultures, 31
Individual psychology, Adler's, 67–70
Inequity, 367
Infant features, and maternal care, 7
Inferiority, 67–38
Inhibition, 47, 53–54
Innate behavior, 5–7
Insecure attachment, 225, 227
Instinct(s)
    of aggression, 48, 384
    behavior patterns, 5–7
    defined, 5
    Freud on, 48
    as "urges," 5
Institutionalization, 77
Institutions, total, 37
Instrumental aggression, 357
Instrumental behaviors, 356
Integrated personality theory, 386–387
Integration, neural structures, 53
Intellectualization, 57
Intelligence, heritability and, 19–20
Intensity, 170
Intentionality, 367
Interactional perspective on personality, 26
Interactionism, 166–167, 377–380
Internal consistency, of tests, 134
Internal control, 99, 320–321
Internal-External Control Scale (I-E Scale), 321, 322
Internalization, 78, 79, 80
International Psychoanalytic Association, 46, 63
Interview, 153–154
Intimacy, 347–349
    and attachment styles, 351–353
Intrinsic aggression, 359
Intrinsic motivation, 327–329
Introversion, 18, 65–66, 159, 160, 161
Intuiting, sensing vs., 66
Isolation, 57

Kibbutz, 37
Kin selection, 235

Language, and repression, 90–91
Latency period, 49, 50
Lawfulness, and control, 92–93
Learned helplessness, 322–325
    and depression, 324
    individual differences in, 325
Learning
    avoidance, 93
    without awareness, 303
    escape, 93
    heritability and, 12–13
    observational, 99
Learning theories of personality, 85–86, 217, 270. *See also* Social learning theory
    associationist (stimulus-response), 86–91
    cognitive behavior modification, 104–105
    main concepts of, 39–40, 41
    models of aggression, 365–371
    reinforcement theory, 91–98
    social learning theory, 98–104
Levelers, 76
Level of aspiration, 335
Lexical hypothesis, 161
Libido, 47, 52, 53, 59, 77
    and developmental stages, 49–51
    theory, 61–62, 63, 77
Life-event stress, 287–291
Life instincts, 48
Life structure, 251–252
Life tasks, 273–274
Liking Scale, 347
Locus of causality, 336
Locus of control, 99, 320–322
Longitudinal study, 244
Love
    companionate, 350–351
    and hate, 354–356
    and intimacy, 351–353
    passionate, 349–350
    research on, 347
    Scales, 347
    and sex, 353–354
    triangular model of, 347–349
    varieties of, 346
Lunacy, and the moon, 36

Mandala, 64
Manic-depressive psychoses, 21, 29
Manifest Anxiety Scale (MAS), 58, 145
Masculine protest, 67
Masculinity, 206
Mastery, 72, 76
Maternal care, infant features and, 6
Maze learning, 12–13
Meaning, 115
Mean level stability, 242
Measurement error, 131, 169
Mediated generalization, 89–90
Mediating responses, 88–89
Menstruation, 247
Mental health, culture and, 32–33
Mental illness, 20–21, 29
Mesomorphic physiques, 158
Meta-analysis, 203
Middle vs. working class, 28
Midlife crisis, 251–252
Mindlessness, 299–300
Mindset, 339–340
Minnesota Multiphasic Personality Inventory (MMPI), 32, 58, 137, 144–145, 147–148, 150, 168–169
    MMPI-2, 144
Misattribution, 281

MMPI. *See* Minnesota Multiphasic Personality Inventory (MMPI)
Modeling, 40, 100–101
    influence of, on aggression, 368–369
Moderator variables, 167–168
Molecular genetics, 22
Monozygotic (MZ) twins, studies of, 13–19
Mood, 278, 286–287
Moon, lunacy and the, 36
Moral development, 231–234
    social learning approach to, 233–234
    stages of (cognitive approach), 232–233
    superego and (psychoanalytic approach), 231
Moratorium, 195
Motivation, Self-Determination Theory, 329–330.
    See also Achievement motivation
Motoric orientation, 28
Multidimensionality, of the person, 380–381

Narcissism, 80–81, 373–374
Narcissistic personality disorder, 80
Narcolepsy, 305
Narcotics, 312–313
Narrative identity, 209–212
National Merit Scholarship Qualifying Test, 18
Natural environment, 33–36
    climate and aggression, 35–36
    climate, subsistence, and settlement patterns, 33–34
Natural selection, 12
Nature-nurture controversy, 1, 17–18, 215, 216–217, 377–380, 383
Need hierarchy, 112–114
Needs, 10, 12, 71–72, 99, 147, 148, 112–114, 150–152
Need value, 99
Negative reinforcement, 93
NEO-PI-r (Revised NEO Personality Inventory), 147, 161, 162, 253
Neural structures, integration of, 53
Neurosis, 69–70
Neuroticism, 160–163
Neurotic patterns, 70
Noise, and aggression, 362–363
Nomothetic data, 98
Nonconscious information processing
    define, 297
    controversy over, 303–304
    relationship of consciousness to, 298–304
Non-rapid eye movement (NREM), 306
Nonshared environment effect, 16–17, 21–22

Obedience, 370
Object, self as, 176–177
Object constancy, 79
Objective personality tests, 125, 142–148
    based on face validity, 143–144
    empirical approaches, 144–145
    factor analysis, 146
    theoretical model, 147–148
Object permanence, 177–178
Object relations theory, 72, 77–80
Object representations, 79
Observation, of behavior, 154
Observational learning, 40, 99
Observed score, 131
Oedipal conflict, 50–51, 53, 81, 231
Old age, 29, 254–257
    aging and health, 255–256
    competence and survival, 256
    demography, 257
    disengagement, 256–257
    trait stability into, 254–255
Openness to experience, 161–162
Operant conditioning and reinforcement, 91–98, 319–320
Oppositional bias, 143–144
Optimism, 325–326
Oral stage, 49–50
Organismic humanism, 112–114
    actualized person, 114
    need hierarchy, 112–114

Ought self, 182
Outcome expectancies, 103
Ovulatory shift, 8

Pain, 88, 94, 95, 104, 311
Parenting styles, 228–231
    authoritarian, 229–231
    authoritative, 229–231
    permissive, 229–230
Parents, continuity between adolescents and, 248–249
Partial reinforcement, 93–94
Passion component, 347
Passionate love, 349–350
Peak experience, 114
Penis envy, 50, 70
Perceived control, 320–330
    efforts to preserve sense of personal control, 326–329
    integrating, with achievement motivation and competence, 340
    learned helplessness, 322–325
    locus of control, 320–322
    optimism, 325–326
    self-determination theory, 329–330
Perceptual constancy, 79
Perceptual defense, 57, 58
Permissiveness-strictness, degree of, 228
Persona, 64
Personal and social development, processes of. *See* Attachment
Personal construct theory, 116–122
    constructive alternativism, 118–119
    emotions, 121–122
    formal theory, 119–120
    human as scientist, 117–118
    overview of, 123
    Role Construct Repertory (REP) Test, 120–121
Personal helplessness, 324
Personality, genetic aspects of, 13–23
Personality assessment, 39, 40, 41, 141–142, 152–155. *See also* Behavioral
    assessment; Interview; Objective personality tests; Physiological assessment;
    Projective personality tests
Personality coefficients, 163–164
Personality coherence, 242–243
Personality continuity and change, 39, 40, 241–245
Personality development, 39, 40, 88–91, 215
    birth order and, 69
    issues in, 216–218
    processes of, 218–227
Personality dynamics, 261, 263–264, 385–386. *See also* Conflict; Emotion;
    Frustration; Impulse control and delay of gratification; Psychodynamics;
    Stress; Substitution
Personality measurement, 127–128. *See also* Reliability; Validity
    prescientific era of, 128–129
    scientific era of, 129–130
Personality structure(s), 103–104, 125, 261, 384–385
    achievement needs as, 331–332
    Freud's, 51–53
    prescientific era, 128–129
    scientific era, 130
Personality tests
    objective, 142–148
    projective, 148–152
Personality theory(ies), 31, 386–387. *See also* Learning theories; Phenomenological
    theories; Psychoanalytic theory
    and antecedents of aggression, 364–371
    integrated, 386–387
    and self, 190
Personality types, 158–159
    Jung's, 65–66
Personal unconscious, 64
Person-centered theory, 109–112
    client-centered therapy, 111–112
    self-actualization, 109–110
Personological tradition, 210
Phallic stage, 49–50
Phenomenological theories of personality, 107–108, 122–123
    existential humanism, 115–116
    humanistic theory, 108–109

implicit psychology, 122–123
main concepts of, 40, 41
organismic humanism, 112–114
personal construct theory, 116–122
person-centered theory, 109–112
Phenomenology, 107
Phenotype, 16
Philia, 346
Physical world, influence on personality of, 33, 37
behavior settings, 36–37
constructed environments, 36
natural environment, 33–36
privacy, 37
summary of environmental effects, 37
Physiological assessment, 154–155
Pity, 284, 337
Pleasure principle, 47, 51, 53, 263
Polymorphism, 18
Positive reinforcement, 93
Possible selves, 182
Postconventional stage, 232
Preconventional stage, 232
Predictive validity, 137
Premsia, 159
Preoccupied style, 226, 227
Press, 151
Primary appraisal, 292
Primary autonomy, 76
Primary drives, 88
Primary emotions, 285
Primary process thought, 52
Priming, 301–302
Privacy, 37
Problem-focused coping, 292
Process, self as, 178
Projection, 57
Projective personality tests and methods, 125, 127, 148–152
Rorschach Inkblot Test, 148–150
Thematic Apperception Test (TAT), 150–153
Prosocial behaviors, 234–238
cooperation, 236
in dolphins, 235
empathy, 237–238
evolution of, 234–235
generosity and caring, 237
Prototype, cognitive, 103
Psychiatric wards, 36
Psychoanalytic ego psychology, 72, 75–77, 79
Psychoanalytic theory/psychoanalysis, 43, 108, 112, 115, 217
of aggression, 364–365
and anxiety, 53–54
basic theoretical concepts of, 46–53
and defense mechanisms, 54–59
evaluation of, 59
influx, 81–82
learning theory compared with, 90
main concepts of, 39, 41
modifications of, 60–72
of moral development, 231
narrative approaches to, 82
since Freud, 72–81
Psychodynamics, 261–264. *See also* Personality dynamics
and behaviorism, 262–263
and Gestalt psychology, 263
from psychoanalytic perspective, 261–262
Psychological determinism, 48–49
Psychological energy, Freud's concept of, 47–48
Psychological reactance, 326
Psychological resilience, 253
Psychopathology, 29, 39, 227
Psychosocial stages, in personality formation, 74–75
Public speaking, 10
Punishment, 40, 95

Q-sort, 111–112

Rapid eye movement (REM), 306–308
Racial identity, 197–198
Radical behaviorism, 92
Range corollary, 119
Range of convenience, 119
Rank order stability, 242
Rapprochement, 79
RAS (ascending reticular activating system), 160
Rationalization, 57
Reactance, 326–327
Reaction formation, 57
Reciprocal determination, 99
Reciprocal inhibition, 104
Regression
and frustration, 273
hypnotic, 311
Reification, 81
Reinforcement, 85, 90–91
and aggression, 369–370
and attachment, 221, 222
learning without awareness and, 303
and operant conditioning, 91–98, 319–320
negative, 93
positive, 93
Reinforcement schedule, 91, 94–95
Reinforcement theory, 91–98
applications of, 95–96
limitations of, 97–98
Reinforcement values, 98
Reinforcer, 92
Relationship Scales Questionnaire (RSQ), 226
Reliability, 125, 127, 131–135
effect of low, on validity, 139
evaluating, 133–134
of observations, 135
sources of error, 132
split-half, 134
test-retest, 134
variability, 132–133
REM (rapid eye movements), 306–308
Repression, 53–54, 107, 112, 262, 269
childhood sexual abuse and, 56–57
experimental study of, 55–56
language and, 90–91
-sensitization, 58
and unconscious, 54–56
Repression-sensitization continuum, 58
Repression-Sensitization (R-S) scale, 58, 138–139, 145
REP (Role Construct Repertory) Test, 120–121, 122
Resilience, 120–121, 253
Respondents, 88
Response(s), 88–89
acquisition and performance of, 101
Response bias, 143
Responsibility, 115, 367–368
attributions of, 340–342
Reticular activating system (RAS), 18
Revised NEO Personality Inventory (NEO-PI-r), 147, 161, 162, 253
Rewards, 40
Ribonucleic acid (RNA), 4–5
Ritualization, 75
RNA (ribonucleic acid), 4–5
Role modeling, 40
Role Construct Repertory (REP) Test, 120–121, 122
Rorschach Inkblot Test, 148–150
Rosenberg Self-Esteem Inventory, 148
RSQ (Relationship Scales Questionnaire), 226
Rules, verbalization and, 101

Sample, heritability studies, 19–20
Scale, 142
Schemas, 301–302
chronically accessible, 302
Schizophrenia, genetics of, 20–21
Scholastic Aptitude Test (SAT), 136–137

Science
    vs. ethnoscience, 122
    personality as, 382–383
    psychology as, 262
Scientist, human as, 117–118
Secondary appraisal, 292
Secondary autonomy, 76
Secondary drives, 88, 89
Secondary process thought, 53
Secure attachment, 225, 226–227
Security, 69–70, 71, 79, 80
Selective breeding, 12–13
Self, 175, 176–178, 381–382. *See also* Self-concept(s)
    actual self, 112, 182, 191, 282
    as agent, 178
    archetype of, 64
    beginnings of, 178–179
    consciousness and, 302–303
    culture and, 176
    defined, 111–112, 176–177
    divided, 313–315
    ideal, 111–112, 182
    and individualism and mental health, 32–33
    interpersonal sense of, 194–196
    narcissism and, 80–81
    ought, 182
    personality theories and, 190
    possible, 182
    protection and enhancement of, 187–189
    relationship of, to consciousness, 302–303
    sociocentric view of, 31
    Western view of, 30–32, 33
Self-actualization, 40, 64, 108–110, 112–114, 115
Self-awareness, 178–179, 303, 304
    positive and negative effects of, 186–187
Self-complexity, 182–183
Self-concept(s), 40, 111–112, 175, 176, 177, 193. *See also* Self
    complexity and clarity of, 182–183
    development of, 178–184
    multiple, 181–182
    working, 181
Self-consciousness, 187
Self-consistency, 189–190
Self-control, 186
    development of, 186
Self-Determination Theory, 329–330
Self-disclosure, and expression, 292–293
Self-efficacy, 102–103, 327
Self-enhancement, 187–189
Self-esteem, 40, 183–184
    assessment of, 148
    and negative affect, 184
    social belonging and, 10, 12
Self-evaluation maintenance, 188–189
Self-discrepancy, 112
Self-identity, 75
Self-images, 212
Self-instruction, 105
Self-monitoring, 26, 185
    and self-control, 186
Self-processes, 184–187
Self-protection, 187–189
Self-reinforcement, 101–102
Self-report, behavior, 154
Self-schemata, 180–181
Sensing vs. intuiting, 66
Sensitive periods, 218
SES (socioeconomic status), intelligence heritability and, 19–20
Settlement patterns, 33–35
Sex, love and, 353–354
Sex differences, 201, 202–205. *See also* Gender differences
    and sex typing, 205–209
    studies of, 203–205
Sex hormones, and aggression, 360
Sex typing, 201, 205–209

Sexual abuse, childhood, and repression, 56–57
Sexual instincts, 39, 48
Sexual motivation, 8–9, 48, 61–62
Shadow, 64
Shame, 284, 285
Shaping, 96
Sharpeners, 76
Shyness, 17–18
Siblings
    nonshared environment effect, 21–22
    twin studies, 13–19
Single nucleotide polymorphism (SNP), 22
Situation
    and discriminative cues, 103
    and traits, 164–165
Situational assessment, 163–164
Situational critique, 164
Situational selection, 26
Situational theories of traits, 163–166
Sixteen Personality-Factor Questionnaire (16 P-F), Cattell's, 144, 147–148
Skin conductance, 154–155
Sleep, 304–305
    disorders, 304
Slips of the tongue, 49271
SNP (single nucleotide polymorphism), 22
Social belonging, need for, 10, 12
Social class, influence on personality of, 27–28
Social desirability, 143, 147
Social influence, and aggression, 370–371
Socialization, 34, 228–231
    child-rearing patterns, 228–231
Social learning theory, 98–104, 270–271. *See also* Learning theories
        of personality
    Bandura's, 99–103
    limitations of, 103–104
    of moral development, 233–234
Social loafing, 29
Social problems, mental illness and, 20–21
Social stratification, 27
Social support, 292–294
Social world, influence on personality of, 27
    culture, 28–33
    social class, 27–28
Society, personality and, 71
Sociobiology, 7
Socioeconomic status (SES), intelligence heritability and, 19–20
Sociometer, 10
Source traits, 146–147, 159
    constitutional, 159
Spatial conflict, 265
Species-spacing, 5
Specific responses, 160
Specific source traits, 159
Split-brain experiments, 313–315
Split-half reliability, 134
Stability, 242, 336
Stable conflicts, 265
Stages, developmental, 49–51, 73–75, 217–218, 232–233
    adult, 250–251
    anal, 49–50
    continuity vs., 217–215
    genital, 49–50
    moral, 232–233
    oral, 49–50
    phallic, 49–50
States vs. traits, 170–171
State-Trait Anxiety Inventory, 148
Stereotypes, 28
Stimulus meaning, aggression and altering of, 375
Strange Situation, 222, 226
Strategies, cognitive, 103
Stress, 171, 287–294
    coping with, 291
    effects of, on thinking, 291
    individual differences in reactions to, 294

life-event, 287–291
  multicultural aspects of, 293–294
  social support and, 292–294
Stressor, cultural interpretation of, 293–294
Struggle, 115
Style of life, 68
Sublimation, 58, 271
Subliminal perception, 262, 301–302
Subsistence, 33–35
Substitution, 271–272
Suicide, 127–128, 136, 186–187, 200, 201
Superego, 51, 53, 72, 75, 77
  and moral development, 231
Superiority, striving for, 67
Superstition, 87
Suppression, 55
Surface traits, 146, 159
Survival
  and competence, 256
  and need for belonging, 10, 12
Symbiosis, 79
Systematic desensitization, 104

TAT (Thematic Apperception Test), 79, 150–152, 262, 331, 332, 333, 335
Temperament, 12, 15, 21, 216–217
  defined, 17
  elements and, 158
  heritability, 17
  physique and, 129, 158–159
  theory of, 128–129
Temperature, and aggression, 35–36
Template-matching technique, 168
Temporal conflict, 265
Temporal consistency, 103
Territoriality, 37
Test-retest reliability, 134
Texas Social Behavior Inventory, 148
Thanatos, 48
Thematic Apperception Test (TAT), 79, 150–152, 262, 331, 332, 333, 335
Theoretical model, of objective personality assessment, 147–148
Theory of mind, 237
Therapeutic processes, 112
Thinking
  effects of stress on, 291
  vs. feeling, 66
Threat, 121–122
Time binding, 269
Toilet training, 228
Token economies, 96
Total institutions, 37
Training, 104
Trait(s), 18, 141, 157
  aggregation techniques, 168–169
  aggression as personality, 372–374
  attack on, 163–166
  broad band personality, 162
  conceptualizing, 177
  constitutional source, 159
  critique of, 163–166
  environment mold, 159
  Eysenck's hierarchy, 159–161
  general source, 159

interactionist position, 166–167
  level changes, 248
  moderator variable approach, 167–168
  review of approaches to, 169–171
  situational assessment, 163–164
  situational theories of, 163–166
  source, 146–147, 159
  specific source, 159
  states vs., 170–171
  surface, 146, 159
  template-matching technique, 168
  theories, 159–163
  twin studies, 13–19
Trance logic, 309
Transactional approach, 166
Transitional objects, 80
True score, 131
True variability, 133
Twins, studies of, 13–19
Two-factor model, emotions, 280–281
Type(s), 158
  Eysenck's, 160
  personality, 65–66, 158–159

Unconditional positive regard, 110, 112
Unconscious, 39, 45–46, 48–49, 52, 54, 55, 57, 59, 90, 298. See also Nonconscious
    information processing
  collective, 64–65
  personal, 64
  repression and, 54–56
Undermanning, 37
Unexpected-reward condition, 328
Universal helplessness, 324
Unstable conflicts, 265

Validity, 125, 127, 131, 132, 135–139
  concurrent, 137
  construct, 138–139
  content, 136
  convergent, 139
  criterion, 136–138
  discriminant, 139
  effect of low reliability on, 139
  predictive, 137
  tests based on face, 143–144
Values, D vs. B, 114
Variability, 132–133
  error, 132
  true, 133
Variables, correlation, 14
Verbalization, and rules, 101
Vicarious punishment, 101
Vicarious reward, 101
Violence, temperature and, 35–36

Warmth-hostility, degree of, 228
Weschler Intelligence Scale for Children, 19–20
Woodworth Personal Data Sheet, 143, 153
Word association technique, 56
Working class, middle vs., 28
Working model, 220
Working self-concept, 181